Preface

Programming with Microsoft Visual Basic .NET is designed for a beginning programming course. This book uses Visual Basic .NET, an object-oriented/event-driven language, to teach programming concepts. This book capitalizes on the energy and enthusiasm students naturally have for Windows-based applications and clearly teaches students how to take full advantage of the power of Visual Basic .NET. It assumes students have learned basic Windows skills and file management from Course Technology's *New Perspectives on Microsoft Windows 2000 Brief*, *New Perspectives on Microsoft Windows XP Brief*, or from an equivalent book.

Organization and Coverage

Programming with Microsoft Visual Basic .NET contains an Overview and 11 tutorials that present hands-on instruction. In these tutorials, students with no previous programming experience learn how to plan and create their own interactive Windows applications. Using this book, students will be able to master more advanced tasks sooner than they would using other introductory texts; a perusal of the table of contents affirms this. By the end of the book, students will have learned how to work with controls and write If...Then...Else, Select Case, Do...Loop, and For...Next statements, as well as how to create and manipulate variables, constants, sequential access files, random access files, and arrays. Students also will learn how to manipulate strings and include multiple forms in a project. GUI design skills are emphasized, and advanced skills such as creating and printing reports, referencing objects, and accessing information in a database using a Windows form and a Web form are taught. The text also introduces students to OOP concepts and terminology.

Approach

Programming with Microsoft Visual Basic .NET distinguishes itself from other Windows textbooks because of its unique two-pronged approach. First, it motivates students by demonstrating why they need to learn the concepts and skills. This book teaches programming concepts using a task-driven rather than a command-driven approach. By working through the tutorials—which are each motivated by a realistic case—students learn how to use programming applications they are likely to encounter in the workplace. This is much more effective than memorizing a list of commands out of context. Second, the content, organization, and pedagogy of this book exploit the Windows environment. The material presented in the tutorials capitalizes on the power of Visual Basic .NET to perform complex programming tasks earlier and more easily than was possible under DOS.

Features

Programming with Microsoft Visual Basic .NET is an exceptional textbook because it also includes the following features:

- **"Read This Before You Begin" Section** This section is consistent with Course Technology's unequaled commitment to helping instructors introduce technology into the classroom. Technical considerations and assumptions about hardware, software, and default settings are listed in one place to help instructors save time and eliminate unnecessary aggravation.

- **Tutorial Cases** Each tutorial begins with a programming-related problem that students could reasonably expect to encounter in business, followed by a demonstration of an application that could be used to solve the problem. Showing the students the completed application before they learn how to create it is motivational and instructionally sound. By allowing the students to see the type of application they will be able to create after completing the tutorial, the students will be more motivated to learn because they can see how the programming concepts they are about to learn can be used and, therefore, why the concepts are important.

- **Lessons** Each tutorial is divided into three lessons—A, B, and C. Lesson A introduces the programming concepts that will be used in the completed application. In Lessons B and C, the student creates the application required to solve the problem specified in the Tutorial Case.

- **Step-by-Step Methodology** The unique Course Technology methodology keeps students on track. They click or press keys always within the context of solving the problem posed in the Tutorial Case. The text constantly guides students, letting them know where they are in the process of solving the problem. The numerous illustrations include labels that direct students' attention to what they should look at on the screen.

- **Help?** Help? notes anticipate the problems students are likely to encounter and help them resolve these problems on their own. This feature facilitates independent learning and frees the instructor to focus on substantive conceptual issues rather than on common procedural errors.

- **Tip** Tip notes provide additional information about a procedure—for example, an alternative method of performing the procedure. They also relate the OOP terminology learned in the Overview to applications created in Visual Basic .NET.

- **GUI Design Tips** GUI Design Tips contain guidelines and recommendations for designing applications that follow Windows standards.

- **Summary** Following each lesson is a Summary, which recaps the programming concepts, commands, and objects covered in the lesson.

- **Questions and Exercises** Each lesson concludes with meaningful, conceptual Questions that test students' understanding of what they learned in the lesson. The Questions are followed by Exercises, which provide students with additional practice of the skills and concepts they learned in the lesson.

- **Discovery Exercises** The Windows environment allows students to learn by exploring and discovering what they can do. The Discovery Exercises are designated by the word "discovery" in the margin. They encourage students to challenge and independently develop their own programming skills while exploring the capabilities of Visual Basic .NET.

- **Debugging Exercises** One of the most important programming skills a student can learn is the ability to find and fix problems in an existing application. The Debugging Exercises are designated by the word "debugging" in the margin and provide an opportunity for students to detect and correct errors in an existing application.

Teaching Tools

The following supplemental materials are available when this book is used in a classroom setting. All of the teaching tools available with this book are provided to the instructor on a single CD-ROM.

Electronic Instructor's Manual—The Instructor's Manual that accompanies this textbook includes:

- Additional instructional material to assist in class preparation, including suggestions for lecture topics.
- Solutions to all end-of-lesson Questions and Exercises.

ExamView® This textbook is accompanied by ExamView, a powerful testing software package that allows instructors to create and administer printed, computer (LAN-based), and Internet exams. ExamView includes hundreds of questions that correspond to the topics covered in this text, enabling students to generate detailed study guides that include page references for further review. The computer-based and Internet testing components allow students to take exams at their computers, and also save the instructor time by grading each exam automatically.

PowerPoint Presentations This book comes with Microsoft PowerPoint slides for each tutorial. These are included as a teaching aid for classroom presentation, to make available to students on the network for tutorial review, or to be printed for classroom distribution. Instructors can add their own slides for additional topics they introduce to the class.

Data Files Data Files, containing all of the data necessary for steps within the tutorials and the end-of-lesson Exercises, are provided through the Course Technology Web site at **www.course.com**, and are also available on the Teaching Tools CD-ROM.

Solution Files Solutions to end-of-lesson questions and exercises are provided on the Teaching Tools CD-ROM and may also be found on the Course Technology Web site at **www.course.com**. The solutions are password protected.

Distance Learning Course Technology is proud to present online courses in WebCT and Blackboard, to provide the most complete and dynamic learning experience possible. When you add online content to one of your courses, you're adding a lot: self tests, links, glossaries, and, most of all, a gateway to the 21st century's most important information resource. We hope you will make the most of your course, both online and offline. For more information on how to bring distance learning to your course, contact your local Course Technology sales representative.

Acknowledgments

Writing a book is a team effort rather than an individual one. I would like to take this opportunity to thank my team, especially Jennifer Muroff (Senior Editor) and Amanda Brodkin (Development Editor). Thank you for your support, enthusiasm, patience, and hard work. I could not have completed this project without the two of you. I also want to thank Karen Jacot (Production Editor), John Freitas (Quality Assurance), Jennifer Locke (Managing Editor), Janet Aras (Associate Product Manager), and Christy Urban (Editorial Assistant) for their contributions. Last, but certainly not least, I want to thank the following reviewers for their invaluable ideas and comments: Dave Fullerton, Yeshiva University; David Grebner, Lansing Community College; Joseph Otto, California State University Los Angeles; and Von Plessner, Northwest State Community College.

Diane Zak

Brief Contents

PREFACE   **iii**

READ THIS BEFORE YOU BEGIN   **xix**

overview

AN OVERVIEW OF VISUAL BASIC .NET *1*

tutorial 1

AN INTRODUCTION TO VISUAL BASIC .NET *15*

tutorial 2

DESIGNING APPLICATIONS *83*

tutorial 3

USING VARIABLES AND CONSTANTS *153*

tutorial 4

THE SELECTION STRUCTURE *217*

tutorial 5

MORE ON THE SELECTION STRUCTURE *281*

tutorial 6

THE REPETITION STRUCTURE *359*

tutorial 7

SUB AND FUNCTION PROCEDURES *433*

tutorial 8

MANIPULATING STRINGS *491*

tutorial 9

SEQUENTIAL ACCESS FILES AND PRINTING *547*

tutorial 10

RANDOM ACCESS FILES *613*

tutorial 11

ARRAYS *665*

appendix A

BASIC TOOLS INCLUDED IN THE WINDOWS FORMS DESIGNER TOOLBOX *721*

appendix B

DATABASE ACCESS USING A WINDOWS FORM *724*

appendix C

DATABASE ACCESS USING A WEB FORM *742*

index *761*

Contents

PREFACE iii

READ THIS BEFORE YOU BEGIN xix

overview

AN OVERVIEW OF VISUAL BASIC .NET *1*

A History and a Demonstration *1*

A Brief History of Programming Languages *1*

Machine Languages *2*

Assembly Languages *2*

High-Level Languages *3*

Procedure-Oriented High-Level Languages *3*

The Introduction of Windows *4*

Object-Oriented/Event-Driven High-Level Languages *4*

OOP Terminology *5*

A Visual Basic .NET Demonstration *7*

Using the Tutorials Effectively *10*

Questions *10*

tutorial 1

AN INTRODUCTION TO VISUAL BASIC .NET *15*

case ▶ Creating a Copyright Screen *15*

Previewing the Copyright Screen *16*

Lesson A: Creating a Windows-Based Application in Visual Basic .NET *17*

Starting and Customizing Visual Studio .NET *17*

Creating the Copyright Screen Application *21*

Managing the Windows in the IDE *26*

The Windows Form Designer Window *28*

The Solution Explorer Window *29*

The Properties Window *31*

Properties of the Windows Form Object *33*

The Name Property *34*

The Text Property *35*

The StartPosition Property *35*

The BackgroundImage Property *35*

The Size Property *36*

Saving a Solution *37*

Closing the Current Solution *38*

Opening an Existing Solution *38*

Exiting Visual Studio .NET *39*

Summary *39*

Questions *41*

Exercises *43*

Lesson B: Working with Controls 45
  The Toolbox Window 45
  Using the Label Tool 49
    Setting the Text and AutoSize Properties 51
    Setting the Location Property 52
  Changing the Property for More Than One Control at a Time 52
  Using the Format Menu 54
  Using the PictureBox Tool 55
  Using the Button Tool 56
  Starting and Ending an Application 57
  Writing Visual Basic .NET Code 59
  Summary 64
  Questions 66
  Exercises 69
Lesson C: Completing the Copyright Screen 72
  Using the Timer Tool 72
  Setting the FormBorderStyle Property 75
  The MinimizeBox, MaximizeBox, and ControlBox Properties 76
  Printing Your Code 77
  Summary 78
  Questions 78
  Exercises 80

t u t o r i a l 2

DESIGNING APPLICATIONS 83

case ▶ Creating an Order Screen 83
  Solving the Problem Using a Procedure-Oriented Approach 84
  Solving the Problem Using an Object-Oriented/Event-Driven (OOED)
    Approach 86
Lesson A: Planning an OOED Application in Visual Basic .NET 90
  Creating an OOED Application 90
  Planning an OOED Application 91
    Identifying the Application's Tasks 91
    Identifying the Objects 93
    Identifying the Events 95
    Drawing a Sketch of the User Interface 96
  Summary 99
  Questions 99
  Exercises 102
Lesson B: Building the User Interface 104
  Preparing to Create the User Interface 104
    Including Graphics in the User Interface 106
    Including Different Fonts in the User Interface 106
    Including Color in the User Interface 107
    The BorderStyle Property 109
    Setting the Text Property 109
  Adding a Text Box Control to the Form 110
  Locking the Controls on a Form 111
  Assigning Access Keys 112
  Setting the TabIndex Property 114

Summary *119*
Questions *120*
Exercises *121*
Lesson C: Coding, Testing, Debugging, and Documenting the Application *125*
Coding the Application *125*
Coding the Clear Screen Button *126*
Assigning a Value to a Property During Run Time *127*
Using the Focus Method *129*
Internally Documenting the Program Code *130*
Writing Arithmetic Expressions *131*
Coding the Calculate Order Button *132*
The Val Function *136*
Using the Format Function *137*
Testing and Debugging the Application *139*
Assembling the Documentation *140*
Summary *141*
Questions *141*
Exercises *142*

t u t o r i a l 3

USING VARIABLES AND CONSTANTS *153*

case ▶ Revising the Skate-Away Sales Application *153*
Previewing the Completed Application *154*
Lesson A: Creating Variables and Named Constants *156*
Using Variables to Store Information *156*
Selecting a Data Type for a Variable *157*
Selecting a Name for a Variable *159*
Declaring a Variable *160*
Assigning Data to an Existing Variable *161*
The Scope of a Variable *162*
Creating a Local Variable *163*
Creating a Form-Level Variable *166*
Named Constants *168*
Summary *170*
Questions *171*
Exercises *172*
Lesson B: Modifying the Skate-Away Sales Application *175*
Storing Information Using Variables *175*
Modifying the Calculate Order Button's Code *177*
Concatenating Strings *183*
The InputBox Function *185*
The Newline Character *190*
The Object Browser *190*
Designating a Default Button *193*
Summary *194*
Questions *195*
Exercises *196*
Lesson C: Modifying the Skate-Away Sales Application's Code *201*
Modifying the Code in the Load Event and CalcButton
Click Event Procedures *201*

Static Variables *205*
Coding the TextChanged Event Procedure *207*
Associating a Procedure With Different Objects or Events *208*
Summary *209*
Questions *210*
Exercises *211*

tutorial 4

THE SELECTION STRUCTURE *217*

case ▶ Creating a Monthly Payment Calculator Application *217*
Previewing the Completed Application *218*
Lesson A: The If...Then...Else Statement *220*
The Selection Structure *220*
Writing Pseudocode for If and If/Else Selection Structures *221*
Flowcharting the If and If/Else Selection Structures *222*
Coding the If and If/Else Selection Structures *224*
Comparison Operators *225*
Using Comparison Operators in an If...Then...Else Statement *226*
Logical Operators *230*
Using the Truth Tables *232*
Using Logical Operators in an If...Then...Else Statement *234*
The UCase and LCase Functions *236*
Using UCase and LCase in a Procedure *238*
Summary *239*
Questions *240*
Exercises *243*
Lesson B: The Monthly Payment Calculator Application *245*
Completing the User Interface *245*
Adding a Group Box Control to the Form *246*
Locking the Controls and Setting the TabIndex Property *249*
Coding the CalcPayButton Click Event Procedure *250*
Using the Pmt Function *252*
The MessageBox.Show Method *255*
Coding the TextChanged Event *261*
Summary *262*
Questions *263*
Exercises *265*
Lesson C: Completing the Monthly Payment Calculator Application *267*
Coding the KeyPress Event *267*
Aligning the Text in a Label Control *272*
Summary *273*
Questions *273*
Exercises *274*

tutorial 5

MORE ON THE SELECTION STRUCTURE *281*

case ▶ Creating a Math Practice Application *281*
Previewing the Completed Application *282*
Lesson A: Nested, If/ElseIf/Else, and Case Selection Structures *284*
Nested Selection Structures *284*

Logic Errors in Selection Structures *288*
   Using a Logical Operator Rather Than a Nested Selection Structure *290*
   Reversing the Primary and Secondary Decisions *292*
   Using an Unnecessary Nested Selection Structure *293*
The If/ElseIf/Else Selection Structure *294*
The Case Selection Structure *296*
   Desk-Checking the Grade Procedure *298*
   Using To and Is in an ExpressionList *299*
The Is, TypeOf...Is, and Like Comparison Operators *300*
   The Is Comparison Operator *300*
   The TypeOf...Is Comparison Operator *302*
   The Like Comparison Operator *303*
Summary *305*
Questions *306*
Exercises *309*
Lesson B: The Math Practice Application *315*
Completing the User Interface *315*
   Adding a Radio Button to the Form *317*
   Adding a Check Box Control to the Form *319*
   Locking the Controls and Setting the TabIndex Property *320*
Coding the Math Practice Application *322*
Creating a User-Defined Sub Procedure *323*
   Generating Random Numbers *325*
Coding the Grade1RadioButton and Grade2RadioButton Click Event
   Procedures *327*
Coding the AdditionRadioButton and SubtractionRadioButton Click Event
   Procedures *330*
Coding the Form's Load Event Procedure *333*
Summary *334*
Questions *335*
Exercises *337*
Lesson C: Completing the Math Practice Application *340*
Coding the CheckAnswerButton Click Event Procedure *340*
Coding the SummaryCheckBox Click Event Procedure *345*
Summary *347*
Questions *348*
Exercises *348*

tutorial 6

THE REPETITION STRUCTURE *359*

case ▶ Creating a Grade Calculator Application *359*

Previewing the Completed Application *360*
Lesson A: The Repetition Structure (Looping) *361*
The Repetition Structure *361*
The For...Next Statement *361*
   Example 1 Button *364*
   Example 2 Button *366*
   Example 3 Button *367*
The Do...Loop Statement *370*
   Pretest Loop Button *373*
   Posttest Loop Button *374*

Using Counters and Accumulators 376
   The Sales Express Application 376
   Pretest Button 378
   Posttest Button 382
Summary 383
Questions 385
Exercises 389
Lesson B: Using Collections 393
The Controls Collection 393
Object Variables 395
The For Each...Next Statement 398
   Including the For Each...Next Loop in a Flowchart and Pseudocode 400
Creating a User-Defined Collection 403
The Grade Calculator Application 405
Coding the GradeForm's Load Event Procedure 407
   Parallel Collections 407
Coding the Check Boxes' Click Event Procedures 408
   The Enabled Property 409
Summary 411
Questions 413
Exercises 415
Lesson C: Completing the Grade Calculator Application 418
Coding the DisplayButton's Click Event Procedure 418
Coding the Text Boxes' Enter Event Procedures 422
Coding the GradeForm's Closing Event Procedure 423
Summary 424
Questions 425
Exercises 425

tutorial 7

SUB AND FUNCTION PROCEDURES 433

case ▶ Creating a Payroll Application 433
Previewing the Completed Application 434
Lesson A: Creating Sub and Function Procedures 435
Procedures 435
Sub Procedures 435
Including Parameters in a User-Defined Sub Procedure 436
Passing Variables 437
   Passing Variables by Value 438
   Passing Variables by Reference 440
Function Procedures 443
Summary 445
Questions 446
Exercises 449
Lesson B: Using a List Box Control
Completing the Payroll Application's User Interface 452
Adding a List Box to a Form 453
   Adding Items to a List Box 454
   The SelectedItem and SelectedIndex Properties 457

Coding the CalculateButton Click Event Procedure 461
Coding the GetFwtTax Function 463
Completing the CalculateButton Click Event Procedure 468
Clearing the Contents of the Label Controls 471
Summary 472
Questions 473
Exercises 474
Lesson C: Completing the Payroll Application 477
Adding an Existing Form to a Solution 478
Coding the Sub Main Procedure 480
Creating an Instance of a Form 481
Using a Form Object's ShowDialog Method 482
Summary 483
Questions 484
Exercises 485

t u t o r i a l   8

MANIPULATING STRINGS 491

case ▶ Creating a Hangman Game Application 491
Previewing the Completed Application 492
Lesson A: String Manipulation 494
Manipulating Strings in Visual Basic .NET 494
Determining the Number of Characters Contained in a String 494
Removing Characters from a String 495
The Remove Method 498
Determining Whether a String Begins or Ends with a Specific Sequence
of Characters 499
Accessing Characters Contained in a String 501
Replacing Characters in a String 502
The Mid Statement 504
Inserting Characters within a String 505
Searching a String 506
Summary 508
Questions 510
Exercises 513
Lesson B: Using a Main Menu Control 516
Completing the Hangman Game Application's User Interface 516
Adding a Main Menu Control to a Form 517
Assigning Shortcut Keys 520
Coding the Click Event Procedure for the Exit Menu Item 521
Summary 522
Questions 523
Exercises 524
Lesson C: Completing the Hangman Game Application 527
The Hangman Game Application 527
Coding the Click Event Procedure for the FileNewMenuItem 529
Coding the Label Controls that Contain the Letters of the Alphabet 532
Summary 538
Questions 538
Exercises 539

t u t o r i a l 9

SEQUENTIAL ACCESS FILES AND PRINTING 547

case ▶ Creating the Carriage House Application 547
  Previewing the Completed Application 548
  Lesson A: Sequential Access Files 551
    File Types 551
    Using Sequential Access Files 551
    Using StreamWriter and StreamReader Objects 552
    Opening a Sequential Access File 553
      Determining Whether a File Exists 556
    Writing Information to a Sequential Access File 556
      Using the PadLeft and PadRight Methods 558
    Reading Information from a Sequential Access File 561
    Closing a Sequential Access File 562
    The File Application 563
    Summary 566
    Questions 568
    Exercises 570
  Lesson B: Using a DateTimePicker Control 573
    Completing the Carriage House Application's User Interface 573
    Adding a DateTimePicker Control to a Form 574
      The ShowUpDown Property 577
      The Format Property 578
    The Value Property 579
      Retrieving the Information Stored in the Value Property 581
    The Text Property 582
    Retrieving the System Date and Time 583
    Coding the CarriageForm Load Event Procedure 585
    Coding the AddButton Click Event Procedure 589
    Summary 591
    Questions 592
    Exercises 593
  Lesson C: Completing the Carriage House Application 598
    The Carriage House Application 598
    Adding a PrintDocument Control to the Form 598
    Coding the Print Report Button's Click Event Procedure 599
    Coding the PrintPage Event Procedure 600
      The e.Graphics.DrawString Method 601
    Summary 604
    Questions 604
    Exercises 605

t u t o r i a l 10

RANDOM ACCESS FILES 613

case ▶ Creating a Seminar Application 613
  Previewing the Seminar Application 614
  Lesson A: Random Access Files 616
    Random Access Files Versus Sequential Access Files 616

Creating a Record Structure *617*

Declaring a Record Variable *619*

Opening a Random Access File 619

Writing Records to a Random Access File 620

Initializing a Random Access File 621

Reading Records from a Random Access File 623

Testing for the End of a Random Access File 623

Closing a Random Access File 625

Summary 625

Questions 626

Exercises 629

Lesson B: Using a Random Access File in an Application 632

The Seminar Application 632

Coding the InitializeButton Click Event Procedure 634

Coding the AddButton Click Event Procedure 637

Coding the DisplayButton Click Event Procedure 640

Summary 644

Questions 645

Exercises 646

Lesson C: Completing the Seminar Application 649

Coding the Remaining Procedures in the Seminar Application 649

Coding the RemoveButton Click Event Procedure 649

Coding the PrintButton Click Event Procedure 653

Coding the SeminarPrintDocument PrintPage Event Procedure 653

Summary 656

Questions 657

Exercises 657

t u t o r i a l 11

ARRAYS *665*

case ▶ Creating a Tax Calculator Application 665

Previewing the Tax Calculator Application 666

Lesson A: Using a One-Dimensional Array 668

Arrays 668

One-Dimensional Arrays 668

Storing Data in a One-Dimensional Array 671

Manipulating One-Dimensional Arrays 672

Displaying the Contents of a One-Dimensional Array 672

Using the Subscript to Access an Element in a One-Dimensional Array 674

Searching a One-Dimensional Array 675

Calculating the Average Amount Stored in a One-Dimensional Numeric Array 676

Determining the Highest Value Stored in a One-Dimensional Array 677

Updating the Values Stored in a One-Dimensional Array 678

Sorting the Data Stored in a One-Dimensional Array 679

Summary 681

Questions 682

Exercises 686

Lesson B: More on One-Dimensional Arrays 691

Parallel One-Dimensional Arrays 691

Storing Records in a One-Dimensional Array 693

Summary *695*

Questions *696*

Exercises *696*

Lesson C: Using a Two-Dimensional Array *700*

Two-Dimensional Arrays *700*

Storing Data in a Two-Dimensional Array *702*

Calculating the Sum of the Numbers Stored in a Two-Dimensional Array *703*

The Tax Calculator Application *704*

Coding the CalculateButton Click Event Procedure *707*

Summary *710*

Questions *710*

Exercises *713*

appendix A

BASIC TOOLS INCLUDED IN THE WINDOWS FORMS DESIGNER TOOLBOX *721*

appendix B

DATABASE ACCESS USING A WINDOWS FORM *724*

Accessing Data Stored in a Database *724*

Adding an OleDbDataAdapter Object to a Windows Form *726*

SQL *731*

Creating a Data Set *736*

Adding a DataGrid Control to the Form *739*

Customizing the Appearance of the DataGrid Control's Data *740*

appendix C

DATABASE ACCESS USING A WEB FORM *742*

Creating a Web-Based Application *742*

Accessing Data Stored in a Database *745*

Adding an OleDbDataAdapter Object to a Web Form *746*

SQL *750*

Creating a Data Set *755*

Adding a DataGrid Control to the Form *757*

Customizing the Appearance of the DataGrid Control's Data *759*

index *761*

Read This Before You Begin

To the User

Data Files

To complete the steps and exercises in this book, you will need data files that have been created for this book. Your instructor will provide the data files to you. You also can obtain the files electronically from the Course Technology Web site by connecting to **http://www.course.com**, and then searching for this book title.

Each tutorial in this book has its own set of data files, which are stored in a separate folder within the VBNET folder. For example, the files for Tutorial 1 are stored in the VBNET\Tut01 folder. Similarly, the files for Tutorial 2 are stored in the VBNET\Tut02 folder. Throughout this book, you will be instructed to open files from or save files to these folders.

You can use a computer in your school lab or your own computer to complete the tutorials and exercises in this book.

Using Your Own Computer

To use your own computer to complete the tutorials and exercises in this book, you will need the following:
- A 486-level or higher personal computer running Microsoft Windows 2000 or Microsoft Windows XP.
- **To start the Visual Basic .NET applications from the Visual Studio .NET environment, the user must have Debugger or Administrator status.**
- **Microsoft Visual Studio .NET Professional Edition, or Enterprise Edition must be installed on your computer.**
  - After Microsoft Visual Studio .NET is installed, start Microsoft Visual Studio .NET. Click Tools on the menu bar, and then click Options to open the Options dialog box. If necessary, click the Environment folder to open it, and then click General. If necessary, click the Close button affects active tab only check box to select it. If necessary, also click the Auto Hide button affects active tab only check box to select it. Click the OK button, and then close Microsoft Visual Studio .NET.
- **Data files.** You will not be able to complete the tutorials and exercises in this book using your own computer unless you have the data files. You can get the data files from your instructor, or you can obtain the data files electronically from the Course Technology Web site by connecting to **http://www.course.com**, and then searching for this book title.

Figures

Many of the figures in this book reflect how your screen will look if you are using a Microsoft Windows 2000 system. Your screen will look similar to these figures if you are using a Microsoft Windows XP system.

Visit Our World Wide Web Site

Additional materials designed especially for you might be available for your course on the World Wide Web. Go to **http://www.course.com**. Periodically search this site for more details.

To the Instructor

To complete the tutorials and exercises in this book, your users must use a set of data files. These files are included in the Instructor's Resource Kit. They also may be obtained electronically through the Course Technology Web site at **http://www.course.com**. Follow the instructions in the Help file to copy the data files to your server or standalone computer. You can view the Help file using a text editor such as WordPad or Notepad. Once the files are copied, you should instruct your users how to copy the files to their own computers or workstations.

The tutorials and exercises in this book were tested using the final version of Visual Studio .NET on both a Microsoft Windows 2000 and a Microsoft Windows XP system.

Course Technology Data Files

You are granted a license to copy the data files to any computer or computer network used by individuals who have purchased this book.

An Overview of Visual Basic .NET:

A History and a Demonstration

A Brief History of Programming Languages

Although computers appear to be amazingly intelligent machines, they cannot yet think on their own. Computers still rely on human beings to give them directions. These directions are called **programs**, and the people who write the programs are called **programmers**.

Just as human beings communicate with each other through the use of languages such as English, Spanish, Hindi, and Chinese, programmers use a variety of special languages, called **programming languages**, to communicate with the computer. Some popular programming languages are Visual Basic, Visual Basic .NET, C# .NET, C++, Java, Perl (Practical Extraction and Report Language), C, and COBOL (Common Business Oriented Language). In the next sections, you follow the progression of programming languages from machine languages to assembly languages, then to procedure-oriented high-level languages, and finally to object-oriented high-level languages.

Machine Languages

Within a computer, all data is represented by microscopic electronic switches that can be either off or on. The off switch is designated by a 0, and the on switch is designated by a 1. Because computers can understand only these on and off switches, the first programmers had to write the program instructions using nothing but combinations of 0s and 1s. Instructions written in 0s and 1s are called **machine language** or **machine code**. The machine languages (each type of machine has its own language) represent the only way to communicate directly with the computer. Figure 1 shows a segment of a program written in a machine language.

```
0100
001101   100000   001101   110001
00101    10001    10000
01110
111001
111001   001   11000   001
11000
0011100
100010   00110
```

Figure 1: A segment of a program written in a machine language

As you can imagine, programming in machine language is very tedious and error-prone and requires highly trained programmers.

Assembly Languages

Slightly more advanced programming languages are called **assembly languages**. Figure 2 shows a segment of a program written in an assembly language.

```
main proc pay
     mov ax, dseg
     mov ax, 0b00h
     add ax, dx
     mov al, bl
     mul bl, ax
     mov bl, 04h
```

Figure 2: A segment of a program written in an assembly language

The assembly languages simplify the programmer's job by allowing the programmer to use mnemonics in place of the 0s and 1s in the program. **Mnemonics** are memory aids—in this case, alphabetic abbreviations for instructions. For example, most assembly languages use the mnemonic ADD to represent an add operation and the mnemonic MUL to represent a multiply operation. The mnemonic MOV is used to move data from one area of the computer's memory to another. Programs written in an assembly language require an **assembler**, which also is a program, to convert the assembly instructions into machine code—the 0s and 1s the computer can understand. Although it is much easier to write programs in assembly language than in machine language, programming in assembly language still is tedious and requires highly trained programmers.

High-Level Languages

High-level languages, which allow the programmer to use instructions that more closely resemble the English language, represent the next major development in programming languages. Programs written in a high-level language require either an interpreter or a compiler to convert the English-like instructions into the 0s and 1s the computer can understand. Like assemblers, both interpreters and compilers are separate programs. An **interpreter** translates the high-level instructions into machine code, line by line, as the program is running, whereas a **compiler** translates the entire program into machine code before running the program. Like their predecessors, the first high-level languages were procedure-oriented.

Procedure-Oriented High-Level Languages

In **procedure-oriented high-level languages**, the emphasis of a program is on *how* to accomplish a task. The programmer must instruct the computer every step of the way, from the start of the task to its completion. The programmer determines and controls the order in which the computer processes the instructions. Examples of procedure-oriented high-level languages include COBOL, BASIC (Beginner's All-Purpose Symbolic Instruction Code), and C.

Figure 3 shows a segment of a program written in BASIC. Notice how closely most of the instructions resemble the English language. Even if you do not know the BASIC language, it is easy to see that the program shown in Figure 3 tells the computer, step by step, *how* to compute and display an employee's net pay.

```
input "Enter name";names$
input "Enter hours worked";hours
input "Enter pay rate";rate
grossPay = hours * rate
federalTax = .2 * grossPay
socSecTax = .07 * grossPay
stateTax = .06 * grossPay
netPay = grossPay - federalTax - socSecTax - stateTax
print names$, netPay
end
```

Figure 3: A program written in BASIC—a procedure-oriented high-level language

In all procedure-oriented programs, the order of the instructions is extremely important. For example, in the program shown in Figure 3, you could not put the instruction to display the net pay before the instruction to calculate the net pay, and then expect the computer to display the correct results. When writing programs in a procedure-oriented language, the programmer must determine not only the proper instructions to give the computer, but the correct sequence of those instructions as well.

Procedure-oriented high-level languages are a vast improvement over machine and assembly languages. Some of the procedure-oriented high-level languages—for example, the BASIC language—do not require a great amount of technical expertise to write simple programs.

The Introduction of Windows

As you know, Windows software provides an easy-to-use **graphical user interface**, referred to as a **GUI**, with which a user can interact. This GUI is common to all applications written for the Windows environment. It is this standard interface that makes Windows applications so popular: once you learn one Windows application, it is very easy to learn another.

Although the standard interface found in all Windows applications makes the user's life much easier, it complicates the programmer's life a great deal. In the beginning, writing programs for the Windows environment was extremely tedious. Programmers found themselves spending countless hours writing instructions to create the buttons, scroll bars, dialog boxes, and menus needed in all Windows applications. Because the programmer has no control over which button the user will click in a Windows application, or which scroll bar the user will employ, the first Windows programmers had to write instructions that could handle any combination of actions the user might take. Tasks that used to take a few lines of program code now needed pages. Because programming Windows applications required a great amount of expertise, it appeared that the beginning of the Windows environment meant the end of the do-it-yourself, nonprofessional programmer. But then a new category of high-level languages emerged—the object-oriented/event-driven high-level programming languages.

Object-Oriented/Event-Driven High-Level Languages

The object-oriented/event-driven high-level languages simplified the task of programming applications for Windows. In **object-oriented/event-driven languages**, the emphasis of a program is on the *objects* included in the user interface (such as scroll bars and buttons) and the *events* (such as scrolling and clicking) that occur when those objects are used.

Unlike the procedure-oriented method of programming, the object-oriented method allows the programmer to use familiar objects to solve problems. The ability to use objects that model things found in the real world makes problem solving much easier. For example, assume that the manager of a flower shop asks you to create a program that keeps track of the shop's daily sales revenue. Thinking in terms of the objects used to represent revenue—cash, checks, credit card receipts, and so on—makes the sales revenue problem easier to solve. Additionally, because each object is viewed as an independent unit, an object can be used in more than one program, usually with little or no modification. A check object used in the sales revenue program, for example, also can be used in a payroll program (which issues checks to employees) and an accounts payable program (which issues checks to creditors). The ability to use an object for more than one purpose saves programming time and money—an advantage that contributes to the popularity of object-oriented programming.

Visual Basic .NET is an object-oriented/event-driven programming language that is easy enough for a nonprogrammer to use, yet sophisticated enough to be used by professional programmers. (Visual C++, C# .NET, Java, and Smalltalk also are object-oriented/event-driven programming languages.) With Visual Basic .NET it takes just a few clicks of the mouse to include standard Windows objects such as buttons, list boxes, scroll bars, and icons in your Windows application. You also can use Visual Basic .NET to create your own objects, such as the check object mentioned in the previous paragraph. Once the objects are created, the programmer then concentrates on writing the specific instructions telling each object how to respond when clicked, double-clicked, scrolled, and so on. For example, Figure 4 shows the Visual Basic .NET instructions that direct an object to close the application when the user clicks the object. (In this case the object is an Exit button.)

```
Private Sub ExitButton_Click(ByVal sender As Object, ⊋
    ByVal e As System.EventArgs) Handles ExitButton.Click
        Me.Close()
End Sub
```

Figure 4: A segment of a program written in Visual Basic .NET—an object-oriented/event-driven language

Before running a sample object-oriented/event-driven application, you learn about the terminology used by object-oriented programmers.

OOP Terminology

Although you may have either heard or read that object-oriented languages are difficult to learn, do not be intimidated. Admittedly, creating object-oriented programs does take some practice. However, you already are familiar with many of the concepts upon which object-oriented programming is based. Much of the anxiety of object-oriented programming stems from the terminology used when discussing it. Many of the terms are unfamiliar, because they typically are not used in everyday conversations. This section will help to familiarize you with the terms used in discussions about object-oriented programming. Do not be concerned if you do not understand everything right away; you will see further explanations and examples of these terms throughout this book.

When discussing object-oriented programs, you will hear programmers use the terms OOP (pronounced like *loop*) and OOD (pronounced like *mood*). **OOP** is an acronym for object-oriented programming and simply means that you are using an object-oriented language to create a program that contains one or more objects. OOD, on the other hand, is an acronym for object-oriented design. Like top-down design, which is used to plan procedure-oriented programs, **OOD** also is a design methodology, but it is used to plan object-oriented programs. Unlike top-down design, which breaks up a problem into one or more tasks, OOD divides a problem into one or more objects.

An **object** is anything that can be seen, touched, or used; in other words, an object is nearly any *thing*. The objects used in an object-oriented program can take on many different forms. The menus, radio buttons, and buttons included in most Windows programs are objects. An object also can represent something encountered in real life—such as a wristwatch, a car, a credit card receipt, and an employee.

Every object has attributes and behaviors. The **attributes** are the characteristics that describe the object. When you tell someone that your wristwatch is a Farentino Model 35A, you are describing the watch (an object) in terms of some of its attributes—in this case, its maker and model number. A watch also has many other attributes, such as a crown, dial, hour hand, minute hand, and movement.

An object's **behaviors**, on the other hand, are the operations (actions) that the object is capable of performing. A watch, for example, can keep track of the time. Some watches also can keep track of the date. Still others can illuminate their dials when a button on the watch is pushed.

You also will hear the term "class" in OOP discussions. A **class** is a pattern or blueprint used to create an object. Every object used in an object-oriented program comes from a class. A class contains—or, in OOP terms, it **encapsulates**—all of the attributes and behaviors that describe the object the class creates. The blueprint for the Farentino Model 35A watch, for example, encapsulates all of the watch's attributes and behaviors. Objects created from a class are referred to as **instances** of the class, and are said to be "instantiated" from the class. All Farentino Model 35A watches are instances of the Farentino Model 35A class.

"Abstraction" is another term used in OOP discussions. **Abstraction** refers to the hiding of the internal details of an object from the user; hiding the internal details helps prevent the user from making inadvertent changes to the object. The internal mechanism of a watch, for example, is enclosed (hidden) in a case to protect the mechanism from damage. Attributes and behaviors that are not **hidden** are said to be **exposed** to the user. Exposed on a Farentino Model 35A watch are the crown used to set the hour and minute hands, and the button used to illuminate the dial. The idea behind abstraction is to expose to the user only those attributes and behaviors that are necessary to use the object, and to hide everything else.

Another OOP term, **inheritance**, refers to the fact that you can create one class from another class. The new class, called the **derived class**, inherits the attributes and behaviors of the original class, called the **base class**. For example, the Farentino company might create a blueprint of the Model 35B watch from the blueprint of the Model 35A watch. The Model 35B blueprint (the derived class) will inherit all of the attributes and behaviors of the Model 35A blueprint (the base class), but it then can be modified to include an additional feature, such as an alarm.

Finally, you also will hear the term "polymorphism" in OOP discussions. **Polymorphism** is the object-oriented feature that allows the same instruction to be carried out differently depending on the object. For example, you open a door, but you also open an envelope, a jar, and your eyes. You can set the time, date, and alarm on a Farentino watch. Although the meaning of the verbs "open" and "set" are different in each case, you can understand each instruction because the combination of the verb and the object makes the instruction clear. Figure 5 uses the wristwatch example to illustrate most of the OOP terms discussed in this section.

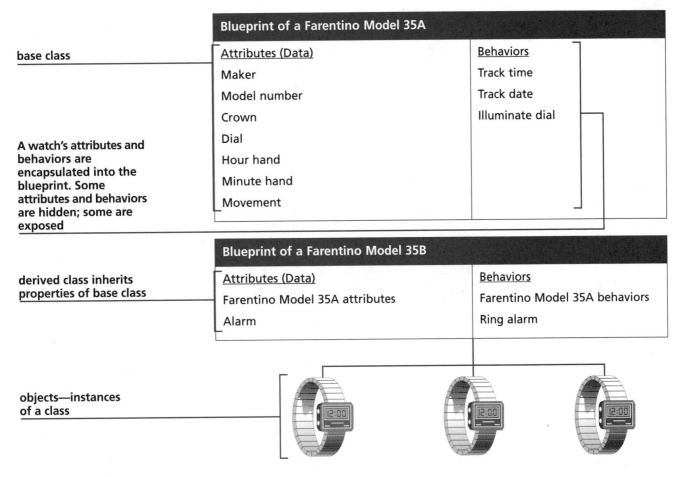

base class

A watch's attributes and behaviors are encapsulated into the blueprint. Some attributes and behaviors are hidden; some are exposed

derived class inherits properties of base class

objects—instances of a class

Figure 5: Illustration of OOP terms

In the next section, you run a Visual Basic .NET application that gives you a quick look at some of the objects you learn how to create in the following tutorials.

A Visual Basic .NET Demonstration

The Visual Basic .NET application you are about to run shows you only some of the objects you learn how to create in the tutorials. For now, it is not important for you to understand how these objects were created or why the objects perform the way they do. Those questions will be answered in the tutorials.

To run the Visual Basic .NET application:

1   Click the **Start** button on the Windows taskbar, and then click **Run** on the Start menu to open the Run dialog box. Click the **Browse** button in the Run dialog box. The Browse dialog box opens.

2   Locate and then open the VBNET\Overview folder on your computer's hard disk. Click **Month** (Month.exe) in the list of filenames, and then click the **Open** button. The Browse dialog box closes and the Run dialog box appears again. Click the **OK** button. After a few moments, Visual Basic .NET displays the Monthly Payment Calculator application shown in Figure 6.

menu

radio buttons

text box

list box

labels

button

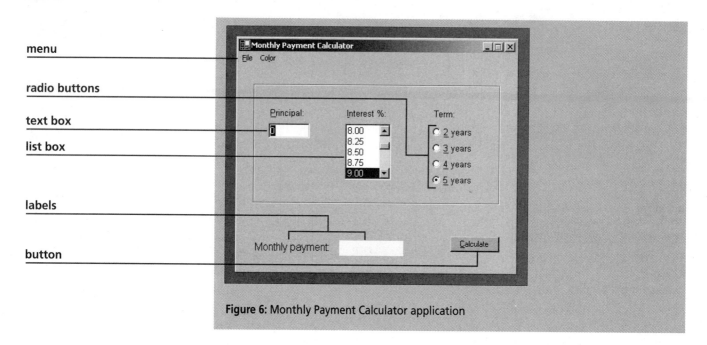

Figure 6: Monthly Payment Calculator application

Figure 6 identifies some of the different objects appearing in the application's interface. Notice that the interface contains a text box, a list box, a button, radio buttons, labels, and a menu. You can use this application to calculate the monthly payment for a car loan. For example, determine the monthly payment for a $30,000 loan at 8% interest for five years.

To compute the monthly car payment:

1 Type **30000** in the Principal text box, and then click **8.00** in the Interest % list box. The radio button corresponding to the five-year term is already selected, so you just need to click the **Calculate** button to compute the monthly payment. The Monthly Payment Calculator application indicates that your monthly payment would be $608.29, as shown in Figure 7.

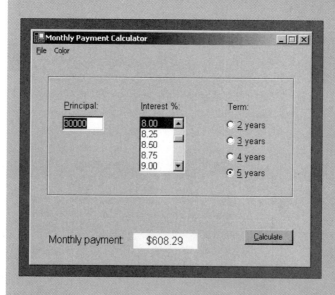

Figure 7: Computed monthly payment

Now determine what your monthly payment would be if you borrowed $10,000 at 7.25% interest for four years.

2   Type **10000** in the Principal text box.

3   Scroll up the Interest % list box until the 7.25 rate is visible, and then click **7.25**.

4   Click the **4 years** radio button, and then click the **Calculate** button to compute the monthly payment. The Monthly Payment Calculator application computes and displays the monthly payment of $240.62.

Notice that the application's menu bar has two menus: File and Color. View the options on both menus.

To view the options on the Color and File menus:

1   Click **Color** on the menu bar. The Color menu opens and displays two options: Background and Information Box.

You use the Background option to change the background color of the application's interface.

2   Click **Background**. The Color dialog box opens. Click a color of your choice, and then click the **OK** button. The color of the application's background changes accordingly.

If you don't like the current color, you can use the Background option on the Color menu to select a different color. Now see what the Information Box option on the Color menu does.

3   Click **Color** on the menu bar, and then click **Information Box**. The Color dialog box opens. Click a color of your choice, and then click the **OK** button. The color of the information box changes accordingly. (The information box is the box in which you enter the principal, interest, and term information.)

If you don't like the current color, you can use the Information Box option on the Color menu to select a different color. Now view the option on the File menu.

4   Click **File** on the menu bar. The File menu opens and shows one option: Exit. You can use the Exit option to end the Monthly Payment Calculator application.

5   Click **Exit** to close the Monthly Payment Calculator application.

As you can see, programming languages have come a long way since the first machine languages. This brief history and demonstration should give you a better appreciation for the Visual Basic .NET programming language.

Using the Tutorials Effectively

The tutorials in this book will help you learn about Microsoft Visual Basic .NET, the newest version of the Visual Basic programming language. The tutorials are designed to be used at your computer. Begin by reading the text that explains the concepts. Then when you come to the numbered steps, follow the steps on your computer. Read each step carefully and completely before you try it.

As you work, compare your screen with the figures to verify your results. Don't worry if your screen display differs slightly from the figures. The important parts of the screen display are labeled in each figure. Just be sure you have these parts on your screen. Important note: Many of the figures in this book reflect how your screen will look if you are using a Microsoft Windows 2000 system. Your screen will look similar to these figures if you are using a Microsoft Windows XP system.

Do not worry about making mistakes; that's part of the learning process. Help? notes identify common problems and explain how to get back on track. You should complete the steps in the Help? notes only if you are having the problem described. Tip notes provide additional information about a procedure—for example, an alternative method of performing the procedure.

Each tutorial is divided into three lessons. You might want to take a break between lessons. Following each lesson is a Summary section that lists the important elements of the lesson. After the Summary section are questions and exercises designed to review and reinforce that lesson's concepts. You should complete all of the end-of-lesson questions and exercises before going on to the next lesson. You cannot learn Visual Basic .NET without a lot of practice, and future tutorials assume that you have mastered the information found in the previous tutorials. Some of the end-of-lesson exercises are Discovery exercises, which allow you to both "discover" the solutions to problems on your own and experiment with material that is not covered in the tutorial.

In each tutorial you will find one or more Debugging exercises. In programming, the term **debugging** refers to the process of finding and fixing any errors in a program. Debugging exercises provide debugging tips and allow you to practice debugging applications.

Throughout the book you will find GUI (Graphical User Interface) design tips. These tips contain guidelines and recommendations for designing applications. You should follow these guidelines and recommendations so that your applications follow the Windows standard.

Before you begin the tutorials, you should know how to use Microsoft Windows 2000 or Microsoft Windows XP. This book assumes you have learned basic Windows-navigation and file-management skills from Course Technology's *New Perspectives on Microsoft Windows 2000 Brief*, *New Perspectives on Microsoft Windows XP Brief*, or an equivalent book.

QUESTIONS

1. The set of directions given to a computer is called _____.
   a. computerese
   b. commands
   c. instructions
   d. a program
   e. rules

2. Instructions written in 0s and 1s are called _____.
   a. assembly language
   b. booleans
   c. computerese
   d. machine code
   e. mnemonics

3. _____ languages allow the programmer to use mnemonics, which are alphabetic abbreviations for instructions.
   a. Assembly
   b. High-level
   c. Machine
   d. Object
   e. Procedure

4. _____ languages allow the programmer to use instructions that more closely resemble the English language.
   a. Assembly
   b. High-level
   c. Machine
   d. Object
   e. Procedure

5. A(n) _____ translates high-level instructions into machine code, line by line, as the program is running.
   a. assembler
   b. compiler
   c. interpreter
   d. program
   e. translator

6. A(n) _____ translates the entire high-level program into machine code before running the program.
   a. assembler
   b. compiler
   c. interpreter
   d. program
   e. translator

7. A(n) _____ converts assembly instructions into machine code.
   a. assembler
   b. compiler
   c. interpreter
   d. program
   e. translator

8. Visual Basic .NET is a(n) _____ language.
   a. assembler
   b. machine
   c. mnemonic
   d. object-oriented/event-driven
   e. procedure-oriented

9. In procedure-oriented languages, the emphasis of a program is on *how* to accomplish a task.
   a. True
   b. False

10. In object-oriented languages, the emphasis of a program is on the objects included in the user interface and the events that occur on those objects.
    a. True
    b. False

11. A(n) _____ is a pattern or blueprint.
    a. attribute
    b. behavior
    c. class
    d. instance
    e. object

12. Which of the following is not an attribute that can be used to describe a human being?
    a. brown eyes
    b. female
    c. red hair
    d. talk
    e. thin

13. The object that you create from a class is called a(n) _____.
    a. abstraction
    b. attribute
    c. instance
    d. procedure
    e. subclass

14. In the context of OOP, the combining of an object's attributes and behaviors into one package is called _____.
    a. abstraction
    b. combining
    c. encapsulation
    d. exposition
    e. inheritance

15. In the context of OOP, the hiding of the internal details of an object from the user is called _____.
    a. abstraction
    b. combining
    c. encapsulation
    d. exposition
    e. inheritance

16. Alcon Toys manufactures several versions of a basic doll. Assume that the basic doll is called Model A and the versions are called Models B, C, and D. In the context of OOP, the Model A doll is called the _____ class; the other dolls are called the _____ class.
    a. base, derived
    b. base, inherited
    c. derived, base
    d. exposed, hidden
    e. inherited, derived

17. In the context of OOP, _____ refers to the fact that you can create one class from another class.
    a. abstraction
    b. combining
    c. encapsulation
    d. exposition
    e. inheritance

18. Use Figure 8 to answer the following questions

Dog class	
Head	Eat
Body	Run
Legs	Play
Heart	Walk
Lungs	Bark

Figure 8

    a. What are the attributes (data or properties) associated with a dog class?

    b. What are the behaviors associated with a dog class?

    c. How many instances (objects) of the dog class are shown in Figure 8?

An Introduction to Visual Basic .NET

Creating a Copyright Screen

case ▶ Interlocking Software Company, a small firm specializing in custom programs, hires you as a programmer trainee. In that capacity, you learn to write applications using Visual Basic .NET, Microsoft's newest version of the Visual Basic programming language.

On your second day of work, Chris Statton, the senior programmer at Interlocking Software, assigns you your first task: create a copyright screen. The copyright screen will serve as a splash screen for each custom application created by Interlocking Software. A **splash screen** is the first image that appears when an application is run. It is used to introduce the application and to hold the user's attention while the application is being read into the computer's memory. The copyright screen you create will identify the application's author and copyright year and include the Interlocking Software Company logo. Although this first task is small, creating the copyright screen will give you an opportunity to learn the fundamentals of Visual Basic .NET without having to worry about the design issues and programming concepts necessary for larger applications.

Previewing the Copyright Screen

Before starting the first lesson, you preview a completed copyright screen. The copyright screen is stored in the VBNET\Tut01\Copy.exe file on your computer's hard disk.

To preview a completed copyright screen:

1   Click the **Start** button on the taskbar, and then click **Run** on the Start menu. When the Run dialog box opens, click the **Browse** button. The Browse dialog box opens. Locate and then open the **VBNET\Tut01** folder.

2   Click **Copy** (Copy.exe) in the list of filenames. (Depending on how Windows is set up on your computer, you may see the .exe extension on the filename. If you do, click the Copy.exe filename.) Click the **Open** button. The Browse dialog box closes and the Run dialog box appears again.

3   Click the **OK** button in the Run dialog box. The copyright screen appears. The author's name and the copyright year appear on the copyright screen, as shown in Figure 1-1. Shortly thereafter, the copyright screen closes.

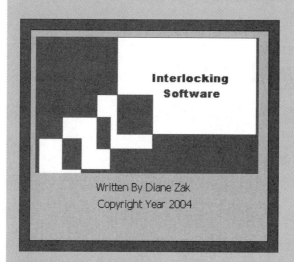

Figure 1-1: Copyright screen

In this tutorial, you learn how to create your own copyright screen.

Tutorial 1 is designed to help you get comfortable with the Visual Studio .NET integrated development environment. You also learn about the Visual Basic .NET language. Remember that each tutorial contains three lessons. You should complete a lesson in full and do the end-of-lesson questions and exercises before moving on to the next lesson.

After completing this lesson, you will be able to:

- Start and customize Visual Studio .NET
- Create a Visual Studio .NET solution
- Add a Visual Basic .NET project to a solution
- Set the properties of an object
- Save a solution, project, and form
- Close a solution
- Open an existing solution

Creating a Windows-Based Application in Visual Basic .NET

Starting and Customizing Visual Studio .NET

Before you can use Visual Basic .NET to create your copyright screen, you must start Visual Studio .NET. Visual Studio .NET is Microsoft's newest **integrated development environment (IDE)** and includes programming languages such as Visual Basic .NET, C++ .NET, and C# .NET. You can use the languages available in Visual Studio .NET to create Windows-based or Web-based applications. A **Windows-based application** has a Windows user interface and runs on a desktop computer. A **user interface** is what you see and interact with when using an application. Graphics programs, data-entry systems, and games are examples of Windows-based applications. A **Web-based application**, on the other hand, has a Web user interface and runs on a server. You access a Web-based application using your computer's browser. Examples of Web-based applications include e-commerce applications available on the Internet and employee handbook applications accessible on a company's intranet.

Microsoft licenses the Visual Studio .NET IDE to other vendors, who also can add languages to the IDE.

You also can create console applications in Visual Studio .NET; however, this type of application is not covered in this book. Console applications do not have a graphical user interface and are run from the DOS command line.

To start Visual Studio .NET:

1   Click the **Start** button on the Windows taskbar to open the Start menu.

2   Point to **Programs**, then point to **Microsoft Visual Studio .NET**, and then click **Microsoft Visual Studio .NET**. The Microsoft Visual Studio .NET copyright screen appears momentarily, and then the Microsoft Development Environment window opens.

   HELP? If you are using Windows XP, point to All Programs.

3   If necessary, maximize the Microsoft Development Environment window.

4   If necessary, click the **My Profile** link on the Start Page. The My Profile pane appears in the Start Page window, as shown in Figure 1-2. (Your screen might not look identical to Figure 1-2, but it should show the Start Page.)

Start Page window

links

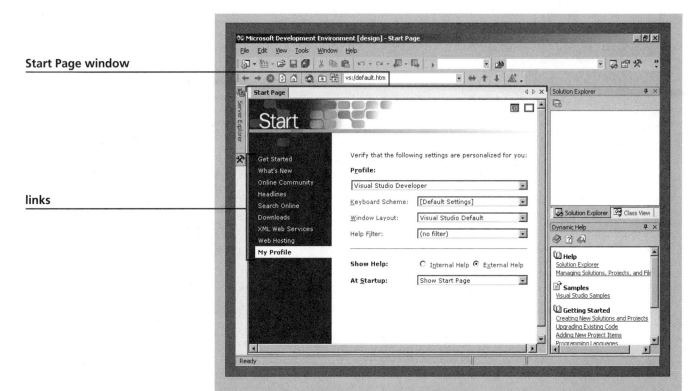

Figure 1-2: Microsoft Development Environment window

HELP? If the Start Page window is not open, click Help on the menu bar, and then click Show Start Page.

The My Profile pane allows you to customize various program settings in the IDE, such as the keyboard scheme, window layout, and help filter. A collection of customized preferences is called a **profile**. Visual Studio .NET provides a set of predefined profiles for your convenience. The default profile is Visual Studio Developer, which is the profile that the steps and figures in this book assume you are using.

5 If necessary, click the **Profile** list arrow, and then click **Visual Studio Developer** in the list.

6 If necessary, change the Keyboard Scheme, Window Layout, Help Filter, and At Startup list box selections on your screen to match those shown in Figure 1-2.

7 If necessary, click the **External Help** radio button to select it. The message "Changes will not take effect until Visual Studio is restarted" appears in a dialog box. Click the OK button to close the dialog box.

8 Click **Tools** on the menu bar, and then click **Options**. The Options dialog box opens. If necessary, click the **Environment** folder to open it, and then click **General**.

9 If necessary, click the **Close button affects active tab only** and **Auto Hide button affects active tab only** check boxes to select each one. See Figure 1-3.

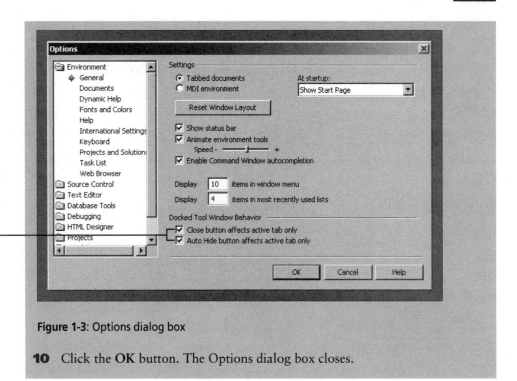

Figure 1-3: Options dialog box

10 Click the **OK** button. The Options dialog box closes.

select these check boxes

> **tip**
> • • • • • • • • • • • • • • • •
>
> ► You can use the Reset Window Layout button in the Options dialog box to return the layout of the windows in the IDE to the default layout that was provided during the initial setup of Visual Studio .NET.

In addition to the My Profile link, the Start Page window contains eight other links. Each link displays information in a pane in the Start Page window. Figure 1-4 describes the purpose of each link.

Link	Purpose
Get Started	create new projects and open existing projects
What's New	access information about the new features in Visual Studio.NET and check for Visual Studio.NET updates
Online Community	contact fellow developers online
Headlines	view links to the latest news from the MSDN Online Library, including information on seminars, trade shows, and conferences, as well as training opportunities offered by Microsoft
Search Online	search the MSDN Online Library
Downloads	access the latest product updates and sample code available for download
XML Web Services	search for XML Web Services to include in your applications, and publish your own XML Web services
Web Hosting	post Web applications, for a fee, on servers provided by third-party Internet Service Providers
My Profile	customize various program settings in the IDE

Figure 1-4: Purpose of the links included on the Start Page

Notice that the What's New, Headlines, Search Online, and Downloads links allow you to access the most current information about Visual Studio .NET. You can use the Online Community link to contact fellow developers online, and the

Web Hosting link to post Web applications on a server. The XML Web Services link allows you to search for and publish XML Web services. The My Profile link allows you to customize the IDE, and the Get Started link provides options for creating and opening projects. View the pane displayed by the Get Started link.

To view the pane displayed by the Get Started link:

1   Click the **Get Started** link on the Start Page. The Get Started pane appears in the Start Page window, as shown in Figure 1-5. (Do not be concerned if your Get Started pane shows project names and dates.)

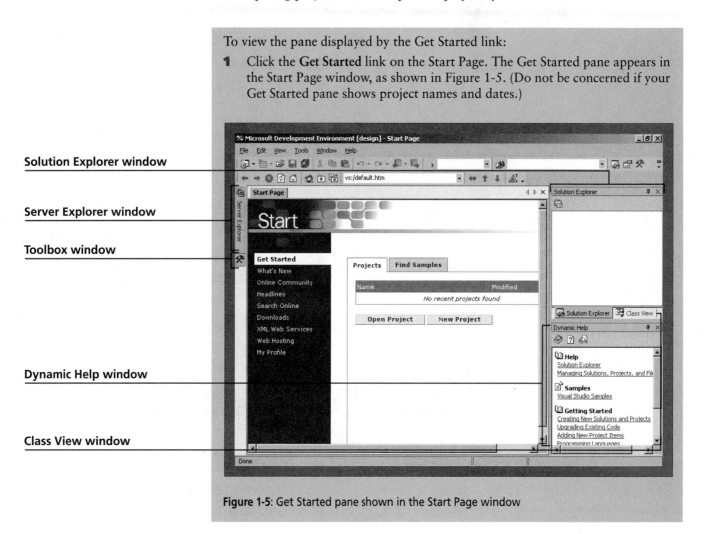

Solution Explorer window

Server Explorer window

Toolbox window

Dynamic Help window

Class View window

Figure 1-5: Get Started pane shown in the Start Page window

As Figure 1-5 indicates, the IDE contains five windows in addition to the Start Page window: Server Explorer, Toolbox, Solution Explorer, Class View, and Dynamic Help. Figure 1-6 briefly describes the purpose of each window.

Window	Purpose
Class View	display the classes, methods, and properties included in a solution
Dynamic Help	display links to context-sensitive help
Server Explorer	display data connections and servers
Solution Explorer	display the names of projects and files included in a solution
Start Page	display the panes associated with the Start Page links
Toolbox	display items that you can use when creating a project

Figure 1-6: Purpose of the windows included in the IDE

You learn more about the Solution Explorer and Dynamic Help windows later in this lesson, and about the Toolbox window in Lesson B. The Server Explorer and Class View windows are not covered in this book.

Recall that your task in this tutorial is to create a simple application: a copyright screen.

Creating the Copyright Screen Application

You create an application by first creating a blank Visual Studio .NET solution, and then you add one or more projects to the solution. A **solution** is simply a container that stores the projects and files for an entire application. A **project** also is a container, but it stores files associated with only a specific piece of the application. Although the idea of solutions, projects, and files may sound confusing, the concept of placing things in containers is nothing new to you. Think of a solution as being similar to a drawer in a filing cabinet. A project then is similar to a file folder that you store in the drawer, and a file is similar to a document that you store in the file folder. You can place many file folders in a filing cabinet drawer, just as you can place many projects in a solution. You also can store many documents in a file folder, similar to the way you can store many files in a project. Figure 1-7 illustrates this analogy.

file

project

solution

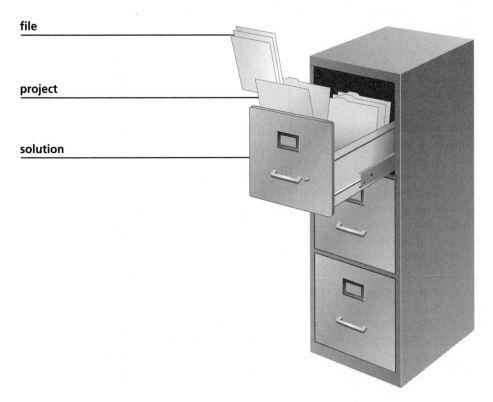

Figure 1-7: Illustration of a solution, project, and file

You can create a blank Visual Studio .NET solution by clicking File on the menu bar, pointing to New, and then clicking Blank Solution. You also can create a blank solution by clicking the New Blank Solution button 🖼️ on the Standard toolbar.

tip
• • • • • • • • • • • • • • • • • •
▶ If the New Blank Solution button 🔲 ▾ is not displayed on the Standard toolbar, click the list arrow on the New Project button 🔲 ▾, which also is located on the Standard toolbar, and then click New Blank Solution in the list.

To create a blank Visual Studio .NET solution:

1   Click **File** on the menu bar, point to **New**, and then click **Blank Solution**. The New Project dialog box opens with Visual Studio Solutions selected in the Project Types list box, and Blank Solution selected in the Templates list box. The message located below the Project Types list box indicates that the Blank Solution template creates an empty solution containing no projects.

A **template** is simply a pattern that Visual Studio .NET uses to create solutions and projects. Each template listed in the Templates list box includes a set of standard folders and files appropriate for the solution or project. The Blank Solution template, for example, contains one folder and two files. The folder and files are automatically created on your computer's hard disk when you click the OK button in the New Project dialog box.

2   Change the name entered in the Name text box to **Copyright Solution**. If necessary, use the Browse button, which appears to the right of the Location text box, to open the **VBNET\Tut01** folder on your computer's hard disk. See Figure 1-8.

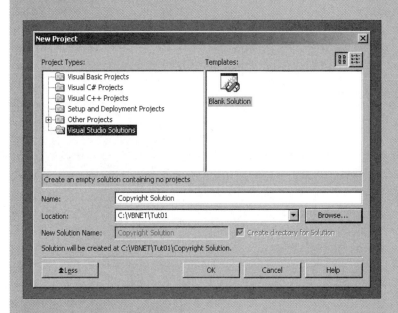

Figure 1-8: New Project dialog box used to create a blank solution

HELP?   If the Less button is not displayed, click the More button.

Notice that the message "Solution will be created at C:\VBNET\Tut01\Copyright Solution." appears above the Less button in the dialog box.

3   Click the **OK** button to close the New Project dialog box. Visual Studio .NET creates a blank solution on your computer's hard disk. It also records in the Solution Explorer window the solution's name (Copyright Solution) and the number of projects contained in the solution (0 projects). See Figure 1-9.

Figure 1-9: Solution Explorer window showing the name of a blank solution

HELP? You might need to widen the Solution Explorer window to view its contents. To do so, position your mouse pointer ⬉ on the window's left border until ⬉ becomes ╢╟, then drag the border to the left.

When a solution's name appears in the Solution Explorer window, it indicates that the solution is open and ready for you to add information to it. (You also can delete information from a solution.)

To view the names of hidden files, start Windows Explorer, then click Tools on the menu bar, and then click Folder Options. When the Folder Options dialog box appears, click the View tab, then click the Show hidden files and folders radio button, and then click the OK button.

Recall that when you use the Blank Solution template to create a solution, Visual Studio .NET automatically creates one folder and two files on your computer's hard disk. The folder has the same name as the solution; in this case, the folder is named Copyright Solution. The two files, which are stored in the folder, also bear the solution's name. However, one file has .sln (which stands for "solution") as its filename extension, and the other has .suo (which stands for "solution user options"). The Copyright Solution.sln file keeps track of the projects and files included in the solution. The Copyright Solution.suo file, which is a hidden file, records the options associated with your solution so that each time you open the solution, it includes any customizations you made.

After you create a blank solution, you then add one or more projects to it. The number of projects in a solution depends on the application you are creating. Most simple applications require one project only, while complex applications usually involve several projects. The copyright screen you are working on is a simple application and requires just one project, which you will create using Visual Basic .NET.

You can add a new project to the current solution by clicking File on the menu bar, pointing to Add Project, and then clicking New Project. You also can right-click the solution's name in the Solution Explorer window, point to Add, and then click New Project. Additionally, you can click either the New Project button on the Get Started pane in the Start Page window, or the New Project button 🗗 on the Standard toolbar.

If the New Project button is not displayed on the Standard toolbar, click the list arrow on the New Blank Solution button, which also is located on the Standard toolbar, and then click New Project in the list.

To add a new Visual Basic .NET project to the current solution:

1   Right-click **Solution 'Copyright Solution' (0 projects)** in the Solution Explorer window. Point to **Add** and then click **New Project**. The Add New Project dialog box opens.

The Project Types list box lists the various types of projects you can add to a solution.

2   If necessary, click **Visual Basic Projects** in the Project Types list box.

The Templates list box lists the project templates available in Visual Basic .NET.

3   If necessary, click **Windows Application** in the Templates list box. This is the appropriate template to use for the copyright screen application, because you want the application to have a Windows user interface.

4   Change the name in the Name text box to **Copyright Project**.

5   Verify that the Location text box contains the location of the Copyright Solution folder. The completed Add New Project dialog box is shown in Figure 1-10. Notice that the message "Project will be created at C:\VBNET\Tut01\Copyright Solution\Copyright Project." appears below the Location text box in the dialog box.

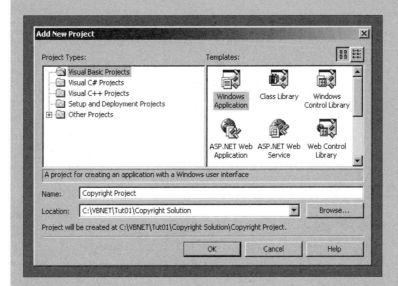

Figure 1-10: Completed Add New Project dialog box

As you learned earlier, a template contains a set of standard folders and files. The folders and files included in the Windows Application template are automatically created on your computer's hard disk when you click the OK button in the Add New Project dialog box.

6   Click the **OK** button to close the Add New Project dialog box. Visual Studio .NET adds a new Visual Basic .NET Windows Application project to the current solution. It also records the project's name (Copyright Project), as well as other information pertaining to the project, in the Solution Explorer window. See Figure 1-11.

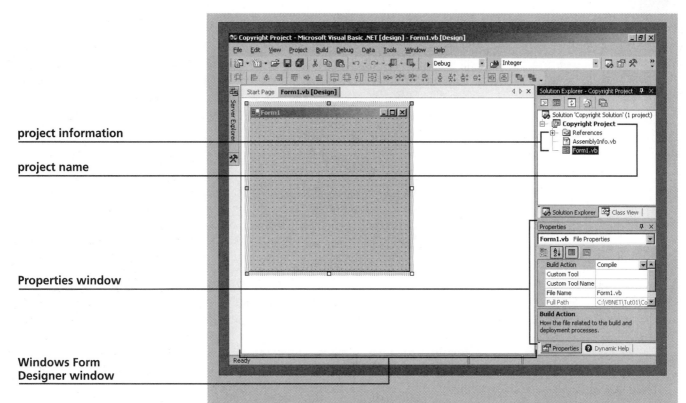

project information

project name

Properties window

Windows Form Designer window

Figure 1-11: New Visual Basic .NET project added to the solution

HELP? If the Windows Form Designer window does not appear in the IDE, click Form1.vb in the Solution Explorer window, if necessary. Then click View on the menu bar, and then click Designer.

HELP? If the Output window appears in the IDE, click the Close button ☒ on its title bar.

HELP? If the Properties window does not appear in the IDE, click View on the menu bar, and then click Properties Window.

HELP? If a plus box ⊞ appears next to the project name in the Solution Explorer window, click the plus box .

HELP? If a minus box ⊟ appears next to the References folder in the Solution Explorer window, click the minus box.

HELP? If the Solution Explorer window displays more folders and files than are shown in Figure 1-11, click the Show All Files button 🗐 on the Solution Explorer window's toolbar.

HELP? If a Misc row appears in the Properties window, click the Alphabetic button 🔠 on the Properties window's toolbar.

Notice that, in addition to the six windows discussed earlier, two new windows appear in the development environment: the Windows Form Designer window and the Properties window. Having eight windows open at the same time can be confusing, especially when you are first learning the IDE. In most cases, you will find it easier to work in the IDE if you either close or auto-hide the windows you are not currently using. In the next section, you learn how to manage the windows in the IDE.

Managing the Windows in the IDE

The easiest way to close an open window in the IDE is to click the Close button ⊠ on the window's title bar. You also can close a window by right-clicking its title bar and then clicking Hide on the context menu; or you can click the window's title bar, then click Window on the menu bar, and then click Hide on the menu. In most cases, the View menu provides an appropriate option for opening a closed window. To open the Toolbox window, for instance, you click View on the menu bar, and then click Toolbox on the menu. The options for opening the Start Page and Dynamic Help windows, however, are located on the Help menu rather than on the View menu.

You can use the Auto Hide button 📌 on a window's title bar to auto-hide a window. You also can auto-hide a window by right-clicking its title bar, and then clicking Auto Hide on the context menu; or you can click the window's title bar, then click Window on the menu bar, and then click Auto Hide on the menu. When you **auto-hide** a window and then move the mouse pointer away from the window, the window is minimized and appears as a tab on the edge of the IDE. Additionally, the 📌 button on the window's title bar is replaced by the 📍 button, which indicates that the window is auto-hidden. The Server Explorer and Toolbox windows shown in Figure 1-11 are examples of auto-hidden windows.

To temporarily display a window that has been auto-hidden, you simply place your mouse pointer on the window's tab; doing so slides the window into view. You can permanently display an auto-hidden window by clicking the 📍 button on the window's title bar. When you click the 📍 button, the button is replaced by the 📌 button, which indicates that the window is not auto-hidden.

In the next set of steps, you close the Server Explorer, Start Page, Class View, and Dynamic Help windows, because you will not need these windows to create the copyright screen. You also practice auto-hiding and displaying the Solution Explorer window.

To close some of the windows in the IDE, and then auto-hide and display the Solution Explorer window:

1. Place your mouse pointer on the **Server Explorer** tab. (The Server Explorer tab is usually located on the left edge of the IDE.) When the Server Explorer window slides into view, which may take several moments, click the **Close** button ⊠ on its title bar.

Now close the Start Page and Class View windows.

2. Click the **Start Page** tab to make the Start Page window the active window, then click the **Close** button ⊠ on its title bar.

3. Click the **Class View** tab to make the Class View window the active window, then click the **Close** button ⊠ on its title bar.

You close the Dynamic Help window next. The **Dynamic Help window** is a context-sensitive system. As you are working in the IDE, the window is constantly being updated with links pertaining to whatever is appropriate for what you are doing at the time. An advantage of keeping the Dynamic Help window open is that it allows you to conveniently access help as you are working in the IDE. A disadvantage is that an open Dynamic Help window consumes computer memory and processor time, both of which are required to keep the window updated.

4 Click the **Dynamic Help** tab to make the Dynamic Help window the active window, then click the **Close** button ⊠ on its title bar.

Next, auto-hide the Solution Explorer window.

5 Click the **Auto Hide** button ⊞ on the Solution Explorer window's title bar, then move the mouse pointer away from the window. The Solution Explorer window is minimized and appears as a tab on the right edge of the IDE.

> **HELP?** If the Solution Explorer window remains on the screen when you move your mouse pointer away from the window, click another window's title bar.

Now temporarily display the Solution Explorer window.

6 Place your mouse pointer on the **Solution Explorer** tab. The Solution Explorer window slides into view.

7 Move your mouse pointer away from the Solution Explorer window. The window is minimized and appears as a tab again.

Next, remove the Auto Hide feature from the Solution Explorer window; this will permanently display the window on the screen.

8 Place your mouse pointer on the **Solution Explorer** tab. When the Solution Explorer window slides into view, click the **Auto Hide** button ⊞ on its title bar. The ⊞ button is replaced by the ⊞ button.

9 Move your mouse pointer away from the Solution Explorer window. The window remains displayed on the screen. Figure 1-12 shows the current status of the windows in the development environment.

Toolbox window (auto-hidden)

Solution Explorer window

Properties window

Windows Form Designer window

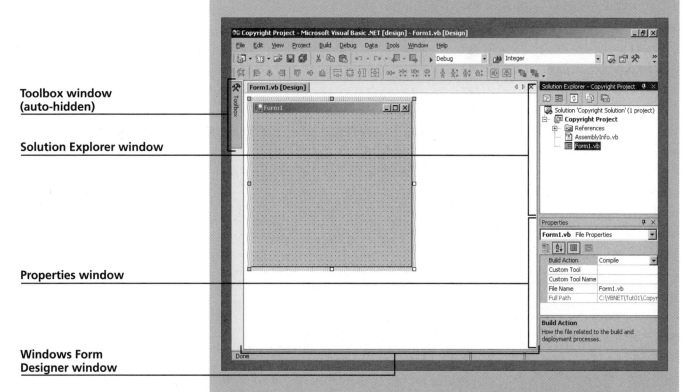

Figure 1-12: Current status of the windows in the development environment

Notice that only four (rather than eight) windows are open: the Toolbox window (which is auto-hidden), the Windows Form Designer window, the Solution Explorer window, and the Properties window.

In the next several sections, you take a closer look at the Windows Form Designer, Solution Explorer, and Properties windows. (Recall that the Toolbox window is covered in Lesson B.)

The Windows Form Designer Window

Figure 1-13 shows the **Windows Form Designer window**, where you create (or design) the user interface for your project. Recall that a user interface is what you see and interact with when using an application.

name of the disk file
that contains the
Windows Form object

title bar

Windows Form object

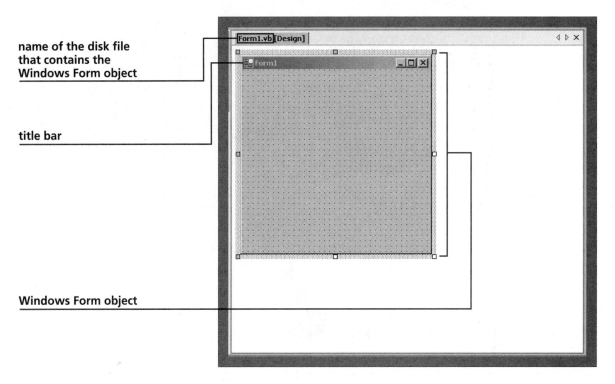

Figure 1-13: Windows Form Designer window

Currently, only a Windows Form object appears in the designer window. A **Windows Form object** is the foundation for the user interface in a Windows-based application. You create the user interface by adding other objects, such as buttons and text boxes, to the form. Dots are displayed in the form to assist you in aligning the objects. The dots will not be visible when you run the application.

Notice that a title bar appears at the top of the Windows Form object. The title bar contains a default caption—in this case, Form1—as well as Minimize ▬, Maximize ☐, and Close ☒ buttons.

At the top of the designer window is a tab labeled Form1.vb [Design]. [Design] simply identifies the window as the designer window. Form1.vb is the name of the file (on your computer's hard disk) that contains the Visual Basic .NET code required to create a Windows Form object. The Form1.vb filename also appears in the Solution Explorer window and in the Properties window.

Next, take a closer look at the Solution Explorer window.

tip

In the context of OOP, the Windows Form object is an instance of the Windows Form class. Recall that a class is a pattern or blueprint that is used to create, or instantiate, an object.

The Solution Explorer Window

The **Solution Explorer window** displays a list of the projects contained in the current solution, and the items contained in each project. Figure 1-14 shows the Solution Explorer window for the Copyright Solution.

Figure 1-14: Solution Explorer window

The Solution Explorer window indicates that the Copyright Solution contains one project named Copyright Project. Within the Copyright Project is a References folder, which contains information needed by the project, and two files named AssemblyInfo.vb and Form1.vb. View the contents of the References folder.

To view the contents of the References folder:

1 Click the **plus box** ⊞ next to the References folder. The contents of the References folder appear. See Figure 1-15.

Figure 1-15: Contents of the References folder

The References folder contains **references**, which are simply addresses of memory cells within the computer's internal memory; each reference points to a namespace. You can picture a namespace as a block of internal memory cells. A **namespace** contains the code that defines a group of related classes. The System.Windows.Forms namespace, for instance, contains the definition of the Windows Form class, which is the class used to create—or, using OOP terminology, instantiate—a Windows Form object. When a project contains a reference to a namespace, it can use the classes that are defined in the namespace to create objects.

Recall that the Copyright Project also contains two files named AssemblyInfo.vb and Form1.vb; both files are source files. A **source file** is a file that contains program code. The AssemblyInfo.vb source file, for example, stores the code needed to **deploy** (install and configure) the project. Currently, the Form1.vb file contains the code that creates (instantiates) the Windows Form object displayed in the designer window. As you add objects (such as buttons and text boxes) to the form, the code to instantiate those objects is automatically added to the Form1.vb file. The Form1.vb file also will contain the code you enter in the Code editor; you learn how to use the Code editor in Lesson B.

In addition to the References folder and two source files, the Copyright Project contains other folders and files as well. Currently, the names of the additional folders and files are not displayed in the Solution Explorer window. You can display the names using the Show All Files button 🖻 on the Solution Explorer window's toolbar.

To view the names of the additional folders and files contained in the current project:

1   Click the **Auto Hide** button 🖈 on the Properties window's title bar, then move the mouse pointer away from the window. Auto-hiding the Properties window allows you to view more of the Solution Explorer window.

2   Click the **Show All Files** button 🖻 on the Solution Explorer window's toolbar. Click any **plus boxes** 田 in the window. See Figure 1-16.

Figure 1-16: Additional folders and files displayed in the Solution Explorer window

The Show All Files button 🖻 acts like a toggle switch: clicking it once turns the folder and file display on, and clicking it again turns the display off.

3   Click the **Show All Files** button 🖻 to hide the names of the additional folders and files.

4   Click the **minus box** 曰 next to the References folder to hide the reference names.

5   Place your mouse pointer on the **Properties** tab. When the Properties window slides into view, click the **Auto Hide** button 🖈 to display the window.

As you learned earlier, the code to create a Windows Form object is stored in a source file on your computer's hard disk. The source file is referred to as a **form file**, because it contains the code associated with the form. The code associated with the first Windows Form object included in a project is automatically stored in a form file named Form1.vb. The code associated with the second Windows Form object in the same project is stored in a form file named Form2.vb, and so on. Because a project can contain many Windows Form objects and, therefore, many form files, it is a good practice to give each form file a more meaningful name; this will help you keep track of the various form files in the project. You can use the Properties window to change the filename.

The Properties Window

As is everything in an object-oriented language, a form file is an object. Each object in Visual Basic .NET has a set of characteristics, called **properties**, associated with it. The properties, which determine an object's appearance and behavior, are listed in the **Properties window**. When an object is created, a default value is assigned to each of its properties. The Properties window shown in Figure 1-17, for example, lists the default values assigned to the properties of the Form1.vb form file.

Object box

Properties list

Description pane

Settings box

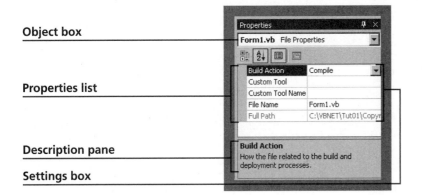

Figure 1-17: Properties window showing the properties of the Form1.vb file object

The OOP term for properties is attributes. The form file object, for example, has a File Name attribute (or property). The Properties window exposes the object's attributes to the programmer.

As indicated in Figure 1-17, the Properties window includes an Object box and a Properties list. The Object box is located immediately below the Properties window's title bar. The **Object box** contains the name of the selected object; in this case, it contains Form1.vb, which is the name of the form file selected in the Solution Explorer window. When an object is selected, its properties appear in the Properties window.

The **Properties list**, which can be displayed either alphabetically or by category, has two columns. The left column displays all the properties associated with the selected object. The right column, called the **Settings box**, displays the current value, or setting, of each of the properties. For example, the current value of the Build Action property shown in Figure 1-17 is Compile. Notice that a brief description of the selected property appears in the Description pane located at the bottom of the Properties window.

Use the Properties window to change the name of the form file object from Form1.vb to Copyright Form.vb.

> **tip**
>
> • • • • • • • • • • • • • • •
>
> You also can change the form file object's name by right-clicking the name in the Solution Explorer window, and then clicking Rename on the context menu.

To change the name of the form file object:

1   Verify that Form1.vb File Properties appears in the Object box in the Properties window.

> **HELP?** If Form1.vb File Properties does not appear in the Object box, click Form1.vb in the Solution Explorer window.

2   Click **File Name** in the Properties window. The Description pane indicates that the File Name property is used to set the name of the file or folder.

> **HELP?** If the Description pane is not displayed in the Properties window, right-click anywhere on the Properties window (except on the title bar), and then click Description on the context menu.

3   Type **Copyright Form.vb** and press **Enter**. (Be sure to include the .vb extension on the filename; otherwise, Visual Basic .NET will not recognize the file as a source file.) Copyright Form.vb appears in the Solution Explorer and Properties windows and on the designer window's tab, as shown in Figure 1-18.

form file object's name

Description pane

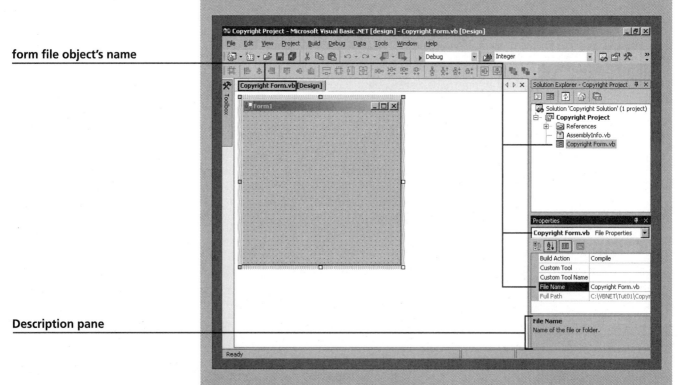

Figure 1-18: Form file object's name displayed in the designer, Solution Explorer, and Properties windows

Notice that you do not have to erase the old text in the Settings box before entering the new text. You need simply to select the appropriate property and then type the new value; the new value replaces the old value for the selected property.

Next, view the properties of the Windows Form object.

Properties of the Windows Form Object

Like the form file object, the Windows Form object also has a set of properties. The properties will appear in the Properties window when you select the Windows Form object in the designer window.

> It is easy to confuse the Windows Form object with the form file object. The Windows Form object is the form itself. A Windows Form object can be viewed in the designer window and appears on the screen when the application is running. The form file object, on the other hand, is the disk file that contains the code to create the Windows Form object.

To view the properties of the Windows Form object:

1 Click the **Auto Hide** button 📌 on the Solution Explorer window's title bar, then move the mouse pointer away from the window. Auto-hiding the Solution Explorer window allows you to view more of the Properties window.

2 Click the **Windows Form** object in the designer window. The properties of the Windows Form object appear in the Properties window.

The properties can be listed either alphabetically or by category.

3 If the properties in your Properties window are listed by category, click the **Alphabetic** button ⬇. If the properties are listed alphabetically, click the **Categorized** button 🔲 to view the category display, then click the **Alphabetic** button ⬇. See Figure 1-19.

location of the Windows Form object class

Windows Form object name

class

Windows Form object

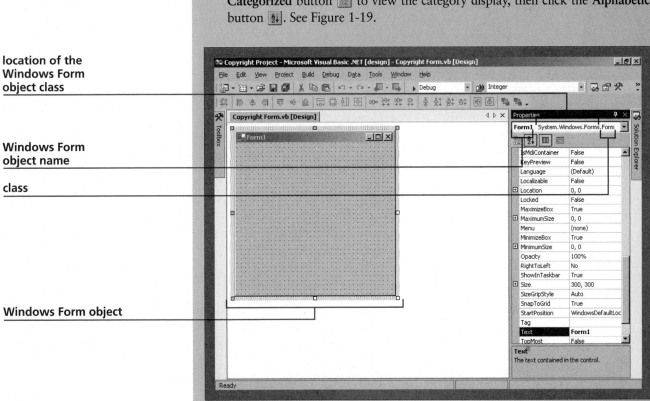

Figure 1-19: Windows Form object properties listed alphabetically in the Properties window

Notice that Form1 System.Windows.Forms.Form appears in the Object box. Form1 is the name of the Windows Form object. The name was automatically assigned to the form when you created the Copyright Project. System.Windows.Forms.Form is the name (Form) and location (System.Windows.Forms) of the class used to create (instantiate) the Windows Form object. The period that separates each word in the name is called the **dot member selection operator**. Similar to the backslash (\) in a folder path, the dot member selection operator indicates a hierarchy, but of namespaces rather than folders. In other words, the backslash in the path C:\VBNET\Tut01\Copyright Solution\Copyright Solution.sln indicates that the Copyright Solution.sln file is contained in (or is a member of) the Copyright Solution folder, which is a member of the Tut01 folder, which is a member of the VBNET folder, which is a member of the C: drive. Likewise, the name System.Windows.Forms.Form indicates that the Form class is a member of the Forms namespace, which is a member of the Windows namespace, which is a member of the System namespace. The dot member selection operator allows the computer to locate the Form class in the computer's internal memory, similar to the way the backslash (\) allows the computer to locate the Copyright Solution.sln file on your computer's hard disk.

The vertical scroll bar on the Properties window indicates that there are more properties to view.

4   Drag the scroll box in the Properties window to the bottom of the vertical scroll bar, then drag it to the top of the vertical scroll bar. As you scroll, notice the various properties associated with a Windows Form object.

As you did with the form file object, you should assign a more meaningful name to the Windows Form object; this will help you keep track of the various forms in a project.

The Name Property

Unlike a form file object, the Windows Form object has a **Name property** rather than a File Name property. You use the name entered in an object's Name property to refer to the object in code. The name must begin with a letter and contain only letters, numbers, and the underscore character. You cannot use punctuation characters or spaces in the name. One popular naming convention is to have the first three characters in the name represent the object's type (form, button, and so on), and the remainder of the name represent the object's purpose. For example, a more descriptive name for the current form would be frmCopyright. The "frm" identifies the object as a form, and "Copyright" reminds you of the form's purpose. Another popular naming convention is to record the object's purpose at the beginning of the name, and then include the object's type at the end of the name. Using this naming convention, you would name the form CopyrightForm. You will use the latter naming convention in this book.

tip

You also can scroll the Properties window using the ↓, ↑, Home, End, Page Down, and Page Up keys on your keyboard, but you first must make the Properties window the active window.

tip

The names of the forms within the same project must be unique.

To change the name of the Windows Form object:

1   Click (**Name**) in the Properties list.

2   Type **CopyrightForm** and press **Enter**. Notice that the designer window's tab now includes an asterisk (*) after [Design]. The asterisk indicates that you have made a change to the form, and the change has not yet been saved to the form file. You learn how to save the form file later in this lesson.

You set the Text property of the Windows Form object next.

The Text Property

Programmers who create applications for the Windows environment need to be aware of the conventions used in Windows applications. One such convention is that the name of the application (for example, Microsoft Visual Basic .NET or Microsoft Word) usually appears in the application window's title bar. Because the Windows Form object in the designer window will become your application's window when the application is run, its title bar should display an appropriate name.

The **Text property** controls the caption displayed in the form's title bar. The content of the Text property also is displayed on the application's button on the taskbar while the application is running. The default caption, Form1, is automatically assigned to the first form in a project. A better, more descriptive caption would be "Interlocking Software Company"—the name of the company responsible for the copyright screen application.

To set the Text property of the Windows Form object:

1 Scroll the Properties window until you see the Text property in the Properties list. Click **Text** in the Properties list.

2 Type **Interlocking Software Company** and press **Enter**. The new text appears in the Settings box to the right of the Text property, and also in the Windows Form object's title bar.

Next, you set the StartPosition property of the Windows Form object.

The StartPosition Property

You use the **StartPosition property** to determine where the Windows Form object is positioned when it first appears on the screen. A Windows Form object that represents a splash screen should be positioned in the middle of the screen.

To center a Windows Form object on the screen:

1 Click **StartPosition** in the Properties list. The list arrow button in the Settings box indicates that the StartPosition property has predefined settings. When you click the list arrow button, a list appears containing the valid settings for the StartPosition property. You then select the setting you want from the list.

2 Click the **list arrow** button in the Settings box, then click **CenterScreen** in the list.

Next, you make the copyright screen more interesting by adding a background image to it.

The BackgroundImage Property

You can use the **BackgroundImage property** to display a graphic as the background of a Windows Form object.

tip

For some properties—such as the BackColor property—a color palette rather than a list appears when you click the list arrow button in the Settings box.

To display a graphic as the background of a Windows Form object:

1 Click **BackgroundImage** in the Properties list. When you click the ellipsis (...) button in the Settings box, a dialog box will open. You use the dialog box to select the file that contains the graphic you want to display.

2 Click the **...** (ellipsis) button in the Settings box. The Open dialog box opens.

Visual Studio .NET comes with a variety of graphics files, which typically are located in the Program Files\Microsoft Visual Studio .NET\Common7\Graphics folder on either the local hard drive or the network drive.

3 Locate and then open the **Program Files\Microsoft Visual Studio .NET\ Common7\Graphics** folder.

The various graphics files are grouped by type. You will use an icon file.

4 Open the **icons** folder. The icon you will use is located in the Misc folder. Open the **Misc** folder. Click **FACE05.ICO** in the list of filenames, and then click the **Open** button. A smiling face icon fills the background of the form.

You can restore the BackgroundImage property to its default setting, which is (none), by right-clicking the property and then clicking Reset on the context menu.

5 Right-click **BackgroundImage** in the Properties list, and then click **Reset** on the context menu. The graphic is removed from the form, and the BackgroundImage property is reset to its default setting.

Next you set the Size property of the Windows Form object.

The Size Property

tip

••••••••••••••••
▶ You also can size a form by selecting it and then pressing and holding down the Shift key as you press either the ↑, ↓, →, or ← key on your keyboard.

As you can with any Windows object, you can size a Windows Form object by selecting it and then dragging the sizing handles that appear around it. You also can set its **Size property**.

To set the Size property of the Windows Form object:

1 Click **Size** in the Properties list. Notice that the Size property contains two numbers, which are separated by a comma and a space. The first number represents the width of the Windows Form object, measured in pixels; the second number represents the height, also measured in pixels.

A **pixel**, which is short for "picture element", is one spot in a grid of thousands of such spots that form an image produced on the screen by a computer or printed on a page by a printer. You can click the plus box ⊞ that appears next to the Size property to verify that the first number listed in the property represents the width and the second number represents the height.

2 Click the **plus box** ⊞ that appears next to the Size property. The Width and Height properties appear below the Size property in the Properties window.

Assume you want to change the Width property to 370 pixels and the Height property to 315 pixels. You can do so by entering 370 in the Width property's Settings box and 315 in the Height property's Settings box; or, you can simply enter 370, 315 in the Size property's Settings box.

3 Type **370, 315** and press **Enter**. Figure 1-20 shows the current status of the copyright screen.

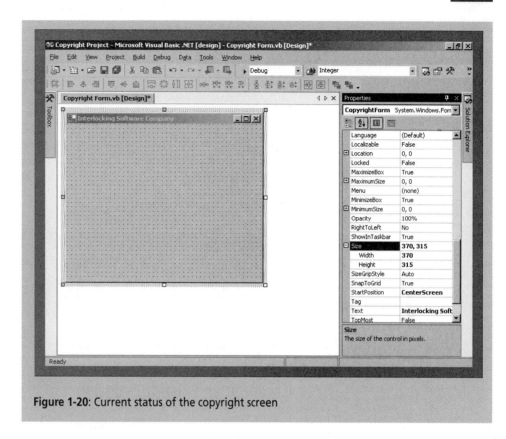

Figure 1-20: Current status of the copyright screen

Next, you learn how to save the work you have done so far.

Saving a Solution

It is a good practice to save the current solution every 10 or 15 minutes so that you will not lose a lot of work if the computer loses power. One way to save the solution is to click File on the menu bar, and then click Save All. Doing so saves any changes made to the files included in the solution. You also can click the Save All button 🖫 on the Standard toolbar.

To save your work:

1   Click **File** on the menu bar, and then click **Save All**.

tip

You also can save the solution by right-clicking its name in the Solution Explorer window, and then clicking Save *<solution filename>* on the context menu. Or you can click the solution's name in the Solution Explorer window, click File on the menu bar, and then click Save *<solution filename>* on the menu.

You also can use the Save button 🖫 on the Standard toolbar to save the solution, but you first must select the solution's name in the Solution Explorer window, because the Save button saves only the changes made to the selected item. For example, if the form file is selected, then the Save button saves only the changes made to the form file. Similarly, if the project name is selected, then only changes made to the files included in the project will be saved. The tooltip box that appears when you rest your mouse pointer on the Save button indicates which files will be saved. In this case, the tooltip box will say Save Copyright Form.vb if the form file's name is selected in the Solution Explorer window, Save Copyright Project if the project name is selected, and Save Copyright Solution.sln if the solution name is selected.

Next, you learn how to close the current solution, and how to open an existing solution. Both of these skills will help you complete the end-of-lesson exercises.

Closing the Current Solution

You close a solution using the Close Solution option on the File menu. When you close a solution, all projects and files contained in the solution also are closed. If unsaved changes were made to the solution, project, or form, a dialog box opens and prompts you to save the appropriate files. The dialog box contains Yes, No, Cancel, and Help buttons. You click the Yes button to save the files before the solution is closed. You click the No button to close the solution without saving the files. You click the Cancel button to leave the solution open, and you click the Help button to display Help pertaining to the dialog box. Use the File menu to close the Copyright Solution.

To close the Copyright Solution:

1 Click **File** on the menu bar, and then click **Close Solution**.

2 Temporarily display the Solution Explorer window to verify that the entire Copyright Solution is closed.

Now you learn how to open a solution that was saved previously.

Opening an Existing Solution

If you want to open an existing solution, you simply click File on the menu bar, and then click Open Solution. You then select the appropriate solution file in the Open Solution dialog box. (Recall that names of solution filenames have an .sln filename extension.) If a solution is already open in the IDE, it is closed before another solution is opened. In other words, only one solution can be open in the IDE at any one time. Use the File menu to open the Copyright Solution.

To open the Copyright Solution:

1 Click **File** on the menu bar, and then click **Open Solution**. The Open Solution dialog box opens.

2 Locate and then open the **VBNET\Tut01\Copyright Solution** folder on your computer's hard disk.

3 If necessary, click **Copyright Solution** (Copyright Solution.sln) in the list of filenames, and then click the **Open** button.

4 If the Windows Form Designer window is not displayed, click **View** on the menu bar, and then click **Designer**.

5 Temporarily display the Solution Explorer window to verify that the entire solution is open.

You will complete the copyright screen in the remaining two lessons. Next, you learn how to exit Visual Studio .NET.

Exiting Visual Studio .NET

As in most Windows applications, you exit an application using either the Close button ☒ on the application window's title bar, or the Exit option on the File menu.

To exit Visual Studio .NET:

1   Click the **Close** button ☒ on the IDE title bar.

You have now completed Lesson A. You can either take a break or complete the end-of-lesson questions and exercises before moving on to the next lesson.

S U M M A R Y

To start Visual Studio .NET:

■   Click the Start button on the Windows taskbar. Point to Programs (All Programs in Windows XP), then point to Microsoft Visual Studio .NET, and then click Microsoft Visual Studio .NET.

To customize the IDE:

■   Use the My Profile pane in the Start Page window.

To create a blank solution:

■   Click File on the menu bar, point to New, and then click Blank Solution. Or, click the New Blank Solution button 🗔 on the toolbar.

To add a new project to the current solution:

■   Click File on the menu bar, point to Add Project, and then click New Project. You also can right-click the solution's name in the Solution Explorer window, point to Add, and then click New Project. Additionally, you can click either the New Project button on the Get Started pane in the Start Page window, or the New Project button 🗔 on the toolbar.

To close a window in the IDE:

■   Click the window's Close button ☒. You also can right-click the window's title bar and then click Hide on the context menu; or you can click the window's title bar, then click Window on the menu bar, and then click Hide on the menu.

To open a closed window in the IDE:

■   Use the Help menu for the Start Page and Dynamic Help windows. Use the View menu for all other windows.

To auto-hide a window in the IDE:

■   Click the Auto Hide button 📌 on the window's title bar. You also can right-click the window's title bar, and then click Auto Hide on the context menu; or you can click the window's title bar, then click Window on the menu bar, and then click Auto Hide on the menu.

To set the value of a property:

■ Select the object whose property you want to set, then select the appropriate property in the Properties list. Type the new property value in the selected property's Settings box, or choose the value from the list, color palette, or dialog box.

To give a more meaningful name to an object:

■ Set the object's Name property.

To control the text appearing in the form's title bar, and on the application's button on the Windows taskbar when the application is running:

■ Set the Windows Form object's Text property.

To control the starting location of the Windows Form object:

■ Set the Windows Form object's StartPosition property.

To display a graphic as the background of a Windows Form object:

■ Set the Windows Form object's BackgroundImage property.
■ Visual Studio .NET comes with a variety of graphics files, which typically are located in the Program Files\Microsoft Visual Studio .NET\Common7\Graphics folder on either the local hard drive or the network drive.

To size a Windows Form object:

■ Drag the form's sizing handles. You also can set the form's Size, Height, and Width properties in the Properties window. Additionally, you can select the form and then press and hold down the Shift key as you press either the ↑, ↓, →, or ← key on your keyboard.

To save a solution:

■ Click File on the menu bar, and then click Save All. You also can click the Save All button 🗗 on the Standard toolbar. You also can click the solution's name in the Solution Explorer window, and then click either the Save *<solution filename>* button 🖫 on the Standard toolbar or the Save *<solution filename>* option on the File menu. Addition-, ally you can right-click the solution's name in the Solution Explorer window, and then click Save *<solution filename>* on the context menu.

To open an existing solution:

■ Click File on the menu bar, and then click Open Solution.

To exit Visual Studio .NET:

■ Click the Close button ☒ on the IDE title bar. You also can click File on the IDE menu bar, and then click Exit.

QUESTIONS

1. A _____ is a pattern that Visual Studio .NET uses to create solutions and projects.
   a. design
   b. profile
   c. solution
   d. template
   e. user interface

2. A _____ is a container that stores the projects and files for an entire application.
   a. form file
   b. profile
   c. solution
   d. template
   e. None of the above.

3. You use the _____ window to set the characteristics that control an object's appearance and behavior.
   a. Characteristics
   b. Object
   c. Properties
   d. Toolbox
   e. Windows Form Designer

4. The _____ window lists the projects and files included in a solution.
   a. Object
   b. Project
   c. Properties
   d. Solution Explorer
   e. Windows Form Designer

5. Solution files in Visual Studio .NET have a(n) _____ extension on their filenames.
   a. .frm
   b. .prg
   c. .sln
   d. .src
   e. .vb

6. Which of the following statements is false?
   a. You can auto-hide a window by clicking the 🔲 button on its title bar.
   b. An auto-hidden window appears as a tab on the edge of the IDE.
   c. You temporarily display an auto-hidden window by placing your mouse pointer on its tab.
   d. You permanently display an auto-hidden window by clicking the 🔲 on its title bar.
   e. None of the above.

7. Visual Basic .NET source files have a(n) _____ extension on their filenames.
   a. .frm
   b. .prg
   c. .sln
   d. .src
   e. .vb

8. The code that creates a Windows Form object is stored in a file whose filename extension is _____.
    a. .frm
    b. .prg
    c. .sln
    d. .src
    e. .vb

9. The _____ property controls the text appearing in the title bar on a Windows Form object.
    a. Caption
    b. FormCaption
    c. Text
    d. Title
    e. TitleBar

10. You give an object a more meaningful name by setting the object's _____ property.
    a. Application
    b. Caption
    c. Form
    d. Name
    e. Text

11. You can size a Windows Form object by _____.
    a. dragging its sizing handles
    b. setting its Height property
    c. setting its Size property
    d. setting its Width property
    e. All of the above.

12. The _____ property determines the position of a Windows Form object when it first appears.
    a. InitialLocation
    b. Location
    c. Start
    d. StartLocation
    e. StartPosition

13. The _____ property allows you to display a graphic as the background of a Windows Form object.
    a. BackgroundImage
    b. BackgroundPicture
    c. GraphicBackground
    d. IconBackground
    e. Image

14. When you close a solution, all projects and files included in the solution also are closed.
    a. True
    b. False

15. A project can contain one or more Windows Form objects.
    a. True
    b. False

16. Explain the difference between a Windows-based application and a Web-based application.

17. Explain the difference between a Windows Form object's Text property and its Name property.

18. Explain the difference between a form file object and a Windows Form object.

19. Define the terms "reference" and "namespace".

20. What does the dot member selection operator indicate in the text System.Windows.Forms.Label?

E X E R C I S E S

1. In this exercise, you change the properties of an existing Windows Form object.
   a. If necessary, start Visual Studio .NET and permanently display the Solution Explorer window.
   b. Click File on the menu bar, and then click Open Solution. Open the Charities Solution (Charities Solution.sln) file, which is contained in the VBNET\Tut01\Charities Solution folder. If the designer window is not open, click the form file's name in the Solution Explorer window, then use the View menu to open the designer window.
   c. Change the following properties of the Windows Form object:

Name:	CharityForm
BackColor:	Select a light blue square on the Custom tab (This property determines the background color of the form.)
Size:	300, 350
StartPosition:	CenterScreen
Text:	Charities Unlimited

   d. Click File on the menu bar, and then click Save All to save the solution.
   e. Close the solution.

2. In this exercise, you create a Visual Basic .NET Windows-based application.
   a. If necessary, start Visual Studio .NET and permanently display the Solution Explorer window.
   b. Create a blank solution named Photo Solution. Save the solution in the VBNET\Tut01 folder.
   c. Add a Visual Basic .NET Windows Application project to the solution. Name the project Photo Project.
   d. Assign the filename Photo Form.vb to the form file object.
   e. Assign the name MyPhotoForm to the Windows Form object.
   f. The Windows Form object's title bar should say Photos Incorporated. Set the appropriate property.
   g. The Windows Form object should be centered on the screen when it first appears. Set the appropriate property.
   h. Include a background image on the form.
   i. Save and then close the solution.

3. In this exercise, you create a Visual Basic .NET Windows-based application.
   a. If necessary, start Visual Studio .NET and permanently display the Solution Explorer window.
   b. Create a blank solution named Yorktown Solution. Save the solution in the VBNET\Tut01 folder.
   c. Add a Visual Basic .NET Windows Application project to the solution. Name the project Yorktown Project.
   d. Assign the filename Yorktown Form.vb to the form file object.
   e. Assign the name ShoppingForm to the Windows Form object.
   f. Include a background image on the form.

g. The Windows Form object's title bar should say Yorktown Shopping Center. Set the appropriate property.

h. The Windows Form object should be centered on the screen when it first appears. Set the appropriate property.

i. Remove the background image from the form. (You included the background image in Step f.)

j. Save and then close the solution.

Exercises 4 and 5 are Discovery Exercises. Discovery Exercises, which may include topics that are not covered in this lesson, allow you to "discover" the solutions to problems on your own.

discovery ▶ 4. In this exercise, you learn about the ControlBox, MaximizeBox, and MinimizeBox properties of a Windows Form object.

a. If necessary, start Visual Studio .NET and permanently display the Solution Explorer window.

b. Open the Greenwood Solution (Greenwood Solution.sln) file, which is contained in the VBNET\Tut01\Greenwood Solution folder. If the designer window is not open, click the form file's name in the Solution Explorer window, then use the View menu to open the designer window.

c. View the properties of the Windows Form object.

d. Click the ControlBox property. What is the purpose of this property? (Refer to the Description pane in the Properties window.)

e. Set the ControlBox property to False. How does this setting affect the Windows Form object?

f. Set the ControlBox property to True.

g. Click the MaximizeBox property. What is the purpose of this property?

h. Set the MaximizeBox property to False. How does this setting affect the Windows Form object?

i. Set the MaximizeBox property to True.

j. Click the MinimizeBox property. What is the purpose of this property?

k. Set the MinimizeBox property to False. How does this setting affect the Windows Form object?

l. Set the MinimizeBox property to True.

m. Close the solution without saving it.

discovery ▶ 5. In this exercise, you use the Description pane in the Properties window to research two properties of a Windows Form object.

a. If necessary, start Visual Studio .NET and permanently display the Solution Explorer window.

b. Open the Greenwood Solution (Greenwood Solution.sln) file, which is contained in the VBNET\Tut01\Greenwood Solution folder. If the designer window is not open, click the form file's name in the Solution Explorer window, then use the View menu to open the designer window.

c. View the properties of the Windows Form object.

d. What property allows you to remove the dots (referred to as the positioning grid) from the form?

e. What property determines whether the value stored in the form's Text property appears on the Windows taskbar when the application is running?

f. Close the solution without saving it.

Working with Controls

The Toolbox Window

In Lesson A, you learned about the Windows Form Designer, Solution Explorer, and Properties windows. In this lesson, you learn about the Toolbox window. First, however, you open the Copyright Solution you created in Lesson A.

To open the Copyright Solution:

1 If necessary, start Visual Studio .NET.

You will not need the Start Page window, so you can close it.

2 Close the Start Page window.

3 Click **File** on the menu bar, and then click **Open Solution**. The Open Solution dialog box opens. Open the **Copyright Solution** (Copyright Solution.sln) file, which is contained in the VBNET\Tut01\Copyright Solution folder.

4 If the designer window is not open, click **Copyright Form.vb** in the Solution Explorer window, then use the View menu to open the designer window.

5 Permanently display the Toolbox and Properties windows. Auto-hide the Solution Explorer window.

6 If necessary, size the Toolbox window so that the entire form appears in the designer window. See Figure 1-21.

tabs

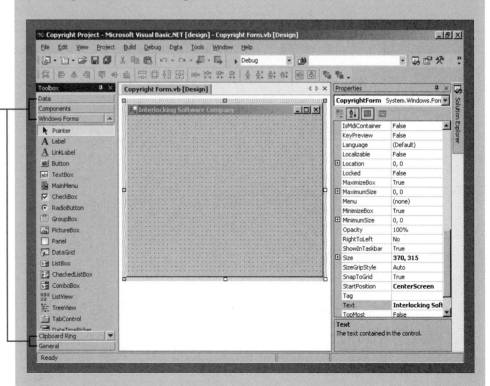

Figure 1-21: Copyright Solution opened in the IDE

> **HELP?** To size the Toolbox window, position your mouse pointer ▷ on the Toolbox window's right border until ▷ becomes ╢╟, then drag the border until the window is the desired size.

The **Toolbox window**, or **toolbox**, contains the tools and other components you use when designing a user interface. The contents of the toolbox vary depending on the designer in use. The toolbox shown in Figure 1-21 appears when you are using the Windows Form designer. Notice that the toolbox contains five tabs, which are labeled Data, Components, Windows Forms, Clipboard Ring, and General. In the next set of steps, you view the contents of each toolbox tab.

To view the contents of the toolbox tabs:

1 Click the **Data** tab on the toolbox. The Components and Windows Forms tabs slide down to reveal the contents of the Data tab. The Data tab provides components that allow you to access data and data sources. Examples of these components include DataSet, OleDbDataAdaptor, and OleDbConnection.

2 Click the **Components** tab on the toolbox. The Components tab slides up to reveal its contents. The Components tab contains items that allow you to perform tasks such as monitoring the file system and recording information pertaining to errors that occur while an application is running. Examples of these components include FileSystemWatcher and EventLog.

3 Click the **Clipboard Ring** tab on the toolbox. The Clipboard Ring tab, which currently contains only the Pointer tool, stores the last few items that you cut or copied to the system clipboard using the Cut or Copy commands. An item on this tab can be dragged and then dropped onto the active design or editing surface.

4 Click the **General** tab on the toolbox. You can use the General tab, which currently contains only the Pointer tool, to store items such as objects or program code. Like items stored on the Clipboard Ring tab, items stored on the General tab can be dragged and then dropped onto the active design or editing surface.

The toolbox tab that you will use most often is the Windows Forms tab.

5 Click the **Windows Forms** tab on the toolbox to view its contents. See Figure 1-22.

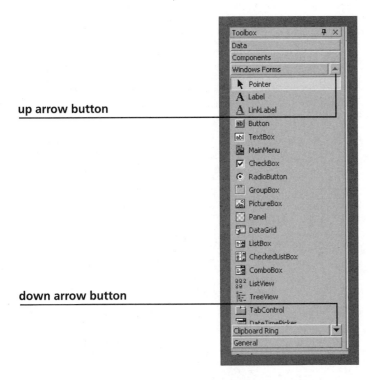

up arrow button

down arrow button

Figure 1-22: Windows Forms tab

tip

. . . .

▶ In the context of OOP, each tool in the toolbox represents a class—a pattern from which one or more objects are created. The object's attributes and behaviors are encapsulated (combined) in the tool.

The Windows Forms tab contains the tools you use when designing your user interface. The tools allow you to place objects such as text boxes, list boxes, and radio buttons on the form. Each tool on the tab is identified by both an icon and a name. For example, the tool you use to include a radio button on a form is identified by the ⊙ icon and the name RadioButton.

The Windows Forms tab contains 47 basic tools; however, you can add new tools or delete existing tools by right-clicking the tab and then clicking Customize Toolbox on the context menu. Depending on the number of tools contained on the tab, and how you have the tools displayed, you may not be able to view all of the tools at the same time. The Windows Forms tab provides up and down arrow buttons that you can use to scroll the list of tools. You also can scroll the list using the up and down arrow keys, as well as the Page Up and Page Down keys on your keyboard. (To use the keys on your keyboard to scroll the list, the Toolbox window must be the active, or current, window.)

By default, the tools on the Windows Forms tab are listed in order by their estimated frequency of use, with the most used tools listed first. If you prefer, you can list the tools alphabetically by name. Or, you can drag a tool to another location on the tab. You also can choose to view the tool icons only, rather than the icons and names; this creates a more compact display of the tools and allows you to view all of the tools at the same time. Try these display variations next.

To change the display of the tools on the Windows Forms tab:

1   Right-click the **Windows Forms** tab, and then click **Sort Items Alphabetically** on the context menu. The tools appear in alphabetical order by name, with one exception: the Pointer tool appears first in the list.

View the various tools included on the tab.

2 Use the down arrow button to scroll to the bottom of the list, then use the up arrow button to scroll to the top of the list.

Now display only the tool icons.

3 Right-click the **Windows Forms** tab. A checkmark appears next to the List View option, which indicates that the option is selected. When the List View option is selected, the Windows Form tab displays both the tool icons and names.

4 Click **List View** to deselect the option; this will remove the checkmark. Now only the tool icons appear on the tab, as shown in Figure 1-23.

RadioButton tool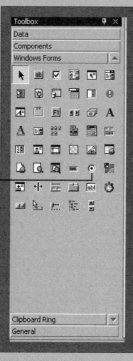

Figure 1-23: Tool icons displayed on the Windows Forms tab

You can display a tool's name by resting the mouse pointer on the tool's icon.

5 Place your mouse pointer on the **RadioButton** tool icon . The tool name, RadioButton, appears in a tooltip box.

You also can move a tool to another location on the Windows Forms tab simply by dragging it. Move the RadioButton tool so that it is the second tool on the tab.

6 Click the **RadioButton** tool to select it, but do not release the mouse button. Drag the tool until it obscures the Button tool, then release the mouse button. The tool appears as the second tool on the tab.

You can use the Customize Toolbox dialog box to restore the Windows Forms tab to its original state.

7 Right-click the **Windows Forms** tab, then click **Customize Toolbox** on the context menu. The Customize Toolbox dialog box opens.

tip

· · · · · · · · · · · · · · · ·
▶ The Customize Toolbox option also is located on the Tools menu.

8 Click the **.NET Framework Components** tab. It may take a few moments for the tab's contents to appear in the dialog box. When the tab's contents appear, click the **Reset** button. A dialog box opens and informs you that the Toolbox default settings will be restored and all custom Toolbox items will be removed. The message in the dialog box asks if you want to continue. Click the **Yes** button. (It will take the computer several moments to restore the default settings.)

9 Click the **OK** button to close the Customize Toolbox dialog box, then click the **Windows Forms** tab in the toolbox. The Windows Forms tab appears in its original state, with the tools listed in order by their frequency of use.

As mentioned earlier, the Windows Forms tab contains 47 basic tools. Appendix A lists the basic tools and provides a brief description of each. You learn about many of these tools throughout this book. You begin with the Label tool.

Using the Label Tool

The tools in the toolbox allow you to create objects, called **controls**, that can be displayed on a form. You use the **Label tool** **A**, for example, to create a label control. The purpose of a **label control** is to display text that the user is not allowed to edit while the application is running. In this application, for example, you do not want the user to change the author name and copyright year on the copyright screen. Therefore, you will display the information using two label controls: one for the name of the application's author and the other for the copyright year.

To use the Label tool to create two label controls:

1 Click the **Label** tool **A** in the toolbox, but do not release the mouse button. Hold down the mouse button as you drag the mouse pointer to the center of the form. (You do not need to worry about the exact size or location of the control.) As you drag the mouse pointer, both an outline of a rectangle and a plus box **+** follow the mouse pointer.

2 Release the mouse button. A label control appears on the form. Notice that sizing handles appear around the label control. You can use the sizing handles to size the control. Also notice that Label1 System.Windows.Forms.Label appears in the Object box in the Properties window. Label1 is the default name assigned to the label control. System.Windows.Forms.Label indicates that the control is an instance of the Label class, which is defined in the System.Windows.Forms namespace. See Figure 1-24. (Do not be concerned if your label control is a different size than the one shown in the figure.)

tip

You also can add a control to the form by clicking the control's tool in the toolbox and then clicking the form. Additionally, you can click the control's tool in the toolbox, then place the mouse pointer on the form, and then press the left mouse button and drag the mouse pointer until the control is the desired size.

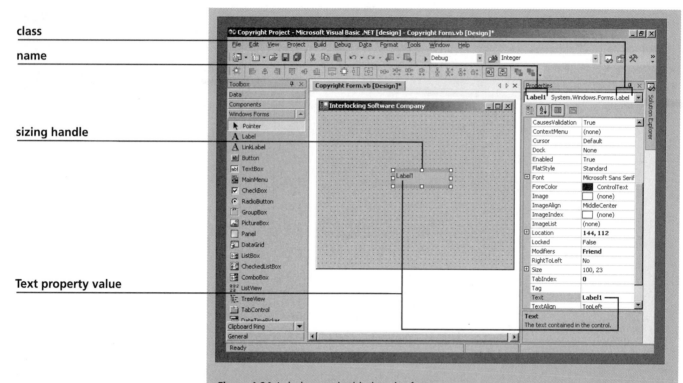

Figure 1-24: Label control added to the form

Recall that, in the context of OOP, each tool in the toolbox represents a class. The label control shown in Figure 1-24 is an instance of the Label class.

tip

To delete a control from the form, you simply select it and then press Delete. In order to delete the selected control, the designer window must be the active window.

Recall from Lesson A that a default value is assigned to each of an object's properties when the object is created. Label1, for example, is the default value assigned to the Text and Name properties of the first label control added to a form. The value of the Text property appears inside the label control, as indicated in Figure 1-24. (You can verify that the Name property also contains Label1 by scrolling to the top of the Properties window.)

3 Click the **Label** tool in the toolbox, and then drag another label control onto the form. Position the new label control below the existing one. (Do not worry about the exact location.) Notice that Label2 is assigned to the Text property of the second label control added to the same form. Label2 also is assigned to the control's Name property.

Now assign a more meaningful name to each label control. Assigning meaningful names to the controls on a form will help you keep track of the various controls in the user interface. Recall that the naming convention used in this book records the object's purpose at the beginning of the name, and then includes the object's type at the end of the name.

To assign a more meaningful name to the label controls:

1 Click the **Label1** control to select it. Scroll to the top of the Properties list, and then click (**Name**).

The Label1 control will display the application author's name, so you will name it AuthorLabel.

class

name

sizing handle

Text property value

2   Type **AuthorLabel** in the Settings box and press **Enter**.

The Label2 control will display the copyright year, so you will name it YearLabel.

3   Click the **Label2** control to select it. Click (**Name**) in the Properties list, then type **YearLabel** in the Settings box and press **Enter**.

Next, set the Text and AutoSize properties of both label controls.

Setting the Text and AutoSize Properties

As you learned earlier, a label control's Text property determines the value that appears inside the control. In this application, you want the words "Written by" and your name to appear in the AuthorLabel control, and the words "Copyright Year" and the year 2004 to appear in the YearLabel control. Therefore, you will need to set the Text property of both controls.

To set the Text property of the two label controls:

1   Currently, the YearLabel control is selected on the form. Scroll down the Properties window until you locate the control's Text property. Click **Text** in the Properties list, then type **Copyright Year 2004** and press **Enter**. The new text appears in the Text property's Settings box and in the YearLabel control.

Because the text is longer than the width of the label control, some of the information wraps around to the next line. You can use the control's sizing handles to adjust the size of the control. You also can use the control's AutoSize property. The **AutoSize property** does just what its name implies: it automatically sizes the control to fit its current contents.

2   Click **AutoSize** in the Properties list, then click the **list arrow** button in the Settings box.

Notice that the AutoSize property can be set to either True or False. Many of the other properties shown in the Properties list also have only these two settings. (The settings are called **Boolean** values, named after the English mathematician George Boole.) The True setting turns the property on, and the False setting turns the property off. You use the True setting to automatically size a control.

3   Click **True** in the list. The YearLabel control stretches automatically to fit the contents of its Text property. Notice that a thin line, rather than sizing handles, surrounds the control. The thin line indicates that the control's AutoSize property is set to True.

4   Click the **AuthorLabel** control on the form. Sizing handles appear around the control to indicate that it is selected, and that its AutoSize property is currently set to False. Notice that the thin line that surrounded the YearLabel control in the previous step disappears when you click another control. This is because the thin line appears only when an auto-sized control is selected.

5   Set the AuthorLabel control's AutoSize property to **True**. A thin line replaces the sizing handles around the control.

6   Click **Text** in the Properties list. Type **Written By** and press the **spacebar**, then type your name and press **Enter**. The AuthorLabel control stretches automatically to fit the contents of its Text property.

tip

You also can size a control by selecting it and then pressing and holding down the Shift key as you press either the ↑, ↓, →, or ← key on your keyboard. Additionally, you can set the control's Size, Height, and Width properties.

Now specify the placement of the two label controls on the form.

Setting the Location Property

You can move a control to a different location on the form by placing your mouse pointer ⍄ on the control until ⍄ becomes ✛, and then dragging the control to the desired location. You also can set the control's Location property, because the property specifies the position of the upper-left corner of the control.

> **To set the Location property of the two label controls:**
>
> **1** Click the **YearLabel** control to select it.
>
> **2** Click **Location** in the Properties list, then click the **plus box** ⊞ next to the property's name. Two additional properties, X and Y, appear below the Location property in the Properties list.
>
> The **X property** specifies the number of pixels from the left border of the form to the left border of the control. The **Y property**, on the other hand, specifies the number of pixels between the top border of the form and the top border of the control. Change the X value to 175, and change the Y value to 250.
>
> **3** Type **175, 250** in the **Location** property and press **Enter**. The YearLabel control moves to its new location.
>
> **4** Click the **minus box** ⊟ next to the Location property's name.
>
> Now select the AuthorLabel control and then set its Location property. In addition to selecting a control by clicking it on the form, you also can select a control by clicking its entry (name and class) in the Object box in the Properties window. Try this now.
>
> **5** Click the **list arrow** button in the Properties window's Object box, and then click **AuthorLabel System.Windows.Forms.Label** in the list. Set the control's Location property to **175, 225**. The AuthorLabel control moves to its new location.
>
> **6** Click **File** on the menu bar, and then click **Save All** to save the solution.

Now set the Font property of the two label controls. As you will see in the next section, you can set the Font property for both controls at the same time.

Changing the Property for More Than One Control at a Time

You can use the Font property to change the appearance of many of the objects in your user interface. The **Font property** allows you to change the type of font used to display the text in the object, as well as the style and size of the font. A **font** is the general shape of the characters in the text. Courier, Tahoma, and Microsoft Sans Serif are examples of font types; font styles include regular, bold, and italic. The numbers 8, 10, and 18 are examples of font sizes, which typically are measured in points, with one **point** equaling 1/72 of an inch.

One reason for changing a font is to bring attention to a specific part of the screen. In the copyright screen, for example, you can make the text in the two label controls more noticeable by increasing the size of the font used to display the text. You can change the font size for both controls at the same time by clicking one control and then pressing and holding down the Control key as you click the other control in the form. You can use the Control+click method to select as many controls as you want. To cancel the selection of one of the selected controls, press and hold down the Control key as you click the control. To cancel the selection of all of the selected controls, release the Control key, then click the form or an unselected control on the form.

The Font property allows you to change the unit of measurement from Point to World, Pixel, Inch, Document, and Millimeter.

You also can select a group of controls on the form by placing the mouse pointer ▷ slightly above and to the left of the first control you want to select, then pressing the left mouse button and dragging. A dotted rectangle appears as you drag. When all of the controls you want to select are within (or at least touched by) the dotted rectangle, release the mouse button. All of the controls surrounded or touched by the dotted rectangle will be selected.

To select both label controls, and then set their Font property:

1 Verify that a thin line surrounds the AuthorLabel control, indicating that the control is selected.

2 Press and hold down the **Ctrl** (or Control) key as you click the **YearLabel** control, then release the Ctrl key. The thin line that surrounds each label control indicates that both controls are selected. (Recall that the thin line appears only when an auto-sized control is selected, and both label controls are auto-sized.) If the label controls were not auto-sized—in other words, if their AutoSize property was set to False—sizing handles (rather than a thin line) would appear around each control to indicate that each is selected. See Figure 1-25.

both label controls are selected

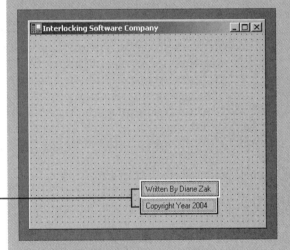

Figure 1-25: Both label controls selected

3 Click **Font** in the Properties list, then click the **...** (ellipsis) button in the Settings box. The Font dialog box opens. See Figure 1-26.

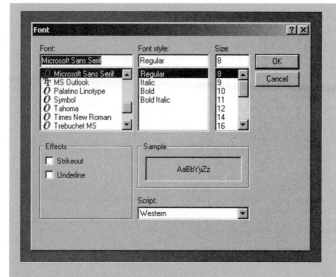

Figure 1-26: Font dialog box

Typically, the default font is the regular style of the Microsoft Sans Serif font, and the default font size is 8 points, or 1/9 of an inch. (Recall that one point is 1/72 of an inch.) Change the font type to Tahoma, and increase the font size to 12 points (1/6 of an inch).

4   Scroll the Font list box and click **Tahoma**, then click **12** in the Size list box. Click the **OK** button. The Font dialog box closes, and the text in the two label controls appears in the new font and font size. (Depending on the number of characters in your name, the AuthorLabel might extend beyond the right border of the form. You fix that problem in the next section.)

Next, you learn how to use the Format menu to center the label controls, horizontally, on the form.

Using the Format Menu

The Format menu provides options that allow you to manipulate the controls in the user interface. The Align option, for example, allows you to align two or more controls by their left, right, top, or bottom borders. You can use the Make Same Size option to make two or more controls the same width or height, or both width and height. The Format menu also has a Center in Form option that centers one or more controls either horizontally or vertically on the form. Use the Center in Form option to center the two label controls on the form.

To center the AuthorLabel and YearLabel controls horizontally on the form:
1   Click the **Copyright Form.vb [Design]*** tab to make the designer window the active window. The two label controls should still be selected. Click **Format** on the menu bar. Point to **Center in Form**, then click **Horizontally**. The two label controls are centered horizontally on the form.
2   Click the **form** to deselect the label controls.

Next, you use the PictureBox tool to add a picture box control to the form.

tip
• • • • • • • • • • • • • • • • •
To use a different unit of measurement for the font size, click the plus box ⊞ in the Font property's Settings box, and then click Unit. Click the list arrow button, and then click the desired unit of measurement.

tip
• • • • • • • • • • • • • • • •
You practice with the Align and Make Same Size options in Discovery Exercise 4 at the end of this lesson.

Using the PictureBox Tool

According to the application you previewed at the beginning of this tutorial, you need to include the Interlocking Software Company logo on your copyright screen. You can do so by displaying the logo in a **picture box control**, which you create using the **PictureBox tool** .

To add a picture box control to the form:

1 Click the **PictureBox** tool in the toolbox, then drag a picture box control to the form. (You do not need to worry about the exact location.) An empty rectangular box with sizing handles appears on the form, and PictureBox1 System.Windows.Forms.PictureBox appears in the Object box in the Properties window. PictureBox1 is the default name assigned to the first picture box control added to a form. System.Windows.Forms.PictureBox indicates that the control is an instance of the PictureBox class, which is defined in the System.Windows.Forms namespace.

2 Set the picture box control's Name property to **LogoPictureBox**.

3 Set the picture box control's Location property to **8, 10**.

You use the picture box control's **Image property** to specify the image you want displayed inside the control.

4 Click **Image** in the Properties list, then click the **...** (ellipsis) button in the Settings box. The Open dialog box opens.

The Interlocking Software Company logo is stored in the Logo file, which is contained in the VBNET\Tut01 folder.

5 Open the **VBNET\Tut01** folder. Click **Logo** (Logo.bmp) in the list of file-names, and then click the **Open** button. Only a small portion of the logo appears in the picture box control.

You can make the picture box control larger by dragging its sizing handles; or you can simply set its **SizeMode property**.

6 Set the picture box control's SizeMode property to **AutoSize**. The picture box control automatically sizes to fit its current contents.

7 Click the **form's title bar** to deselect the picture box control. See Figure 1-27.

Figure 1-27: Picture box control added to the form

The last tool you learn about in this lesson is the Button tool.

Using the Button Tool

Every Windows application should give the user a way to exit the program. Most Windows applications provide either an Exit option on a File menu or an Exit button for this purpose. When the user clicks the menu option or button, the application ends and the user interface is removed from the screen. In this lesson, the copyright screen will provide an Exit button.

In Windows applications, a **button control** performs an immediate action when clicked. Examples of button controls used in most Windows applications include the OK and Cancel buttons, as well as the Open and Save buttons. You create a button using the **Button tool** in the toolbox.

> Recall that the copyright screen will serve as a splash screen for each custom application created by Interlocking Software. Splash screens typically do not contain an Exit button; rather, they use a Timer control to automatically remove the splash screen after a set period of time. You learn how to include a Timer control in a splash screen in Lesson C. For this lesson, you use an Exit button.

To add a button control to the form:

1 Click the **Button** tool in the toolbox, then drag a button control to the form. Position the button control to the immediate right of the label controls. (You do not need to worry about the exact location.)

Notice that Button1 System.Windows.Forms.Button appears in the Object box in the Properties window. Button1 is the default name assigned to the first button control added to a form. System.Windows.Forms.Button tells you that the control is an instance of the Button class, which is defined in the System.Windows.Forms namespace.

First, assign a more meaningful name to the button control. Then change the button control's font and location.

2 Set the button control's Name property to **ExitButton**.

3 Set the button control's Font property to **Tahoma**.

4 Set the button control's Location property to **270, 256**.

The button control's Text property determines the caption that appears on the button. Change the Text property from Button1 to Exit.

5 Set the button control's Text property to **Exit**. Figure 1-28 shows the button control added to the form.

Figure 1-28: Button control added to the form

You will not need the Toolbox and Properties windows, so you can auto-hide them.

6 Auto-hide the Toolbox and Properties windows.

7 Click **File** on the menu bar, and then click **Save All** to save your work.

Now that the user interface is complete, you can start the copyright screen application to see how it will look to the user.

Starting and Ending an Application

You can start an application by clicking Debug on the menu bar, and then clicking Start; or you can simply press the F5 key on your keyboard. When you start an application, Visual Studio .NET automatically creates a file that can be run outside of the Visual Studio .NET IDE. The file, referred to as an **executable file**, has the same name as the project, but with an .exe filename extension. In the next set of steps, you learn how to change the name of the executable file and select the form that will first appear when the application is started. You then start and stop the application.

To change the project's properties, and then start and stop the copyright screen application:

1 Right-click **Copyright Project** in the Solution Explorer window, and then click **Properties**. The Copyright Project Property Pages dialog box opens. If necessary, click the **Common Properties** folder to open it, then click **General**.

First, change the name of the application's executable file.

2 Change the filename in the Assembly name text box to **Copyright**. The Output name in the Information section of the dialog box now says Copyright.exe.

When the application is started, the CopyrightForm should be the first form that appears on the screen.

3 Click the **Startup object** list arrow, and then click **CopyrightForm** in the list. See Figure 1-29.

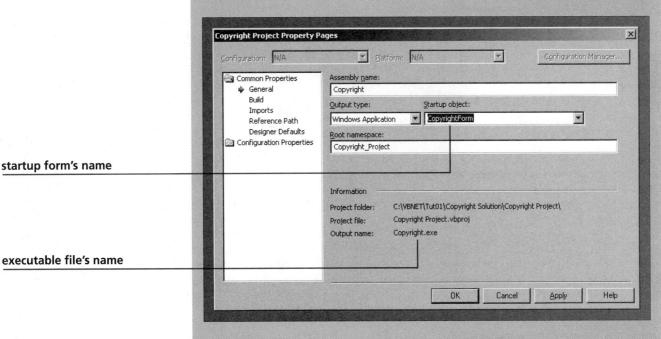

startup form's name

executable file's name

Figure 1-29: Copyright Project Property Pages dialog box

4   Click the **OK** button to close the Copyright Project Property Pages dialog box. Now save and then start the application.

5   Click **File** on the menu bar, and then click **Save All**. Click **Debug** on the menu bar, and then click **Start**. See Figure 1-30. (Do not be concerned about the windows that appear at the bottom of the screen.)

form's Close button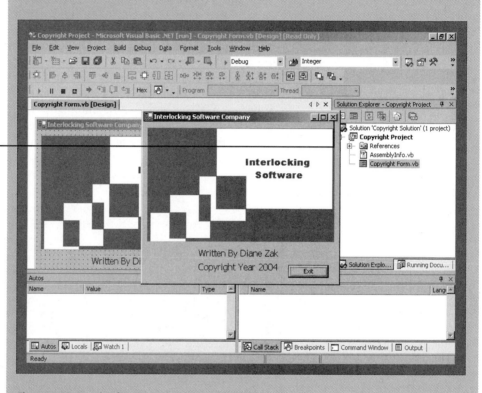

Figure 1-30: Result of starting the copyright screen application

> **HELP?**   If the "Access is denied. Verify that you are an administrator or a member of the 'Debugger Users' group on the machine you are trying to debug." message appears in a dialog box, click the OK button. Have your computer's administrator change your group membership to Debugger Users.

Recall that the purpose of the Exit button is to allow the user to end the application. Currently, the button will not work as intended, because you have not yet entered the instructions that tell the button how to respond when clicked. You can verify that the Exit button does not work by clicking it.

6   Click the **Exit** button on the copyright screen. Notice that it does not end the application.

At this point, you can stop the application by clicking the Close button ⊠ on the form's title bar. You also can click the designer window to make it the active window, then click Debug on the menu bar, and then click Stop Debugging; another option is to press Shift+F5.

7   Click the **Close** button ⊠ on the form's title bar. When the application ends, you are returned to the IDE, and an Output window appears at the bottom of the screen. See Figure 1-31.

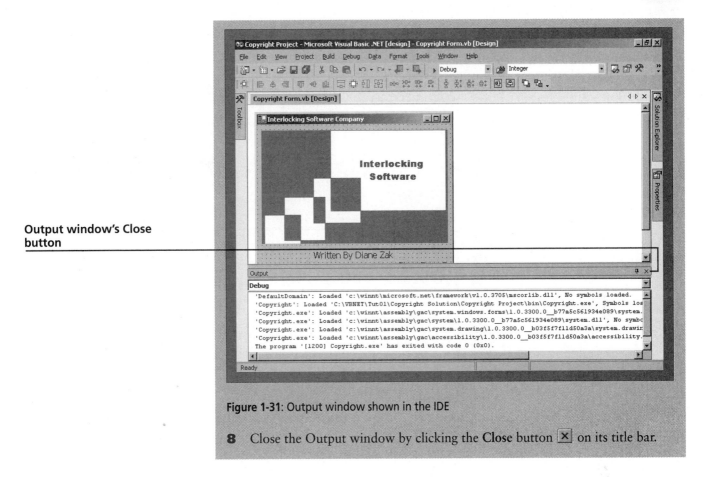

Output window's Close button

Figure 1-31: Output window shown in the IDE

8 Close the Output window by clicking the **Close** button ☒ on its title bar.

Next, you learn how to instruct the Exit button to stop the copyright screen application when the button is clicked.

Writing Visual Basic .NET Code

Think about the Windows environment for a moment. Did you ever wonder why the OK and Cancel buttons respond the way they do when you click them, or how the Exit option on the File menu knows to close the application? The answer to these questions is very simple: a programmer gave the buttons and menu option explicit instructions on how to respond to the actions of the user. Those actions— such as clicking, double-clicking, and scrolling—are called **events**. The set of Visual Basic .NET instructions, or code, that tells an object how to respond to an event is called an **event procedure**.

At this point, the Exit button in the copyright screen does not know what it is supposed to do. You tell the button what to do by writing an event procedure for it. You write the event procedure in the Code editor window, which is a window you have not yet seen. You can use various methods to open the Code editor window. For example, you can right-click anywhere on the form (except the form's title bar), and then click View Code on the context menu. You also can click View on the menu bar, and then click Code; or you can press the F7 key on your keyboard. (To use the View menu or the F7 key, the designer window should be the active window.)

tip

You also can open the Code editor window by double-clicking the form or a control on the form. Doing so displays (in the Code editor window) a default event procedure for the object you double-clicked.

To open the Code editor window:

1   Verify that the Windows Form object's title bar is highlighted, indicating that the designer window is the active window.

2   Click **View** on the menu bar, and then click **Code**. The Code editor window opens in the IDE, as shown in Figure 1-32. Notice that the Code editor window already contains some Visual Basic .NET code (instructions).

Code editor window's tab

designer window's tab

class definition

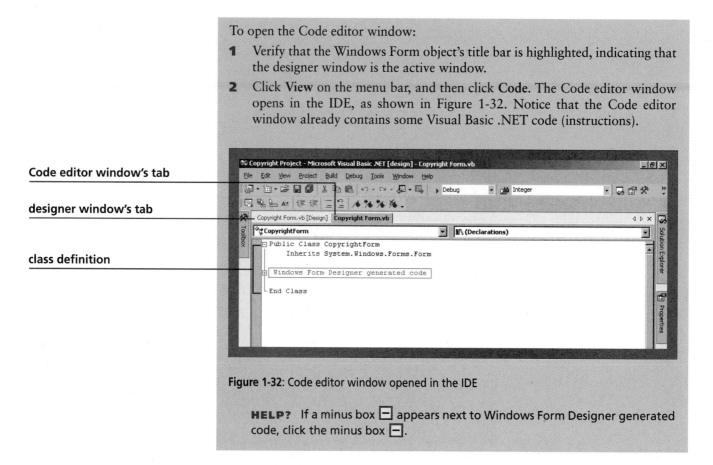

Figure 1-32: Code editor window opened in the IDE

HELP? If a minus box ⊟ appears next to Windows Form Designer generated code, click the minus box ⊟.

As Figure 1-32 indicates, the block of code that begins with the `Public Class CopyrightForm` instruction and ends with the `End Class` instruction is a class definition. A **class definition** is simply a block of code that specifies (or defines) the attributes and behaviors of an object. The CopyrightForm class definition, for example, specifies the attributes and behaviors of a CopyrightForm object. When you start the application, Visual Basic .NET uses the class definition to create the object.

Notice the `Inherits System.Windows.Forms.Form` instruction included in the CopyrightForm class definition. As you learned in the Overview, you can create one class (called the derived class) from another class (called the base class). The derived class inherits all of the attributes and behaviors of the base class, but then can be modified to, for instance, include an additional feature. The `Inherits System.Windows.Forms.Form` instruction allows the CopyrightForm class (the derived class) to inherit the attributes and behaviors of the Form class (the base class), which is provided by Visual Studio .NET and defined in the System.Windows.Forms namespace. In other words, rather than you having to write all of the code necessary to create a Windows Form object, Visual Studio .NET provides the basic code in the Form class. As you add controls to your Windows Form object, the Windows Form designer makes the appropriate modifications to the base class. You can view the additional code generated by the designer by clicking the plus box ⊞ next to the `Windows Form Designer generated code` entry in the Code editor window.

To view the code generated by the designer:

1 Click the **plus box** ⊞ next to the Windows Form Designer generated code entry in the Code editor window. Do not be overwhelmed by the code generated by the designer. In most cases, you do not need to concern yourself with this code.

2 Scroll the Code editor window as shown in Figure 1-33.

Class Name list box

Method Name list box

creates the AuthorLabel control

assigns the True value to the AuthorLabel's AutoSize property

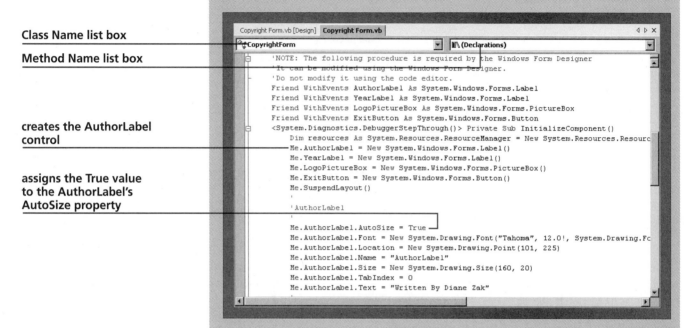

Figure 1-33: Code generated by the Windows Form Designer

Each time you added a control to the CopyrightForm and then set the control's properties, the designer entered the appropriate code in the CopyrightForm class definition. For example, when you used the toolbox to add the AuthorLabel control to the form, the designer entered the instruction `Me.AuthorLabel = New System.Windows.Forms.Label()` in the CopyrightForm class definition. The `Me` in the instruction refers to the current form, which, in this case, is the CopyrightForm. Similarly, when you set the AuthorLabel's AutoSize property to True in the Properties window, the designer recorded the instruction `Me.AuthorLabel.AutoSize = True` in the CopyrightForm class definition. The instruction, called an **assignment statement**, assigns the value `True` to the AutoSize property of the AuthorLabel control on the CopyrightForm.

3 Click the **minus box** ⊟ next to the Windows Form Designer generated code entry in the Code editor window. This collapses the code to one line.

As Figure 1-33 indicates, the Code editor window also contains a Class Name list box and a Method Name list box. The **Class Name list box** lists the names of the objects included in the user interface. The **Method Name list box**, on the other hand, lists the events to which the selected object is capable of responding. You use the Class Name and Method Name list boxes to select the object and event, respectively, that you want to code. In this case, you want the Exit button to end the application when the button is clicked. Use the list boxes to select the ExitButton object and Click event.

In OOP, the events to which an object can respond are considered the object's behaviors, because they represent actions that the object can have performed on it. The Code editor window exposes the object's behaviors to the programmer.

ExitButton's Click event procedure

you enter your instructions here

To select both the ExitButton object and Click event:

1 Click the **Class Name** list arrow, then click **ExitButton** in the list. Click the **Method Name** list arrow, then click **Click** in the list. See Figure 1-34. (Do not be concerned if you cannot view all of the ExitButton's code. The font used to display the text in the Code editor window shown in Figure 1-34 was changed to 10-point Microsoft Sans Serif so that you could view all of the code in the figure. It is not necessary for you to change the font.)

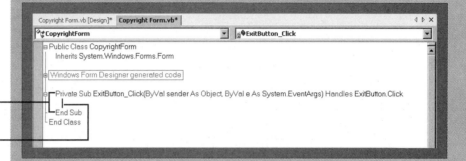

Figure 1-34: ExitButton's Click event procedure shown in the Code editor window

To change the font used to display text in the Code editor window, click Tools on the menu bar, and then click Options. When the Options dialog box appears, click the Environment folder to open it, then click Fonts and Colors. Select Text Editor from the Show settings for list box, and Text from the Display items list box.

The `Public` keyword in the class definition indicates that the class can be used by code defined outside of the class.

Notice that, when you select an object and event, additional code automatically appears in the Code editor window. To help you follow the rules of the Visual Basic .NET programming language, called **syntax**, the Code editor provides you with a **code template** for every event procedure. The first line in the Code template is called the **procedure header**, and the last line is called the **procedure footer**.

The procedure header begins with the two keywords `Private Sub`. A **keyword** is a word that has a special meaning in a programming language. The **Sub** keyword is an abbreviation of the term **sub procedure**, which, in programming terminology, refers to a block of code that performs a specific task. The **Private** keyword indicates that the procedure can be used only within the class in which it is defined—in this case, only within the CopyrightForm class.

Following the `Sub` keyword is the name of the object (`ExitButton`), an underscore (_), the name of the event (`Click`), and parentheses containing `ByVal sender as Object, ByVal e As System.EventArgs`. The items within the parentheses are called **parameters** and represent information that is passed to the procedure when it is invoked. For now, you do not need to worry about the parameters; you learn more about parameters later in this book.

Following the items in parentheses in the procedure header is `Handles ExitButton.Click`. This part of the procedure header indicates that the procedure handles (or is associated with) the ExitButton's Click event. In other words, the procedure will be processed when the ExitButton is clicked. As you learn later in this book, you can associate the same procedure with more than one event. To do so, you list each event, separated by commas, in the `Handles` section of the procedure header.

The code template ends with the procedure footer, which contains the keywords `End Sub`. You enter your Visual Basic .NET instructions between the `Private Sub` and `End Sub` lines. In this case, the instructions in the Code window tell the ExitButton how to respond to the Click event.

If you are using a color monitor, the keywords in the code appear in a different color from the rest of the code. The Code editor window displays keywords in a different color to help you quickly identify these elements. In this case, the color-coding helps you easily locate the procedure header and footer.

The insertion point located in the event procedure indicates where you enter your code for the ExitButton. Notice that the Code editor automatically indents the line between the procedure header and footer. Indenting the lines within a procedure makes the instructions easier to read and is a common programming practice.

In this case, you want to instruct the button to end the application whenever the button is clicked; you can use the `Me.Close` method to do so. A **method** is simply a predefined Visual Basic .NET procedure that you can call (or invoke) when needed. When you call the **Me.Close method**, for example, Visual Basic .NET terminates the current application. You call the `Me.Close` method by entering the instruction `Me.Close()` in a procedure. Notice the empty set of parentheses after the method's name in the instruction. The parentheses are required when calling any of Visual Basic .NET's methods; however, depending on the method, the parentheses may or may not be empty.

To code the ExitButton's Click event procedure, then save and start the application:

1 Type **me.close()** in the Code editor window, and then press **Enter**. See Figure 1-35.

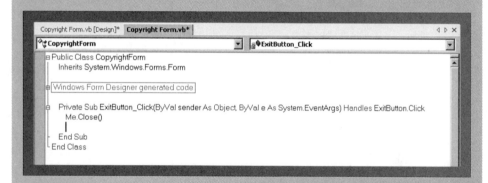

Figure 1-35: `Me.Close` method entered in the ExitButton's Click event procedure

When the user clicks the Exit button on the copyright screen, the computer reads and processes the instructions entered in the button's Click event procedure. It is probably no surprise to you that the instructions are processed, one after another, in the order in which they are entered in the procedure. In programming, this is referred to as **sequential processing** or as the **sequence structure**. (You learn about two other programming structures [selection and repetition] in future tutorials.) You are finished with the Code editor window, so you can close it.

2 Click the **Close** button ☒ on the Code editor window's title bar.

3 Click **File** on the menu bar, and then click **Save All**.

Now start the application to verify that the Exit button ends the application.

4 Click **Debug** on the menu bar, and then click **Start**. The copyright screen appears.

5 Click the **Exit** button to end the application. The application ends and you are returned to the designer window.

6 Close the Output window, then use the File menu to close the solution.

7 Permanently display the Toolbox and Solution Explorer windows.

tip

If you forget to enter the parentheses after a method's name, the Code editor will enter them for you when you move the insertion point to another line in the Code editor window.

Now you can either take a break or complete the end-of-lesson questions and exercises before moving on to the next lesson. You will complete the copyright screen in Lesson C.

SUMMARY

To sort the tools in the toolbox alphabetically by name:

■ Right-click the Windows Forms tab, and then click Sort Items Alphabetically.

To display the tool icons and tool names in the toolbox:

■ Right-click the Windows Forms tab, and then click List View to select it.

To display only the tool icons in the toolbox:

■ Right-click the Windows Forms tab, and then click List View to deselect it.
■ You can display the tool's name by resting your mouse pointer on the tool's icon.

To move a tool to a different location in the toolbox:

■ Click the tool to select it, then drag the tool to the new location.

To restore the Windows Forms tab to its original state:

■ Right-click the Windows Forms tab, then click Customize Toolbox. Click the .NET Framework Components tab in the Customize Toolbox dialog box. Click the Reset button, then click the Yes button, and then click the OK button.

To add a control to a form:

■ Click the appropriate tool in the toolbox, but do not release the mouse button. Drag the mouse pointer to the form. As you drag, both an outline of a rectangle and a plus box follow the mouse pointer. When you release the mouse button, the control appears on the form.
■ You also can add a control to a form by clicking the appropriate tool in the toolbox and then clicking the form. Additionally, you can click the control's tool in the toolbox, then place the mouse pointer on the form, and then press the left mouse button and drag the mouse pointer until the control is the desired size.

To delete a control from a form:

■ Select the control you want to delete, then press the Delete key. To delete a control, the designer window must be the active window.

To display text that the user cannot edit while the application is running:

■ Use the Label tool **A** to create a label control. Then set the label control's Text property.

To automatically size a label control to fit its current contents:

■ Set the label control's AutoSize property to True.

To move a control to a different location on the form:

■ Drag the control to the desired location. You also can set the control's Location property. Additionally, you can select the control and then press and hold down the Control key as you press either the ↑, ↓, →, or ← key on your keyboard.

To size a control:

■ Drag the control's sizing handles. You also can set the control's Size, Height, and Width properties. Additionally, you can select the control and then press and hold down the Shift key as you press either the ↑, ↓, →, or ← key on your keyboard.

To control the type, style, and size of the font used to display text in a control:

■ Set the control's Font property.

To select multiple controls:

■ Click the first control you want to select, then Control+click each of the other controls you want to select.
■ You also can select a group of controls on the form by placing the mouse pointer ⬉ slightly above and to the left of the first control you want to select, then pressing the left mouse button and dragging. A dotted rectangle appears as you drag. When all of the controls you want to select are within (or at least touched by) the dotted rectangle, release the mouse button. All of the controls surrounded or touched by the dotted rectangle will be selected.
■ You cancel the selection of one of the selected controls by pressing and holding down the Control key as you click the control. You cancel the selection of all of the selected controls by releasing the Control key and then clicking the form or an unselected control on the form.

To center one or more controls on the form:

■ Select any controls you want to center. Click Format on the menu bar, point to Center in Form, and then click either Horizontally or Vertically.

To align the borders of two or more controls on the form:

■ Select the controls you want to align. Click Format on the menu bar, point to Align, and then click the appropriate option.

To make two or more controls on the form the same size:

■ Select the controls you want to size. Click Format on the menu bar, point to Make Same Size, and then click the appropriate option.

To display a graphic in a control in the user interface:

■ Use the PictureBox tool 🖻 to create a picture box control, then set the control's Image and SizeMode properties.

To display a standard button that performs an action when clicked:

■ Use the Button tool 🔳 to create a button control.

To change a project's properties:

■ Right-click the project's name in the Solution Explorer window, then click Properties.

To start and stop an application:

■ Click Debug on the menu bar, and then click Start to start the application. You also can press the F5 key on your keyboard.

■ Click Debug on the menu bar, and then click Stop Debugging to stop the application. You also can press Shift+F5.

To open the Code editor window:

■ Right-click anywhere on the form (except the form's title bar), and then click View Code on the context menu. You also can click View on the menu bar, and then click Code; or you can press the F7 key on your keyboard. (To use the View menu or the F7 key, the designer window should be the active window.) You also can open the Code editor window by double-clicking the form or a control on the form. Doing so brings up a default event procedure for the object you double-clicked.

To display an object's event procedure in the Code editor window:

■ Open the Code editor window. Use the Class Name list box to select the desired object, then use the Method Name list box to select the desired event.

To allow the user to end a running application:

■ One way of allowing the user to end a running application is to include the `Me.Close` method in the Click event procedure of a button control.

QUESTIONS

1. The tools you use when designing your user interface are found on the _____ tab on the Toolbox window.
   a. Clipboard Ring
   b. Components
   c. Data
   d. General
   e. Windows Forms

2. Which of the following statements is false?
   a. When the List View option on the Windows Forms tab context menu is selected, the tool icons and names appear on the tab.
   b. You can sort the tools on the Windows Forms tab alphabetically by name.
   c. When only the tool icons appear on the Windows Forms tab, you can display a tool's name by resting your mouse pointer on the tool's icon.
   d. You can drag a tool to another location on the Windows Forms tab.
   e. None of the above.

3. The purpose of the _____ control is to display text that the user is not allowed to edit while the application is running.
    a. Button
    b. DisplayBox
    c. Label
    d. PictureBox
    e. TextBox

4. Which of the following properties automatically adjusts the size of a label control to fit the control's current contents?
    a. AutoSize
    b. AutoSizeControl
    c. AutoSizeLabel
    d. Size
    e. SizeAuto

5. The text displayed in a label control is stored in the control's _____ property.
    a. Caption
    b. Display
    c. Label
    d. Name
    e. Text

6. How can you tell when a button control is selected in the designer window?
    a. A thin line surrounds the control.
    b. Sizing handles appear around the control.
    c. The Object box in the Properties window contains the control's name and class.
    d. Both a and c.
    e. Both b and c.

7. How can you tell when an auto-sized label control is selected in the designer window?
    a. A thin line surrounds the control.
    b. Sizing handles appear around the control.
    c. The Object box in the Properties window contains the control's name and class.
    d. Both a and c.
    e. Both b and c.

8. The first value stored in the Location property specifies the number of _____.
    a. pixels from the left border of the form to the left border of the control
    b. pixels from the right border of the form to the right border of the control
    c. pixels between the top border of the form and the top border of the control
    d. pixels between the bottom border of the form and the bottom border of the control

9. The Font property allows you to change the _____ of the font used to display text in an object.
    a. type
    b. style
    c. size
    d. measurement unit
    e. All of the above.

10. The Format menu contains options that allow you to _____.
    a. align two or more controls
    b. center one or more controls horizontally within the form
    c. center one or more controls vertically within the form
    d. make two or more controls the same size
    e. All of the above.

11. The _____ property determines the graphic to display in a picture box control.
    a. DisplayImage
    b. Graphic
    c. Image
    d. Picture
    e. PictureBox

12. You can size a picture box control to fit its current contents by setting the control's _____ property.
    a. AutoSize
    b. ImageSize
    c. PictureSize
    d. Size
    e. SizeMode

13. The Button class is defined in the _____ namespace.
    a. System.Forms
    b. System.Windows.Forms
    c. System.Windows.Forms.Button
    d. Windows.Button
    e. Windows.Forms

14. The caption that appears on a button is stored in the button control's _____ property.
    a. Caption
    b. Command
    c. Control
    d. Label
    e. Text

15. Which of the following statements is false?
    a. You can start an application by clicking Debug on the menu bar, and then clicking Start.
    b. The executable file that Visual Studio .NET automatically creates when you start an application has the same name as the solution, but with an .exe extension.
    c. You can use the Project Properties dialog box to change the executable file's name.
    d. You can use the Project Properties dialog box to select the form that will first appear when the application is started.
    e. None of the above.

16. The _____ method terminates the application.
    a. Me.Close
    b. Me.Done
    c. Me.Finish
    d. Me.Stop
    e. None of the above.

17. Actions such as clicking, double-clicking, and scrolling are called _____.
    a. actionEvents
    b. events
    c. happenings
    d. procedures
    e. None of the above.

18. Define the term "syntax".

19. Explain the purpose of the Class Name and Method Name list boxes in the Code editor window.

20. Define the term "keyword".

E X E R C I S E S

1. In this exercise, you add controls to a Windows Form. You also change the properties of the form and its controls.

    a.   If necessary, start Visual Studio .NET and permanently display the Solution Explorer window.

    b.   Click File on the menu bar, and then click Open Solution. Open the Mechanics Solution (Mechanics Solution.sln) file, which is contained in the VBNET\Tut01\Mechanics Solution folder. If the designer window is not open, click the form file's name in the Solution Explorer window, then use the View menu to open the designer window.

    c.   Assign the filename Mechanics Form.vb to the form file object.

    d.   Assign the name MechForm to the Windows Form object.

    e.   The Windows Form object's title bar should say IMA. Set the appropriate property.

    f.   The Windows Form object should be centered on the screen when it first appears. Set the appropriate property.

    g.   Add a label control to the form. Change the label control's name to CompanyLabel.

    h.   The label control should stretch to fit its current contents. Set the appropriate property.

    i.   The label control should display the text "International Mechanics Association" (without the quotation marks). Set the appropriate property.

    j.   Display the label control's text in italics using the Tahoma font. Change the size of the text to 12 points.

    k.   The label control should be located 16 pixels from the top of the form.

    l.   Center the label control horizontally on the form.

    m.   Add a button control to the form. Change the button control's name to ExitButton.

    n.   The button control should display the text "Exit" (without the quotation marks). Set the appropriate property.

    o.   Display the button control's text using the Tahoma font. Change the size of the text to 12 points.

    p.   The button control should be located 200 pixels from the left border of the form, and 240 pixels from the top of the form.

    q.   Open the Code editor window. Enter the `Me.Close` method in the ExitButton's Click event procedure.

    r.   Display the Mechanics Project Properties Pages dialog box. Open the Common Properties folder, then click General. Use the Assembly name text box to change the executable file's name to IMA. Change the startup form to MechForm.

    s.   Save the solution. Start the application, then use the Exit button to stop the application.

    t.   Close the Output window, then close the solution.

2. In this exercise, you create the user interface shown in Figure 1-36.
   a. If necessary, start Visual Studio .NET and permanently display the Solution Explorer window.
   b. Create a blank solution named Costello Solution. Save the solution in the VBNET\Tut01 folder.
   c. Add a Visual Basic .NET Windows Application project to the solution. Name the project Costello Project.
   d. Assign the filename Costello Form.vb to the form file object.
   e. Create the interface shown in Figure 1-36. Name the Windows Form object and controls appropriately. You can use any font type, style, and size for the label controls.

Figure 1-36

   f. Code the Exit button so that it terminates the application when it is clicked.
   g. Change the executable file's name to Costello Motors. Change the startup form to the name of your Windows Form object.
   h. Save the solution. Start the application, then use the Exit button to stop the application.
   i. Close the Output window, then close the solution.

3. In this exercise, you create the user interface shown in Figure 1-37.
   a. If necessary, start Visual Studio .NET and permanently display the Solution Explorer window.
   b. Create a blank solution named Tabatha Solution. Save the solution in the VBNET\Tut01 folder.
   c. Add a Visual Basic .NET Windows Application project to the solution. Name the project Tabatha Project.
   d. Assign the filename Tabatha Form.vb to the form file object.
   e. Create the interface shown in Figure 1-37. Name the Windows Form object and controls appropriately. You can use any font type, style, and size for the label controls.

Figure 1-37

    f.   Code the Exit button so that it terminates the application when it is clicked.

    g.   Change the executable file's name to Tabatha. Change the startup form to the name of your Windows Form object.

    h.   Save the solution. Start the application, then use the Exit button to stop the application.

    i.   Close the Output window, then close the solution.

Exercise 4 is a Discovery Exercise. Discovery Exercises, which may include topics that are not covered in this lesson, allow you to "discover" the solutions to problems on your own.

discovery ▶

4.   In this exercise, you learn about the Format menu's Align and Make Same Size options.

    a.   If necessary, start Visual Studio .NET and permanently display the Solution Explorer window.

    b.   Open the Jerrods Solution (Jerrods Solution.sln) file, which is contained in the VBNET\Tut01\Jerrods Solution folder. If the designer window is not open, click the form file's name in the Solution Explorer window, then use the View menu to open the designer window.

    c.   Click one of the button controls on the form, then press and hold down the Ctrl (or Control) key as you click the remaining two button controls.

Notice that the sizing handles on the last button selected are black, whereas the sizing handles on the other two button controls are white. The Align and Make Same Size options on the Format menu use the control with the black sizing handles as the reference control when aligning and sizing the selected controls. First, practice with the Align option by aligning the three button controls by their left borders.

    d.   Click Format, point to Align, and then click Lefts. The left borders of the first two controls you selected are aligned with the left border of the last control you selected.

The Make Same Size option makes the selected objects the same height, width, or both. Here again, the last object you select determines the size.

    e.   Click the form to deselect the three buttons. Click Button2, then Ctrl+click Button3, and then Ctrl+click Button1. Click Format, point to Make Same Size, and then click Both. The height and width of the first two controls you selected now match the height and width of the last control you selected. Click the form to deselect the button controls.

    f.   Save and then close the solution.

After completing this lesson, you will be able to:

- Set the properties of a timer control
- Delete a control from the form
- Delete code from the Code editor window
- Code the timer control's Tick event
- Remove and/or disable the Minimize, Maximize, and Close buttons
- Prevent the user from sizing a form
- Print the project's code

Completing the Copyright Screen

Using the Timer Tool

Recall that the copyright screen will serve as a splash screen for each custom application created by Interlocking Software. Splash screens typically do not contain an Exit button; rather, they use a timer control to automatically remove the splash screen after a set period of time. You create a timer control using the **Timer tool** in the toolbox. In this lesson, you remove the Exit button from the copyright screen and replace it with a timer control. First, open the Copyright Solution.

To open the Copyright Solution:

1   If necessary, start Visual Studio .NET and close the Start Page window.
2   If necessary, permanently display the Toolbox and Solution Explorer windows.
3   Click **File** on the menu bar, and then click **Open Solution**. The Open Solution dialog box opens. Open the **Copyright Solution** (Copyright Solution.sln) file, which is contained in the VBNET\Tut01\Copyright Solution folder.
4   If necessary, open the designer window to view the copyright screen.

You can use a **timer control** to process code at regular time intervals. You simply set the control's **Interval property** to the length of the desired time interval, in milliseconds. You also set its Enabled property to True. The **Enabled property** determines whether an object can respond to an event—in this case, whether it can respond to the Tick event. You then enter the code you want processed into the control's Tick event procedure. The Tick event procedure tells the computer what to do after each time interval has elapsed. Use the Timer tool to add a timer control to the copyright screen.

To add a timer control to the copyright screen, and then change its properties:

1   Auto-hide the Solution Explorer window. If necessary, permanently display the Properties window.
2   Click the **Timer** tool in the toolbox, then drag a timer control to the form. (Do not worry about the exact location.) When you release the mouse button, a timer control appears in the component tray, as shown in Figure 1-38.

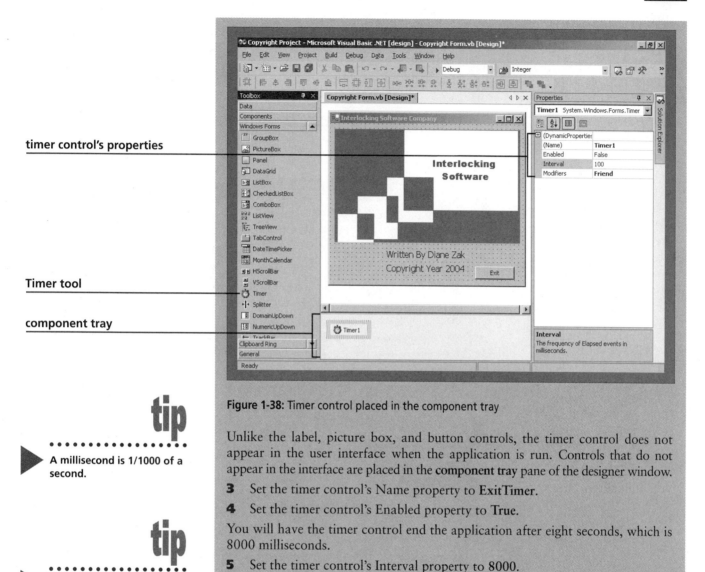

timer control's properties

Timer tool

component tray

Figure 1-38: Timer control placed in the component tray

Unlike the label, picture box, and button controls, the timer control does not appear in the user interface when the application is run. Controls that do not appear in the interface are placed in the **component tray** pane of the designer window.

3   Set the timer control's Name property to **ExitTimer**.

4   Set the timer control's Enabled property to **True**.

You will have the timer control end the application after eight seconds, which is 8000 milliseconds.

5   Set the timer control's Interval property to **8000**.

6   Auto-hide the Toolbox and Properties windows.

Now that you have a timer control on the form, you no longer need the Exit button, so you can delete it and its associated code. You then will enter the `Me.Close` method in the timer control's Tick event procedure.

To delete the ExitButton and its code, then code the ExitTimer control:

1   Click the **ExitButton** to select it, then press **Delete** to delete the control from the Windows form.

Note that deleting a control from the form does not delete the control's code, which remains in the Code editor window.

2   Click **View** on the menu bar, and then click **Code**. Select the entire Click event procedure for the ExitButton, as shown in Figure 1-39. (Do not be concerned if you cannot view all of the ExitButton's code. The font used to display the text in the Code editor window shown in Figure 1-39 was changed to 10-point Microsoft Sans Serif so that you could view all of the code in the figure. It is not necessary for you to change the font.)

---

tip

• • • • • • • • • • • • • • • •

▶ A millisecond is 1/1000 of a second.

---

tip

• • • • • • • • • • • • • • • •

▶ You can delete a control from the component tray by right-clicking it and then clicking Delete.

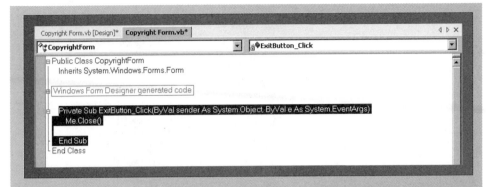

Figure 1-39: ExitButton's Click event procedure selected in the Code editor window

3 Press **Delete** to delete the selected code from the Code editor window.

Now enter the `Me.Close` method in the ExitTimer's Tick event procedure.

4 Click the **Class Name** list arrow, and then click **ExitTimer** in the list. Click the **Method Name** list arrow, and then click **Tick** in the list. The ExitTimer's Tick event procedure appears in the Code editor window.

5 Type **me.close()** and press **Enter**. See Figure 1-40. (Recall that the font used to display the text shown in the Code editor was changed to 10-point Microsoft Sans Serif so that you could view all of the code.)

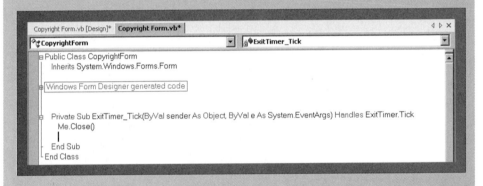

Figure 1-40: ExitTimer's Tick event procedure

Now save the solution and then start the application.

6 Click **File** on the menu bar, and then click **Save All**.

7 Click **Debug** on the menu bar, and then click **Start**. Place your mouse pointer ⇘ on the right border of the form until ⇘ becomes ↔, then drag the form's border to the left. Notice that you can size the form while the application is running. As a general rule, the user typically is not allowed to change the size of a splash screen. You can prevent the user from sizing the form by changing the form's FormBorderStyle property.

After eight seconds elapse, the application ends and the copyright screen is removed from view.

8 Close the Output window. Click the **Copyright Form.vb [Design]** tab to make the designer window the active window.

Now learn about the FormBorderStyle property of a Windows Form object.

Setting the FormBorderStyle Property

The **FormBorderStyle property** determines the border style of a Windows Form object. Figure 1-41 lists the valid settings for the FormBorderStyle property and provides a brief description of the border provided by each setting.

FormBorderStyle setting	Description of the border
Fixed3D	fixed, three-dimensional
FixedDialog	fixed, thick dialog-style
FixedSingle	fixed, thin line
FixedToolWindow	fixed, tool window style
None	no border
Sizable	sizable, normal style (default setting)
SizableToolWindow	sizable, tool window style

Figure 1-41: FormBorderStyle settings

For most applications, you will want to leave the FormBorderStyle setting at its default value, Sizable. When the FormBorderStyle property is set to Sizable, the user can drag the form's borders to change the form's size while the application is running. If you want to prevent the user from sizing the form, you can set the FormBorderStyle property to any of the fixed settings shown in Figure 1-41; splash screens typically use either the None setting or the FixedSingle setting. When the FormBorderStyle property is set to None, no border is drawn around the form. Setting the FormBorderStyle property to FixedSingle, on the other hand, draws a fixed, thin line around the form. You will set the copyright screen's FormBorderStyle property to FixedSingle.

To change the FormBorderStyle property, then save and start the application:

1 Click the **form's title bar** to select the form.

2 Set the FormBorderStyle property to **FixedSingle**.

3 Click **File** on the menu bar, and then click **Save All**.

4 Click **Debug** on the menu bar, and then click **Start**. Try to size the form by dragging one of its borders. You will notice that you cannot size the form using its border.

5 When the application ends, click **Debug** on the menu bar, and then click **Start** to display the splash screen again. Notice that the copyright screen's title bar contains a Minimize button, a Maximize button, and a Close button. As a general rule, most splash screens do not contain these elements. You learn how to remove the elements, as well as the title bar itself, in the next section.

6 If necessary, click the **Close** button ☒ on the splash screen's title bar.

7 When the application ends, close the Output window.

Now learn about a Windows Form object's MinimizeBox, MaximizeBox, and ControlBox properties.

The MinimizeBox, MaximizeBox, and ControlBox Properties

You can use a Windows Form object's MinimizeBox property to disable the Minimize button that appears on the form's title bar. Similarly, you can use the MaximizeBox property to disable the Maximize button. You experiment with both properties in the next set of steps.

To experiment with the MinimizeBox and MaximizeBox properties:

1   If necessary, click the **form's title bar** to select the form.

First, disable the Minimize button.

2   Set the MinimizeBox property to **False**. Notice that the Minimize button appears dimmed (grayed-out) on the title bar. This indicates that the button is not available for use.

Now enable the Minimize button and disable the Maximize button.

3   Set the MinimizeBox property to **True**, then set the MaximizeBox property to **False**. Now the Maximize button appears dimmed (grayed-out) on the title bar.

Now observe what happens if both the MinimizeBox and MaximizeBox properties are set to False.

4   Set the MinimizeBox property to **False**. (The MaximizeBox property is already set to False.) Notice that when both properties are set to False, the buttons are not disabled; rather, they are removed from the title bar.

Now return the buttons to their original state.

5   Set the MinimizeBox and MaximizeBox properties to **True**.

Unlike most applications, splash screens typically do not contain a title bar. You can remove the title bar by setting the Windows Form object's ControlBox property to False, and then removing the text from its Text property. You try this next.

To remove the title bar from the copyright screen:

1   If necessary, click the **form's title bar** to select the form.

2   Set the ControlBox property to **False**. Notice that setting this property to False removes the title bar elements (icon and buttons) from the form; however, it does not remove the title bar itself. To remove the title bar, you must delete the contents of the form's Text property.

3   Delete the contents of the form's Text property.

4   Click **File** on the menu bar, and then click **Save All**.

5   Click **Debug** on the menu bar, and then click **Start**. The copyright screen appears without a title bar. See Figure 1-42.

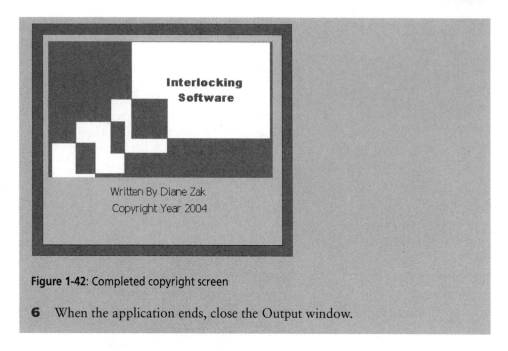

Interlocking Software

Written By Diane Zak
Copyright Year 2004

Figure 1-42: Completed copyright screen

6 When the application ends, close the Output window.

Before ending this lesson you learn how to print the application.

Printing Your Code

You always should print a copy of the code entered in the Code editor window, because the printout will help you understand and maintain the application in the future. To print the code, the Code editor window must be the active, or current, window.

To print the copyright screen's code:

1 Click the **Copyright Form.vb** tab to make the Code editor window the active window.

Only the code that is not collapsed will be sent to the printer for printing.

2 Verify that the only plus box ⊞ in the Code editor window appears next to the Windows Form Designer generated code entry. If a plus box appears anywhere else in the Code editor window, click ⊞. (You typically do not need to print the code generated by the designer.)

3 Click **File** on the menu bar, then click **Print**. The Print dialog box opens.

4 If your computer is connected to a printer, click the **OK** button to begin printing; otherwise, click the **Cancel** button. If you clicked the OK button, your printer prints the code.

5 Click **File** on the menu bar, and then click **Close Solution**.

6 Click **File** on the menu bar, and then click **Exit** to exit Visual Studio .NET.

You now have completed Tutorial 1. You can either take a break or complete the end-of lesson questions and exercises.

S U M M A R Y

To perform code at specified intervals of time:

■ Use the Timer tool 🕐 to add a timer control to the form. Set the timer control's Interval property to the number of milliseconds for each interval. Set the timer control's Enabled property to True to turn the timer control on. Enter the code in the timer control's Tick event procedure.

To delete a control that contains code:

■ Select the control you want to delete, then press Delete. Open the Code editor window and delete the control's event procedures.

To enable/disable the Minimize button on the form's title bar:

■ Set the form's MinimizeBox property.

To enable/disable the Maximize button on the form's title bar:

■ Set the form's MaximizeBox property.

To control whether the icon, as well as the Minimize, Maximize, and Close buttons, appear in the form's title bar:

■ Set the form's ControlBox property.

To control the border style of the form:

■ Set the form's FormBorderStyle property.

To print the Visual Basic .NET code:

■ Open the Code editor window. Click File on the menu bar, and then click Print. Click the OK button in the Print dialog box.

Q U E S T I O N S

1. You can use a _____ control to process code at regular time intervals.
    a. clock
    b. stopwatch
    c. timer
    d. watch
    e. None of the above.

2. The _____ property determines whether an object can respond to an event.
    a. Enabled
    b. Event
    c. PermitResponse
    d. Respond
    e. Response

3. After each time interval has elapsed, the code in a timer control's _____ is processed.
    a. Interval property
    b. Interval event procedure
    c. Tick property
    d. Tick event procedure
    e. Timer event procedure

4. Ten seconds equals _____ milliseconds.
    a. 100
    b. 1000
    c. 10,000
    d. 100,000
    e. 1,000,000

5. Which of the following is false?
    a. When you add a timer control to a form, the control appears in the component tray.
    b. The user can see a timer control while the application is running.
    c. You can delete a control from the component tray by right-clicking it and then clicking Delete.
    d. The number entered in a timer control's Interval property represents the number of milliseconds for each interval.
    e. None of the above.

6. To disable the Minimize button on a form's title bar, set the form's _____ property to False.
    a. ButtonMin
    b. ButtonMinimize
    c. Minimize
    d. MinimizeBox
    e. MinimizeButton

7. The _____ property determines whether the user can drag a form's borders while the application is running.
    a. BorderStyle
    b. Drag
    c. FormBorder
    d. StyleBorder
    e. None of the above.

8. You can remove the Minimize, Maximize, and Close buttons from a form's title bar by setting the form's _____ property to False.
    a. ControlBox
    b. ControlButton
    c. Elements
    d. TitleBar
    e. TitleBarElements

9. Explain how you print a project's code.

10. Explain how you delete a control that contains code.

E X E R C I S E S

1. In this exercise, you modify an existing form by replacing its button control with a timer control.

    a. If necessary, start Visual Studio .NET and permanently display the Solution Explorer window.

    b. Click File on the menu bar, and then click Open Solution. Open the Jefferson Solution (Jefferson Solution.sln) file, which is contained in the VBNET\Tut01\Jefferson Solution folder. If the designer window is not open, click the form file's name in the Solution Explorer window, then use the View menu to open the designer window.

    c. Delete the ExitButton from the form, then delete the ExitButton's code from the Code editor window.

    d. Return to the designer window. Add a timer control to the form. Change the timer control's name to ExitTimer.

    e. Set the timer control's Enabled property to True.

    f. The timer control should end the application after 10 seconds have elapsed. Set the appropriate property. Then, enter the `Me.Close` method in the appropriate event procedure in the Code editor window.

    g. Save the solution. Start the application. After 10 seconds, the application should end.

    h. Remove the elements (icon and buttons) from the form's title bar.

    i. Delete the text that appears in the form's title bar.

    j. Set the form's FormBorderStyle property to FixedSingle.

    k. Save the solution. Start the application. After 10 seconds, the application should end.

    l. Close the Output window, then close the solution.

2. In this exercise, you design your own user interface.

    a. If necessary, start Visual Studio .NET and permanently display the Solution Explorer window.

    b. Create a blank solution named My Interface Solution. Save the solution in the VBNET\Tut01 folder.

    c. Add a Visual Basic .NET Windows Application project to the solution. Name the project My Interface Project.

    d. Assign the filename My Interface Form.vb to the form file object.

    e. Use one or more label and picture box controls in your interface. Include a button that the user can click to end the application. You can use any font type, style, and size for the label control(s). You also can use any graphic for the picture box.

    f. Be sure to name the Windows Form object and controls appropriately.

    g. Change the executable file's name to My Interface. Change the startup form to the name of your Windows Form object.

    h. Disable the Minimize and Maximize buttons on the form.

    i. Save the solution. Start the application, then use the Exit button to stop the application.

    j. Close the Output window, then close the solution.

    Exercises 3 through 5 are Discovery Exercises. Discovery Exercises, which may include topics that are not covered in this lesson, allow you to "discover" the solutions to problems on your own.

discovery ▶
3. In this exercise, you learn how to enter an assignment statement in an event procedure.

    a. If necessary, start Visual Studio .NET and permanently display the Solution Explorer window.

    b. Create a blank solution named Icon Solution. Save the solution in the VBNET\Tut01 folder.

    c. Add a Visual Basic .NET Windows Application project to the solution. Name the project Icon Project.

d. Assign the filename Icon Form.vb to the form file object.

e. Add a picture box control and three buttons to the form. (The location and size of the controls is not important.) Name the controls IconPictureBox, OnButton, OffButton, and ExitButton.

f. Include any graphic in the picture box control.

g. The captions for the three buttons should be On, Off, and Exit. Change the appropriate property for each button.

h. The Exit button should end the application when clicked. Enter the appropriate code in the Code editor window.

i. Display the OffButton's Click event procedure in the Code editor window. In the procedure, enter the instruction `Me.IconPictureBox.Visible = False`. This instruction is called an assignment statement, because it assigns a value to a container; in this case, the container is the Visible property of the IconPictureBox control. When you click the OffButton, the `Me.IconPictureBox.Visible = False` instruction will hide the picture box from view.

j. Display the OnButton's Click event procedure in the Code editor window. In the procedure, enter an instruction that will display the picture box.

k. Save the solution, then start the application. Use the OffButton to hide the picture box, then use the OnButton to display the picture box. Finally, use the ExitButton to end the application.

l. Close the Output window, then close the solution.

discovery ▶ 4. In this exercise, you learn how to display a graphic on the face of a button control. (This exercise assumes that you have completed Discovery Exercise 3.)

a. If necessary, start Visual Studio .NET and permanently display the Solution Explorer window.

b. Click File on the menu bar, and then click Open Solution. Open the Icon Solution (Icon Solution.sln) file, which is contained in the VBNET\Tut01\Icon Solution folder. If the designer window is not open, click the form file's name in the Solution Explorer window, then use the View menu to open the designer window.

You use a button's Image property to specify the graphic you want displayed on the face of the button. You use a button's ImageAlign property to specify the graphic's alignment on the button.

c. Click the OnButton. Set the Image property using any of the Visual Studio .NET icons. The icons are usually stored in the Program Files\Microsoft Visual Studio .NET\Common7\Graphics\icons folder on either the local hard drive or the network drive.

d. Set the OnButton's ImageAlign property to TopLeft. (Hint: When you click the ImageAlign property's list arrow, nine buttons will appear in the list. Select the button in the top left.)

e. Set the Image and ImageAlign properties of the OffButton and ExitButton.

f. Close the solution.

discovery ▶ 5. In this exercise, you learn how to display a tooltip.

a. If necessary, start Visual Studio .NET and permanently display the Solution Explorer window.

b. Click File on the menu bar, and then click Open Solution. Open the Tooltip Solution (Tooltip Solution.sln) file, which is contained in the VBNET\Tut01\Tooltip Solution folder. If the designer window is not open, click the form file's name in the Solution Explorer window, then use the View menu to open the designer window.

c. Locate the ToolTip tool [image] in the toolbox. Drag a tooltip control to the form. Notice that the control appears in the component tray rather than on the form.

d. Click the ExitButton to select it. Set the button's ToolTip on ToolTip1 property to "Ends the application." (without the quotation marks).

e. Save the solution, then start the application. Hover your mouse pointer over the Exit button. The tooltip "Ends the application." appears in a tooltip box.

f.   Click the Exit button to end the application.

g.   Close the Output window, then close the solution.

Exercise 6 is a Debugging Exercise. Debugging Exercises provide an opportunity for you to detect and correct errors in an existing application.

debugging

6.   In this exercise, you debug an existing application.

a.   If necessary, start Visual Studio .NET and permanently display the Solution Explorer window.

b.   Click File on the menu bar, and then click Open Solution. Open the Debug Solution (Debug Solution.sln) file, which is contained in the VBNET\Tut01\Debug Solution folder. If the designer window is not open, click the form file's name in the Solution Explorer window, then use the View menu to open the designer window.

c.   Start the application. Click the Exit button. Notice that the Exit button does not end the application.

d.   Click the Close button ✖ on the form's title bar to end the application.

e.   Locate and then correct the error.

f.   Start the application. Click the Exit button, which should end the application.

g.   Close the Output window, then close the solution.

Designing Applications

Creating an Order Screen

case ▶ During your second week at Interlocking Software, you and Chris Statton, the senior programmer, meet with the sales manager of Skate-Away Sales. The sales manager, Jacques Cousard, tells you that his company sells skateboards by phone. The skateboards are priced at $100 each and are available in two colors—yellow and blue. He further explains that Skate-Away Sales employs 20 salespeople to answer the phones. The salespeople record each order on a form that contains the customer's name, address, and the number of blue and yellow skateboards ordered. They then calculate the total number of skateboards ordered and the total price of the skateboards, including a 5% sales tax.

Mr. Cousard feels that having the salespeople manually perform the necessary calculations is much too time-consuming and prone to errors. He wants Interlocking to create a computerized application that will solve the problems of the current order-taking system.

Solving the Problem Using a Procedure-Oriented Approach

As you learned in the Overview, procedure-oriented languages preceded OOED (object-oriented/event-driven) languages. Recall that in procedure-oriented languages, the emphasis of a program is on *how* to accomplish a task. The programmer must instruct the computer every step of the way, from the start of the task to the completion of the task. The procedure-oriented approach to problem solving requires a programmer to think in a step-by-step, top-to-bottom fashion. Planning tools such as flowcharts and pseudocode make this approach easier. A **flowchart** uses standardized symbols to show the steps needed to solve a problem. **Pseudocode** uses English phrases to describe the required steps. Some programmers prefer to use flowcharts, while others prefer pseudocode. (You learn more about pseudocode in Lesson C of this tutorial, and about flowcharts in Tutorial 4, as these planning tools also are useful in object-oriented/event-driven programming.) Take a look at a procedure-oriented approach to solving Skate-Away's problem. Figure 2-1 shows the solution written in pseudocode.

---

1. get customer name, street address, city, state, ZIP, number of blue skateboards, number of yellow skateboards

2. calculate total skateboards = number of blue skateboards + number of yellow skateboards

3. calculate total price = total skateboards * $100 * 105%

4. print customer name, street address, city, state, ZIP, number of blue skateboards, number of yellow skateboards, total skateboards, total price

5. end

Figure 2-1: Pseudocode for the procedure-oriented solution

Notice that the pseudocode indicates the sequence of steps the computer must take to process an order. Using the pseudocode as a guide, the programmer then translates the solution into a language that the computer can understand. Figure 2-2 shows the pseudocode translated into Microsoft's QuickBASIC language. QuickBASIC, a procedure-oriented language, is a predecessor of the Visual Basic programming language.

```
Ans$ = "Y"
While Ans$ = "Y" or Ans$ = "y"
        Input "Enter the customer's name", Names$
        Input "Enter the street address:", Address$
        Input "Enter the city:", City$
        Input "Enter the state:", State$
        Input "Enter the zip code:", Zip$
        Input "Enter the number of blue skateboards:", Blue
        Input "Enter the number of yellow skateboards:", Yellow
        Totboards = Blue + Yellow
        Totprice = Totboards * 100 * 1.05
        Print "Customer name:", Names$
        Print "Address:", Address$
        Print "City:", City$
        Print "State:", State$
        Print "Zip:", Zip$
        Print "Blue skateboards:", Blue
        Print "Yellow skateboards:", Yellow
        Print "Total skateboards:", Totboards
        Print "Total price: $", Totprice
        Input "Do you want to enter another order? Enter Y if you
        do, or N if you don't.", Ans$
Wend
End
```

Figure 2-2: Procedure-oriented program written in QuickBASIC

Practice entering an order using this procedure-oriented program.

To use the procedure-oriented program to enter an order:

1 Use the Run command on the Windows Start menu to run the **Procedur** (**Procedur.exe**) file, which is contained in the VBNET\Tut02 folder on your computer's hard disk. A prompt requesting the customer's name appears on the screen.

Assume that Sport Warehouse wants to place an order for 10 blue skateboards and 20 yellow skateboards.

2 Type **Sport Warehouse** and press **Enter**. A prompt requesting the street address appears on the screen.

3 Type **123 Main** and press **Enter**, then type **Glendale** for the city and press **Enter**, then type **IL** for the state and press **Enter**, and then type **60134** for the ZIP code and press **Enter**. The program now prompts you to enter the number of blue skateboards ordered.

4 Type **10** as the number of blue skateboards ordered, then press **Enter**. A prompt requesting the number of yellow skateboards ordered appears next.

5 Type **20** as the number of yellow skateboards ordered, then press **Enter**. The program computes and displays the total skateboards ordered (30) and the total price of the order ($3,150.00). (Recall that skateboards are $100 each and there is a 5% sales tax.) See Figure 2-3.

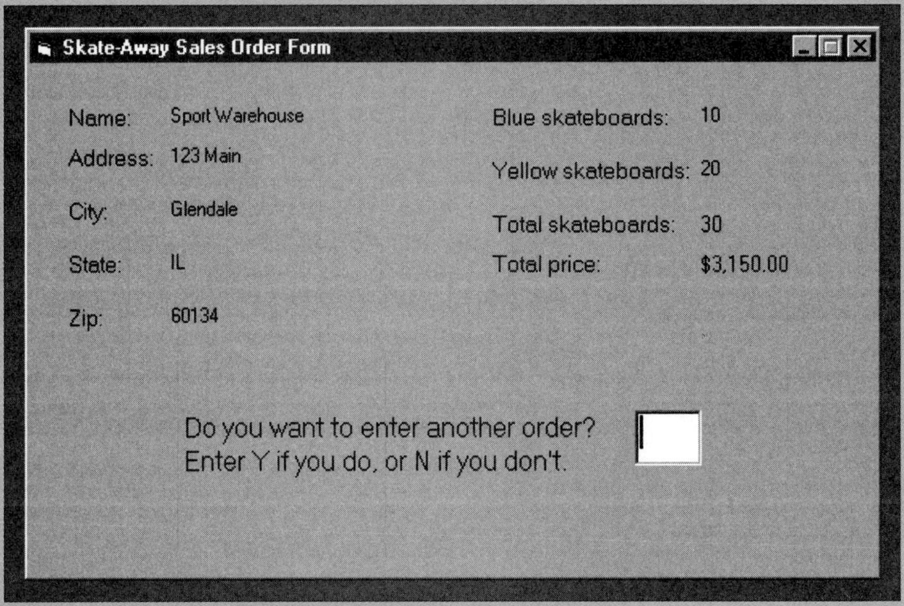

Skate-Away Sales Order Form

Name:	Sport Warehouse	Blue skateboards:	10
Address:	123 Main	Yellow skateboards:	20
City:	Glendale	Total skateboards:	30
State:	IL	Total price:	$3,150.00
Zip:	60134		

Do you want to enter another order?
Enter Y if you do, or N if you don't.

Figure 2-3: Results of the procedure-oriented program

Notice that the screen also contains a prompt that asks if you want to enter another order.

6 Type **n** and press **Enter** to end the program.

Although Skate-Away Sales could use this procedure-oriented program to record its phone orders, the program has one very important limitation that is inherent in all procedure-oriented programs: the user has little, if any, control over the processing of the program. Recall, for example, that you could not control the sequence in which the order information was entered. What if the customer wants to order the yellow skateboards before the blue skateboards? Also recall that you could not change the information once you entered it. What if the customer changes his or her mind about how many blue skateboards to order? And, finally, recall that you had no control over when the program calculated the total order and the total price. What if the customer wants to know the total price of the blue skateboards before placing the yellow skateboard order?

Now look at the object-oriented/event-driven approach to programming.

Solving the Problem Using an Object-Oriented/Event-Driven (OOED) Approach

As you learned in the Overview, in object-oriented/event-driven languages, the emphasis of a program is on the *objects* included in the user interface (such as scroll bars or buttons) and the *events* that occur on those objects (such as scrolling or clicking). Unlike the procedure-oriented approach to problem solving, the OOED approach does not view the solution as a step-by-step, top-to-bottom process. Instead, the OOED programmer's goal is to give the user as much control over the program as possible.

When using the OOED approach to problem solving, the programmer begins by identifying the tasks the application needs to perform. Then the programmer decides on the appropriate objects to which those tasks will be assigned and on any events necessary to trigger those objects to perform their assigned task(s). For example, the copyright screen you created in Tutorial 1 had to provide the user with a way to end the application. Recall that you assigned that task to the Exit button in Lesson B. The event that triggered the Exit button to perform its assigned task was the Click event. In this book, you will use a **TOE** (Task, Object, Event) **chart** to assist you in planning your object-oriented/event-driven programs.

Before learning how to plan an OOED application, run an OOED application written in Visual Basic .NET and designed to solve Skate-Away's problem.

To run the OOED application:

1 Use the Run command on the Start menu to run the **OOED** (OOED.exe) file, which is contained in the VBNET\Tut02 folder on your computer's hard disk. The order screen shown in Figure 2-4 appears.

text box

label control

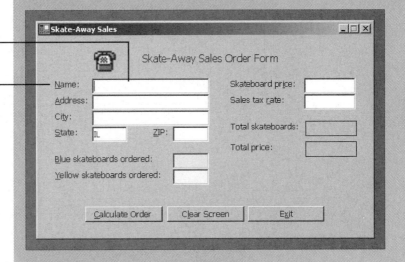

Figure 2-4: Order screen created by the OOED application

The order screen contains a new control: a text box. You use a **text box** to provide areas in the form where the user can enter information.

Notice that Visual Basic .NET displays an insertion point in the first text box. The label control to the left of the text box identifies the information the user should enter; in this case, the user should enter the customer's name. Enter Sport Warehouse's information.

2 Type **Sport Warehouse** as the customer's name, then press **Tab** twice. The insertion point appears in the City text box.

3 Type **Glendale** as the city, then press **Shift+Tab** (press and hold down the Shift key as you press the Tab key) to move the insertion point to the Address text box.

Notice that the OOED application allows you to enter the order information in any order.

tip

• • • • • • • • • • • • • • •

▶ You also can click inside a text box to place the insertion point in the text box.

4 Type **123 Main** as the address, then press **Tab** twice. Because most of Skate-Away's customers reside in Illinois, the OOED application already contains IL in the State box.

5 Press **Tab**, then type **60134** as the ZIP code, and then press **Tab**. The insertion point appears in the Blue skateboards ordered text box.

6 Type **10** as the number of blue skateboards ordered and press **Tab** twice. Type **100** as the skateboard price and press **Tab**, then type **.05** as the sales tax rate and press **Tab**. Click the **Calculate Order** button. The Calculate Order button calculates the total skateboards (10) and the total price ($1,050.00). Notice that the OOED application allows you to tell the customer how much the blue skateboards will cost before the yellow skateboard order is placed.

7 Click the **Yellow skateboards ordered** text box, type **20**, then click the **Calculate Order** button. The application recalculates the total skateboards (30) and the total price ($3,150.00).

Now assume that Sport Warehouse wants to change the number of blue skateboards ordered to 20.

8 Change the number of blue skateboards ordered from 10 to **20**, then click the **Calculate Order** button. The application recalculates the total skateboards (40) and the total price ($4,200.00). See Figure 2-5.

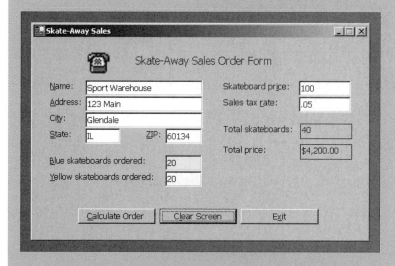

Figure 2-5: Completed order using the OOED program

Notice that the captions that identify each button and text box in the interface have an underlined letter, which is called an access key. An **access key** allows the user to select a control using the Alt key in combination with a character, such as a letter or number. For example, when the salesperson is finished with an order, he or she can clear the screen either by clicking the Clear Screen button or by pressing the Alt key along with the letter l—the Clear Screen button's access key.

9   Press **Alt+l** (the letter "l") to clear the screen for the next order. The previous customer's information (except the state, skateboard price, and sales tax rate) disappears, and the insertion point appears in the Name text box.

    HELP? Pressing Alt+l means to press and hold down the Alt key as you type the letter l. Be sure to type the letter l, and not the number 1.

You learn more about access keys in Lesson B.

10 Press **Alt + x** (or click the **Exit** button) to end the application.

Unlike the procedure-oriented program, the OOED program gives users a great deal of control. Users can enter information in any order, change what they entered at any time, and calculate a subtotal whenever they like.

In Lesson A, you learn how a Visual Basic .NET programmer plans an OOED application. Then, in Lessons B and C, you create the OOED application that you just viewed.

LESSON A

objectives

After completing this lesson, you will be able to:

■ Plan an OOED application in Visual Basic .NET

■ Complete a TOE (Task, Object, Event) chart

■ Follow the Windows standards regarding the layout and labeling of controls

Planning an OOED Application in Visual Basic .NET

Creating an OOED Application

The process a programmer follows when creating an OOED application is similar to the process a builder follows when building a home. Both processes are shown in Figure 2-6.

A builder's process	A programmer's process
1. Meet with the client	1. Meet with the client
2. Plan the home (blueprint)	2. Plan the application (TOE chart)
3. Build the frame	3. Build the user interface
4. Complete the home	4. Code the application
5. Inspect the home and fix any problems	5. Test and debug the application
6. Assemble the documentation	6. Assemble the documentation

Figure 2-6: Processes used by a builder and a programmer

As Figure 2-6 shows, both the builder and the programmer first meet with the client to discuss the client's wants and needs. They then create a plan (blueprint) for the project. After the plan is approved by the client, the builder builds the home's frame; likewise, the programmer builds the user interface, which is the application's frame. Once the frame is built, the builder completes the home by adding the electrical wiring, walls, and so on. Similarly, the programmer completes the application by adding the necessary code (instructions) to the user interface. When the home is complete, the builder makes a final inspection and corrects any problems before the customer moves in. Likewise, the completed application is tested by the programmer, and any problems, called **bugs**, are fixed before the application is given to the user. The final step in both processes is to assemble the project's documentation (paperwork), which then is given to the customer/user.

You learn how to plan an OOED application in this lesson. Steps three through six of the process are covered in Lessons B and C.

Planning an OOED Application

As any builder will tell you, the most important aspect of a home is not its beauty; rather, it is how closely the home matches the buyer's wants and needs. For example, a large dining room may be appropriate for someone who frequently entertains; for someone who does not, it may be a waste of space. The same is true for an OOED application. For an application to meet the user's needs, therefore, it is essential for the programmer to plan the application jointly with the user. It cannot be stressed enough that the only way to guarantee the success of an application is to actively involve the user in the planning phase. Planning an OOED application requires the following four steps:

1. Identify the tasks the application needs to perform.
2. Identify the objects to which you will assign those tasks.
3. Identify the events required to trigger an object into performing its assigned tasks.
4. Draw a sketch of the user interface.

You can use a TOE (Task, Object, Event) chart to record the application's tasks, objects, and events. In the next section, you begin completing a TOE chart for the Skate-Away Sales application. The first step is to identify the application's tasks.

Identifying the Application's Tasks

Realizing that it is essential to involve the user when planning the application, you meet with the sales manager of Skate-Away Sales, Mr. Cousard, to determine his requirements. You ask Mr. Cousard to bring the form the salespeople currently use to record the orders. Viewing the current forms and procedures will help you gain a better understanding of the application. You also can use the current form as a guide when designing the user interface. Figure 2-7 shows the current order form used by Skate-Away Sales.

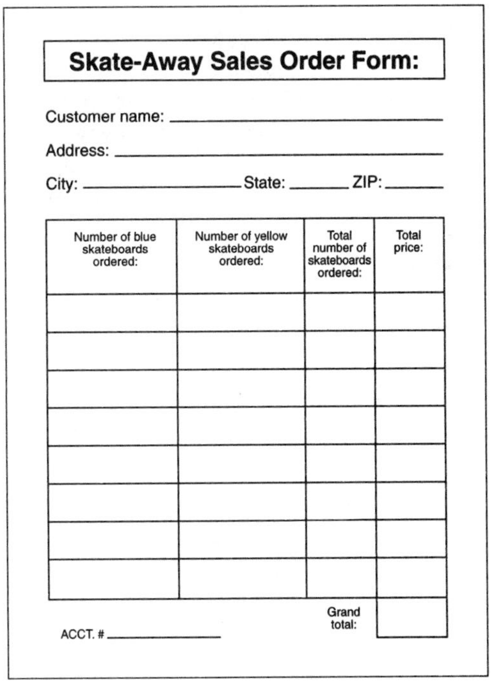

Figure 2-7: Current order form used by Skate-Away Sales

When identifying the tasks an application needs to perform, it is helpful to ask the following questions:

- What information, if any, will the application need to display on the screen and/or print on the printer?
- What information, if any, will the user need to enter into the user interface to display and/or print the desired information?
- What information, if any, will the application need to calculate to display and/or print the desired information?
- How will the user end the application?
- Will previous information need to be cleared from the screen before new information is entered?

The answers to these questions will help you identify the application's major tasks. The answers for each question for the Skate-Away Sales application are as follows.

What information, if any, will the application need to display on the screen and/or print on the printer? (Notice that "display" refers to the screen, and "print" refers to the printer.) The Skate-Away Sales application should display the customer's name, street address, city, state, ZIP code, skateboard price, sales tax rate, the number of blue skateboards ordered, the number of yellow skateboards ordered, the total number of skateboards ordered, and the total price of the order. In this case, the application does not need to print anything on the printer.

What information, if any, will the user need to enter into the user interface to display and/or print the desired information? In the Skate-Away Sales application, the salesperson (the user) must enter the customer's name, street address, city, state, ZIP code, skateboard price, sales tax rate, and the number of blue and yellow skateboards ordered.

What information, if any, will the application need to calculate to display and/or print the desired information? The Skate-Away Sales application needs to calculate the total number of skateboards ordered and the total price of the order.

How will the user end the application? In Tutorial 1, you learned that all applications should give the user a way to exit the program. The Skate-Away Sales application needs to provide a way to end the application.

Will previous information need to be cleared from the screen before new information is entered? After Skate-Away's salesperson enters and calculates an order, he or she will need to clear the order's information from the screen before entering the next order.

Figure 2-8 shows the Skate-Away Sales application's tasks listed in a TOE chart. Unlike procedure-oriented planning, OOED planning does not require the TOE chart tasks to be listed in any particular order. In this case, the data entry tasks are listed first, followed by the calculation tasks, display tasks, application ending task, and screen clearing task.

Task	Object	Event

Get the following order information from the user:
   Customer's name
   Street address
   City
   State
   ZIP code
   Price of a skateboard
   Sales tax rate
   Number of blue skateboards ordered
   Number of yellow skateboards ordered		

Calculate the total skateboards ordered and the total price		

Display the following information:
   Customer's name
   Street address
   City
   State
   ZIP code
   Price of a skateboard
   Sales tax rate
   Number of blue skateboards ordered
   Number of yellow skateboards ordered
   Total skateboards ordered
   Total price		

End the application		
Clear the screen for the next order		

Figure 2-8: Tasks entered in a TOE chart

Next, identify the objects that will perform the tasks listed in the TOE chart.

tip

You can draw a TOE chart by hand, or you can use the table feature in a word processor (such as Microsoft Word) to draw one.

Identifying the Objects

After completing the Task column of the TOE chart, you then assign each task to an object in the user interface. For this application, the only objects you will use, besides the Windows form itself, are the button, label, and text box controls. As you learned in Tutorial 1, you use a label control to display information that you do not want the user to change while your application is running, and you use a button control to perform an action immediately after it is clicked by the user. As you learned earlier, you use a text box to give the user an area in which to enter data. Now assign each of the tasks in the TOE chart to an object.

The first task listed in Figure 2-8 is to get the order information from the user. For each order, the salesperson will need to enter the customer's name, address, city, state, and ZIP code, as well as the skateboard price, sales tax rate, and the number of blue and yellow skateboards ordered. Because you need to provide the salesperson with areas in which to enter the information, you assign the first task to nine text boxes—one for each item of information. The names of the text boxes will be NameTextBox, AddressTextBox, CityTextBox, StateTextBox, ZipTextBox, PriceTextBox, RateTextBox, BlueTextBox, and YellowTextBox.

The second task listed in the TOE chart is to calculate both the total number of skateboards ordered and the total price. So that the salesperson can calculate these amounts at any time, you assign the task to a button named CalcButton.

The third task listed in the TOE chart is to display the order information, the total number of skateboards ordered, and the total price. The order information will be displayed automatically when the user enters that information in the nine text boxes. The total skateboards ordered and the total price, however, are not entered by the user; rather, those amounts are calculated by the CalcButton. Because the user should not be allowed to change the calculated results, you will have the CalcButton display the total skateboards ordered and the total price in two label controls named TotalBoardsLabel and TotalPriceLabel. Recall from Tutorial 1 that a user cannot access the contents of a label control while the application is running. Notice that the task of displaying the total skateboards ordered involves two objects (CalcButton and TotalBoardsLabel). The task of displaying the total price also involves two objects (CalcButton and TotalPriceLabel).

The last two tasks listed in the TOE chart are "End the application" and "Clear the screen for the next order." You assign these tasks to buttons so that the user has control over when the tasks are performed. You name the buttons ExitButton and ClearButton. Figure 2-9 shows the TOE chart with the Task and Object columns completed.

Task	Object	Event
Get the following order information from the user:		
Customer's name	NameTextBox	
Street address	AddressTextBox	
City	CityTextBox	
State	StateTextBox	
ZIP code	ZipTextBox	
Price of a skateboard	PriceTextBox	
Sales tax rate	RateTextBox	
Number of blue skateboards ordered	BlueTextBox	
Number of yellow skateboards ordered	YellowTextBox	
Calculate the total skateboards ordered and the total price	CalcButton	
Display the following information:		
Customer's name	NameTextBox	
Street address	AddressTextBox	
City	CityTextBox	
State	StateTextBox	
ZIP code	ZipTextBox	
Price of a skateboard	PriceTextBox	
Sales tax rate	RateTextBox	
Number of blue skateboards ordered	BlueTextBox	
Number of yellow skateboards ordered	YellowTextBox	
Total skateboards ordered	CalcButton, TotalBoardsLabel	
Total price	CalcButton, TotalPriceLabel	
End the application	ExitButton	
Clear the screen for the next order	ClearButton	

Figure 2-9: Tasks and objects entered in a TOE chart

After defining the application's tasks and assigning those tasks to objects in the user interface, you then determine which objects need an event (such as clicking or double-clicking) to occur for the object to do its assigned task. Identify the events required by the objects listed in Figure 2-9's TOE chart.

tip

• • • • • • • • • • • • • •

▶ Not all objects in a user interface will need an event to occur in order for the object to perform its assigned tasks.

Identifying the Events

The nine text boxes listed in the TOE chart in Figure 2-9 are assigned the task of getting and displaying the order information. Text boxes accept and display information automatically, so no special event is necessary for them to do their assigned task.

The two label controls listed in the TOE chart are assigned the task of displaying the total number of skateboards ordered and the total price of the order. Label controls automatically display their contents so, here again, no special event needs to occur. (Recall that the two label controls will get their values from the CalcButton.)

The remaining objects listed in the TOE chart are the three buttons: CalcButton, ClearButton, and ExitButton. You will have the buttons perform their assigned tasks when they are clicked by the user. Figure 2-10 shows the TOE chart with the tasks, objects, and events necessary for the Skate-Away Sales application.

Task	Object	Event
Get the following order information from the user:		
Customer's name	NameTextBox	None
Street address	AddressTextBox	None
City	CityTextBox	None
State	StateTextBox	None
ZIP code	ZipTextBox	None
Price of a skateboard	PriceTextBox	None
Sales tax rate	RateTextBox	None
Number of blue skateboards ordered	BlueTextBox	None
Number of yellow skateboards ordered	YellowTextBox	None
Calculate the total skateboards ordered and the total price	CalcButton	Click
Display the following information:		
Customer's name	NameTextBox	None
Street address	AddressTextBox	None
City	CityTextBox	None
State	StateTextBox	None
ZIP code	ZipTextBox	None
Price of a skateboard	PriceTextBox	None
Sales tax rate	RateTextBox	None
Number of blue skateboards ordered	BlueTextBox	None
Number of yellow skateboards ordered	YellowTextBox	None
Total skateboards ordered	CalcButton, TotalBoardsLabel	Click, None
Total price	CalcButton, TotalPriceLabel	Click, None
End the application	ExitButton	Click
Clear the screen for the next order	ClearButton	Click

Figure 2-10: Completed TOE chart ordered by task

If the application you are creating is small, as is the Skate-Away Sales application, you can use the TOE chart in its current form to help you write the code. When the application you are creating is large, however, it is helpful to rearrange the TOE chart so that it is ordered by object instead of by task. To do so, you simply list all of the objects in the Object column, being sure to list each object only once. Then list the tasks you have assigned to each object in the Task column, and list the event in the Event column. Figure 2-11 shows the rearranged TOE chart, ordered by object rather than by task.

Task	Object	Event
1. Calculate the total skateboards ordered and the total price 2. Display the total skateboards ordered and the total price in the TotalBoardsLabel and TotalPriceLabel	CalcButton	Click
Clear the screen for the next order	ClearButton	Click
End the application	ExitButton	Click
Display the total skateboards ordered (from CalcButton)	TotalBoardsLabel	None
Display the total price (from CalcButton)	TotalPriceLabel	None
Get and display the order information	NameTextBox, AddressTextBox, CityTextBox, StateTextBox, ZipTextBox, PriceTextBox, RateTextBox, BlueTextBox, YellowTextBox	None

Figure 2-11: Completed TOE chart ordered by object

After completing the TOE chart, the next step is to draw a rough sketch of the user interface.

Drawing a Sketch of the User Interface

Although the TOE chart lists the objects you need to include in the application's user interface, it does not tell you *where* to place those objects in the interface. While the design of an interface is open to creativity, there are some guidelines to which you should adhere so that your application is consistent with the Windows standards. This consistency will make your application easier to both learn and use, because the user interface will have a familiar look to it.

In Western countries, you should organize the user interface so that the information flows either vertically or horizontally, with the most important information always located in the upper-left corner of the screen. In a vertical arrangement the information flows from top to bottom; the essential information is located in the first column of the screen, while secondary information is placed in subsequent columns. In a horizontal arrangement, on the other hand, the information flows from left to right; the essential information is placed in the first row of the screen, with secondary information placed in subsequent rows. You can use white space, a GroupBox control, or a Panel control to group related controls together.

If buttons appear in the interface, they should be positioned either in a row along the bottom of the screen, or stacked in either the upper-right or lower-right corner. Limit to six the number of buttons in the interface, and place the most commonly used button first—either on the left when the buttons are along the bottom of the screen, or on the top when the buttons are stacked in either the upper-right or lower-right corner.

Figures 2-12 and 2-13 show two different sketches of the Skate-Away Sales interface. In Figure 2-12, the information is arranged vertically; white space is used to group the related controls together and the buttons are positioned along the bottom of the screen. In Figure 2-13, the information is arranged horizontally; a GroupBox control is used to group the related controls together, and the buttons are stacked in the upper-right corner of the screen.

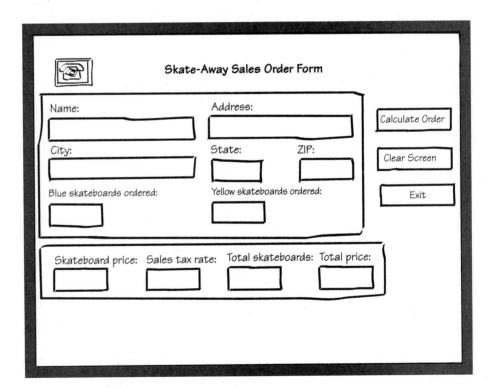

Figure 2-12: Vertical arrangement of the Skate-Away Sales interface

Figure 2-13: Horizontal arrangement of the Skate-Away Sales interface

Notice that each text box and button control in the interface is labeled so the user knows the control's purpose. Labels that identify text boxes should be left-aligned and positioned either above or to the left of the text box. As you learned in Tutorial 1, buttons are identified by a caption that appears on the button itself. Identifying labels and captions should be from one to three words only, and each should appear on one line.

Labels and captions should be meaningful. The label identifying a text box, for example, should tell the user the type of information to enter. A button's caption, on the other hand, should tell the user what action the button will perform when the button is clicked.

Notice that each text box's identifying label ends with a colon (:). The colon distinguishes an identifying label from other text in the user interface. The Windows standard is to use sentence capitalization for identifying labels. **Sentence capitalization** means you capitalize only the first letter in the first word and in any words that are customarily capitalized. The Windows standard for button captions is to use book title capitalization. When using **book title capitalization**, you capitalize the first letter in each word, except for articles, conjunctions, and prepositions that do not occur at either the beginning or the end of the caption.

When laying out the controls in the interface, try to minimize the number of different margins so that the user can more easily scan the information. You can do so by aligning the borders of the controls wherever possible, as shown in Figures 2-12 and 2-13.

In this section you learned some basic guidelines to follow when sketching a GUI (Graphical User Interface). You will learn more GUI guidelines as you progress through this book. For now, however, you have completed the second of the six steps involved in creating an application: plan the application. Recall that the planning step requires you to:

1. Identify the tasks the application needs to perform.
2. Identify the objects to which you will assign those tasks.
3. Identify the events required to trigger an object into performing its assigned tasks.
4. Draw a sketch of the user interface.

In Lesson B you use the sketch shown in Figure 2-12 as a guide when building the Skate-Away Sales interface. Recall that building the user interface is the third of the six steps involved in creating an OOED application. For now, you can either take a break or complete the end-of-lesson questions and exercises before moving on to the next lesson. In Lesson C, you will complete the fourth (code the application), fifth (test and debug the application), and sixth (assemble the documentation) steps.

Layout and Organization of Your Interface

GUI Design Tips

- Organize the user interface so that the information flows either vertically or horizontally, with the most important information always located in the upper-left corner of the screen.

- Group related controls together using white space, a GroupBox control, or a Panel control.

- Position buttons in a row along the bottom of the screen, or stack them in either the upper-right or lower-right corner. Use no more than six buttons on a screen. Place the most commonly used button first (either on the left or on the top).

- Use meaningful captions in buttons. Place the caption on one line and use from one to three words only. Use book title capitalization for button captions.

- Use a label to identify each text box in the user interface. The label text should be from one to three words only, and entered on one line. Left-justify the label text, and position the label either above or to the left of the control. Follow the label text with a colon (:) and use sentence capitalization.

- Align the borders of the controls in the user interface to minimize the number of different margins.

S U M M A R Y

To create an OOED application:

■ Follow these six steps:
   1. Meet with the client.
   2. Plan the application.
   3. Build the user interface.
   4. Code the application.
   5. Test and debug the application.
   6. Assemble the documentation.

To plan an OOED application in Visual Basic .NET:

■ Follow these four steps:
   1. Identify the tasks the application needs to perform.
   2. Identify the objects to which you will assign those tasks.
   3. Identify the events required to trigger an object into performing its assigned tasks.
   4. Draw a sketch of the user interface.

To assist you in identifying the tasks an application needs to perform, ask the following questions:

■ What information, if any, will the application need to display on the screen and/or print on the printer?
■ What information, if any, will the user need to enter into the user interface to display and/or print the desired information?
■ What information, if any, will the application need to calculate to display and/or print the desired information?
■ How will the user end the application?
■ Will prior information need to be cleared from the screen before new information is entered?

Q U E S T I O N S

1. You use a _____ control to display information you do not want the user to change.
   a. button
   b. form
   c. label
   d. text box
   e. user

2. You use a _____ control to accept or display information you will allow the user to change.
   a. button
   b. changeable
   c. form
   d. label
   e. text box

3. You use a _____ control to perform an immediate action when it is clicked by the user.
    a. button
    b. form
    c. label
    d. text box

4. You can use a _____ chart to plan your OOED applications.
    a. EOT
    b. ETO
    c. OET
    d. OTE
    e. TOE

5. When designing a user interface, you should organize the information _____.
    a. either horizontally or vertically
    b. horizontally only
    c. vertically only

6. When designing a user interface, the most important information should be placed in the _____ of the screen.
    a. center
    b. lower-left corner
    c. lower-right corner
    d. upper-left corner
    e. upper-right corner

7. You can use _____ to group related controls together in an interface.
    a. a GroupBox control
    b. a Panel control
    c. white space
    d. All of the above.
    e. None of the above.

8. Buttons in an interface should be _____.
    a. positioned in a row along the bottom of the screen
    b. stacked in either the upper-left or lower-left corner of the screen
    c. stacked in either the upper-right or lower-right corner of the screen
    d. either a or b
    e. either a or c

9. Use no more than _____ buttons on a screen.
    a. five
    b. four
    c. seven
    d. six
    e. two

10. If more than one button appears in an interface, the most commonly used button should be placed _____.
    a. first
    b. in the middle
    c. last
    d. either a or c

11. Which of the following statements is false?
    a. A button's caption should appear on one line.
    b. A button's caption should be from one to three words only.
    c. A button's caption should be entered using book title capitalization.
    d. A button's caption should end with a colon (:).

12. The labels that identify text boxes should be entered using _____.
    a. book title capitalization
    b. sentence capitalization
    c. either a or b

13. Which of the following statements is false?
    a. Labels that identify text boxes should be aligned on the left.
    b. An identifying label should be positioned either above or to the left of the text box it identifies.
    c. Labels that identify text boxes should be entered using book title capitalization.
    d. Labels that identify text boxes should end with a colon (:).

14. _____ means you capitalize only the first letter in the first word and in any words that are customarily capitalized.
    a. Book title capitalization
    b. Sentence capitalization

15. Button captions should be entered using _____, which means you capitalize the first letter in each word, except for articles, conjunctions, and prepositions that do not occur at either the beginning or the end of the caption.
    a. book title capitalization
    b. sentence capitalization

16. Listed below are the four steps you should follow when planning an OOED application. Put them in the proper order by placing a number (1 through 4) on the line to the left of the step.

    _____ Identify the objects to which you will assign those tasks.

    _____ Draw a sketch of the user interface.

    _____ Identify the tasks the application needs to perform.

    _____ Identify the events required to trigger an object into performing its assigned tasks.

17. Listed below are the six steps you should follow when creating an OOED application. Put them in the proper order by placing a number (1 through 6) on the line to the left of the step.

    _____ Test and debug the application.

    _____ Build the user interface.

    _____ Code the application.

    _____ Assemble the documentation.

    _____ Plan the application.

    _____ Meet with the client.

EXERCISES

The following list summarizes the GUI design guidelines you have learned so far. You can use this list to verify that the interfaces you create in the following exercises adhere to the GUI standards outlined in the book.

- Information should flow either vertically or horizontally, with the most important information always located in the upper-left corner of the screen.

- Related controls should be grouped together using white space, a GroupBox control, or a Panel control.

- Set the form's FormBorderStyle, ControlBox, MaximizeBox, MinimizeBox, and StartPosition properties appropriately:

  - A splash screen should not have a Minimize, Maximize, or Close button, and its borders should not be sizable.

  - A form that is not a splash screen should always have a Minimize button and a Close button, but you can choose to disable the Maximize button. Typically, the FormBorderStyle property is set to Sizable, but also can be set to FixedSingle.

- Buttons should be positioned either in a row along the bottom of the screen, or stacked in either the upper-right or lower-right corner.

- Use no more than six buttons on a screen.

- The most commonly used button should be placed first.

- Button captions should:

  - be meaningful
  - be from one to three words
  - appear on one line
  - be entered using book title capitalization

- Use labels to identify the text boxes in the interface, and position the label either above or to the left of the text box.

- Label text should:

  - be from one to three words
  - appear on one line
  - be left-justified
  - end with a colon (:)
  - be entered using sentence capitalization

- Align controls to minimize the number of different margins.

1. In this exercise, you prepare a TOE chart and create two sketches of the application's user interface. (Refer to the list at the beginning of the Exercises section.)

   Scenario: Sarah Brimley is the accountant at Paper Products. The salespeople at Paper Products are paid a commission, which is a percentage of the sales they make. The current commission rate is 10%. (In other words, if you have sales totaling $2,000, your commission is $200.) Sarah wants you to create an application that will compute the commission after she enters the salesperson's name, territory number, and sales.

   a. Prepare a TOE chart ordered by task.

   b. Rearrange the TOE chart created in Step a so that it is ordered by object.

   c. Draw two sketches of the user interface—one using a horizontal arrangement and the other using a vertical arrangement.

2. In this exercise, you prepare a TOE chart and create two sketches of the application's user interface. (Refer to the list at the beginning of the Exercises section.)

   Scenario: RM Sales divides its sales territory into four regions: North, South, East, and West. Robert Gonzales, the sales manager, wants an application in which he can enter the current year's sales for each region and the projected increase (expressed as a percentage) in sales for each region. He then wants the application to compute the following year's projected sales for each region. (For example, if Robert enters 10000 as the current sales for the South region, and then enters a 10% projected increase, the application should display 11000 as next year's projected sales.)

   a. Prepare a TOE chart ordered by task.

   b. Rearrange the TOE chart created in Step a so that it is ordered by object.

   c. Draw two sketches of the user interface—one using a horizontal arrangement and the other using a vertical arrangement.

3. In this exercise, you modify an existing application's user interface so that the interface follows the GUI design guidelines covered in Tutorial 2's Lesson A. (Refer to the list at the beginning of the Exercises section.)

   a. If necessary, start Visual Studio .NET. Open the Time Solution (Time Solution.sln) file, which is contained in the VBNET\Tut02\Time Solution folder. If the designer window is not open, right-click the form file's name in the Solution Explorer window, then click View Designer.

   b. Lay out and organize the interface so it follows all of the GUI design guidelines specified in Lesson A.

   c. Save and start the application, then click the Exit button to end the application. (The Exit button contains the code to end the application.)

LESSON B

objectives

After completing this lesson, you will be able to:

- Build the user interface using your TOE chart and sketch
- Follow the Windows standards regarding the use of graphics, color, and fonts
- Set the BorderStyle property
- Add a text box to a form
- Lock the controls on the form
- Assign access keys to controls
- Use the TabIndex property

Building the User Interface

Preparing to Create the User Interface

In Lesson A, you completed the second of the six steps involved in creating an OOED application: plan the application. You now are ready to tackle the third step, which is to build the user interface. You use the TOE chart and sketch you created in the planning step as guides when building the interface, which involves placing the appropriate controls on the form and setting the applicable properties of those controls. Recall that a property controls the appearance and behavior of an object, such as the object's font, size, and so on. Some programmers create the entire interface before setting the properties of each object; other programmers change the properties of each object as it is added to the form. Either way will work, so it's really just a matter of personal preference.

To save you time, your computer's hard disk contains a partially completed application for Skate-Away Sales. When you open the application, you will notice that most of the user interface has been created and most of the properties have been set. Only one control—a text box—is missing from the form. You add the missing control and set its properties later in this lesson.

To open the partially completed application:

1. Start Microsoft Visual Studio .NET, if necessary. Close the Start Page window.
2. Click **File** on the menu bar, then click **Open Solution**. Open the **Order Solution** (Order Solution.sln) file, which is contained in the VBNET\Tut02\Order Solution folder on your computer's hard disk.
3. If the designer window is not open, right-click **Order Form.vb** in the Solution Explorer window, then click **View Designer**.

Figure 2-14 identifies the controls already included in the application. (You won't see the names of the controls on your screen. The names are included in Figure 2-14 for your reference only.)

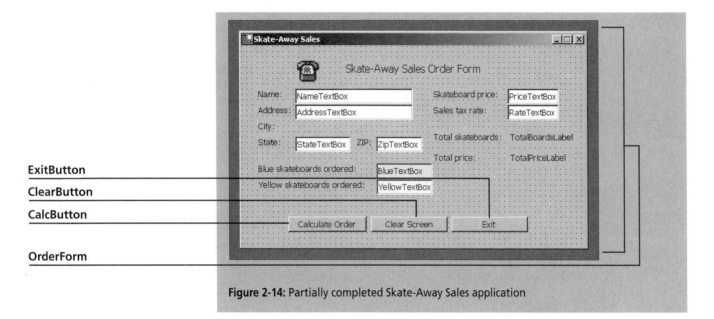

Figure 2-14: Partially completed Skate-Away Sales application

The user interface shown in Figure 2-14 resembles the sketch shown in Lesson A's Figure 2-12. Recall that the sketch was created using the guidelines you learned in Lesson A. For example, the information is arranged vertically, with the most important information located in the upper-left corner of the screen. The buttons are positioned along the bottom of the screen, with the most commonly used button placed first. The buttons contain meaningful captions, which are entered using book title capitalization. Each caption appears on one line, and no caption exceeds the three-word limit. The labels that identify text boxes are left-aligned and positioned to the left of their respective control; each uses sentence capitalization and each ends with a colon.

Notice that the controls are aligned wherever possible to minimize the number of different margins appearing in the user interface. You can use the dots that Visual Basic .NET displays on the form during design time to help you align the various controls in the interface. As you learned in Tutorial 1, you also can use the Align option on the Format menu.

When positioning the controls, be sure to maintain a consistent margin from the edge of the form; two or three dots is recommended. For example, notice in Figure 2-14 that three dots separate the bottom border of the three buttons from the bottom edge of the form. Also notice that three dots appear between the left edge of the form and the left border of the six labels located in the first column.

As illustrated in Figure 2-14, related controls typically are placed on succeeding dots. For example, notice that the top of the AddressTextBox control is placed on the horizontal line of dots found immediately below the NameTextBox control. Also notice that the left edge of the Clear Screen button is placed on the vertical line of dots found to the immediate right of the Calculate Order button. Controls that are not part of any logical grouping may be positioned from two to four dots away from other controls.

Always size the buttons in the interface relative to each other. When the buttons are positioned on the bottom of the screen, as they are in Figure 2-14, all the buttons should be the same height; their widths, however, may vary if necessary. If the buttons are stacked in either the upper-right or lower-right corner of the screen, on the other hand, all the buttons should be the same height and the same width.

When building the user interface, keep in mind that you want to create a screen that no one notices. Snazzy interfaces may get "oohs" and "aahs" during their initial use, but they become tiresome after a while. The most important point to remember is that the interface should not distract the user from doing his or her work. Unfortunately, it is difficult for some application developers to refrain from using the many different colors, fonts, and graphics available in Visual Basic .NET; actually, using these elements is not the problem—overusing them is. So that you do not overload your user interfaces with too much color, too many fonts, and too many graphics, the next three sections provide some guidelines to follow regarding these elements. Consider the graphics first.

Placing and Sizing Design Elements

- Maintain a consistent margin of two or three dots from the edge of the form.
- Position related controls on succeeding dots. Controls that are not part of any logical grouping may be positioned from two to four dots away from other controls.
- Buttons in the user interface should be sized relative to each other. If the buttons are positioned at the bottom of the screen, then each button should be the same height; their widths, however, may vary. If the buttons are stacked in either the upper-right or lower-right corner of the screen, then each should be the same height and the same width.
- Try to create a user interface that no one notices.

Including Graphics in the User Interface

The human eye is attracted to pictures before text, so include a graphic only if it is necessary to do so. Graphics typically are used to either emphasize or clarify a portion of the screen. You also can use a graphic for aesthetic purposes, as long as the graphic is small and placed in a location that does not distract the user. The small graphic in the Skate-Away Sales interface, for example, is included for aesthetics only. The graphic is purposely located in the upper-left corner of the interface, which is where you want the user's eye to be drawn first anyway. The graphic adds a personal touch to the Skate-Away Sales order form without being distracting to the user.

In the next section you will learn some guidelines pertaining to the use of different fonts in the interface.

Including Different Fonts in the User Interface

As you learned in Tutorial 1, you can change the type, style, and size of the font used to display the text in an object. Recall that Microsoft Sans Serif, Tahoma, and Courier are examples of font types; regular, bold, and italic are examples of font styles; and 8, 10, and 18 points are examples of font sizes.

Some fonts are serif, and some are sans serif. A **serif** is a light cross stroke that appears at the top or bottom of a character. The characters in a serif font have the light strokes, whereas the characters in a sans serif font do not. ("Sans" is a French

GUI
Design Tips

Adding Graphics

- Include a graphic only if it is necessary to do so. If the graphic is used solely for aesthetics, use a small graphic and place it in a location that will not distract the user.

word meaning "without.") Books use serif fonts, because those fonts are easier to read on the printed page. Sans serif fonts, on the other hand, are easier to read on the screen, so you should use a sans serif font for the text in a user interface. The default font type used for interface elements in Windows is Microsoft Sans Serif. However, for applications that will run on systems running Windows 2000 or Windows XP, it is recommended that you use the Tahoma font, because it offers improved readability and globalization support. You should use only one font type for all of the text in the interface. The Skate-Away Sales interface, for example, uses only the Tahoma font.

You can use 8-, 9-, 10-, 11-, or 12-point fonts for the elements in the user interface, but be sure to limit the number of font sizes used to either one or two. The Skate-Away Sales application uses two font sizes: 12 point for the heading at the top of the interface, and 10 point for everything else.

Avoid using italics and underlining in an interface, because both make text difficult to read. Additionally, limit the use of bold text to titles, headings, and key items that you want to emphasize.

tip

· · · · · · · · · · · · · · ·
► As you learned in Tutorial 1, a point is 1/72 of an inch.

GUI Design Tips

Selecting Appropriate Font Types, Styles, and Sizes

- Use only one font type for all of the text in the interface. Use a sans serif font— preferably the Tahoma font. If the Tahoma font is not available, use either Microsoft Sans Serif or Arial.

- Use 8-, 9-, 10-, 11-, or 12-point fonts for the elements in the user interface.

- Limit the number of font sizes used to either one or two.

- Avoid using italics and underlining, because both make text difficult to read.

- Limit the use of bold text to titles, headings, and key items.

In addition to overusing graphics and fonts, many application developers make the mistake of using either too much color or too many different colors in the user interface. In the next section you learn some guidelines pertaining to the use of color.

Including Color in the User Interface

Just as the human eye is attracted to graphics before text, it also is attracted to color before black and white, so use color sparingly. It is a good practice to build the interface using black, white, and gray first, then add color only if you have a good reason to do so. Keep the following four points in mind when deciding whether to include color in an interface:

1. Some users will be working on monochrome monitors.
2. Many people have some form of either color-blindness or color confusion, so they will have trouble distinguishing colors.
3. Color is very subjective; a pretty color to you may be hideous to someone else.
4. A color may have a different meaning in a different culture.

Usually, it is best to follow the Windows standard of using black text on a white, off-white, or light gray background. The Skate-Away Sales interface, for example, displays black text on a light gray background. If you want to add some color to the interface, you also can use black text on either a pale blue or a pale yellow background. Because dark text on a light background is the easiest to read, never use a dark color for the background or a light color for the text; a dark background is hard on the eyes, and light-colored text can appear blurry.

If you are going to include color in the interface, limit the number of colors to three, not including white, black, and gray. Be sure that the colors you choose complement each other.

Although color can be used to identify an important element in the interface, you should never use it as the only means of identification. In the Skate-Away Sales application, for example, the colors blue and yellow help the salesperson quickly identify where to enter the order for blue and yellow skateboards, respectively. Notice, however, that color is not the only means of identifying those areas in the interface; the labels to the left of the controls also tell the user where to enter the orders for blue and yellow skateboards.

GUI Design Tips

Selecting Appropriate Colors

- The human eye is attracted to color before black and white. Build the interface using black, white, and gray first, then add color only if you have a good reason to do so.

- Use white, off-white, or light gray for an application's background, and black for the text. You also can use black text on either a pale blue or a pale yellow background. Dark text on a light background is the easiest to read.

- Never use a dark color for the background or a light color for the text. A dark background is hard on the eyes, and light-colored text can appear blurry.

- Limit the number of colors to three, not including white, black, and gray. The colors you choose should complement each other.

- Never use color as the only means of identification for an element in the user interface.

Now you begin completing the Skate-Away Sales user interface. First, observe how the interface looks with a white background instead of a gray one.

To change the background color of the form:

1 Click the **form** to select it. Click **BackColor** in the Properties list, then click the **Settings box list arrow**. Click the **Custom** tab, then click a **white color square**. The background color of the form changes to white. Notice that the background color of most of the controls on the form also changes to white.

Unlike in previous versions of Visual Basic, if you do not explicitly set the BackColor property of a control in Visual Basic .NET, the control inherits the color setting of its parent. In this case, the form is the parent of each control in the Skate-Away Sales interface; however, the BackColor properties of the BlueTextBox and YellowTextBox controls were explicitly set to blue and yellow, respectively.

Now explicitly set the background color of the Calculate Order button.

2 Click the **Calculate Order** button. Click **BackColor** in the Properties list, then click the **Settings box list arrow**. Click the **System** tab, then click **Control**. The background color of the Calculate Order button changes to gray.

Assume you prefer the way the interface originally looked. You can use the Undo option to cancel the changes you just made.

3 Click **Edit** on the menu bar, then click **Undo** to change the background color of the Calculate Order button to white, which is the color of its parent form.

4 Click **Edit** on the menu bar, then click **Undo** to change the background color of the form to its original color, gray.

Next, you learn about the BorderStyle property.

In Windows applications, a control that contains data that the user is not allowed to edit does not usually appear three-dimensional. Therefore, you should avoid setting a label control's BorderStyle property to Fixed3D.

The BorderStyle Property

The **BorderStyle property** determines the style of a control's border and can be set to None, FixedSingle, or Fixed3D. Controls with a BorderStyle property set to None have no border. Setting the BorderStyle property to FixedSingle surrounds the control with a thin line, and setting it to Fixed3D gives the control a three-dimensional appearance. Currently, the BorderStyle property of the label controls on the Skate-Away Sales form is set to None, which is the default for a label control. The BorderStyle property of the text boxes is set to Fixed3D—the default for a text box.

Text boxes and label controls that identify other controls (such as those that identify text boxes) should have their BorderStyle property left at the default of Fixed3D and None, respectively. However, you typically set to FixedSingle the BorderStyle property of label controls that display program output, such as the result of a calculation. In the Skate-Away Sales application, you will set the BorderStyle property of the TotalBoardsLabel and TotalPriceLabel controls to FixedSingle, because both controls display calculated results.

GUI Design Tips

Setting the BorderStyle Property of a Text Box and Label

- Set to Fixed3D (the default) the BorderStyle property of text boxes.
- Set to None (the default) the BorderStyle property of labels that identify other controls.
- Set to FixedSingle the BorderStyle property of labels that display program output, such as the result of a calculation.

To change the BorderStyle property of the TotalBoardsLabel and TotalPriceLabel controls:

1   Select the **TotalBoardsLabel** and **TotalPriceLabel** controls.

   HELP?   To select both controls, click the TotalBoardsLabel control, then Ctr+click the TotalPriceLabel control. If necessary, refer back to Figure 2-14 for the location of these two controls.

2   Set the selected controls' BorderStyle property to **FixedSingle**, then click the **form** to deselect the controls. Notice that both label controls appear as flat boxes on the screen.

Next you learn about the Text property.

Setting the Text Property

Recall that most of Skate-Away's customers are in Illinois. Instead of having the salesperson enter IL in the StateTextBox control for each order, it would be more efficient to have IL appear automatically in the State text box when the application is run. If the user needs to change the state entry while the application is running, he or she can simply click the State text box, then delete the current entry and retype the new one. You can display IL in the StateTextBox control by setting the control's Text property to IL.

To set the StateTextBox control's Text property:

1   Click the **StateTextBox** control.

2   Click **Text** in the Properties list, then type **IL** and press **Enter**. IL appears in the StateTextBox control.

Recall that, in the context of OOP, each tool in the toolbox is a class—a pattern from which one or more objects, called controls, are created. Each control you create is an instance of the class. The TextBox1 text box, for example, is an instance of the TextBox class.

Be sure to use either the Delete key or the Backspace key to delete the highlighted text in the Properties list. Do not use the Spacebar to delete the highlighted text. Pressing the Spacebar does not clear the property's contents; rather, it replaces the highlighted text with a space.

Notice that the text box control in which the user enters the city is missing from the interface. You add the control next.

Adding a Text Box Control to the Form

A **text box control** provides an area in the form where the user can enter data. Add the missing text box control to the form and then set its properties.

To add a text box control to the form, and then set its properties:

1 Click the **TextBox tool** in the toolbox, then drag a text box control to the form. Position the text box control to the right of the City: label, immediately below the AddressTextBox control. For now, do not worry about the exact location and size of the control.

The TextBox1 text that appears inside the text box is the current setting of the control's Text property. You should delete the contents of the Text property so that it does not appear when the application is run.

2 Double-click **Text** in the Properties list. This highlights the TextBox1 text in the Settings box.

   HELP? If the TextBox1 text is not highlighted in the Settings box, double-click the Text property again until the TextBox1 text is highlighted. You also can drag in the Settings box to highlight the TextBox1 text.

3 Press **Delete**, then press **Enter** to remove the highlighted text. The text box is now empty.

Now change the text box's default name (TextBox1) to CityTextBox. Also change the font size to 10 points.

4 Set the following two properties for the text box control:

   Name: **CityTextBox**

   Font: **10 points**

   HELP? Recall that the Name property is listed third when the properties are listed alphabetically in the Properties list. It is listed in the Design category when the properties are listed by category.

Now use the Align option on the Format menu to align the left border of the CityTextBox control with the left border of the AddressTextBox control.

5 Press and hold down the **Control** (or **Ctrl**) key as you click the **AddressTextBox** control. The CityTextBox and AddressTextBox controls should now be selected.

6 Click **Format** on the menu bar, point to **Align**, and then click **Lefts** to align the left border of both controls.

Next, use the Make Same Size option on the Format menu to size the CityTextBox control appropriately.

7 Click **Format** on the menu bar, point to **Make Same Size**, and then click **Both** to make the CityTextBox control's height and width the same as the AddressTextBox control's height and width.

8 Click the **form** to deselect the controls. See Figure 2-15.

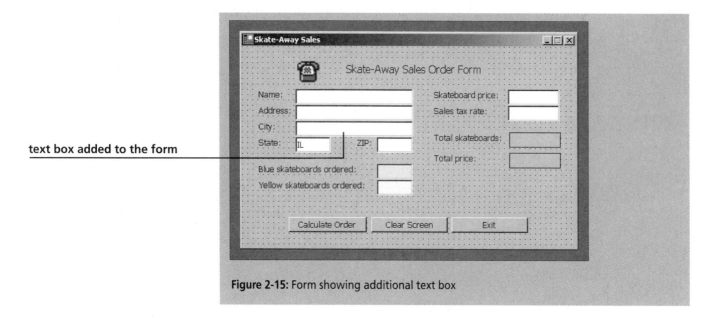

text box added to the form

Figure 2-15: Form showing additional text box

Before saving the solution, you learn how to lock the controls on the form.

Locking the Controls on a Form

Once you have placed all of the controls in the desired locations on the form, it is a good idea to lock the controls in their current positions so you do not inadvertently move them. Once the controls are locked, you will not be able to move them until you unlock them; you can, however, delete them.

You also can use the Lock Controls option on the format menu to lock and unlock the controls on a form.

To lock the controls on the form, and then save the solution:

1 Right-click the **form** (or any control on the form), then click **Lock Controls** on the shortcut menu.

2 Try dragging one of the controls to a different location on the form. You will not be able to.

If you need to move a control after you have locked the controls in place, you can either change the control's Location property setting in the Properties list or unlock the controls by selecting the Lock Controls option again. The Lock Controls option is a toggle option: selecting it once activates it, and selecting it again deactivates it.

You also can save the solution by clicking the Save All button 📄 on the Standard toolbar.

3 Click **File** on the menu bar, and then click **Save All** to save the solution.

Next you learn how to assign access keys to the controls that can accept user input.

Assigning Access Keys

An **access key** allows the user to select an object using the Alt key in combination with a letter or number. For example, you can select Visual Basic .NET's File menu by pressing Alt+F, because the letter "F" is the File menu's access key. Access keys are not case sensitive—in other words, you can select the File menu by pressing either Alt+F or Alt+f.

You should assign access keys to each of the controls (in the interface) that can accept user input. Examples of such controls include text boxes and buttons, because the user can enter information in a text box and he or she can click a button. It is important to assign access keys to these controls for the following three reasons:

1. Access keys allow a user to work with the application even if the mouse becomes inoperative.
2. Access keys allow users who are fast typists to keep their hands on the keyboard.
3. Access keys allow people with disabilities, which may prevent them from working with a mouse, to use the application.

You assign an access key by including an ampersand (&) in the control's caption or identifying label. For example, to assign an access key to a button, you include the ampersand in the button's Text property, which is where a button's caption is stored. To assign an access key to a text box, on the other hand, you include the ampersand in the Text property of the label control that identifies the text box. (As you learn later in this lesson, you also must set the identifying label's TabIndex property to a value that is one number less than the value stored in the text box's TabIndex property.) You enter the ampersand to the immediate left of the character you want to designate as the access key. For example, to assign the letter C as the access key for the Calculate Order button, you enter &Calculate Order in the button's Text property. To assign the letter N as the access key for the NameTextBox control, you enter &Name: in the Text property of its identifying label control.

Each access key appearing in the interface should be unique. The first choice for an access key is the first letter of the caption or identifying label, unless another letter provides a more meaningful association. For example, the letter X typically is the access key for an Exit button, because the letter X provides a more meaningful association than does the letter E. If you can't use the first letter (perhaps because it already is used as the access key for another control) and no other letter provides a more meaningful association, then use a distinctive consonant in the caption or label. The last choices for an access key are a vowel or a number. Assign an access key to each button and text box in the Skate-Away Sales interface.

To assign an access key to each button and text box in the interface:

1   Click the **Calculate Order** button, then click **Text** in the Properties list.
Use the letter C as the access key for the Calculate Order button.

2   Place the mouse pointer in the Text property's Settings box. The mouse pointer becomes an I-bar ⌶.

3   Place the ⌶ to the left of the C in Calculate, then click at that location. The insertion point appears before the word Calculate.

4 Type & (ampersand), then press **Enter**. The Text property should now say &Calculate Order, and the interface should show the letter C underlined in the button's caption.

HELP? If you are using Windows 2000 and the letter C does not appear underlined in the button's caption, click Start on the Windows taskbar, point to Settings, then click Control Panel. Double-click the Display icon to open the Display Properties dialog box, then click the Effects tab. Click the Hide keyboard navigation indicators until I use the Alt key check box to remove the checkmark. Click the OK button to close the Display Properties dialog box, then close the Control Panel window.

If you are using Windows XP and the letter C does not appear underlined in the button's caption, click Start on the Windows taskbar, click Control Panel, click Appearance and Themes, and then click Display to open the Display Properties dialog box. Click the Appearance tab, and then click the Effects button. Click the Hide underlined letters for keyboard navigation until I press the Alt key check box to remove the checkmark. Click the OK button twice, then close the Control Panel window.

Now assign the letter "l" as the access key for the Clear Screen button. (In this case, you cannot use the letter "C" for the Clear Screen button, because the letter is the access key for the Calculate Order button and access keys should be unique.)

5 Click the **Clear Screen** button, then change its Text property to **C&lear Screen**.

As mentioned earlier, the letter "X" is customarily the access key for an Exit button.

6 Click the **Exit** button, then change its Text property to **E&xit**.

7 Use the information in Figure 2-16 to include an access key in the label controls that identify text boxes in the interface.

Control name	Text	Access key
IdNameLabel	Name:	N
IdAddressLabel	Address:	A
IdCityLabel	City:	T
IdStateLabel	State:	S
IdZipLabel	ZIP:	Z
IdBlueLabel	Blue skateboards ordered:	B
IdYellowLabel	Yellow skateboards ordered:	Y
IdPriceLabel	Skateboard price:	I
IdRateLabel	Sales tax rate	R

Figure 2-16: Access keys included in the label controls that identify text boxes

The last step in completing an interface is to set the TabIndex property of the controls.

tip

You should not include an access key in the Text property of the Total skateboards: and Total price: labels, because these labels do not identify text boxes; rather, they identify other label controls. Recall that users cannot access label controls while an application is running, so it is inappropriate to assign an access key to them.

tip

The ampersand in a label control's Text property designates an access key only if the label control's UseMnemonic property is set to True, which is the default for that property. In the rare cases where you do not want the ampersand to designate an access key—for example, you want the label control's Text property to say, literally, J & M Sales—then you need to set the label control's UseMnemonic property to False.

Setting the TabIndex Property

The **TabIndex property** determines the order in which a control receives the focus when the user presses either the Tab key or an access key while the application is running. A control having a TabIndex of 2, for instance, will receive the focus immediately after the control whose TabIndex is 1. Likewise, a control with a TabIndex of 18 will receive the focus immediately after the control whose TabIndex is 17. When a control has the **focus**, it can accept user input.

When you add to a form a control that has a TabIndex property, Visual Basic .NET sets the control's TabIndex property to a number that represents the order in which the control was added to the form. The TabIndex property for the first control added to a form is 0 (zero), the TabIndex property for the second control is 1, and so on. In most cases, you will need to change the TabIndex values, because the order in which the controls were added to the form rarely represents the order in which each should receive the focus.

To determine the appropriate TabIndex settings for an application, you first make a list of the controls (in the interface) that can accept user input. The list should reflect the order in which the user will want to access the controls. For example, in the Skate-Away Sales application, the user typically will want to access the NameTextBox control first, then the AddressTextBox control, the CityTextBox control, and so on. If a control that accepts user input is identified by a label control, you also include the label control in the list. (A text box is an example of a control that accepts user input and is identified by a label control.) You place the name of the label control immediately above the name of the control it identifies. For example, in the Skate-Away Sales application, the IdNameLabel control (which contains Name:) identifies the NameTextBox control; therefore, IdNameLabel should appear immediately above NameTextBox in the list. The names of controls that do not accept user input, and those that are not identifying controls, should be listed at the bottom of the list; these names do not need to appear in any specific order.

After listing the controls, you then assign each control in the list a TabIndex value, beginning with the number 0. Figure 2-17 shows the list of controls for the Skate-Away Sales interface, along with the appropriate TabIndex values. Rows pertaining to controls that accept user input are shaded in the figure.

Not all controls have a TabIndex property; PictureBox, MainMenu, and Timer controls, for example, do not have a TabIndex property.

Controls that accept user input, along with their identifying label controls	TabIndex setting
IdNameLabel (Name:)	0
NameTextBox	1
IdAddressLabel (Address:)	2
AddressTextBox	3
IdCityLabel (City:)	4
CityTextBox	5
IdStateLabel (State:)	6
StateTextBox	7
IdZipLabel (ZIP:)	8
ZipTextBox	9

identifying label

text box

Figure 2-17: List of controls and TabIndex settings

Controls that accept user input, along with their identifying label controls	TabIndex setting
IdBlueLabel (Blue skateboards ordered:)	10
BlueTextBox	11
IdYellowLabel (Yellow skateboards ordered:)	12
YellowTextBox	13
IdPriceLabel (Skateboard price:)	14
PriceTextBox	15
IdRateLabel (Sales tax rate:)	16
RateTextBox	17
CalcButton	18
ClearButton	19
ExitButton	20
Other controls	**TabIndex setting**
IdHeadingLabel (Skate-Away Sales Order Form)	21
IdTotalBoardsLabel (Total skateboards:)	22
IdTotalPriceLabel (Total price:)	23
TotalBoardsLabel	24
TotalPriceLabel	25
PhonePictureBox	This control does not have a TabIndex property.

Figure 2-17: List of controls and TabIndex settings (continued)

If a control does not have a TabIndex property, you do not assign it a TabIndex value. You can tell if a control has a TabIndex property by viewing its Properties list.

As Figure 2-17 indicates, 12 controls in the Skate-Away Sales interface—nine text boxes and three buttons—can accept user input. Notice that each text box in the list is associated with an identifying label control, whose name appears immediately above the text box name in the list. Also notice that the TabIndex value assigned to each text box's identifying label control is one number less than the value assigned to the text box itself. For example, the IdNameLabel control has a TabIndex value of 0, and its corresponding text box (NameTextBox) has a TabIndex value of 1. Likewise, the IdAddressLabel control and its corresponding text box have TabIndex values of 2 and 3, respectively. For a text box's access key (which is defined in the identifying label) to work appropriately, you must be sure to set the identifying label control's TabIndex property to a value that is one number less than the value stored in the text box's TabIndex property.

You can use the Properties list to set the TabIndex property of each control; or, you can use the Tab Order option on the View menu. You already know how to set a property using the Properties list. In the next set of steps, you learn how to use the Tab Order option on the View menu.

tip

· · · · · · · · · · · · · · · · ·

▶ The Tab Order option on the View menu is available only when the designer window is the active window.

To set the TabIndex values:

1 Click **View** on the menu bar, then click **Tab Order.** The current TabIndex value for each control except the PictureBox control appears in blue boxes on the form. (PictureBox controls do not have a TabIndex property.) The TabIndex values reflect the order in which each control was added to the form.

HELP? If the Tab Order option does not appear on the View menu, click the form, then repeat Step 1.

According to Figure 2-17, the first control in the tab order should be the IdNameLabel control, which contains the text Name:. Currently, this control has a TabIndex value of 2, which indicates that it was the third control added to the form.

2 Place the mouse pointer on the Name: label. (You cannot see the entire label, because the box containing the number 2 covers the letters Na.) A rectangle surrounds the label and the mouse pointer becomes a crosshair ┼, as shown in Figure 2-18.

crosshair

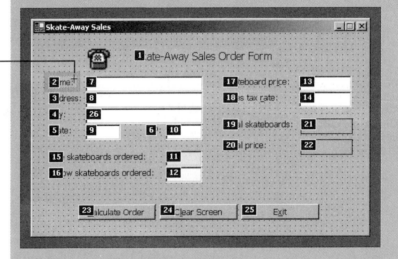

Figure 2-18: Crosshair positioned on the Name: label

3 Click the Name: label (or click the box containing the number 2). The number 0 replaces the number 2 in the box, and the color of the box changes from blue to white to indicate that you have set the TabIndex value.

4 Click the NameTextBox text box, which appears to the immediate right of the Name: label. The number 1 replaces the number 7 in the box, and the color of the box changes from blue to white.

5 Use the information in Figure 2-19 to set the TabIndex values for the remaining controls—the controls with TabIndex values of 2 through 25. Be sure to set the values in numerical order. If you make a mistake, press the Esc key to remove the TabIndex boxes from the form, then repeat Steps 1 through 5. When you have finished setting all of the TabIndex values, the color of the boxes will automatically change from white to blue, as shown in Figure 2-19.

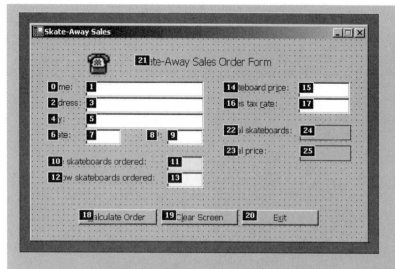

Figure 2-19: Correct TabIndex values shown in the form

6 Verify that the TabIndex values shown on your screen agree with those shown in Figure 2-19, then press **Esc** to remove the TabIndex boxes from the form.

tip
....

You also can remove the TabIndex boxes by clicking View, and then clicking Tab Order.

GUI Design Tips

Rules for Assigning Access Keys and Controlling the Focus

- When assigning an access key to a control, use the first letter of the caption or identifying label, unless another letter provides a more meaningful association. If you can't use the first letter and no other letter provides a more meaningful association, then use a distinctive consonant. Lastly, use a vowel or a number.

- Access keys should be unique.

- Assign a TabIndex value to each control in the interface, except for controls that do not have a TabIndex property. The TabIndex values should reflect the order in which the user will want to access the controls.

- To give users keyboard access to text boxes, assign an access key to the text box control's identifying label. Set the TabIndex property of the label control so that its value is one number less than the value in the TabIndex property of the corresponding text box. (In other words, the TabIndex value of the text box should be one number greater than the TabIndex value of its identifying label control.)

Now save the solution and start the application to verify that it is working correctly.

To save the solution and then start the application:

1 Click the **Save All** button [🖫] on the Standard toolbar to save the solution. Click the **Start** button [▸] on the Standard toolbar to start the application. See Figure 2-20.

insertion point

Figure 2-20: Completed user interface for the Skate-Away Sales application

tip

• • • • • • • • • • • • • • • • • •

You also can start the application by pressing the F5 key, or by clicking Debug on the menu bar, and then clicking Start.

When you start an application, Visual Basic .NET places the focus in the control whose TabIndex value is 0—in this case, that control is the IdNameLabel (Name:) control. However, because label controls cannot receive the focus, Visual Basic .NET sends the focus to the next control in the tab order sequence—in this case, that control is the NameTextBox. Notice that an insertion point appears in the NameTextBox control. The insertion point indicates that the text box has the focus and is ready to receive input from you.

2 Type **Sport Warehouse** in the NameTextBox. Notice that a text box displays the information it receives from you. The information is recorded in the text box's Text property. In this case, for example, the information is recorded in the Text property of the NameTextBox.

In Windows applications, the Tab key moves the focus forward, and the Shift + Tab key combination moves the focus backward.

3 Press **Tab** to move the focus to the AddressTextBox, then press **Shift + Tab** to move the focus back to the NameTextBox.

Use the Tab key to verify the tab order of the controls in the interface.

4 Press **Tab**, slowly, nine times. The focus moves to the following controls: AddressTextBox, CityTextBox, StateTextBox, ZipTextBox, BlueTextBox, YellowTextBox, PriceTextBox, RateTextBox, and CalcButton.

Notice that, when the focus moves to the Calculate Order button, the button's border is highlighted and a dotted rectangle appears around its caption. Pressing the Enter key when a button has the focus invokes the button's Click event and causes the computer to process any code contained in the event procedure.

5 Press **Tab** three times. The focus moves to the ClearButton, then to the ExitButton, and finally back to the NameTextBox.

You also can move the focus using a text box's access key.

6 Press **Alt+b** to move the focus to the BlueTextBox, then press **Alt+n** to move the focus to the NameTextBox.

7 On your own, try the access keys for the remaining text boxes in the interface.

Unlike pressing a text box's access key, which moves the focus, pressing a button's access key invokes the button's Click event procedure; any code contained in the event procedure will be processed by the computer.

8 Press **Alt+x** to invoke the Exit button's Click event procedure, which contains the `Me.Close()` instruction. The application ends, and you are returned to the designer window.

9 Close the Output window, then use the File menu to close the solution.

You now have finished planning the application and building the user interface. For now, you can either take a break or complete the end-of-lesson questions and exercises before moving on to the next lesson. You will complete the remaining steps involved in creating an OOED application in Lesson C.

S U M M A R Y

To control the border around a label control:

■ Set the label control's BorderStyle property to None, FixedSingle, or Fixed3D.

To lock/unlock the controls on the form:

■ Right-click the form or any control on the form, then select Lock Controls on the short-cut menu. To unlock the controls, simply select the Lock Controls option again. You also can lock/unlock controls by using the Lock Controls option on the Format menu.

To assign an access key to a control:

■ Type an ampersand (&) in the Text property of the control's caption or identifying label. The ampersand should appear to the immediate left of the letter or number that you want to designate as the access key. (The ampersand in a label control's Text property designates an access key only if the label control's UseMnemonic property is set to True, which is the default for that property.)

To give users keyboard access to a text box:

■ Assign an access key to the text box control's identifying label control. Set the label control's TabIndex property so that its value is one number less than the TabIndex value of the text box.

To access a control that has an access key:

■ Press and hold down the Alt key as you press the control's access key.

To set the tab order:

■ Set each control's TabIndex property to a number that represents the order in which you want the control to receive the focus. Remember to begin with 0 (zero). You can use the Properties list to set the TabIndex values. Or, you can use the Tab Order option on the View menu.

QUESTIONS

1. The _____ property determines the order in which a control receives the focus when the user presses the Tab key or an access key.
   a. OrderTab
   b. SetOrder
   c. TabIndex
   d. TabOrder
   e. TabStop

2. When placing controls on a form, you should maintain a consistent margin of _____ dots from the edge of the window.
   a. one or two
   b. two or three
   c. two to five
   d. three to 10
   e. 10 to 20

3. If the buttons are positioned on the bottom of the screen, then each button should be _____.
   a. the same height
   b. the same width
   c. the same height and the same width

4. If the buttons are stacked in either the upper-right or the lower-right corner of the screen, then each button should be _____.
   a. the same height
   b. the same width
   c. the same height and the same width

5. The human eye is attracted to _____.
   a. black and white before color
   b. color before black and white
   c. graphics before text
   d. text before graphics
   e. both b and c

6. When building an interface, always use _____.
   a. dark text on a dark background
   b. dark text on a light background
   c. light text on a dark background
   d. light text on a light background
   e. either b or c

7. Use _____ fonts for the elements in the user interface.
   a. 6-, 8-, or 10-point
   b. 8-, 9-, 10-, 11-, or 12-point
   c. 10-, 12-, or 14-point
   d. 12-, 14-, or 16-point

8. Limit the number of font sizes used in an interface to _____.
   a. one or two
   b. two or three
   c. three or four

9. Use a _____ font for the text in the user interface.
   a. sans serif
   b. serif

10. Limit the number of font types used in an interface to _____.
    a. one
    b. two
    c. three
    d. four

11. To put a border around a label control, you set the label control's _____ property to FixedSingle.
    a. Appearance
    b. BackStyle
    c. Border
    d. BorderStyle
    e. Text

12. You use the _____ character to assign an access key to a control.
    a. &
    b. *
    c. @
    d. $
    e. ^

13. You assign an access key using a control's _____ property.
    a. Access
    b. Caption
    c. Key
    d. KeyAccess
    e. Text

14. Explain the procedure for choosing a control's access key.

15. Explain how you give users keyboard access to a text box.

EXERCISES

The following list summarizes the GUI design guidelines you have learned so far. You can use this list to verify that the interfaces you create in the following exercises adhere to the GUI standards outlined in the book.

■ Information should flow either vertically or horizontally, with the most important information always located in the upper-left corner of the screen.

■ Maintain a consistent margin of two or three dots from the edge of the window.

■ Try to create a user interface that no one notices.

■ Related controls should be grouped together using white space, a GroupBox control, or a Panel control.

■ Set the form's FormBorderStyle, ControlBox, MaximizeBox, MinimizeBox, and StartPosition properties appropriately:

    ■ A splash screen should not have a Minimize, Maximize, or Close button, and its borders should not be sizable.

    ■ A form that is not a splash screen should always have a Minimize button and a Close button, but you can choose to disable the Maximize button. Typically, the FormBorderStyle property is set to Sizable, but also can be set to FixedSingle.

- Position related controls on succeeding dots. Controls that are not part of any logical grouping may be positioned from two to four dots away from other controls.

- Buttons should be positioned either in a row along the bottom of the screen, or stacked in either the upper-right or lower-right corner.

- If the buttons are positioned at the bottom of the screen, then each button should be the same height; their widths, however, may vary.

- If the buttons are stacked in either the upper-right or lower-right corner of the screen, then each should be the same height and the same width.

- Use no more than six buttons on a screen.

- The most commonly used button should be placed first.

- Button captions should:

  - be meaningful
  - be from one to three words
  - appear on one line
  - be entered using book title capitalization

- Use labels to identify the text boxes in the interface, and position the label either above or to the left of the text box.

- Label text should:

  - be from one to three words
  - appear on one line
  - be left-justified
  - end with a colon (:)
  - be entered using sentence capitalization

- Labels that identify controls should have their BorderStyle property set to None.

- Labels that display program output, such as the result of a calculation, should have their BorderStyle property set to FixedSingle.

- Align controls to minimize the number of different margins.

- If you use a graphic in the interface, use a small one and place it in a location that will not distract the user.

- Use the Tahoma font for applications that will run on systems running Windows 2000 or Windows XP.

- Use no more than two different font sizes, which should be 8, 9, 10, 11, or 12 point.

- Use only one font type, which should be a sans serif font, in the interface.

- Avoid using italics and underlining.

- Limit the use of bold text to titles, headings, and key items.

- Build the interface using black, white, and gray first, then add color only if you have a good reason to do so.

- Use white, off-white, light gray, pale blue, or pale yellow for an application's background, and black for the text.

- Limit the number of colors to three, not including white, black, and gray. The colors you choose should complement each other.

- Never use color as the only means of identification for an element in the user interface.

- Set each control's TabIndex property to a number that represents the order in which you want the control to receive the focus (begin with 0).

- A text box's TabIndex value should be one more than the TabIndex value of its identifying label.

- Assign a unique access key to each control (in the interface) that can receive user input (text boxes, buttons, and so on).

- When assigning an access key to a control, use the first letter of the caption or identifying label, unless another letter provides a more meaningful association. If you can't use the first letter and no other letter provides a more meaningful association, then use a distinctive consonant. Lastly, use a vowel or a number.

- Lock the controls in place on the form.

1. In this exercise, you finish building a user interface.
   a. If necessary, start Visual Studio .NET. Open the Paper Solution (Paper Solution.sln) file, which is contained in the VBNET\Tut02\Paper Solution folder. If the designer window is not open, right-click the form file's name in the Solution Explorer window, then click View Designer.
   b. Finish building the user interface shown in Figure 2-21 by adding a text box named NameTextBox. Assign access keys to the text boxes and buttons, as shown in the figure. Also, adjust the TabIndex values appropriately. (The user will enter the name, then the territory number, and then the sales.)

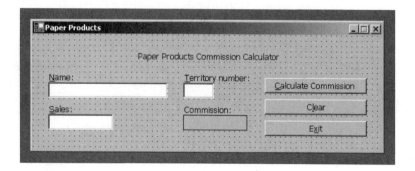

Figure 2-21

   c. Lock the controls on the form.
   d. Change the background color of the form to pale yellow. Change the background color of the buttons to gray (use the Control setting on the System tab).
   e. Save the solution, then start the application. Verify that the tab order is correct, and that the access keys work appropriately. Click the Exit button to end the application. (The Exit button has already been coded for you. You will code the Calculate Commission and Clear buttons in Lesson C's Exercise 1.)

2. In this exercise, you finish building a user interface.
   a. If necessary, start Visual Studio .NET. Open the RMSales Solution (RMSales Solution.sln) file, which is contained in the VBNET\Tut02\RMSales Solution folder. If the designer window is not open, right-click the form file's name in the Solution Explorer window, then click View Designer.
   b. Finish building the user interface shown in Figure 2-22 by adding a text box named NsalesTextBox. Adjust the TabIndex values appropriately. (The user will enter the North region's sales and increase percentage before entering the South region's sales and increase percentage.)

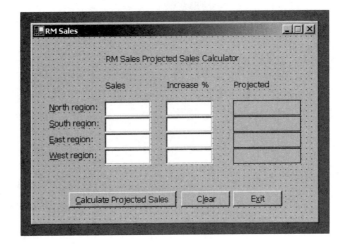

Figure 2-22

   c. Lock the controls on the form.
   d. Change the BorderStyle property of the label controls appropriately.
   e. Save the solution, then start the application. Verify that the tab order is correct, and that the access keys work appropriately. Click the Exit button to end the application. (The Exit button has already been coded for you. You will code the Calculate Projected Sales and Clear buttons in Lesson C's Exercise 2.)

3. In this exercise, you modify the application that you saved in Lesson A's Exercise 3.
   a. If necessary, start Visual Studio .NET. Open the Time Solution (Time Solution.sln) file, which is contained in the VBNET\Tut02\Time Solution folder. If the designer window is not open, right-click the form file's name in the Solution Explorer window, then click View Designer.
   b. Lock the controls on the form.
   c. Assign access keys to the controls that can accept user input.
   d. Set each control's TabIndex property appropriately.
   e. Save the solution, then start the application. Verify that the tab order is correct, and that the access keys work appropriately. Click the Exit button to end the application.

LESSON C
objectives

After completing this lesson, you will be able to:

- Use the TOE chart to code the application
- Use pseudocode to plan an object's code
- Write an assignment statement
- Use the Focus method
- Include internal documentation in the code
- Write arithmetic expressions
- Use the Val and Format functions

Coding, Testing, Debugging, and Documenting the Application

Coding the Application

After meeting with the client, planning the application, and building the user interface, you then write the Visual Basic .NET instructions to tell the objects in the interface how to respond to events. The instructions are called **code**, and the process of writing the instructions is called **coding**. You will need to write code for each object that has an event listed in the third column of the TOE chart you created in Lesson A. For your reference while coding, the TOE chart is shown in Figure 2-23.

Task	Object	Event
1. Calculate the total skateboards ordered and the total price 2. Display the total skateboards ordered and the total price in the TotalBoardsLabel and TotalPriceLabel	CalcButton	Click
Clear the screen for the next order	ClearButton	Click
End the application	ExitButton	Click
Display the total skateboards ordered (from CalcButton)	TotalBoardsLabel	None
Display the total price (from CalcButton)	TotalPriceLabel	None
Get and display the order information	NameTextBox, AddressTextBox, CityTextBox, StateTextBox, ZipTextBox, PriceTextBox, RateTextBox, BlueTextBox, YellowTextBox	None

Figure 2-23: Completed TOE chart ordered by object

According to the TOE chart, only the three buttons require coding, as they are the only objects with an event listed in the third column of the chart. The Exit button has already been coded for you, so you need to write the code for only the Clear Screen and Calculate Order buttons. First, however, open the Order application that you created in Lesson B.

To open the Order application:

1   Start Microsoft Visual Studio .NET, if necessary. Close the Start Page window.

2   Click **File** on the menu bar, then click **Open Solution**. Open the **Order Solution** (Order Solution.sln) file, which is contained in the VBNET\Tut02\Order Solution folder on your computer's hard disk.

3   If the designer window is not open, right-click **Order Form.vb** in the Solution Explorer window, then click **View Designer**.

Figure 2-24 identifies the objects included in the user interface. (You won't see the names of the controls on your screen. The names are included in Figure 2-24 for your reference only.)

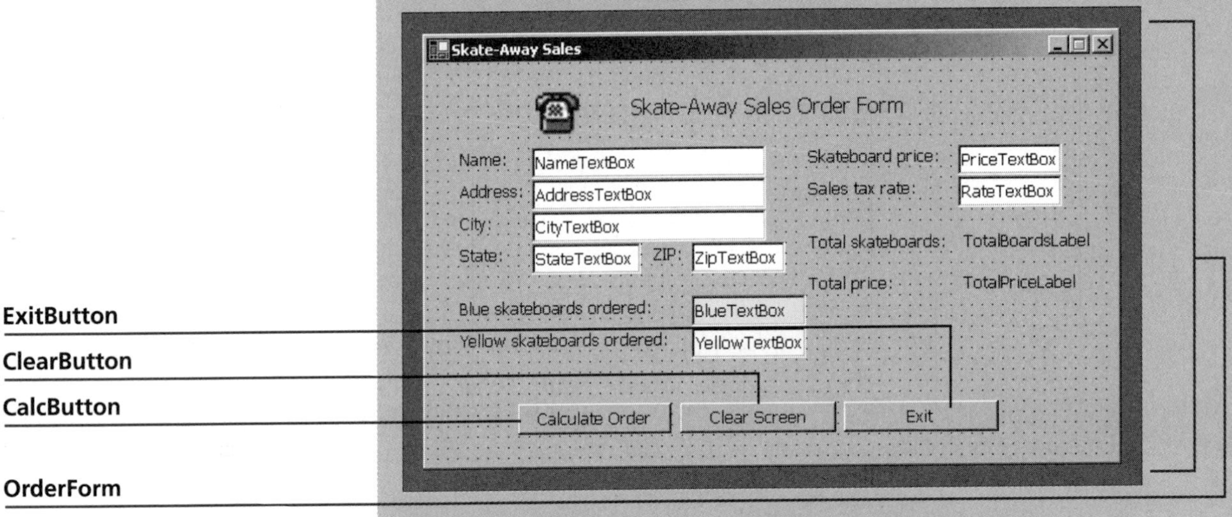

Figure 2-24: Skate-Away Sales user interface

Recall that the controls are locked on the form. You code the Clear Screen button first.

Coding the Clear Screen Button

According to the TOE chart, the Clear Screen button is assigned the task of clearing the screen for the next order. Clearing the screen involves assigning a zero-length string to the Text property of the NameTextBox, AddressTextBox, CityTextBox, ZipTextBox, BlueTextBox, YellowTextBox, TotalBoardsLabel, and TotalPriceLabel controls, and assigning the string "IL" to the Text property of the StateTextBox control. A **string** is simply a group of characters enclosed in quotation marks. The word "Jones", for example, is a string. Likewise, "45" is a string, but 45 is not; 45 is a number. "Jones" is a string with a length of five, because there are five characters between the quotation marks. "45" is a string with a length of two, because there are two characters between the quotation marks. Following this logic, a **zero-length string**, also called an **empty string**, is a set of quotation marks with nothing between them, like this: "". Assigning a zero-length string to the Text property of a control removes the contents of the control. Figure 2-25 lists what you want the Clear Screen button to do when the button is clicked by the user.

You are assigning "IL" to the StateTextBox control in case the user changed the state when he or she entered an order. Remember that most, but not all, of Skate-Away's customers are in Illinois.

Clear Screen button
1. assign a zero-length string to the Text property of the NameTextBox, AddressTextBox, CityTextBox, ZipTextBox, BlueTextBox, and YellowTextBox
2. assign "IL" to the StateTextBox's Text property
3. assign a zero-length string to the Text property of the TotalBoardsLabel and TotalPriceLabel
4. send the focus to the NameTextBox

Figure 2-25: Steps for the Clear Screen button

Notice that the list shown in Figure 2-25 is composed of short statements in English. The statements represent the steps the Clear Screen button needs to follow in order to prepare the screen for the next order. In programming terms, the list of steps shown in Figure 2-25 is called pseudocode. As you learned in Lesson A, pseudocode is a tool programmers use to help them plan the steps that an object needs to take in order to perform its assigned task. Even though the word *pseudocode* might be unfamiliar to you, you already have written pseudocode without even realizing it. Think about the last time you gave directions to someone. You wrote each direction down on paper, in your own words; your directions were a form of pseudocode.

The programmer uses the pseudocode as a guide when coding the application. For example, you will use the pseudocode shown in Figure 2-25 to write the appropriate Visual Basic .NET instructions for the Clear Screen button. The first three steps in the pseudocode assign either a zero-length string or the string "IL" to the Text property of various controls in the interface. You use an **assignment statement**, which is simply a Visual Basic .NET instruction, to set the value of a property while an application is running.

Assigning a Value to a Property During Run Time

The period that appears in an assignment statement is called the dot member selection operator. It tells Visual Basic .NET that what appears to the right of the dot is a member of what appears to the left of the dot. For example, the assignment statement `Me.NameTextBox.Text` indicates that the Text property is a member of the NameTextBox control, which is a member of the current form.

You use the syntax [**Me.**]*object.property* = *expression* to set the value of an object's property while an application is running. In the syntax, **Me** refers to the current form; notice that Me. is optional, as indicated by the square brackets ([]) in the syntax. *Object* and *property* are the names of the object and property, respectively, to which you want the value of the *expression* assigned. Notice that you use a period to separate the form reference (Me) from the object name, and the object name from the property name. Also notice that you use an equal sign (=) to separate the [**Me.**]*object.property* information from the *expression*. When it appears in an assignment statement, the equal sign (=) is often referred to as the **assignment operator**.

When an assignment statement is encountered in a program, the computer assigns the value of the expression appearing on the right side of the assignment operator (=) to the object and property that appears on the left side of the assignment operator. For example, the assignment statement `Me.NameTextBox.Text = ""` assigns a zero-length string to the Text property of the NameTextBox control.

Similarly, the assignment statement `Me.StateTextBox.Text = "IL"` assigns the string "IL" to the Text property of the StateTextBox control. As you learn later in this lesson, the assignment statement `Me.SumTextBox.Text = 3 + 5` assigns the value 8 to the Text property of the SumTextBox control. You will use assignment statements to code the Clear Screen button.

tip

You also can open the Code editor window by pressing the F7 key, or by clicking View on the menu bar, and then clicking Code.

tip

The easiest way to enter the instruction in Step 3 is to type `me.namet.te` and press Enter.

To begin coding the Clear Screen button:

1 Right-click the **form** (or a control on the form), and then click **View Code** to open the Code editor window.

2 Click the **Class Name** list arrow in the Code editor window, and then click **ClearButton** in the list. Click the **Method Name** list arrow in the Code editor window, and then click **Click** in the list. The code template for the ClearButton object's Click event procedure appears in the Code editor window.

Step 1 in the pseudocode shown in Figure 2-25 is to assign a zero-length string to the Text property of six of the text boxes.

3 Type **me.nametextbox.text = ""** (be sure you do not type any spaces between the quotation marks) and press **Enter**. The Code editor changes the instruction to `Me.NameTextBox.Text = ""`. (Notice the capitalization.)

When entering code, you can type the names of commands, objects, and properties in lowercase letters. When you move to the next line, the Code editor automatically changes your code to reflect the proper capitalization of those elements. This provides a quick way of verifying that you entered an object's name and property correctly, and that you entered the code using the correct syntax. If the capitalization does not change, then the Code editor does not recognize the object, command, or property.

4 Copy the `Me.NameTextBox.Text = ""` assignment statement to the clipboard, then paste the assignment statement into the Code editor window five times, between the original assignment statement and the `End Sub` instruction.

> **HELP?** To copy the `Me.NameTextBox.Text = ""` statement to the clipboard, highlight the statement, then press Ctrl+c. To paste the `Me.NameTextBox.Text = ""` statement into the Code editor window, first click at the location where you want to begin pasting, then press Ctrl+v. You also can use the Copy option on the Edit menu to copy the statements to the clipboard, and the Paste option on the Edit menu to paste the statements into the Code editor window.

5 Change the names of the controls in the copied assignment statements to match Figure 2-26, then position the insertion point as shown in the figure.

```
OrderForm                                          ClearButton_Click
Public Class OrderForm
    Inherits System.Windows.Forms.Form

    Windows Form Designer generated code

    Private Sub ExitButton_Click(ByVal sender As Object, ByVal e As System.EventArgs) Ha
        Me.Close()
    End Sub

    Private Sub ClearButton_Click(ByVal sender As Object, ByVal e As System.EventArgs) I
        Me.NameTextBox.Text = ""
        Me.AddressTextBox.Text = ""
        Me.CityTextBox.Text = ""
        Me.ZipTextBox.Text = ""
        Me.BlueTextBox.Text = ""
        Me.YellowTextBox.Text = ""

    End Sub
End Class
```

change the control names as shown

position the insertion point here

Figure 2-26: Assignment statements entered in the Clear Screen button's Click event procedure

The second step in the pseudocode is to assign the string "IL" to the Text property of the StateTextBox.

6 Type **me.statetextbox.text = "IL"** and press **Enter**.

Step 3 in the pseudocode is to assign a zero-length string to the TotalBoardsLabel and TotalPriceLabel controls.

7 Type **me.totalboardslabel.text = " "** and then press **Enter**, then type **me.totalpricelabel.text = " "** and press **Enter**.

The last step in the pseudocode shown in Figure 2-25 is to send the focus to the NameTextBox. You can accomplish this using the Focus method. A **method** is a predefined Visual Basic .NET procedure.

Using the Focus Method

The **Focus method** allows you to move the focus to a specified control while the application is running. The syntax of the Focus method is **[Me.]**_object_**.Focus()**, where _object_ is the name of the object to which you want the focus sent.

To enter the Focus method in the Clear Screen button's Click event procedure, then save the solution:

1 Type **me.nametextbox.focus()** and press **Enter**.

2 Click **File** on the menu bar, and then click **Save All**.

tip

Methods and events constitute an object's behaviors. An event is a behavior that can be performed on an object—for example, a button can be clicked. A method is a behavior that an object can perform—for example, a text box can send the focus to itself.

It is a good practice to leave yourself some comments as reminders in the Code editor window. Programmers refer to this as **internal documentation**.

Internally Documenting the Program Code

Visual Basic .NET provides an easy way to document a program internally. You simply place an apostrophe (') before the statement you want treated as a comment. Visual Basic .NET ignores everything that appears after the apostrophe on that line. Add some comments to the Clear Screen button's code.

To internally document the Clear Screen button's code, then test the code to verify that it is working correctly:

1   Position the I-bar ⌶ at the beginning of the `Me.NameTextBox.Text = ""` line in the ClearButton object's Click event procedure, then click at that location. The insertion point appears at that location.

2   Press **Enter** to insert a blank line, then click the blank line. Press **Tab** twice to indent the code you are about to type, then type '**prepare screen for next order** (be sure to type the apostrophe).

Notice that the internal documentation appears in a different color from the rest of the code. Recall from Tutorial 1 that the Code editor displays keywords and key symbols in a different color to help you quickly identify these elements in your code. In this case, the color coding helps you easily locate the comments.

3   Position ⌶ after the `Me.TotalPriceLabel.Text = ""` instruction, then click at that location. Press **Enter** to insert a blank line below the instruction, then type '**send focus to the Name text box**. Figure 2-27 shows the completed Click event procedure for the Clear Screen button.

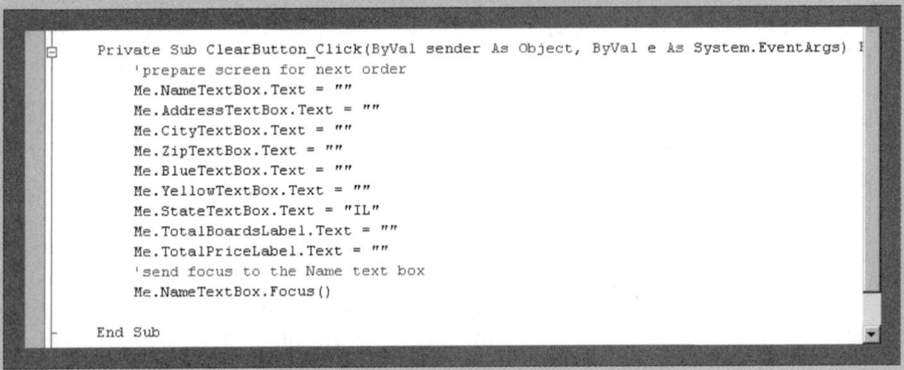

```
Private Sub ClearButton_Click(ByVal sender As Object, ByVal e As System.EventArgs)
    'prepare screen for next order
    Me.NameTextBox.Text = ""
    Me.AddressTextBox.Text = ""
    Me.CityTextBox.Text = ""
    Me.ZipTextBox.Text = ""
    Me.BlueTextBox.Text = ""
    Me.YellowTextBox.Text = ""
    Me.StateTextBox.Text = "IL"
    Me.TotalBoardsLabel.Text = ""
    Me.TotalPriceLabel.Text = ""
    'send focus to the Name text box
    Me.NameTextBox.Focus()

End Sub
```

Figure 2-27: Completed Click event procedure for the Clear Screen button

It is a good programming practice to write the code for one object at a time, and then test and debug that object's code before coding the next object. This way, if something is wrong with the program, you know exactly where to look for the error.

4   Save the solution, then start the application.

5   Enter your name and address information (including the city, state, and ZIP) in the appropriate text boxes, then enter **10** for the number of blue skateboards ordered and **10** for the number of yellow skateboards ordered. Enter **100** for the skateboard price and **.05** for the sales tax rate.

6 Click the **Clear Screen** button. Following the instructions you entered in the Clear Screen button's Click event procedure, Visual Basic .NET removes the contents of the NameTextBox, AddressTextBox, CityTextBox, ZipTextBox, BlueTextBox, YellowTextBox, TotalBoardsLabel, and TotalPriceLabel controls. It also places the string "IL" in the StateTextBox control, and sends the focus to the Name text box. Notice that the PriceTextBox control still contains 100, and the RateTextBox control still contains .05. Recall that you did not instruct the Clear Screen button to clear the contents of those controls.

7 Click the **Exit** button to end the application. You are returned to the Code editor window.

8 Close the Output window.

The Calculate Order button is the only object that still needs to be coded. However, before coding the button, you learn how to write arithmetic expressions in Visual Basic .NET.

Writing Arithmetic Expressions

The difference between the negation and subtraction operators shown in Figure 2-28 is that the negation operator is unary, whereas the subtraction operator is binary. *Unary* and *binary* refer to the number of operands required by the operator. Unary operators require one operand; binary operators require two operands.

Most applications require the computer to perform one or more calculations. You instruct the computer to perform a calculation by writing an arithmetic expression that contains one or more arithmetic operators. Figure 2-28 lists the arithmetic operators available in Visual Basic .NET, along with their precedence numbers. The **precedence numbers** indicate the order in which Visual Basic .NET performs the operation in an expression. Operations with a precedence number of 1 are performed before operations with a precedence number of 2, which are performed before operations with a precedence number of 3, and so on. However, you can use parentheses to override the order of precedence, because operations within parentheses always are performed before operations outside of parentheses.

Operator	Operation	Precedence number
^	exponentiation (raises a number to a power)	1
–	negation	2
*, /	multiplication and division	3
\	integer division	4
Mod	modulus arithmetic	5
+, –	addition and subtraction	6

Important Note: You can use parentheses to override the order of precedence. Operations within parentheses are always performed before operations outside parentheses.

Figure 2-28: Arithmetic operators and their order of precedence

Notice that some operators shown in Figure 2-28 have the same precedence number. For example, both the addition and subtraction operator have a precedence number of 6. If an expression contains more than one operator having the same priority, those operators are evaluated from left to right. In the expression 3 + 12 / 3 - 1, for instance, the division (/) is performed first, then the addition (+), and then the subtraction (-). In other words, Visual Basic .NET first divides 12 by 3, then adds the result of the division (4) to 3, and then subtracts 1 from the result of the addition (7). The expression evaluates to 6.

You can use parentheses to change the order in which the operators in an expression are evaluated. For example, the expression 3 + 12 / (3 - 1) evaluates to 9, not 6. This is because the parentheses tell Visual Basic .NET to subtract 1 from 3 first, then divide the result of the subtraction (2) into 12, and then add the result of the division (6) to 3.

Two of the arithmetic operators listed in Figure 2-28 might be less familiar to you; these are the integer division operator (\) and the modulus arithmetic operator (Mod). You use the **integer division operator** (\) to divide two integers (whole numbers), and then return the result as an integer. For example, the expression 211\4 results in 52—the integer result of dividing 211 by 4. (If you use the standard division operator (/) to divide 211 by 4, the result is 52.75 rather than simply 52.)

The modulus arithmetic operator also is used to divide two numbers, but the numbers do not have to be integers. After dividing the numbers, the **modulus arithmetic operator** returns the remainder of the division. For example, 211 Mod 4 equals 3, which is the remainder of 211 divided by 4. One use for the modulus arithmetic operator is to determine whether a year is a leap year—one that has 366 days rather than 365 days. As you may know, if a year is a leap year, then its year number is evenly divisible by the number 4. In other words, if you divide the year number by 4 and the remainder is 0 (zero), then the year is a leap year. You can determine whether the year 2004 is a leap year by using the expression 2004 Mod 4. This expression evaluates to 0 (the remainder of 2004 divided by 4), so the year 2004 is a leap year. Similarly, you can determine whether the year 2005 is a leap year by using the expression 2005 Mod 4. This expression evaluates to 1 (the remainder of 2005 divided by 4), so the year 2005 is not a leap year.

When entering an arithmetic expression in code, you do not enter the dollar sign ($) or the percent sign (%). If you want to enter a percentage in an arithmetic expression, you first must convert the percentage to its decimal equivalent; for example, you would convert 5% to .05.

In addition to the arithmetic operators, Visual Basic .NET also allows you to use comparison operators and logical operators in an expression. You learn about comparison and logical operators in Tutorial 4. For now, you need to know only the arithmetic operators in order to code the Calculate Order button in the Skate-Away Sales application.

Coding the Calculate Order Button

According to the TOE chart for the Skate-Away Sales application (shown earlier in Figure 2-23), the Calculate Order button is responsible for calculating both the total number of skateboards ordered and the total price of the order, and then displaying the calculated amounts in the TotalBoardsLabel and TotalPriceLabel controls. The instructions to accomplish the Calculate Order button's tasks should be placed in the button's Click event procedure, because you want the instructions processed when the user clicks the button. Figure 2-29 shows the pseudocode for the Calculate Order button Click event procedure. The pseudocode lists the steps the button needs to take in order to accomplish its tasks.

Calculate Order button
1. calculate total skateboards = blue skateboards + yellow skateboards
2. calculate total price =
   total skateboards * skateboard price * (1 + sales tax rate)
3. display total skateboards and total price in TotalBoardsLabel and
   TotalPriceLabel controls
4. send the focus to the Clear Screen button

Figure 2-29: Pseudocode for the Calculate Order button

The first step listed in the pseudocode shown in Figure 2-29 is to calculate the total number of skateboards ordered. This is accomplished by adding the number of blue skateboards ordered to the number of yellow skateboards ordered. Recall that the number of blue skateboards ordered is recorded in the BlueTextBox control's Text property as the user enters that information in the interface. Likewise, the number of yellow skateboards ordered is recorded in the YellowTextBox control's Text property. You can use an assignment statement to add together the Text property of the two text boxes, and then assign the sum to the Text property of the TotalBoardsLabel control, which is where the TOE chart indicates the sum should be displayed. The total skateboards calculation is illustrated in Figure 2-30.

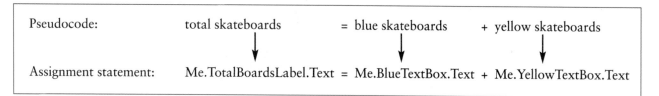

Figure 2-30: Illustration of the total skateboards calculation

The next step shown in the pseudocode is to compute the total price of the order. This is accomplished by multiplying the total number of skateboards ordered by the skateboard price ($100), and then adding a 5% sales tax to the result. The total number of skateboards ordered is recorded in the TotalBoardsLabel control, the price is entered in the PriceTextBox control, and the sales tax rate is entered in the RateTextBox control. The TOE chart indicates that the total price should be displayed in the TotalPriceLabel control. The total price calculation is illustrated in Figure 2-31.

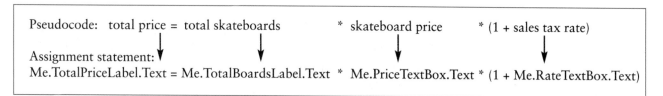

Figure 2-31: Illustration of the total price calculation

Step 3 in the pseudocode is to display the total skateboards and total price in the TotalBoardsLabel and TotalPriceLabel controls. This step was accomplished in the assignment statements shown in Figures 2-30 and 2-31.

The last step in the Calculate Order button's pseudocode is to send the focus to the Clear Screen button. After calculating an order, the salesperson typically will want to clear the screen for the next order. Sending the focus to the Clear Screen button after a calculation is made allows the user to select the button simply by pressing the Enter key. Begin coding the Calculate Order button's Click event procedure.

To begin coding the Calculate Order button's Click event procedure:

1 Click the **Class Name** list arrow in the Code editor window, and then click **CalcButton** in the list. Click the **Method Name** list arrow in the Code editor window, and then click **Click** in the list. The code template for the CalcButton Click event procedure appears in the Code editor window.

2 Type **'calculate total number of skateboards and total price** and press **Enter.**

3 Type **me.totalboardslabel.text = me.bluetextbox.text + me.yellowtextbox.text** and press **Enter.** Recall that this instruction calculates the total number of skateboards ordered.

The instruction that calculates the total price of the order is quite long. You can use the **line continuation character,** which is a space followed by an underscore, to break up a long instruction into two or more physical lines in the Code editor window; this makes the instruction easier to read and understand.

4 Type **me.totalpricelabel.text = me.totalboardslabel.text * me.pricetextbox.text _** (be sure to include a space before the underscore) and press **Enter.**

5 Press **Tab** to indent the line, then type ***(1 + me.ratetextbox.text)** and press **Enter.**

Finally, enter the instruction to send the focus to the Clear Screen button.

6 Enter the additional two lines of code indicated in Figure 2-32.

enter these two lines of code

```
Private Sub CalcButton_Click(ByVal sender As Object, ByVal e As System.EventArgs) Ha
    'calculate total number of skateboards and total price
    Me.TotalBoardsLabel.Text = Me.BlueTextBox.Text + Me.YellowTextBox.Text
    Me.TotalPriceLabel.Text = Me.TotalBoardsLabel.Text * Me.PriceTextBox.Text _
        * (1 + Me.RateTextBox.Text)
    'send the focus to the Clear Screen button
    Me.ClearButton.Focus()

End Sub
```

Figure 2-32: Code entered in the Calculate Order button's Click event procedure

7 Save the solution, then start the application.

8 Press **Tab** five times to move the focus to the BlueTextBox control. Type **5** as the number of blue skateboards ordered, then press **Tab.** Type **10** as the number of yellow skateboards ordered, then press **Tab.** Type **100** as the skateboard price, then press **Tab.** Type **.05** as the sales tax rate, then click the **Calculate Order** button. The Calculate Order button calculates, incorrectly, the total skateboards and the total price, then moves the focus to the Clear Screen button, as shown in Figure 2-33.

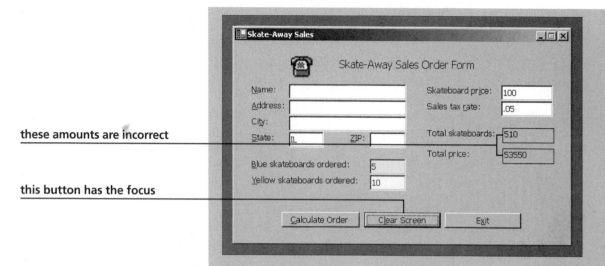

Figure 2-33: Screen showing the incorrect amounts calculated by the Calculate Order button

Notice that the screen shows 510 as the total number of skateboards ordered. Rather than mathematically adding the two order quantities together, which should have resulted in a total of 15, Visual Basic .NET appended the second order quantity to the end of the first order quantity, giving 510. When the total skateboards ordered figure is incorrect, it follows that the total price figure also will be incorrect, as the total skateboards ordered figure is used in the total price calculation.

9 Click the **Exit** button to end the application. You are returned to the Code editor window.

10 Close the Output window.

The `Me.TotalBoardsLabel.Text = Me.BlueTextBox.Text + Me.YellowTextBox.Text` equation you entered in the Calculate Order button's Click event procedure is supposed to calculate the total skateboards ordered, but the equation is not working correctly. Instead of the plus sign (+) adding the blue skateboard quantity to the yellow skateboard quantity, the plus sign appends the latter quantity to the end of the first one. This occurs because the plus sign in Visual Basic .NET performs two roles: it adds numbers together and it concatenates (links together) strings. You learn about string concatenation in Tutorial 3. (Recall that strings are groups of characters enclosed in quotation marks.)

In Visual Basic .NET, a value stored in the Text property of an object is treated as a string rather than as a number, even though you do not see the quotation marks around the value. Adding strings together does not give you the same result as adding numbers together. As you observed in the Skate-Away Sales application, adding the string "5" to the string "10" results in the string "510," whereas adding the number 5 to the number 10 results in the number 15. To fix the problem, you need to instruct Visual Basic .NET to treat the entries in the Text property of both the BlueTextBox and YellowTextBox controls as numbers rather than as strings; you can use the Val function to do so.

The Val Function

Like a method, a **function** is a predefined procedure that performs a specific task. However, unlike a method, a function returns a value after performing its task. The **Val function**, for instance, temporarily converts a string to a number, and then returns the number. (The number is stored in the computer's memory only while the function is processing.)

The syntax of the Val function is **Val**(*string*), where *string* is the string you want treated as a number. Because Visual Basic .NET must be able to interpret the *string* as a numeric value, the *string* cannot include a letter or a special character, such as the dollar sign, the comma, or the percent sign (%); it can, however, include a period and a space. When Visual Basic .NET encounters an invalid character in the Val function's *string*, Visual Basic .NET stops converting the *string* to a number at that point. Figure 2-34 shows some examples of how the Val function converts various strings. Notice that the Val function converts the "$56.88", the "Abc", and the "" (zero-length string) to the number 0.

This Val function:	Would be converted to:
Val("456")	456
Val("24,500")	24
Val("123X")	123
Val("$56.88")	0
Val("Abc")	0
Val("")	0
Val("25%")	25
Val("24 500")	24500

Figure 2-34: Examples of the Val function

You will use the Val function in the Calculate Order button's Click event procedure to temporarily convert to numbers the Text property of the controls included in calculations.

To include the Val function in the Calculate Order button's code:

1 Change the Me.TotalBoardsLabel.Text = Me.BlueTextBox.Text + Me.YellowTextBox.Text statement to Me.TotalBoardsLabel.Text = Val(Me.BlueTextBox.Text) + Val(Me.YellowTextBox.Text). Be sure to watch the placement of the parentheses.

2 Change the instruction that calculates the total price as shown in Figure 2-35. Be sure to watch the placement of the parentheses in the instruction. Also, notice that there are two parentheses at the end of the instruction. (Do not be concerned if you cannot view all of the CalcButton's code. The font used to display the text in the Code editor window shown in Figure 2-35 was changed to 11-point Microsoft Sans Serif so that you could view all of the total price equation in the figure. It is not necessary for you to change the font.)

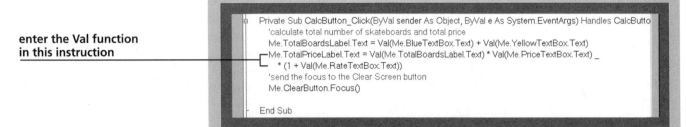

**enter the Val function
in this instruction**

```
Private Sub CalcButton_Click(ByVal sender As Object, ByVal e As System.EventArgs) Handles CalcButto
    'calculate total number of skateboards and total price
    Me.TotalBoardsLabel.Text = Val(Me.BlueTextBox.Text) + Val(Me.YellowTextBox.Text)
    Me.TotalPriceLabel.Text = Val(Me.TotalBoardsLabel.Text) * Val(Me.PriceTextBox.Text) _
        * (1 + Val(Me.RateTextBox.Text))
    'send the focus to the Clear Screen button
    Me.ClearButton.Focus()

End Sub
```

Figure 2-35: Val function entered in the Calculate Order button's code

3   Save the solution, then start the application.

4   Click the **BlueTextBox** control, type **5** as the number of blue skateboards ordered, then press **Tab**. Type **10** as the number of yellow skateboards ordered, **100** as the skateboard price, and **.05** as the sales tax rate. Click the **Calculate Order** button. The application correctly calculates the total skateboards (15) and the total price (1575), then sends the focus to the Clear Screen button.

In the next section, you will improve the appearance of the interface by including a dollar sign, a comma thousand separator, and two decimal places in the total price amount.

5   Press **Enter** to clear the screen, then click the **Exit** button. You are returned to the Code editor window. Close the Output window.

Next, learn about the Format function.

Using the Format Function

You can use the **Format function** to improve the appearance of the numbers displayed in an interface. The syntax of the Format function is **Format**(*expression, style*). *Expression* specifies the number, date, time, or string whose appearance you want to format. *Style* is either the name of a predefined Visual Basic .NET format style or, if you want more control over the appearance of the *expression*, a string containing special symbols that indicate how you want the *expression* displayed. (You can display the Help screen for the Format function to learn more about these special symbols.) In this case, you will use one of the predefined Visual Basic .NET format styles, some of which are explained in Figure 2-36.

tip

If you are thinking that the instructions are getting a bit unwieldy, you are correct. In Tutorial 3 you learn how to write more compact assignment statements.

tip

You could have included the Format function in the equation that calculates the total price, but then the equation would be so long that it would be difficult to understand.

Format style	Description
Currency	Displays a number with a dollar sign and two decimal places; if appropriate, displays a number with a thousand separator; negative numbers are enclosed in parentheses
Fixed	Displays a number with at least one digit to the left and two digits to the right of the decimal point
Standard	Displays a number with at least one digit to the left and two digits to the right of the decimal point; if appropriate, displays a number with a thousand separator
Percent	Multiplies a number by 100 and displays the number with a percent sign (%); displays two digits to the right of the decimal point

Figure 2-36: Some of the predefined format styles in Visual Basic .NET

You will use the Currency format style to display the total price amount with a dollar sign, a comma thousand separator, and two decimal places.

To format the total price amount:

1 Insert a blank line below the total price equation, then enter the additional line of code shown in Figure 2-37.

enter this line of code

```
Private Sub CalcButton_Click(ByVal sender As Object, ByVal e As System.EventArgs) Ha
    'calculate total number of skateboards and total price
    Me.TotalBoardsLabel.Text = Val(Me.BlueTextBox.Text) + Val(Me.YellowTextBox.Text)
    Me.TotalPriceLabel.Text = Val(Me.TotalBoardsLabel.Text) * Val(Me.PriceTextBox.Te
        * (1 + Val(Me.RateTextBox.Text))
    Me.TotalPriceLabel.Text = Format(Me.TotalPriceLabel.Text, "currency")
    'send the focus to the Clear Screen button
    Me.ClearButton.Focus()

    End Sub
```

Figure 2-37: Format function entered in the Calculate Order button's Click event procedure

2 Save the solution, start the application, then enter the following order:
Sport Warehouse, 123 Main, Glendale, IL, 60134, 10 blue skateboards, 15 yellow skateboards

3 Enter **100** as the skateboard price and **.05** as the sales tax rate.

4 Click the **Calculate Order** button. The application calculates the total skateboards and total price. The total price appears formatted, as shown in Figure 2-38.

total price appears with a $, a comma thousand separator, and two decimal places

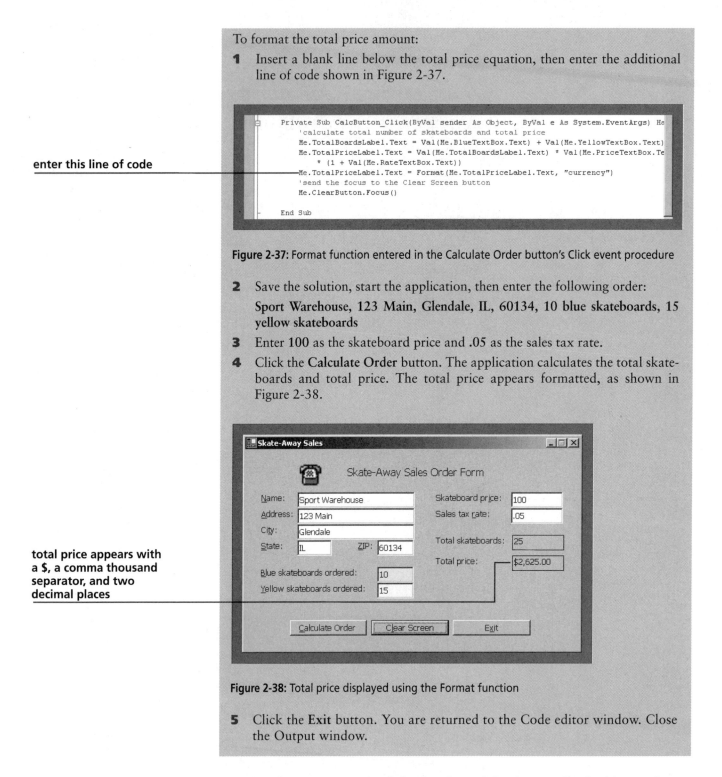

Figure 2-38: Total price displayed using the Format function

5 Click the **Exit** button. You are returned to the Code editor window. Close the Output window.

You have now completed the first four of the six steps involved in creating an OOED application: meeting with the client, planning the application, building the user interface, and coding the application. The fifth step is to test and debug the application.

Testing and Debugging the Application

You test an application by starting it and entering some sample data. You should use both valid and invalid test data. **Valid data** is data that the application is expecting. For example, the Skate-Away Sales application is expecting the user to enter a numeric value as the skateboard price. **Invalid data**, on the other hand, is data that the application is not expecting. The Skate-Away Sales application, for example, is not expecting the user to enter a letter for the number of either blue or yellow skateboards ordered. You should test the application as thoroughly as possible, because you don't want to give the user an application that ends abruptly when invalid data is entered.

Debugging refers to the process of locating errors in the program. Program errors can be either syntax errors or logic errors. Most **syntax errors** are simply typing errors that occur when entering instructions; for example, typing `Me.Clse()` instead of `Me.Close()` results in a syntax error. Most syntax errors are detected by the Code editor as you enter the instructions. An example of a much more difficult type of error to find, and one that the Code editor cannot detect, is a logic error. You create a **logic error** when you enter an instruction that does not give you the expected results. An example of a logic error is the instruction `Me.AverageLabel.Text = Val(Me.Num1TextBox.Text) + Val(Me.Num2TextBox.Text) / 2`, which is supposed to calculate the average of two numbers. Although the instruction is syntactically correct, it is logically incorrect. The instruction to calculate the average of two numbers, written correctly, is `Me.AverageLabel.Text = (Val(Me.Num1TextBox.Text) + Val(Me.Num2TextBox.Text)) / 2`. Because division has a higher precedence number than does addition, you must place parentheses around the `Val(Me.Num1TextBox.Text) + Val(Me.Num2TextBox.Text)` part of the equation.

To test and debug the Skate-Away Sales application with both valid and invalid data:

1 Start the application. First, test the application by clicking the **Calculate Order** button without entering any data. The application displays 0 as the total number of skateboards ordered, and $0.00 as the total price.

2 Next, enter the letter **r** for the number of blue skateboards ordered and the letter **p** for the number of yellow skateboards ordered. Enter **100** for the skateboard price and .05 for the sales tax rate. Click the **Calculate Order** button. The application displays 0 as the total number of skateboards ordered, and $0.00 as the total price. (Recall that the Val function converts letters to the number 0.)

3 Click the **Clear Screen** button. Enter **10** as the number of blue skateboards ordered, and **10** as the number of yellow skateboards ordered. Now highlight the 100 in the PriceTextBox control, then type the letters **xyz**. Click the **Calculate Order** button. The application displays 20 as the total number of skateboards ordered, and $0.00 as the total price.

4 Click the **Clear Screen** button, then enter an order that is correct. Click the **Calculate Order** button.

5 Click the **Clear Screen** button, then practice with other entries to see how the application responds.

6 When you are finished, click the **Exit** button to end the application.

7 When you are returned to the Code editor window, close the Output window.

After you have tested the application to verify that it is working correctly, you can move to the last step involved in creating an OOED application, which is to assemble the documentation.

Assembling the Documentation

Assembling the documentation refers to putting in a safe place your planning tools and a printout of the application's interface and code, so you can refer to them if you need to change the application in the future. Your planning tools include the TOE chart, sketch of the user interface, and either the flowcharts or pseudocode.

To print the application's code and interface:

1 While viewing the Code editor window, click **File** on the menu bar, then click **Print**. When the Print dialog box appears, click the **OK** button to print the code.

Now print the interface.

2 Start the application. The Skate-Away Sales interface appears on the screen.

3 Press **Alt + Print Screen** (or Prt Sc) to place a picture of the interface on the clipboard.

4 Click the **Exit** button to end the application.

5 Close the Output window.

6 Start Microsoft Word (or any application that can display a picture) and open a new document. Click **Edit** on the Word menu bar, then click **Paste** to paste the contents of the clipboard in the document. (You also can press Ctrl + v.)

7 Click **File** on the Word menu bar, and then click **Print**. When the Print dialog box appears, click the **OK** button to print the document.

8 Click **File** on the Word menu bar, and then click **Exit**. When you are asked if you want to save the changes made to the document, click the **No** button.

9 Click **File** on the Visual Basic .NET menu bar, and then click **Close Solution**.

You now have completed the six steps involved in creating an application:
1. Meet with the client.
2. Plan the application.
3. Build the user interface.
4. Code the application.
5. Test and debug the application.
6. Assemble the documentation.

You now have completed Tutorial 2. You can either take a break or complete the end-of-lesson questions and exercises.

S U M M A R Y

To assign a value to the property of an object while an application is running:

■ Use an assignment statement that follows the syntax [**Me.**]*object*.*property* = *expression*.

To move the focus to an object while the program is running:

■ Use the Focus method. The method's syntax is **Me.***object*.**Focus**().

To document Visual Basic code with comments:

■ Begin the comment with an apostrophe (').

To divide two integers, and then return the result as an integer:

■ Use the integer division operator (\).

To divide two numbers, and then return the remainder as an integer:

■ Use the modulus arithmetic operator (Mod).

To temporarily convert a string to a number:

■ Use the Val function. The function's syntax is **Val**(*string*).

To improve the appearance of numbers in the user interface:

■ Use the Format function. The function's syntax is **Format**(*expression*, *style*).

Q U E S T I O N S

1. Which of the following is a valid assignment statement?
    a. `Me.NameTextBox = 'Jones'`
    b. `Me.NameTextBox.Caption = "Jones"`
    c. `Me.NameTextBox.Text = 'Jones'`
    d. `Me.NameTextBox.Text = "Jones"`
    e. None of the above is valid.

2. Which of the following assignment statements will not calculate correctly?
    a. `Me.TotalLabel.Text = Val(Me.Sales1TextBox.Text) +`
       `Val(Me.Sales2TextBox.Text)`
    b. `Me.TotalLabel.Text = Val(Me.Sales1Label.Text) +`
       `Val(Me.Sales2Label.Text)`
    c. `Me.TotalLabel.Text = Val(Me.RedTextBox.Text) * 2`
    d. `Me.TotalLabel.Text = Val(Me.BlueLabel.Text) * 1.1`
    e. All of the above are correct.

3. You use the _____ function to display a dollar sign and a thousand separator in numbers.
   a. Display
   b. Focus
   c. Format
   d. Style
   e. Val

4. The _____ function temporarily converts a string to a number.
   a. Convert
   b. Format
   c. String
   d. StringToNum
   e. Val

5. Listed below are the six steps you should follow when creating an OOED application. Put them in the proper order by placing a number (1 to 6) on the line to the left of the step.
   _____ Assemble the documentation.
   _____ Plan the application.
   _____ Code the application.
   _____ Build the user interface.
   _____ Test and debug the application.
   _____ Meet with the client.

6. The instruction `Me.TotalLabel.Text = Val(Me.NumTextBox.Text) / 2`, which should multiply the contents of the NumTextBox by 2 and then assign the result to the TotalLabel, is an example of _____.
   a. a logic error
   b. a syntax error
   c. a correct instruction

7. The instruction `Me.SalesLabel.Text = Format(Me.SalesLabel.Text, "curency")` is an example of _____.
   a. a logic error
   b. a syntax error
   c. a correct instruction

8. What value is assigned to the Me.NumLabel control when the `NumLabel.Text = 73 / 25` instruction is processed?

9. What value is assigned to the Me.NumLabel control when the `NumLabel.Text = 73 \ 25` instruction is processed?

10. What value is assigned to the Me.NumLabel control when the `NumLabel.Text = 73 Mod 25` instruction is processed?

E X E R C I S E S

NOTE: In Exercises 4 through 11, and in Exercises 13 through 19, you perform the second through sixth steps involved in creating an OOED application. Recall that the six steps are:

1. Meet with the client.

2. Plan the application. (Prepare a TOE chart that is ordered by object, and draw a sketch of the user interface.)

3. Build the user interface. (To help you remember the names of the controls as you are coding, print the application's interface and then write the names next to each object.)

4. Code the application. (Be sure to write pseudocode for each of the objects that will be coded.)

5. Test and debug the application. (Use the sample data provided in each of the exercises.)

6. Assemble the documentation (your planning tools and a printout of the interface and code).

The following list summarizes the GUI design guidelines you have learned so far. You can use this list to verify that the interfaces you create in the following exercises adhere to the GUI standards outlined in the book.

■ Information should flow either vertically or horizontally, with the most important information always located in the upper-left corner of the screen.

■ Maintain a consistent margin of two or three dots from the edge of the window.

■ Try to create a user interface that no one notices.

■ Related controls should be grouped together using white space, a GroupBox control, or a Panel control.

■ Set the form's FormBorderStyle, ControlBox, MaximizeBox, MinimizeBox, and StartPosition properties appropriately:

   ■ A splash screen should not have a Minimize, Maximize, or Close button, and its borders should not be sizable.

   ■ A form that is not a splash screen should always have a Minimize button and a Close button, but you can choose to disable the Maximize button. Typically, the FormBorderStyle property is set to Sizable, but also can be set to FixedSingle.

■ Position related controls on succeeding dots. Controls that are not part of any logical grouping may be positioned from two to four dots away from other controls.

■ Buttons should be positioned either in a row along the bottom of the screen, or stacked in either the upper-right or lower-right corner.

■ If the buttons are positioned at the bottom of the screen, then each button should be the same height; their widths, however, may vary.

■ If the buttons are stacked in either the upper-right or lower-right corner of the screen, then each should be the same height and the same width.

■ Use no more than six buttons on a screen.

■ The most commonly used button should be placed first.

■ Button captions should:

   ■ be meaningful

   ■ be from one to three words

   ■ appear on one line

   ■ be entered using book title capitalization

- Use labels to identify the text boxes in the interface, and position the label either above or to the left of the text box.

- Label text should:

    - be from one to three words
    - appear on one line
    - be left-justified
    - end with a colon (:)
    - be entered using sentence capitalization

- Labels that identify controls should have their BorderStyle property set to None.

- Labels that display program output, such as the result of a calculation, should have their BorderStyle property set to FixedSingle.

- Align controls to minimize the number of different margins.

- If you use a graphic in the interface, use a small one and place it in a location that will not distract the user.

- Use the Tahoma font for applications that will run on Windows 2000 or Windows XP.

- Use no more than two different font sizes, which should be 8, 9, 10, 11, or 12 point.

- Use only one font type, which should be a sans serif font, in the interface.

- Avoid using italics and underlining.

- Limit the use of bold text to titles, headings, and key items.

- Build the interface using black, white, and gray first, then add color only if you have a good reason to do so.

- Use white, off-white, light gray, pale blue, or pale yellow for an application's background, and black for the text.

- Limit the number of colors to three, not including white, black, and gray. The colors you choose should complement each other.

- Never use color as the only means of identification for an element in the user interface.

- Set each control's TabIndex property to a number that represents the order in which you want the control to receive the focus (begin with 0).

- A text box's TabIndex value should be one more than the TabIndex value of its identifying label.

- Assign a unique access key to each control (in the interface) that can receive user input (text boxes, buttons, and so on).

- When assigning an access key to a control, use the first letter of the caption or identifying label, unless another letter provides a more meaningful association. If you can't use the first letter and no other letter provides a more meaningful association, then use a distinctive consonant. Lastly, use a vowel or a number.

- Lock the controls in place on the form.

- Document the program internally.

- Use the Val function on any Text property involved in a calculation.

- Use the Format function to improve the appearance of numbers in the interface.

- Test the application with both valid and invalid data (for example, test the application without entering any data, and test it by entering letters where numbers are expected).

1. In this exercise, you complete the application that you saved in Lesson B's Exercise 1.
   a. If necessary, start Visual Studio .NET. Open the Paper Solution (Paper Solution.sln) file, which is contained in the VBNET\Tut02\Paper Solution folder. If the designer window is not open, right-click the form file's name in the Solution Explorer window, then click View Designer.
   b. Code the Calculate Commission button appropriately. Recall that the commission rate is 10%. Be sure to use the Val function. Use the Format function to display the commission with a dollar sign, a comma thousand separator, and two decimal places. Use the Focus method to send the focus to the Clear button.
   c. Code the Clear button appropriately. Send the focus to the Name text box.
   d. Save the solution, then start the application. Test the application with both valid and invalid data. Use the following information for the valid data:

Name:	Pat Brown
Territory number:	10
Sales:	2500

2. In this exercise, you complete the application that you saved in Lesson B's Exercise 2.
   a. If necessary, start Visual Studio .NET. Open the RMSales Solution (RMSales Solution.sln) file, which is contained in the VBNET\Tut02\RMSales Solution folder. If the designer window is not open, right-click the form file's name in the Solution Explorer window, then click View Designer.
   b. Code the Calculate Projected Sales button appropriately. Be sure to use the Val function. Use the Format function to display the projected sales using the Standard format. Send the focus to the Clear button.
   c. Code the Clear button appropriately. Send the focus to the NsalesTextBox control.
   d. Save the solution, then start the application. Test the application with both valid and invalid data. Use the following information for the valid data:

North sales and percentage:	25000, .05
South sales and percentage:	30000, .07
East sales and percentage:	10000, .04
West sales and percentage:	15000, .11

3. In this exercise, you complete the application that you saved in Lesson B's Exercise 3.
   a. If necessary, start Visual Studio .NET. Open the Time Solution (Time Solution.sln) file, which is contained in the VBNET\Tut02\Time Solution folder. If the designer window is not open, right-click the form file's name in the Solution Explorer window, then click View Designer.
   b. Code the Calculate button appropriately. Be sure to use the Val function. Send the focus to the Monday text box.
   c. Save the solution, then start the application. Test the application with both valid and invalid data. Use the following information for the valid data:

Monday hours:	7
Tuesday hours:	8
Wednesday hours:	6
Thursday hours:	5
Friday hours:	4
Saturday hours:	2
Sunday hours:	0

4. Scenario: In previous versions of Visual Basic, the location of a control on a form was measured in twips. A twip is 1/1440 of an inch; in other words, 1440 twips equal one inch. Create an application that allows you to enter the number of twips, and then converts the twips to inches.

   a. If necessary, start Visual Studio .NET. Create a blank solution named Twips Solution. Save the solution in the VBNET\Tut02 folder.

   b. Add a Visual Basic .NET Windows Application project to the solution. Name the project Twips Project.

   c. Perform the steps involved in creating an OOED application. (See the NOTE and list at the beginning of the Exercises section.)

   d. Test the application two times, using the following data.

   Twips: 2880   Twips: abc

5. Scenario: John Lee wants an application in which he can enter the following three pieces of information: his cash balance at the beginning of the month, the amount of money he earned during the month, and the amount of money he spent during the month. He wants the application to compute his ending balance.

   a. If necessary, start Visual Studio .NET. Create a blank solution named JohnLee Solution. Save the solution in the VBNET\Tut02 folder.

   b. Add a Visual Basic .NET Windows Application project to the solution. Name the project JohnLee Project.

   c. Perform the steps involved in creating an OOED application. (See the NOTE and list at the beginning of the Exercises section.)

   d. Test the application twice using the following data.

   Beginning cash balance: 5000   Earnings: 2500   Expenses: 3000
   Beginning cash balance: xyz   Earnings: xyz   Expenses: xyz

6. Scenario: Lana Jones wants an application that will compute the average of any three numbers she enters.

   a. If necessary, start Visual Studio .NET. Create a blank solution named LanaJones Solution. Save the solution in the VBNET\Tut02 folder.

   b. Add a Visual Basic .NET Windows Application project to the solution. Name the project LanaJones Project.

   c. Perform the steps involved in creating an OOED application. (See the NOTE and list at the beginning of the Exercises section.)

   d. Test the application twice, using the following data.

   First Number: 27   Second Number: 9   Third Number: 18
   First Number: A   Second Number: B   Third Number: C

7. Scenario: Martha Arenso, manager of Bookworms Inc., needs an inventory application. Martha will enter the title of a book, the number of paperback versions of the book currently in inventory, the number of hardcover versions of the book currently in inventory, the cost of the paperback version, and the cost of the hardcover version. Martha wants the application to compute the value of the paperback versions of the book, the value of the hardcover versions of the book, the total number of paperback and hardcover versions, and the total value of the paperback and hardcover versions.

   a. If necessary, start Visual Studio .NET. Create a blank solution named Bookworms Solution. Save the solution in the VBNET\Tut02 folder.

   b. Add a Visual Basic .NET Windows Application project to the solution. Name the project Bookworms Project.

   c. Perform the steps involved in creating an OOED application. (See the NOTE and list at the beginning of the Exercises section.) Format the dollar amounts to show a dollar sign, comma thousand separator, and two decimal places.

   d. Test the application twice, using the following data.

   Book Title: An Introduction to Visual Basic .NET

   Paperback versions: 100   Paperback cost: 40
   Hardcover versions: 50   Hardcover cost: 75

Book Title: Advanced Visual Basic .NET

Paperback versions: A   Paperback cost: B

Hardcover versions: C   Hardcover cost: D

8. Scenario: Jackets Unlimited is having a 25% off sale on all its merchandise. The store manager asks you to create an application that requires the clerk simply to enter the original price of a jacket. The application should then compute the discount and new price.

   a. If necessary, start Visual Studio .NET. Create a blank solution named Jackets Solution. Save the solution in the VBNET\Tut02 folder.

   b. Add a Visual Basic .NET Windows Application project to the solution. Name the project Jackets Project.

   c. Perform the steps involved in creating an OOED application. (See the NOTE and list at the beginning of the Exercises section.) Format the discount and new price using the Standard format style.

   d. Test the application twice, using the following data.

       Jacket's original price: 50

       Jacket's original price: ***

9. Scenario: Typing Salon charges $.10 per typed envelope and $.25 per typed page. The company accountant wants an application to help her prepare bills. She will enter the customer's name, the number of typed envelopes, and the number of typed pages. The application should compute the total bill.

   a. If necessary, start Visual Studio .NET. Create a blank solution named TypingSalon Solution. Save the solution in the VBNET\Tut02 folder.

   b. Add a Visual Basic .NET Windows Application project to the solution. Name the project TypingSalon Project.

   c. Perform the steps involved in creating an OOED application. (See the NOTE and list at the beginning of the Exercises section.) Format the total bill using the Currency format style.

   d. Test the application twice, using the following data.

       Customer's name: Alice Wong

       Number of typed envelopes: 250   Number of typed pages: 200

       Customer's name: Alice Wong

       Number of typed envelopes: $4   Number of typed pages: AB

10. Scenario: Management USA, a small training center, plans to run two full-day seminars on December 1. The seminars are called "How to Be an Effective Manager" and "How to Run a Small Business." Each seminar costs $200. Registration for the seminars will be done by phone. When a company calls to register its employees, the phone representative will ask for the following information: the company's name, address (including city, state, and ZIP), the number of employees registering for the "How to Be an Effective Manager" seminar, and the number of employees registering for the "How to Run a Small Business" seminar. Claire Jenkowski, the owner of Management USA, wants the application to calculate the total number of employees the company is registering and the total cost.

   a. If necessary, start Visual Studio .NET. Create a blank solution named Management Solution. Save the solution in the VBNET\Tut02 folder.

   b. Add a Visual Basic .NET Windows Application project to the solution. Name the project Management Project.

   c. Perform the steps involved in creating an OOED application. (See the NOTE and list at the beginning of the Exercises section.) Format the total cost using the Currency format style.

   d. Test the application twice, using the following data.

       Company Name: ABC Company

       Address: 345 Main St.

       City, State, ZIP: Glen, TX 70122

Registrants for "How to Be an Effective Manager": 10
Registrants for "How to Run a Small Business": 5

Company Name: 1
Address: 2
City, State, ZIP: 3
Registrants for "How to Be an Effective Manager": A
Registrants for "How to Run a Small Business": B

11. Scenario: Suman Gadhari, the payroll clerk at Sun Projects, wants an application that will compute the net pay for each of the company's employees. Suman will enter the employee's name, hours worked, and rate of pay. For this application, you do not have to worry about overtime, as this company does not allow anyone to work more than 40 hours. Suman wants the application to compute the gross pay, the federal withholding tax (FWT), the Social Security tax (FICA), the state income tax, and the net pay. Use the following information when computing the three taxes:

FWT: 20% of gross pay

FICA: 8% of gross pay

state income tax: 2% of gross pay

    a. If necessary, start Visual Studio .NET. Create a blank solution named SunProjects Solution. Save the solution in the VBNET\Tut02 folder.
    b. Add a Visual Basic .NET Windows Application project to the solution. Name the project SunProjects Project.
    c. Perform the steps involved in creating an OOED application. (See the NOTE and list at the beginning of the Exercises section.) Format the dollar amounts to the Standard format style.
    d. Test the application twice, using the following data.
     Employee's name: Susan Reha
     Hours worked: 40
     Rate of pay: 12

     Employee's name: Susan Reha
     Hours worked: X
     Rate of pay: Y

Exercises 12 through 19 are Discovery Exercises. Discovery Exercises, which may include topics that are not covered in this lesson, allow you to "discover" the solutions to problems on your own.

discovery ▶   **12.** In this exercise, you learn about the TabStop property.
    a. Open the Order Solution (Order Solution.sln) file that you completed in Lesson C. The file is located in the VBNET\Tut02\Order Solution folder. The **TabStop property** allows you to bypass a control in the tab order when the user is tabbing. You can use the TabStop property in the Skate-Away Sales application to bypass the StateTextBox control. Because most of Skate-Away's customers are located in Illinois, there is no need for the user to tab into the StateTextBox control when entering data. Should the user want to change the State value, he or she needs simply to click the control or use the control's access key.
    b. Change the StateTextBox control's TabStop property to False, then save the solution and start the application. Verify that the StateTextBox control is bypassed when you tab through the controls in the interface.

discovery ▶ 13. Scenario: Colfax Industries needs an application that allows the shipping clerk to enter the quantity of an item in inventory and the number of the items that can be packed in a box for shipping. When the shipping clerk clicks a button, the application should compute and display the number of full boxes that can be packed and how many of the item are left over.

    a. If necessary, start Visual Studio .NET. Create a blank solution named Colfax Solution. Save the solution in the VBNET\Tut02 folder.

    b. Add a Visual Basic .NET Windows Application project to the solution. Name the project Colfax Project.

    c. Perform the steps involved in creating an OOED application. (See the NOTE and list at the beginning of the Exercises section.)

    d. Test the application using the following information. Colfax has 45 skateboards in inventory. If six skateboards can fit into a box for shipping, how many full boxes could the company ship, and how many skateboards will remain in inventory?

discovery ▶ 14. Scenario: Perry Brown needs an application that will allow him to enter the length of four sides of a polygon. The application should compute and display the perimeter of the polygon.

    a. If necessary, start Visual Studio .NET. Create a blank solution named PerryBrown Solution. Save the solution in the VBNET\Tut02 folder.

    b. Add a Visual Basic .NET Windows Application project to the solution. Name the project PerryBrown Project.

    c. Perform the steps involved in creating an OOED application. (See the NOTE and list at the beginning of the Exercises section.)

    d. Test the application using the following information. Each day Perry rides his bike around a park that has side lengths of 1/2 mile, 1 mile, 1/2 mile, and 1 mile. How far does Perry ride his bike each day?

discovery ▶ 15. Scenario: Builders Inc. needs an application that will allow its salesclerks to enter both the diameter of a circle and the price of railing material per foot. The application should compute and display the circumference of the circle and the total price of the railing material. (Use 3.14 as the value of pi.)

    a. If necessary, start Visual Studio .NET. Create a blank solution named Builders Solution. Save the solution in the VBNET\Tut02 folder.

    b. Add a Visual Basic .NET Windows Application project to the solution. Name the project Builders Project.

    c. Perform the steps involved in creating an OOED application. (See the NOTE and list at the beginning of the Exercises section.) Display the total price with a dollar sign, a comma thousand separator, and two decimal places.

    d. Test the application using the following information. Jack Jones, one of Builders Inc.'s customers, is building a railing around a circular deck having a diameter of 36 feet. The railing material costs $2 per foot. What is the circumference of the deck and the total price of the railing material?

discovery ▶ 16. Scenario: Temp Employers wants an application that will allow its employees to enter the number of hours worked. The application should compute and display the number of weeks (assume a 40-hour week), days (assume an eight-hour day), and hours worked. For example, if the user enters the number 70, the application should display 1 week, 3 days, and 6 hours.

    a. If necessary, start Visual Studio .NET. Create a blank solution named Temp Solution. Save the solution in the VBNET\Tut02 folder.

    b. Add a Visual Basic .NET Windows Application project to the solution. Name the project Temp Project.

    c. Perform the steps involved in creating an OOED application. (See the NOTE and list at the beginning of the Exercises section.)

    d. Test the application three times, using the following data.

    Hours worked: 88

    Hours worked: 111

    Hours worked: 12

discovery ▶ 17. Scenario: Tile Limited wants an application that will allow its salesclerks to enter the length and width (in feet) of a rectangle, and the price of a square foot of tile. The application should compute and display the area of the rectangle and the total price of the tile.

a. If necessary, start Visual Studio .NET. Create a blank solution named Tile Solution. Save the solution in the VBNET\Tut02 folder.

b. Add a Visual Basic .NET Windows Application project to the solution. Name the project Tile Project.

c. Perform the steps involved in creating an OOED application. (See the NOTE and list at the beginning of the Exercises section.) Display the total price with a dollar sign, comma thousand separator, and two decimal places.

d. Test the application using the following data. Susan Caper, one of Tile Limited's customers, is tiling a floor in her home. The floor is 12 feet long and 14 feet wide. The price of a square foot of tile is $1.59. What is the area of the floor and how much will the tile cost?

discovery ▶ 18. Scenario: Willow Pools wants an application that will allow its salespeople to enter the length, width, and height of a rectangle. The application should compute and display the volume of the rectangle.

a. If necessary, start Visual Studio .NET. Create a blank solution named Willow Solution. Save the solution in the VBNET\Tut02 folder.

b. Add a Visual Basic .NET Windows Application project to the solution. Name the project Willow Project.

c. Perform the steps involved in creating an OOED application. (See the NOTE and list at the beginning of the Exercises section.)

d. Test the application using the following data. The swimming pool at a health club is 100 feet long, 30 feet wide, and 4 feet deep. How many cubic feet of water will the pool contain?

discovery ▶ 19. Scenario: Quick Loans wants an application that will allow its clerks to enter the amount of a loan, the interest rate, and the term of the loan (in years). The application should compute and display the total amount of interest and the total amount to be repaid. Use the Pmt function. (Hint: Use the Help menu to display the Pmt function's Help window.)

a. If necessary, start Visual Studio .NET. Create a blank solution named Loan Solution. Save the solution in the VBNET\Tut02 folder.

b. Add a Visual Basic .NET Windows Application project to the solution. Name the project Loan Project.

c. Perform the steps involved in creating an OOED application. (See the NOTE and list at the beginning of the Exercises section.) Format the total interest and total repaid using the Standard format style.

d. Test the application using the following data. You visit Quick Loans because you want to borrow $9000 to buy a new car. The loan is for three years at an annual interest rate of 12%. How much will you pay in interest over the three years, and what is the total amount you will repay?

Exercise 20 is a Debugging Exercise. Debugging Exercises provide an opportunity for you to detect and correct errors in an existing application.

debugging   20. In this exercise, you debug an existing application. The purpose of the exercise is to demonstrate the importance of using the Val function in calculations that include the Text property.

a. If necessary, start Visual Studio .NET. Open the Debug Solution (Debug Solution.sln) file, which is contained in the VBNET\Tut02\Debug Solution folder. If the designer window is not open, right-click the form file's name in the Solution Explorer window, then click View Designer. The application allows you to enter a number. It then multiplies the number by 3 and displays the result.

b. Start the application. When the interface appears, type the number 4 in the Enter a number text box, then click the Triple Number button. The number 12 appears in the Number tripled label control.

c. Delete the number 4 from the Enter a number text box, then type the letter R in the text box. Click the Triple Number button. An error message appears in a dialog box, and the instruction causing the error appears highlighted in the Code editor window. See Figure 2-39.

error message dialog box

the instruction that caused the error is highlighted in the Code editor window

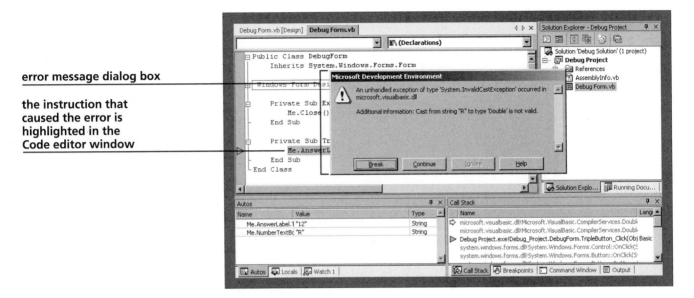

Figure 2-39

The error message first informs you that an unhandled exception occurred. It then gives you some additional information about the error—in this case, that a "Cast from String ('R') to Double is not valid." The "Cast from String ('R') to Double is not valid." message means that Visual Basic .NET is unable to convert the letter R to a number. ("Double" is a numeric data type; you learn about data types in Tutorial 3.)

d. Click the Break button in the dialog box. The dialog box closes. Highlighted in the Code editor window is the `Me.AnswerLabel.Text = Me.NumberTextBox.Text * 3` instruction, which is causing the error. See Figure 2-40.

you use the Val function to correct this instruction

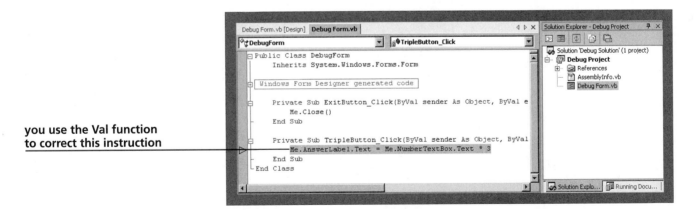

Figure 2-40

e. Click Debug on the menu bar, then click Stop Debugging.

f. Use the Val function to tell Visual Basic .NET to treat the contents of the NumberTextBox control's Text property as a number rather than as a string.

g. Save the solution, then start the application. Type the letter R in the Enter a number text box, then click the Triple Number button. Rather than displaying an error message, the application displays the number 0 in the Number tripled control.

h. Close the Output window, then close the solution.

Using Variables and Constants

Revising the Skate-Away Sales Application

case ▶ Mr. Cousard, the manager of Skate-Away Sales, informs you that he wants to make a change to the Skate-Away Sales application that you created in Tutorial 2. He now wants to include a message on the order form. The message should say "The sales tax was", followed by the sales tax amount and the name of the salesperson who recorded the order. In this tutorial, you modify the application's code to accommodate this change.

Previewing the Completed Application

Before you begin modifying the Skate-Away Sales application, you first preview the completed application.

To preview the completed application:

1 Use the Run command on the Windows Start menu to run the **Skate** (Skate.exe) file, which is contained in the VBNET\Tut03 folder on your computer's hard disk. An order form similar to the one that you created in Tutorial 2 appears on the screen.

2 Enter the following customer information on the order form: **Skaters Inc., 34 Plum Drive, Chicago, IL, 60654.**

3 Click the **Skateboard price** text box, then type **100** and press **Tab**. Type **.05** for the sales tax rate.

4 Click the **Blue skateboards ordered** text box, then type **25** as the number of blue skateboards ordered.

Although the Calculate Order button does not have the focus, you still can select it by pressing the Enter key, because the Calculate Order button is the default button in the user interface. You learn how to designate a default button in Lesson B.

5 Press **Enter** to calculate the order. A Name Entry dialog box appears and requests the salesperson's name, as shown in Figure 3-1.

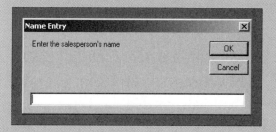

Figure 3-1: Name Entry dialog box

6 Type your name in the dialog box's text box and press **Enter**. The application calculates the order. The completed order form is shown in Figure 3-2.

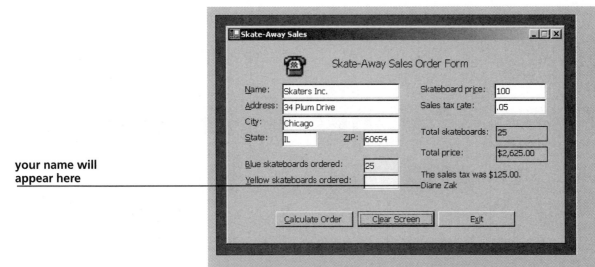

**your name will
appear here**

Figure 3-2: Completed order form

Notice that the sales tax amount and the salesperson's name (your name) appear on the order form. The application uses string concatenation, which you learn about in Lesson B, to display the information.

7 Click the **Yellow skateboards ordered** text box, then type **5**. The application clears the contents of the label controls that display the total skateboards ordered, total price, and message. In Lesson C, you learn how to clear the contents of a control when the value stored in a different control changes.

8 Click the **Calculate Order** button to calculate the order. The Name Entry dialog box appears and displays your name in its text box. Press **Enter**. The application recalculates the total skateboards ordered, total price, and sales tax amount.

9 Click the **Exit** button to end the application.

In Lesson A, you learn how to store information, temporarily, in memory locations inside the computer. You modify the Skate-Away Sales application in Lessons B and C.

After completing this lesson, you will be able to:

- Create a local and form-level variable
- Select an appropriate data type for a variable
- Select an appropriate name for a variable
- Assign data to an existing variable
- Create a named constant

Creating Variables and Named Constants

Using Variables to Store Information

Recall that all of the skateboard information in the Skate-Away Sales application is temporarily stored in the properties of various controls on the order form. For example, the number of blue skateboards ordered is stored in the Text property of the BlueTextBox control, and the number of yellow skateboards ordered is stored in the Text property of the YellowTextBox control. Also recall that the assignment statement `Me.TotalBoardsLabel.Text = Val(Me.BlueTextBox.Text) + Val(Me.YellowTextBox.Text)` calculates the total skateboards ordered by adding the value stored in the BlueTextBox control's Text property to the value stored in the YellowTextBox control's Text property, and then assigns the sum to the Text property of the TotalBoardsLabel control. Similarly, the total price equation, `Me.TotalPriceLabel.Text = Val(Me.TotalBoardsLabel.Text) * Val(Me.PriceTextBox.Text) * (1 + Val(Me.RateTextBox.Text))`, calculates the total price of the order and assigns the result to the TotalPriceLabel control.

Besides storing data in the properties of controls, a programmer also can store data, temporarily, in memory locations inside the computer. The memory locations are called **variables**, because the contents of the locations can change as the program is running. It may be helpful to picture a variable as a small box inside the computer. You can enter and store data in the box, but you cannot actually see the box.

One use for a variable is to hold information that is not stored in a control on the user interface. For example, if you did not need to display the total number of skateboards ordered on the Skate-Away Sales order form, you could eliminate the TotalBoardsLabel control from the form and store the total number of skateboards in a variable instead. You then would use the value stored in the variable, rather than the value stored in the Text property of the TotalBoardsLabel control, in the total price equation.

You also can store the data contained in a control's property in a variable. For example, you can store the data in the Text property of a text box or label control in a variable. Programmers typically do so when the data is a numeric amount that will be used in a calculation. As you will learn in the next section, assigning numeric data to a variable allows you to control the preciseness of the data. It also makes your code run more efficiently, because the computer can process data stored in a variable much faster than it can process data stored in the property of a control.

Before learning how to create a variable in a Visual Basic .NET application, you learn how to select an appropriate data type and name for the variable.

Selecting a Data Type for a Variable

Each variable (memory location) used in an application must be assigned a data type by the programmer. The **data type** determines the type of data the variable can store. Figure 3-3 describes the basic data types available in Visual Basic .NET.

Type	Stores	Memory required	Values
Boolean	logical value	2 bytes	True, False
Byte	binary number	1 byte	0 to 255 (unsigned)
Char	one character	2 bytes	one character
Date	date and time information	8 bytes	dates from January 1, 0001 to December 31, 9999, and times from 0:00:00 to 23:59:59
Decimal	fixed-point number	16 bytes	+/-79,228,162,514,264,337,593,543,950,335 with no decimal point; +/-7.9228162514264337593543950335 with a decimal point; smallest non-zero number is +/-0.0000000000000000000000000001
Double	floating-point number	8 bytes	+/- 4.94065645841247E-324 to 1.79769313486231E308
Integer	integer	4 bytes	-2,147,483,648 to 2,147,483,647
Long	integer	8 bytes	-9,223,372,036,854,775,808 to 9,223,372,036,854,775,807
Object	object reference	4 bytes	N/A
Short	integer	2 bytes	-32,768 to 32,767
Single	floating-point number	4 bytes	+/- 1.401298E-45 to 3.402823E38
String	text	varies	0 to approximately 2 billion characters

Figure 3-3: Basic data types in Visual Basic .NET

tip

Each data type is a class, which means that each data type is a pattern from which one or more objects—in this case, variables—are created (instantiated).

As Figure 3-3 indicates, variables assigned the Integer, Long, or Short data type can store **integers**, which are whole numbers—numbers without any decimal places. The differences among these three data types are in the range of integers each type can store and the amount of memory each type needs to store the integer. The memory requirement of a data type is an important consideration when coding an application. If you want to reduce the amount of internal memory that an application consumes, thereby improving the application's efficiency, you should use variables with smaller memory requirements wherever possible. For example, although an Integer variable can store numbers in the Short range of -32768 to 32767, the Integer data type takes twice as much memory as the Short data type to do so. Therefore, you can conserve internal memory by storing a person's age in a Short variable.

Keep in mind, however, that memory usage is not the only important factor in determining an application's efficiency; the speed at which the application executes also is important. Although a Short variable uses less internal memory than does an Integer variable, a calculation containing Integer variables takes less time to process than the equivalent calculation containing Short variables. This is because the computer must convert a Short variable to the Integer data type before the calculation is performed.

Figure 3-3 indicates that Single and Double variables can store a **floating-point number**, which is a number that is expressed as a multiple of some power of 10. Floating-point numbers are written in E (exponential) notation, which is similar to scientific notation. For example, the number 3,200,000 written in E (exponential) notation is 3.2E6; written in scientific notation it is 3.2×10^6. Notice that exponential notation simply replaces "$\times 10^6$" with the letter E followed by the power number—in this case, 6.

Another way of viewing 3.2E6 is that the positive number after the E indicates how many places to the right to move the decimal point. In this case, E6 means to move the decimal point six places to the right; so 3.2E6 becomes 3,200,000. Moving the decimal point six places to the right is the same as multiplying the number by 10 to the sixth power.

Floating-point numbers also can have a negative number after the E. For example, 3.2E-6 means 3.2 divided by 10 to the sixth power, or .0000032. The negative number after the E tells you how many places to the left to move the decimal point. In this case, E-6 means to move the decimal point six places to the left.

tip

∙∙∙∙∙∙∙∙∙∙∙∙∙∙∙∙

▶ A number such as 4.5 can be written as either 4.5 or 4.5E0.

Floating-point numbers, which can be stored in either Single or Double variables, are used to represent both extremely small and extremely large numbers. The differences between the Single and Double types are in the range of numbers each type can store and the amount of memory each type needs to store the numbers. Although a Double variable can store numbers in a Single variable's range, a Double variable takes twice as much memory to do so.

Variables declared using the Decimal data type store numbers with a fixed decimal point. Unlike floating-point numbers, fixed-point numbers are not expressed as a multiple of some power of 10. For example, the number 32000 expressed as a floating-point number is 3.2E4, but that same number expressed as a fixed-point number is simply 32000. Calculations involving fixed-point numbers are not subject to the small rounding errors that may occur when floating-point numbers are used. In most cases, these small rounding errors do not create any problems in an application. One exception, however, is when the application contains complex equations dealing with money, where you need accuracy to the penny. In those cases, the Decimal data type is the best type to use.

Also listed in Figure 3-3 are the Char data type, which can store one character, and the String data type, which can store from zero to approximately two billion characters. As you learned in Tutorial 2, a string is a group of characters enclosed in quotation marks. "Desk" and "AB345" are two examples of strings.

You use a Boolean variable to store the Boolean values True and False, and a Date variable to store date and time information. The Byte data type is used to store binary numbers.

If you do not assign a specific data type to a variable, Visual Basic .NET assigns the Object type to it. Unlike other variables, an Object variable can store many different types of data, and it also can freely change the type of stored data while the application is running. For example, you can store the number 40 in an Object variable at the beginning of the application and then, later on in the application, store the string

"John Smith" in that same variable. Although the Object data type is the most flexible data type, it is less efficient than the other data types. At times it uses more memory than necessary to store a value and, because the computer has to determine which type of data is currently stored in the variable, your application will run more slowly.

In addition to assigning a data type to the variables used in an application, the programmer also must assign a name to each variable.

Selecting a Name for a Variable

You should assign a descriptive name to each variable used in an application. The name should help you remember the variable's data type and purpose. One popular naming convention is to have the first three characters in the name represent the data type, and the remainder of the name represent the variable's purpose. Figure 3-4 lists the three characters typically associated with the Visual Basic .NET data types.

Type	ID
Boolean	bln
Byte	byt
Char	cha
Date	dtm
Decimal	dec
Double	dbl
Integer	int
Long	lng
Object	obj
Short	shr
Single	sng
String	str

Figure 3-4: Data types and their three-character IDs

> Pascal is a programming language that was created by Niklaus Wirth in the late 1960s. It was named in honor of the seventeenth-century French mathematician Blaise Pascal, and is used to develop scientific applications.

In addition to the three-character ID, many programmers also include the lower-case letter "m"—which stands for "module scope"—at the beginning of form-level variable names, because this helps to distinguish the form-level variables from the local variables used in an application. For example, you would use intScore to name a local Integer variable, but use mintScore to name a form-level Integer variable. You learn about module-scope and form-level and local variables later in this lesson.

It is a common practice to type the letter m and the three-character ID using lowercase letters, and then use Pascal-case for the remainder of the variable's name. Using **Pascal-case**, you capitalize the first letter in each word in the name. For example, a good name for a variable that stores a sales amount is sngSalesAmount. Although S also could be used as the variable's name, it is not as descriptive as the name sngSalesAmount. In the latter case, the name reminds you that the variable is a Single variable that stores a sales amount.

In addition to being descriptive, the name that a programmer assigns to a variable must follow several specific rules, which are listed in Figure 3-5. Also included in the figure are examples of valid and invalid variable names.

Rules for naming variables
1. The name must begin with a letter.
2. The name must contain only letters, numbers, and the underscore character. No punctuation characters or spaces are allowed in the name.
3. The name cannot contain more than 255 characters. (32 characters is the recommended maximum number of characters to use.)
4. The name cannot be a reserved word, such as Val or Print.

Valid variable names	Invalid variable names	
blnPrint	Print	(the name cannot be a reserved word)
dec2002Sales	2002SalesDec	(the name must begin with a letter)
intRegionWest	intRegion West	(the name cannot contain a space)
mstrFirstName	mstrFirst.Name	(the name cannot contain punctuation)

Figure 3-5: Rules for variable names along with examples of valid and invalid names

Now that you know how to select an appropriate data type and name for a variable, you can learn how to declare a variable in code. Declaring a variable tells Visual Basic .NET to set aside a small section of the computer's internal memory.

Declaring a Variable

tip

A declaration statement also can begin with a keyword other than Dim or Private—for example, it can begin with Static or Public. You learn about the Static keyword in Discovery Exercise 15 at the end of this lesson and in Lesson C, and about the Public keyword in Tutorial 7. The other keywords found at the beginning of declaration statements are beyond the scope of this book.

tip

Dim comes from the word "dimension", which is how programmers in the 1960s referred to the process of allocating the computer's memory.

You use a declaration statement to declare, or create, a variable. The declaration statement you enter in your code will follow the syntax *accessibility variablename* [**As** *datatype*][= *initialvalue*]. In the syntax, *accessibility* is typically either the keyword Dim or the keyword Private. The appropriate keyword to use depends on whether the variable is a local (Dim) or form-level (Private) variable. As mentioned earlier, you learn about local and form-level variables later in this lesson.

Variablename in the syntax is the variable's name, and *datatype* is the variable's data type. *Initialvalue* is the value you want stored in the variable when it is created in the computer's internal memory.

Although the "**As** *datatype*" part of a declaration statement is optional, as indicated by the square brackets in the syntax, you always should assign a specific data type to each variable you declare. If you do not assign a data type to a variable, Visual Basic .NET assigns the Object type to the variable, which may not be the most efficient data type.

Notice that the "= *initialvalue*" part of a declaration statement also is optional. If you do not assign an initial value to a variable when it is declared, Visual Basic .NET stores a default value in the variable; the default value depends on the variable's data type. A variable declared using one of the numeric data types is automatically initialized to—in other words, given a beginning value of—the number 0. Visual Basic .NET automatically initializes a Boolean variable to False, and a Date variable to 12:00 AM January 1, 0001. Object and String variables are automatically initialized using the keyword Nothing. Variables initialized to Nothing do not actually contain the word "Nothing"; rather, they contain no data at all. Figure 3-6 shows examples of statements used to declare variables.

tip

A variable is considered an object in Visual Basic .NET and is an instance of the class specified in the *datatype* information. The `Dim intHours as Integer` statement, for example, creates an object named intHours, which is an instance of the Integer class.

Statement and explanation
`Dim intHours As Integer` declares an Integer variable named intHours; the variable is automatically initialized to 0
`Dim sngRate As Single = .03` declares a Single variable named sngRate and initializes it to .03
`Dim decPrice, decDiscount As Decimal` declares two Decimal variables named decPrice and decDiscount; the variables are automatically initialized to 0
`Private mblnDataOk As Boolean` declares a Boolean variable named mblnDataOk; the variable is automatically initialized to False
`Dim strName As String, intAge As Integer` declares a String variable named strName and an Integer variable named intAge; the String variable is automatically initialized to Nothing, and the Integer variable is automatically initialized to 0

Figure 3-6: Examples of variable declaration statements

After a variable is created, you can use an assignment statement to store other data in the variable.

Assigning Data to an Existing Variable

The syntax of an assignment statement that stores a value in a variable is *variable-name = value*. The two instructions `intNumber = 500` and `strName = "Mary"` are examples of assignment statements that assign values to variables. The `intNumber = 500` assignment statement stores the number 500 in an Integer variable named intNumber. The `strName = "Mary"` assignment statement stores the string "Mary" (without the quotation marks) in the strName variable. The number 500 and the string "Mary" are called literal constants. A **literal constant** is simply an item of data whose value does not change while the application is running. The number 500 is a numeric literal constant, and the string "Mary" is a string literal constant. Notice that you can store literal constants in variables. Also notice that string literal constants are enclosed in quotation marks, but numeric literal constants and variable names are not. The quotation marks differentiate a string from both a number and a variable name. In other words, "500" is a string, but 500 is a number. Similarly, "Mary" is a string, but Mary (without the quotation marks) would be interpreted by Visual Basic .NET as the name of a variable.

It is important to remember that a variable can store only one item of data at any one time. When you use an assignment statement to assign another item to the variable, the new data replaces the existing data. For example, assume that a button's Click event procedure contains the following three lines of code:

```
Dim intNumber As Integer
intNumber = 500
intNumber = intNumber * 2
```

When you run the application and click the button, the three lines of code are processed as follows:

- The Dim statement creates the intNumber variable in memory and automatically initializes it to the number 0. Here again, you may want to picture the intNumber variable as a small box inside the computer; the box contains the number 0.
- The `intNumber = 500` assignment statement removes the zero from the intNumber variable and stores the number 500 there instead. The variable (box) now contains the number 500 only.
- The `intNumber = intNumber * 2` assignment statement first multiplies the contents of the intNumber variable (500) by the number 2, giving 1000. The assignment statement then replaces the current contents of the intNumber variable (500) with 1000. Notice that the calculation appearing on the right side of the assignment operator (=) is performed first, and then the result is assigned to the variable whose name appears on the left side of the assignment operator.

As you can see, after data is stored in a variable, you can use the data in calculations, just as you can with the data stored in the properties of controls. When a statement contains the name of a variable, the computer uses the value stored inside the variable to process the statement.

You now know how to use a variable declaration statement to declare a variable. Recall that the statement allows you to assign a name, data type, and initial value to the variable you are declaring. You also know how to use an assignment statement to store data in an existing variable. There is just one more thing about variables that you need to learn to complete this tutorial's application: in addition to a name and a data type, every variable also has a scope.

The Scope of a Variable

A variable's **scope** indicates which procedures in an application can use the variable. The scope is determined by where you declare the variable—in other words, where you enter the variable's declaration statement. In most cases, you will enter the declaration statement either in a procedure, such as an event procedure, or in the Declarations section of a form.

When you declare a variable in a procedure, the variable is called a **local variable** and is said to have **procedure scope**, because only that procedure can use the variable. For example, if you enter the `Dim intNumber As Integer` statement in the CalcButton Click event procedure, only the CalcButton Click event procedure can use the intNumber variable. No other procedures in the application are allowed to use the intNumber variable. As a matter of fact, no other procedures in the application will even know that the intNumber variable exists. Local variables retain their values only while the procedure in which they are declared is running. When a procedure ends, Visual Basic .NET removes the procedure's local variables from the computer's internal memory. Most of the variables in your applications will be local variables.

When you declare a variable in the form's Declarations section, the variable is called a **form-level variable** and is said to have **module scope**. A form-level variable can be used by all of the procedures in the form, including the procedures associated with the controls contained on the form. For example, if you enter the `Private mintNumber As Integer` statement in a form's Declarations section, every procedure in the form can use the mintNumber variable. Form-level variables retain their values and remain in the computer's internal memory until the application ends.

As you will learn in Lesson C, you can use the Static keyword to declare a local variable that remains in the computer's memory, and therefore retains its value, when the procedure in which it is declared ends.

Form-level variables also are referred to as module-level variables.

The Scope application contained in the VBNET\Tut03\Scope Solution folder on your computer's hard disk is designed to help clarify the difference between a local variable and a form-level variable.

To open the Scope application:

1   Start Microsoft Visual Studio .NET, if necessary.

You will not need the Start Page window, so you can close it.

2   Close the Start Page window.

3   Click **File** on the menu bar, and then click **Open Solution**. The Open Solution dialog box opens. Open the **Scope Solution** (Scope Solution.sln) file, which is contained in the VBNET\Tut03\Scope Solution folder.

4   If the designer window is not open, right-click **Scope Form.vb** in the Solution Explorer window, then click **View Designer**.

5   Auto-hide the Toolbox, Solution Explorer, and Properties windows, if necessary. The Scope application's user interface is shown in Figure 3-7.

SalesButton

Comm2Button

SalesLabel

CommissionLabel

Comm5Button

ExitButton

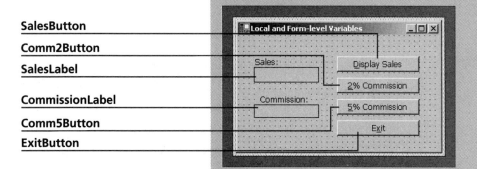

Figure 3-7: Scope application's user interface

The Scope application allows the user to calculate either a 2% or 5% commission on a sales amount. It displays the sales and commission amounts in the SalesLabel and CommissionLabel controls, respectively.

You will use the Scope application to experiment with creating local and form-level variables.

Creating a Local Variable

The first procedure you code in the Scope application is the SalesButton Click event procedure. The procedure will declare a local variable named intSales. It then will assign the number 500 to the intSales variable, and display the contents of the variable in the SalesLabel control on the form.

To code the SalesButton Click event procedure, then test the procedure:

1 Right-click the **form**, and then click **View Code** to open the Code editor window.

2 Click the **Class Name** list arrow, and then click **SalesButton** in the list. Click the **Method Name** list arrow, and then click **Click** in the list. The SalesButton Click event procedure appears in the Code editor window.

First, create a local Integer variable to store a sales amount. It is customary to enter variable declaration statements at the beginning of the procedure, immediately below the Private Sub instruction.

3 Type **dim intSales as integer** and press **Enter**.

Now store the number 500 in the local intSales variable.

4 Type **intsales = 500** and press **Enter**.

Finally, display the contents of the intSales variable in the SalesLabel control.

5 Type **me.saleslabel.text = intsales** and press **Enter**. Figure 3-8 shows the SalesButton Click event procedure.

```
Private Sub SalesButton_Click(ByVal sender As Object, ByVal e As System.EventArgs) H
    Dim intSales As Integer
    intSales = 500
    Me.SalesLabel.Text = intSales
    |
End Sub
```

Figure 3-8: SalesButton Click event procedure

Now test the SalesButton Click event procedure.

6 Click **File** on the menu bar, and then click **Save All**. Click **Debug** on the menu bar, and then click **Start**.

7 Click the **Display Sales** button. The `Dim intSales As Integer` instruction in the SalesButton Click event procedure creates and initializes (to the number 0) a local Integer variable named intSales. The `intSales = 500` instruction assigns the number 500 to the intSales variable, and the `Me.SalesLabel.Text = intSales` instruction displays the contents of the intSales variable (500) in the SalesLabel control. When the Click event procedure ends, which is when the computer processes the procedure's `End Sub` statement, the local intSales variable is removed from the computer's internal memory.

8 Click the **Exit** button to end the application. When you return to the Code editor window, close the Output window.

Next, code the Comm2Button Click event procedure, which should calculate a 2% commission on the sales amount stored in the intSales variable, and then display the result in the CommissionLabel control.

To code the Comm2Button Click event procedure, then test the procedure:

1 Click the **Class Name** list arrow, and then click **Comm2Button** in the list. Click the **Method Name** list arrow, and then click **Click** in the list. The Comm2Button Click event procedure appears in the Code editor window.

2 Type **me.commissionlabel.text = intsales * .02** and press **Enter**. Notice the jagged line that appears below the variable's name (intSales) in the instruction. The jagged line indicates that there is something wrong with the code. To determine the problem, you need simply to rest your mouse pointer somewhere on the word (or words) immediately above the jagged line. In this case, for example, you need to rest your mouse pointer on the variable name, intSales.

HELP? If a jagged line does not appear below the intSales variable name in the Comm2Button Click event procedure, right-click Scope Project in the Solution Explorer window, and then click Properties. When the Scope Project Property Pages dialog box opens, open the Common Properties folder, if necessary, and then click Build. Click the Option Explicit list arrow, and then click On. Click the OK button to close the dialog box.

3 Rest your mouse pointer I on the variable's name, as shown in Figure 3-9. Notice that a message appears in a box.

local variable
declaration statement

mouse pointer

```
Private Sub SalesButton_Click(ByVal sender As Object, ByVal e As System.EventArgs) H
      Dim intSales As Integer
      intSales = 500
      Me.SalesLabel.Text = intSales

End Sub

Private Sub Comm2Button_Click(ByVal sender As Object, ByVal e As System.EventArgs) H
      Me.CommissionLabel.Text = intsales * 0.02
      |                         The name 'intsales' is not declared.
End Sub
```

Figure 3-9: Result of resting your mouse pointer on the variable's name

The message in the box indicates that the intSales variable is not declared; in other words, the Comm2Button Click event procedure cannot locate the variable's declaration statement, which you previously entered in the SalesButton Click event procedure. As you learned earlier, only the procedure in which a variable is declared can use the variable. No other procedure even knows that the variable exists. Observe what happens if you use the same name to declare a variable in more than one procedure.

4 Insert a blank line above the assignment statement in the Comm2Button Click event procedure. In the blank line, type **dim intSales as integer,** and then click the assignment statement to move the insertion point away from the current line. Notice that the jagged line disappears from the assignment statement. If necessary, change intsales in the assignment statement to **intSales.**

5 Save the solution, and then start the application.

6 Click the **Display Sales** button. The contents of the SalesButton control's local intSales variable (500) appears in the SalesLabel control.

When the SalesButton Click event procedure ends, its local intSales variable is removed from the computer's internal memory.

7 Click the **2% Commission** button. The number 0 appears in the CommissionLabel control. The correct commission, however, should be 10 (2% of the $500 sales amount).

The zero appears because the `Dim intSales As Integer` instruction in the Comm2Button Click event procedure creates and initializes (to the number 0) its own local Integer variable named intSales. The `Me.CommissionLabel.Text = intSales * 0.02` instruction multiplies the contents of the intSales variable (0) by 0.02, and then assigns the result (0) to the Text property of the CommissionLabel control. When the Comm2Button Click event procedure ends, which is when the computer processes the procedure's `End Sub` statement, its local intSales variable is removed from the computer's internal memory.

8   Click the **Exit** button to end the application. When you return to the Code editor window, close the Output window.

As this example shows, when you use the same name to declare a variable in more than one procedure, each procedure creates its own local variable. Although the variables have the same name, each refers to a different location (box) in memory. But what if you want the SalesButton Click event procedure, the Comm2Button Click event procedure, and the Comm5Button Click event procedure to use the same intSales variable (box) in memory? In that case, you need to declare the variable as a form-level variable.

Creating a Form-Level Variable

In the Scope application, the Click event procedures for the SalesButton, Comm2Button, and Comm5Button need to use the same location in memory. If you want more than one procedure in the *same* form to use the *same* variable, you need to declare the variable as a form-level variable rather than as a local variable. You declare a form-level variable by entering a declaration statement in the Declarations section of the form. Code entered in the Declarations section is automatically processed when the application is started.

To declare a form-level variable:

1   Position the mouse pointer ⌶ immediately above the ExitButton Click event procedure, then click at that location. When you do so, the Class Name list box will contain ScopeForm and the Method Name list box will contain (Declarations).

2   Press **Enter** to insert a blank line, then type **'declare form-level variable** and press **Enter**.

As mentioned earlier, many programmers include the lowercase letter "m"— which stands for "module scope"—at the beginning of form-level variable names, because this helps to distinguish the form-level variables from the local variables used in an application. In this case, for example, you would name the form-level variable mintSales rather than intSales.

3   Type **private mintSales as integer** and press **Enter**.

Now remove the Dim statement from the SalesButton and Comm2Button Click event procedures.

4   Highlight the `Dim intSales As Integer` statement in the SalesButton Click event procedure, then press **Delete** two times.

5   Highlight the `Dim intSales As Integer` statement in the Comm2Button Click event procedure, then press **Delete** two times.

tip

You also can use the Dim keyword rather than the Private keyword to declare a form-level variable; both keywords produce the same result.

Now change intSales to mintSales.

6 Change intSales in the Comm2Button Click event procedure to **mintSales**, then click the **next line in the procedure** to remove the jagged line from the statement.

7 Change intSales in the two assignment statements in the SalesButton Click event procedure to **mintSales**.

Now code the Comm5Button Click event procedure.

8 Click the **Class Name** list arrow, and then click **Comm5Button** in the list. Click the **Method Name** list arrow, and then click **Click** in the list. The Comm5Button Click event procedure appears in the Code editor window.

9 Type **me.commissionlabel.text = mintsales * .05** and press **Enter**. The application's modified code is shown in Figure 3-10.

form-level variable declaration statement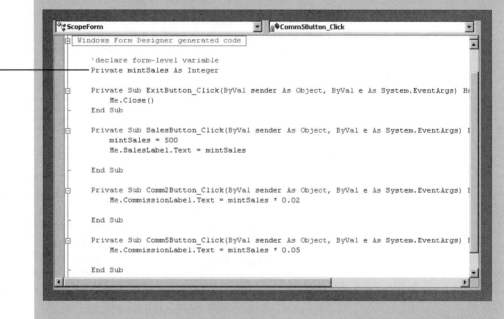

```
ScopeForm                                    Comm5Button_Click

   Windows Form Designer generated code

     'declare form-level variable
     Private mintSales As Integer

     Private Sub ExitButton_Click(ByVal sender As Object, ByVal e As System.EventArgs) Ha
          Me.Close()
     End Sub

     Private Sub SalesButton_Click(ByVal sender As Object, ByVal e As System.EventArgs) H
          mintSales = 500
          Me.SalesLabel.Text = mintSales

     End Sub

     Private Sub Comm2Button_Click(ByVal sender As Object, ByVal e As System.EventArgs) H
          Me.CommissionLabel.Text = mintSales * 0.02

     End Sub

     Private Sub Comm5Button_Click(ByVal sender As Object, ByVal e As System.EventArgs) H
          Me.CommissionLabel.Text = mintSales * 0.05

     End Sub
```

Figure 3-10: Modified code using a form-level variable

Now test the code to verify that it works correctly.

To test the application's code:

1 Save the solution, then start the application. The `Private mintSales As Integer` statement in the form's Declarations section creates and initializes (to the number 0) an Integer variable named mintSales.

2 Click the **Display Sales** button. The `mintSales = 500` instruction in the SalesButton Click event procedure stores the number 500 in the form-level mintSales variable. The `Me.SalesLabel.Text = mintSales` statement then displays the contents of the form-level variable (500) in the SalesLabel control.

3   Click the **2% Commission** button. The `Me.CommissionLabel.Text = mintSales * 0.02` instruction in the Comm2Button Click event procedure multiplies the contents of the form-level mintSales variable (500) by 0.02, and then displays the result (10) in the CommissionLabel control.

4   Click the **5% Commission** button. The `Me.CommissionLabel.Text = mintSales * 0.05` instruction in the Comm5Button Click event procedure multiplies the contents of the form-level mintSales variable (500) by 0.05, and then displays the result (25) in the CommissionLabel control.

As this example shows, when you declare a form-level variable, any procedure in the form can use the variable.

5   Click the **Exit** button to end the application. The computer removes the form-level mintSales variable from its internal memory.

6   When you return to the Code editor window, close the Output window.

You are finished with this application, so you can close it.

7   Click **File** on the menu bar, and then click **Close Solution**.

In addition to literal constants and variables, you also can use named constants in your code.

Named Constants

Like a variable, a **named constant** is a memory location inside the computer. However, unlike a variable, the contents of a named constant cannot be changed while the program is running. You create a named constant using the **Const statement**. The syntax of the Const statement is **Const** *constantname* [**As** *datatype*] = *expression*, where *constantname* and *datatype* are the constant's name and data type, respectively, and *expression* is the value you want assigned to the named constant. The *expression* can be a literal constant or another named constant; it also can contain arithmetic and logical operators. The *expression* cannot, however, contain variables or functions (such as Val).

The square brackets in the Const statement's syntax indicate that the "**As** *datatype*" portion is optional. If you do not assign a data type to a constant, Visual Basic .NET assigns a data type based on the *expression*, which may not be the most efficient type. For example, if you create a named constant for the number 45.6 and do not assign a data type to the constant, Visual Basic .NET assigns the Double data type to it, even though a Single data type is more efficient.

The rules for naming a named constant are the same as for naming a variable, except the customary practice is to precede the named constant's name with the three letters "con". Beginning the constant's name with "con", which is short for "constant," allows you to distinguish the named constants from the variables used in an application. Figure 3-11 shows examples of using the Const statement to create named constants.

tip

Recall that, if you do not specify a data type when creating a variable, Visual Basic .NET assigns the Object data type to the variable.

Const statement	Explanation
`Const conPi As Single = 3.141593`	creates a Single named constant named conPi and assigns the literal constant 3.141593 to it
`Const conMsg As String = "Great!"`	creates a String named constant named conMsg and assigns the literal constant "Great!" to it
`Const conPrice As Integer = 25`	creates an Integer named constant named conPrice and assigns the literal constant 25 to it

Figure 3-11: Examples of the Const statement

Similar to creating local and form-level variables, you create a local constant by entering the Const statement in the appropriate procedure, and you create a form-level constant by entering the Const statement in the form's Declarations section.

Named constants make code more self-documenting and, therefore, easier to modify, because they allow you to use meaningful words in place of values that are less clear. The named constant conPi, for example, is much more meaningful than is the number 3.141593, which is the value of pi rounded to six decimal places. Once you create a named constant, you then can use the constant's name rather than its value in the code. Unlike variables, named constants cannot be inadvertently changed while your program is running.

You will declare a named constant in the Constant application, which is contained in the VBNET\Tut03\Constant Solution folder on your computer's hard disk.

To open the Constant application:

1 Click **File** on the menu bar, and then click **Open Solution**.

2 Open the **Constant Solution** (Constant Solution.sln) file, which is contained in the VBNET\Tut03\Constant Solution folder.

3 If the designer window is not open, right-click **Constant Form.vb** in the Solution Explorer window, then click **View Designer**. The Constant application's user interface is shown in Figure 3-12.

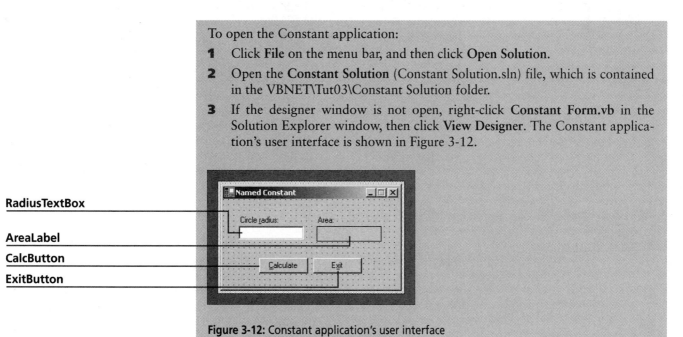

Figure 3-12: Constant application's user interface

The Constant application calculates and displays the area of a circle, using the radius entered in the RadiusTextBox.

4 Right-click the **form**, then click **View Code** to open the Code editor window.

The formula for calculating the area of a circle is Area = Πr^2.

5 In the CalcButton Click event procedure, enter the Const statement and the assignment statement shown in Figure 3-13.

enter these two statements

```
Private Sub CalcButton_Click(ByVal sender As Object, ByVal e As System.EventArgs) Ha
    'declare constant and variable
    Const conPi As Single = 3.141593
    Dim sngRadius, sngArea As Single
    'assign value to sngRadius variable
    sngRadius = Val(Me.RadiusTextBox.Text)
    'calculate the area
    sngArea = conPi * sngRadius ^ 2
    'display the area
    Me.AreaLabel.Text = Format(sngArea, "standard")

End Sub
```

Figure 3-13: The completed CalcButton Click event procedure

The `Const conPi as Single = 3.141593` statement creates a named constant in memory, and assigns the 3.141593 value to it. The `sngArea = conPi * sngRadius ^ 2` statement calculates the area of a circle.

6 Save the solution, then start the application.

7 Type 5 in the Circle radius text box, and then click the **Calculate** button. The CalcButton Click event procedure displays 78.54 as the area of the circle.

8 Click the **Exit** button to end the application. When you return to the Code editor window, close the Output window.

You are finished with the Constant application, so you can close it.

9 Click **File** on the menu bar, and then click **Close Solution**.

You now have completed Lesson A. You will use local and form-level variables in the Skate-Away Sales application, which you will modify in Lessons B and C. Now you can either take a break or complete the end-of-lesson questions and exercises before moving on to the next lesson.

SUMMARY

To create a variable:

■ See naming rules in Figures 3-4 and 3-5, and data types listed in Figure 3-3.

■ To create a local variable, enter the variable declaration statement in a procedure. To create a form-level variable, enter the variable declaration statement in a form's Declarations section. The syntax of a variable declaration statement is *accessibility variablename* [**As** *datatype*] [= *initialvalue*], where *accessibility* is typically either the keyword Dim (for a local variable) or the keyword Private (for a form-level variable). *Variablename* in the syntax is the variable's name, and *datatype* is the variable's data type. *Initialvalue* is the value you want stored in the variable when it is created in the computer's internal memory.

To use an assignment statement to assign data to a variable:

■ Use the syntax *variablename = value.*

To create a named constant:

■ Use the Const statement, whose syntax is **Const** *constantname* [**As** *datatype*] = *expression.*
■ The rules for naming constants are the same as for naming variables, except you precede the constant's name with the three letters "con", which is short for "constant."
■ Use the Const statement to declare local and form-level constants in a procedure and form's Declarations section, respectively.

QUESTIONS

1. _____ are memory locations in which you store information, temporarily.
   a. Boxes
   b. Literal constants
   c. Named constants
   d. Variables
   e. Both c and d.

2. Which of the following are valid variable names?
   a. dec94Income
   b. decIncome
   c. decInc_94
   d. decIncomeTax
   e. All of the above.

3. Which of the following is the correct data type to use for a variable that will always contain a whole number less than 50,000?
   a. Decimal
   b. Integer
   c. Long
   d. Single
   e. Object

4. A(n) _____ variable is known only to the procedure in which it is declared.
   a. current
   b. event
   c. form-level
   d. local
   e. None of the above.

5. A _____ is a data item whose value does not change while the program is running.
   a. literal constant
   b. literal variable
   c. named constant
   d. symbolic variable
   e. variable

6. A _____ is a memory location whose value can change while the program is running.
    a. literal constant
    b. literal variable
    c. named constant
    d. symbolic variable
    e. variable

7. A _____ is a memory location whose value cannot change while the program is running.
    a. literal constant
    b. literal variable
    c. named constant
    d. symbolic variable
    e. variable

8. If you do not provide a data type in a variable declaration statement, Visual Basic .NET assigns the _____ data type to the variable.
    a. Decimal
    b. Integer
    c. Object
    d. String
    e. None of the above

9. Many programmers begin a form-level variable's name with the _____.
    a. letter f
    b. letter m
    c. letters fl
    d. letters frm
    e. letters mod

10. Data stored in a variable can be processed much faster than data stored in the property of a control.
    a. True
    b. False

E X E R C I S E S

1. Assume a procedure needs to store an item's name and its price. The price may have a decimal place. Write the appropriate Dim statement to create the necessary local variables.

2. Assume a procedure needs to store the name of an item in inventory and its height and weight. The height may have decimal places; the weight will be whole numbers only. Write the appropriate Dim statement to create the necessary local variables.

3. Assume a procedure needs to store the name of an inventory item, the number of units in stock at the beginning of the current month, the number of units purchased during the current month, the number of units sold during the current month, and the number of units in stock at the end of the current month. (The number of units is always a whole number.) Write the appropriate Dim statement to create the necessary local variables.

4. Assume a procedure needs to store the name and the population of a city. Write the appropriate Dim statement to create the necessary local variables.

5. Assume your application needs to store the part number of an item and its cost. (An example of a part number for this application is A103.) Write the appropriate Private statement to create the necessary form-level variables.

6. Write an assignment statement that assigns Miami to an existing variable named strCity.

7. Write an assignment statement that assigns the part number AB103 to an existing variable named strPartNo.

8. Write an assignment statement that assigns the word Desk to an existing variable named strName, the number 40 to an existing variable named intInStock, and the number 20 to an existing variable named intOnOrder.

9. Write an assignment statement that adds the contents of the decSales1 variable to the contents of the decSales2 variable, and then assigns the sum to an existing variable named decTotalSales.

10. Write an assignment statement that multiplies the contents of the sngSalary variable by the number 1.5, and then assigns the result to the sngSalary variable.

11. Assume a form contains two buttons named SalaryButton and BonusButton. Both buttons' Click event procedures need to use the mstrEmpName variable. Write the appropriate statement to declare the mstrEmpName variable. Also specify where you will need to enter the statement and whether the variable is a local or form-level variable.

12. Assume a form contains two buttons named WestButton and SouthButton. The Click event procedure for the WestButton needs to use a variable named sngWestSales. The Click event procedure for the SouthButton needs to use a variable named sngSouthSales. Both buttons' Click event procedures need to use the msngCompanySales variable. Write the appropriate statements to declare the sngWestSales, sngSouthSales, and msngCompanySales variables. Also specify where you will need to enter each statement and whether each variable is a local or form-level variable.

13. Write the statement to declare a local named constant named conTaxRate whose value is .05.

14. Assume two procedures in a form need to use the mconAge named constant, whose value is 21. Write the statement to declare the constant. Also specify where you will need to enter the statement and whether the constant is a local or form-level constant.

Exercise 15 is a Discovery Exercise. Discovery Exercises, which may include topics that are not covered in the tutorial, allow you to "discover" the solutions to problems on your own.

discovery ▶ 15. In this exercise, you learn how to declare a Static variable.
  a. If necessary, start Visual Studio .NET. Open the Static Solution (Static Solution.sln) file, which is contained in the VBNET\Tut03\Static Solution folder. If the designer window is not open, right-click the form file's name in the Solution Explorer window, then click View Designer.

  The application is supposed to count the number of times the Count button is pressed, but it is not working correctly.

  b. Start the application. Click the Count button. The message indicates that you have pressed the Count button once, which is correct.
  c. Click the Count button several more times. Notice that the message still displays the number 1.

d. Click the Exit button to end the application. Close the Output window.

e. Open the Code editor window. The CountButton Click event procedure first uses a Dim statement to declare a local variable named intCounter. It then adds 1 to the intCounter variable, and then displays the variable's value in the CounterLabel control on the form.

f. Change the Dim in the variable declaration statement to Static.

g. Save the solution, then start the application.

h. Click the Count button several times. Each time you click the Count button, the message changes to indicate the number of times the button was clicked.

i. Click the Exit button to end the application.

j. Close the Output window, then close the solution.

After completing this lesson, you will be able to:

- Include local and form-level variables in an application
- Concatenate strings
- Get user input using the InputBox function
- Locate the Visual Basic .NET intrinsic constants in the Object Browser
- Include the vbNewLine constant in code
- Designate the default button for a form

Modifying the Skate-Away Sales Application

Storing Information Using Variables

Recall that Mr. Cousard, the manager of Skate-Away Sales, has asked you to modify the order form that you created in Tutorial 2. The order form should now display the message "The sales tax was" followed by the sales tax amount and the name of the salesperson who recorded the order. Before making modifications to an application's existing code, you should review the application's documentation and revise the necessary documents. In this case, you need to revise the Skate-Away Sales application's TOE chart and also the pseudocode for the Calculate Order button, which is responsible for making the application's calculations. The revised TOE chart is shown in Figure 3-14. Changes made to the original TOE chart, which is shown in Tutorial 2's Figure 2-11, are shaded in the figure. (You will view the revised pseudocode for the Calculate Order button later in this lesson.)

Task	Object	Event
1. Calculate the total skateboards ordered and the total price 2. Display the total skateboards ordered and the total price in the TotalBoardsLabel and TotalPriceLabel 3. Calculate the sales tax 4. Display the message, sales tax, and salesperson's name in the MessageLabel	CalcButton	Click
Clear the screen for the next order	ClearButton	Click
End the application	ExitButton	Click
Display the total skateboards ordered (from CalcButton)	TotalBoardsLabel	None
Display the total price (from CalcButton)	TotalPriceLabel	None
Get and display the order information	NameTextBox, AddressTextBox, CityTextBox, StateTextBox, ZipTextBox, PriceTextBox, RateTextBox, BlueTextBox, YellowTextBox	None
Get the salesperson's name	OrderForm	Load
Display the message, sales tax, and salesperson's name (from CalcButton)	MessageLabel	None

Figure 3-14: Revised TOE chart for the Skate-Away Sales application

Notice that the CalcButton control's Click event procedure now has two more tasks to perform: it must calculate the sales tax and also display the message, sales tax, and salesperson's name in the MessageLabel control. Two additional objects (OrderForm and MessageLabel) also are included in the revised TOE chart. The OrderForm's Load event procedure, which occurs before the OrderForm is displayed the first time, is responsible for getting the salesperson's name when the application is started. The MessageLabel control will display the message, sales tax, and salesperson's name. As the revised TOE chart indicates, you need to change the code in the CalcButton's Click event procedure, and you also need to code the form's Load event procedure. The MessageLabel control, however, does not need to be coded.

Before you can begin modifying its code, you need to open the Skate-Away Sales application.

To open the Skate-Away Sales application:

1 Start Microsoft Visual Studio .NET, if necessary.

You will not need the Start Page window, so you can close it.

2 Close the Start Page window.

3 Click **File** on the menu bar, and then click **Open Solution**. The Open Solution dialog box opens. Open the **Order Solution** (Order Solution.sln) file, which is contained in the VBNET\Tut03\Order Solution folder.

4 If the designer window is not open, right-click **Order Form.vb** in the Solution Explorer window, then click **View Designer**.

5 Auto-hide the Toolbox, Solution Explorer, and Properties windows, if necessary. The Skate-Away Sales order form is shown in Figure 3-15.

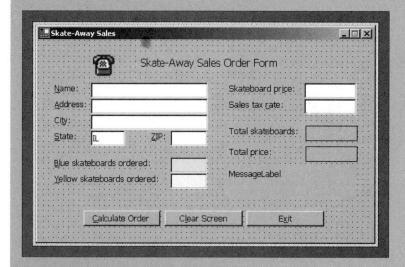

Figure 3-15: Skate-Away Sales order form

Two minor modifications were made to the order form that you created in Tutorial 2. First, the order form now contains a label control named MessageLabel. You will use the MessageLabel control to display the message that contains both the sales tax amount and the name of the salesperson. Second, the instruction `Me.MessageLabel.Text = ""` was added to the Clear Screen button's Click event procedure. The instruction will remove the message from the MessageLabel control when the user clicks the Clear Screen button.

6 Click the **MessageLabel** control to select it.

The MessageLabel control should be empty when the order form first appears on the screen.

7 Delete the contents of the MessageLabel control's Text property.

> **HELP?** To delete the contents of the Text property, double-click Text in the Properties list; this will highlight the contents of the Text property in the Settings box. Press the Delete key to delete the highlighted text, then press Enter.

8 Click the **form's title bar** to select the form.

Now begin modifying the Skate-Away Sales application so that it displays the sales tax amount on the order form.

Modifying the Calculate Order Button's Code

Currently, the Calculate Order button calculates the amount of sales tax as part of the total price equation. Recall that the total price equation from Tutorial 2 is `Me.TotalPriceLabel.Text = Val(Me.TotalBoardsLabel.Text) * Val(Me.PriceTextBox.Text) * (1+ Val(Me.RateTextBox.Text))`. Now that Mr. Cousard wants the sales tax amount to appear on the order form, you need to include a separate equation for the sales tax amount in the Calculate Order button's code. In this lesson, you first remove the existing code from the Calculate Order button's Click event procedure. You then recode the procedure using variables (rather than control properties) in the equations. Figure 3-16 shows the revised pseudocode for the Calculate Order button's Click event procedure. Changes made to the original pseudocode, which is shown in Tutorial 2's Figure 2-29, are shaded in the figure.

Calculate Order button

1. declare variables

2. assign values to variables

3. calculate total skateboards = blue skateboards + yellow skateboards

4. calculate subtotal = total skateboards * skateboard price

5. calculate sales tax = subtotal * sales tax rate

6. calculate total price = subtotal + sales tax

7. display total skateboards and total price in TotalBoardsLabel and TotalPriceLabel controls

8. display "The sales tax was" message, sales tax, and salesperson's name in the MessageLabel control

9. send the focus to the Clear Screen button

Figure 3-16: Revised pseudocode for the Calculate Order button's Click event procedure

Notice that, in addition to using variables, the Click event procedure now includes two additional calculations—one for a subtotal and the other for the sales tax. The subtotal amount is computed by multiplying the total skateboards ordered by the skateboard price. The sales tax amount is computed by multiplying the subtotal amount by the sales tax rate. Also notice that the total price equation has changed; it now simply adds the subtotal amount to the sales tax amount. Before sending the focus to the Clear Screen button, the Click event procedure displays a message, the sales tax amount, and the salesperson's name in the MessageLabel control.

In the next set of steps, you open the Code editor window and review the code contained in the Calculate Order button's Click event procedure.

To open the Code editor window, and then review the code in the Calculate Order button's Click event procedure:

1 Right-click the **form** and then click **View Code**. The Code editor window opens.

2 Scroll down the Code editor window until the entire CalcButton Click event procedure is visible. See Figure 3-17.

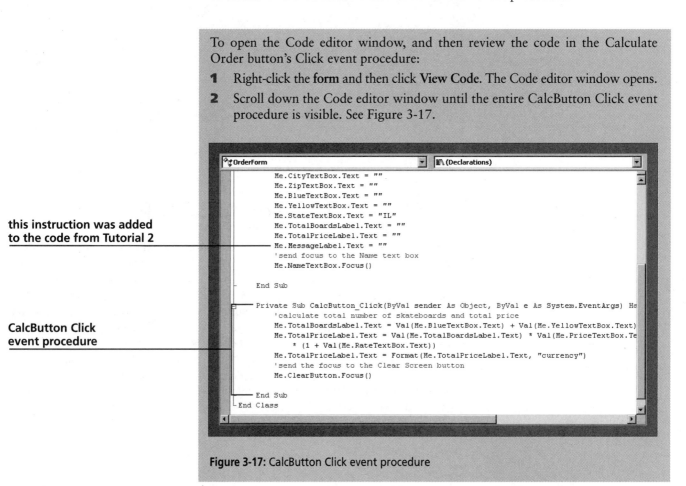

this instruction was added to the code from Tutorial 2

CalcButton Click event procedure

Figure 3-17: CalcButton Click event procedure

The equations that calculate the total skateboards ordered and the total price use the Text property of various controls included on the interface. The Val function in the equations is necessary because the Text property of a control is treated as a string rather than as a number. As you learned in Tutorial 2, the Val function returns the numeric equivalent of a string. What you did not learn in Tutorial 2, however, is that the Val function returns a number whose data type is Double. Therefore, when the computer processes the total skateboard equation, it first converts the contents of both the BlueTextBox.Text and YellowTextBox.Text properties to Double type numbers, then adds the Double numbers together and assigns the sum to the TotalBoardsLabel control. As you may remember, the Double data type consumes 8 bytes of the computer's internal memory. In this case, because a customer can order only a whole number of blue and yellow skateboards, and the number of skateboards ordered is typically under 1,000 for each color, it would be more efficient to store the blue and yellow skateboard information in either Short (2 bytes of memory) or Integer (4 bytes of memory) variables. You will use Integer variables, because a calculation containing Integer variables takes less time to process than the equivalent calculation containing Short variables. Assigning the Text property of the BlueTextBox and YellowTextBox controls to Integer variables allows you to control the data type of the numbers used in the total skateboards equation. You will assign the result of the total skateboards equation to an Integer variable named intTotalBoards. Figure 3-18 lists the names of the variables you will use in the Calculate Order button's Click event procedure and what will be assigned to each variable.

Variable	Assign to variable
intBlue	contents of BlueTextBox.Text
intYellow	contents of YellowTextBox.Text
intTotalBoards	sum of intBlue + intYellow
sngPrice	contents of PriceTextBox.Text
sngRate	contents of RateTextBox.Text
sngSubtotal	product of intTotalBoards * sngPrice
sngSalesTax	product of sngSubtotal * sngRate
sngTotalPrice	sum of sngSubtotal + sngSalesTax

Figure 3-18: List of variables and what you will assign to each

tip

You are using Single (4 bytes of memory) rather than Decimal (16 bytes of memory) variables for the price, subtotal, sales tax, and total price amounts because these variables will not need to store large money values. Also, the equations that use these variables are not complex, so rounding errors will not be a problem. Recall that it is best to use a smaller data type whenever possible.

Now remove the existing code from the CalcButton Click event procedure.

To remove the code from the CalcButton Click event procedure:

1 Highlight all of the instructions between the `Private Sub` and the `End Sub` instructions, as shown in Figure 3-19. Be sure that you do not highlight the `Private Sub` and `End Sub` instructions.

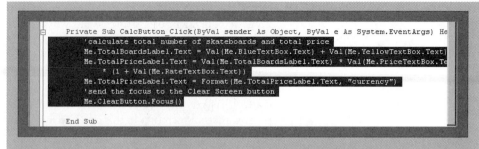

Figure 3-19: Instructions highlighted in the CalcButton Click event procedure

2   Press **Delete** to remove the highlighted code.

HELP? If you inadvertently deleted the `Private Sub` and `End Sub` instructions, click the Class Name list arrow, then click CalcButton in the list. Click the Method Name list arrow, and then click Click in the list.

The first step listed in the pseudocode shown in Figure 3-16 is to declare the variables. Because only the Calculate Order button's Click event procedure will need to use the eight variables listed in Figure 3-18, you will declare the variables as local variables.

To begin coding the Calculate Order button's Click event procedure:

1   Enter the two Dim statements shown in Figure 3-20.

Type the variable names in the Dim statement using the exact capitalization you want. Then, any time you want to refer to the variables in the code, you can enter their names using any case and the Code editor will adjust the name to match the case used in the Dim statement.

```
Private Sub CalcButton_Click(ByVal sender As Object, ByVal e As System.EventArgs) He
    Dim intBlue, intYellow, intTotalBoards As Integer
    Dim sngPrice, sngRate, sngSubtotal, sngSalesTax, sngTotalPrice As Single

End Sub
```

Figure 3-20: Dim statements entered in the procedure

The next step in the pseudocode is to assign values to the variables. The intBlue, intYellow, sngPrice, and sngRate variables will get their values from the BlueTextBox, YellowTextBox, PriceTextBox, and RateTextBox controls, respectively. The remaining variables will get their values from the equations that calculate the total skateboards, subtotal, sales tax, and total price amounts.

2 Enter the one line of documentation and four assignment statements shown in Figure 3-21, then position the insertion point as shown in the figure.

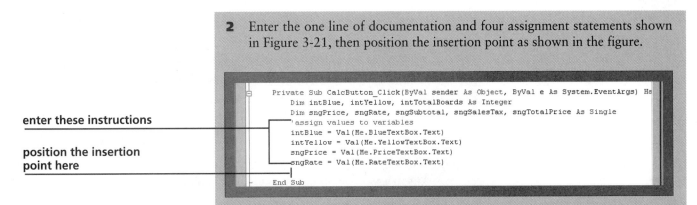

enter these instructions

position the insertion
point here

```
Private Sub CalcButton_Click(ByVal sender As Object, ByVal e As System.EventArgs) Ha
    Dim intBlue, intYellow, intTotalBoards As Integer
    Dim sngPrice, sngRate, sngSubtotal, sngSalesTax, sngTotalPrice As Single
    'assign values to variables
    intBlue = Val(Me.BlueTextBox.Text)
    intYellow = Val(Me.YellowTextBox.Text)
    sngPrice = Val(Me.PriceTextBox.Text)
    sngRate = Val(Me.RateTextBox.Text)

End Sub
```

Figure 3-21: Documentation and assignment statements entered in the procedure

The `intBlue = Val(Me.BlueTextBox.Text)` and `intYellow = Val(Me.YellowTextBox.Text)` statements first convert the contents of the BlueTextBox and YellowTextBox controls to Double type numbers. The statements then convert the Double numbers to Integer numbers before storing them in the intBlue and intYellow variables. Similarly, the `sngPrice = Val(Me.PriceTextBox.Text)` and `sngRate = Val(Me.RateTextBox.Text)` statements first convert the values in the Text properties of the PriceTextBox and RateTextBox controls to Double type numbers. These statements then convert the Double numbers to Single numbers before storing them in the sngPrice and sngRate variables.

The next step in the pseudocode is to calculate the total number of skateboards ordered by adding the number of blue skateboards ordered to the number of yellow skateboards ordered. When entering the total skateboards equation, you will use the variables that you declared in the procedure, rather than the control properties that you used in Tutorial 2's equation. In other words, you will enter `intTotalBoards = intBlue + intYellow` instead of `Me.TotalBoardsLabel.Text = Val(Me.BlueTextBox.Text) + Val(Me.YellowTextBox.Text)`. Notice how, in addition to making your application run more efficiently and allowing you to control the preciseness of the numbers used in the calculations, variables also make the lines of code much shorter and easier to understand.

To continue coding the CalcButton Click event procedure:

1 Type **'perform calculations** and press **Enter**, then type **inttotalboards = intblue + intyellow** and press **Enter**.

The next steps in the pseudocode are to calculate the subtotal, sales tax, and total price amounts. You calculate the subtotal amount by multiplying the number of skateboards ordered (which is stored in the intTotalBoards variable) by the skateboard price (which is stored in the sngPrice variable).

2 Type **sngsubtotal = inttotalboards * sngprice** and press **Enter**.

You calculate the sales tax amount by multiplying the subtotal amount (which is stored in the sngSubtotal variable) by the sales tax rate (which is stored in the sngRate variable).

3 Type **sngsalestax = sngsubtotal * sngrate** and press **Enter**.

To calculate the total price amount, you simply add the sales tax amount to the subtotal amount. The subtotal amount is stored in the sngSubtotal variable, and the sales tax amount is stored in the sngSalesTax variable.

4   Type **sngtotalprice = sngsubtotal + sngsalestax** and press **Enter**.

The next step in the pseudocode is to display the total skateboards and the total price in the TotalBoardsLabel and TotalPriceLabel controls on the form. As you did in Tutorial 2, you will use the Format function to format the total price as currency, which will display a dollar sign ($), a comma thousand separator, and two decimal places.

5   Type **'display total amounts in controls** and press **Enter**.

6   Type **me.totalboardslabel.text = inttotalboards** and press **Enter**, then type **me.totalpricelabel.text = format(sngtotalprice, "currency")** and press **Enter**.

The next step in the pseudocode is to display a message, the sales tax, and the salesperson's name in the MessageLabel control. For now, just display the sales tax so you can verify that the sales tax equation is working correctly. Use the Format function to display the sales tax in the currency format.

7   Type **me.messagelabel.text = format(sngsalestax, "currency")** and press **Enter**.

The last step in the pseudocode is to send the focus to the Clear Screen button. As you learned in Tutorial 2, you can use the Focus method to send the focus to a control.

8   Type **me.clearbutton.focus**() and press **Enter**.

9   Compare your code to the code shown in Figure 3-22. Make any necessary corrections before continuing.

```
Private Sub CalcButton_Click(ByVal sender As Object, ByVal e As System.EventArgs) Ha
    Dim intBlue, intYellow, intTotalBoards As Integer
    Dim sngPrice, sngRate, sngSubtotal, sngSalesTax, sngTotalPrice As Single
    'assign values to variables
    intBlue = Val(Me.BlueTextBox.Text)
    intYellow = Val(Me.YellowTextBox.Text)
    sngPrice = Val(Me.PriceTextBox.Text)
    sngRate = Val(Me.RateTextBox.Text)
    'perform calculations
    intTotalBoards = intBlue + intYellow
    sngSubtotal = intTotalBoards * sngPrice
    sngSalesTax = sngSubtotal * sngRate
    sngTotalPrice = sngSubtotal + sngSalesTax
    'display total amounts in controls
    Me.TotalBoardsLabel.Text = intTotalBoards
    Me.TotalPriceLabel.Text = Format(sngTotalPrice, "currency")
    Me.MessageLabel.Text = Format(sngSalesTax, "currency")
    Me.ClearButton.Focus()

End Sub
```

Figure 3-22: Calculate Order button's Click event procedure

Now test the code entered in the CalcButton's Click event procedure.

To test the CalcButton's Click event procedure:

1 Click **File** on the menu bar, and then click **Save All**. Click **Debug** on the menu bar, and then click **Start**.

2 Enter the following order:

blue skateboards ordered:	10
yellow skateboards ordered:	10
skateboard price:	100
sales tax rate:	.05

3 Click the **Calculate Order** button. The application displays the total number of skateboards ordered in the TotalBoardsLabel control, the total price in the TotalPriceLabel control, and the sales tax in the MessageLabel control, then sends the focus to the Clear Screen button, as shown in Figure 3-23.

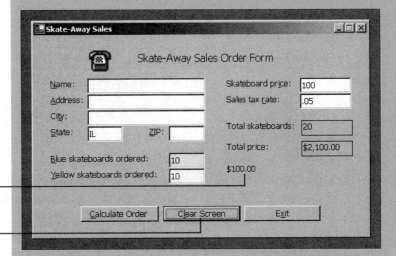

sales tax amount

this button has the focus

Figure 3-23: Order form showing sales tax amount

4 Click the **Exit** button. When you return to the Code editor window, close the Output window.

In addition to displaying the sales tax, the MessageLabel control also must display the message "The sales tax was" and the name of the salesperson recording the order. Before you can accomplish this task, you need to learn how to concatenate (link together) strings.

Concatenating Strings

Connecting (or linking) strings together is called **concatenating**. You use the **concatenation operator**, which is the ampersand (&), to concatenate strings in Visual Basic .NET. Figure 3-24 shows some examples of string concatenation. Notice that you also can concatenate a number with a string; in those cases, Visual Basic .NET treats the number as though it were a string.

tip
· · · · · · · · · · · · · · · ·

You also can use the plus sign (+) to concatenate strings. To avoid confusion, however, you should use the plus sign for addition and the ampersand for concatenation.

Assume you have the following variables:		
Variables	**Data type**	**Contents**
strFirstName	String	Sue
strLastName	String	Chen
intAge	Integer	21

Using the above variables, this concatenated string:	Would result in:
strFirstName & strLastName	SueChen
strFirstName & " " & strLastName	Sue Chen
strLastName & ", " & strFirstName	Chen, Sue
"She is " & intAge & "!"	She is 21!

Figure 3-24: Examples of string concatenation

When concatenating strings, you must be sure to include a space before and after the concatenation operator—the ampersand (&). If you do not enter a space before and after the ampersand, Visual Basic .NET will not recognize the ampersand as the concatenation operator.

You will use the concatenation operator to link the string "The sales tax was" to the sales tax stored in the sngSalesTax variable, and then concatenate the sales tax to a period, which will mark the end of the sentence. Using the examples shown in Figure 3-24 as a guide, the correct syntax for the MessageLabel control's assignment statement would be `Me.MessageLabel.Text = "The sales tax was " & Format(sngSalesTax, "currency") & "."`.

To concatenate a message, the sales tax amount, and a period, and then save and start the application:

1 Change the `Me.MessageLabel.Text = Format(sngSalesTax, "currency")` assignment statement as shown in Figure 3-25.

include a space here

modify this statement

line continuation character

```
Private Sub CalcButton_Click(ByVal sender As Object, ByVal e As System.EventArgs) Ha
    Dim intBlue, intYellow, intTotalBoards As Integer
    Dim sngPrice, sngRate, sngSubtotal, sngSalesTax, sngTotalPrice As Single
    'assign values to variables
    intBlue = Val(Me.BlueTextBox.Text)
    intYellow = Val(Me.YellowTextBox.Text)
    sngPrice = Val(Me.PriceTextBox.Text)
    sngRate = Val(Me.RateTextBox.Text)
    'perform calculations
    intTotalBoards = intBlue + intYellow
    sngSubtotal = intTotalBoards * sngPrice
    sngSalesTax = sngSubtotal * sngRate
    sngTotalPrice = sngSubtotal + sngSalesTax
    'display total amounts in controls
    Me.TotalBoardsLabel.Text = intTotalBoards
    Me.TotalPriceLabel.Text = Format(sngTotalPrice, "currency")
    Me.MessageLabel.Text = "The sales tax was " _
        & Format(sngSalesTax, "currency") & "."
    Me.ClearButton.Focus()
End Sub
```

Figure 3-25: Modified assignment statement entered in the procedure

2 Save and then start the application.

3 Enter the following order:

blue skateboards ordered	10
yellow skateboards ordered	10
skateboard price	100
sales tax rate	.05

4 Click the **Calculate Order** button. The application displays the total number of skateboards ordered, the total price, and the message, including the sales tax, as shown in Figure 3-26.

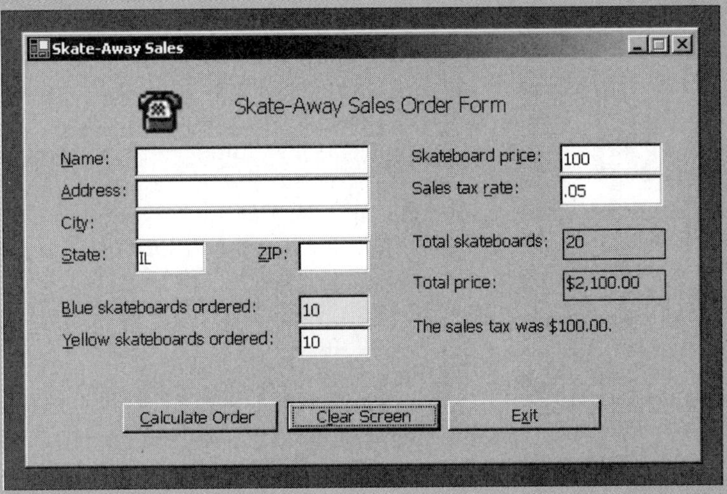

Figure 3-26: Order form showing the message and sales tax amount

5 Click the **Exit button.** When you return to the Code editor window, close the Output window.

Now that you have the message and sales tax amount displaying correctly in the MessageLabel control, you just need to get the salesperson's name and then concatenate it to the end of the message. You can use the InputBox function to obtain the name from the user.

The InputBox Function

The **InputBox function** displays one of Visual Basic .NET's predefined dialog boxes. The dialog box contains a message, along with an OK button, a Cancel button, and an input area in which the user can enter information. The message that you display in the dialog box should prompt the user to enter the appropriate information in the input area of the dialog box. The user then needs to click either the OK button or the Cancel button to continue working in the application. Figure 3-27 shows an example of a dialog box created by the InputBox function.

title

prompt

defaultResponse

input area

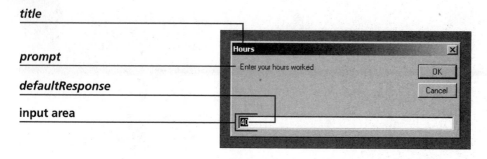

Figure 3-27: Example of a dialog box created by the InputBox function

The InputBox function's syntax also includes *XPos* and *YPos* arguments, which allow you to specify the horizontal and vertical position of the dialog box on the screen. Both arguments are optional; if omitted, the dialog box appears centered on the screen.

You learned about both sentence and book title capitalization in Tutorial 2's Lesson A.

The syntax of the InputBox function is **InputBox(***prompt*[, *title*][, *defaultResponse*]), where *prompt* is the message you want displayed inside the dialog box, *title* is the text you want displayed in the dialog box's title bar, and *defaultResponse* is the text you want displayed in the input area of the dialog box. In Figure 3-27, "Enter your hours worked" is the *prompt*, "Hours" is the *title*, and "40" is the *defaultResponse*.

When entering the InputBox function in the Code editor window, the *prompt*, *title*, and *defaultResponse* arguments must be enclosed in quotation marks, unless that information is stored in a variable or named constant. The standard is to use sentence capitalization for the *prompt*, but book title capitalization for the *title*. The capitalization (if any) you use for the *defaultResponse* will depend on the text itself.

Notice that the *title* and *defaultResponse* arguments are optional, as indicated by the square brackets in the syntax. If you omit the *title*, the application name appears in the title bar. If you omit the *defaultResponse* argument, a blank input area appears when the dialog box opens.

Recall that a function is a predefined procedure that returns a value. The value returned by the InputBox function depends on whether the user clicks the dialog box's OK, Cancel, or Close button ⊠. If the user clicks the OK button, the InputBox function returns the value contained in the input area of the dialog box. However, if the user clicks either the Cancel button or the Close button, the InputBox function returns a zero-length (or empty) string. Figure 3-28 shows some examples of the InputBox function used in assignment statements.

the additional comma is required when using the *defaultResponse* argument without the *title* argument

use the Val function when assigning the return value to a numeric variable

InputBox function examples
strName = InputBox("Enter your name")
strCity = InputBox("City name", "City")
strState = InputBox("State name", "State", "Alaska")
strState = InputBox("State name",, "Alaska")
intAge = Val(InputBox("How old are you?", "Age"))
sngHours = Val(InputBox(conPrompt, conTitle, "0"))

Figure 3-28: Examples of the InputBox function in assignment statements

GUI
Design Tips

InputBox Function's Prompt and Title Capitalization

- In the InputBox function, use sentence capitalization for the *prompt*, and book title capitalization for the *title*.

You will use the InputBox function in the Skate-Away Sales application to prompt the salesperson to enter his or her name. You will create named constants for the *prompt* and *title* arguments, and store the function's return value in a String variable named mstrSalesPerson. The InputBox function will be entered in the OrderForm's Load event procedure because, according to the revised TOE chart (shown earlier in Figure 3-14), that is the procedure responsible for getting the salesperson's name. Recall that a form's Load event occurs before the form is displayed the first time. After the Load event procedure obtains the salesperson's name, you then can have the CalcButton Click event procedure concatenate the name to the message displayed in the MessageLabel control. Figure 3-29 shows the pseudocode for the form's Load event procedure.

Order Form

1. declare named constants

2. get the salesperson's name and assign the name to the form-level mstrSalesPerson variable

---

Figure 3-29: Pseudocode for the OrderForm's Load event procedure

Before entering the InputBox function in the Load event procedure, you must decide where to declare the variable that will store the function's return value. In other words, should the mstrSalesPerson variable be a local or form-level variable? When deciding, consider the fact that the form's Load event procedure needs to assign a value—in this case, the value returned by the InputBox function—to the mstrSalesPerson variable. The Calculate Order button's Click event procedure also needs to use the mstrSalesPerson variable, because the procedure must concatenate the variable to the message displayed in the MessageLabel control. Recall from Lesson A that when two procedures in the *same* form need to use the *same* variable, you declare the variable as a form-level variable by entering the variable declaration statement in the form's Declarations section.

To continue coding the Skate-Away Sales application, then save and start the application:

1 Scroll to the top of the Code editor window. Position the mouse pointer I immediately above the ExitButton Click event procedure, then click at that location. When you do so, the Class Name list box will say OrderForm and the Method Name list box will say (Declarations).

First, declare the mstrSalesPerson variable as a form-level String variable.

2 Press **Enter** to insert a blank line, then type **'declare form-level variable** and press **Enter**. Type **private mstrSalesPerson as string** and press **Enter**. See Figure 3-30.

Declarations section

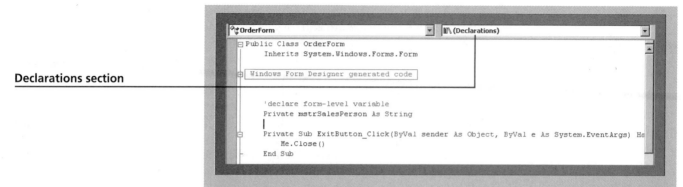

```
OrderForm                                    ▼   ║▌\ (Declarations)                              ▼
⊟ Public Class OrderForm
       Inherits System.Windows.Forms.Form

⊟  Windows Form Designer generated code


        'declare form-level variable
        Private mstrSalesPerson As String

⊟       Private Sub ExitButton_Click(ByVal sender As Object, ByVal e As System.EventArgs) Ha
            Me.Close()
        End Sub
```

Figure 3-30: Form-level variable declared in the Declarations section

Now enter the InputBox function in the form's Load event procedure, so the function will be processed as soon as the salesperson starts the application. You access the form's procedures by selecting (Base Class Events) in the Class Name list box.

3   Click the **Class Name** list arrow, and then click (**Base Class Events**) in the list.

4   Click the **Method Name** list arrow to view a list of the form's procedures. Scroll down the list until you see Load, then click **Load** in the list. The OrderForm's Load event procedure appears in the Code editor window.

To make the assignment statement that contains the InputBox function shorter and easier to understand, you create named constants for the function's *prompt* ("Enter the salesperson's name") and *title* ("Name Entry") arguments, and then use the named constants rather than the longer strings in the function. You are using named constants rather than variables because the *prompt* and *title* will not change as the program is running.

5   Type the documentation and code shown in Figure 3-31.

enter these instructions

```
⊟    Private Sub OrderForm_Load(ByVal sender As Object, ByVal e As System.EventArgs) Hand
         'declare named constants
         Const conPrompt As String = "Enter the salesperson's name"
         Const conTitle As String = "Name Entry"
         'get the salesperson's name, assign return value to form-level variable
         mstrSalesPerson = InputBox(conPrompt, conTitle)

     End Sub
```

Figure 3-31: Form's Load event procedure

The InputBox function will prompt the user to enter the salesperson's name, and then store the response in the form-level mstrSalesPerson variable. Recall that form-level variables remain in memory until the application ends.

Now modify the Calculate Order button's Click event procedure by concatenating the mstrSalesPerson variable to the message assigned to the MessageLabel control.

6   Locate the CalcButton Click event procedure in the Code editor window, then modify the MessageLabel control's assignment statement as shown in Figure 3-32.

```
Private Sub CalcButton_Click(ByVal sender As Object, ByVal e As System.EventArgs) Ha
    Dim intBlue, intYellow, intTotalBoards As Integer
    Dim sngPrice, sngRate, sngSubtotal, sngSalesTax, sngTotalPrice As Single
    'assign values to variables
    intBlue = Val(Me.BlueTextBox.Text)
    intYellow = Val(Me.YellowTextBox.Text)
    sngPrice = Val(Me.PriceTextBox.Text)
    sngRate = Val(Me.RateTextBox.Text)
    'perform calculations
    intTotalBoards = intBlue + intYellow
    sngSubtotal = intTotalBoards * sngPrice
    sngSalesTax = sngSubtotal * sngRate
    sngTotalPrice = sngSubtotal + sngSalesTax
    'display total amounts in controls
    Me.TotalBoardsLabel.Text = intTotalBoards
    Me.TotalPriceLabel.Text = Format(sngTotalPrice, "currency")
    Me.MessageLabel.Text = "The sales tax was " _
        & Format(sngSalesTax, "currency") & "." & mstrSalesPerson
    Me.ClearButton.Focus()
End Sub
```

add this to the assignment statement

Figure 3-32: Modified assignment statement

Next, save the solution and start the application to test the code in the form's Load event procedure and in the Calculate Order button's Click event procedure.

7 Save the solution and then start the application. The Name Entry dialog box created by the InputBox function appears first. See Figure 3-33.

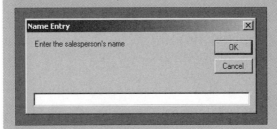

Figure 3-33: Dialog box created by the InputBox function

8 Type your name in the input area of the dialog box, then click the **OK** button. The order form appears.

9 Click the **Calculate Order** button. Your name appears in the MessageLabel control; however, it appears much too close to the period.

At this point you could replace the period (".") in the MessageLabel control's assignment statement with a period and two spaces (". "). Or, you could display the salesperson's name on the next line in the MessageLabel control. You will use the newline character, which you learn about in the next section, to place the name on a separate line.

10 Click the **Exit** button. When you return to the Code editor window, close the Output window.

tip
....
Chr, which stands for "character," is a function.

The Newline Character

The newline character, which is Chr(13) & Chr(10), instructs the computer to issue a carriage return followed by a line feed. The combination of the carriage return followed by a line feed will advance the insertion point to the next line in the MessageLabel control. Whenever you want to start a new line, you simply type the newline character at that location in your code. In this case, for example, you want to advance to a new line after displaying the period—in other words, before displaying the salesperson's name.

You could include the newline character in the MessageLabel control's assignment statement, like this: Me.MessageLabel.Text = "The sales tax was " & Format (sngSalesTax, "currency") & "." & Chr(13) & Chr(10) & mstrSalesPerson. The disadvantage of using Chr(13) & Chr(10) in your code is that it forces you and the next programmer looking at your code to remember that this combination of the Chr function displays a new line. A better way of displaying a new line is to use one of the Visual Basic .NET intrinsic constants in your code. An **intrinsic constant** is a named constant that is built into Visual Basic .NET itself. In other words, although you could create your own named constant for the Chr(13) & Chr(10) combination, you do not have to because Visual Basic .NET already has created one for you. You can use the Object Browser window to view the names of the intrinsic constants available in Visual Basic .NET.

The Object Browser

The **Object Browser** is a window that provides information about the various objects available to your application. The information includes properties, methods, events, and intrinsic constants. You open the Object Browser window by clicking View on the menu bar, pointing to Other Windows, and then clicking Object Browser.

To use the Object Browser window to view the intrinsic constants available in Visual Basic .NET:

1   Click **View** on the menu bar, point to **Other Windows**, and then click **Object Browser**. The Object Browser window opens.

2   If necessary, expand the Microsoft Visual Basic .NET Runtime node by clicking its plus box ⊞. If necessary, expand the Microsoft.VisualBasic node by clicking its plus box ⊞.

3   Click **Constants** in the Objects list. The names of the intrinsic constants available in Visual Basic .NET appear in the Members of 'Constants' list, as shown in Figure 3-34. (You may need to scroll up the Objects list box to view the Microsoft Visual Basic .NET Runtime entry in the list.)

Close button

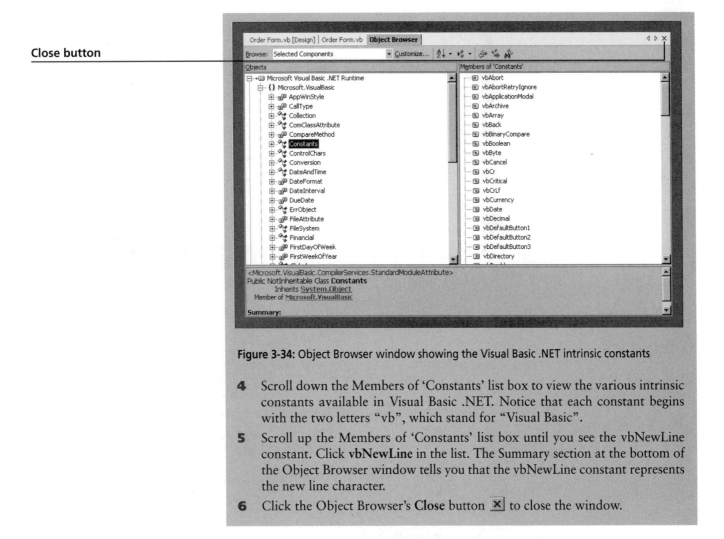

Figure 3-34: Object Browser window showing the Visual Basic .NET intrinsic constants

4   Scroll down the Members of 'Constants' list box to view the various intrinsic constants available in Visual Basic .NET. Notice that each constant begins with the two letters "vb", which stand for "Visual Basic".

5   Scroll up the Members of 'Constants' list box until you see the vbNewLine constant. Click **vbNewLine** in the list. The Summary section at the bottom of the Object Browser window tells you that the vbNewLine constant represents the new line character.

6   Click the Object Browser's **Close** button ☒ to close the window.

You will use the vbNewLine constant to display the salesperson's name on a separate line in the MessageLabel control.

To use the vbNewLine constant to display the salesperson's name on a separate line:

1   Modify the MessageLabel control's assignment statement as indicated in Figure 3-35. This will complete the CalcButton Click event procedure.

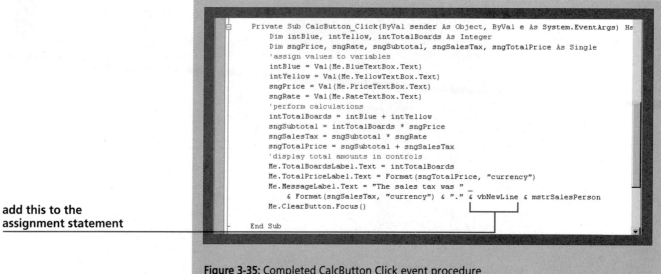

```
Private Sub CalcButton_Click(ByVal sender As Object, ByVal e As System.EventArgs) Ha
    Dim intBlue, intYellow, intTotalBoards As Integer
    Dim sngPrice, sngRate, sngSubtotal, sngSalesTax, sngTotalPrice As Single
    'assign values to variables
    intBlue = Val(Me.BlueTextBox.Text)
    intYellow = Val(Me.YellowTextBox.Text)
    sngPrice = Val(Me.PriceTextBox.Text)
    sngRate = Val(Me.RateTextBox.Text)
    'perform calculations
    intTotalBoards = intBlue + intYellow
    sngSubtotal = intTotalBoards * sngPrice
    sngSalesTax = sngSubtotal * sngRate
    sngTotalPrice = sngSubtotal + sngSalesTax
    'display total amounts in controls
    Me.TotalBoardsLabel.Text = intTotalBoards
    Me.TotalPriceLabel.Text = Format(sngTotalPrice, "currency")
    Me.MessageLabel.Text = "The sales tax was " _
        & Format(sngSalesTax, "currency") & "." & vbNewLine & mstrSalesPerson
    Me.ClearButton.Focus()
End Sub
```

add this to the assignment statement

Figure 3-35: Completed CalcButton Click event procedure

2   Save the solution and then start the application. The Name Entry dialog box created by the InputBox function appears first. See Figure 3-36.

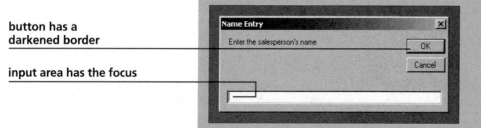

button has a darkened border

input area has the focus

Figure 3-36: Focus and default button shown in the dialog box

Notice that the OK button in the dialog box has a darkened border, even though it does not have the focus; the input area has the focus, as indicated by the position of the insertion point. In Windows terminology, a button that has a darkened border when it does not have the focus is called the default button. You can select a default button by pressing Enter at any time. You try this next.

3   Type your name in the input area of the dialog box. Then, instead of clicking the OK button, simply press **Enter**. The order form appears.

4   Click the **Calculate Order** button. Your name now appears on a separate line in the MessageLabel control.

5   Click the **Exit** button to end the application. When you return to the Code editor window, close the Output window.

In the next section, you designate a default button for the order form.

A Windows form also has a CancelButton property, which determines which button's Click event procedure is processed when the user presses the Esc key.

GUI
Design Tips

Rules for Assigning the Default Button

- The default button should be the button that is most often selected by the user, except in cases where the tasks performed by the button are both destructive and irreversible. The default button typically is the first button.

Designating a Default Button

As you already know from using Windows applications, you can select a button by clicking it or by pressing Enter when the button has the focus. If you make a button the **default button**, you also can select it by pressing Enter even when the button does not have the focus. When a button is selected, the computer processes the code contained in the button's Click event procedure.

The default button in an interface should be the button that is most often selected by the user, except in cases where the tasks performed by the button are both destructive and irreversible; for example, a button that deletes information should not be designated as the default button. If you assign a default button in an interface, it typically is the first button, which means that it is on the left when the buttons are positioned along the bottom of the screen, and on the top when the buttons are stacked in either the upper-right or lower-right corner.

You specify the default button (if any) by setting the Windows form's **AcceptButton property**. The property's initial value is (none), which indicates that the form does not have a default button. In the next set of steps, you use the AcceptButton property to make the Calculate Order button the default button on the order form.

To make the Calculate Order button the default button, then save the solution and start the application:

1 Click the **Order Form.vb [Design]** tab to return to the designer window.

2 Click the **form's title bar**, if necessary, to select the form, then set the form's AcceptButton property to **CalcButton**. A darkened border appears around the Calculate Order button, as shown in Figure 3-37.

default button has a darkened border

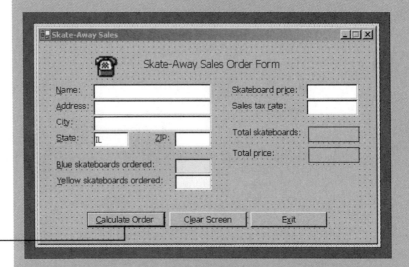

Figure 3-37: Darkened border shown around the Calculate Order button

3 Save the solution, and then start the application. When prompted for the salesperson's name, type your name and press **Enter**.

4 When the order form appears, enter **10** as the number of blue skateboards ordered, **100** as the skateboard price, and **.1** as the sales tax rate. Press **Enter** to calculate the order. "The sales tax was $100.00." and your name appear in the MessageLabel control.

5 Click the **Exit** button. When you return to the Code editor window, close the Output window.

6 Click **File** on the menu bar, then click **Close Solution**.

You now have completed Lesson B. In Lesson C you modify the Skate-Away Sales application so that it requests the salesperson's name before each order is calculated. Now you can either take a break or complete the end-of-lesson questions and exercises before moving on to the next lesson.

SUMMARY

To concatenate strings:

■ Use the concatenation operator—the ampersand (&). Be sure to put a space before and after the ampersand.

To display a dialog box containing a prompt, an input area, an OK button, and a Cancel button:

■ Use the InputBox function, whose syntax is **InputBox**(*prompt*[, *title*][, *default-Response*]). The *prompt*, *title*, and *defaultResponse* arguments must be enclosed in quotation marks, unless the information is stored in a variable or named constant. Use sentence capitalization for the *prompt*, but book title capitalization for the *title*.

■ If the user clicks the OK button, the InputBox function returns the value contained in the input area of the dialog box. If the user clicks either the Cancel button or the Close button ☒, the InputBox function returns a zero-length (or empty) string.

To view information about the various objects available to an application:

■ Use the Object Browser window. To open the Object Browser, click View on the menu bar, point to Other Windows, and then click Object Browser.

To advance the insertion point to the next line:

■ Use the vbNewLine constant in code. Its value is `Chr(13)` & `Chr(10)`.

To make a button the default button:

■ Set the Windows form's AcceptButton property to the name of the button.

QUESTIONS

1. The InputBox function displays a dialog box containing which of the following?
   a. Cancel button
   b. input area
   c. OK button
   d. prompt
   e. All of the above.

2. Which of the following is the concatenation operator?
   a. @
   b. #
   c. $
   d. &
   e. *

3. Assume the strRegion1 variable contains the string "North" and the strRegion2 variable contains the string "West". Which of the following will display the string "NorthWest" (one word) in the RegionLabel control?
   a. `Me.RegionLabel.Text = strRegion1 & strRegion2`
   b. `Me.RegionLabel.Text = "strRegion1" & "strRegion2"`
   c. `Me.RegionLabel.Text = strRegion1 $ strRegion2`
   d. `Me.RegionLabel.Text = strRegion1 # strRegion2`
   e. `Me.RegionLabel.Text = strRegion1 @ strRegion2`

4. Assume the strCity variable contains the string "Boston" and the strState variable contains the string "MA". Which of the following will display the string "Boston, MA" (the city, a comma, a space, and the state) in the AddressLabel control?
   a. `Me.AddressLabel.Text = strCity #, & strState`
   b. `Me.AddressLabel.Text = "strCity" & ", " & "strState"`
   c. `Me.AddressLabel.Text = strCity $ ", " $ strState`
   d. `Me.AddressLabel.Text = strCity & ", " & strState`
   e. `Me.AddressLabel.Text = "strCity," & "strState"`

5. Which of the following intrinsic constants advances the insertion point to the next line?
   a. Advance
   b. Next
   c. vbAdvance
   d. vbNewLine
   e. None of the above.

6. If you want to give the user the ability to select a specific button when the button does not have the focus, set the form's _____ property to the name of the button.
   a. AcceptButton
   b. DefaultButton
   c. EnterButton
   d. FocusButton
   e. None of the above.

7. You can use the _____ window to view the Visual Basic .NET intrinsic constants.
   a. Constant Browser
   b. Constant Finder
   c. Find Constant
   d. Object Browser
   e. Object Finder

8. Which of the following prompts the user for a number, and then correctly assigns the user's response to the sngNum variable?
   a. `InputBox("Enter a number:", "Number") = sngNum`
   b. `sngNum = Chr(InputBox("Enter a number:", "Number"))`
   c. `sngNum = InputBox("Enter a number:", "Number")`
   d. `sngNum = Val(InputBox("Enter a number:", "Number")`
   e. `sngNum = Val(InputBox("Enter a number:", "Number"))`

9. Which of the following prompts the user for the name of a city, and then correctly assigns the user's response to the strCity variable?
   a. `InputBox("Enter the city:", "City") = strCity`
   b. `strCity = Chr(InputBox("Enter the city:", "City"))`
   c. `strCity = InputBox("Enter the city:", "City")`
   d. `strCity = Val(InputBox("Enter the city:", "City")`
   e. `strCity = Val(InputBox("Enter the city:", "City"))`

EXERCISES

1. In this exercise, you modify the code in an existing application so that it uses variables rather than control properties. The application calculates the commission earned on a salesperson's sales using a commission rate of 10%.
   a. If necessary, start Visual Studio .NET. Open the Commission Solution (Commission Solution.sln) file, which is contained in the VBNET\Tut03\Commission Solution folder. If the designer window is not open, right-click the form file's name in the Solution Explorer window, then click View Designer.
   b. Make the Calculate Commission button the default button.
   c. Review the code in the Calculate Commission button's Click event procedure. Recode the procedure so that it uses variables rather than control properties in the equation that calculates the commission.
   d. Save the solution, then start the application. Test the application by calculating the commission for Mary Smith, whose sales are 7500.
   e. Click the Exit button to end the application.
   f. Close the Output window, then close the solution.

2. In this exercise, you code an application that calculates the square root of a number.
   a. If necessary, start Visual Studio .NET. Open the Square Root Solution (Square Root Solution.sln) file, which is contained in the VBNET\Tut03\Square Root Solution folder. If the designer window is not open, right-click the form file's name in the Solution Explorer window, then click View Designer.
   b. Make the Calculate Square Root button the default button.

c. Code the Calculate Square Root button so that it calculates and displays the square root of a whole number. Be sure to assign the numeric equivalent of the NumberTextBox.Text property to an Integer variable. Assign the square root of the number to a Single variable. You can use the Math.Sqrt function, whose syntax is **Math.Sqrt(*number*)**, to calculate the square root.

d. Save the solution, then start the application. Test the application by calculating the square root of 144.

e. Click the Exit button to end the application.

f. Close the Output window, then close the solution.

3. In this exercise, you code an application for Mingo Sales. The application allows the sales manager to enter the sales made in three states. It should calculate both the total sales made and the total commission earned in the three states.

a. If necessary, start Visual Studio .NET. Open the Mingo Solution (Mingo Solution.sln) file, which is contained in the VBNET\Tut03\Mingo Solution folder. If the designer window is not open, right-click the form file's name in the Solution Explorer window, then click View Designer.

b. Make the Commission button the default button.

c. Code the Exit button so that it ends the application when it is clicked.

d. Use the pseudocode shown in Figure 3-38 to code the Commission button's Click event procedure. (Be sure to use variables.) Format the total sales and the commission using the Standard format style.

Commission button

1. declare variables for the three state sales, the total sales, and the commission

2. assign values to variables

3. calculate total sales = New York sales + Maine sales + Florida sales

4. calculate commission = total sales * 5%

5. display total sales and commission in the TotalSalesLabel and CommissionLabel controls

6. send the focus to the New York sales text box

Figure 3-38

e. Save the solution, then start the application. Test the application by calculating the total sales and commission for the following sales amounts:

New York sales: 15000

Maine sales: 25000

Florida sales: 10500

f. Click the Exit button to end the application, then close the Output window.

g. Code the form's Load event procedure so that it uses the InputBox function to ask the user for the commission rate before the form appears.

h. Save the solution, then start the application. When you are prompted to enter the commission rate, type .1 (the decimal equivalent of 10%) and then click the OK button. Test the application by calculating the total sales and commission for the following sales amounts:

New York sales: 26000

Maine sales: 34000

Florida sales: 17000

i. Click the Exit button to end the application.

j. Close the Output window, then close the solution.

4. In this exercise, you code an application for IMY Industries. The application should calculate the new hourly pay for each of three job codes, given the current hourly pay for each job code and the raise percentage (entered as a decimal number). The application should display the message "Raise percentage: XX" in a label control on the form. The XX in the message should be replaced by the actual raise percentage, formatted using the Percent format style.

    a. If necessary, start Visual Studio .NET. Open the IMY Solution (IMY Solution.sln) file, which is contained in the VBNET\Tut03\IMY Solution folder. If the designer window is not open, right-click the form file's name in the Solution Explorer window, then click View Designer.

    b. Code the Exit button so that it ends the application when it is clicked.

    c. Before the form appears, use the InputBox function to prompt the personnel clerk to enter the raise percentage. You will use the raise percentage to calculate the new hourly pay for each job code.

    d. Use the pseudocode shown in Figure 3-39 to code the New Hourly Pay button's Click event procedure. Create a named constant for the "Raise percentage: " message. Format the new hourly pay using the Standard format style. Format the raise rate (in the message) using the Percent format style.

New Hourly Pay button

1. declare variables and constant

2. assign values to variables

3. calculate new hourly pay = current hourly pay * raise rate + current hourly pay

4. display new hourly pay in appropriate label controls

5. display message and raise rate in MessageLabel control

6. send the focus to the Job Code 1 text box

Figure 3-39

    e. Save the solution, then start the application. When you are prompted to enter the raise percentage, type .05 (the decimal equivalent of 5%) and then click the OK button. Use the following information to calculate the new hourly pay for each job code:

    Current hourly pay for job code 1:   5
    Current hourly pay for job code 2:   6.5
    Current hourly pay for job code 3:   8.75

    f. Click the Exit button to end the application.

    g. Close the Output window, then close the solution.

5. In this exercise, you modify the application that you coded in Exercise 4. The application now will allow the user to enter a separate raise percentage for each job code.

    a. If necessary, start Visual Studio .NET. Open the IMY Solution (IMY Solution.sln) file, which is contained in the VBNET\Tut03\IMY Solution folder. If the designer window is not open, right-click the form file's name in the Solution Explorer window, then click View Designer.

    b. Modify the application's code so that it asks the personnel clerk to enter the raise for each job code separately. (*Hint*: Use three InputBox functions in the form's Load event procedure.)

c. Display the following information on separate lines in the MessageLabel control (be sure to replace XX with the appropriate raise percentage):
Job Code 1: XX%
Job Code 2: XX%
Job Code 3: XX%

d. Save the solution, then start the application. When you are prompted to enter the raise percentages for the job codes, use .03 for job code 1, .05 for job code 2, and .045 for job code 3.

e. Use the following information to calculate the new hourly pay for each job code:
Current hourly pay for job code 1:   5
Current hourly pay for job code 2:   6.5
Current hourly pay for job code 3:   8.75

f. Click the Exit button to end the application.

g. Close the Output window, then close the solution.

Use the information shown in Figure 3-40 to complete Exercises 6 through 8.

Variable/Constant name	Contents
strCity	Madison
strState	WI
strZip	53711
conMessage	The capital of

Figure 3-40

6. Using the information shown in Figure 3-40, write an assignment statement that displays the string "Madison, WI" in the AddressLabel control.

7. Using the information shown in Figure 3-40, write an assignment statement that displays the string "The capital of WI is Madison." in the AddressLabel control.

8. Using the information shown in Figure 3-40, write an assignment statement that displays the string "My ZIP code is 53711." in the AddressLabel control.

Exercises 9 and 10 are Discovery Exercises. Discovery Exercises, which may include topics that are not covered in this lesson, allow you to "discover" the solutions to problems on your own.

discovery ▶ 9. In this exercise, you learn about the CancelButton property of a Windows form.

a. If necessary, start Visual Studio .NET. Open the Cancel Solution (Cancel Solution.sln) file, which is contained in the VBNET\Tut03\Cancel Solution folder. If the designer window is not open, right-click the form file's name in the Solution Explorer window, then click View Designer.

b. Open the Code editor window and view the existing code.

c. Start the application. Type your first name in the text box, then press Enter to select the Clear button, which is the form's default button. The Clear button removes your name from the text box.

d. Click the Undo button. Your name reappears in the text box.

e. Click the Exit button to end the application, then close the Output window.

f. Return to the designer window. Set the form's CancelButton property to UndoButton. This tells the computer to process the code in the Undo button's Click event procedure when the user presses Esc.

g. Save the solution, then start the application.

h. Type your first name in the text box, then press Enter to select the Clear button.

i. Press Esc to select the Undo button. Your name reappears in the text box.

j. Click the Exit button to end the application.

k. Close the Output window, then close the solution.

discovery ▶   **10.** In this exercise, you practice using the Object Browser.

a. If necessary, start Visual Studio .NET. Open the Order Solution (Order Solution.sln) file, which is contained in the VBNET\Tut03\Order Solution folder.

b. Open the Object Browser window. Click the Find Symbol ⚇ button. (If you cannot locate the Find Symbol button, refer to Figure 3-41.) When the Find Symbol dialog box opens, type math in the Find what box, as shown in Figure 3-41.

Find Symbol button

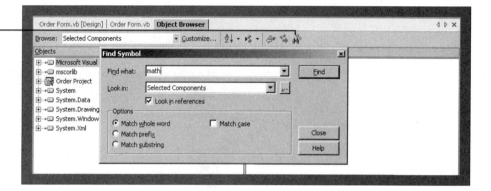

Figure 3-41

c. Click the Find button in the dialog box. The Find Symbol Results window opens. Click the Close button in the Find Symbol dialog box.

d. Right-click Math (System) in the Find Symbol Results window, then click Browse Definition. Close the Find Symbol Results window.

e. Scroll to the bottom of the Members of 'Math' list box. What is the value assigned to the E named constant? What is the value assigned to the PI named constant?

f. Click the Find Symbol ⚇ button. Use the Find Symbol dialog box to find the word *color*. When the Find Symbol Results window opens, close the Find Symbol dialog box. Right-click Color (System.Drawing) in the Find Symbol Results window, then click Browse Definition. Close the Find Symbol Results window.

g. Scroll the Members of 'Color' list box to view the various color settings.

h. Close the Object Browser window, then close the solution.

After completing this lesson, you will be able to:

■ Include a static variable in code

■ Code the TextChanged event procedure

■ Create a procedure that handles more than one event

Modifying the Skate-Away Sales Application's Code

Modifying the Code in the Load Event and CalcButton Click Event Procedures

Mr. Cousard, the sales manager at Skate-Away Sales, asks you to make an additional change to the order form that you completed in Lesson B. Currently, the order form allows the user to enter the salesperson's name only once, when the application first starts. Mr. Cousard would like to have the order form ask for the salesperson's name each time an order is calculated. This way, while a salesperson is at lunch or on a break, another salesperson can use the same computer to take an order, without having to start the application again.

As you learned in Lesson B, before making modifications to an application's existing code, you should review the application's documentation and revise the necessary documents. First, view the revised TOE chart, which is shown in Figure 3-42. Changes made to the TOE chart from Lesson B are shaded in the figure. (Lesson B's TOE chart is shown in Figure 3-14.) Notice that the Calculate Order button's Click event procedure, rather than the OrderForm's Load event procedure, now is responsible for getting the salesperson's name.

Task	Object	Event
1. Get the salesperson's name 2. Calculate the total skateboards ordered and the total price 3. Display the total skateboards ordered and the total price in the TotalBoardsLabel and TotalPriceLabel 4. Calculate the sales tax 5. Display the message, sales tax, and salesperson's name in the MessageLabel	CalcButton	Click
Clear the screen for the next order	ClearButton	Click
End the application	ExitButton	Click
Display the total skateboards ordered (from CalcButton)	TotalBoardsLabel	None
Display the total price (from CalcButton)	TotalPriceLabel	None
Get and display the order information	NameTextBox, AddressTextBox, CityTextBox, StateTextBox, ZipTextBox, PriceTextBox, RateTextBox, BlueTextBox, YellowTextBox	None
~~Get the salesperson's name~~	~~OrderForm~~	~~Load~~
Display the message, sales tax, and salesperson's name (from CalcButton)	MessageLabel	None

you can remove this line because you no longer need to code the Load event

Figure 3-42: Revised TOE chart

Next, view the revised pseudocode for the Calculate Order button's Click event procedure, which is shown in Figure 3-43. Changes made to the pseudocode from Lesson B are shaded in the figure. (Lesson B's pseudocode is shown in Figure 3-16.)

Calculate Order button

1. declare variables and named constants

2. assign values to variables

3. get the salesperson's name

4. calculate total skateboards = blue skateboards + yellow skateboards

5. calculate subtotal = total skateboards * skateboard price

6. calculate sales tax = subtotal * sales tax rate

7. calculate total price = subtotal + sales tax

8. display total skateboards and total price in TotalBoardsLabel and TotalPriceLabel controls

9. display "The sales tax was" message, sales tax, and salesperson's name in the MessageLabel control

10. send the focus to the Clear Screen button

Figure 3-43: Revised pseudocode for the Calculate Order button

First, open the Skate-Away Sales application and move the code contained in the OrderForm's Load event procedure to the CalcButton's Click event procedure.

To open the application and move the code:

1 Start Microsoft Visual Studio .NET, if necessary. Close the Start Page window.

2 Click **File** on the menu bar, and then click **Open Solution**. Open the **Order Solution** (Order Solution.sln) file, which is contained in the VBNET\Tut03\Order Solution folder.

3 If the Code editor window is not open, right-click **Order Form.vb** in the Solution Explorer window, then click **View Code**.

4 Locate the OrderForm Load event procedure. Highlight the first comment and the two Const instructions in the procedure. Click **Edit** on the menu bar, and then click **Cut**.

It is customary to place any local constant declaration statements at the beginning of the procedure, below the Dim statements.

5 Locate the CalcButton Click event procedure. Insert a blank line below the second Dim statement in the procedure. With the insertion point in the blank line, click **Edit** on the menu bar, and then click **Paste** to paste the comment and two Const statements into the procedure.

6 Return to the OrderForm Load event procedure. Highlight the remaining comment and assignment statement. Click **Edit** on the menu bar, and then click **Cut**.

7 Return to the CalcButton Click event procedure. Insert a blank line below the `sngRate = Val(Me.RateTextBox.Text)` instruction. With the insertion point in the blank line, click **Edit** on the menu bar, and then click **Paste** to paste the comment and assignment statement into the procedure.

8 Highlight **form-level** in the comment, and then press **Delete** twice. If necessary, remove the blank line above the `'perform calculations` comment. The modified CalcButton Click event procedure is shown in Figure 3-44. (The procedure's `End Sub` statement does not appear in the figure.)

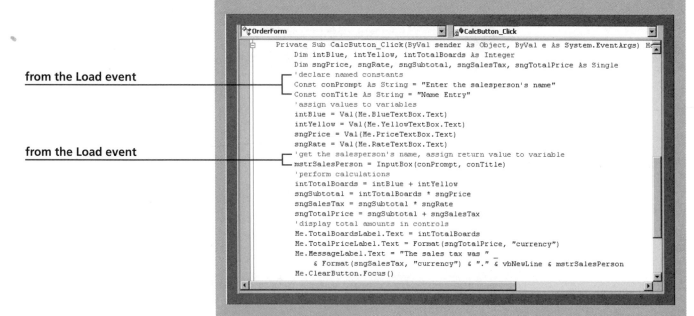

```
OrderForm                                    CalcButton_Click
        Private Sub CalcButton_Click(ByVal sender As Object, ByVal e As System.EventArgs) H
            Dim intBlue, intYellow, intTotalBoards As Integer
            Dim sngPrice, sngRate, sngSubtotal, sngSalesTax, sngTotalPrice As Single
            'declare named constants
            Const conPrompt As String = "Enter the salesperson's name"
            Const conTitle As String = "Name Entry"
            'assign values to variables
            intBlue = Val(Me.BlueTextBox.Text)
            intYellow = Val(Me.YellowTextBox.Text)
            sngPrice = Val(Me.PriceTextBox.Text)
            sngRate = Val(Me.RateTextBox.Text)
            'get the salesperson's name, assign return value to variable
            mstrSalesPerson = InputBox(conPrompt, conTitle)
            'perform calculations
            intTotalBoards = intBlue + intYellow
            sngSubtotal = intTotalBoards * sngPrice
            sngSalesTax = sngSubtotal * sngRate
            sngTotalPrice = sngSubtotal + sngSalesTax
            'display total amounts in controls
            Me.TotalBoardsLabel.Text = intTotalBoards
            Me.TotalPriceLabel.Text = Format(sngTotalPrice, "currency")
            Me.MessageLabel.Text = "The sales tax was " _
                & Format(sngSalesTax, "currency") & "." & vbNewLine & mstrSalesPerson
            Me.ClearButton.Focus()
```

from the Load event

from the Load event

Figure 3-44: Modified CalcButton Click event procedure

9 Return to the OrderForm Load event procedure. Highlight the remaining lines in the procedure, beginning with the `Private Sub` line and ending with the `End Sub` line. Press **Delete** to delete the lines from the Code editor window.

Now that you have moved the InputBox function from the OrderForm Load event procedure to the CalcButton Click event procedure, only one procedure—the CalcButton Click event procedure—needs to use the mstrSalesPerson variable. Therefore, you can move the statement that declares the mstrSalesPerson variable from the form's Declarations section to the CalcButton Click event procedure. Additionally, you will need to change the keyword Private to the keyword Dim, and you should change the variable's name from mstrSalesPerson to strSalesPerson to indicate that it no longer is a form-level variable.

To move the mstrSalesPerson variable declaration statement, then modify the statement, and then save the solution and start the application:

1 Locate the form's Declarations section. Highlight the `'declare form-level variable` comment, then press **Delete** to delete the comment.

2 Highlight the `Private mstrSalesPerson As String` statement in the Declarations section. Click **Edit** on the menu bar, and then click **Cut**.

3 Locate the CalcButton Click event procedure. Insert a blank line below the second Dim statement in the CalcButton Click event procedure. With the insertion point in the blank line, click **Edit** on the menu bar, and then click **Paste** to paste the Private statement in the procedure.

4 Change Private in the variable declaration statement to **Dim**, and change mstrSalesPerson to **strSalesPerson**. Notice that a jagged line appears below the variable name, mstrSalesPerson, in two assignment statements in the procedure.

5 Change mstrSalesPerson to **strSalesPerson** in both assignment statements, as indicated in Figure 3-45.

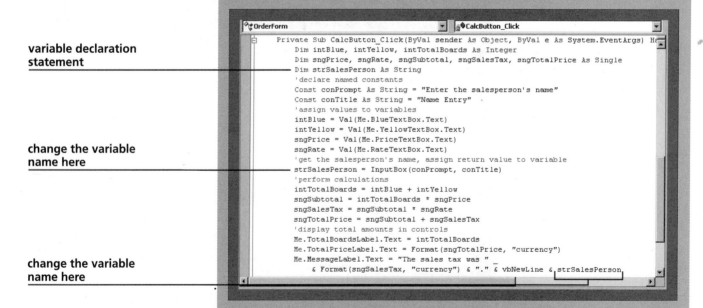

variable declaration statement

change the variable name here

change the variable name here

```
OrderForm                              CalcButton_Click
      Private Sub CalcButton_Click(ByVal sender As Object, ByVal e As System.EventArgs) H
            Dim intBlue, intYellow, intTotalBoards As Integer
            Dim sngPrice, sngRate, sngSubtotal, sngSalesTax, sngTotalPrice As Single
            Dim strSalesPerson As String
            'declare named constants
            Const conPrompt As String = "Enter the salesperson's name"
            Const conTitle As String = "Name Entry"
            'assign values to variables
            intBlue = Val(Me.BlueTextBox.Text)
            intYellow = Val(Me.YellowTextBox.Text)
            sngPrice = Val(Me.PriceTextBox.Text)
            sngRate = Val(Me.RateTextBox.Text)
            'get the salesperson's name, assign return value to variable
            strSalesPerson = InputBox(conPrompt, conTitle)
            'perform calculations
            intTotalBoards = intBlue + intYellow
            sngSubtotal = intTotalBoards * sngPrice
            sngSalesTax = sngSubtotal * sngRate
            sngTotalPrice = sngSubtotal + sngSalesTax
            'display total amounts in controls
            Me.TotalBoardsLabel.Text = intTotalBoards
            Me.TotalPriceLabel.Text = Format(sngTotalPrice, "currency")
            Me.MessageLabel.Text = "The sales tax was " _
                & Format(sngSalesTax, "currency") & "." & vbNewLine & strSalesPerson
```

Figure 3-45: Changes made to the variable declaration and two assignment statements

Now save the solution and start it to verify that the application works correctly.

6   Click **File** on the menu bar, and then click **Save All**. Click **Debug** on the menu bar, and then click **Start**. The order form appears.

7   Enter 10 as the number of yellow skateboards ordered, **100** as the skateboard price, and **.1** as the sales tax rate. Press **Enter** to calculate the order. The Name Entry dialog box created by the InputBox function appears.

8   Type your name in the Name Entry dialog box, then press **Enter**. "The sales tax was $100.00." and your name appear in the MessageLabel control.

9   Click the **Calculate Order** button. Notice that the Name Entry dialog box requires the user to enter the salesperson's name again. It would be more efficient for the user if the salesperson's name appeared as the default response the second and subsequent times the Calculate Order button is clicked.

10 Click the **Cancel** button in the dialog box, then click the **Exit** button on the order form. When you return to the Code editor window, close the Output window.

Recall that the InputBox function allows you to specify a default response, which appears in the input area of the dialog box when the dialog box is opened. Observe the effect of using the contents of the strSalesPerson variable as the default response.

▶ Recall that when you click the Cancel button in the InputBox function's dialog box, the function returns a zero-length (empty) string.

To modify the InputBox function:

1   Change the `strSalesPerson = InputBox(conPrompt, conTitle)` statement in the CalcButton Click event procedure to **strSalesPerson = InputBox(conPrompt, conTitle, strSalesPerson)**.

2   Save the solution, then start the application.

3   Click the **Calculate Order** button to calculate the order. Type your name in the Name Entry dialog box, then press **Enter**. "The sales tax was $0.00." and your name appear in the MessageLabel control.

4   Click the **Calculate Order** button again. Notice that your name still does not appear in the input area of the dialog box. This is because the strSalesPerson variable is both created in and removed from the computer's internal memory each time you click the Calculate Order button. (Recall that the Dim statement creates the variable in memory, and the variable is removed from memory when the End Sub statement is processed.)

To display the salesperson's name in the dialog box when the Calculate Order button is clicked the second and subsequent times, you need to use a static variable.

5   Click the **Cancel** button in the dialog box, then click the **Exit** button on the order form to end the application. When you return to the Code editor window, close the Output window.

Static Variables

A **static variable** is a local variable that retains its value even when the procedure in which it is declared ends. Similar to a form-level variable, a static variable is not removed from memory until the application ends. You declare a static variable using the syntax **Static** *variablename* [**As** *datatype*] [= *initialvalue*].

To declare the strSalesPerson variable as a static variable, then test the application:

1   Change the `Dim strSalesPerson As String` statement in the CalcButton Click event procedure to **Static strSalesPerson As String**. See Figure 3-46. (The Code editor's font type and size were changed so that you could view more of the code in the figure.)

static variable declaration

```
OrderForm                                    CalcButton_Click

Private Sub CalcButton_Click(ByVal sender As Object, ByVal e As System.EventArgs) Handles CalcButton.Click
    Dim intBlue, intYellow, intTotalBoards As Integer
    Dim sngPrice, sngRate, sngSubtotal, sngSalesTax, sngTotalPrice As Single
    Static strSalesPerson As String
    'declare named constants
    Const conPrompt As String = "Enter the salesperson's name"
    Const conTitle As String = "Name Entry"
    'assign values to variables
    intBlue = Val(Me.BlueTextBox.Text)
    intYellow = Val(Me.YellowTextBox.Text)
    sngPrice = Val(Me.PriceTextBox.Text)
    sngRate = Val(Me.RateTextBox.Text)
    'get the salesperson's name, assign return value to variable
    strSalesPerson = InputBox(conPrompt, conTitle, strSalesPerson)
    'perform calculations
    intTotalBoards = intBlue + intYellow
    sngSubtotal = intTotalBoards * sngPrice
    sngSalesTax = sngSubtotal * sngRate
    sngTotalPrice = sngSubtotal + sngSalesTax
    'display total amounts in controls
    Me.TotalBoardsLabel.Text = intTotalBoards
    Me.TotalPriceLabel.Text = Format(sngTotalPrice, "currency")
    Me.MessageLabel.Text = "The sales tax was " _
        & Format(sngSalesTax, "currency") & "." & vbNewLine & strSalesPerson
    Me.ClearButton.Focus()
```

Figure 3-46: Static variable declared in the completed CalcButton Click event procedure

2   Save the solution, then start the application.

3   Press **Enter** to calculate the order. Type your name in the Name Entry dialog box, and then press **Enter**. "The sales tax was $0.00." and your name appear in the MessageLabel control.

4   Press **Enter** to clear the screen.

5   Enter **10** as the number of yellow skateboards ordered, **100** as the skateboard price, and **.05** as the sales tax rate. Press **Enter** to calculate the order. Notice that your name appears highlighted in the input area of the Name Entry dialog box. Press **Enter** to select the OK button in the dialog box. The application calculates the total skateboards ordered (10), total price ($1,050.00), and sales tax ($50.00).

6   Enter **20** as the number of blue skateboards ordered. Notice that, at this point, the total skateboards ordered, the total price, and the sales tax amount shown on the order form are incorrect, because they do not reflect the additional order of 20 blue skateboards. To display the correct amounts, you will need to recalculate the order by selecting the Calculate Order button.

7   Press **Enter** to recalculate the order, then press **Enter** to select the OK button in the Name Entry dialog box. The application calculates the total skateboards ordered (30), total price ($3,150.00), and sales tax ($150.00).

8   Click the **Exit** button to end the application. When you return to the Code editor window, close the Output window.

Having the previously calculated figures remain on the screen when a change is made to the interface could be misleading. A better approach is to clear the total skateboards ordered, total price, and sales tax message when a change is made to one of the following input items: the number of blue skateboards ordered, the number of yellow skateboards ordered, the skateboard price, or the sales tax rate.

Coding the TextChanged Event Procedure

A control's **TextChanged event** occurs when the contents of a control's Text property change. This can happen as a result of either the user entering data into the control, or the application's code assigning data to the control's Text property. In the next set of steps, you code the BlueTextBox TextChanged event procedure so that it clears the contents of the TotalBoardsLabel, TotalPriceLabel, and MessageLabel controls when the user changes the number of blue skateboards ordered.

To code the BlueTextBox TextChanged event procedure, then test the procedure:

1   Click the **Class Name** list arrow in the Code editor window, then click **BlueTextBox** in the list. Click the **Method Name** list arrow. Scroll the list until you see TextChanged, and then click **TextChanged**. The BlueTextBox TextChanged event procedure appears in the Code editor window.

2   Enter the three assignment statements shown in Figure 3-47.

```
Private Sub BlueTextBox_TextChanged(ByVal sender As Object, ByVal e As System.EventA
    Me.TotalBoardsLabel.Text = ""
    Me.TotalPriceLabel.Text = ""
    Me.MessageLabel.Text = ""

End Sub
```

Figure 3-47: Assignment statements entered in the BlueTextBox TextChanged event procedure

Now test the procedure to verify that it is working correctly.

3   Save the solution, then start the application.

4   Enter 5 as the number of blue skateboards ordered, 100 as the skateboard price, and .05 as the sales tax rate. Press **Enter** to calculate the order.

5   Type your name in the Name Entry dialog box, then press **Enter** to select the OK button. The application calculates the total skateboards ordered (5), total price ($525.00), and sales tax ($25.00).

6   Change the number of blue skateboards ordered to 3. Notice that when you make a change to the number of blue skateboards ordered, the application clears the total skateboards ordered, total price, and message information from the form.

7   Click the **Exit** button to end the application. When you return to the Code editor window, close the Output window.

Recall that you also want to clear the total skateboards ordered, total price, and message information when a change is made to the number of yellow skateboards ordered, skateboard price, or sales tax rate. You could code the TextChanged event procedure for the YellowTextBox, PriceTextBox, and RateTextBox controls separately, as you did with the BlueTextBox control. However, an easier way is simply to create one procedure for the computer to process when the TextChanged event of any of these controls occurs.

Associating a Procedure With Different Objects or Events

As you learned in Tutorial 1, the keyword Handles appears in a procedure header and indicates the object and event associated with the procedure. For example, the `Handles BlueTextBox.TextChanged` that appears at the end of the procedure header shown in Figure 3-48 indicates, not surprisingly, that the BlueTextBox_TextChanged procedure is associated with the TextChanged event of the BlueTextBox control. In other words, the BlueTextBox_TextChanged procedure will be processed when the TextChanged event of the BlueTextBox control occurs.

procedure name

Handles keyword

names of object and event

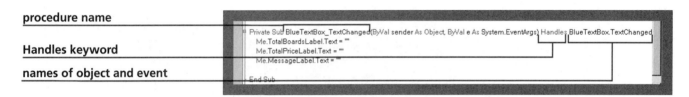

```
Private Sub BlueTextBox_TextChanged(ByVal sender As Object, ByVal e As System.EventArgs) Handles BlueTextBox.TextChanged
    Me.TotalBoardsLabel.Text = ""
    Me.TotalPriceLabel.Text = ""
    Me.MessageLabel.Text = ""
End Sub
```

Figure 3-48: Handles keyword shown in the procedure

Although the procedure name (BlueTextBox_TextChanged) shown in Figure 3-48 contains the object name (BlueTextBox) and event name (TextChanged), both of which appear after the Handles keyword, that is not a requirement. You can change the name of the procedure to anything you like. You also can associate a procedure with more than one object and event; to do so, you simply list each object and event, separated by commas, in the Handles section of the procedure header. In the Skate-Away Sales application, you will change the name of the BlueTextBox_TextChanged procedure to Clear. You then will associate the Clear procedure with the BlueTextBox.TextChanged, YellowTextBox.TextChanged, PriceTextBox.TextChanged, and RateTextBox.TextChanged events.

To change the BlueTextBox_TextChanged procedure's name to Clear, and then associate the procedure with different objects and events:

1 Change BlueTextBox_TextChanged, which appears after Private Sub in the procedure header, to **Clear**.

2 In the Clear procedure header, position your mouse pointer Ⅰ immediately before the letter H in the word **Handles**, and then click at that location. Type _ (the underscore, which is the line continuation character). Be sure there is a space between the ending parenthesis and the underscore.

3 Press **Enter** to move the Handles portion of the procedure header to the next line in the procedure. Press **Tab** two times to indent the line.

4 Position your mouse pointer Ⅰ immediately after `Handles BlueTextBox.TextChanged`, and then click at that location.

The Clear procedure is already associated with the BlueTextBox.TextChanged event. You just need to associate it with the YellowTextBox.TextChanged, PriceTextBox.TextChanged, and RateTextBox.TextChanged events.

5   Type , (a comma). Scroll the list of object names until you see YellowTextBox. Click **YellowTextBox** in the list, and then press **Tab** to enter the object name in the procedure.

6   Type . (a period), then scroll the list of event names until you see TextChanged. Click **TextChanged**, and then press **Tab**. Type , _ (a comma, a space, and an underscore) and press **Enter**.

7   Press the **Spacebar** to display the listing of object names, then enter the additional code shown in Figure 3-49.

enter this code

```
Private Sub Clear(ByVal sender As Object, ByVal e As System.EventArgs) _
        Handles BlueTextBox.TextChanged, YellowTextBox.TextChanged, _
        PriceTextBox.TextChanged, RateTextBox.TextChanged
    Me.TotalBoardsLabel.Text = ""
    Me.TotalPriceLabel.Text = ""
    Me.MessageLabel.Text = ""

End Sub
```

Figure 3-49: Completed Clear procedure

Now test the Clear procedure to verify that it is working correctly.

To test the Clear procedure:

1   Save the solution, then start the application.

2   Enter **5** as the number of blue skateboards ordered, **10** as the number of yellow skateboards ordered, **100** as the skateboard price, and **.05** as the sales tax rate. Press **Enter** to calculate the order.

3   Type your name in the Name Entry dialog box, then press **Enter** to select the OK button. The application calculates the total skateboards ordered (15), total price ($1,575.00), and sales tax ($75.00).

4   Change the skateboard price to **50**. When you do so, the application clears the total skateboards ordered, total price, and message information from the form.

5   Click the **Calculate Order** button, then click the **OK** button in the Name Entry dialog box.

6   On your own, verify that the Clear procedure clears the appropriate information when a change is made to the number of blue skateboards ordered, the number of yellow skateboards ordered, or the sales tax rate.

7   When you have finished testing the application, click the **Exit** button. When you return to the Code editor window, close the Output window.

8   Click **File** on the menu bar, and then click **Close Solution** to close the solution.

S U M M A R Y

To create a static variable:

■   Use a declaration statement that follows the syntax **Static** *variablename* [**As** *datatype*] [= *initialvalue*].

To process code when the contents of a control have changed:

■ Enter the code in the control's TextChanged event.

To create a procedure for more than one object or event:

■ List each object and event (using the syntax *object.event*) after the Handles keyword in the procedure.

Q U E S T I O N S

1. A _____ variable is a local variable that retains its value after the procedure in which it is declared ends.
   a. consistent
   b. constant
   c. static
   d. stationary
   e. term

2. Which of the following statements declares a local variable that retains its value after the procedure in which it is declared ends?
   a. `Const conCount As Integer`
   b. `Dim conCount As Constant`
   c. `Dim intCount As Integer`
   d. `Static intCount As Integer`
   e. None of the above.

3. The _____ event occurs when the contents of a text box have changed.
   a. Change
   b. Changed
   c. Text
   d. TextChange
   e. TextChanged

4. Assume you have a procedure named GetNumber. Which of the following instructions indicates that the procedure should be processed when the user clicks either the Num1TextBox or the Num2TextBox control?
   a. `Private Sub GetNumber(ByVal sender As Object, ByVal e As System.EventArgs) Handles Num1TextBox.Click, Num2TextBox.Click`
   b. `Private Sub GetNumber(ByVal sender As Object, ByVal e As System.EventArgs) Handles Num1TextBox, Num2TextBox`
   c. `Private Sub GetNumber(ByVal sender As Object, ByVal e As System.EventArgs) Handles Num1TextBox.Click and Num2TextBox.Click`
   d. `Private Sub GetNumber(ByVal sender As Object, ByVal e As System.EventArgs) Handles Click for Num1TextBox, Num2TextBox`
   e. None of the above.

E X E R C I S E S

The following list summarizes the GUI design guidelines you have learned so far. You can use this list to verify that the interfaces you create in the following exercises adhere to the GUI standards outlined in the book.

- ■ Information should flow either vertically or horizontally, with the most important information always located in the upper-left corner of the screen.

- ■ Maintain a consistent margin of two or three dots from the edge of the window.

- ■ Try to create a user interface that no one notices.

- ■ Related controls should be grouped together using white space, a GroupBox control, or a Panel control.

- ■ Set the form's FormBorderStyle, ControlBox, MaximizeBox, MinimizeBox, and StartPosition properties appropriately:

  - ■ A splash screen should not have a Minimize, Maximize, or Close button, and its borders should not be sizable.

  - ■ A form that is not a splash screen should always have a Minimize button and a Close button, but you can choose to disable the Maximize button. Typically, the FormBorderStyle property is set to Sizable, but also can be set to FixedSingle.

- ■ Position related controls on succeeding dots. Controls that are not part of any logical grouping may be positioned from two to four dots away from other controls.

- ■ Buttons should be positioned either in a row along the bottom of the screen, or stacked in either the upper-right or lower-right corner.

- ■ If the buttons are positioned at the bottom of the screen, then each button should be the same height; their widths, however, may vary.

- ■ If the buttons are stacked in either the upper-right or lower-right corner of the screen, then each should be the same height and the same width.

- ■ Use no more than six buttons on a screen.

- ■ The most commonly used button should be placed first.

- ■ The default button should be the button that is most often selected by the user, except in cases where the tasks performed by the button are both destructive and irreversible. The default button typically is the first button.

- ■ Button captions should:

  - ■ be meaningful
  - ■ be from one to three words
  - ■ appear on one line
  - ■ be entered using book title capitalization

- ■ Use labels to identify the text boxes in the interface, and position the label either above or to the left of the text box.

- Label text should:
  - be from one to three words
  - appear on one line
  - be left-justified
  - end with a colon (:)
  - be entered using sentence capitalization
- Labels that identify controls should have their BorderStyle property set to None.
- Labels that display program output, such as the result of a calculation, should have their BorderStyle property set to FixedSingle.
- Align controls to minimize the number of different margins.
- If you use a graphic in the interface, use a small one and place it in a location that will not distract the user.
- Use the Tahoma font for applications that will run on Windows 2000 or Windows XP.
- Use no more than two different font sizes, which should be 8, 9, 10, 11, or 12 point.
- Use only one font type, which should be a sans serif font, in the interface.
- Avoid using italics and underlining.
- Limit the use of bold text to titles, headings, and key items.
- Build the interface using black, white, and gray first, then add color only if you have a good reason to do so.
- Use white, off-white, light gray, pale blue, or pale yellow for an application's background, and black for the text.
- Limit the number of colors to three, not including white, black, and gray. The colors you choose should complement each other.
- Never use color as the only means of identification for an element in the user interface.
- Set each control's TabIndex property to a number that represents the order in which you want the control to receive the focus (begin with 0).
- A text box's TabIndex value should be one more than the TabIndex value of its identifying label.
- Assign a unique access key to each control (in the interface) that can receive user input (text boxes, buttons, and so on).
- When assigning an access key to a control, use the first letter of the caption or identifying label, unless another letter provides a more meaningful association. If you can't use the first letter and no other letter provides a more meaningful association, then use a distinctive consonant. Lastly, use a vowel or a number.
- Lock the controls in place on the form.
- Document the program internally.
- Use the Val function on any Text property involved in a calculation.

> ■ Use the Format function to improve the appearance of numbers in the interface.
>
> ■ In the InputBox function, use sentence capitalization for the *prompt,* and book title capitalization for the *title.*
>
> ■ Test the application with both valid and invalid data (for example, test the application without entering any data, and test it by entering letters where numbers are expected).

1. In this exercise, you code an application that allows the user to enter a person's first name and last name, and then uses string concatenation to display the last name, a comma, a space, and the first name in a label control.
    a. If necessary, start Visual Studio .NET. Open the Name Solution (Name Solution.sln) file, which is contained in the VBNET\Tut03\Name Solution folder. If the designer window is not open, right-click the form file's name in the Solution Explorer window, then click View Designer.
    b. Code the form's Load event procedure so that it uses two InputBox functions to prompt the user to enter his or her first name and last name. Assign the results of both functions to variables.
    c. Code the Display button's Click event procedure so that it displays the user's last name, a comma, a space, and the user's first name in the NameLabel control.
    d. Save the solution, then start the application. Test the application by entering your first and last names, and then clicking the Display button.
    e. Click the Exit button to end the application.
    f. Close the Output window, then close the solution.

2. In this exercise, you create an application that allows the user to enter a number of pennies. The application then calculates the number of dollars, quarters, dimes, nickels, and pennies that the user would receive if he or she cashed in the pennies at a bank.
    a. If necessary, start Visual Studio .NET. Create a blank solution named Pennies Solution. Save the solution in the VBNET\Tut03 folder.
    b. Add a Visual Basic .NET Windows Application project to the solution. Name the project Pennies Project.
    c. Assign the filename Pennies Form.vb to the form file object.
    d. Assign the name MoneyForm to the Windows Form object.
    e. The design of the interface is up to you. Code the application appropriately. (*Hint:* Review the arithmetic operators listed in Figure 2-28 in Tutorial 2.)
    f. Save the solution, then start the application. Test the application twice, using the following data: 2311 pennies and 7333 pennies.
    g. Stop the application.
    h. Close the Output window, then close the solution.

3. In this exercise, you create an application that can help students in grades 1 through 6 learn how to make change. The application should allow the student to enter the amount of money the customer owes and the amount of money the customer paid. It then should calculate the amount of change, as well as how many dollars, quarters, dimes, nickels, and pennies to return to the customer. For now, you do not have to worry about the situation where the price is greater than what the customer pays. You can assume that the customer paid either the exact amount or more than the exact amount.
    a. If necessary, start Visual Studio .NET. Create a blank solution named Change Solution. Save the solution in the VBNET\Tut03 folder.

b. Add a Visual Basic .NET Windows Application project to the solution. Name the project Change Project.

c. Assign the filename Change Form.vb to the form file object.

d. Assign the name ChangeForm to the Windows Form object.

e. The design of the interface is up to you. Code the application appropriately. (*Hint*: Review the arithmetic operators listed in Figure 2-28 in Tutorial 2.)

f. Save the solution, then start the application. Test the application three times, using the following data:

    75.33 as the amount owed and 80.00 as the amount paid

    39.67 as the amount owed and 50.00 as the amount paid

    45.55 as the amount owed and 45.55 as the amount paid

g. Stop the application.

h. Close the Output window, then close the solution.

Exercise 4 is a Discovery Exercise. Discovery Exercises, which may include topics that are not covered in this lesson, allow you to "discover" the solutions to problems on your own.

discovery ▶ 4. In this exercise, you discover the difference between the Val function and the CType function, which is one of the conversion functions. Unlike the Val function, which returns a Double number, the CType function allows you to convert a string or number to a specified data type.

a. If necessary, start Visual Studio .NET. Open the Function Solution (Function Solution.sln) file, which is contained in the VBNET\Tut03\Function Solution folder. If the designer window is not open, right-click the form file's name in the Solution Explorer window, then click View Designer.

b. Click Help on the menu bar, and then click Index. Type ctype in the Look for text box, and then click CType function in the list. Read and then close the Help window.

c. Open the Code editor window. Print and then review the code.

d. Start the application. Click the Display button. The interface lists the original value, the value returned by the Val function, and the value returned by the CType function.

e. Click the Exit button to end the application, then close the Output window.

f. Use the Function application to answer the following questions:

    What value (if any) will the expression Val("") return?

    What value (if any) will the expression CType("", Integer) return?

    What value (if any) will the expression Val("A") return?

    What value (if any) will the expression CType("A", Integer) return?

Exercise 5 is a Debugging Exercise. Debugging Exercises provide an opportunity for you to detect and correct errors in an existing application.

debugging 🖼 5. In this exercise, you debug an existing application. The purpose of this exercise is to demonstrate the problems that can occur when using the InputBox function.

a. If necessary, start Visual Studio .NET. Open the Debug Solution (Debug Solution.sln) file, which is contained in the VBNET\Tut03\Debug Solution folder. If the designer window is not open, click the form file's name in the Solution Explorer window, then use the View menu to open the designer window.

b. Start the application. Click the Compute Sum button, then click the OK button in the First Number dialog box without entering a number. Read the error message that appears in a message box.

c. Click the Break button. Notice that the first assignment statement is causing the problem. Click Debug on the menu bar, and then click Stop Debugging.

d. Start the application again. Click the Compute Sum button. Type 3 in the input area of the First Number dialog box, then click the OK button. When the Second Number dialog box appears, click the Cancel button. Read the error message that appears in a message box.

e. Click the Break button. Notice that the second assignment statement is causing the problem. Click Debug on the menu bar, and then click Stop Debugging.

f. Use the Val function to correct the code so that the application does not result in an error message when the user clicks the OK button without entering any data, or when he or she clicks the Cancel button.

g. Start the application. Click the Compute Sum button, then click the OK button in the First Number dialog box without entering any data. Click the Cancel button in the second dialog box. The application should not result in an error message.

h. Stop the application. Close the output window, then close the solution.

The Selection Structure

Creating a Monthly Payment Calculator Application

case ▶ After weeks of car shopping, Herman Juarez still has not decided on what car to purchase. Recently, Herman has noticed that many auto dealers, in an effort to boost sales, are offering buyers a choice of either a large cash rebate or an extremely low financing rate, much lower than the rate Herman would pay by financing the car through his local credit union. Herman is not sure whether to take the lower financing rate from the dealer, or take the rebate and then finance the car through the credit union. He has asked you to create an application that he can use to calculate and display the monthly payment on a car loan.

Previewing the Completed Application

Before creating the Monthly Payment Calculator application, you first preview the completed application.

To preview the completed application:

1   Use the Run command on the Windows Start menu to run the **Payment** (Payment.exe) file, which is contained in the VBNET\Tut04 folder on your computer's hard disk. The Monthly Payment Calculator application's user interface appears on the screen.

Calculate the monthly payment on a $9,000 loan at 5% interest for 3 years.

2   Type **9000** in the Principal text box, then press **Tab**.

3   Type **5** in the Rate text box, then press **Enter** to select the Calculate Monthly Payment button, which is the default button on the form. A message box containing the message "The term must be greater than or equal to 1." appears on the screen, as shown in Figure 4-1. You learn how to create a message box in Lesson B.

message box

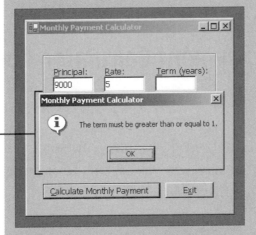

Figure 4-1: Monthly Payment Calculator application's user interface

4   Press **Enter** to select the OK button in the message box.

5   Press **Tab** to move the insertion point into the Term text box. Type **3** in the Term text box, then press **Enter**. The application calculates and displays a monthly payment amount of $268.62, as shown in Figure 4-2.

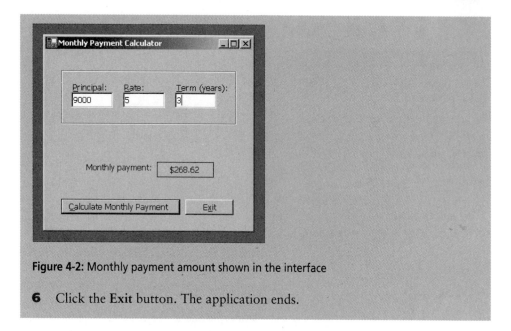

Figure 4-2: Monthly payment amount shown in the interface

6 Click the **Exit** button. The application ends.

Before you can begin coding the Monthly Payment Calculator application, you need to learn about the selection structure; you learn that structure in Lesson A. In Lesson B, you complete the Monthly Payment Calculator application's interface as you learn how to use a GroupBox control. You begin coding the application in Lesson B, and complete the application in Lesson C.

After completing this lesson, you will be able to:

- Write pseudocode for the selection structure
- Create a flowchart to help you plan an application's code
- Write an If...Then...Else statement
- Write code that uses comparison operators and logical operators
- Use the UCase and LCase functions

The If...Then...Else Statement

The Selection Structure

The applications you created in the previous three tutorials used only the sequence programming structure. In the sequence programming structure, the program instructions were processed, one after another, in the order in which each appeared in the Code editor window. In many applications, however, the next instruction to be processed will depend on the result of a decision or comparison that the program must make. For example, a payroll program typically will need to compare the number of hours the employee worked with the number 40 to determine whether the employee should receive overtime pay in addition to regular pay. Based on the result of that comparison, the program then will select either an instruction that computes regular pay only, or an instruction that computes regular pay plus overtime pay.

You use the **selection structure**, also called the **decision structure**, when you want a program to make a decision or comparison and then, based on the result of that decision or comparison, select a particular set of tasks to perform. Although the idea of using the selection structure in a program is new, the concept of the selection structure is one with which you already are familiar, because you use it each day to make hundreds of decisions. For example, every morning you have to decide if you are hungry and, if you are, what you are going to eat. Figure 4-3 shows other examples of selection structures you might use today.

tip

As you may remember from Tutorial 1, the selection structure is one of three programming structures. The other two programming structures are sequence, which was covered in the previous tutorials, and repetition, which is covered in Tutorial 6.

	Example 1	Example 2
condition	if *it is raining*	if *you have a test tomorrow*
condition	wear a raincoat	study tonight
	bring an umbrella	otherwise
		watch a movie

Figure 4-3: Selection structures you might use today

In the examples shown in Figure 4-3, the portion in *italics*, called the **condition**, specifies the decision you are making and is phrased so that it results in either a true or false answer only. For example, either it is raining (true) or it is not raining (false). Likewise, either you have a test tomorrow (true) or you do not have a test tomorrow (false).

If the condition is true, you perform a specific set of tasks. If the condition is false, on the other hand, you might or might not need to perform a different set of tasks. For instance, look at the first example shown in Figure 4-3. If it is raining (a true condition), then you will wear a raincoat and bring an umbrella. Notice that you do not have anything in particular to do if it is not raining (a false condition). Compare this with the second example shown in Figure 4-3. If you have a test tomorrow (a true condition), then you will study tonight. However, if you do not have a test tomorrow (a false condition), then you will watch a movie.

Like you, the computer also can evaluate a condition and then select the appropriate tasks to perform based on that evaluation. When using the selection structure in a program, the programmer must be sure to phrase the condition so that it results in either a true or a false answer only. The programmer also must specify the tasks to be performed when the condition is true and, if necessary, the tasks to be performed when the condition is false.

Visual Basic .NET provides four forms of the selection structure: If, If/Else, If/ElseIf/Else, and Case. You learn about If and If/Else selection structures in this tutorial. If/ElseIf/Else and Case selection structures are covered in Tutorial 5. (Tutorial 5 also covers nested selection structures. A nested selection structure is a selection structure that is contained entirely within another selection structure.)

Writing Pseudocode for If and If/Else Selection Structures

An **If structure** contains only one set of instructions, which are processed when the condition is true. An **If/Else structure**, on the other hand, contains two sets of instructions: one set is processed when the condition is true and the other set is processed when the condition is false. Figure 4-4 shows examples of both the If and the If/Else structures written in pseudocode.

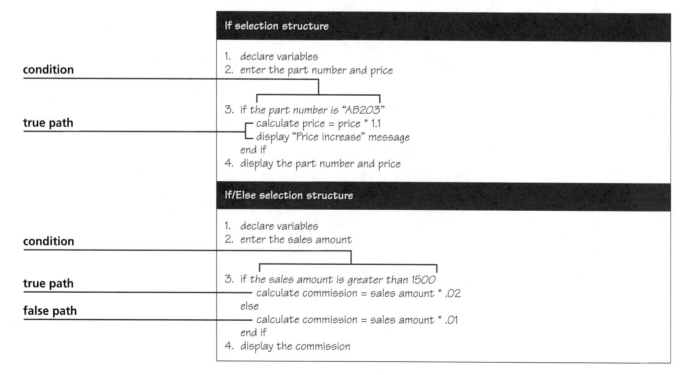

Figure 4-4: Examples of the If and If/Else structures written in pseudocode

Although pseudocode is not standardized—every programmer has his or her own version—you will find some similarities among the various versions. For example, many programmers begin the selection structure with the word "if" and end the structure with the two words "end if"; they also use the word "else" to designate the instructions to be performed when the condition is false.

In the examples shown in Figure 4-4, the italicized portion of the instruction indicates the condition to be evaluated. Notice that each condition results in either a true or a false answer only. In Example 1, either the part number is "AB203" or it isn't. In Example 2, either the sales amount is greater than the number 1500 or it isn't.

When the condition is true, the set of instructions following the condition is selected for processing. The instructions following the condition are referred to as the **true path**—the path you follow when the condition is true. The true path ends when you come to the "else" or, if there is no "else", when you come to the end of the selection structure (the "end if"). After the true path instructions are processed, the instruction following the "end if" is processed. In the examples shown in Figure 4-4, the display instructions are processed after the instructions in the true path.

The instructions processed when the condition is false depend on whether the selection structure contains an "else". When there is no "else", as in the first example shown in Figure 4-4, the selection structure ends when its condition is false, and processing continues with the instruction following the "end if". In the first example, for instance, the "display the part number and price" instruction is processed when the part number is not "AB203." In cases where the selection structure contains an "else", as in the second example shown in Figure 4-4, the instructions between the "else" and the "end if"—referred to as the **false path**—are processed before the instruction after the "end if" is processed. In the second example, the "calculate commission = sales amount * .01" instruction is processed first, followed by the "display the commission" instruction.

Recall from Tutorial 2 that, in addition to using pseudocode to plan algorithms, programmers also use flowcharts. In the next section, you learn how to show the If and If/Else selection structures in a flowchart.

Flowcharting the If and If/Else Selection Structures

Unlike pseudocode, which consists of English statements, a flowchart uses standardized symbols to show the steps the computer needs to take to accomplish a task. Figure 4-5 shows Figure 4-4's examples in flowchart form.

The flowcharts shown in Figure 4-5 contain four different symbols: an oval, a rectangle, a parallelogram, and a diamond. The symbols are connected with lines, called **flowlines**. The oval symbol is called the **start/stop symbol**. The start oval indicates the beginning of the flowchart, and the stop oval indicates the end of the flowchart. The rectangles that appear between the start and the stop ovals are called **process symbols**. You use the process symbol to represent tasks such as declaring variables and making calculations. The first rectangle in each example represents a declaration task, and the remaining rectangles represent calculation tasks.

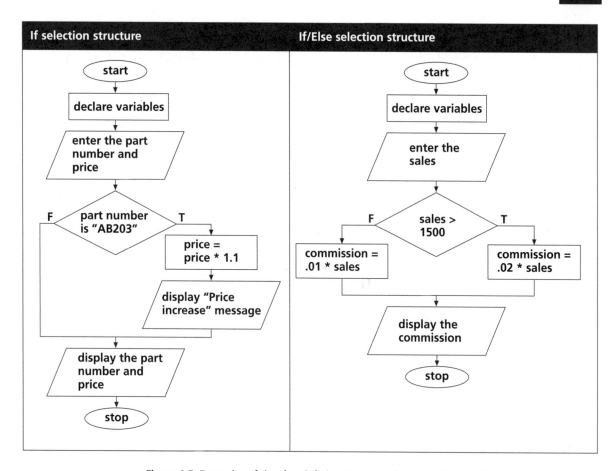

Figure 4-5: Examples of the If and If/Else structures drawn in flowchart form

The parallelogram in a flowchart is called the **input/output symbol** and is used to represent input tasks, such as getting information from the user, and output tasks, such as displaying information. The first parallelogram in each example shown in Figure 4-5 represents an input task, and the last parallelogram represents an output task.

The diamond in a flowchart is called the **selection/repetition symbol**, because it is used to represent both selection and repetition. In Figure 4-5's flowcharts, the diamonds represent the selection structure. (You learn how to use the diamond to represent the repetition structure in Tutorial 6.) Notice that inside each diamond is a comparison that evaluates to either true or false only. Each diamond also has one flowline entering the symbol and two flowlines leaving the symbol. The two flowlines leading out of the diamond should be marked so that anyone reading the flowchart can distinguish the true path from the false path. You mark the flowline leading to the true path with a "T" (for true), and you mark the flowline leading to the false path with an "F" (for false).

You also can mark the flowlines leading out of the diamond with a "Y" and an "N" (for yes and no).

To translate the flowchart into Visual Basic .NET code, you simply start at the top of the flowchart and write the code for each symbol as you follow the flowlines down to the bottom of the flowchart. Keep in mind that some symbols in a flowchart may require more than one line of code.

Next, learn how to code the If and If/Else selection structures in Visual Basic .NET.

Coding the If and If/Else Selection Structures

You use the **If...Then...Else statement** to code the If and If/Else selection structures in Visual Basic .NET. The syntax of the If...Then...Else statement is shown in Figure 4-6.

If *condition* **Then**

   statement block containing one or more statements to be processed when the condition is true

[Else

   statement block containing one or more statements to be processed when the condition is false]

End If

Figure 4-6: Syntax of the If...Then...Else statement used to code the If and If/Else structures

The items in square brackets ([ ]) in the syntax are optional. For example, you do not always need to include the `Else` portion of the syntax, referred to as the **Else clause**, in an If...Then...Else statement. Words in **bold**, however, are essential components of the statement. The words `If`, `Then`, and `End If`, for instance, must be included in the If...Then...Else statement. (The word `Else` must be included only if the statement uses the Else clause.) Items in *italics* indicate where the programmer must supply information pertaining to the current application. For instance, the programmer must supply the *condition* to be evaluated. The *condition* must be a Boolean expression, which is an expression that results in a Boolean value (True or False). In addition to supplying the *condition*, the programmer also must supply the statements to be processed when the *condition* evaluates to true and, optionally, when the *condition* evaluates to false. The set of statements contained in the true path, as well as the set of statements contained in the false path, are referred to as a **statement block**.

The If...Then...Else statement's *condition* can contain variables, literal constants, named constants, properties, functions, arithmetic operators, comparison operators, and logical operators. You already know about variables, literal constants, named constants, properties, functions, and arithmetic operators. You learn about comparison operators and logical operators in the following sections.

Comparison Operators

Visual Basic .NET provides nine **comparison operators**, also referred to as **relational operators**. Figure 4-7 lists the six most commonly used comparison operators. You learn about the remaining three comparison operators—Is, TypeOf...Is, and Like—in Tutorial 5.

Operator	Operation
=	equal to
>	greater than
>=	greater than or equal to
<	less than
<=	less than or equal to
<>	not equal to

Figure 4-7: Most commonly used comparison operators

Unlike arithmetic operators, comparison operators do not have an order of precedence in Visual Basic .NET. If an expression contains more than one comparison operator, Visual Basic .NET evaluates the comparison operators from left to right in the expression. Keep in mind, however, that comparison operators are evaluated after any arithmetic operators in the expression. In other words, in the expression 5 – 2 > 1 + 2, the two arithmetic operators (–, +) are evaluated before the comparison operator (>). The result of the expression is the Boolean value False, as shown in Figure 4-8.

Evaluation steps	Result
Original expression	5 – 2 > 1 + 2
5 – 2 is evaluated first	3 > 1 + 2
1 + 2 is evaluated second	3 > 3
3 > 3 is evaluated last	False

Figure 4-8: Evaluation steps for an expression containing arithmetic and comparison operators

Figure 4-9 shows examples of using comparison operators in the If…Then…Else statement's *condition*.

If…Then…Else statement's *condition*	Meaning
`If sngPrice < 45.75 Then`	Compares the contents of the sngPrice variable to the number 45.75. The *condition* evaluates to True if the sngPrice variable contains a number that is less than 45.75; otherwise, it evaluates to False.
`If intAge >= 21 Then`	Compares the contents of the intAge variable to the number 21. The *condition* evaluates to True if the intAge variable contains a number that is greater than or equal to 21; otherwise, it evaluates to False.
`If intNum1 = intNum2 Then`	Compares the contents of the intNum1 variable to the contents of the intNum2 variable. The *condition* evaluates to True if the contents of both variables are equal; otherwise, it evaluates to False.
`If strState <> "MA" Then`	Compares the contents of the strState variable to the string "MA". The *condition* evaluates to True if the strState variable does not contain the string "MA"; otherwise, it evaluates to False.

Figure 4-9: Examples of comparison operators in the If…Then…Else statement's *condition*

Notice that the expression contained in each *condition* shown in Figure 4-9 evaluates to one of two Boolean values—either True or False. All expressions containing a comparison operator will result in an answer of either True or False only.

In the next section, you view the pseudocode, flowchart, and Visual Basic .NET code for two procedures that contain comparison operators in an If…Then…Else statement. The first procedure uses the If selection structure, and the second procedure uses the If/Else selection structure.

Using Comparison Operators in an If…Then…Else Statement

Assume you want to swap the values in two variables, but only if the first value is greater than the second value. Figure 4-10 shows the pseudocode, flowchart, and Visual Basic .NET code for a procedure that will accomplish this task.

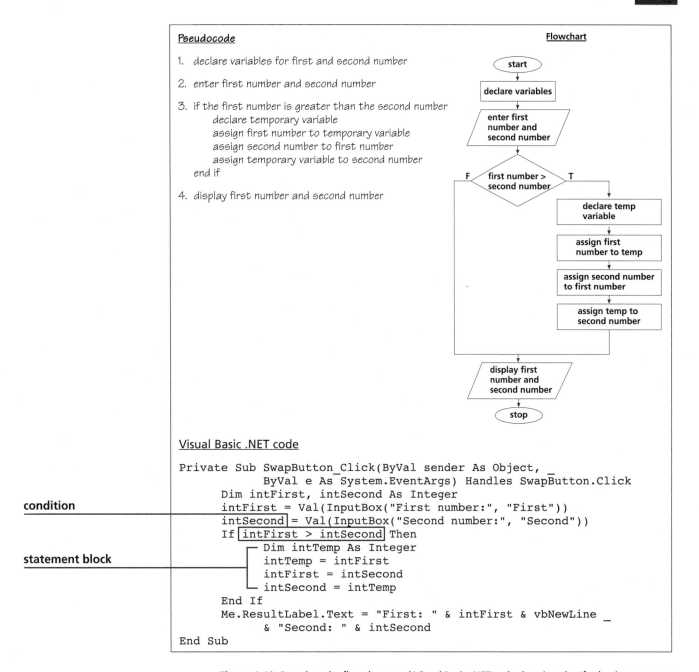

Figure 4-10: Pseudocode, flowchart, and Visual Basic .NET code showing the If selection structure

The `intFirst > intSecond` *condition* in the Visual Basic .NET code shown in Figure 4-10 tells the computer to compare the contents of the intFirst variable to the contents of the intSecond variable. If the *condition* is true, which means that the value in the intFirst variable is greater than the value in the intSecond variable, then the four instructions contained in the If...Then...Else statement's true path swap the values contained in those variables. Study closely the instructions used to swap the two values. The first instruction, `Dim intTemp As Integer`, declares a variable named intTemp. Like the variables declared at the beginning of a procedure, variables declared within a statement block are local variables and remain in memory until the procedure ends. However, unlike variables declared at the beginning of a procedure, variables declared within a statement block have block scope rather than procedure scope. Recall that when a variable has procedure scope, it can be used anywhere within the procedure. A variable that has **block scope**, on the other hand, can be used only within the statement block in which it is declared. In this case, for example, the intFirst and intSecond variables can be used anywhere within the SwapButton's Click event procedure, but the intTemp variable can be used only within the If...Then...Else statement's true path. You may be wondering why the intTemp variable was not declared at the beginning of the procedure, along with the intFirst and intSecond variables. Although that would have been correct, the intTemp variable is not needed unless a swap is necessary, so there is no reason to create the variable until it is needed.

The second instruction in the If...Then...Else statement's true path, `intTemp = intFirst`, assigns the value in the intFirst variable to the intTemp variable. In other words, it stores a copy of the intFirst variable's contents in the intTemp variable. Next, the `intFirst = intSecond` instruction assigns the value in the intSecond variable to the intFirst variable. Finally, the `intSecond = intTemp` instruction assigns the value in the intTemp variable to the intSecond variable. The intTemp variable is necessary to store the contents of the intFirst variable temporarily so that the swap can be made. If you did not store the intFirst variable's value in the intTemp variable, the intSecond variable's value would write over the value in the intFirst variable, and the value in the intFirst variable would be lost. Figure 4-11 illustrates the process of swapping.

	intTemp	intFirst	intSecond
values stored in the variables after the InputBox functions and the `Dim intTemp As Integer` instruction are processed	0	8	4
result of the `intTemp = intFirst` instruction	8	8	4
result of the `intFirst = intSecond` instruction	8	4	4
result of the `intSecond = intTemp` instruction (completes the swapping process)	8	4	8

Figure 4-11: Illustration of the swapping process

In the next example, assume you want to give the user the option of displaying either the sum of two numbers that he or she enters, or the difference between the two numbers. Figure 4-12 shows the pseudocode, flowchart, and Visual Basic .NET code for a procedure that will accomplish this task.

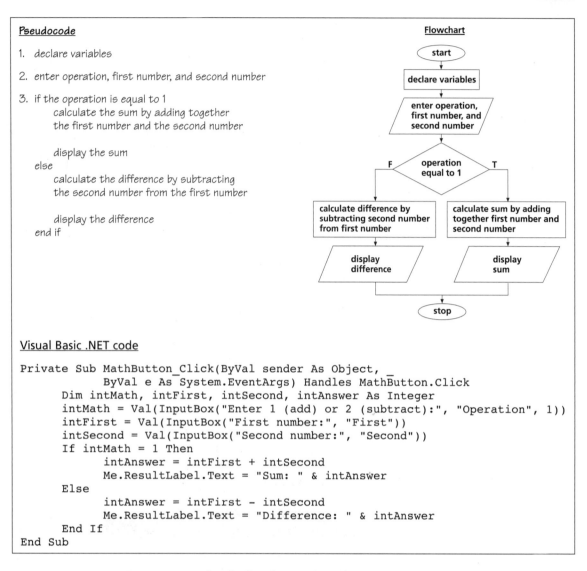

Pseudocode

1. declare variables

2. enter operation, first number, and second number

3. if the operation is equal to 1
       calculate the sum by adding together
       the first number and the second number

       display the sum
   else
       calculate the difference by subtracting
       the second number from the first number

       display the difference
   end if

Visual Basic .NET code

```
Private Sub MathButton_Click(ByVal sender As Object, _
        ByVal e As System.EventArgs) Handles MathButton.Click
    Dim intMath, intFirst, intSecond, intAnswer As Integer
    intMath = Val(InputBox("Enter 1 (add) or 2 (subtract):", "Operation", 1))
    intFirst = Val(InputBox("First number:", "First"))
    intSecond = Val(InputBox("Second number:", "Second"))
    If intMath = 1 Then
        intAnswer = intFirst + intSecond
        Me.ResultLabel.Text = "Sum: " & intAnswer
    Else
        intAnswer = intFirst - intSecond
        Me.ResultLabel.Text = "Difference: " & intAnswer
    End If
End Sub
```

Figure 4-12: Pseudocode, flowchart, and Visual Basic .NET code showing the If/Else selection structure

The intMath = 1 *condition* in the Visual Basic .NET code shown in Figure 4-12 tells the computer to compare the contents of the intMath variable to the number 1. If the *condition* is true, then the selection structure calculates and displays the sum of the two numbers entered by the user. If the *condition* is false, however, the selection structure calculates and displays the difference between the two numbers.

Recall that you also can use logical operators in the If…Then…Else statement's *condition*.

Logical Operators

Logical operators, sometimes referred to as **Boolean operators,** allow you to combine two or more *conditions* into one compound *condition*. Visual Basic .NET has six logical operators, which are listed along with their order of precedence in Figure 4-13.

Operator	Operation	Precedence number
Not	reverses the value of the *condition*; True becomes False, and False becomes True	1
And	all conditions must be true for the compound condition to be true	2
AndAlso	same as the And operator, except performs short-circuit evaluation	2
Or	only one of the conditions must be true for the compound condition to be true	3
OrElse	same as the Or operator, except performs short-circuit evaluation	3
Xor	one and only one condition can be true for the compound condition to be true	4

Figure 4-13: Logical operators

The tables shown in Figure 4-14, called **truth tables,** summarize how Visual Basic .NET evaluates the logical operators in an expression. Like expressions containing comparison operators, expressions containing logical operators always evaluate to a Boolean value.

Truth table for the Not operator	
value of *condition*	value of Not *condition*
True	False
False	True

Truth table for the And operator		
value of *condition1*	value of *condition2*	value of *condition1* And *condition2*
True	True	True
True	False	False
False	True	False
False	False	False

Truth table for the AndAlso operator		
value of *condition1*	value of *condition2*	value of *condition1* AndAlso *condition2*
True	True	True
True	False	False
False	(not evaluated)	False

Figure 4-14: Truth tables for the logical operators

Truth table for the Or operator		
value of *condition1*	value of *condition2*	value of *condition1* Or *condition2*
True	True	True
True	False	True
False	True	True
False	False	False

Truth table for the OrElse operator		
value of *condition1*	value of *condition2*	value of *condition1* OrElse *condition2*
True	(not evaluated)	True
False	True	True
False	False	False

Truth table for the Xor operator		
value of *condition1*	value of *condition2*	value of *condition1* Xor *condition2*
True	True	False
True	False	True
False	True	True
False	False	False

Figure 4-14: Truth tables for the logical operators (continued)

As Figure 4-14 indicates, the Not operator reverses the truth-value of the *condition*. If the value of the *condition* is True, then the value of Not *condition* is False. Likewise, if the value of the *condition* is False, then the value of Not *condition* is True. As you can see, the Not operator can be confusing, so it is best to avoid using it if possible. In Tutorial 10, which covers random access files, you learn a useful purpose for the Not operator. For now you do not need to worry about the Not operator; just be aware that it exists.

Now look at the truth tables for the And and AndAlso logical operators. When you use the And or AndAlso operators to combine two conditions, the resulting compound condition is True only when both conditions are True. If either condition is False or if both conditions are False, then the compound condition is False. The difference between the And and AndAlso operators is that the And operator always evaluates both conditions, while the AndAlso operator performs a **short-circuit evaluation**, which means that it does not always evaluate *condition2*. Because both conditions combined with the AndAlso operator need to be True for the compound condition to be True, the AndAlso operator does not evaluate *condition2* if *condition1* is False. Although the And and AndAlso operators produce the same results, the AndAlso operator is more efficient.

Now look at the truth tables for the Or and OrElse logical operators. When you combine conditions using the Or or OrElse operators, the compound condition is False only when both conditions are False. If either condition is True or if both conditions are True, then the compound condition is True. The difference between the Or and OrElse operators is that the Or operator always evaluates both conditions, while the OrElse operator performs a short-circuit evaluation. Because only one of the conditions combined with the OrElse operator needs to be True for the compound condition to be True, the OrElse operator does not evaluate *condition2* if *condition1* is True. Although the Or and OrElse operators produce the same results, the OrElse operator is more efficient.

Finally, look at the truth table for the Xor operator. When you combine conditions using the Xor operator, the compound condition is True only when one and only one condition is True. If both conditions are True or both conditions are False, then the compound condition is False. In the next section, you use the truth tables to determine which logical operator is appropriate for the If...Then...Else statement's compound condition.

Using the Truth Tables

Assume that you want to pay a bonus to every A-rated salesperson whose monthly sales total more than $10,000. To receive a bonus, the salesperson must be rated A and he or she must sell more than $10,000 in product. Assuming the two variables strRate and sngSales contain the salesperson's rating and sales amount, you can phrase *condition1* as `strRate = "A"` and *condition2* as `sngSales > 10000`. Now the question is, which logical operator should you use to combine both conditions into one compound condition? You can use the truth tables shown in Figure 4-14 to answer this question.

For a salesperson to receive a bonus, remember that both *condition1* (`strRate = "A"`) and *condition2* (`sngSales > 10000`) must be True at the same time. If either condition is False, or if both conditions are False, then the compound condition should be False, and the salesperson should not receive a bonus. According to the truth tables, the And, AndAlso, Or, and OrElse operators evaluate the compound condition as True when both conditions are True. However, only the And and AndAlso operators evaluate the compound condition as False when either one or both of the conditions are False. The Or and OrElse operators, you will notice, evaluate the compound condition as False only when *both* conditions are False. Therefore, the correct compound condition to use here is either `strRate = "A" And sngSales > 10000` or `strRate = "A" AndAlso sngSales > 10000`. Recall, however, that the AndAlso operator is more efficient than the And operator.

Now assume that you want to send a letter to all A-rated salespeople and all B-rated salespeople. Assuming the rating is stored in the strRate variable, you can phrase *condition1* as `strRate = "A"` and *condition2* as `strRate = "B"`. Now which operator do you use?

At first it might appear that either the And or the AndAlso operator is the correct one to use, because the example says to send the letter to "all A-rated salespeople and all B-rated salespeople." In everyday conversations, you will find that people sometimes use the word *and* when what they really mean is *or*. Although both words do not mean the same thing, using *and* instead of *or* generally does not cause a problem because we are able to infer what another person means. Computers, however, cannot infer anything; they simply process the directions you give them, word for word. In this case, you actually want to send a letter to all salespeople with either an A or a B rating (a salesperson cannot have both an A rating and a B rating), so you will need to use either the Or or the OrElse operator. As the truth tables indicate, the Or and OrElse operators are the only operators that evaluate the compound condition as True if one or more of the conditions is True. Therefore, the correct compound condition to use here is either `strRate = "A" Or strRate = "B"` or `strRate = "A" OrElse strRate = "B"`. Recall, however, that the OrElse operator is more efficient than the Or operator.

Finally, assume that, when placing an order, a customer is allowed to use only one of two coupons. Assuming the program uses the variables strCoupon1 and strCoupon2 to keep track of the coupons, you can phrase *condition1* as `strCoupon1 = "Use"` and *condition2* as `strCoupon2 = "Use"`. Now which operator should you use to combine both conditions? According to the truth tables, the Xor operator is the only operator that evaluates the compound condition as True when one and only one condition is True. Therefore, the correct compound condition to use here is `strCoupon1 = "Use" Xor strCoupon2 = "Use"`.

Figure 4-15 shows the order of precedence for the arithmetic, comparison, and logical operators you have learned so far.

Operator	Operation	Precedence number
^	exponentiation	1
–	negation	2
*, /	multiplication and division	3
\	integer division	4
Mod	modulus arithmetic	5
+, –	addition and subtraction	6
&	concatenation	7
=, >, >=, <, <=, <>	equal to, greater than, greater than or equal to, less than, less than or equal to, not equal to	8
Not	reverses truth value of condition	9
And, AndAlso	all conditions must be true for the compound condition to be true	10
Or, OrElse	only one condition needs to be true for the compound condition to be true	11
Xor	one and only one condition can be true for the compound condition to be true	12

Figure 4-15: Order of precedence for arithmetic, comparison, and logical operators

Notice that the logical operators are evaluated after any arithmetic operators or comparison operators in the expression. In other words, in the expression `12 > 0 AndAlso 12 < 10 * 2`, the arithmetic operator (*) is evaluated first, followed by the two comparison operators (> and <), followed by the logical operator (AndAlso). The expression evaluates to True, as shown in Figure 4-16.

Evaluation steps	Result
Original expression	12 > 0 AndAlso 12 < 10 * 2
10 * 2 is evaluated first	12 > 0 AndAlso 12 < 20
12 > 0 is evaluated second	True AndAlso 12 < 20
12 < 20 is evaluated third	True AndAlso True
True AndAlso True is evaluated last	True

Figure 4-16: Evaluation steps for an expression containing arithmetic, comparison, and logical operators

In the next section, you view the Visual Basic .NET code for three procedures that contain a logical operator in an If...Then...Else statement.

Using Logical Operators in an If...Then...Else Statement

Assume you want to create a procedure that calculates and displays an employee's gross pay. To keep this example simple, assume that no one at the company works more than 40 hours per week, and everyone earns the same hourly rate, $10.65. Before making the gross pay calculation, the procedure should verify that the number of hours entered by the user is greater than or equal to zero, but less than or equal to 40. Programmers refer to the process of verifying that the input data is within the expected range as **data validation**. In this case, if the number is valid, the procedure should calculate and display the gross pay; otherwise, it should display an error message alerting the user that the input data is incorrect. Figure 4-17 shows two ways of writing the Visual Basic .NET code for this procedure. Notice that the If...Then...Else statement in the first example uses the AndAlso logical operator, whereas the If...Then...Else statement in the second example uses the OrElse logical operator.

Example 1: using the AndAlso operator

```
Dim sngHours, sngGross As Single
sngHours = Val(InputBox("Enter hours worked", "Hours", "0"))
If sngHours >= 0 AndAlso sngHours <= 40 Then
    sngGross = sngHours * 10.65
    Me.ResultLabel.Text = Format(sngGross, "currency")
Else
    Me.ResultLabel.Text = "Input Error"
End If
```

Example 2: using the OrElse operator

```
Dim sngHours, sngGross As Single
sngHours = Val(InputBox("Enter hours worked", "Hours", "0"))
If sngHours < 0 OrElse sngHours > 40 Then
    Me.ResultLabel.Text = "Input Error"
Else
    sngGross = sngHours * 10.65
    Me.ResultLabel.Text = Format(sngGross, "currency")
End If
```

Figure 4-17: AndAlso and OrElse logical operators in the If...Then...Else statement

The `sngHours >= 0 AndAlso sngHours <= 40` compound condition in the first example shown in Figure 4-17 tells the computer to determine whether the value stored in the sngHours variable is greater than or equal to the number 0 and, at the same time, less than or equal to the number 40. If the compound condition evaluates to True, then the selection structure calculates and displays the gross pay; otherwise, it displays the "Input Error" message.

The `sngHours < 0 OrElse sngHours > 40` compound condition in the second example shown in Figure 4-17 tells the computer to determine whether the value stored in the sngHours variable is less than the number 0 or greater than the number 40. If the compound condition evaluates to True, then the selection structure displays the "Input Error" message; otherwise, it calculates and displays the gross pay. Both If…Then…Else statements shown in Figure 4-17 produce the same results, and simply represent two different ways of performing the same task.

In the next procedure, assume you want to display the word "Pass" if the user enters the letter P, and the word "Fail" if the user enters anything else. Figure 4-18 shows three ways of writing the Visual Basic .NET code for this procedure.

Example 1: using the OrElse operator

```
Dim strLetter As String
strLetter = Me.LetterTextBox.Text
If strLetter = "P" OrElse strLetter = "p" Then
    Me.ResultLabel.Text = "Pass"
Else
    Me.ResultLabel.Text = "Fail"
End If
```

Example 2: using the AndAlso operator

```
Dim strLetter As String
strLetter = Me.LetterTextBox.Text
If strLetter <> "P" AndAlso strLetter <> "p" Then
    Me.ResultLabel.Text = "Fail"
Else
    Me.ResultLabel.Text = "Pass"
End If
```

Example 3: correct, but less efficient, solution

```
Dim strLetter As String
strLetter = Me.LetterTextBox.Text
If strLetter = "P" OrElse strLetter = "p" Then
    Me.ResultLabel.Text = "Pass"
End If
If strLetter <> "P" AndAlso strLetter <> "p" Then
    Me.ResultLabel.Text = "Fail"
End If
```

Figure 4-18: More examples of using the OrElse and AndAlso logical operators

tip

The uppercase letter P is stored in the computer's internal memory using the eight bits 01010000 (ASCII code 80), whereas the lowercase letter p is stored using the eight bits 01110000 (ASCII code 112). ASCII stands for American Standard Code for Information Interchange and is the coding scheme used by microcomputers to represent the numbers, letters, and symbols on the keyboard.

The `strLetter = "P" OrElse strLetter = "p"` compound condition in the first example shown in Figure 4-18 tells the computer to determine whether the value stored in the strLetter variable is either the uppercase letter P or the lowercase letter p. If the compound condition evaluates to True, which means that the variable contains one of those two letters, then the selection structure displays the word "Pass"; otherwise, it displays the word "Fail". You may be wondering why you needed to tell the computer to compare the contents of the strLetter variable to both the uppercase and lowercase version of the letter P. As is true in many programming languages, string comparisons in Visual Basic .NET are case sensitive. That means that the uppercase version of a string is not the same as its lowercase counterpart. So, although a human recognizes P and p as being the same letter, a computer does not; to a computer, a P is different from a p. The reason for this differentiation is that each character on the computer's keyboard is stored differently in the computer's internal memory.

The `strLetter <> "P" AndAlso strLetter <> "p"` compound condition in the second example shown in Figure 4-18 tells the computer to determine whether the value stored in the strLetter variable is not equal to either the uppercase letter P or the lowercase letter p. If the compound condition evaluates to True, which means that the variable does not contain either of those two letters, then the selection structure displays the word "Fail"; otherwise, it displays the word "Pass".

Rather than using one If...Then...Else statement with an Else clause, as in Examples 1 and 2, Example 3 in Figure 4-18 uses two If...Then...Else statements with no Else clause in either one. Although the If...Then...Else statement in Example 3 produces the same results as the If...Then...Else statements in Examples 1 and 2, it does so less efficiently. For example, assume that the user enters the letter P in the LetterTextBox control. The compound condition in the first If...Then...Else statement shown in Example 3 determines whether the value stored in the strLetter variable is equal to either P or p; in this case, the compound condition evaluates to True, because the strLetter variable contains the letter P. The first If...Then...Else statement's true path displays the word "Pass" in the ResultLabel control, and then the first If...Then...Else statement ends. Although the appropriate word ("Pass") already appears in the ResultLabel control, the procedure instructs the computer to evaluate the second If...Then...Else statement's compound condition to determine whether to display the "Fail" message. The second evaluation is unnecessary and makes Example 3's code less efficient than the code shown in Examples 1 and 2.

Visual Basic .NET provides two functions that you can use, instead of a compound condition containing a logical operator, to perform a case-insensitive comparison of two strings.

The UCase and LCase Functions

As you learned earlier, string comparisons in Visual Basic .NET are case-sensitive, which means that the string "P" is not the same as the string "p". A problem occurs when you need to include a string, entered by the user, in a comparison, because you cannot control the case in which the user enters the string.

In the last section, you viewed examples that used two conditions connected by a logical operator to solve the string comparison problem. But what if, unlike the strings used in those examples, the strings you want to compare contain more than one character? For example, what if the strings represent a state abbreviation, which contains two characters? To perform a case-insensitive comparison of two-character strings, you would need to use four conditions connected by three logical operators, like this: strState = "CA" OrElse strState = "Ca" OrElse strState = "cA" OrElse strState = "ca". Imagine what the compound condition would look like if the string had 10 characters!

The simplest way to perform a case-insensitive comparison of two strings is to use either the **UCase** (uppercase) **function** or the **LCase** (lowercase) **function** in the If...Then...Else statement's *condition*. The syntax of the UCase function is **UCase**(*string*), and the syntax of the LCase function is **LCase**(*string*). Both functions temporarily convert the *string* to the appropriate case. Figure 4-19 shows six examples of using the UCase and LCase functions. In the first four examples, the functions are used to compare two strings in an If...Then...Else statement. The last two examples show how you can use the UCase function to assign the uppercase equivalent of a string to the Text property of a control and to a variable.

tip
. . . .

The UCase and LCase functions do not actually change the *string* to uppercase or lowercase letters, respectively. For example, `UCase(strName)` simply returns the uppercase equivalent of the strName variable's contents, but it does not change the variable's contents to uppercase letters. To change the variable's contents to uppercase letters, you would need to use the last statement shown in Figure 4-19.

Examples	Results
`If UCase(strLetter) = "P" Then`	compares the uppercase version of the string stored in the strLetter variable to the uppercase letter "P"
`If LCase(strState) = "ca" Then`	compares the lowercase version of the string stored in the strState variable to the lowercase letters "ca"
`If UCase(strItem1) <> UCase(strItem2) Then`	compares the uppercase version of the string stored in the strItem1 variable to the uppercase version of the string stored in the strItem2 variable
`If "reno" = LCase(Me.CityTextBox.Text) Then`	compares the lowercase letters "reno" to the lowercase version of the string stored in the CityTextBox control
`Me.StateTextBox.Text = UCase(strState)`	assigns the uppercase version of the string stored in the strState variable to the Text property of the StateTextBox control
`strName = UCase(strName)`	changes the contents of the strName variable to uppercase

Figure 4-19: Examples of using the UCase and LCase functions

When using the UCase function, be sure that everything you are comparing is uppercase. In other words, the clause `If UCase(strLetter) = "p" Then` will not work correctly: the *condition* will always evaluate to False, because the lowercase version of a letter will never be equal to its uppercase counterpart. Likewise, when using the LCase function, be sure that everything you are comparing is lowercase.

In the next section, you view the Visual Basic .NET code for three procedures that contain the UCase and LCase functions.

Using UCase and LCase in a Procedure

Assume you want to create a procedure that displays the message "We have a store in this state." if the user enters any of the following three state IDs: Il, In, Ky. If the user enters an ID other than these, you want to display the message "We do not have a store in this state." Figure 4-20 shows three ways of writing the Visual Basic .NET code for this procedure.

Example 1: using the UCase function

```
Dim strState As String
strState = Me.StateTextBox.Text
If UCase(strState) = "IL" OrElse UCase(strState) = "IN" _
    OrElse UCase(strState) = "KY"
   Me.ResultLabel.Text = "We have a store in this state."
Else
   Me.ResultLabel.Text = "We do not have a store in this state."
End If
```

Example 2: using the UCase function

```
Dim strState As String
strState = UCase(Me.StateTextBox.Text)
If strState = "IL" OrElse strState = "IN" OrElse strState = "KY"
   Me.ResultLabel.Text = "We have a store in this state."
Else
   Me.ResultLabel.Text = "We do not have a store in this state."
End If
```

Example 3: using the LCase function

```
Dim strState As String
strState = LCase(Me.StateTextBox.Text)
If strState <> "il" AndAlso strState <> "in" AndAlso strState <> "ky"
   Me.ResultLabel.Text = "We do not have a store in this state."
Else
   Me.ResultLabel.Text = "We have a store in this state."
End If
```

Figure 4-20: Examples of using the UCase and LCase functions in a procedure

When the computer processes the `UCase(strState) = "IL" OrElse UCase(strState ) = "IN" OrElse UCase(strState) = "KY"` compound condition, which is shown in Example 1 in Figure 4-20, it first temporarily converts the contents of the strState variable to uppercase, and then compares the result to the string "IL". If the comparison evaluates to False, the computer again temporarily converts the contents of the strState variable to uppercase, this time comparing the result to the string "IN". If the comparison evaluates to False, it again converts the contents of the strState variable to uppercase, and compares the result to the string "KY". Notice that, depending on the result of each condition, the computer might have to convert the contents of the strState variable to uppercase three times. A more efficient way of writing Example 1's code is shown in Example 2 in Figure 4-20.

The `strState = UCase(Me.StateTextBox.Text)` instruction in Example 2 tells the computer to assign to the strState variable the uppercase equivalent of the StateTextBox control's Text property. The `strState = "IL" OrElse strState = "IN" OrElse strState = "KY"` compound condition first compares the contents of the strState variable (which now contains uppercase letters) to the string "IL". If the condition evaluates to False, the computer compares the contents of the strState variable to the string "IN". If this condition evaluates to False, the computer compares the contents of the strState variable to the string "KY". Notice that the computer has to convert the contents of the strState variable to uppercase only once rather than three times.

The `strState = LCase(Me.StateTextBox.Text)` instruction in Example 3 tells the computer to assign to the strState variable the lowercase equivalent of the StateTextBox control's Text property. Similar to the conditions shown in Example 2, the conditions in Example 3 also compare the contents of the `strState` variable (which, in this case, contains lowercase letters) to each of the three state IDs. However, rather than testing for equality, the conditions in Example 3 test for inequality. The three examples shown in Figure 4-20 produce the same results, and simply represent different ways of performing the same task.

S U M M A R Y

To evaluate an expression containing arithmetic, comparison, and logical operators:

■ Evaluate the arithmetic operators first, then evaluate the comparison operators, and then evaluate the logical operators. Figure 4-15 shows the order of precedence for the arithmetic, comparison, and logical operators.

To create a flowchart:

■ Use the start/stop oval to mark the beginning and end of the flowchart.
■ Use the input/output parallelogram to represent input tasks, such as getting information from the user, and output tasks, such as displaying information.
■ Use the process rectangle to represent tasks such as declaring variables and making calculations.
■ Use the selection/repetition diamond to represent the selection and repetition programming structures.
■ Connect the flowchart symbols with flowlines.

To code a selection structure:

■ Use the If...Then...Else statement. The statement's syntax is shown in Figure 4-6.

To compare two values:

■ Use the comparison operators listed in Figure 4-7.

To swap the values contained in two variables:

■ Assign the value stored in the first variable to a temporary variable, then assign the value stored in the second variable to the first variable, and then assign the value stored in the temporary variable to the second variable.

To create a compound condition:

■ Use the logical operators listed in Figure 4-13, and the truth tables listed in Figure 4-14.

To return the uppercase equivalent of a string:

■ Use the UCase function. The function's syntax is **UCase**(*string*).

To return the lowercase equivalent of a string:

■ Use the LCase function. The function's syntax is **LCase**(*string*).

QUESTIONS

1. Which of the following is a valid condition for an If...Then...Else statement?
   a. `Val(Me.AgeTextBox.Text > 65)`
   b. `Val(Me.PriceLabel.Text) > 0 AndAlso < 10`
   c. `sngSales > 500 AndAlso < 800`
   d. `sngCost > 100 AndAlso sngCost <= 1000`
   e. `UCase(strState) = "Alaska" OrElse UCase(strState) = "Hawaii"`

2. You can use the _____ function to return the uppercase equivalent of a string.
   a. Caseupper
   b. CaseU
   c. LCase
   d. UCase
   e. Upper

3. Assume you want to compare the string contained in the Text property of the NameTextBox control with the name Bob. Which of the following conditions should you use in the If...Then...Else statement? (Be sure the condition will handle Bob, BOB, bob, and so on.)
   a. `Me.NameTextBox.Text = "BOB"`
   b. `Me.NameTextBox.Text = UCase("BOB")`
   c. `Me.NameTextBox.Text = UCase("Bob")`
   d. `UCase(Me.NameTextBox.Text) = "Bob"`
   e. `UCase(Me.NameTextBox.Text) = "BOB"`

4. Which of the following will change the contents of the NameTextBox control to uppercase?
   a. `Me.NameTextBox.Text = UCase(Me.NameTextBox.Text)`
   b. `Me.NameTextBox.Text = ME.NAMETEXTBOX.TEXT`
   c. `UCase(Me.NameTextBox.Text) = UCase(Me.NameTextBox.Text)`
   d. `UCase(Me.NameTextBox.Text) = Me.NameTextBox.Text`
   e. `Upper(Me.NameTextBox.Text) = "Me.NameTextBox.Text"`

5. The six logical operators are listed below. Indicate their order of precedence by placing a number (1, 2, and so on) on the line to the left of the operator. (If two or more operators have the same precedence, assign the same number to each.)

_____   Xor

_____   And

_____   Not

_____   Or

_____   AndAlso

_____   OrElse

6. An expression can contain arithmetic, comparison, and logical operators. Indicate the order of precedence for the three types of operators by placing a number (1, 2, or 3) on the line to the left of the operator type.

_____   Arithmetic

_____   Logical

_____   Comparison

7. The expression 3 > 6 AndAlso 7 > 4 evaluates to _____.
   a.   True
   b.   False

8. The expression 4 > 6 OrElse 10 < 2 * 6 evaluates to _____.
   a.   True
   b.   False

9. The expression 7 >= 3 + 4 Or 6 < 4 And 2 < 5 evaluates to _____.
   a.   True
   b.   False

Use the following information to answer Questions 10–17:

   X=5, Y=3, Z=2, A=True, B=False

10. The expression X – Y = Z evaluates to _____.
   a.   True
   b.   False

11. The expression X * Z > X * Y AndAlso A evaluates to _____.
   a.   True
   b.   False

12. The expression: X * Z < X * Y Or A evaluates to _____.
   a.   True
   b.   False

13. The expression A AndAlso B evaluates to _____.
   a.   True
   b.   False

14. The expression A OrElse B evaluates to _____.
   a.   True
   b.   False

15. The expression X * Y > Y ^ Z evaluates to _____.
    a. True
    b. False

16. The expression X * Y > Y ^ Z And A Or B evaluates to _____.
    a. True
    b. False

17. The expression A Xor B evaluates to _____.
    a. True
    b. False

Use the following selection structure to answer Questions 18 and 19:

```
If intNumber <= 100 Then
    intNumber = intNumber * 2
Else
    intNumber = intNumber * 3
End If
```

18. Assume the intNumber variable contains the number 90. What value will be in the intNumber variable after the above selection structure is processed?
    a. 0
    b. 90
    c. 180
    d. 270
    e. None of the above.

19. Assume the intNumber variable contains the number 1000. What value will be in the intNumber variable after the above selection structure is processed?
    a. 0
    b. 1000
    c. 2000
    d. 3000
    e. None of the above.

20. Which of the following flowchart symbols is used to represent the If...Then...Else selection structure?
    a. diamond
    b. hexagon
    c. oval
    d. parallelogram
    e. rectangle

21. The _____ symbol is used in a flowchart to represent a calculation task.
    a. input/output
    b. process
    c. selection/repetition
    d. start
    e. stop

22. The _____ symbol is used in a flowchart to represent an input task.
    a. input/output
    b. process
    c. selection/repetition
    d. start
    e. stop

23. The process symbol in a flowchart is the _____.
    a. diamond
    b. oval
    c. parallelogram
    d. rectangle
    e. square

24. The input/output symbol in a flowchart is the _____.
    a. diamond
    b. oval
    c. parallelogram
    d. rectangle
    e. square

25. The selection/repetition symbol in a flowchart is the _____.
    a. diamond
    b. oval
    c. parallelogram
    d. rectangle
    e. square

EXERCISES

1. Draw the flowchart that corresponds to the following pseudocode.

    ```
    if hours > 40
            display "Overtime pay"
    else
            display "Regular pay"
    end if
    ```

2. Write an If...Then...Else statement that displays the string "Pontiac" in the CarMakeLabel control if the CarTextBox control contains the string "Grand Am" (in any case).

3. Write an If...Then...Else statement that displays the string "Entry error" in the MessageLabel control if the intUnits variable contains a number that is less than 0; otherwise, display the string "Valid Number".

4. Write an If...Then...Else statement that displays the string "Reorder" in the MessageLabel control if the sngPrice variable contains a number that is less than 10; otherwise, display the string "OK".

5. Write an If...Then...Else statement that assigns the number 10 to the sngBonus variable if the sngSales variable contains a number that is less than or equal to $250; otherwise, assign the number 15.

6. Write an If...Then...Else statement that displays the number 25 in the ShippingLabel control if the strState variable contains the string "Hawaii" (in any case); otherwise, display the number 50.

7. Assume you want to calculate a 3% sales tax if the strState variable contains the string "Colorado" (in any case); otherwise, you want to calculate a 4% sales tax. You can calculate the sales tax by multiplying the tax rate by the contents of the sngSales variable. Display the sales tax in the SalesTaxLabel control. Draw the flowchart, then write the Visual Basic .NET code.

8. Assume you want to calculate an employee's gross pay. Employees working more than 40 hours should receive overtime pay (time and one-half) for the hours over 40. Use the variables sngHours, sngRate, and sngGross. Display the contents of the sngGross variable in the GrossLabel control. Write the pseudocode, then write the Visual Basic .NET code.

9. Write the If...Then...Else statement that displays the string "Dog" in the AnimalLabel control if the strAnimal variable contains the letter "D" (in any case); otherwise, display the string "Cat". Draw the flowchart, then write the Visual Basic .NET code.

10. Assume you want to calculate a 10% discount on desks sold to customers in Colorado. Use the variables strItem, strState, sngSales, and sngDiscount. Format the discount using the Standard format style and display it in the DiscountLabel control. Write the pseudocode, then write the Visual Basic .NET code.

11. Assume you want to calculate a 2% price increase on all red shirts, but a 1% price increase on all other items. In addition to calculating the price increase, also calculate the new price. You can use the variables strColor, strItem, sngOrigPrice, sngIncrease, and sngNewPrice. Format the original price, price increase, and new price using the Standard format style. Display the original price, price increase, and new price in the OriginalLabel, IncreaseLabel, and NewLabel controls, respectively. Write the Visual Basic .NET code.

12. Write the Visual Basic .NET code that swaps the values stored in the sngMarySales and sngJeffSales variables, but only if the value stored in the sngMarySales variable is less than the value stored in the sngJeffSales variable.

After completing this lesson, you will be able to:

- Group objects using a GroupBox control
- Calculate a periodic payment using the Pmt function
- Create a message box using the MessageBox.Show method
- Determine the value returned by a message box

The Monthly Payment Calculator Application

Completing the User Interface

Recall that Herman Juarez has asked you to create an application that he can use to calculate the monthly payment on a car loan. To make this calculation, the application will need to know the loan amount (principal), the annual percentage rate (APR) of interest, and the life of the loan (term) in years. The sketch of the application's user interface is shown in Figure 4-21.

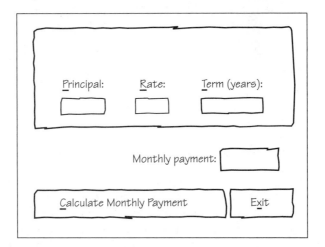

Figure 4-21: Sketch of the Monthly Payment Calculator user interface

The user interface contains a group box, three text boxes, five labels, and two buttons. To save you time, your computer's hard disk contains a partially completed Monthly Payment Calculator application. When you open the application, you will notice that most of the user interface has already been created and the properties of the existing objects have been set. You complete the user interface in this lesson.

To open the partially completed application:

1 Start Microsoft Visual Studio .NET, if necessary, then close the Start Page window.

> **2** Click **File** on the menu bar, and then click **Open Solution**. The Open Solution dialog box opens. Open the **Payment Solution** (Payment Solution.sln) file, which is contained in the VBNET\Tut04\Payment Solution folder.
>
> **3** If the designer window is not open, right-click **Payment Form.vb** in the Solution Explorer window, then click **View Designer**.
>
> **4** Auto-hide the Toolbox, Solution Explorer, and Properties windows, if necessary. The partially completed user interface is shown in Figure 4-22.

IdTermLabel

RateTextBox

IdRateLabel

IdPrincipalLabel

PrincipalTextBox

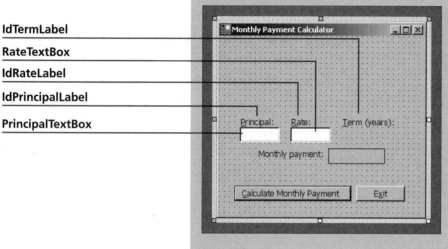

Figure 4-22: Partially completed Monthly Payment Calculator user interface

Only two controls are missing from the interface: a group box and a text box. You add the group box control first, and then you add the text box.

Adding a Group Box Control to the Form

You use the **GroupBox tool** in the Toolbox window to add a group box control to the interface. A **group box control** serves as a container for other controls. You can use a group box control to visually separate related controls from other controls on the form. In the Monthly Payment Calculator interface, for example, the group box control will visually separate the controls relating to the principal, rate, and term information from the rest of the controls.

Visual Basic .NET treats the group box and the controls contained in the group box as one unit. When you move the group box, the controls inside the group box also move, and when you delete the group box, the controls inside the group box also are deleted.

You can include an identifying label on a group box by setting the group box control's Text property. Labeling a group box is optional, but if you do, you should use sentence capitalization for the identifying label.

tip

> You also can use a panel control to group related controls together. You use the Panel tool in the toolbox to add a panel control to the interface. The difference between a panel control and a group box control is that, unlike a group box control, a panel control can have scroll bars. Additionally, a group box control, unlike a panel control, has a Text property.

GUI Design Tips

Labeling a Group Box Control

- Use sentence capitalization for the optional identifying label, which is entered in the control's Text property.

To add a group box to the interface, and then drag several of the existing controls into the group box:

1 Click the **GroupBox** tool in the toolbox, and then drag a group box control onto the form.

2 Set the following properties for the group box control:

Name:	**InfoGroupBox**
Location:	**24, 24**
Size:	**272, 88**

The group box control will not need an identifying label in this interface, so you can delete the contents of its Text property.

3 Delete the contents of the group box control's Text property.

Now drag the IdPrincipalLabel, PrincipalTextBox, IdRateLabel, RateTextBox, and IdTermLabel controls into the group box control.

4 Select the following five controls: IdPrincipalLabel, PrincipalTextBox, IdRateLabel, RateTextBox, and IdTermLabel.

HELP? As you learned in Tutorial 1, you can select more than one control by clicking the first control and then pressing and holding down the Ctrl (Control) key as you click the other controls you want to select.

5 Place your mouse pointer on one of the selected controls. The mouse pointer turns into ✥. Press and hold down the left mouse button as you drag the selected controls into the group box, then release the mouse button. (The controls will not appear in the group box until you release the mouse button.) See Figure 4-23.

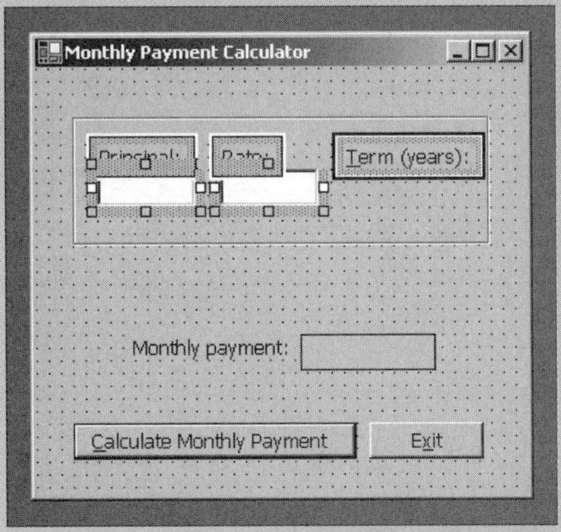

Figure 4-23: Controls dragged into the group box

6 Click the **form** to deselect the controls.

Also missing from the interface is a text box in which the user can enter the term information.

As you learned in Tutorial 1, the last control selected is used as the reference control when aligning and sizing controls.

To add the missing text box:

1 Click the **TextBox** tool [abl] in the toolbox, and then drag a text box control into the group box, immediately below the IdTermLabel.

2 Change the text box's Name property from TextBox1 to **TermTextBox**.

3 Delete the contents of the TermTextBox control's Text property.

4 With the TermTextBox control selected, press and hold down the Ctrl key as you click the **RateTextBox** control on the form. Both controls now should be selected.

5 Click **Format** on the menu bar, point to **Align**, and then click **Tops** to align the top border of the TermTextBox control with the top border of the RateTextBox control.

6 Click **Format** on the menu bar, point to **Make Same Size**, and then click **Both** to make the TermTextBox control the same size as the RateTextBox control.

7 Ctrl+click the **RateTextBox** control to deselect the control. The TermTextBox control should still be selected.

8 With the TermTextBox control selected, Ctrl+click the **IdTermLabel** control. Both controls should now be selected.

9 Click **Format** on the menu bar, point to **Align**, and then click **Lefts** to align the left border of the TermTextBox control with the left border of the IdTermLabel control.

10 Click the **form** to deselect the controls. Figure 4-24 shows the completed user interface.

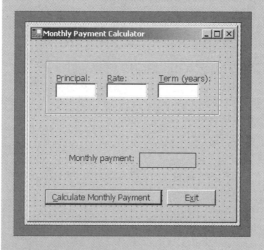

Figure 4-24: Completed user interface

Now that you have completed the user interface, you can lock the controls in place, and then set each control's TabIndex property appropriately.

Locking the Controls and Setting the TabIndex Property

As you learned in Tutorial 2, when you have completed a user interface, you should lock the controls in place, and then set each control's TabIndex property appropriately.

To lock the controls, and then set each control's TabIndex property:

1   Right-click the **form**, and then click **Lock Controls** on the shortcut menu.

2   Click **View** on the menu bar, and then click **Tab Order**. The current TabIndex value for each control appears in blue boxes on the form.

Notice that the TabIndex values of the controls contained within the group box begin with the number 9, which is the TabIndex value of the group box itself; this indicates that the controls belong to the group box rather than to the form. As mentioned earlier, if you move or delete the group box, the controls that belong to the group box also will be moved or deleted. The numbers that appear after the period in the controls' TabIndex values indicate the order in which each control was added to the group box.

3   Click the **InfoGroupBox** control. The number 0 replaces the number 9 in the TabIndex box, and the color of the box changes from blue to white to indicate that you have set the TabIndex value.

4   Click the **IdPrincipalLabel** control. The number 0.0 appears in the control's TabIndex box.

5   Click the **PrincipalTextBox** control. The number 0.1 appears in the control's TabIndex box.

6   Use the information in Figure 4-25 to set the TabIndex values for the remaining controls on the form.

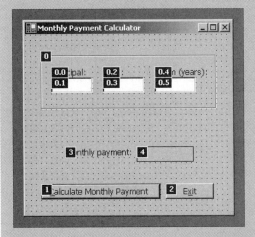

Figure 4-25: Correct TabIndex values

7   Press **Esc** to remove the TabIndex boxes from the form.

8   Click **File** on the menu bar, and then click **Save All** to save the solution.

tip

Recall that you also can click View on the menu bar and then click Tab Order to remove the TabIndex boxes.

Now you can begin coding the application. The TOE chart for the Monthly Payment Calculator application is shown in Figure 4-26.

Task	Object	Event
1. Calculate the monthly payment amount 2. Display the monthly payment amount in the PaymentLabel control	CalcPayButton	Click
End the application	ExitButton	Click
Display the monthly payment amount (from CalcPayButton)	PaymentLabel	None
Get and display the principal, rate, and term amounts	PrincipalTextBox, RateTextBox, TermTextBox	None
Clear the contents of the PaymentLabel control	PrincipalTextBox, RateTextBox, TermTextBox	TextChanged
Prevent the user from typing a minus sign, dollar sign, percent sign, comma, or space in a text box	PrincipalTextBox, RateTextBox, TermTextBox	KeyPress

Figure 4-26: TOE chart for the Monthly Payment Calculator application

According to the TOE chart, the Click event procedures for the two buttons, and the TextChanged and KeyPress events for the three text boxes, need to be coded. When you open the Code editor window, you will notice that the ExitButton's Click event procedure already has been coded for you. In this lesson, you first code the CalcPayButton Click event procedure, and then you code the TextChanged event for the text boxes. You code the KeyPress event in Lesson C.

Coding the CalcPayButton Click Event Procedure

According to the TOE chart shown in Figure 4-26, the CalcPayButton's Click event procedure is responsible for calculating the monthly payment amount, and then displaying the result in the PaymentLabel control. The pseudocode for the CalcPayButton's Click event procedure is shown in Figure 4-27.

```
CalcPayButton
1. declare variables

2. assign principal, rate, and term to variables

3. if rate >= 1
       rate = rate /100
   end if

4. if term >= 1
       calculate the monthly payment
       display the monthly payment in the PaymentLabel control
   else
       display the message "The term must be greater than or equal to 1." in a message box
   end if
```

Figure 4-27: Pseudocode for the CalcPayButton Click event procedure

To begin coding the CalcPayButton Click event procedure:

1 Right-click the **form**, and then click **View Code** to open the Code editor window. Notice that the ExitButton Click event procedure already contains the `Me.Close()` statement.

2 Click the **Class Name** list arrow, and then click **CalcPayButton** in the list. Click the **Method Name** list arrow, and then click **Click** in the list. The template for the CalcPayButton Click event procedure appears in the Code editor window.

The first step in the pseudocode shown in Figure 4-27 is to declare the necessary variables. The CalcPayButton Click event procedure will need to use four variables. The sngPrincipal, sngRate, and intTerm variables will store the information entered by the user, and the sngPayment variable will store the monthly payment amount.

3 Type **dim sngPrincipal, sngRate, sngPayment as single** and press **Enter**. Then type **dim intTerm as integer** and press **Enter** twice. It is a good programming practice to use a blank line to separate related blocks of code in the Code editor window; this makes your code more readable and easier to understand.

Step 2 in the pseudocode is to assign the principal, rate, and term information to the appropriate variables.

4 Enter the comment and three assignment statements shown in Figure 4-28, then position the insertion point as shown in the figure.

```
Private Sub CalcPayButton_Click(ByVal sender As Object, ByVal e As System.EventArgs)
    Dim sngPrincipal, sngRate, sngPayment As Single
    Dim intTerm As Integer

    'assign text box values to variables
    sngPrincipal = Val(Me.PrincipalTextBox.Text)
    sngRate = Val(Me.RateTextBox.Text)
    intTerm = Val(Me.TermTextBox.Text)

    I
End Sub
```

enter these four lines of code

position the insertion point here

Figure 4-28: Comment and three assignment statements entered in the procedure

Now use a selection structure to handle step 3 in the pseudocode—determining whether the application needs to convert the interest rate entered by the user to its decimal equivalent. This is necessary because the user might enter the rate as a percentage, or he or she might enter it as a decimal number. For example, an interest rate of 5% might be entered as either 5 or .05.

5 Type **'convert the rate to decimal, if necessary** and press **Enter**.

6 Type **if sngrate >= 1 then** and press **Enter**. Notice that, when you press Enter, the Code editor automatically enters the `End If` statement in the window. Type **sngrate = sngrate / 100** between the `If` and `End If` statements.

7 Position the mouse pointer I after the `End If` statement, and then click at that location. Press **Enter** twice to insert two blank lines after the `End If` statement.

Step 4 in the pseudocode is to determine whether the term amount entered by the user is greater than or equal to one year.

8 Type **'verify that the term is valid** and press **Enter**.

9 Type **if intterm >= 1 then** and press **Enter**. Figure 4-29 shows the current status of the procedure.

```
Private Sub CalcPayButton_Click(ByVal sender As Object, ByVal e As System.EventArgs)
    Dim sngPrincipal, sngRate, sngPayment As Single
    Dim intTerm As Integer

    'assign text box values to variables
    sngPrincipal = Val(Me.PrincipalTextBox.Text)
    sngRate = Val(Me.RateTextBox.Text)
    intTerm = Val(Me.TermTextBox.Text)

    'convert the rate to decimal, if necessary
    If sngRate >= 1 Then
        sngRate = sngRate / 100
    End If

    'verify that the term is valid
    If intTerm >= 1 Then

    End If
End Sub
```

Figure 4-29: Current status of the CalcPayButton Click event procedure

According to the pseudocode, if the term is valid, the procedure should calculate the monthly payment, and then display the monthly payment in the PaymentLabel control. You can use the Pmt function to calculate the monthly payment.

Using the Pmt Function

You can use the Visual Basic .NET **Pmt function** to calculate a periodic payment on either a loan or an investment. Figure 4-30 shows the syntax of the Pmt function and lists the meaning of each argument included in the function. The figure also includes three examples of using the function.

Syntax	
Pmt(*Rate, NPer, PV*[, *FV, Due*]**)**	
Argument	**Meaning**
Rate	interest rate per period
NPer	total number of payment periods (the term)
PV	present value of the loan or investment; the present value of a loan is the loan amount, whereas the present value of an investment is zero
FV	future value of the loan or investment; the future value of a loan is zero, whereas the future value of an investment is the amount you want to accumulate; if omitted, the number 0 is assumed
Due	due date of payments; can be either the intrinsic constant `DueDate.EndOfPeriod` or the intrinsic constant `DueDate.BegOfPeriod`; if omitted, `DueDate.EndOfPeriod` is assumed

Figure 4-30: Syntax, arguments, and examples of the Pmt function

---

Example 1 – Calculates the annual payment for a loan of $9,000 for 3 years at 5% interest. The payments are due at the end of each period (year).

Rate: .05
NPer: 3
PV: 9000
FV: 0
Due: DueDate.EndOfPeriod
Function: Pmt(.05, 3, 9000, 0, DueDate.EndOfPeriod)
                    or
          Pmt(.05, 3, 9000)
Annual payment (rounded to the nearest cent): -3,304.88

Example 2 – Calculates the monthly payment for a loan of $12,000 for 5 years at 6% interest. The payments are due at the beginning of each period (month).

Rate: .06/12
NPer: 5 * 12
PV: 12000
FV: 0
Due: DueDate.BegOfPeriod
Function: Pmt(.06/12, 5 * 12, 12000, 0, DueDate.BegOfPeriod)
Monthly payment (rounded to the nearest cent): -230.84

Example 3 – Calculates the amount you need to save each month to accumulate $40,000 at the end of 20 years. The interest rate is 6%, and deposits are due at the beginning of each period (month).

Rate: .06/12
NPer: 20 * 12
PV: 0
FV: 40000
Due: DueDate.BegOfPeriod
Function: Pmt(.06/12, 20 * 12, 0, 40000, DueDate.BegOfPeriod)
Monthly payment (rounded to the nearest cent): -86.14

Figure 4-30: Syntax, arguments, and examples of the Pmt function (continued)

Notice that the Pmt function contains five arguments. Three of the arguments (*Rate*, *NPer*, and *PV*) are required, and two (*FV* and *Due*) are optional. If the *FV* (future value) argument is omitted, the Pmt function uses the default value, 0. If the *Due* argument is omitted, the Pmt function uses the constant DueDate.EndOfPeriod as the default value. The DueDate.EndOfPeriod constant indicates that payments are due at the end of each period.

Study closely the three examples shown in Figure 4-30. Example 1 uses the Pmt function to calculate the annual payment for a loan of $9,000 for 3 years at 5% interest, where payments are due at the end of each period; in this case, a period is a year. As the example indicates, the annual payment returned by the Pmt function and rounded to the nearest cent is -3,304.88. In other words, if you borrow $9,000 for 3 years at 5% interest, you would need to make three annual payments of $3,304.88 to pay off the loan. Notice that the Pmt function returns a negative number.

When calculating an annual payment, the *Rate* argument should specify the annual interest rate, and the *NPer* argument should specify the life of the loan or investment in years. In Example 1, the *Rate* argument is .05, which is the annual interest rate, and the *NPer* argument is the number 3, which is the number of years you have to pay off the loan. As the example indicates, you can use the function Pmt(.05, 3, 9000, 0, DueDate.EndOfPeriod) to calculate the annual payment. You also can use the function Pmt(.05, 3, 9000), because the default values for the optional *FV* and *Due* arguments are 0 and DueDate.EndOfPeriod, respectively.

The *Rate* and *NPer* arguments in the Pmt function must be expressed using the same units. For example, if *Rate* is a monthly interest rate, then *NPer* must specify the number of monthly payments. If *Rate* is an annual interest rate, then *NPer* must specify the number of annual payments.

You learned about the negation operator in Tutorial 2. The negation operator reverses the sign of the number: a negative number becomes a positive number and vice versa.

The Pmt function shown in Example 2 in Figure 4-30 calculates the monthly payment for a loan of $12,000 for 5 years at 6% interest, where payments are due at the beginning of each period; in this case, a period is a month. Notice that the *Rate* and *NPer* arguments are expressed in monthly terms rather than in annual terms. The monthly payment for this loan, rounded to the nearest cent, is -230.84.

In addition to using the Pmt function to calculate the payments required to pay off a loan, you also can use the Pmt function to calculate the amount you would need to save each period to accumulate a specific sum. The function `Pmt( .06/12, 20 * 12, 0, 40000, DueDate.BegOfPeriod)` shown in Example 3 in Figure 4-30, for instance, indicates that you need to save 86.14 (rounded to the nearest cent) each month to accumulate $40,000 at the end of 20 years, assuming a 6% interest rate and the appropriate amount deposited at the beginning of each period.

In the current application, you will use the Pmt function to calculate a monthly payment on a car loan. When entering the Pmt function, you must convert the annual interest rate, which is stored in the sngRate variable, to a monthly rate; you do so by dividing the annual rate by 12. You also must multiply by 12 the term of the loan, which is expressed in years and stored in the intTerm variable, to convert the number of years to the number of months. Additionally, because you want the monthly payment amount to appear as a positive number, you will precede the Pmt function with the negation operator (–).

To continue coding the CalcPayButton Click event procedure:

1 In the blank line below the `If intTerm >= 1 Then` instruction, type **'calculate and display the monthly payment** and press **Enter**.

2 Type **sngpayment = -pmt(sngrate/12, intterm * 12, sngprincipal, 0, duedate.begofperiod)** and press **Enter**.

Now format the monthly payment amount using the Currency format style, and then display the formatted amount in the PaymentLabel control.

3 Type **me.paymentlabel.text = format(sngpayment, "currency")** and press **Enter**. See Figure 4-31. (The size of the font used in the Code editor window was changed so that you could view more of the code in the figure.)

```
Private Sub CalcPayButton_Click(ByVal sender As Object, ByVal e As System.EventArgs) Handles Calc
    Dim sngPrincipal, sngRate, sngPayment As Single
    Dim intTerm As Integer

    'assign text box values to variables
    sngPrincipal = Val(Me.PrincipalTextBox.Text)
    sngRate = Val(Me.RateTextBox.Text)
    intTerm = Val(Me.TermTextBox.Text)

    'convert the rate to decimal, if necessary
    If sngRate >= 1 Then
        sngRate = sngRate / 100
    End If

    'verify that the term is valid
    If intTerm >= 1 Then
        'calculate and display the monthly payment
        sngPayment = -Pmt(sngRate / 12, intTerm * 12, sngPrincipal, 0, DueDate.BegOfPeriod)
        Me.PaymentLabel.Text = Format(sngPayment, "currency")

    End If
End Sub
```

true path

Figure 4-31: Selection structure's true path coded in the procedure

4 Save the solution.

According to the pseudocode shown in Figure 4-27, if the term entered by the user is not greater than or equal to 1, the CalcPayButton Click event procedure should display an appropriate message in a message box. You can display the message using the MessageBox.Show method.

The MessageBox.Show Method

You can use the **MessageBox.Show method** to display a message box that contains text, one or more buttons, and an icon. Figure 4-32 shows the syntax of the MessageBox.Show method. It also lists the meaning of each argument used by the method, and includes two examples of using the method to create a message box.

In previous versions of Visual Basic, programmers used the MsgBox function to display a message box. Although the MsgBox function still is available in Visual Basic .NET, the MessageBox.Show method is the recommended way to display a message box.

Syntax	
MessageBox.Show(*text, caption, buttons, icon[, defaultButton]***)**	
Argument	**Meaning**
text	text to display in the message box
caption	text to display in the title bar of the message box
buttons	buttons to display in the message box; can be one of the following constants: MessageBoxButtons.AbortRetryIgnore MessageBoxButtons.OK MessageBoxButtons.OKCancel MessageBoxButtons.RetryCancel MessageBoxButtons.YesNo MessageBoxButtons.YesNoCancel
icon	icon to display in the message box; typically, one of the following constants: MessageBoxIcon.Exclamation ⚠ MessageBoxIcon.Information ⓘ MessageBoxIcon.Stop ⊗
defaultButton	button automatically selected when the user presses Enter; can be one of the following constants: MessageBoxDefaultButton.Button1 (default setting) MessageBoxDefaultButton.Button2 MessageBoxDefaultButton.Button3

Example 1 – Displays an informational message box that contains the message "Record deleted.".
```
MessageBox.Show("Record deleted.", "Payroll", _
    MessageBoxButtons.OK, MessageBoxIcon.Information)
```

Example 2 – Displays a warning message box that contains the message "Delete this record?".
```
MessageBox.Show("Delete this record?", "Payroll", _
    MessageBoxButtons.YesNo, MessageBoxIcon.Exclamation, _
    MessageBoxDefaultButton.Button2)
```

Figure 4-32: Syntax, arguments, and examples of the MessageBox.Show method

As Figure 4-32 indicates, the *text* argument specifies the text to display in the message box. The *text* argument can be a String literal constant, String named constant, or String variable. The message in the *text* argument should be concise but clear, and should be entered using sentence capitalization. You should avoid using the words "error," "warning," or "mistake" in the message, as these words imply that the user has done something wrong.

The *caption* argument specifies the text to display in the title bar of the message box, and typically is the application's name. Like the *text* argument, the *caption* argument can be a String literal constant, String named constant, or String variable. Unlike the *text* argument, however, the *caption* argument is entered using book title capitalization.

The *buttons* argument indicates the buttons to display in the message box and can be one of six different constants. For example, a *buttons* argument of `MessageBoxButtons.AbortRetryIgnore` displays the Abort, Retry, and Ignore buttons in the message box. A *buttons* argument of `MessageBoxButtons.OK`, on the other hand, displays only the OK button in the message box.

The *icon* argument specifies the icon to display in the message box and typically is one of the following constants: `MessageBoxIcon.Exclamation`, `MessageBoxIcon.Information`, or `MessageBoxIcon.Stop`. A message box's icon indicates the type of message being sent to the user. The `MessageBoxIcon.Exclamation` constant, for example, displays the Warning Message icon ⚠, which alerts the user to a condition or situation that requires him or her to make a decision before the application can proceed. The message to the user can be phrased as a question, such as "Save changes to the document?"

The `MessageBoxIcon.Information` constant displays the Information Message icon ⓘ. The Information Message icon indicates that the message in the message box is for information only and does not require the user to make a decision. An example of an informational message is "The changes were saved." A message box with an Information Message icon should contain only an OK button; in other words, you always use `MessageBoxButtons.OK` for the *buttons* argument when using `MessageBoxIcon.Information` for the *icon* argument. The user acknowledges the informational message by clicking the OK button.

The `MessageBoxIcon.Stop` constant displays the Stop Message icon ⊗, which alerts the user to a serious problem that requires intervention or correction before the application can continue. You would use the Stop Message icon in a message box that alerts the user that the disk in the disk drive is write-protected.

The *defaultButton* argument in the MessageBox.Show method identifies the default button, which is the button that is selected automatically when the user presses Enter. To designate the first button in the message box as the default button, you either set the *defaultButton* argument to `MessageBoxDefaultButton.Button1`, or you simply omit the argument. To have the second or third button be the default button, you set the *defaultButton* argument to `MessageBoxDefaultButton.Button2` or `MessageBoxDefaultButton.Button3`, respectively. The default button should be the button that represents the user's most likely action, as long as that action is not destructive.

Study closely the two examples shown in Figure 4-32. The `MessageBox.Show("Record deleted.", "Payroll", MessageBoxButtons.OK, MessageBoxIcon.Information)` instruction in Example 1 displays the informational message box shown in Figure 4-33. Similarly, the `MessageBox.Show("Delete this record?", "Payroll", MessageBoxButtons.YesNo, MessageBoxIcon.Exclamation, MessageBoxDefaultButton.Button2)` instruction in Example 2 displays the warning message box shown in Figure 4-34.

Figure 4-33: Message box displayed by the MessageBox.Show method shown in Example 1 in Figure 4-32

default button

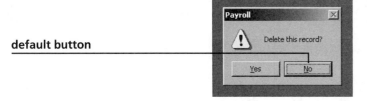

Figure 4-34: Message box displayed by the MessageBox.Show method shown in Example 2 in Figure 4-32

MessageBox.Show Method Standards

- Use sentence capitalization for the *text* argument, but book title capitalization for the *caption* argument. The name of the application typically appears in the *caption* argument.
- Avoid using the words "error," "warning," or "mistake" in the message, as these words imply that the user has done something wrong.
- Display the Warning Message icon ⚠ in a message box that alerts the user that he or she must make a decision before the application can continue. You can phrase the message as a question.
- Display the Information Message icon ⓘ in a message box that displays an informational message along with an OK button only.
- Display the Stop Message icon ⊗ when you want to alert the user of a serious problem that must be corrected before the application can continue.
- The default button in the dialog box should be the one that represents the user's most likely action, as long as that action is not destructive.

After displaying the message box, the MessageBox.Show method waits for the user to choose one of the buttons displayed in the message box. It then closes the message box and returns a number—an integer—that indicates which button the user chose. Figure 4-35 lists the numbers associated with the various buttons. It also lists the constant values assigned to each number, and the meaning of the numbers and constants.

Number	Constant	Meaning
1	DialogResult.OK	user chose the OK button
2	DialogResult.Cancel	user chose the Cancel button
3	DialogResult.Abort	user chose the Abort button
4	DialogResult.Retry	user chose the Retry button
5	DialogResult.Ignore	user chose the Ignore button
6	DialogResult.Yes	user chose the Yes button
7	DialogResult.No	user chose the No button

Figure 4-35: Values returned by the MessageBox.Show method

As Figure 4-35 indicates, the MessageBox.Show method returns the number 6 when the user selects the Yes button. The number 6 is represented by the constant `DialogResult.Yes`. When referring to the MessageBox.Show method's return value in code, you should use the constants listed in Figure 4-35 rather than the numbers, because the constants make the code easier to understand.

Sometimes you are not interested in the value returned by the MessageBox.Show method. This is the case when the message box is for informational purposes only. Recall that the only button in an informational message box is the OK button. Many times, however, the button selected by the user determines the next task performed by an application. For example, selecting the Yes button in the message box shown earlier in Figure 4-34 tells the application to delete the record; selecting the No button tells the application not to delete the record. Figure 4-36 shows examples of using the value returned by the MessageBox.Show method. In each example, the MessageBox.Show method displays a message box that contains Yes and No buttons.

Examples

Example 1
```
Dim intButton As Integer
intButton = MessageBox.Show("Delete this record?", _
            "Payroll", MessageBoxButtons.YesNo, _
            MessageBoxIcon.Exclamation, _
            MessageBoxDefaultButton.Button2)
If intButton = DialogResult.Yes Then
     instructions to delete the record
End If
```

Example 2
```
If MessageBox.Show("Delete this record?", _
     "Payroll", MessageBoxButtons.YesNo, _
     MessageBoxIcon.Exclamation, _
     MessageBoxDefaultButton.Button2) = DialogResult.Yes Then
          instructions to delete the record
End If
```

Figure 4-36: Examples of using the value returned by the MessageBox.Show method

Examples

Example 3
```
Dim intButton As Integer
intButton = MessageBox.Show("Play another game?", _
              "Math Monster", MessageBoxButtons.YesNo, _
              MessageBoxIcon.Exclamation)
If intButton = DialogResult.Yes Then
     instructions to start another game
Else   'DialogResult.No ─────────────────
       instructions to close the game application
End If
```

documentation

Figure 4-36: Examples of using the value returned by the MessageBox.Show method (continued)

In Example 1, the value returned by the MessageBox.Show method is assigned to an Integer variable named intButton. If the user selects the Yes button in the message box, the number 6 is stored in the intButton variable; otherwise, the number 7 is stored in the variable to indicate that the user selected the No button. The selection structure in the example then compares the contents of the intButton variable to the constant `DialogResult.Yes`. If the intButton variable contains the number 6, which is the value of the `DialogResult.Yes` constant, then the instructions to delete the record are processed; otherwise, the deletion instructions are skipped.

You do not have to store the value returned by the MessageBox.Show method in a variable, although doing so can make your code more readable. In Example 2 in Figure 4-36, for instance, the method's return value is not stored in a variable. Instead, the method appears in the selection structure's condition, where its return value is compared to the `DialogResult.Yes` constant.

The selection structure shown in Example 3 in Figure 4-36 performs one set of tasks when the user selects the Yes button, and another set of tasks when the user selects the No button. It is a good programming practice to document the Else portion of the selection structure as shown in the figure, because it makes it clear that the Else portion is processed only when the user selects the No button.

Recall that the CalcPayButton Click event procedure should display the message "The term must be greater than or equal to 1." if the term entered by the user is not greater than or equal to 1. The message box is for informational purposes only; therefore, it should contain the Information Message icon and the OK button, and you do not need to be concerned with its return value.

To complete the CalcPayButton Click event procedure:

1 Enter the additional code shown in Figure 4-37, which shows the completed CalcPayButton Click event procedure. (The size of the font used in the Code editor window was changed so that you could view more of the code in the figure.)

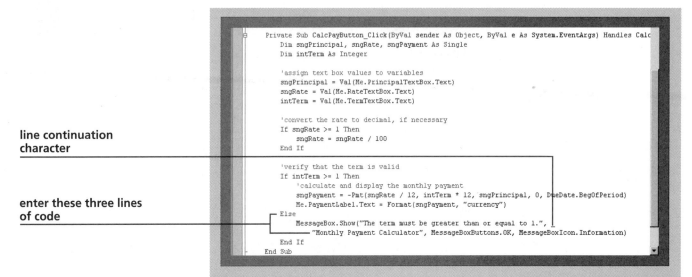

line continuation character

enter these three lines of code

```
Private Sub CalcPayButton_Click(ByVal sender As Object, ByVal e As System.EventArgs) Handles Calc
    Dim sngPrincipal, sngRate, sngPayment As Single
    Dim intTerm As Integer

    'assign text box values to variables
    sngPrincipal = Val(Me.PrincipalTextBox.Text)
    sngRate = Val(Me.RateTextBox.Text)
    intTerm = Val(Me.TermTextBox.Text)

    'convert the rate to decimal, if necessary
    If sngRate >= 1 Then
        sngRate = sngRate / 100
    End If

    'verify that the term is valid
    If intTerm >= 1 Then
        'calculate and display the monthly payment
        sngPayment = -Pmt(sngRate / 12, intTerm * 12, sngPrincipal, 0, DueDate.BegOfPeriod)
        Me.PaymentLabel.Text = Format(sngPayment, "currency")
    Else
        MessageBox.Show("The term must be greater than or equal to 1.", _
            "Monthly Payment Calculator", MessageBoxButtons.OK, MessageBoxIcon.Information)
    End If
End Sub
```

Figure 4-37: Completed CalcPayButton Click event procedure

2   Save the solution, then start the application. The Monthly Payment Calculator user interface appears on the screen.

Calculate the monthly payment for a loan of $12,000 for 5 years at 6% interest, where payments are due at the beginning of each month. (Recall that the *Due* argument in the Pmt function is `DueDate.BegOfPeriod`.)

3   Type **12000** in the Principal text box and press **Tab**. Type **6** in the Rate text box and press **Enter** to select the Calculate Monthly Payment button, which is the default button on the form. The message box created by the MessageBox.Show method appears on the screen, as shown in Figure 4-38.

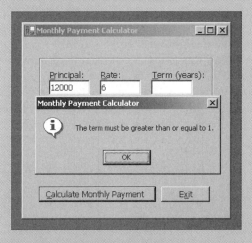

Figure 4-38: Message box created by the MessageBox.Show method

4   Press **Enter** to select the OK button in the message box. The message box closes.

5   Click the **Term** text box, then type **5** and press **Enter**. The CalcPayButton Click event procedure calculates and displays the monthly payment formatted using the Currency format style, as shown in Figure 4-39.

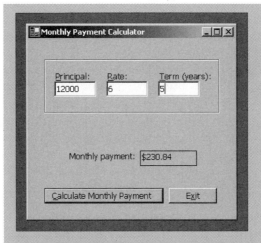

Figure 4-39: Monthly payment displayed in the interface

6 Click the **Exit** button to end the application.

Now verify that the application works correctly when the user enters the interest rate as a decimal number.

7 Start the application. Enter **12000** in the Principal text box, **.06** in the Rate text box, and **5** in the Term text box. Press **Enter**. The CalcPayButton Click event procedure calculates and displays a monthly payment of **$230.84**, which is the same monthly payment shown in Figure 4-39.

8 Click the **Exit** button to end the application. When you return to the Code editor window, close the Output window.

According to the TOE chart shown earlier in Figure 4-26, you also need to code the TextChanged event for the three text boxes.

Coding the TextChanged Event

As you learned in Tutorial 3, a control's TextChanged event occurs when the contents of a control's Text property have changed. This can happen as a result of either the user entering data into the control, or the application's code assigning data to the control's Text property. In this case, when the user makes a change to the information entered in the PrincipalTextBox, RateTextBox, and TermTextBox controls, the Monthly Payment Calculator application should delete the monthly payment displayed in the PaymentLabel control.

To code the TextChanged event for the three text boxes:

1 Click the **Class Name** list arrow in the Code editor window, and then click **PrincipalTextBox** in the list. Click the **Method Name** list arrow in the Code editor window, and then click **TextChanged** in the list. The template for the PrincipalTextBox control's TextChanged event appears in the Code editor window.

2 Type **me.paymentlabel.text = " "** and press **Enter**. This instruction tells the computer to remove the contents of the PaymentLabel control.

Next, assign the procedure a more meaningful name, and then tell the computer to process the procedure when the TextChanged event occurs for any of the three text boxes.

3 Change PrincipalTextBox_TextChanged, which appears after the words `Private Sub`, to **ClearLabel**.

4 Type _ (an underscore, which is the line continuation character) immediately before the letter H in the word `Handles`, and then press **Enter**.

5 Press **Tab** twice to indent the `Handles` line, and then make the additional changes noted in Figure 4-40.

enter this additional code ────────────►

```
Private Sub ClearLabel(ByVal sender As Object, ByVal e As System.EventArgs) _
        Handles PrincipalTextBox.TextChanged, RateTextBox.TextChanged, TermTextBox.TextChanged
    Me.PaymentLabel.Text = ""

End Sub
```

Figure 4-40: Completed ClearLabel procedure

Now test the ClearLabel procedure to verify that it is working correctly.

To test the ClearLabel procedure:

1 Save the solution, then start the application.

2 Enter **30000** in the Principal text box, **8** in the Rate text box, and **5** in the Term text box. Press **Enter**. $604.26 appears in the Monthly payment label.

3 Change the term from 5 to 3. Notice that the $604.26 no longer appears in the Monthly payment label. This is because when you make a change to the Term text box, the text box's TextChanged event processes the `Me.PaymentLabel.Text = ""` instruction contained in the ClearLabel procedure.

4 Press **Enter**. $933.87 appears in the Monthly payment label.

5 On your own, verify that the monthly payment amount is removed from the interface when the user changes the principal and rate amounts.

6 Click the **Exit** button to end the application. When you return to the Code editor window, close the Output window, then close the Code editor window.

7 Click **File** on the menu bar, and then click **Close Solution** to close the solution.

You now have completed Lesson B. In Lesson C you complete the Monthly Payment Calculator application by coding the KeyPress event for the three text boxes. For now, you can either take a break or complete the end-of-lesson questions and exercises before moving on to the next lesson.

SUMMARY

To use a group box control to group controls together:

■ Use the GroupBox tool 🔲 to add a group box control to the form. Drag controls from either the form or the Toolbox window into the group box control.

■ To include an optional identifying label on a group box control, set the group box control's Text property.

■ The TabIndex value of a control contained within a group box control is composed of two numbers separated by a period. The number to the left of the period is the TabIndex value of the group box itself. The number to the right of the period indicates the order in which the control was added to the group box.

To calculate a periodic payment on either a loan or an investment:

■ Use the Pmt function. The function's syntax is **Pmt**(*Rate, NPer, PV*[, *FV, Due*]). Refer to Figure 4-30 for a description of each argument and examples of using the function to calculate a periodic payment.

To display a message box that contains text, one or more buttons, and an icon:

■ Use the MessageBox.Show method. The method's syntax is **MessageBox.Show**(*text, caption, buttons, icon*[, *defaultButton*]). Refer to Figure 4-32 for a description of each argument and examples of using the method to display a message box.

■ Figure 4-35 lists the values returned by the MessageBox.Show method.

QUESTIONS

1. Which of the following statements is false?
   a. When you delete a group box control, the controls contained within the group box remain on the form.
   b. Use sentence capitalization for the group box control's identifying label.
   c. When you move a group box control, the controls contained within the group box also move.
   d. You can include an identifying label on a group box by setting the group box control's Text property.
   e. You can drag a control from the Toolbox window into a group box control.

2. Assume that the TabIndex value of a group box control is 5. If the NameTextBox control was the first control added to the group box, then its TabIndex value will be
   _____.
   a. 0.5
   b. 1
   c. 1.5
   d. 5.0
   e. 5.1

3. Which of the following calculates the monthly payment on a loan of $5,000 for 2 years at 4% interest? Payments are due at the end of the month and should be expressed as a positive number.
   a. `-Pmt(.04/12, 2 * 12, 5000)`
   b. `-Pmt(.04/12, 24, 5000)`
   c. `-Pmt(.04/12, 2 * 12, 5000, 0)`
   d. `-Pmt(.04/12, 24, 5000, 0, DueDate.EndOfPeriod)`
   e. All of the above.

4. Which of the following calculates the quarterly payment on a loan of $6,000 for 3 years at 9% interest? Payments are due at the beginning of the quarter and should be expressed as a negative number.
   a. `Pmt(.09/4, 3 * 12, 6000, 0, DueDate.BegOfPeriod)`
   b. `Pmt(.09/4, 3 * 4, 6000, 0, DueDate.BegOfPeriod)`
   c. `Pmt(.09/12, 3 * 12, 6000, 0, DueDate.BegOfPeriod)`
   d. `Pmt(.09/12, 12, 6000, 0, DueDate.BegOfPeriod)`
   e. None of the above.

5. Which of the following calculates the amount you need to save each month to accumulate $50,000 at the end of 10 years? The interest rate is 3% and deposits, which should be expressed as a positive number, are due at the beginning of the month.
   a. `Pmt(.03/12, 10 * 12, 0, 50000, DueDate.BegOfPeriod)`
   b. `-Pmt(.03/12, 10 * 12, 0, 50000, DueDate.BegOfPeriod)`
   c. `-Pmt(.03/12, 10 * 12, 50000, 0)`
   d. `Pmt(.03/12, 10 * 12, 50000, 0, DueDate.BegOfPeriod)`
   e. `-Pmt(.03/12, 120, 50000, 0, DueDate.BegOfPeriod)`

6. A message box's _____ argument indicates the type of message being sent.
   a. *buttons*
   b. *caption*
   c. *icon*
   d. *text*
   e. Both b and c.

7. You use the _____ constant to include the Warning Message icon in a message box.
   a. `MessageBox.Exclamation`
   b. `MessageBox.IconExclamation`
   c. `MessageBoxIcon.Exclamation`
   d. `MessageBox.IconWarning`
   e. `MessageBox.WarningIcon`

8. If a message is for informational purposes only and does not require the user to make a decision, the message box should display which of the following?
   a. an OK button and the ⓘ icon
   b. an OK button and the ⚠ icon
   c. a Yes button and the ⓘ icon
   d. any button and the ⓘ icon
   e. an OK button and any icon

9. You can use the _____ method to display a message in a message box.
   a. MessageBox.Display
   b. MessageBox.Open
   c. Message.Open
   d. Message.Show
   e. None of the above.

10. If the user clicks the OK button in a message box, the message box returns the number 1, which is equivalent to which constant?
    a. `DialogResult.OK`
    b. `DialogResult.OKButton`
    c. `Message.OK`
    d. `MessageBox.OK`
    e. `MessageResult.OK`

E X E R C I S E S

1. In this exercise, you code an application that uses the Pmt function to calculate the amount of money you need to save each week to accumulate a specific sum.

   a. If necessary, start Visual Studio .NET. Open the Weekly Savings Solution (Weekly Savings Solution.sln) file, which is contained in the VBNET\Tut04\Weekly Savings Solution folder. If the designer window is not open, right-click the form file's name in the Solution Explorer window, then click View Designer.

   b. Add a group box control to the interface. Name the group box control InfoGroupBox. Drag the IdGoalLabel, IdRateLabel, IdTermLabel, GoalTextBox, RateTextBox, and TermTextBox controls into the group box.

   c. Lock the controls, then set the TabIndex property appropriately.

   d. The user will enter the amount he or she wants to accumulate in the GoalTextBox. He or she will enter the annual interest rate and term (in years) in the RateTextBox and TermTextBox controls, respectively. Code the Calculate button so that it calculates the amount of money the user will need to save each week. Assume that each year has exactly 52 weeks, and that deposits are made at the end of the week. Format the weekly payment using the Standard format style, and display it in the SavingsLabel control.

   e. Save the solution, then start the application. Test the application by calculating the amount the user needs to save to accumulate $10,000 at the end of two years, assuming a 4.5% interest rate.

   f. Click the Exit button to end the application.

   g. Close the Output window, then close the solution.

2. In this exercise, you code an application for Mingo Sales. The application calculates a 10% discount if the customer is a wholesaler.

   a. If necessary, start Visual Studio .NET. Open the Discount Solution (Discount Solution.sln) file, which is contained in the VBNET\Tut04\Discount Solution folder. If the designer window is not open, right-click the form file's name in the Solution Explorer window, then click View Designer.

   The user will enter the product number, quantity ordered, and price in the ProductTextBox, QuantityTextBox, and PriceTextBox controls, respectively.

   b. Code the Calculate button so that it displays the message "Are you a wholesaler?" in a message box. If the user is a wholesaler, calculate a 10% discount on the total due, and then display the discount (formatted using the Standard format style) in the DiscountLabel control; otherwise, display 0.00 in the DiscountLabel control. Display the total due in the TotalLabel control, formatted using the Currency format style.

   c. Have the application remove the contents of the DiscountLabel and TotalLabel controls when a change is made to the contents of a text box on the form.

   d. Save the solution, then start the application. Test the application by calculating the total due for a wholesaler ordering four units of product number BCX12 at $10 per unit. Then test the application by calculating the total due for a non-wholesaler ordering two units of product number ABC34 at $5 per unit.

   e. Click the Exit button to end the application.

   f. Close the Output window, then close the solution.

Exercise 3 is a Discovery Exercise. Discovery Exercises, which may include topics that are not covered in this lesson, allow you to "discover" the solutions to problems on your own.

discovery ▶   3.   In this exercise, you research the constants you can use to display an icon in a message box.

a.   If necessary, start Visual Studio .NET. Click Help on the menu bar, and then click Index. Click the Filtered by list arrow, and then click Visual Basic and Related in the list (this may take several seconds to load).

b.   Type MessageBoxIcon in the Look for text box, then click MessageBoxIcon enumeration in the list of topics. An enumeration is simply a set of related constants. In this case, the MessageBoxIcon enumeration contains the constants you can use in the MessageBox.Show method's *icon* argument.

c.   Read the MessageBoxIcon Enumeration Help screen. In addition to the `MessageBoxIcon.Exclamation` constant, what other constant displays the Warning Message icon ⚠ in a message box? Which constants display the Information Message icon ⓘ? Which constants display the Stop Message icon ⊗? Which constant displays a symbol consisting of a question mark in a circle?

d.   Close the Help window.

LESSON C
objectives

After completing this lesson, you will be able to:

■ Specify the keys that a text box will accept

■ Display the ControlChars constants

■ Align the text in a label control

Completing the Monthly Payment Calculator Application

Coding the KeyPress Event

Recall that you still need to code the KeyPress event for the three text box controls in the Monthly Payment Calculator application. Before learning more about this event, open the Monthly Payment Calculator application that you worked on in Lesson B, and then view the template for the PrincipalTextBox control's KeyPress event procedure.

To open the Monthly Payment Calculator application, then view the template for the KeyPress event procedure:

1 Start Microsoft Visual Studio .NET, if necessary, and then close the Start Page window.

2 Click **File** on the menu bar, and then click **Open Solution**. The Open Solution dialog box opens. Open the **Payment Solution** (Payment Solution.sln) file, which is contained in the VBNET\Tut04\Payment Solution folder.

3 If the designer window is not open, right-click **Payment Form.vb** in the Solution Explorer window, then click **View Designer**.

4 Auto-hide the Toolbox, Solution Explorer, and Properties windows, if necessary. See Figure 4-41.

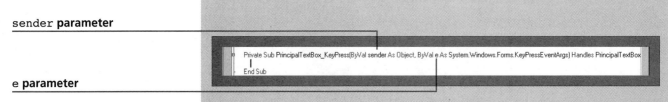

Figure 4-41: Monthly Payment Calculator application

5 If the Code editor window is not open, right-click **Payment Form.vb** in the Solution Explorer window, then click **View Code.**

6 Click the **Class Name** list arrow, and then click **PrincipalTextBox** in the list. Click the **Method Name** list arrow, and then click **KeyPress** in the list. Figure 4-42 shows the template for the PrincipalTextBox KeyPress event procedure. The items contained within parentheses in the procedure are called **parameters** and represent information passed to the procedure when the event occurs. (The font size in the Code editor window was changed so that you could view more of the code in the figure. `PrincipalTextBox.KeyPress` appears after the `Handles` keyword in the procedure.)

`sender` **parameter**

```
Private Sub PrincipalTextBox_KeyPress(ByVal sender As Object, ByVal e As System.Windows.Forms.KeyPressEventArgs) Handles PrincipalTextBox
End Sub
```

`e` **parameter**

Figure 4-42: Template for the PrincipalTextBox control's KeyPress event procedure

A control's KeyDown event also occurs when the user presses a key while the control has the focus. The KeyDown event occurs before the KeyPress event. When the user releases the key, the control's KeyUp event occurs.

A control's **KeyPress event** occurs when the user presses a key while the control has the focus. When the KeyPress event occurs, the memory address of the control receiving the event is sent to the event's `sender` parameter. In this case, for example, the memory address of the PrincipalTextBox is sent to the `sender` parameter. You learn more about the `sender` parameter in Tutorial 5. Additionally, a character corresponding to the key that was pressed is sent to the KeyPress event's `e` parameter. For example, when you press the period (.) on your keyboard, a period is sent to the `e` parameter. Similarly, when you press the Shift key along with a letter key on your keyboard, the uppercase version of the letter is sent to the `e` parameter.

One popular use for the KeyPress event is to prevent users from entering inappropriate characters in a text box. For example, a text box for entering a person's age should contain numbers only; it should not contain letters or special characters, such as the dollar sign or percent sign. To prevent a text box from accepting inappropriate characters, you first use the `e` parameter's **KeyChar property** to determine the key that the user pressed. You then use the `e` parameter's **Handled property** to cancel the key if it is an inappropriate one. Figure 4-43 shows examples of using the KeyChar and Handled properties in the KeyPress event procedure.

tip

· · · · · · · · · · · · · · · · ·

▶ KeyChar stands for "key character".

Examples

Example 1 - prevents the text box from accepting the dollar sign

```
Private Sub SalesTextBox_KeyPress(ByVal sender As Object, _
        ByVal e As System.Windows.Forms.KeyPressEventArgs) _
        Handles SalesTextBox.KeyPress
    If e.KeyChar = "$" Then
            e.Handled = True
    End If
End Sub
```

Example 2 – allows the text box to accept only numbers

```
Private Sub AgeTextBox_KeyPress(ByVal sender As Object, _
        ByVal e As System.Windows.Forms.KeyPressEventArgs) _
        Handles AgeTextBox.KeyPress
    If e.KeyChar < "0" OrElse e.KeyChar > "9" Then
            e.Handled = True
    End If
End Sub
```

Example 3 – allows the text box to accept only numbers and the Backspace key

```
Private Sub AgeTextBox_KeyPress(ByVal sender As Object, _
        ByVal e As System.Windows.Forms.KeyPressEventArgs) _
        Handles AgeTextBox.KeyPress
    If (e.KeyChar < "0" OrElse e.KeyChar > "9") _
        AndAlso e.KeyChar <> ControlChars.Back Then
            e.Handled = True
    End If
End Sub
```

Figure 4-43: Examples of using the KeyChar and Handled properties

The selection structure shown in Example 1 in Figure 4-43 prevents the SalesTextBox control from accepting the dollar sign. The `e.KeyChar = "$"` condition in the selection structure compares the contents of the `e` parameter's KeyChar property with a dollar sign ($). If the condition evaluates to True, which means that a dollar sign is stored in the KeyChar property, the `e.Handled = True` instruction cancels the key before it is entered in the SalesTextBox control.

You can use the selection structure shown in Example 2 in Figure 4-43 to prevent a text box from accepting a character that is not a number. However, keep in mind that Example 2's selection structure also prevents the text box from accepting the Backspace key. In other words, when entering text in the AgeTextBox control, you will not be able to use the Backspace key to delete a character entered in the text box. You can, however, use the left and right arrow keys to position the insertion point immediately before the character you want to delete, and then use the Delete key to delete the character.

Like Example 2's selection structure, the selection structure shown in Example 3 in Figure 4-43 also prevents the AgeTextBox control from accepting a character that is not a number. However, unlike Example 2's selection structure, Example 3's selection structure allows the user to employ the Backspace key, which is represented by the constant **ControlChars.Back**. Basically, Example 3's selection structure tells the KeyPress event to cancel a key if it is not a number and, at the same time, it is not the Backspace key.

Before entering the appropriate code in the PrincipalTextBox KeyPress event procedure, use the Object Browser to view the other ControlChars constants.

To view a list of ControlChars constants:

1 Click **View** on the menu bar, point to **Other Windows**, and then click **Object Browser**. Click the Find Symbol button 🔍. (If you cannot locate the Find Symbol button, refer to Figure 4-44.)

2 When the Find Symbol dialog box opens, type **controlchars** in the Find what box. Click the **Match whole word** option button, if necessary, and then click the **Find** button in the dialog box. The Find Symbol Results window opens. Click the **Close** button in the dialog box.

3 Right-click **ControlChars (Microsoft.VisualBasic)** in the Find Symbol Results window, then click **Browse Definition**. Close the Find Symbol Results window. The ControlChars constants appear in the Members of 'ControlChars' list box, as shown in Figure 4-44.

Find Symbol button

constants

Close button

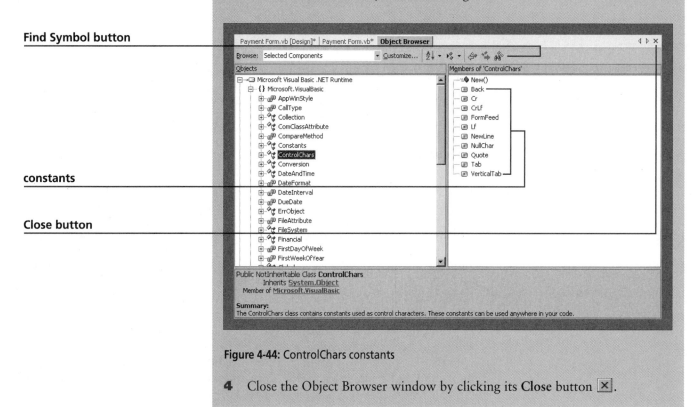

Figure 4-44: ControlChars constants

4 Close the Object Browser window by clicking its **Close** button ✕.

In the Monthly Payment Calculator application, you want the three text boxes to accept the numbers 0 through 9, the Backspace key, and the period; keys other than these should be canceled.

To allow the three text boxes to accept numbers, the Backspace key, and the period:

1 Change `PrincipalTextBox_KeyPress`, which appears in the procedure header, to **CancelKeys**.

2 Position your mouse pointer I immediately before the letter H in the word `Handles`, which also appears in the procedure header, and then click at that location.

3 Type _ (the underscore, which is the line continuation character), and then press **Enter** to move `Handles  PrincipalTextBox.KeyPress` to the next line in the procedure.

4 Press **Tab** twice. Change `Handles PrincipalTextBox.KeyPress` to **Handles   PrincipalTextBox.KeyPress,   RateTextBox.KeyPress, TermTextBox.KeyPress.**

5 Enter the additional code shown in Figure 4-45. (The font size in the Code editor window was changed so that you could view more of the code in the figure.)

enter these five lines of code

line continuation character

```
Private Sub CancelKeys(ByVal sender As Object, ByVal e As System.Windows.Forms.KeyPressEventArgs) _
        Handles PrincipalTextBox.KeyPress, RateTextBox.KeyPress, TermTextBox.KeyPress
    'allow numbers, the Backspace key, and the period
    If (e.KeyChar < "0" OrElse e.KeyChar > "9") _
        AndAlso e.KeyChar <> ControlChars.Back AndAlso e.KeyChar <> "." Then
        e.Handled = True
    End If
End Sub
```

Figure 4-45: Completed CancelKeys procedure

Now save the solution, then start the application and test the CancelKeys procedure.

To save the solution, then start the application and test the CancelKeys procedure:

1 Save the solution, then start the application.

2 Try entering a letter in the Principal text box, then try entering a special character, such as a dollar sign.

3 Type **30000** in the Principal text box, then press **Backspace** to delete the last zero. The text box now contains 3000.

4 On your own, try entering a letter in the Rate text box, then try entering a special character.

5 Type **.045** in the Rate text box, then press **Backspace** to delete the number 5. The text box now contains .04.

6 On your own, try entering a letter in the Term text box, then try entering a special character.

7 Type **20** in the Term text box, then press **Backspace** to delete the zero. The text box now contains 2.

8 Press **Enter** to calculate the monthly payment amount. The number $129.84 appears in the PaymentLabel control.

Notice that the monthly payment amount aligns on the top and left sides of the label control. You can improve the appearance of the interface by centering the amount in the control. You learn how to align the text contained in a label control in the next section.

9   Click the **Exit** button to end the application. When you return to the Code editor window, close the Output window.

You have finished coding the Monthly Payment Calculator application, so you can close the Code editor window.

10   Click the Code editor window's **Close** button ⊠.

Aligning the Text in a Label Control

The **TextAlign property** controls the placement of the text in a label control and can be set to TopLeft (the default), TopCenter, TopRight, MiddleLeft, MiddleCenter, MiddleRight, BottomLeft, BottomCenter, or BottomRight. In this case, you will change the PaymentLabel control's TextAlign property to MiddleCenter.

To change the TextAlign property to MiddleCenter, then test the application:

1   Click the **PaymentLabel** control on the form, then click **TextAlign** in the Properties window.

2   Click the list arrow in the Settings box. Buttons corresponding to the valid settings for the TextAlign property appear, as shown in Figure 4-46.

MiddleCenter setting ————————————

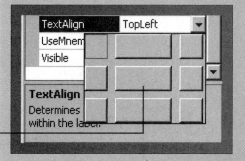

Figure 4-46: TextAlign property settings

3   Click the center button. MiddleCenter appears in the TextAlign property.

4   Save the solution, then start the application.

5   Type **9000** in the Principal text box, 5 in the Rate text box, and 3 in the Term text box. Press **Enter**. The monthly payment amount, $268.62, appears centered in the PaymentLabel control, as shown in Figure 4-47.

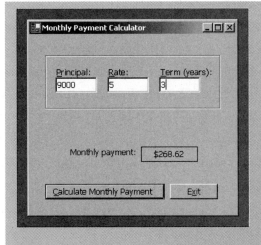

Figure 4-47: Monthly payment amount centered in the label control

6 Click the **Exit** button to end the application, then close the Output window and the Code editor window.

7 Click **File** on the menu bar, and then click **Close Solution.**

You now have completed Tutorial 4. You can either take a break or complete the end-of-lesson questions and exercises.

SUMMARY

To allow a text box to accept only certain keys:

- Code the text box's KeyPress event.
- The key the user pressed is stored in the KeyChar property of the KeyPress event procedure's e parameter. The `e.Handled = True` instruction cancels the key pressed by the user.

To align the text in a control:

- Set the control's TextAlign property.

QUESTIONS

1. A control's _____ event occurs when a user presses a key while the control has the focus.

   a. Key

   b. KeyPress

   c. Press

   d. PressKey

   e. None of the above.

2. When entered in the appropriate event, which of the following statements cancels the key pressed by the user?

    a.   `Cancel = True`

    b.   `e.Cancel = True`

    c.   `e.Handled = True`

    d.   `Handled = True`

    e.   `Key = Null`

3. Which of the following can be used in an If...Then...Else statement to determine whether the user pressed the Backspace key?

    a.   `If ControlChars.Back = True Then`

    b.   `If e.KeyChar = Backspace Then`

    c.   `If e.KeyChar = ControlChars.Backspace Then`

    d.   `If KeyChar.ControlChars = Back Then`

    e.   None of the above.

4. Which of the following can be used in an If...Then...Else statement to determine whether the user pressed the $ (dollar sign) key?

    a.   `If ControlChars.DollarSign = True Then`

    b.   `If e.KeyChar = "$" Then`

    c.   `If e.KeyChar = Chars.DollarSign Then`

    d.   `If KeyChar.ControlChars = "$" Then`

    e.   None of the above.

5. You can center the contents of a label control by setting the control's _____ property to MiddleCenter.

    a.   Align

    b.   AlignLabel

    c.   AlignText

    d.   LabelAlign

    e.   TextAlign

EXERCISES

The following list summarizes the GUI design guidelines you have learned so far. You can use this list to verify that the interfaces you create in the following exercises adhere to the GUI standards outlined in the book.

- Information should flow either vertically or horizontally, with the most important information always located in the upper-left corner of the screen.

- Maintain a consistent margin of two or three dots from the edge of the window.

- Try to create a user interface that no one notices.

- Related controls should be grouped together using white space, a GroupBox control, or a Panel control.

- Set the form's FormBorderStyle, ControlBox, MaximizeBox, MinimizeBox, and StartPosition properties appropriately:

    - A splash screen should not have a Minimize, Maximize, or Close button, and its borders should not be sizable.

- A form that is not a splash screen should always have a Minimize button and a Close button, but you can choose to disable the Maximize button. Typically, the FormBorderStyle property is set to Sizable, but also can be set to FixedSingle.

- Position related controls on succeeding dots. Controls that are not part of any logical grouping may be positioned from two to four dots away from other controls.

- Buttons should be positioned either in a row along the bottom of the screen, or stacked in either the upper-right or lower-right corner.

- If the buttons are positioned at the bottom of the screen, then each button should be the same height; their widths, however, may vary.

- If the buttons are stacked in either the upper-right or lower-right corner of the screen, then each should be the same height and the same width.

- Use no more than six buttons on a screen.

- The most commonly used button should be placed first.

- The default button should be the button that is most often selected by the user, except in cases where the tasks performed by the button are both destructive and irreversible. The default button typically is the first button.

- Button captions should:
  - be meaningful
  - be from one to three words
  - appear on one line
  - be entered using book title capitalization

- Use labels to identify the text boxes in the interface, and position the label either above or to the left of the text box.

- Label text should:
  - be from one to three words
  - appear on one line
  - be left-justified
  - end with a colon (:)
  - be entered using sentence capitalization

- Labels that identify controls should have their BorderStyle property set to None.

- Labels that display program output, such as the result of a calculation, should have their BorderStyle property set to FixedSingle.

- Align controls to minimize the number of different margins.

- If you use a graphic in the interface, use a small one and place it in a location that will not distract the user.

- Use the Tahoma font for applications that will run on Windows 2000 or Windows XP.

- Use no more than two different font sizes, which should be 8, 9, 10, 11, or 12 point.

- Use only one font type, which should be a sans serif font, in the interface.

- Avoid using italics and underlining.

- Limit the use of bold text to titles, headings, and key items.

- Build the interface using black, white, and gray first, then add color only if you have a good reason to do so.

- Use white, off-white, light gray, pale blue, or pale yellow for an application's background, and black for the text.

- Limit the number of colors to three, not including white, black, and gray. The colors you choose should complement each other.

- Never use color as the only means of identification for an element in the user interface.

- Set each control's TabIndex property to a number that represents the order in which you want the control to receive the focus (begin with 0).

- A text box's TabIndex value should be one more than the TabIndex value of its identifying label.

- Assign a unique access key to each control (in the interface) that can receive user input (text boxes, buttons, and so on).

- When assigning an access key to a control, use the first letter of the caption or identifying label, unless another letter provides a more meaningful association. If you can't use the first letter and no other letter provides a more meaningful association, then use a distinctive consonant. Lastly, use a vowel or a number.

- Lock the controls in place on the form.

- Document the program internally.

- Use the Val function on any Text property involved in a calculation.

- Use the Format function to improve the appearance of numbers in the interface.

- In the InputBox function, use sentence capitalization for the *prompt*, and book title capitalization for the *title*.

- Use sentence capitalization for the optional identifying label in a group box control.

- MessageBox.Show method:

  - Use sentence capitalization for the *text* argument, but book title capitalization for the *caption* argument. The name of the application typically appears in the *caption* argument.

  - Avoid using the words "error," "warning," or "mistake" in the message.

  - Display the Warning Message icon ⚠ in a message box that alerts the user that he or she must make a decision before the application can continue. You can phrase the message as a question.

  - Display the Information Message icon ⓘ in a message box that displays an informational message along with an OK button only.

- ■ Display the Stop Message icon ⊗ when you want to alert the user of a serious problem that must be corrected before the application can continue.

- ■ The default button in the dialog box should be the one that represents the user's most likely action, as long as that action is not destructive.

■ Use the KeyPress event to prevent a text box from accepting inappropriate keys.

■ Test the application with both valid and invalid data (for example, test the application without entering any data, and test it by entering letters where numbers are expected).

1. In this exercise, you code an application that swaps two values entered by the user.

a. If necessary, start Visual Studio .NET. Open the Swap Solution (Swap Solution.sln) file, which is contained in the VBNET\Tut04\Swap Solution folder. If the designer window is not open, right-click the form file's name in the Solution Explorer window, then click View Designer.

b. Complete the code for the DisplayButton Click event procedure. The procedure should swap the two values entered by the user, but only if the first value is greater than the second value.

c. Save the solution, then start the application. Test the application by clicking the Display button, and then entering the two values 10 and 7. Click the Display button again, then enter the two values 5 and 9.

d. Click the Exit button to end the application.

e. Close the Output window, then close the solution.

2. In this exercise, you code an application that either adds or subtracts two numbers.

a. If necessary, start Visual Studio .NET. Open the Math Solution (Math Solution.sln) file, which is contained in the VBNET\Tut04\Math Solution folder. If the designer window is not open, right-click the form file's name in the Solution Explorer window, then click View Designer.

b. Complete the code for the OperationButton Click event procedure. The procedure should either add or subtract the two numbers entered by the user.

c. Save the solution, then start the application. Test the application by clicking the Add or Subtract button. Use the application to add the two numbers 23 and 13. Click the Add or Subtract button again. Use the application to subtract the two numbers 23 and 13.

d. Click the Exit button to end the application.

e. Close the Output window, then close the solution.

3. In this exercise, you create an application for Micro Seminars. The application displays the total amount a company owes for a seminar. The seminar charge is $80 per person.

a. If necessary, start Visual Studio .NET. Create a blank solution named Seminar Solution. Save the solution in the VBNET\Tut04 folder.

b. Add a Visual Basic .NET Windows Application project to the solution. Name the project Seminar Project.

c. Assign the filename Seminar Form.vb to the form file object.

d. Assign the name SeminarForm to the Windows Form object.

e. When designing the interface, provide a text box into which the user can enter the number of seminar registrants, and a label for displaying the total owed.

f. Code the application appropriately. The number of registrants should be less than 50. Display an appropriate message if the number of registrants is invalid.

g. Allow the user to press only numeric keys and the Backspace key when entering the number of registrants.

h. When a change is made to the number of registrants entered in the text box, clear the contents of the label control that displays the total owed.

i. Center the total owed in the label control, and format it using the Currency format style.

j. Save the solution, then start the application. Test the application with both valid and invalid data.

k. End the application.

l. Close the Output window, then close the solution.

4. In this exercise, you code an application that allows the user to enter a state abbreviation.

a. If necessary, start Visual Studio .NET. Open the State Solution (State Solution.sln) file, which is contained in the VBNET\Tut04\State Solution folder. If the designer window is not open, right-click the form file's name in the Solution Explorer window, then click View Designer.

b. Code the application so that it allows the user to enter only letters in the StateTextBox. Also allow the user to use the Backspace key.

c. Save the solution, then start the application. Test the application with both valid data (uppercase and lowercase letters and the Backspace key) and invalid data (numbers and special characters).

d. Click the Exit button to end the application.

e. Close the Output window, then close the solution.

5. In this exercise, you code an application that calculates a customer's water bill.

a. If necessary, start Visual Studio .NET. Open the Water Solution (Water Solution.sln) file, which is contained in the VBNET\Tut04\Water Solution folder. If the designer window is not open, right-click the form file's name in the Solution Explorer window, then click View Designer.

b. Code the application so that it calculates and displays the gallons of water used and the water charge. Format the water charge using the Currency format style. The charge for water is $1.75 per 1000 gallons, or .00175 per gallon. Before making the calculations, verify that the meter readings entered by the user are valid. To be valid, the current meter reading must be greater than or equal to the previous meter reading. Display an appropriate message if the meter readings are not valid.

c. Allow the user to enter only numbers in the CurrentTextBox and PreviousTextBox controls. Also allow the user to press the Backspace key when entering data in those two text boxes.

d. Clear the contents of the GalUsedLabel and ChargeLabel controls when a change is made to the contents of a text box on the form.

e. Save the solution, then start the application. Test the application with both valid and invalid data.

f. Click the Exit button to end the application.

g. Close the Output window, then close the solution.

Exercises 6 and 7 are Discovery Exercises. Discovery Exercises, which may include topics that are not covered in this lesson, allow you to "discover" the solutions to problems on your own.

discovery ▶ 6. In this exercise, you code an application that calculates a bonus.

a. If necessary, start Visual Studio .NET. Open the Bonus Solution (Bonus Solution.sln) file, which is contained in the VBNET\Tut04\Bonus Solution folder. If the designer window is not open, right-click the form file's name in the Solution Explorer window, then click View Designer.

b. The user will enter the sales amount in the SalesTextBox. The sales amount will always be an integer. Code the CalcButton Click event procedure so that it calculates the salesperson's bonus. Display the bonus, formatted using the Currency format style, in the BonusLabel control. The following rates should be used when calculating the bonus:

Sales amount ($)	Bonus
0-5000	1% of the sales amount
5001-10000	3% of the sales amount
Over 10000	7% of the sales amount

(*Hint*: You can nest an If...Then...Else statement, which means you can place one If...Then...Else statement inside another If...Then...Else statement.)

c. Allow the user to enter only numbers in the SalesTextBox control. Also allow the user to press the Backspace key when entering data in that text box.

d. Clear the contents of the BonusLabel control when a change is made to the contents of the SalesTextBox control.

e. Save the solution, then start the application. Test the application with both valid and invalid data.

f. Click the Exit button to end the application.

g. Close the Output window, then close the solution.

discovery ▶ 7. In this exercise, you learn how to specify the maximum number of characters that can be entered in a text box.

a. If necessary, start Visual Studio .NET. Open the Zip Solution (Zip Solution.sln) file, which is contained in the VBNET\Tut04\Zip Solution folder. If the designer window is not open, right-click the form file's name in the Solution Explorer window, then click View Designer.

b. Click the ZipTextBox. Scan the Properties list, looking for a property that allows you to specify the maximum number of characters that can be entered in the text box. When you locate the property, set its value to 10.

c. Save the solution, then start the application. Test the application by trying to enter more than 10 characters in the text box.

d. Click the Exit button to end the application.

e. Close the Output window, then close the solution.

Exercise 8 is a Debugging Exercise. Debugging Exercises provide an opportunity for you to detect and correct errors in an existing application.

debugging   8. In this exercise, you debug an existing application. The purpose of this exercise is to demonstrate operator order of precedence.

a. If necessary, start Visual Studio .NET. Open the Debug Solution (Debug Solution.sln) file, which is contained in the VBNET\Tut04\Debug Solution folder. If the designer window is not open, right-click the form file's name in the Solution Explorer window, then click View Designer.

b. Open the Code editor window. Review the existing code. The CalcButton Click event procedure should calculate a 10% bonus if the code entered by the user is either 1 or 2 and, at the same time, the sales amount is greater than $10,000. Otherwise, the bonus rate is 5%. Also, the CancelKeys procedure should allow the user to enter only numbers, and also use the Backspace key, when entering data in the two text boxes on the form.

c. Start the application. Type the number 1 in the Code text box, then press Backspace. Notice that the Backspace key is not working correctly.

d. Click the Exit button to end the application.

e. Make the appropriate change to the CancelKeys procedure.

f. Save the solution, then start the application. Type the number 12 in the Code text box, then press Backspace to delete the 2. The Code text box now contains the number 1. Type 200 in the Sales amount text box, then click the Calculate Bonus button. A message box appears and indicates that the bonus amount is $20.00 (10% of $200), which is incorrect; it should be $10.00 (5% of $200).

g. Click the OK button to close the message box. Click the Exit button to end the application.

h. Make the appropriate change to the CalcButton Click event procedure.

i. Save the solution, then start the application. Type the number 1 in the Code text box. Type 200 in the Sales amount text box, then click the Calculate Bonus button. The message box correctly indicates that the bonus amount is $10.00.

j. Click the Exit button to end the application.

k. Close the Output window, then close the solution.

More on the Selection Structure

Creating a Math Practice Application

case ▶ On Monday you meet with Susan Chen, the principal of a local primary school. Ms. Chen needs an application that the first and second grade students can use to practice both adding and subtracting numbers. The application should display the addition or subtraction problem on the screen, then allow the student to enter the answer, and then verify that the answer is correct. If the student's answer is not correct, the application should give him or her as many chances as necessary to answer the problem correctly.

The problems displayed for the first grade students should use numbers from 1 through 10 only; the problems for the second grade students should use numbers from 10 through 99. Because the first and second grade students have not learned about negative numbers yet, the subtraction problems should never ask them to subtract a larger number from a smaller one.

Ms. Chen also wants the application to keep track of how many correct and incorrect responses the student makes; this information will help her assess the student's math ability. Finally, she wants to be able to control the display of this information to keep students from being distracted or pressured by the number of right and wrong answers.

Previewing the Completed Application

Before you begin creating the Math Practice application, you first preview the completed application.

To preview the completed application:

1 Use the Run command on the Windows Start menu to run the **Math** (Math.exe) file, which is contained in the VBNET\Tut05 folder on your computer's hard disk. The Math Practice application's user interface appears on the screen. See Figure 5-1.

your numbers may differ

enter the answer here

check box

radio buttons

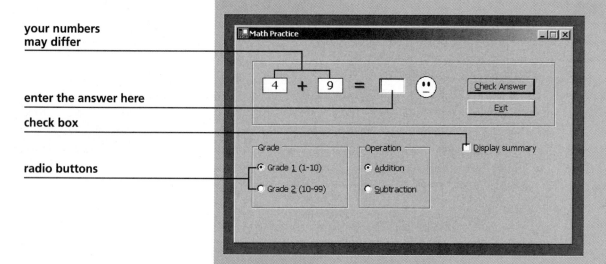

Figure 5-1: Math Practice application's user interface

Do not worry if the numbers on your screen do not match the ones shown in the figure. This application uses the Random object and the Random.Next method to display random numbers in the two label controls. You learn how to use the Random object and the Random.Next method in Lesson B.

The Math Practice application contains two new controls—radio buttons and a check box. You learn about these controls in Lesson B.

2 Type the correct answer to the addition problem appearing in the interface, then press **Enter** to select the Check Answer button, which is the default button on the form.

When you answer the math problem correctly, a happy face icon appears in the picture box control located to the left of the Check Answer button, and a new problem appears in the interface.

3 Click the **Display summary** check box to select it. A check mark appears inside the check box, and a group box control appears below the check box. The label controls contained in the group box display the number of correct and incorrect responses, as shown in Figure 5-2. In this case, you have made one correct response and zero incorrect responses.

new math problem appears

happy face icon appears when the answer is correct

number of correct and incorrect responses

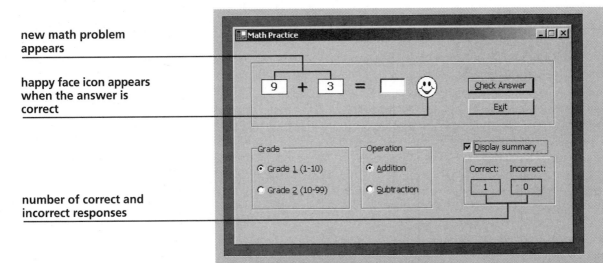

Figure 5-2: Interface showing that a correct response was made to the previous problem

4 Click the **Subtraction** radio button. A black dot appears in the center of the Subtraction radio button to indicate that the radio button is selected. The math problem changes to one involving subtraction.

5 Click inside the text box in which you enter the answer. Type an incorrect answer to the subtraction problem appearing on the screen, then press **Enter**. The application replaces the happy face icon in the picture box control with an icon whose facial expression is neutral. It also displays the "Try again!" message in a message box.

6 Press **Enter** to close the message box. The application highlights the incorrect answer in the text box and gives you another chance to enter a correct response. The interface shows that you have made one correct response and one incorrect response.

7 Type the correct answer to the subtraction problem, then press **Enter**. The happy face icon reappears in the picture box control, and the number of correct responses now says 2. Additionally, a new math problem appears in the interface.

8 Click the **Display summary** check box to deselect it. The application removes the check mark from the check box and hides the group box control that contains the summary information.

9 Click the **Exit** button. The application ends.

Before you can begin coding the Math Practice application, you need to learn how to write nested and extended selection structures, as well as how to use the Is, TypeOf...Is, and Like comparison operators. You learn those structures and operators in Lesson A. In Lesson B you complete the Math Practice application's interface as you learn how to include radio button and check box controls in an interface. You begin coding the application in Lesson B, and complete the application in Lesson C.

After completing this lesson, you will be able to:

- Include a nested selection structure in pseudocode and in a flowchart
- Code a nested selection structure
- Desk-check an algorithm
- Recognize common logic errors in selection structures
- Code an If/ElseIf/Else selection structure
- Include a Case selection structure in pseudocode and in a flowchart
- Code a Case selection structure
- Write code that uses the Is, TypeOf...Is, and Like comparison operators

Nested, If/ElseIf/Else, and Case Selection Structures

Nested Selection Structures

As you learned in Tutorial 4, you use the selection structure when you want a procedure to make a decision and then select one of two paths—either the true path or the false path—based on the result of that decision. Both paths in a selection structure can include instructions that declare and initialize variables, perform calculations, and so on; both also can include other selection structures. When either a selection structure's true path or its false path contains another selection structure, the inner selection structure is referred to as a **nested selection structure**, because it is contained (nested) within the outer selection structure.

You use a nested selection structure if more than one decision needs to be made before the appropriate action can be taken. For example, assume you want to create a procedure that determines whether a person can vote, and then, based on the result of that determination, displays one of three messages. The messages, along with the criteria for displaying each message, are shown here:

Message	Criteria
"You are too young to vote."	person is younger than 18 years old
"You can vote."	person is at least 18 years old and is registered to vote
"You need to register before you can vote."	person is at least 18 years old but is not registered to vote

As the chart indicates, the person's age and voter registration status determine which of the three messages is the appropriate one to display. If the person is younger than 18 years old, the procedure should display the message "You are too young to vote." However, if the person is at least 18 years old, the program should display one of two different messages. The correct message to display is determined

The lines connecting the selection structures in the pseudocode and code shown in Figure 5-3 are included in the figure to help you see which clauses are related to each other.

by the person's voter registration status. If the person is registered, then the appropriate message is "You can vote."; otherwise, it is "You need to register before you can vote." Notice that determining the person's voter registration status is important only *after* his or her age is determined. You can think of the decision regarding the age as being the **primary decision**, and the decision regarding the registration status as being the **secondary decision**, because whether the registration decision needs to be made depends on the result of the age decision. The primary decision is always made by the outer selection structure, while the secondary decision is always made by the inner (nested) selection structure.

Figure 5-3 shows the pseudocode and Visual Basic .NET code for a procedure that determines voter eligibility, and Figure 5-4 shows the corresponding flowchart. In both figures, the outer selection structure determines the age (the primary decision), and the nested selection structure determines the voter registration status (the secondary decision). Notice that the nested selection structure appears in the outer selection structure's true path in both figures.

Pseudocode

1. declare variables

2. get the age

3. if the age is greater than or equal to 18
      get the registration status
      if the registration status is Y
         display "You can vote."
      else
         display "You need to register before you can vote."
      end if
  else
      display "You are too young to vote."
  end if

Visual Basic .NET code

```
Dim intAge As Integer, strStatus As String
intAge = Val(InputBox("Enter your age", "Age"))
If intAge >= 18 Then
      strStatus = InputBox("Are you registered to vote (Y or N)?", _
            "Registration", "Y")

      If UCase(strStatus) = "Y" Then
            Me.MessageLabel.Text = "You can vote."
      Else
            Me.MessageLabel.Text = "You need to register before you can vote."
      End If

Else
      Me.MessageLabel.Text = "You are too young to vote."
End If
```

Figure 5-3: Pseudocode and Visual Basic .NET code showing the nested selection structure in the true path

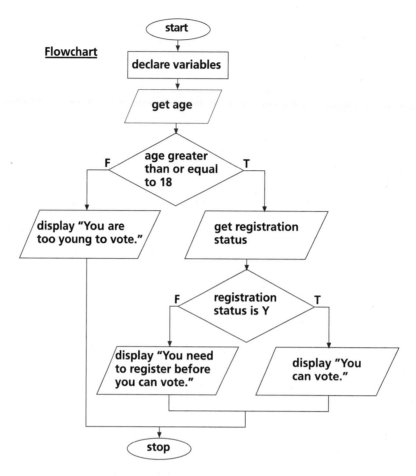

Figure 5-4: Flowchart showing the nested selection structure in the true path

As both figures indicate, the procedure begins by declaring the variables and then getting the age from the user. The condition in the outer selection structure then checks to determine whether the age is greater than or equal to 18. If the condition is false, it means that the person is not old enough to vote. In that case, only one message—the "You are too young to vote." message—is appropriate. After the message is displayed, both the outer selection structure and the procedure end.

If the outer selection structure's condition is true, on the other hand, it means that the person *is* old enough to vote. Before displaying the appropriate message, the instructions in the outer selection structure's true path first get the registration status from the user. A nested selection structure then is used to determine whether the person is registered. If he or she is registered, the instruction in the nested selection structure's true path displays the message "You can vote."; otherwise, the instruction in the nested selection structure's false path displays the message "You need to register before you can vote." After the appropriate message is displayed, both selection structures, as well as the procedure, end. Notice that the nested selection structure in Figure 5-4 is processed only when the outer selection structure's condition is true.

Figure 5-5 shows the pseudocode and Visual Basic .NET code for a different version of the voter eligibility procedure. As in the previous version, the outer selection structure in this version determines the age (the primary decision), and the nested selection structure determines the voter registration status (the secondary decision). In this version of the procedure, however, the nested selection structure appears in the false path of the outer selection structure.

Pseudocode

1. declare variables

2. get the age

3. if the age is less than 18
       display "You are too young to vote."
   else
       get the registration status
       if the registration status is Y
           display "You can vote."
       else
           display "You need to register before you can vote."
       end if
   end if

Visual Basic .NET code

```
Dim intAge As Integer, strStatus As String
intAge = Val(InputBox("Enter your age", "Age"))
If intAge < 18 Then
        Me.MessageLabel.Text = "You are too young to vote."
Else
        strStatus = InputBox("Are you registered to vote (Y or N)?", _
                "Registration", "Y")

        If UCase(strStatus) = "Y" Then
                Me.MessageLabel.Text = "You can vote."
        Else
                Me.MessageLabel.Text = "You need to register before you can vote."
        End If
End If
```

Figure 5-5: Pseudocode and Visual Basic .NET code showing the nested selection structure in the false path

Like the version shown earlier, this version of the voter eligibility procedure first gets the age from the user. However, rather than checking to determine whether the age is greater than or equal to 18, the outer selection structure in this version checks to determine whether the age is less than 18. If the condition is true, the instruction in the outer selection structure's true path displays the message "You are too young to vote." If the condition is false, the instructions in the outer selection structure's false path first get the registration status from the user, and then use a nested selection structure to determine whether the person is registered. If the person is registered, the instruction in the nested selection structure's true path displays the message "You can vote."; otherwise, the instruction in the nested selection structure's false path displays the message "You need to register before you can vote." Unlike in the previous version, the nested selection structure in this version of the procedure is processed only when the outer selection structure's condition is false. Figure 5-6 shows the flowchart for this version of the voter eligibility procedure.

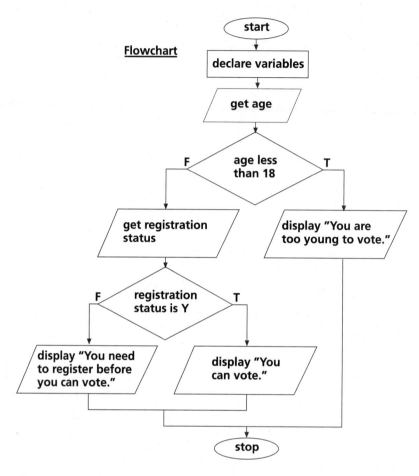

Figure 5-6: Flowchart showing the nested selection structure in the false path

Notice that both versions of the voter eligibility procedure produce the same results. Neither version is better than the other; each simply represents a different way of solving the same problem.

In the next section, you learn some of the common logic errors made when writing selection structures. Being aware of these errors will help to prevent you from making them.

Logic Errors in Selection Structures

Typically, logic errors commonly made when writing selection structures are a result of one of the following mistakes:

1. Using a logical operator when a nested selection structure is needed
2. Reversing the primary and secondary decisions
3. Using an unnecessary nested selection structure

The XYZ Company's vacation procedure can be used to demonstrate each of these logic errors. Assume that the company employs both full-time and part-time employees. Only full-time employees receive a paid vacation, as shown here:

Vacation weeks	Criteria
0	Part-time employees
2	Full-time employees working at the company for 5 years or fewer
3	Full-time employees working at the company for over 5 years

The vacation procedure should allow the user to enter the employee's status—either F for full-time or P for part-time—and the number of years the employee has worked for the company. If the employee is full-time, the procedure should display the number of vacation weeks to which the employee is entitled, and then the procedure should end. If the employee is not full-time, the procedure should simply end without displaying anything.

As the vacation chart indicates, the employee's status—either full-time or part-time—is a factor in determining whether the employee receives any paid vacation. If the employee is entitled to a paid vacation, then the number of years he or she has worked for the company determines the appropriate number of vacation weeks. In this case, the decision regarding the employee's status is the primary decision, and the decision regarding the years employed is the secondary decision, because whether the years employed decision needs to be made depends on the result of the status decision.

The pseudocode shown in Figure 5-7 represents a correct algorithm for the vacation procedure. An **algorithm** is simply the set of step-by-step instructions that accomplish a task.

Correct algorithm for the vacation procedure

```
1. declare variables

2. get the status and years

3. if the status is F
        if the years are greater than 5
                display "3-week vacation"
        else
                display "2-week vacation"
        end if
    end if
```

Figure 5-7: A correct algorithm for the vacation procedure

tip

You also could have written the nested selection structure's condition as follows: *if the years are less than or equal to 5*. The nested structure's true path then would contain the instruction *display "2-week vacation"*, and its false path would contain the instruction *display "3-week vacation"*.

To observe why the algorithm shown in Figure 5-7 is correct, you will desk-check it. **Desk-checking**, also called **hand-tracing**, means that you use sample data to walk through each of the steps in the algorithm manually, just as if you were the computer. Programmers desk-check an algorithm to verify that it will work as intended. If any errors are found in the algorithm, the errors are corrected before the programmer begins coding the algorithm. You will use the following test data to desk-check the algorithm shown in Figure 5-7:

Data for first desk-check	Data for second desk-check	Data for third desk-check
Status: F	Status: F	Status: P
Years: 4	Years: 15	Years: 11

The algorithm should display the message "2-week vacation" for the first set of test data, the message "3-week vacation" for the second set, and nothing for the third set.

Using the first set of test data, the user enters F as the status and 4 as the years. The outer selection structure's condition determines whether the status is F; it is, so the nested selection structure's condition checks whether the years are greater than 5. The years are not greater than 5, so the nested selection structure's false path displays the message "2-week vacation," which is correct. After doing so, both selection structures and the procedure end.

Using the second set of test data, the user enters F as the status and 15 as the years. The outer selection structure's condition determines whether the status is F; it is, so the nested selection structure's condition checks whether the years are greater than 5. The years are greater than 5, so the nested selection structure's true path displays the message "3-week vacation," which is correct. After doing so, both selection structures and the procedure end.

Using the third set of test data, the user enters P as the status and 11 as the years. The outer selection structure's condition determines whether the status is F. The status is not F, so the outer selection structure and the procedure end. Notice that the nested selection structure is not processed when the outer selection structure's condition is false. Figure 5-8 shows the results of desk-checking the correct algorithm shown in Figure 5-7.

Desk-check	Result
First: using F as the status and 4 as the years	"2-week vacation" displayed
Second: using F as the status and 15 as the years	"3-week vacation" displayed
Third: using P as the status and 11 as the years	Nothing is displayed

Figure 5-8: Results of desk-checking the correct algorithm shown in Figure 5-7

In the next section, you view and desk-check another algorithm for the vacation procedure. You will find that the algorithm does not produce the desired results because it contains a logical operator instead of a nested selection structure.

Using a Logical Operator Rather Than a Nested Selection Structure

One common error made when writing selection structures is to use a logical operator in the outer selection structure's condition when a nested selection structure is needed. Figure 5-9 shows an example of this error in the vacation algorithm. The correct algorithm is included in the figure for comparison.

logical operator used rather than a nested selection structure

Correct algorithm	Incorrect algorithm
1. declare variables ·	1. declare variables
2. get the status and years	2. enter the status and years

3. if the status is F
        if the years are greater than 5
            display "3-week vacation"
        else
            display "2-week vacation"
        end if
    end if
	3. if the status is F AndAlso the years are greater than 5
	        display "3-week vacation"
	    else
	        display "2-week vacation"
	    end if

Figure 5-9: Correct algorithm and an incorrect algorithm containing the first logic error

Notice that the incorrect algorithm uses one selection structure rather than two selection structures, and the selection structure's condition contains the AndAlso logical operator. Consider why the selection structure in the incorrect algorithm cannot be used in place of the selection structures in the correct algorithm. In the correct algorithm, the outer and nested selection structures indicate that a hierarchy exists between the status and years employed decisions: the status decision is always made first, followed by the years employed decision (if necessary). In the incorrect algorithm, on the other hand, the logical operator in the selection structure's condition indicates that no hierarchy exists between the status and years employed decisions; each has equal weight and neither is dependent on the other, which is incorrect. To better understand why this algorithm is incorrect, you will desk-check it using the same test data used to desk-check the correct algorithm.

After the user enters the first set of test data—F as the status and 4 as the years—the selection structure's condition in the incorrect algorithm determines whether the status is F and, at the same time, the years are greater than 5. Only one of these conditions is true, so the compound condition evaluates to false and the selection structure's false path displays the message "2-week vacation" before both the selection structure and the procedure end. Even though the algorithm's selection structure is phrased incorrectly, notice that the incorrect algorithm produces the same result as the correct algorithm using the first set of test data.

After the user enters the second set of test data—F as the status and 15 as the years—the selection structure's condition in the incorrect algorithm determines whether the status is F and, at the same time, the years are greater than 5. Both conditions are true, so the compound condition is true and the selection structure's true path displays the message "3-week vacation" before both the selection structure and the procedure end. Here again, using the second set of test data, the incorrect algorithm produces the same result as the correct algorithm.

After the user enters the third set of test data—P as the status and 11 as the years—the selection structure's condition in the incorrect algorithm determines whether the status is F and, at the same time, the years are greater than 5. Only one of these conditions is true, so the compound condition is false and the selection structure's false path displays the message "2-week vacation" before both the selection structure and the procedure end. Notice that the incorrect algorithm produces erroneous results for the third set of test data; according to Figure 5-8, the algorithm should not have displayed anything using this data. It is important to desk-check an algorithm several times using different test data. In this case, if you had used only the first two sets of data to desk-check the incorrect algorithm, you would not have discovered the error.

Figure 5-10 shows the results of desk-checking the incorrect algorithm shown in Figure 5-9. As indicated in the figure, the results of the first and second desk-checks are correct, but the result of the third desk-check is not correct.

As you learned in Tutorial 4, when you use the AndAlso logical operator to combine two conditions in a selection structure, both conditions must be true for the compound condition to be true. If at least one of the conditions is false, then the compound condition is false and the instructions in the selection structure's false path (assuming there is a false path) are processed.

Desk-check	Result
First: using F as the status and 4 as the years	"2-week vacation" displayed
Second: using F as the status and 15 as the years	"3-week vacation" displayed
Third: using P as the status and 11 as the years	"2-week vacation" displayed

correct results

incorrect result

Figure 5-10: Results of desk-checking the incorrect algorithm shown in Figure 5-9

Next, you view and desk-check another algorithm for the vacation procedure. You will find that this algorithm also does not produce the desired results, because the primary and secondary decisions are reversed in the selection structures.

Reversing the Primary and Secondary Decisions

Another common error made when writing a selection structure that contains a nested selection structure is to reverse the primary and secondary decisions—in other words, put the secondary decision in the outer selection structure, and put the primary decision in the nested selection structure. Figure 5-11 shows an example of this error in the vacation algorithm. The correct algorithm is included in the figure for comparison.

primary and secondary decisions reversed

Correct algorithm	Incorrect algorithm
1. declare variables	1. declare variables
2. get the status and years	2. get the status and years

3. if the status is F
        if the years are greater than 5
            display "3-week vacation"
        else
            display "2-week vacation"
        end if
    end if
	3. if the years are greater than 5
	        if the status is F
	            display "3-week vacation"
	        else
	            display "2-week vacation"
	        end if
	    end if

Figure 5-11: Correct algorithm and an incorrect algorithm containing the second logic error

Unlike the selection structures in the correct algorithm, which determine the employment status before determining the number of years employed, the selection structures in the incorrect algorithm determine the number of years employed before determining the employment status. Consider how this difference changes the algorithm. In the correct algorithm, the selection structures indicate that only employees whose status is full-time receive a paid vacation, which is correct. The selection structures in the incorrect algorithm, on the other hand, indicate that all employees who have been with the company for more than five years receive a paid vacation, which is not correct. Desk-check the incorrect algorithm to see the results.

After the user enters the first set of test data—F as the status and 4 as the years—the condition in the outer selection structure determines whether the years are greater than 5. The years are not greater than 5, so both the outer selection structure and the procedure end. Notice that the incorrect algorithm does not display the expected message, "2-week vacation."

After the user enters the second set of test data—F as the status and 15 as the years—the condition in the outer selection structure determines whether the years are greater than 5; they are, so the condition in the nested selection structure checks whether the status is F. The status is F, so the nested selection structure's true path displays the message "3-week vacation," which is correct.

After the user enters the third set of test data—P as the status and 11 as the years—the condition in the outer selection structure determines whether the years are greater than 5; they are, so the condition in the nested selection structure checks whether the status is F. The status is not F, so the nested selection structure's false path displays the message "2-week vacation," which is not correct.

Figure 5-12 shows the results of desk-checking the incorrect algorithm shown in Figure 5-11. As indicated in the figure, only the results of the second desk-check are correct.

only this result is corrrect

Desk-check	Result
First: using F as the status and 4 as the years	Nothing is displayed
Second: using F as the status and 15 as the years	"3-week vacation" displayed
Third: using P as the status and 11 as the years	"2-week vacation" displayed

Figure 5-12: Results of desk-checking the incorrect algorithm shown in Figure 5-11

Next, you view and desk-check another algorithm for the vacation procedure. This one contains the third logic error—using an unnecessary nested selection structure. Like the correct algorithm, this algorithm produces the desired results; however, it does so in a less efficient manner than the correct algorithm.

Using an Unnecessary Nested Selection Structure

Another common error made when writing selection structures is to include an unnecessary nested selection structure. In most cases, a selection structure containing this error still will produce the correct results; the only problem is that it does so less efficiently than selection structures that are properly structured. Figure 5-13 shows an example of this error in the vacation algorithm. The correct algorithm is included in the figure for comparison.

unnecessary nested selection structure

Correct algorithm	Inefficient algorithm
1. declare variables	1. declare variables
2. get the status and years	2. get the status and years

3. if the status is F
     if the years are greater than 5
        display "3-week vacation"
     else
        display "2-week vacation"
     end if
end if
	3. if the status is F
	     if the years are greater than 5
	        display "3-week vacation"
	     else
	        if the years are less than or equal to 5
	           display "2-week vacation"
	        end if
	     end if
	end if

Figure 5-13: Correct algorithm and an inefficient algorithm containing the third logic error

Unlike the correct algorithm, which contains two selection structures, the inefficient algorithm contains three selection structures. Notice that the condition in the third selection structure checks whether the years are less than or equal to 5, and is processed only when the condition in the second selection structure is false; in other words, it is processed only when the years are not greater than 5. However, if the years are not greater than 5, then they would have to be either less than or equal to 5, so the third selection structure is unnecessary. To better understand the error in the inefficient algorithm, you will desk-check it.

After the user enters the first set of test data—F as the status and 4 as the years—the first selection structure's condition determines whether the status is F; it is, so the second selection structure's condition checks whether the years are greater than 5. The years are not greater than 5, so the third selection structure's condition checks whether the years are less than or equal to 5—an unnecessary decision. In this case, the years (4) are less than or equal to 5, so the third selection structure's true path displays the message "2-week vacation," which is correct. After doing so, the three selection structures and the procedure end.

After the user enters the second set of test data—F as the status and 15 as the years—the first selection structure's condition determines whether the status is F; it is, so the second selection structure's condition checks whether the years are greater than 5. The years are greater than 5, so the second selection structure's true path displays the message "3-week vacation," which is correct. After doing so, the first and second selection structures and the procedure end.

After the user enters the third set of test data—P as the status and 11 as the years—the condition in the first selection structure determines whether the status is F; it isn't, so the first selection structure and the procedure end.

Figure 5-14 shows the results of desk-checking the inefficient algorithm shown in Figure 5-13. As indicated in the figure, although the results of the three desk-checks are correct, the result of the first desk-check is obtained in a less efficient manner.

correct result is obtained in a less efficient manner

Desk-check	Result
First: using F as the status and 4 as the years	"2-week vacation" displayed
Second: using F as the status and 15 as the years	"3-week vacation" displayed
Third: using P as the status and 11 as the years	Nothing is displayed

Figure 5-14: Results of desk-checking the inefficient algorithm shown in Figure 5-13

As you learned in Tutorial 4, Visual Basic .NET provides four forms of the selection structure: If, If/Else, If/ElseIf/Else, and Case. You learned about the If and If/Else selection structures in Tutorial 4. In this tutorial, you learn about the If/ElseIf/Else and Case selection structures, which are commonly referred to as **extended selection structures** or **multiple-path selection structures**.

The If/ElseIf/Else Selection Structure

At times, you may need to create a selection structure that can choose from several alternatives. For example, assume you are asked to create a procedure that displays a message based on a letter grade that the user enters. Figure 5-15 shows the valid letter grades and their corresponding messages.

Letter grade	Message
A	Excellent
B	Above Average
C	Average
D	Below Average
F	Below Average

Figure 5-15: Letter grades and messages

As Figure 5-15 indicates, if the letter grade is an A, then the procedure should display the message "Excellent." If the letter grade is a B, then the procedure should display the message "Above Average," and so on. Figure 5-16 shows two versions of the Visual Basic .NET code for the grade procedure. The first version uses nested If/Else structures to display the appropriate message, while the second version uses the If/ElseIf/Else structure. As you do with the If/Else structure, you use the If...Then...Else statement to code the If/ElseIf/Else structure.

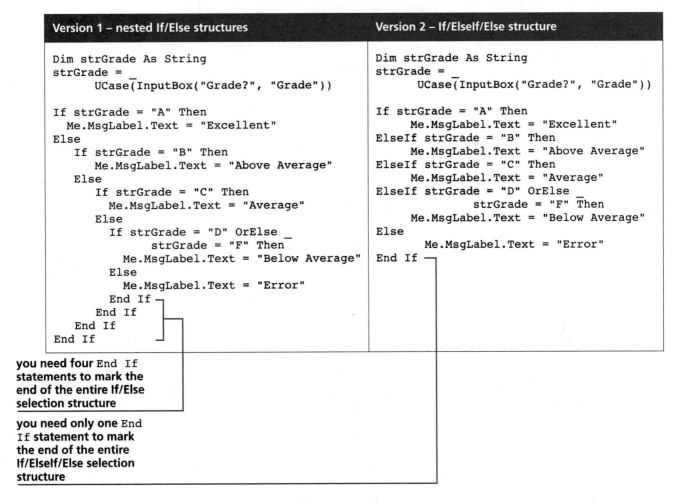

Version 1 – nested If/Else structures

```
Dim strGrade As String
strGrade = _
        UCase(InputBox("Grade?", "Grade"))

If strGrade = "A" Then
  Me.MsgLabel.Text = "Excellent"
Else
    If strGrade = "B" Then
        Me.MsgLabel.Text = "Above Average"
    Else
        If strGrade = "C" Then
          Me.MsgLabel.Text = "Average"
        Else
          If strGrade = "D" OrElse _
                strGrade = "F" Then
            Me.MsgLabel.Text = "Below Average"
          Else
            Me.MsgLabel.Text = "Error"
          End If
        End If
    End If
End If
```

Version 2 – If/ElseIf/Else structure

```
Dim strGrade As String
strGrade = _
        UCase(InputBox("Grade?", "Grade"))

If strGrade = "A" Then
        Me.MsgLabel.Text = "Excellent"
ElseIf strGrade = "B" Then
        Me.MsgLabel.Text = "Above Average"
ElseIf strGrade = "C" Then
        Me.MsgLabel.Text = "Average"
ElseIf strGrade = "D" OrElse _
            strGrade = "F" Then
        Me.MsgLabel.Text = "Below Average"
Else
        Me.MsgLabel.Text = "Error"
End If
```

you need four End If **statements to mark the end of the entire If/Else selection structure**

you need only one End If **statement to mark the end of the entire If/ElseIf/Else selection structure**

Figure 5-16: Two versions of the Visual Basic .NET code for the grade procedure

Although you can write the grade procedure using either nested If/Else selection structures (as shown in Version 1) or the If/ElseIf/Else selection structure (as shown in Version 2), the **If/ElseIf/Else structure** provides a much more convenient way of writing a multiple-path selection structure.

Next, learn about the Case form of the selection structure.

The Case Selection Structure

It is often simpler and clearer to use the Case form of the selection structure, rather than the If/ElseIf/Else form, in situations where the selection structure has many paths from which to choose. Figure 5-17 shows the flowchart and pseudocode for the grade procedure, using the Case selection structure.

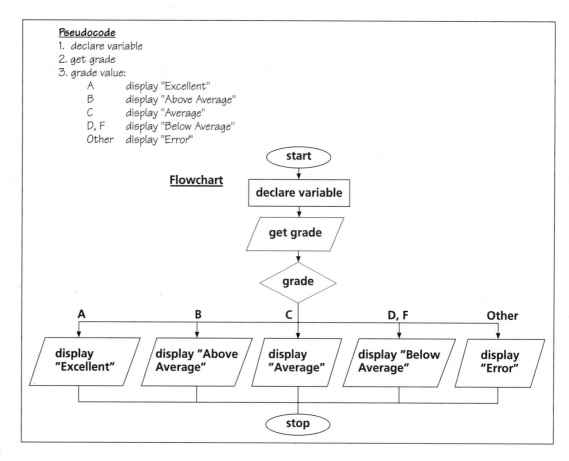

Figure 5-17: Flowchart and pseudocode showing the Case selection structure

The flowchart symbol for the Case selection structure is the same as the flowchart symbol for the If, If/Else, and If/ElseIf/Else structures—a diamond. Unlike the diamonds used in the other selection structures, however, the Case diamond does not contain a condition requiring a true or false answer. Instead, the Case diamond contains an expression—in this case, grade—whose value determines which path is chosen.

Like the If, If/Else, and If/ElseIf/Else diamond, the Case diamond has one flowline leading into the symbol. Unlike the other diamonds, however, the Case diamond has many flowlines leading out of the symbol. Each flowline represents a possible path for the selection structure. The flowlines must be marked appropriately, indicating which value(s) are necessary for each path to be chosen.

In Visual Basic .NET, you use the **Select Case statement** to code the Case selection structure. Figure 5-18 shows the syntax of the Select Case statement. It also shows how you could use the Select Case statement in the grade procedure to display a message based on a letter grade entered by the user.

Syntax	Grade procedure

Select Case *selectorExpression*
   Case *expressionList1*
     [*instructions for the first Case*]
   [**Case** *expressionList2*
     [*instructions for the second Case*]]
   [**Case** *expressionListn*
     [*instructions for the nth case*]]
   [**Case Else**
     [*instructions for when the*
     selectorExpression does not match
     any of the expressionLists]]
End Select
	``
	Dim strGrade As String
	strGrade = _
	    UCase(InputBox("Grade?", "Grade"))
	
	Select Case strGrade
	   Case "A"
	      Me.MsgLabel.Text = "Excellent"
	   Case "B"
	      Me.MsgLabel.Text = "Above Average"
	   Case "C"
	      Me.MsgLabel.Text = "Average"
	   Case "D", "F"
	      Me.MsgLabel.Text = "Below Average"
	   Case Else
	      Me.MsgLabel.Text = "Error"
	End Select
	``

Figure 5-18: Syntax and an example of the Select Case statement

tip

It is customary to indent each Case clause, as well as the instructions within each Case clause, as shown in Figure 5-18.

The Select Case statement begins with the Select Case clause and ends with the two words `End Select`. Between the Select Case clause and the `End Select` are the individual Case clauses. Each Case clause represents a different path that the selection structure can follow. You can have as many Case clauses as necessary in a Select Case statement. If the Select Case statement includes a `Case Else` clause, the `Case Else` clause must be the last clause in the statement.

Notice that the Select Case clause must include a *selectorExpression*. The *selectorExpression* can contain any combination of variables, constants, functions, operators, and properties. In the grade procedure shown in Figure 5-18, the *selectorExpression* is a String variable named strGrade.

Each of the individual Case clauses, except the `Case Else` clause, must contain an *expressionList*, which can include one or more expressions. To include more than one expression in an *expressionList*, you simply separate each expression with a comma, as in the *expressionList* `Case "D", "F"`. The data type of the expressions must be compatible with the data type of the *selectorExpression*. In other words, if the *selectorExpression* is numeric, the expressions in the Case clauses should be numeric. Likewise, if the *selectorExpression* is a string, the expressions should be strings. In the grade procedure shown in Figure 5-18, the *selectorExpression* (strGrade) is a string, and so are the expressions—"A", "B", "C", "D", and "F"—as the quotation marks indicate.

When processing the Select Case statement, the computer first compares the value of the *selectorExpression* with the values listed in *expressionList1*. If a match is found, the computer processes the instructions for the first Case, stopping when it reaches either another Case clause (including the `Case Else` clause) or the `End Select` (which marks the end of the selection structure). It then skips to the instruction following the `End Select`. If a match is not found in *expressionList1*, the computer skips to the second Case clause, where it compares the *selectorExpression* with the values listed in *expressionList2*. If a match is found, the computer processes the instructions for the second Case clause and then skips to the instruction following the

End Select. If a match is not found, the computer skips to the third Case clause, and so on. If the *selectorExpression* does not match any of the values listed in any of the *expressionLists*, the computer then processes the instructions listed in the **Case Else** clause or, if there is no **Case Else** clause, it processes the instruction following the **End Select**. Keep in mind that if the *selectorExpression* matches a value in more than one Case clause, only the instructions in the first match are processed.

To better understand the Select Case statement, you will desk-check the grade procedure shown in Figure 5-18.

Desk-Checking the Grade Procedure

Assume the user enters the letter C in response to the "Grade?" prompt. The grade procedure stores the letter C in the strGrade variable, which then is used as the *selectorExpression* in the procedure's Select Case statement. The computer compares the value of the *selectorExpression* ("C") with the expression listed in *expressionList1* ("A"). "C" does not match "A", so the computer compares the value of the *selectorExpression* ("C") with the expression listed in *expressionList2* ("B"). "C" does not match "B", so the computer compares the value of the *selectorExpression* ("C") with the expression listed in *expressionList3* ("C"). Here there is a match, so the computer processes the **Me.MsgLabel.Text = "Average"** instruction, which displays the string "Average" in the MsgLabel control. The computer then skips the remaining instructions in the Select Case statement and processes the instruction following the **End Select**. (In the grade procedure, the **End Sub**, which is not shown in Figure 5-18, would be processed.)

Now assume the user enters the letter F in response to the "Grade?" prompt. The grade procedure stores the letter F in the strGrade variable, which then is used as the *selectorExpression* in the procedure's Select Case statement. The computer compares the value of the *selectorExpression* ("F") with the expression listed in *expressionList1* ("A"). "F" does not match "A", so the computer compares the value of the *selectorExpression* ("F") with the expression listed in *expressionList2* ("B"). "F" does not match "B", so the computer compares the value of the *selectorExpression* ("F") with the expression listed in *expressionList3* ("C"). "F" does not match "C", so the computer compares the value of the *selectorExpression* ("F") with the expressions listed in *expressionList4* ("D", "F"). Here the computer finds a match, so it processes the **Me.MsgLabel.Text = "Below Average"** instruction, which displays the string "Below Average" in the MsgLabel control. The computer then processes the instruction following the **End Select**.

Finally, assume the user enters the letter X as the grade. In this situation, the computer processes the **Me.MsgLabel.Text = "Error"** instruction contained in the **Case Else** clause, because the *selectorExpression* ("X") does not match any of the expressions listed in the other Case clauses. The computer then processes the instruction following the **End Select**. Figure 5-19 shows the results of desk-checking the grade procedure shown in Figure 5-18.

tip

The *selectorExpression* needs to match only one of the expressions listed in an *expressionList*.

Desk-check	Result
First: using A	"Excellent" displayed
Second: using F	"Below Average" displayed
Third: using X	"Error" displayed

Figure 5-19: Results of desk-checking the grade procedure shown in Figure 5-18

You also can specify a range of values in an *expressionList*—such as the values 1 through 4, and values greater than 10. You can do so using the keywords To and Is.

Using To and Is in an *ExpressionList*

You can use either the keyword To or the keyword Is to specify a range of values in a Case clause's *expressionList*. You use the To keyword when you know both the upper and lower bounds of the range, and you use the Is keyword when you know only one end of the range—either the upper or lower end. For example, assume that the price of an item sold by ABC Corporation depends on the number of items ordered, as shown in the following table:

Number of items ordered	Price per item
1 – 5	$ 25
6 – 10	$ 23
More than 10	$ 20

Figure 5-20 shows the Select Case statement that assigns the appropriate price per item to the intItemPrice variable.

Item price procedure

```
Dim intNumOrdered, intItemPrice As Integer
intNumOrdered = Val(Me.NumOrderedTextBox.Text)
Select Case intNumOrdered
    Case 1 To 5
        intItemPrice = 25
    Case 6 To 10
        intItemPrice = 23
    Case Is > 10
        intItemPrice = 20
    Case Else
        intItemPrice = 0
        MessageBox.Show("Incorrect number ordered", _
            "Pricing", MessageBoxButtons.OK, _
            MessageBoxIcon.Information)
End Select
```

Figure 5-20: Example of using the To and Is keywords in a Select Case statement

tip

When you use the To key-word, the value preceding the To always must be less than the value following the To; in other words, 10 To 6 is not a correct expression. Visual Basic .NET will not display an error message if the value preced-ing the To is greater than the value following the To. Instead, the Select Case statement simply will not give the correct results. This is another reason why it always is important to test your code thoroughly.

According to the ABC Corporation table, the price for one to five items is $25 each. You could, therefore, have written the first Case clause as Case 1, 2, 3, 4, 5. However, a more convenient way of writing that range of numbers is to use the keyword To in the Case clause, but you must follow this syntax to do so: Case *smallest value in the range* To *largest value in the range*. The expression 1 To 5 in the first Case clause, for example, specifies the range of num-bers from one to five, inclusive. The expression 6 To 10 in the second Case clause specifies the range of numbers from six to 10, inclusive. Notice that both Case clauses state both the lower (1 and 6) and upper (5 and 10) ends of each range.

▶ Because intNumOrdered is an Integer variable, you also can write the third Case clause as `Case Is >= 11`, which specifies all numbers that are greater than or equal to the number 11.

▶ If you neglect to type the keyword Is in an expression, the Code editor types it in for you. In other words, if you enter `Case > 10`, the Code editor changes the clause to `Case Is > 10`.

The third Case clause in Figure 5-20, `Case Is > 10`, contains the Is keyword rather than the To keyword. Recall that you use the Is keyword when you know only one end of the range of values—either the upper or lower end. In this case, for example, you know only the lower end of the range, 10. You always use the Is keyword in combination with one of the following comparison (relational) operators: =, <, <=, >, >=, <>. The `Case Is > 10` clause, for example, specifies all numbers that are greater than the number 10.

Notice that the `Case Else` clause shown in Figure 5-20 first assigns the number 0 to the intItemPrice variable and then uses the MessageBox.Show method to display the message "Incorrect number ordered." The `Case Else` clause is processed when the intNumOrdered variable contains a value that is not included in any of the Case clauses—namely, a zero or a negative number.

In Tutorial 4's Lesson A, you learned six of the nine comparison operators available in Visual Basic .NET. You learn the remaining three comparison operators in this lesson. You often will find these operators used in selection structures.

The Is, TypeOf...Is, and Like Comparison Operators

In addition to the =, <>, <, <=, >, >= comparison operators, which you learned about in Tutorial 4, Visual Basic .NET also provides the Is, TypeOf...Is, and Like comparison operators. Figure 5-21 briefly describes these three comparison operators.

Operator	Operation
Is	determine whether two object references refer to the same object
TypeOf...Is	determine whether an object is a specified type
Like	use pattern matching to determine whether one string is equal to another string

Figure 5-21: Is, TypeOf...Is, and Like comparison operators

First, learn about the Is comparison operator.

The Is Comparison Operator

You use the **Is operator** to determine whether two object references refer to the same object. An **object reference** is a memory address within the computer's internal memory; it indicates where in memory the object is stored. If both object references refer to the same object, the Is operator evaluates to True; otherwise, it evaluates to False.

Figure 5-22 shows the syntax of the Is operator. It also shows the CalcComm procedure, which uses the Is operator in a selection structure to determine the button selected by the user.

Is operator

Syntax

objectReference1 **Is** *objectReference2*

The Is operator evaluates to True if *objectReference1* is the same as *objectReference2*; otherwise it evaluates to False.

Example

```
Private Sub CalcComm(ByVal sender As Object, _
        ByVal e As System.EventArgs) _
        Handles Calc2Button.Click, Calc4Button.Click, _
        Calc7Button.Click

    Dim sngSales, sngComm As Single
    sngSales = Val(Me.SalesTextBox.Text)

    If sender Is Calc2Button Then
        sngComm = sngSales * .02
    ElseIf sender Is Calc4Button Then
        sngComm = sngSales * .04
    Else
        sngComm = sngSales * .07
    End If
    Me.CommLabel.Text = Format(sngComm, "currency")
End Sub
```

Handles section — (points to Handles clause)

compares memory addresses — (points to `sender Is Calc2Button`)

Figure 5-22: Syntax and an example of the Is operator

As the Handles section in the procedure header indicates, the CalcComm procedure, which calculates and displays a commission amount, is processed when the user selects the Calc2Button, Calc4Button, or Calc7Button on the form. When one of these buttons is selected, its memory address is sent to the CalcComm procedure's `sender` parameter. In this case, for example, the memory address of the Calc2Button is sent to the `sender` parameter if the user selects the Calc2Button. Likewise, if the user selects the Calc4Button, the Calc4Button's memory address is sent to the `sender` parameter. The Calc7Button's memory address is sent to the `sender` parameter if the user selects the Calc7Button.

Before the commission amount can be calculated, the procedure first must determine which button has been selected by the user, because each button is associated with a different commission rate. The `sender Is Calc2Button` condition in the first If...Then...Else statement compares the memory address stored in the `sender` parameter with the memory address of the Calc2Button. If the condition evaluates to True, it means that both memory addresses are the same. If both memory addresses are the same, then the user selected the Calc2Button and the commission amount should be calculated by multiplying the sales amount by 2 percent.

If the `sender` parameter does not contain the address of the Calc2Button, the `sender Is Calc4Button` condition in the ElseIf clause compares the memory address stored in the `sender` parameter with the memory address of the Calc4Button. If both memory addresses are the same, then the user selected the Calc4Button and the commission amount is 4 percent of the sales amount. If both memory addresses are not the same, then the user must have selected the Calc7Button; in this case, the commission amount is 7 percent of the sales amount.

Next, learn about the TypeOf...Is comparison operator.

tip

The Is operator is not the same as the Is keyword used in the Select Case statement. Recall that the Is keyword is used in combination with one of the following comparison operators: =, <, <=, >, >=, <>.

The TypeOf...Is Comparison Operator

You use the **TypeOf...Is operator** to determine whether an object is a specified type. For example, you can use the operator to determine whether an object is a TextBox or a Button. If the object's type matches the specified type, the TypeOf...Is operator evaluates to True; otherwise, it evaluates to False.

Figure 5-23 shows the syntax of the TypeOf...Is operator. It also shows the DisplayMessage procedure, which uses the TypeOf...Is operator in a selection structure to determine the type of control that invoked the procedure.

Handles section

compares object types

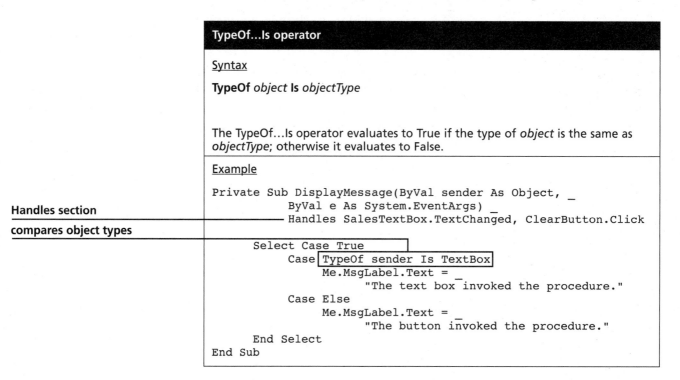

TypeOf...Is operator

Syntax

TypeOf *object* **Is** *objectType*

The TypeOf...Is operator evaluates to True if the type of *object* is the same as *objectType*; otherwise it evaluates to False.

Example

```
Private Sub DisplayMessage(ByVal sender As Object, _
            ByVal e As System.EventArgs) _
            Handles SalesTextBox.TextChanged, ClearButton.Click

        Select Case True
            Case TypeOf sender Is TextBox
                Me.MsgLabel.Text = _
                    "The text box invoked the procedure."
            Case Else
                Me.MsgLabel.Text = _
                    "The button invoked the procedure."
        End Select
End Sub
```

Figure 5-23: Syntax and an example of the TypeOf...Is operator

As the Handles section in the procedure header indicates, the DisplayMessage procedure, which simply displays a message in a label control, is processed when the SalesTextBox control's TextChanged event occurs, and also when the ClearButton control's Click event occurs. When either of these events occurs, the memory address of the control associated with the event is sent to the DisplayMessage procedure's `sender` parameter. In this case, for example, the memory address of the SalesTextBox is sent to the `sender` parameter when the text box's TextChanged event occurs. Likewise, the memory address of the ClearButton is sent to the `sender` parameter when the button's Click event occurs.

The Select Case statement in the procedure displays the appropriate message based on the type of control whose address is stored in the `sender` parameter. Notice that the Select Case statement uses the Boolean value True as the *selectorExpression*. It also uses the TypeOf...Is operator in the first Case clause to compare the `sender` parameter's type to the type, TextBox. If the `TypeOf sender Is TextBox` expression evaluates to True, it means that the `sender` parameter's type is TextBox. In this case, because the value of the expression (True) matches the value of the *selectorExpression* (True), the procedure displays the message "The text box invoked the procedure." in the MsgLabel control. If, on the other hand, the `TypeOf sender Is TextBox` expression evaluates to False, it means that the `sender` parameter's type is not TextBox. Here, because the value of the expression (False) does not match the value of the *selectorExpression* (True), the procedure displays the message "The button invoked the procedure." in the MsgLabel control.

Finally, learn about the Like comparison operator.

The Like Comparison Operator

The **Like operator** allows you to use pattern matching to determine whether one string is equal to another string. To use the Like operator, you must follow the syntax *string* **Like** *pattern*. Both *string* and *pattern* must be String expressions; however, *pattern* can contain one or more of the pattern-matching characters described in Figure 5-24.

Pattern-matching characters	Matches in *string*
?	any single character
*	zero or more characters
#	any single digit (0-9)
[*charlist*]	any single character in the *charlist* (for example, [a-z] matches any lowercase letter)
[!*charlist*]	any single character not in the *charlist* (for example, [!a-z] matches any character that is not a lowercase letter)

Figure 5-24: Pattern-matching characters

Figure 5-25 shows the syntax of the Like operator and contains several examples of using the Like operator and its pattern-matching characters to compare strings.

Like operator	
Syntax	
string **Like** *pattern*	
The Like operator evaluates to True if *string* matches *pattern*; otherwise it evaluates to False.	
Examples	**Results**
Example 1 UCase(strName) Like "B?LL"	evaluates to True if the string stored in the strName variable begins with the letter B, followed by one character and then the two letters LL; otherwise, it evaluates to False
Example 2 strState Like "K*"	evaluates to True if the string stored in the strState variable begins with the letter K, followed by zero or more characters; otherwise, it evaluates to False

Figure 5-25: Syntax and examples of the Like operator

Examples	Results
<u>Example 3</u> `strId Like "###*"`	evaluates to True if the string stored in the strId variable begins with three digits, followed by zero or more characters; otherwise, it evaluates to False
<u>Example 4</u> `UCase(strName) Like "T[OI]M"`	evaluates to True if the string stored in the strName variable begins with the letter T, followed by either the letter O or the letter I, followed by the letter M; otherwise, it evaluates to False
<u>Example 5</u> `strLetter Like "[a-z]"`	evaluates to True if the string stored in the strLetter variable is a lowercase letter; otherwise, it evaluates to False
<u>Example 6</u> `strLetter Like "[!a-zA-Z]"`	evaluates to True if the string stored in the strLetter variable is not a letter; otherwise, it evaluates to False

Figure 5-25: Syntax and examples of the Like operator (continued)

Study closely each example shown in Figure 5-25. The `UCase(strName) Like "B?LL"` expression in Example 1 contains the question mark (?) pattern-matching character, which is used to match one character in the *string*. Examples of *strings* that would make this expression evaluate to True include "Bill", "Ball", "bell", and "bull". Examples of *strings* for which the expression would evaluate to False include "BPL", "BLL", and "billy".

Example 2's expression, `strState Like "K*"`, uses the asterisk (*) pattern-matching character to match zero or more characters. Examples of *strings* that would make this expression evaluate to True include "KANSAS", "Ky", and "Kentucky". Examples of *strings* for which the expression would evaluate to False include "kansas" and "ky".

Example 3's expression, `strId Like "###*"`, contains two different pattern-matching characters: the number sign (#), which matches a digit, and the asterisk (*), which matches zero or more characters. Examples of *strings* that would make this expression evaluate to True include "178" and "983Ab". Examples of *strings* for which the expression would evaluate to False include "X34" and "34Z".

The `UCase(strName) Like "T[OI]M"` expression in Example 4 in Figure 5-25 contains a *charlist* (character list)—in this case, the two letters O and I—enclosed in square brackets ([]). The expression evaluates to True if the string stored in the strName variable is either "Tom" or "Tim" (entered in any case). If the strName variable does not contain "Tom" or "Tim"—for example, if it contains "Tam" or "Tommy"—the expression evaluates to False.

Example 5's expression, `strLetter Like "[a-z]"`, also contains a *charlist* enclosed in square brackets; however, the *charlist* represents a range of values—in this case, the lowercase letters "a" through "z". Notice that you use a hyphen (-) to specify a range of values. In this case, if the string stored in the strLetter variable is a lowercase letter, then the expression evaluates to True; otherwise, it evaluates to False.

tip

When using the hyphen to specify a range of values, the value on the left side of the hyphen must have a lower ASCII value than the value on the right side of the hyphen. For example, you must use [a-z], and not [z-a], to specify the lowercase letters of the alphabet.

The `strLetter Like "[!a-zA-Z]"` expression shown in the last example in Figure 5-25 also contains a *charlist* that specifies a range of values; however, the *charlist* is preceded by an exclamation point (!), which stands for "not". The expression evaluates to True if the string stored in the strLetter variable is *not* a letter; otherwise, it evaluates to False.

You now have completed Lesson A. You can either take a break or complete the end-of-lesson questions and exercises before moving on to the next lesson.

SUMMARY

To create a selection structure that evaluates both a primary and a secondary decision:

■ Place (or nest) the selection structure for the secondary decision within either the true path or false path of the selection structure for the primary decision.

To verify that an algorithm works correctly:

■ Desk-check the algorithm. Desk-checking, also called hand-tracing, means that you use sample data to walk through each of the steps in the algorithm manually, just as if you were the computer.

To code a multiple-path (or extended) selection structure:

■ Use either the If...Then...Else statement or the Select Case statement.

To specify a range of values in a Case clause contained in a Select Case statement:

■ Use the keyword To when you know both the upper and lower bounds of the range. The syntax for using the To keyword is **Case** *smallest value in the range* **To** *largest value in the range*.
■ Use the keyword Is when you know only one end of the range—either the upper or lower end. The Is keyword is used in combination with one of the following comparison operators: =, <, <=, >, >=, <>.

To determine whether two object references refer to the same object:

■ Use the Is comparison operator. The syntax for using the Is operator is *objectReference1* **Is** *objectReference2*. The Is operator returns the Boolean value True if both *objectReferences* contain the same address; otherwise, the operator returns the Boolean value False.

To determine whether an object is a specified type:

■ Use the TypeOf...Is comparison operator. The syntax for using the TypeOf...Is operator is **TypeOf** *object* **Is** *objectType*.

To use pattern matching to determine whether one string is equal to another string:

■ Use the Like comparison operator. The syntax for using the Like operator is *string* **Like** *pattern*, where *pattern* can contain one or more pattern-matching characters. Refer to Figure 5-24 for the pattern-matching characters.

QUESTIONS

Use the following code to answer Questions 1 through 3.

```
If intNumber <= 100 Then
        intNumber = intNumber * 2
ElseIf intNumber > 500 Then
        intNumber = intNumber * 3
End If
```

1. Assume the intNumber variable contains the number 90. What value will be in the intNumber variable after the preceding code is processed?
   a. 0
   b. 90
   c. 180
   d. 270

2. Assume the intNumber variable contains the number 1000. What value will be in the intNumber variable after the preceding code is processed?
   a. 0
   b. 1000
   c. 2000
   d. 3000
   e. None of the above.

3. Assume the intNumber variable contains the number 200. What value will be in the intNumber variable after the preceding code is processed?
   a. 0
   b. 200
   c. 400
   d. 600
   e. None of the above.

Use the following code to answer Questions 4 through 7.

```
If intId = 1 Then
        Me.NameLabel.Text = "Janet"
ElseIf intId = 2 OrElse intId = 3 Then
        Me.NameLabel.Text = "Paul"
ElseIf intId = 4 Then
        Me.NameLabel.Text = "Jerry"
Else
        Me.NameLabel.Text = "Sue"
End If
```

4. What, if anything, will the preceding code display if the intId variable contains the number 2?
   a. Janet
   b. Jerry
   c. Paul
   d. Sue
   e. nothing

5. What, if anything, will the preceding code display if the intId variable contains the number 4?
   a. Janet
   b. Jerry
   c. Paul
   d. Sue
   e. nothing

6. What, if anything, will the preceding code display if the intId variable contains the number 3?
   a. Janet
   b. Jerry
   c. Paul
   d. Sue
   e. nothing

7. What, if anything, will the preceding code display if the intId variable contains the number 8?
   a. Janet
   b. Jerry
   c. Paul
   d. Sue
   e. nothing

8. A nested selection structure can appear in _____ of another selection structure.
   a. only the true path
   b. only the false path
   c. either the true path or the false path

9. Which of the following flowchart symbols represents the Case selection structure?
   a. diamond
   b. hexagon
   c. oval
   d. parallelogram
   e. rectangle

10. If the *selectorExpression* used in the Select Case statement is an Integer variable named intCode, which of the following Case clauses is valid?
   a. `Case 3`
   b. `Case Is > 7`
   c. `Case 3, 5`
   d. `Case 1 To 4`
   e. All of the above.

Use the following Case statement to answer Questions 11 through 13.

```
Select Case intId
      Case 1
              Me.NameLabel.Text = "Janet"
      Case 2 To 4
              Me.NameLabel.Text = "Paul"
      Case 5, 7
              Me.NameLabel.Text = "Jerry"
      Case Else
              Me.NameLabel.Text = "Sue"
End Select
```

11. What will the preceding Case statement display if the intId variable contains the number 2?
    a. Jerry
    b. Paul
    c. Sue
    d. nothing

12. What will the preceding Case statement display if the intId variable contains the number 3?
    a. Jerry
    b. Paul
    c. Sue
    d. nothing

13. What will the preceding Case statement display if the intId variable contains the number 6?
    a. Jerry
    b. Paul
    c. Sue
    d. nothing

14. Which of the following can be used to determine whether the sender parameter contains the address of the NameTextBox?
    a. `If sender Is NameTextBox Then`
    b. `If sender = NameTextBox Then`
    c. `If sender Like NameTextBox Then`
    d. `If sender Is = NameTextBox Then`
    e. `If TypeOf sender Is NameTextBox Then`

15. Which of the following can be used to determine whether the sender parameter contains the address of a label control?
    a. `If sender Is Label Then`
    b. `If sender = Label Then`
    c. `If sender Like Label Then`
    d. `If sender Is = Label Then`
    e. `If TypeOf sender Is Label Then`

16. Which of the following can be used to determine whether the strPartNum variable contains two characters followed by a digit?
    a. `If UCase(strPartNum) = "##?" Then`
    b. `If UCase(strPartNum) Is = "**?" Then`
    c. `If UCase(strPartNum) = "##?" Then`
    d. `If UCase(strPartNum) Like "[0-9]" Then`
    e. None of the above.

17. Which of the following can be used to determine whether the strItem variable contains either the word "shirt" or the word "skirt"?
    a. `If UCase(strItem) = "SHIRT" OrElse UCase(strItem) = "SKIRT" Then`
    b. `If UCase(strItem) = "S[HK]IRT" Then`
    c. `If UCase(strItem) Like "S[HK]IRT" Then`
    d. `If UCase(strItem) Like "S[H-K]IRT" Then`
    e. a and c

18. Which of the following can be used to determine whether the percent sign (%) is the last character entered in the RateTextBox?
    a. `If "%" Like Me.RateTextBox.Text Then`
    b. `If "%" Like [Me.RateTextBox.Text] Then`
    c. `If Me.RateTextBox.Text Like "?%" Then`
    d. `If Me.RateTextBox.Text Like "*%" Then`
    e. `If Me.RateTextBox.Text Like [*%] Then`

19. Which of the following pattern-matching characters represents any single digit (0–9)?
    a. #
    b. *
    c. ?
    d. &
    e. @

20. Which of the following pattern-matching characters represents zero or more characters?
    a. #
    b. *
    c. ?
    d. &
    e. @

21. Assume that you need to create a procedure that displays the appropriate fee to charge a golfer. The fee is based on the following fee schedule:

Fee	Criteria
0	Club members
15	Non-members golfing on Monday through Thursday
25	Non-members golfing on Friday through Sunday

    In this procedure, which is the primary decision and which is the secondary decision? Why?

22. List the three errors commonly made when writing selection structures. Which error makes the selection structure inefficient, but not incorrect?

23. Explain what the term "desk-checking" means.

24. What is an object reference?

25. What is an algorithm?

E X E R C I S E S

1. Write the Visual Basic .NET code for the algorithm shown in Figure 5-7 in the lesson. The employee's status and years employed are entered in the StatusTextBox and YearsTextBox controls, respectively. Store the text box values in the strStatus and intYears variables. Display the appropriate message in the MsgLabel control.

2. Modify the code from Exercise 1 so that it displays the message "No vacation" if the employee's status is part-time.

3. Write the Visual Basic .NET code that displays the message "Highest honors" if a student's test score is 90 or above. If the test score is 70 through 89, display the message "Good job". For all other test scores, display the message "Retake the test". Use the If/ElseIf/Else selection structure. The test score is stored in the intScore variable. Display the appropriate message in the MsgLabel control.

4. Write the Visual Basic .NET code that compares the contents of the intQuantity variable to the number 10. If the intQuantity variable contains a number that is equal to 10, display the string "Equal" in the MsgLabel control. If the intQuantity variable contains a number that is greater than 10, display the string "Over 10". If the intQuantity variable contains a number that is less than 10, display the string "Not over 10". Use the If/ElseIf/Else selection structure.

5. Write the Visual Basic .NET code that corresponds to the flowchart shown in Figure 5-26. Store the salesperson's code, which is entered in the CodeTextBox control, in an Integer variable named intCode. Store the sales amount, which is entered in the SalesTextBox control, in a Single variable named sngSales. Display the result of the calculation, or the error message, in the MsgLabel control.

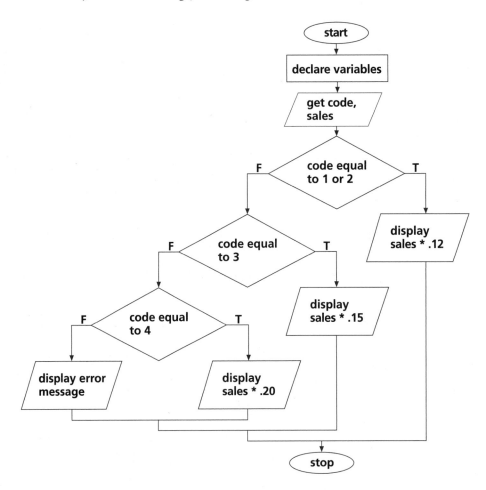

Figure 5-26

6. Write the Visual Basic .NET code that corresponds to the flowchart shown in Figure 5-27. Store the salesperson's code, which is entered in the CodeTextBox control, in an Integer variable named intCode. Store the sales amount, which is entered in the SalesTextBox control, in a Single variable named sngSales. Display the result of the calculation, or the error message, in the MsgLabel control.

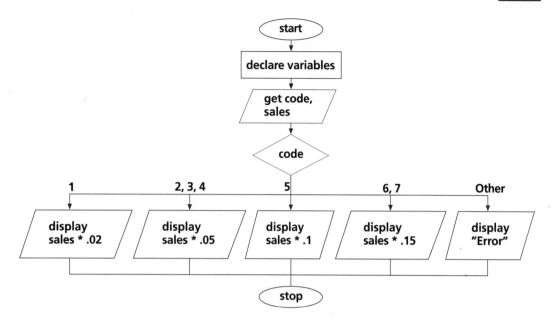

Figure 5-27

7. Assume that a procedure needs to display a shipping charge based on the state name stored in the strState variable. (You can assume that the state name is stored using uppercase letters.) Write a Select Case statement that assigns the shipping charge to the sngShip variable. Use the following table to determine the appropriate shipping charge.

State entered in the strState variable	Shipping charge
HAWAII	$25.00
OREGON	$30.00
CALIFORNIA	$32.50

   Display an appropriate message in the MsgLabel control if the strState variable contains a value that does not appear in the table. Also assign the number 0 to the sngShip variable.

8. Rewrite the code from Exercise 7 using an If...Then...Else statement.

9. The price of a concert ticket depends on the seat location stored in the strSeat variable. (You can assume that the seat location is stored using uppercase letters.) Write a Select Case statement that displays the price in the PriceLabel control. Use the following table to determine the appropriate price.

Seat location	Concert ticket price
BOX	$75.00
PAVILION	$30.00
LAWN	$21.00

   Display an appropriate message in the PriceLabel control if the strSeat variable contains a value that does not appear in the table.

10. Rewrite the code from Exercise 9 using an If...Then...Else statement.

11. Assume that a procedure needs to display a shipping charge based on the ZIP code stored in the strZip variable. The ZIP code should contain five digits. Write an If...Then...Else statement that assigns the shipping charge to the sngShip variable. Use the following table to determine the appropriate shipping charge. (*Hint*: Notice that the first two ZIP codes begin with "605", and the last three ZIP codes begin with "606".)

ZIP code entered in the strZip variable	Shipping charge
60522	$25.00
60534	$25.00
60611	$30.00
60612	$30.00
60634	$30.00

All other ZIP codes are charged $35.00 for shipping.

12. Rewrite the code from Exercise 11 using a Select Case statement.

13. Assume that the DisplayCapital procedure is invoked when the Click event occurs for one of the following buttons: AlabamaButton, AlaskaButton, ArizonaButton, and ArkansasButton. Write an If...Then...Else statement that displays the name of the appropriate state's capital in the CapitalLabel control. Use the following table.

State	Capital
Alabama	Montgomery
Alaska	Juneau
Arizona	Phoenix
Arkansas	Little Rock

14. Rewrite the code from Exercise 13 using a Select Case statement.

15. In this exercise, you complete two procedures that display a message based on a code entered by the user.

    a. If necessary, start Visual Studio .NET. Open the Animal Solution (Animal Solution.sln) file, which is contained in the VBNET\Tut05\Animal Solution folder. If the designer window is not open, right-click the form file's name in the Solution Explorer window, then click View Designer.

    b. Open the Code editor window. Complete the If...Then...Else button's Click event procedure by writing an If...Then...Else statement that displays the string "Dog" if the intAnimal variable contains the number 1. Display the string "Cat" if the intAnimal variable contains the number 2. Display the string "Bird" if the intAnimal variable contains anything other than the number 1 or the number 2. Display the appropriate string in the MsgLabel control.

    c. Save the solution, then start the application. Test the application three times, using the numbers 1, 2, and 5.

    d. Click the Exit button to end the application.

    e. Complete the Select Case button's Click event procedure by writing a Select Case statement that displays the string "Dog" if the strAnimal variable contains either the letter "D" or the letter "d". Display the string "Cat" if the strAnimal variable contains either the letter "C" or the letter "c". Display the string "Bird" if the strAnimal variable contains anything other than the letters "D", "d", "C", or "c". Display the appropriate string in the MsgLabel control.

    f. Save the solution, then start the application. Test the application three times, using the letters D, c, and x.

    g. Click the Exit button to end the application.

    h. Close the Output window, then close the solution.

16. In this exercise, you complete two procedures that display the name of the month corresponding to a number entered by the user.

   a.   If necessary, start Visual Studio .NET. Open the Month Solution (Month Solution.sln) file, which is contained in the VBNET\Tut05\Month Solution folder. If the designer window is not open, right-click the form file's name in the Solution Explorer window, then click View Designer.

   b.   Open the Code editor window. Complete the If...Then...Else button's Click event procedure by writing an If...Then...Else statement that displays the name of the month corresponding to the number entered by the user. For example, if the user enters the number 1, the procedure should display the string "January". If the user enters an invalid number (one that is not in the range 1 through 12), display an appropriate message. Display the appropriate string in the MsgLabel control.

   c.   Save the solution, then start the application. Test the application three times, using the numbers 3, 7, and 20.

   d.   Click the Exit button to end the application.

   e.   Now assume that the user will enter the first three characters of the month's name (rather than the month number) in the text box. Complete the Select Case button's Click event procedure by writing a Select Case statement that displays the name of the month corresponding to the characters entered by the user. For example, if the user enters the three characters "Jan" (in any case), the procedure should display the string "January". If the user enters "Jun", the procedure should display "June". If the three characters entered by the user do not match any of the expressions in the Case clauses, display an appropriate message. Display the appropriate string in the MsgLabel control.

   f.   Save the solution, then start the application. Test the application three times, using the following data: jun, dec, xyz.

   g.   Click the Exit button to end the application.

   h.   Close the Output window, then close the solution.

17. In this exercise, you complete a procedure that calculates and displays a bonus amount.

   a.   If necessary, start Visual Studio .NET. Open the Bonus Solution (Bonus Solution.sln) file, which is contained in the VBNET\Tut05\Bonus Solution folder. If the designer window is not open, right-click the form file's name in the Solution Explorer window, then click View Designer.

   b.   Open the Code editor window. Complete the Calculate button's Click event procedure by writing an If...Then...Else statement that assigns the number 25 to the sngBonus variable if the user enters a sales amount that is greater than or equal to $100, but less than or equal to $250. If the user enters a sales amount that is greater then $250, assign the number 50 to the sngBonus variable. If the user enters a sales amount that is less than 100, assign the number 0 as the bonus.

   c.   Save the solution, then start the application. Test the application three times, using sales amounts of 100, 300, and 40.

   d.   Click the Exit button to end the application.

   e.   Close the Output window, then close the solution.

18. In this exercise, you complete a procedure that calculates and displays the total amount owed by a company.

   a.   If necessary, start Visual Studio .NET. Open the Seminar Solution (Seminar Solution.sln) file, which is contained in the VBNET\Tut05\Seminar Solution folder. If the designer window is not open, right-click the form file's name in the Solution Explorer window, then click View Designer.

b. Open the Code editor window. Assume you offer programming seminars to companies. Your price per person depends on the number of people the company registers. (For example, if the company registers seven people, then the total amount owed is $560, which is calculated by multiplying the number 7 by the number 80.) Use the Select Case statement and the following table to complete the Calculate button's Click event procedure.

Number of registrants	Criteria
1 - 4	$100 per person
5 - 10	$ 80 per person
11 or more	$ 60 per person
Less than 1	$ 0 per person

c. Save the solution, then start the application. Test the application four times, using the following data: 7, 4, 11, and -3.

d. Click the Exit button to end the application.

e. Close the Output window, then close the solution.

The Math Practice Application

Completing the User Interface

Recall that Susan Chen, the principal of a local primary school, wants an application that the first and second grade students can use to practice both adding and subtracting numbers. The application should display the addition or subtraction problem on the screen, then allow the student to enter the answer, and then verify that the answer is correct. If the student's answer is not correct, the application should give him or her as many chances as necessary to answer the problem correctly.

The problems displayed for the first grade students should use numbers from 1 through 10 only, and the problems for the second grade students should use numbers from 10 through 99. Because the students have not learned about negative numbers yet, the subtraction problems should never ask them to subtract a larger number from a smaller one.

Ms. Chen also wants the application to keep track of how many correct and incorrect responses the student makes. Recall that Ms. Chen wants to be able to control the display of this information. The sketch of the Math Practice application's user interface is shown in Figure 5-28.

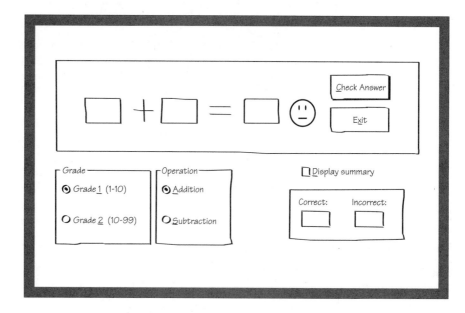

Figure 5-28: Sketch of the Math Practice application's user interface

The user interface contains one text box, four radio buttons, one check box, three picture box controls, four group box controls, and various label controls. To save you time, your computer's hard disk contains a partially completed Math Practice application. When you open the application, you will notice that most of the user interface has already been created and the properties of the existing objects have been set. You complete the user interface in this lesson.

To open the partially completed application:

1   Start Microsoft Visual Studio .NET, if necessary, and then close the Start Page window.

2   Click **File** on the menu bar, and then click **Open Solution**. The Open Solution dialog box opens. Open the **Math Solution** (Math Solution.sln) file, which is contained in the VBNET\Tut05\Math Solution folder.

3   If the designer window is not open, right-click **Math Form.vb** in the Solution Explorer window, then click **View Designer**.

4   Auto-hide the Toolbox, Solution Explorer, and Properties windows, if necessary. Figure 5-29 shows the partially completed user interface for the Math Practice application.

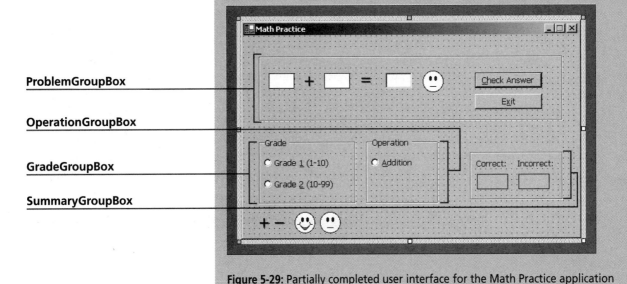

Figure 5-29: Partially completed user interface for the Math Practice application

As Figure 5-29 indicates, the names of the four group boxes are ProblemGroupBox, GradeGroupBox, OperationGroupBox, and SummaryGroupBox. The ProblemGroupBox control contains eight controls; the names of the controls (from left to right) are Num1Label, OperatorPictureBox, Num2Label, EqualPictureBox, AnswerTextBox, AnswerPictureBox, CheckAnswerButton, and ExitButton. As you learned in Tutorial 1, Visual Studio .NET comes with a variety of graphics files, which typically are located in the Program Files\Microsoft Visual Studio .NET\Common7\Graphics folder on either the local hard drive or the network drive. The graphics that appear in the OperatorPictureBox, EqualPictureBox, and AnswerPictureBox controls, for example, are stored in the MISC18.ICO, MISC22.ICO, and FACE01.ICO files within the Graphics\icons\Misc folder.

tip

Recall that you display a graphic in a picture box control by setting the control's **Image** property.

The GradeGroupBox control contains two radio buttons named Grade1RadioButton and Grade2RadioButton, and the OperationGroupBox control contains one radio button named AdditionRadioButton. The SummaryGroupBox control contains four label controls named IdCorrectLabel, CorrectLabel, IdIncorrectLabel, and IncorrectLabel.

In addition to the controls already mentioned, the form also contains four picture box controls positioned at the bottom of the form and named PlusPictureBox, MinusPictureBox, HappyPictureBox, and NeutralPictureBox. The graphics that appear in these controls are stored in the MISC18.ICO, MISC19.ICO, FACE03.ICO, and FACE01.ICO files within the Graphics\icons\Misc folder. For now, do not worry about these four picture box controls; you learn their purpose later in this lesson.

Only two controls are missing from the interface: the Subtraction radio button and the Display summary check box. You add the radio button first, and then you add the check box.

Adding a Radio Button to the Form

You use the **RadioButton tool** in the toolbox to add a radio button control to the interface. A **radio button control** is the appropriate control to use when you want to limit the user to only one choice in a group of two or more related and mutually exclusive choices. In the Math Practice application, for example, you want the user to select one grade level (either Grade 1 or Grade 2) and one mathematical operation (either Addition or Subtraction), so the radio button control is the appropriate control to use in this situation.

Each radio button in an interface should be labeled so that the user knows its purpose. You enter the label using sentence capitalization in the radio button's Text property. Each radio button also should have a unique access key, which allows the user to select the button using the keyboard. Add the missing Subtraction radio button to the interface.

To add a radio button to the interface:

1 Click the **RadioButton** tool in the toolbox, and then drag a radio button control into the OperationGroupBox control, immediately below the AdditionRadioButton. The RadioButton1 control appears in the interface.

2 Set the following properties for the RadioButton1 control:

Name:	**SubtractionRadioButton**
Location:	8, 59
Size:	96, 24
Text:	&Subtraction

3 Click the form's **title bar**. Figure 5-30 shows the Subtraction radio button in the interface.

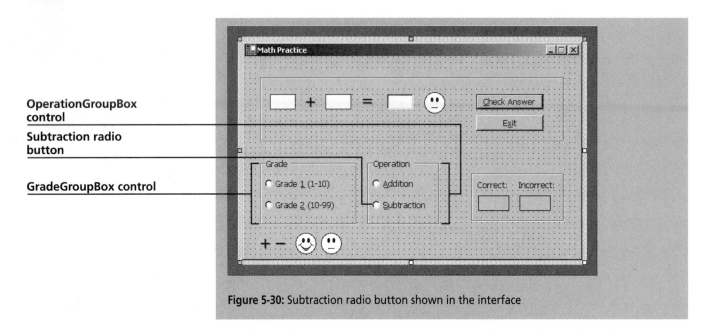

Figure 5-30: Subtraction radio button shown in the interface

OperationGroupBox control

Subtraction radio button

GradeGroupBox control

tip

••••••••••••••••

▶ If you have more than seven choices from which the user can choose, you should consider using a ListBox, CheckedListBox, or ComboBox control rather than radio buttons.

The Math Practice application contains two groups of radio buttons: one group allows the user to select the grade level, and the other allows him or her to select the mathematical operation. The minimum number of radio buttons in a group is two, because the only way to deselect a radio button is to select another radio button. The recommended maximum number of radio buttons in a group is seven. Notice that each group of radio buttons in the Math Practice application contains the minimum number of required radio buttons, two.

To include two groups of radio buttons in an interface, at least one of the groups must be placed within either a group box control or a panel control; otherwise, the radio buttons are considered to be in the same group and only one can be selected at any one time. In this case, the radio buttons pertaining to the grade choice are contained in the GradeGroupBox control, and the radio buttons pertaining to the mathematical operation are contained in the OperationGroupBox control. Placing each group of radio buttons in a separate group box control allows the user to select one button from each group.

It is customary in Windows applications to have one of the radio buttons in each group of radio buttons already selected when the user interface first appears. The selected button is called the **default radio button** and is either the radio button that represents the user's most likely choice or the first radio button in the group. You designate a radio button as the default radio button by setting the button's **Checked property** to the Boolean value True. In the Math Practice application, you will make the first radio button in each group the default radio button.

To designate the first radio button in each group as the default radio button:

1 Click the **Grade 1** radio button to select it, and then set its Checked property to **True**. A black dot appears inside the circle in the Grade 1 radio button.

2 Click the **Addition** radio button to select it, and then set its Checked property to **True**. A black dot appears inside the circle in the Addition radio button.

Radio Button Standards

- Use radio buttons when you want to limit the user to one of two or more related and mutually exclusive choices.
- The minimum number of radio buttons in a group is two, and the recommended maximum is seven.
- The label in the radio button's Text property should be entered using sentence capitalization.
- Assign a unique access key to each radio button in an interface.
- Use a group box control (or a panel control) to create separate groups of radio buttons. Only one button in each group can be selected at any one time.
- Designate a default radio button in each group of radio buttons.

Next, add the missing check box control to the interface.

Adding a Check Box Control to the Form

You use the **CheckBox tool** in the toolbox to add a check box control to the interface. Check boxes work like radio buttons in that they are either selected or deselected only; but that is where the similarity ends. You use radio button controls when you want to limit the user to only one choice from a group of related and mutually exclusive choices. You use **check box controls**, on the other hand, to allow the user to select any number of choices from a group of one or more independent and nonexclusive choices. Unlike radio buttons, where only one button in a group can be selected at any one time, any number of check boxes on a form can be selected at the same time.

As with radio buttons, each check box in an interface should be labeled so that the user knows its purpose. You enter the label using sentence capitalization in the check box's Text property. Each check box also should have a unique access key.

Check Box Standards

- Use check boxes when you want to allow the user to select any number of choices from a group of one or more independent and nonexclusive choices.
- The label in the check box's Text property should be entered using sentence capitalization.
- Assign a unique access key to each check box in an interface.

tip

The SummaryCheckBox control is an instance of the CheckBox class.

To add a check box to the interface:

1   Click the **CheckBox** tool in the toolbox, and then drag a check box control onto the form. Position the check box control immediately above the SummaryGroupBox control. (You can look ahead to Figure 5-31 for the exact location.) The CheckBox1 control appears in the interface.

2   Set the following properties for the CheckBox1 control:

Name:	**SummaryCheckBox**
Location:	**352, 144**
Size:	**136, 32**
Text:	**&Display summary**

3   Click the form's **title bar**. Figure 5-31 shows the Display summary check box in the interface.

**Display summary
check box**

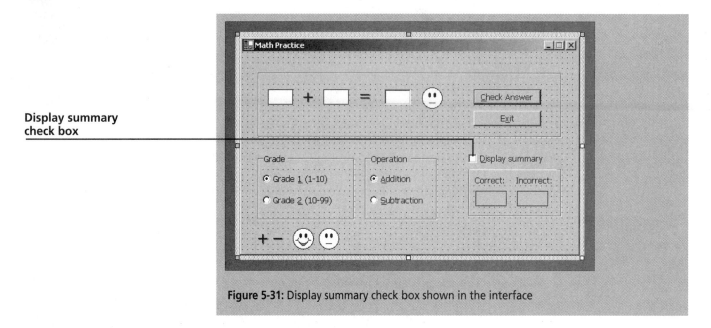

Figure 5-31: Display summary check box shown in the interface

Now that you have completed the user interface, you can lock the controls in place, and then set each control's TabIndex property appropriately.

Locking the Controls and Setting the TabIndex Property

Recall that when you have completed a user interface, you should lock the controls in place and then set each control's TabIndex property appropriately.

To lock the controls, and then set each control's TabIndex property:

1   Right-click the **form**, and then click **Lock Controls** on the shortcut menu.

2   Click **View** on the menu bar, and then click **Tab Order**. Use Figure 5-32 to set the TabIndex values for the controls on the form.

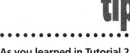

As you learned in Tutorial 2, picture box controls do not have a TabIndex property.

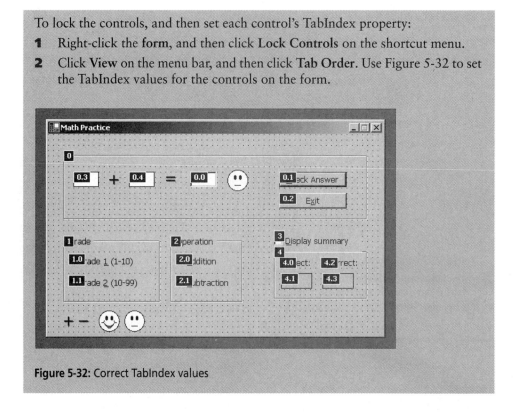

Figure 5-32: Correct TabIndex values

3 Press **Esc** to remove the TabIndex boxes from the form.

Now start the application to observe how you select and deselect radio buttons and check boxes.

To observe how you select and deselect radio buttons and check boxes:

1 Click **File** on the menu bar, and then click **Save All**. Click **Debug** on the menu bar, and then click **Start**. Notice that the Grade 1 and Addition radio buttons already are selected, as the black dot inside each button's circle indicates. Also notice that the four picture box controls located at the bottom of the form, as well as the SummaryGroupBox control and its contents, do not appear in the interface when the application is started. This is because the Visible property of those controls is set to False in the Properties window. You learn more about the Visible property of a control in Lesson C.

You can select a different radio button control by clicking it. You can click either the circle or the text that appears inside the radio button.

2 Click the **Subtraction** radio button. Visual Basic .NET selects the Subtraction radio button as it deselects the Addition radio button. This is because both radio buttons belong to the same group and only one radio button in a group can be selected at any one time.

3 Click the **Grade 2** radio button. Visual Basic .NET selects the Grade 2 radio button as it deselects the Grade 1 radio button. Here again, the Grade 1 and Grade 2 radio buttons belong to the same group; so selecting one deselects the other.

After selecting a radio button in a group, you then can use the ↑ and ↓ keys on your keyboard to select another radio button in the group.

4 Press ↑ to select the Grade 1 radio button, and then press ↓ to select the Grade 2 radio button.

5 Press **Tab**. Notice that the focus moves to the Subtraction radio button rather than to the Addition radio button. In Windows applications, only the selected radio button in a group of radio buttons receives the focus.

You can select a check box control by clicking either the square or the text that appears inside the control.

6 Click the **Display summary** check box to select it. A check mark appears inside the check box. The check mark indicates that the check box is selected.

7 Click the **Display summary** check box to deselect it. Visual Basic .NET removes the check mark from the check box.

When a check box has the focus, you can use the spacebar on your keyboard to select and deselect it.

8 Press the **spacebar** to select the Display summary check box. A check mark appears inside the check box. Press the **spacebar** again to deselect the check box, which removes the check mark.

9 Click the **Exit** button to end the application. When you return to the designer window, close the Output window.

Now you can begin coding the application.

Coding the Math Practice Application

The TOE chart for the Math Practice application is shown in Figure 5-33.

Task	Object	Event
1. Display the plus sign in the OperatorPictureBox control 2. Generate and display two random numbers in the Num1Label and Num2Label controls	AdditionRadioButton	Click
Display either the happy face or the neutral face icon (from CheckAnswerButton)	AnswerPictureBox	None
Get and display the user's answer	AnswerTextBox	None
1. Calculate the correct answer to the math problem 2. Compare the correct answer to the user's answer 3. Display appropriate icon in the AnswerPictureBox 4. If the user's answer is correct, then generate and display two random numbers in the Num1Label and Num2Label controls 5. If the user's answer is incorrect, then display the "Try again!" message 6. Add 1 to the number of either correct or incorrect responses 7. Display the number of correct and incorrect responses in the CorrectLabel and IncorrectLabel controls, respectively	CheckAnswerButton	Click
Display the number of correct responses (from CheckAnswerButton)	CorrectLabel	None
Display the equal sign	EqualPictureBox	None
End the application	ExitButton	Click
Display an addition problem when the form first appears on the screen	MathForm	Load
Generate and display two random numbers in the Num1Label and Num2Label controls	Grade1RadioButton, Grade2RadioButton	Click
Display the number of incorrect responses (from CheckAnswerButton)	IncorrectLabel	None
Display two random numbers (from Grade1RadioButton, Grade2RadioButton, AdditionRadioButton, SubtractionRadioButton, CheckAnswerButton)	Num1Label, Num2Label	None
Display either the plus sign or the minus sign (from AdditionRadioButton and SubtractionRadioButton)	OperatorPictureBox	None
1. Display the minus sign in the OperatorPictureBox control 2. Generate and display two random numbers in the Num1Label and Num2Label controls	SubtractionRadioButton	Click
Display or hide the SummaryGroupBox control	SummaryCheckBox	Click

Figure 5-33: TOE chart for the Math Practice application

According to the TOE chart, the Click event procedures for seven of the controls—namely, the AdditionRadioButton, CheckAnswerButton, ExitButton, Grade1RadioButton, Grade2RadioButton, SubtractionRadioButton, and SummaryCheckBox controls—and the Load event for the MathForm need to be coded. In this lesson, you code all but the Click event procedures for the ExitButton control (which already has been coded for you) and the CheckAnswerButton and SummaryCheckBox controls (which you code in Lesson C).

Notice that the task of generating and displaying two random numbers in the Num1Label and Num2Label controls appears in the Task column for five of the controls. For example, the task is listed as Step 2 for the AdditionRadioButton and SubtractionRadioButton controls. It is listed as the only task for the Grade1RadioButton and Grade2RadioButton controls, and it also appears as Step 4 for the CheckAnswerButton control. Rather than entering the appropriate code in the Click event procedures for each of the five controls, you will enter the code in a user-defined Sub procedure. You then will have the five Click event procedures call (or invoke) the Sub procedure. First, learn how to create a user-defined Sub procedure.

Creating a User-Defined Sub Procedure

A **user-defined Sub procedure** is a collection of code that can be invoked from one or more places in an application. When the code, or a portion of the code, for two or more objects is almost identical, it is more efficient to enter the code once, in a user-defined Sub procedure, instead of duplicating the code in various event procedures throughout the application.

The rules for naming a user-defined Sub procedure are the same as those for naming variables and constants. (The naming rules are listed in Figure 3-5 in Tutorial 3.) You should select a descriptive name for the Sub procedure—one that indicates the task the procedure performs. It is a common practice to begin the name with a verb. For example, a good name for a Sub procedure that generates and displays two random numbers is GenerateAndDisplayNumbers.

To create a user-defined Sub procedure named GenerateAndDisplayNumbers:

1 Right-click the **form** and then click **View Code** to open the Code editor window. Notice that the Exit button's Click event procedure already contains the appropriate code.

2 Click the blank line above the `End Class` statement, and then press **Enter** to insert another blank line.

As you learned in Tutorial 1, every procedure begins with a procedure header and ends with a procedure footer. In this case, you will use `Private Sub GenerateAndDisplayNumbers()` as the procedure header, and `End Sub` as the procedure footer. Recall that the keyword Private indicates that the procedure can be used only within the class in which it is defined—in this case, only within the MathForm class. The keyword Sub indicates that the procedure is a Sub procedure.

In the GenerateAndDisplayNumbers procedure, an empty set of parentheses follows the procedure's name. The empty set of parentheses indicates that no items of information will be passed (sent) to the procedure when it is called. You learn how to pass information to a Sub procedure in Tutorial 7.

3 In the new blank line, type **private sub GenerateAndDisplayNumbers**() and press **Enter**. When you press Enter, the Code editor automatically enters the procedure footer for you, as shown in Figure 5-34.

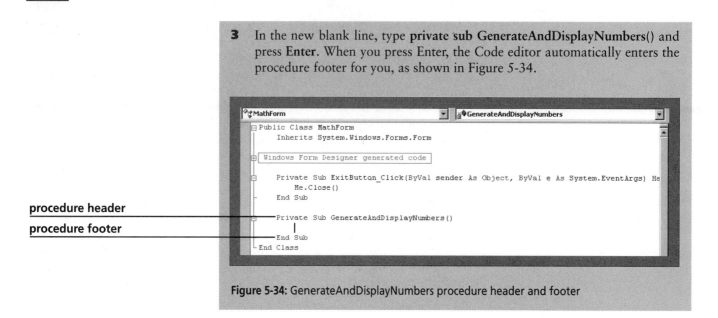

procedure header

procedure footer

Figure 5-34: GenerateAndDisplayNumbers procedure header and footer

Figure 5-35 shows the pseudocode for the GenerateAndDisplayNumbers procedure.

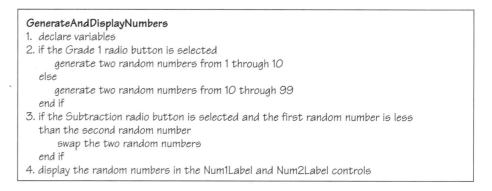

GenerateAndDisplayNumbers
1. declare variables
2. if the Grade 1 radio button is selected
    generate two random numbers from 1 through 10
  else
    generate two random numbers from 10 through 99
  end if
3. if the Subtraction radio button is selected and the first random number is less
  than the second random number
    swap the two random numbers
  end if
4. display the random numbers in the Num1Label and Num2Label controls

Figure 5-35: Pseudocode for the GenerateAndDisplayNumbers procedure

The first step in the pseudocode is to declare the variables. The GenerateAndDisplayNumbers procedure will use two Integer variables to store the two random numbers generated by the procedure.

To begin coding the GenerateAndDisplayNumbers procedure:

1 Type **dim intNum1, intNum2 as integer** and press **Enter**.

Step 2 in the pseudocode is to determine whether the Grade 1 radio button is selected in the interface. You can determine whether a radio button is selected by comparing its Checked property to the Boolean value True. If the Checked property contains the Boolean value True, then the radio button is selected; if it contains the Boolean value False, then the radio button is not selected.

2 Type **'generate random numbers** and press **Enter**, then type **if me.grade1radiobutton.checked = true then** and press **Enter**.

If the Grade 1 radio button is selected, then the GenerateAndDisplayNumbers procedure should generate two random numbers from 1 through 10.

Generating Random Numbers

Pseudo-random numbers are chosen with equal probability from a finite set of numbers. The chosen numbers are not completely random because a definite mathematical algorithm is used to select them, but they are sufficiently random for practical purposes.

Visual Studio .NET provides a **pseudo-random number generator**, which is a device that produces a sequence of numbers that meet certain statistical requirements for randomness. To use the pseudo-random number generator in a procedure, you first create a Random object, typically using the syntax **Dim** *objectname* **As New Random()**. The **Random object** represents the pseudo-random number generator in the procedure.

After creating a Random object, you can generate random integers using the **Random.Next method**. The syntax of the Random.Next method is *randomObject*.**Next**(*minValue*, *maxValue*), where *randomObject* is the name of a Random object. The *minValue* and *maxValue* arguments in the syntax must be integers, and *minValue* must be less than *maxValue*. The Random.Next method returns an integer that is greater than or equal to *minValue*, but less than *maxValue*. Figure 5-36 shows examples of using a Random object and the Random.Next method to generate random integers.

Examples	Result

<u>Example 1</u>
`Dim GeneratorRandom As New Random()`
`Me.NumLabel.Text = GeneratorRandom.Next(0, 51)`
	creates a Random object named GeneratorRandom, then displays (in the NumLabel control) a random integer that is greater than or equal to 0, but less than 51

<u>Example 2</u>
`Dim GeneratorRandom As New Random()`
`Me.NumLabel.Text = GeneratorRandom.Next(50, 100)`
	creates a Random object named GeneratorRandom, then displays (in the NumLabel control) a random integer that is greater than or equal to 50, but less than 100

<u>Example 3</u>
`Dim GeneratorRandom As New Random()`
`Me.NumLabel.Text = GeneratorRandom.Next(-10, 0)`
	creates a Random object named GeneratorRandom, then displays (in the NumLabel control) a random integer that is greater than or equal to -10, but less than 0

Figure 5-36: Examples of generating random integers

In Discovery Exercise 4 at the end of this lesson, you learn how to use the Random.NextDouble method to generate a random floating-point number.

The `Dim GeneratorRandom As New Random()` statement in each example creates a Random object named GeneratorRandom. The GeneratorRandom object represents the pseudo-random number generator in the procedure. The `Me.NumLabel.Text = GeneratorRandom.Next(0, 51)` statement shown in Example 1 displays a random integer that is greater than or equal to 0, but less than 51. In Example 2, the `Me.NumLabel.Text = GeneratorRandom.Next(50, 100)` statement displays a random integer that is greater than or equal to 50, but less than 100. In Example 3, the `Me.NumLabel.Text = GeneratorRandom.Next(-10, 0)` statement displays a random integer that is greater than or equal to -10, but less than 0.

In Discovery Exercise 5 at the end of this lesson, you learn how to generate random numbers using the Randomize statement and the Rnd function.

According to the pseudocode shown in Figure 5-35, if the Grade 1 radio button is selected in the Math Practice interface, then the GenerateAndDisplayNumbers procedure should generate two random numbers from 1 through 10. To generate numbers within that range, you need to use the number 1 as the *minValue* and the number 11 as the *maxValue*. If the Grade 1 radio button is not selected, then the Grade 2 button must be selected. In that case, the GenerateAndDisplayNumbers procedure should generate two random numbers from 10 through 99. To generate numbers within that range, you need to use the numbers 10 and 100 as the *minValue* and *maxValue*, respectively.

To continue coding the GenerateAndDisplayNumbers procedure:

1   Enter the additional code shown in Figure 5-37, then position the insertion point as shown in the figure. (Be sure to declare the Random object in the Dim statement.)

enter this code

enter these five lines of code

position the insertion point here

```
Private Sub GenerateAndDisplayNumbers()
    Dim intNum1, intNum2 As Integer, GeneratorRandom As New Random()
    'generate random numbers
    If Me.Grade1RadioButton.Checked = True Then
        intNum1 = GeneratorRandom.Next(1, 11)
        intNum2 = GeneratorRandom.Next(1, 11)
    Else 'Grade2RadioButton.Checked = True
        intNum1 = GeneratorRandom.Next(10, 100)
        intNum2 = GeneratorRandom.Next(10, 100)
    End If

End Sub
```

Figure 5-37: Random number generation code entered in the GenerateAndDisplayNumbers procedure

Step 3 in the pseudocode is to determine whether the Subtraction radio button is selected and, at the same time, to determine whether the first random number is less than the second random number. If both conditions are true, then the procedure should swap (interchange) the two random numbers, because no subtraction problem should result in a negative number.

2   Enter the additional code shown in Figure 5-38, then position the insertion point as shown in the figure.

enter these seven lines of code

position the insertion point here

```
Private Sub GenerateAndDisplayNumbers()
    Dim intNum1, intNum2 As Integer, GeneratorRandom As New Random()
    'generate random numbers
    If Me.Grade1RadioButton.Checked = True Then
        intNum1 = GeneratorRandom.Next(1, 11)
        intNum2 = GeneratorRandom.Next(1, 11)
    Else 'Grade2RadioButton.Checked = True
        intNum1 = GeneratorRandom.Next(10, 100)
        intNum2 = GeneratorRandom.Next(10, 100)
    End If
    'swap numbers if the subtraction problem would result in a negative number
    If Me.SubtractionRadioButton.Checked = True AndAlso intNum1 < intNum2 Then
        Dim intTemp As Integer
        intTemp = intNum1
        intNum1 = intNum2
        intNum2 = intTemp
    End If

End Sub
```

Figure 5-38: Additional code shown in the GenerateAndDisplayNumbers procedure

The last step in the pseudocode shown in Figure 5-35 is to display the random numbers in the Num1Label and Num2Label controls.

3 Enter the additional code shown in Figure 5-39, which shows the completed GenerateAndDisplayNumbers procedure.

```
Private Sub GenerateAndDisplayNumbers()
    Dim intNum1, intNum2 As Integer, GeneratorRandom As New Random()
    'generate random numbers
    If Me.Grade1RadioButton.Checked = True Then
        intNum1 = GeneratorRandom.Next(1, 11)
        intNum2 = GeneratorRandom.Next(1, 11)
    Else 'Grade2RadioButton.Checked = True
        intNum1 = GeneratorRandom.Next(10, 100)
        intNum2 = GeneratorRandom.Next(10, 100)
    End If
    'swap numbers if the subtraction problem would result in a negative number
    If Me.SubtractionRadioButton.Checked = True AndAlso intNum1 < intNum2 Then
        Dim intTemp As Integer
        intTemp = intNum1
        intNum1 = intNum2
        intNum2 = intTemp
    End If
    'display numbers in the label controls
    Me.Num1Label.Text = intNum1
    Me.Num2Label.Text = intNum2
End Sub
```

enter these three lines of code

Figure 5-39: Completed GenerateAndDisplayNumbers procedure

4 Click **File** on the menu bar, and then click **Save All**.

Next, code the Click event procedures for the Grade 1 and Grade 2 radio buttons.

Coding the Grade1RadioButton and Grade2RadioButton Click Event Procedures

> **tip**
> ● ● ● ● ● ● ● ● ● ● ● ● ● ● ●
> The word "Call" also is optional when calling a Sub procedure. In other words, you can call the GenerateAndDisplay-Numbers procedure using either the statement Call GenerateAndDisplay-Numbers() or the statement GenerateAndDisplay-Numbers().

According to the TOE chart shown in Figure 5-33, the Grade1RadioButton and Grade2RadioButton controls should generate and display two random numbers when clicked. Recall that the code to generate and display the random numbers is entered in the GenerateAndDisplayNumbers procedure. The Grade1RadioButton and Grade2RadioButton controls can use the code entered in the GenerateAndDisplayNumbers procedure simply by calling, or invoking, the procedure.

You can use the Visual Basic .NET **Call statement**, whose syntax is **Call** *procedurename*([*argumentlist*]), to call (invoke) a user-defined Sub procedure. The square brackets in the syntax indicate that the *argumentlist* is optional. If you have no information to pass to the procedure that you are calling, as is the case in the GenerateAndDisplayNumbers procedure, you simply include an empty set of parentheses after the *procedurename*.

Figure 5-40 shows two examples of including the Call GenerateAndDisplayNumbers() statement in the Click event procedures for the Grade1RadioButton and Grade2RadioButton controls.

Example 1

```
Private Sub Grade1RadioButton_Click(ByVal sender As Object, _
        ByVal e As System.EventArgs) Handles Grade1RadioButton.Click
    Call GenerateAndDisplayNumbers()
End Sub

Private Sub Grade2RadioButton_Click(ByVal sender As Object, _
        ByVal e As System.EventArgs) Handles Grade2RadioButton.Click
    Call GenerateAndDisplayNumbers()
End Sub
```

Example 2

```
Private Sub ProcessGradeRadioButtons(ByVal sender As Object, _
        ByVal e As System.EventArgs) _
        Handles Grade1RadioButton.Click, Grade2RadioButton.Click
    Call GenerateAndDisplayNumbers()
End Sub
```

Figure 5-40: Two examples of including the Call statement in the Click event procedures for the grade radio buttons

In the first example shown in Figure 5-40, the Call statement is entered in both Click event procedures. In the second example, the Call statement is entered in a procedure named ProcessGradeRadioButtons, which, according to its Handles section, is processed when the Click event occurs for either the Grade1RadioButton or Grade2RadioButton control. In this case, neither example is better than the other; both simply represent different ways of performing the same task.

To call the GenerateAndDisplayNumbers procedure when the Grade 1 and Grade 2 radio buttons are clicked:

1 Click the **Class Name** list arrow in the Code editor window, and then click **Grade1RadioButton** in the list. Click the **Method Name** list arrow, and then click **Click** in the list. The template for the Grade1RadioButton Click event procedure appears in the Code editor window.

2 Change Grade1RadioButton_Click, which appears after `Private Sub` in the procedure header, to **ProcessGradeRadioButtons**.

3 Click immediately before the word Handles in the procedure header. Type _ (the underscore, which is the line continuation character) and press **Enter**.

4 Press **Tab** twice to indent the line.

5 Enter the additional code shown in Figure 5-41, which shows the completed ProcessGradeRadioButtons procedure. (The size of the font used in the Code editor window was changed so that you could view more of the code in the figure.)

enter this line of code

enter this code

```
Private Sub ProcessGradeRadioButtons(ByVal sender As Object, ByVal e As System.EventArgs) _
        Handles Grade1RadioButton.Click,  Grade2RadioButton.Click
    Call GenerateAndDisplayNumbers()
End Sub
```

Figure 5-41: Completed ProcessGradeRadioButtons procedure

When the user clicks either the Grade 1 radio button or the Grade 2 radio button, the computer processes the `Call GenerateAndDisplayNumbers()` statement contained in the ProcessGradeRadioButtons procedure. When the Call statement is processed, the computer leaves the ProcessGradeRadioButtons procedure, temporarily, to process the instructions contained in the GenerateAndDisplayNumbers procedure. When the GenerateAndDisplayNumbers procedure ends, which is when the computer processes the procedure's `End Sub` statement, the computer returns to the ProcessGradeRadioButtons procedure, to the line below the Call statement. In the ProcessGradeRadioButtons procedure, the line below the Call statement is the `End Sub` statement, which ends the procedure. Figure 5-42 illustrates the concept of calling a procedure.

leave ProcessGradeRadio-Buttons procedure, temporarily

return to ProcessGradeRadio-Buttons procedure

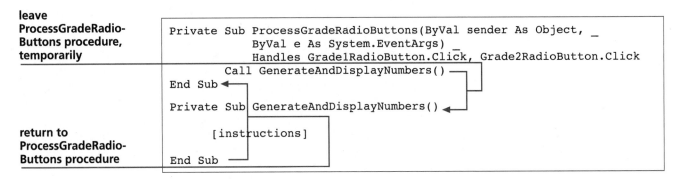

```
Private Sub ProcessGradeRadioButtons(ByVal sender As Object, _
            ByVal e As System.EventArgs) _
            Handles Grade1RadioButton.Click, Grade2RadioButton.Click
        Call GenerateAndDisplayNumbers()
End Sub

Private Sub GenerateAndDisplayNumbers()

        [instructions]

End Sub
```

Figure 5-42: Illustration of calling a procedure

Now test the grade radio buttons to verify that they are working correctly.

To test the grade radio buttons:

1 Click **File** on the menu bar, and then click **Save All**. Click **Debug** on the menu bar, and then click **Start**.

2 Click the **Grade 2** radio button. The computer leaves the ProcessGrade-RadioButtons procedure, temporarily, to process the instructions in the GenerateAndDisplayNumbers procedure. The GenerateAndDisplayNumbers procedure generates and displays two random integers from 10 through 99, as shown in Figure 5-43. (Do not be concerned if the numbers on your screen are different from the ones shown in the figure.)

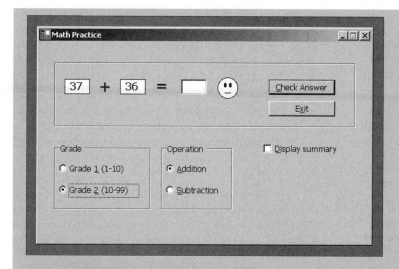

Figure 5-43: Two random numbers displayed in the interface

When the GenerateAndDisplayNumbers procedure ends, the computer returns to the ProcessGradeRadioButtons procedure, to the line immediately below the Call statement. That line is the **End Sub** statement, which ends the ProcessGradeRadioButtons procedure.

3   Click the **Grade 1** radio button. The computer leaves the ProcessGrade-RadioButtons procedure, temporarily, to process the instructions in the GenerateAndDisplayNumbers procedure. The GenerateAndDisplayNumbers procedure generates and displays two random integers from 1 through 10. When the GenerateAndDisplayNumbers procedure ends, the computer returns to the ProcessGradeRadioButtons procedure, to the line immediately below the Call statement. That line is the **End Sub** statement, which ends the ProcessGradeRadioButtons procedure.

4   Click the **Exit** button. When you return to the Code editor window, close the Output window.

Next, code the Click event procedures for the Addition and Subtraction radio buttons.

Coding the AdditionRadioButton and SubtractionRadioButton Click Event Procedures

According to the TOE chart shown in Figure 5-33, when the user clicks either the AdditionRadioButton control or the SubtractionRadioButton control, the control's Click event procedure should display the appropriate mathematical operator (either a plus sign or a minus sign) in the OperatorPictureBox control, and then generate and display two random numbers in the Num1Label and Num2Label controls. Figure 5-44 shows two examples of coding the Click event procedures for these radio buttons.

Example 1

```
Private Sub AdditionRadioButton_Click(ByVal sender As Object, _
        ByVal e As System.EventArgs) Handles AdditionRadioButton.Click
    Me.OperatorPictureBox.Image = Me.PlusPictureBox.Image
    Call GenerateAndDisplayNumbers()
End Sub

Private Sub SubtractionRadioButton_Click(ByVal sender As Object, _
        ByVal e As System.EventArgs) Handles SubtractionRadioButton.Click
    Me.OperatorPictureBox.Image = Me.MinusPictureBox.Image
    Call GenerateAndDisplayNumbers()
End Sub
```

Example 2

```
Private Sub ProcessOperationRadioButtons(ByVal sender As Object, _
        ByVal e As System.EventArgs) _
        Handles AdditionRadioButton.Click, SubtractionRadioButton.Click
    If sender Is AdditionRadioButton Then
        Me.OperatorPictureBox.Image = Me.PlusPictureBox.Image
    Else 'SubtractionRadioButton is sender
        Me.OperatorPictureBox.Image = Me.MinusPictureBox.Image
    End If
    Call GenerateAndDisplayNumbers()
End Sub
```

Figure 5-44: Examples of coding the Click event procedures for the operation radio buttons

In Example 1 in Figure 5-44, both Click event procedures first display the appropriate operator in the OperatorPictureBox control. For example, the Click event procedure for the AdditionRadioButton control displays the plus sign by assigning the Image property of the PlusPictureBox control, which is located at the bottom of the form, to the Image property of the OperatorPictureBox control. Likewise, the Click event procedure for the SubtractionRadioButton control displays the minus sign by assigning the Image property of the MinusPictureBox control, which also is located at the bottom of the form, to the Image property of the OperatorPictureBox control. After assigning the appropriate operator, the Click event procedures shown in Example 1 call the GenerateAndDisplayNumbers procedure to generate and display two random numbers in the Num1Label and Num2Label controls.

In the second example shown in Figure 5-44, the code to display the operator and random numbers is entered in the ProcessOperationRadioButtons procedure, rather than in the individual Click event procedures. According to the Handles section, the ProcessOperationRadioButtons procedure is processed when either the AdditionRadioButton Click event or the SubtractionRadioButton Click event occurs. Notice that the procedure uses a selection structure to determine whether the sender parameter contains the address of the AdditionRadioButton control. If it does, then the procedure displays the plus sign in the OperatorPictureBox control; otherwise, it displays the minus sign in the OperatorPictureBox control. Here again, neither example is better than the other; both simply represent two different ways of performing the same task.

tip

▶ To remove a graphic from a picture box control while a procedure is running, set the picture box control's Image property to the keyword Nothing.

To code the AdditionRadioButton and SubtractionRadioButton Click event procedures, then test the application:

1 Click the **Class Name** list arrow in the Code editor window, and then click **AdditionRadioButton** in the list. Click the **Method Name** list arrow, and then click **Click** in the list. The template for the AdditionRadioButton Click event procedure appears in the Code editor window.

2 Change AdditionRadioButton_Click, which appears after `Private Sub` in the procedure header, to **ProcessOperationRadioButtons**.

3 Click immediately before the word Handles in the procedure header. Type _ (the underscore, which is the line continuation character) and press **Enter**.

4 Press **Tab** twice to indent the line.

5 Enter the additional code shown in Figure 5-45, which shows the completed ProcessOperationRadioButtons procedure. (The size of the font used in the Code editor window was changed so that you could view more of the code in the figure.)

enter these seven lines of code

enter this code

```
Private Sub ProcessOperationRadioButtons(ByVal sender As Object, ByVal e As System.EventArgs) _
    Handles AdditionRadioButton.Click, SubtractionRadioButton.Click
    'display appropriate operator
    If sender Is AdditionRadioButton Then
        Me.OperatorPictureBox.Image = Me.PlusPictureBox.Image
    Else 'SubtractionRadioButton is sender
        Me.OperatorPictureBox.Image = Me.MinusPictureBox.Image
    End If
    Call GenerateAndDisplayNumbers()
End Sub
```

Figure 5-45: Completed ProcessOperationRadioButtons procedure

Now test the application's code.

6 Save the solution, then start the application. Notice that, even though the Grade 1 and Addition radio buttons are selected in the interface, an addition problem does not automatically appear in the interface. You fix that in the next section.

7 Click the **Subtraction** radio button. A minus sign appears in the OperatorPictureBox control, and two new random integers from 1 through 10 appear in the interface.

8 Click the **Addition** radio button. A plus sign appears in the OperatorPictureBox control, and two new random integers from 1 through 10 appear in the interface.

9 Click the **Grade 2** radio button. Two new random integers from 10 through 99 appear in the interface.

10 Click the **Exit** button. When you return to the Code editor window, close the Output window.

In the Math Practice application, you want an addition problem to be displayed automatically when the form first appears on the screen. You can accomplish this task in two ways: either you can use the Call statement to call the GenerateAndDisplayNumbers procedure, or you can use the PerformClick method to invoke the AdditionRadioButton control's Click event procedure. Whichever way you choose, the appropriate code must be entered in the form's Load event procedure, which is the last procedure you will code in this lesson.

Coding the Form's Load Event Procedure

tip

. . . .

▶ You also can use the Button.PerformClick method, whose syntax is *button*.**PerformClick()**, to click a Button control from code.

Instructions entered in the form's **Load event procedure** are processed when the application is started and the form is loaded into memory. The form is not displayed on the screen until all of the instructions in its Load event procedure are processed. To automatically display an addition problem when the Math Practice interface first appears, you can enter either the statement `Call GenerateAndDisplayNumbers()` or the statement `Me.AdditionRadioButton.PerformClick()` in the MathForm's Load event procedure. The latter statement uses the **RadioButton.PerformClick method**, whose syntax is *radiobutton*.**PerformClick()**, to invoke the Addition radio button's Click event, which causes the code in the Click event procedure to be processed by the computer.

To automatically display an addition problem when the Math Practice interface first appears:

1 Click the **Class Name** list arrow in the Code editor window, and then click (**Base Class Events**) in the list. Click the **Method Name** list arrow, and then click **Load** in the list. The template for the MathForm Load event procedure appears in the Code editor window.

2 Enter the Call statement shown in Figure 5-46, which shows the completed Load event procedure.

enter this statement ──────

```
Private Sub MathForm_Load(ByVal sender As Object, ByVal e As System.EventArgs) Handles MyBase.Load
    Call GenerateAndDisplayNumbers()
End Sub
```

Figure 5-46: Completed Load event procedure

3 Save the solution, then start the application. When the Math Practice interface appears on the screen, it displays an addition problem, as shown in Figure 5-47.

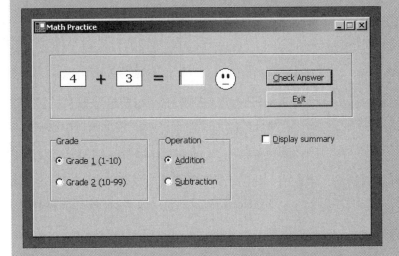

Figure 5-47: Addition problem displayed when the form first appears

4 Click the **Exit** button to end the application. When you return to the Code editor window, close the Output window, then close the Code editor window.

5 Click **File** on the menu bar, and then click **Close Solution** to close the solution.

You now have completed Lesson B. You can either take a break or complete the end-of-lesson questions and exercises before moving on to the next lesson. You complete the Math Practice application in Lesson C.

SUMMARY

To limit the user to only one choice in a group of two or more related and mutually exclusive choices:

- Use the RadioButton tool ⊙ to add a radio button control to the interface.
- To include two groups of radio buttons in an interface, at least one of the groups must be placed within either a group box control or a panel control.

To allow the user to select any number of choices from a group of one or more independent and nonexclusive choices:

- Use the CheckBox tool to add a check box control to the interface.

To create a collection of code that can be invoked from one or more places in a program:

- Create a user-defined Sub procedure. The Sub procedure's name should begin with a verb and indicate the task performed by the procedure.

To generate random numbers that are integers:

- Create a Random object to represent the Visual Studio .NET pseudo-random number generator. Typically, the syntax for creating a Random object is **Dim** *objectname* **As New Random**().
- Use the Random.Next method to generate a random integer. The syntax of the Random.Next method is *randomObject*.**Next**(*minValue, maxValue*), where *randomObject* is the name of the Random object, and *minValue* and *maxValue* are integers. The Random.Next method returns an integer that is greater than or equal to *minValue*, but less than *maxValue*.

To call (invoke) a user-defined Sub procedure:

- Use the Call statement. The syntax of the Call statement is **Call** *procedurename* ([*argumentlist*]), where *procedurename* is the name of the procedure you want to call, and *argumentlist* (which is optional) contains the information you want to send to the Sub procedure.

To process code when the form is loaded into memory:

- Enter the code in the form's Load event procedure.

To invoke a radio button control's Click event procedure from code:

■ Use the RadioButton.PerformClick method. The syntax of the RadioButton.PerformClick method is *radiobutton*.**PerformClick**(), where *radiobutton* is the name of the radio button whose Click event you want invoked.

QUESTIONS

1. The minimum number of radio buttons in a group is _____.
   a. one
   b. two
   c. three
   d. four
   e. seven

2. The minimum number of check boxes in an interface is _____.
   a. one
   b. two
   c. three
   d. four
   e. seven

3. The text appearing in check box and radio button controls should be entered using _____.
   a. book title capitalization
   b. sentence capitalization
   c. either book title capitalization or sentence capitalization

4. It is customary in Windows applications to designate a default check box.
   a. True
   b. False

5. To create three groups of radio buttons in an interface, what is the minimum number of groups that must be placed in a separate group box or panel control?
   a. zero
   b. one
   c. two
   d. three

6. To create three groups of check boxes in an interface, what is the minimum number of groups that must be placed in a separate group box or panel control?
   a. zero
   b. one
   c. two
   d. three

7. Assume that a form contains two group box controls, each containing three radio buttons. How many radio buttons can be selected on the form?
   a. one
   b. two
   c. three
   d. five
   e. six

8. Assume that a form contains two group box controls, each containing three check boxes. How many check boxes can be selected on the form?
    a. one
    b. two
    c. three
    d. five
    e. six

9. If a radio button is selected, its _____ property contains the Boolean value True.
    a. Checked
    b. Dot
    c. On
    d. Selected
    e. Value

10. You can use the radio button control to limit the user to only one choice in a group of two or more related and mutually exclusive choices.
    a. True
    b. False

11. You can use the check box control to allow the user to select any number of independent and nonexclusive choices.
    a. True
    b. False

12. Which of the following statements declares an object that can represent the Visual Studio .NET pseudo-random number generator in a procedure?
    a. `Dim Generator As New RandomNumber()`
    b. `Dim NumberGenerator As New Generator()`
    c. `Dim NumberRandom As New Random()`
    d. `Dim NumberRandom As Random`
    e. `Dim Number As New RandomObject`

13. Which of the following statements generates a random number from 1 to 25, inclusive? (The Random object's name is GeneratorRandom.)
    a. `intNumber = GeneratorRandom(1, 25)`
    b. `intNumber = GeneratorRandom.Get(1, 25)`
    c. `intNumber = GeneratorRandom.Next(1, 25)`
    d. `intNumber = GeneratorRandom.Next(1, 26)`
    e. `intNumber = GeneratorRandom.NextNumber(1, 26)`

14. You can use the _____ statement to invoke a user-defined Sub procedure.
    a. Call
    b. DoProcedure
    c. Get
    d. Invoke
    e. ProcedureCall

15. The _____ event occurs when a form is being read into the computer's internal memory.
    a. BringIn
    b. Change
    c. Load
    d. MemoryInit
    e. Read

16. Which of the following statements invokes the AlaskaRadioButton control's Click event procedure?
    a. `Me.AlaskaRadioButton.Click()`
    b. `Me.AlaskaRadioButton.ClickIt`
    c. `Me.Click.AlaskaRadioButton()`
    d. `Me.PerformClick.AlaskaRadioButton`
    e. None of the above.

E X E R C I S E S

1. In this exercise, you use the RadioButton.PerformClick method to invoke a radio button's Click event procedure.
    a. If necessary, start Visual Studio .NET. Open the Practice Solution (Practice Solution.sln) file, which is contained in the VBNET\Tut05\Practice Solution folder. If the designer window is not open, right-click the form file's name in the Solution Explorer window, then click View Designer.
    b. Modify the form's Load event procedure so that it uses the RadioButton.PerformClick method to invoke the Addition radio button's Click event procedure.
    c. Save the solution, then start the application. An addition problem automatically appears in the interface.
    d. Click the Exit button to end the application.
    e. Close the Output window, then close the solution.

2. In this exercise, you code an application for Woodland School. The application allows a student to select the name of a state and the name of a capital city. After making his or her selections, the student can click the Verify Answer button to verify that the selected city is the capital of the selected state.
    a. If necessary, start Visual Studio .NET. Open the Capitals Solution (Capitals Solution.sln) file, which is contained in the VBNET\Tut05\Capitals Solution folder. If the designer window is not open, right-click the form file's name in the Solution Explorer window, then click View Designer.
    b. Designate the first radio button in each group as the default radio button for the group.
    c. Enter the code to invoke the Click event for the two default radio buttons when the form is read into the computer's internal memory.
    d. Declare two form-level variables named mstrCapital and mstrChoice.
    e. Code the State radio buttons' Click event procedures so that each assigns the appropriate capital to the mstrCapital variable, and each removes the contents of the MsgLabel control.
    f. Code the Capital radio buttons' Click event procedures so that each assigns the selected capital to the mstrChoice variable, and each removes the contents of the MsgLabel control.
    g. Code the Verify Answer button's Click event procedure so that it displays the word "Correct" in the MsgLabel control if the student selected the appropriate capital; otherwise, display the word "Incorrect".
    h. Save the solution, then start the application. Test the application by selecting Illinois from the State group and Salem from the Capital group. Click the Verify Answer button. The word "Incorrect" appears in the MsgLabel control. Now select Wisconsin from the State group and Madison from the Capital group. Click the Verify Answer button. The word "Correct" appears in the MsgLabel control.
    i. Click the Exit button to end the application.
    j. Close the Output window, then close the solution.

3. In this exercise, you code an application for Professor Juarez. The application displays a letter grade based on the average of three test scores entered by the professor.

    a. If necessary, start Visual Studio .NET. Open the Grade Solution (Grade Solution.sln) file, which is contained in the VBNET\Tut05\Grade Solution folder. If the designer window is not open, right-click the form file's name in the Solution Explorer window, then click View Designer.

    b. Code the Display Grade button's Click event procedure so that it displays the appropriate letter grade based on the average of three test scores. Each test is worth 100 points. Use the following information to complete the procedure:

Test average	Grade
90-100	A
80-89	B
70-79	C
60-69	D
below 60	F

    c. When the user makes a change to the contents of a text box, the application should remove the contents of the GradeLabel control. Code the appropriate event procedures.

    d. Save the solution, then start the application. Test the application three times. For the first test, use scores of 90, 95, and 100. For the second test, use scores of 83, 72, and 65. For the third test, use scores of 40, 30, and 20.

    e. Click the Exit button to end the application.

    f. Close the Output window, then close the solution.

Exercises 4 and 5 are Discovery Exercises. Discovery Exercises, which may include topics that are not covered in this lesson, allow you to "discover" the solutions to problems on your own.

discovery ▶

4. In this exercise, you generate and display random floating-point numbers.

    a. If necessary, start Visual Studio .NET. Open the Random Float Solution (Random Float Solution.sln) file, which is contained in the VBNET\Tut05\Random Float Solution folder. If the designer window is not open, right-click the form file's name in the Solution Explorer window, then click View Designer.

    b. You can use the Random.NextDouble method to return a floating-point random number that is greater than or equal to 0.0, but less than 1.0. The syntax of the Random.NextDouble method is *randomObject*.**NextDouble**. Code the Display Random Number button's Click event procedure so that it displays a random floating-point number in the NumberLabel control.

    c. Save the solution, then start the application. Click the Display Random Number button several times. Each time you click the button, a random number that is greater than or equal to 0.0, but less than 1.0, appears in the NumberLabel control.

    d. Click the Exit button to end the application.

    e. You can use the following formula to generate random floating-point numbers within a specified range: (*maxValue – minValue* + **1**) * *randomObject*.**NextDouble** + *minValue*. For example, assuming the Random object's name is GeneratorRandom, the formula (10 − 1 + 1) * GeneratorRandom.NextDouble + 1 generates floating-point numbers that are greater than or equal to 1.0, but less than 11.0. Modify the Display Random Number button's Click event procedure so that it displays a random floating-point number that is greater than or equal to 25.0, but less than 51.0. Format the floating-point number using the Standard format style.

f.   Save the solution, then start the application. Click the Display Random Number button several times. Each time you click the button, a random number that is greater than or equal to 25.0, but less than 51.0, appears in the NumberLabel control.

g.   Click the Exit button to end the application.

h.   Close the Output window, then close the solution.

discovery ▶   5.   In this exercise, you use the Randomize statement and Rnd function, which are used in previous versions of Visual Basic to generate and display random numbers. You also can use the Randomize statement and Rnd function in Visual Basic .NET.

a.   If necessary, start Visual Studio .NET. Open the Randomize Solution (Randomize Solution.sln) file, which is contained in the VBNET\Tut05\Randomize Solution folder. If the designer window is not open, right-click the form file's name in the Solution Explorer window, then click View Designer.

In addition to using a Random object and the Random.Next method to generate random numbers, you also can use the Randomize statement and the Rnd function. The Randomize statement initializes (gives a beginning value to) the random number generator, and the Rnd function generates the random number. The syntax of the Randomize statement is **Randomize**, and the syntax of the Rnd function is **Rnd**. The Rnd function produces floating-point numbers within the 0.0 to 1.0 range, including 0.0 but not including 1.0. For example, the statement `Me.NumberLabel.Text = Rnd` displays a random floating-point number that is greater than or equal to 0.0, but less than 1.0. You can use the following formula to generate random floating-point numbers in a range other than 0.0 to 1.0: (*maxValue – minValue* + 1) * **Rnd** + *minValue*. To generate random integers within a specified range, you simply include the Int function (Int stands for Integer) in the formula, like this: **Int**((*maxValue – minValue* + 1) * **Rnd** + *minValue*). The Int function returns the integer portion of a number. For example, the formula `Int((10 - 1 + 1) * Rnd + 1)` returns random integers from 1 through 10.

b.   Complete the Display Random Number button's Click event procedure by entering the Randomize statement immediately below the Dim statement. Then use the Rnd function to assign, to the intNumber variable, a random integer from 10 through 100.

c.   Save the solution, then start the application. Click the Display Random Number button several times. Each time you click the button, a random number that is greater than or equal to 10, but less than or equal to 100, appears in the NumberLabel control.

d.   Click the Exit button to end the application.

e.   Close the Output window, then close the solution.

LESSON C
objectives

After completing this lesson, you will be able to:

- Select the existing text in a text box control
- Code a check box control's Click event procedure
- Display and hide a control

Completing the Math Practice Application

Coding the CheckAnswerButton Click Event Procedure

Recall that to complete the Math Practice application, you still need to code the Click event procedures for the CheckAnswerButton and the DisplaySummaryCheckBox controls. Before you can code these procedures, you need to open the Math Practice application from Lesson B.

To open the Math Practice application from Lesson B:

1 Start Microsoft Visual Studio .NET, if necessary, and then close the Start Page window.

2 Click **File** on the menu bar, and then click **Open Solution**. The Open Solution dialog box opens. Open the **Math Solution** (Math Solution.sln) file, which is contained in the VBNET\Tut05\Math Solution folder.

3 If the designer window is not open, right-click **Math Form.vb** in the Solution Explorer window, then click **View Designer**.

4 Auto-hide the Toolbox, Solution Explorer, and Properties windows, if necessary. Figure 5-48 shows the user interface for the Math Practice application.

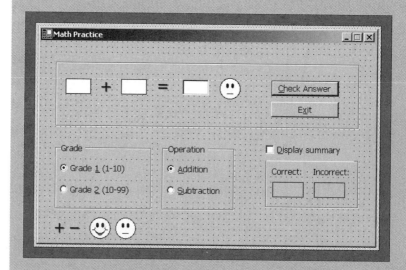

Figure 5-48: User interface for the Math Practice application

The pseudocode for the CheckAnswerButton control's Click event procedure is shown in Figure 5-49.

```
CheckAnswerButton
1. declare variables
2. assign random numbers and user's answer to variables
3. if the Addition radio button is selected
        add the two random numbers together, and assign the result to a variable
   else
        subtract the second random number from the first random number, and assign the
        result to a variable
   end if
4. if the user's answer is correct
        display the happy face icon in the AnswerPictureBox control
        add 1 to the number of correct responses
        clear the contents of the AnswerTextBox control
        call the GenerateAndDisplayNumbers procedure to generate and display two
        random numbers
   else
        display the neutral face icon in the AnswerPictureBox control
        add 1 to the number of incorrect responses
        display the "Try again!" message in a message box
        select the existing text in the AnswerTextBox control
   end if
5. send the focus to the AnswerTextBox control
6. display the number of correct and incorrect responses in the CorrectLabel and
   IncorrectLabel controls
```

Figure 5-49 Pseudocode for the CheckAnswerButton control's Click event procedure

The first step in the pseudocode is to declare the variables. The CheckAnswerButton control's Click event procedure will use the six local Integer variables listed in Figure 5-50.

Name	Purpose
intNum1	store the random number contained in the Num1Label control
intNum2	store the random number contained in the Num2Label control
intUserAnswer	store the user's answer, which is contained in the AnswerTextBox
intCorrectAnswer	store the correct answer
intNumberCorrect	store the number of correct responses made by the user; declare as a static variable
intNumberIncorrect	store the number of incorrect responses made by the user; declare as a static variable

Figure 5-50: Local variables used by the CheckAnswerButton control's Click event procedure

Notice that two of the variables listed in Figure 5-50—namely, intNumberCorrect and intNumberIncorrect—will need to be declared as static variables. As you learned in Tutorial 3, a static variable is a local variable that retains its value even when the procedure in which it is declared ends. In this case, the intNumberCorrect and intNumberIncorrect variables need to be static variables because they must keep a running tally of the number of correct and incorrect responses.

To begin coding the CheckAnswerButton Click event procedure:

1 Right-click the **form** and then click **View Code** to open the Code editor window.

2 Click the **Class Name** list arrow in the Code editor window, and then click **CheckAnswerButton** in the list. Click the **Method Name** list arrow, and then click **Click** in the list. The template for the CheckAnswerButton Click event procedure appears in the Code editor window.

3 Type **dim intNum1, intNum2, intUserAnswer, intCorrectAnswer as integer** and press **Enter**.

4 Type **static intNumberCorrect, intNumberIncorrect as integer** and press **Enter**.

Next, assign the two random numbers and the user's answer—which are stored in the Num1Label, Num2Label, and AnswerTextBox controls—to the appropriate variables.

5 Enter the comment and three assignment statements shown in Figure 5-51.

enter these four lines of code

```
Private Sub CheckAnswerButton_Click(ByVal sender As Object, ByVal e As System.Event)
    Dim intNum1, intNum2, intUserAnswer, intCorrectAnswer As Integer
    Static intNumberCorrect, intNumberIncorrect As Integer
    'assign random numbers and user's answer to variables
    intNum1 = Val(Me.Num1Label.Text)
    intNum2 = Val(Me.Num2Label.Text)
    intUserAnswer = Val(Me.AnswerTextBox.Text)

End Sub
```

Figure 5-51: Comment and assignment statements entered in the procedure

Step 3 in the pseudocode is to determine whether the Addition radio button is selected in the interface. If it is, then the procedure should add the two random numbers together; otherwise, it should subtract the second random number from the first random number. In either case, the result of the calculation should be assigned to a variable.

6 Enter the comment and selection structure shown in Figure 5-52, then position the insertion point as shown in the figure. (You also could use an If...Then...Else statement rather than a Select Case statement to determine whether the Addition radio button is selected.)

```
Private Sub CheckAnswerButton_Click(ByVal sender As Object, ByVal e As System.Event
    Dim intNum1, intNum2, intUserAnswer, intCorrectAnswer As Integer
    Static intNumberCorrect, intNumberIncorrect As Integer
    'assign random numbers and user's answer to variables
    intNum1 = Val(Me.Num1Label.Text)
    intNum2 = Val(Me.Num2Label.Text)
    intUserAnswer = Val(Me.AnswerTextBox.Text)
    'calculate correct answer
    Select Case True
        Case Me.AdditionRadioButton.Checked
            intCorrectAnswer = intNum1 + intNum2
        Case Else 'SubtractionRadioButton is selected
            intCorrectAnswer = intNum1 - intNum2
    End Select

End Sub
```

enter these seven lines of code

position the insertion point here

Figure 5-52: Comment and selection structure entered in the procedure

7 Click **File** on the menu bar, and then click **Save All**.

Step 4 in the pseudocode shown in Figure 5-49 is to determine whether the user's answer is correct. You can do so by comparing the contents of the intUserAnswer variable to the contents of the intCorrectAnswer variable.

To continue coding the CheckAnswerButton Click event procedure:

1 The insertion point should be positioned below the **End Select** statement. Type **'determine whether the user's answer is correct** and press **Enter**, then type **if intuseranswer = intcorrectanswer then** and press **Enter**. (You also could use a Select Case statement to compare the contents of both variables.)

If the user's answer is correct, the procedure should perform the following four tasks: display the happy face icon in the AnswerPictureBox control, add the number 1 to the number of correct responses, clear the contents of the AnswerTextBox control, and call the GenerateAndDisplayNumbers procedure to generate and display two random numbers.

2 Enter the additional code shown in Figure 5-53.

```
Private Sub CheckAnswerButton_Click(ByVal sender As Object, ByVal e As System.Event
    Dim intNum1, intNum2, intUserAnswer, intCorrectAnswer As Integer
    Static intNumberCorrect, intNumberIncorrect As Integer
    'assign random numbers and user's answer to variables
    intNum1 = Val(Me.Num1Label.Text)
    intNum2 = Val(Me.Num2Label.Text)
    intUserAnswer = Val(Me.AnswerTextBox.Text)
    'calculate correct answer
    Select Case True
        Case Me.AdditionRadioButton.Checked
            intCorrectAnswer = intNum1 + intNum2
        Case Else 'SubtractionRadioButton is selected
            intCorrectAnswer = intNum1 - intNum2
    End Select
    'determine whether the user's answer is correct
    If intUserAnswer = intCorrectAnswer Then
        Me.AnswerPictureBox.Image = Me.HappyPictureBox.Image
        intNumberCorrect = intNumberCorrect + 1
        Me.AnswerTextBox.Text = ""
        Call GenerateAndDisplayNumbers()

    End If
End Sub
```

enter these four lines of code

Figure 5-53: Additional code entered in the procedure

If the user's answer is not correct, the procedure should perform the following four tasks: display the neutral face icon in the AnswerPictureBox control, add the number 1 to the number of incorrect responses, display the "Try again!" message in a message box, and select the existing text in the AnswerTextBox control. You can use the **SelectAll method** to select all of the text contained in a text box. The syntax of the SelectAll method is *textbox*.**SelectAll()**, where *textbox* is the name of the text box whose text you want to select.

3   Complete the If...Then...Else statement by entering the additional code shown in Figure 5-54, then position the insertion point as shown in the figure.

```
        'determine whether the user's answer is correct
        If intUserAnswer = intCorrectAnswer Then
            Me.AnswerPictureBox.Image = Me.HappyPictureBox.Image
            intNumberCorrect = intNumberCorrect + 1
            Me.AnswerTextBox.Text = ""
            Call GenerateAndDisplayNumbers()
        Else
            Me.AnswerPictureBox.Image = Me.NeutralPictureBox.Image
            intNumberIncorrect = intNumberIncorrect + 1
            MessageBox.Show("Try again!", "Math Practice", _
                MessageBoxButtons.OK, MessageBoxIcon.Information)
            Me.AnswerTextBox.SelectAll()
        End If

    End Sub
```

enter these six lines of code

position the insertion point here

Figure 5-54: Completed If...Then...Else statement shown in the procedure

The last two steps in the pseudocode shown in Figure 5-49 are to send the focus to the AnswerTextBox control and then display the number of correct and incorrect responses in the CorrectLabel and IncorrectLabel controls.

4   Type **me.answertextbox.focus()** and press **Enter**.

5   Type **me.correctlabel.text = intnumbercorrect** and press **Enter**.

6   Type **me.incorrectlabel.text = intnumberincorrect** and press **Enter**. Figure 5-55 shows the completed CheckAnswerButton Click event procedure.

```
Private Sub CheckAnswerButton_Click(ByVal sender As Object, ByVal e As
System.EventArgs) Handles CheckAnswerButton.Click
        Dim intNum1, intNum2, intUserAnswer, intCorrectAnswer As Integer
        Static intNumberCorrect, intNumberIncorrect As Integer
        'assign random numbers and user's answer to variables
        intNum1 = Val(Me.Num1Label.Text)
        intNum2 = Val(Me.Num2Label.Text)
        intUserAnswer = Val(Me.AnswerTextBox.Text)
        'calculate correct answer
        Select Case True
            Case Me.AdditionRadioButton.Checked
                intCorrectAnswer = intNum1 + intNum2
            Case Else 'SubtractionRadioButton is selected
                intCorrectAnswer = intNum1 - intNum2
        End Select
        'determine whether the user's answer is correct
        If intUserAnswer = intCorrectAnswer Then
            Me.AnswerPictureBox.Image = Me.HappyPictureBox.Image
            intNumberCorrect = intNumberCorrect + 1
            Me.AnswerTextBox.Text = ""
            Call GenerateAndDisplayNumbers()
        Else
            Me.AnswerPictureBox.Image = Me.NeutralPictureBox.Image
            intNumberIncorrect = intNumberIncorrect + 1
            MessageBox.Show("Try again!", "Math Practice", _
                MessageBoxButtons.OK, MessageBoxIcon.Information)
            Me.AnswerTextBox.SelectAll()
        End If
        Me.AnswerTextBox.Focus()
        Me.CorrectLabel.Text = intNumberCorrect
        Me.IncorrectLabel.Text = intNumberIncorrect

End Sub
```

Figure 5-55: Completed CheckAnswerButton Click event procedure

7   Click **File** on the menu bar, and then click **Save All**.

Before testing the code in the Check Answer button's Click event procedure, you will code the SummaryCheckBox control's Click event procedure.

Coding the SummaryCheckBox Click Event Procedure

As you learned in Tutorial 4, Visual Basic .NET treats the group box and the controls contained in the group box as one unit. Hiding the group box also hides the controls contained within the group box.

Recall that the four picture box controls located at the bottom of the form do not appear in the interface when the Math Practice application is started. This is because the Visible property of those controls is set to False in the Properties window. The Visible property of the SummaryGroupBox control is also set to False, which explains why you do not see the control and its contents when the form appears on the screen.

According to the TOE chart shown earlier in Figure 5-33, the SummaryCheckBox control's Click event procedure is responsible for both displaying and hiding the SummaryGroupBox control. The procedure should display the group box control when the user selects the check box, and it should hide the group box control when the user deselects the check box. You can use a check box control's Checked property to determine whether the check box was selected or deselected by the user. If the Checked property contains the Boolean value True, then the check box was selected; if it contains the Boolean value False, then the check box was deselected.

tip

▶ Unlike the Click event procedure for a radio button, the Click event procedure for a check box always will contain a selection structure that determines whether the check box was selected or deselected by the user. The selection structure is not necessary in a radio button's Click event procedure, because clicking a radio button always selects the button; the user cannot deselect a radio button by clicking it.

To code the SummaryCheckBox control's Click event procedure:

1 Click the **Class Name** list arrow in the Code editor window, and then click **SummaryCheckBox** in the list. Click the **Method Name** list arrow, and then click **Click** in the list. The template for the SummaryCheckBox Click event procedure appears in the Code editor window.

2 Type **if me.summarycheckbox.checked = true then** and press **Enter**. (You also could use the Select Case statement rather than the If...Then...Else statement to compare the Checked property to the Boolean value True.)

If the user selected the SummaryCheckBox control, then the procedure should display the SummaryGroupBox control. You can do so by setting the SummaryGroupBox control's Visible property to the Boolean value True.

3 Type **me.summarygroupbox.visible = true** and press **Enter**.

If the user deselected the SummaryCheckBox control, then the procedure should hide the SummaryGroupBox control. You can do so by setting the SummaryGroupBox control's Visible property to the Boolean value False.

4 Enter the additional code shown in Figure 5-56, which shows the completed SummaryCheckBox Click event procedure.

enter these two lines of code

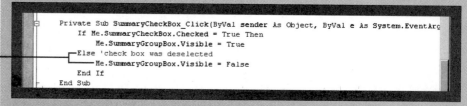

```
    Private Sub SummaryCheckBox_Click(ByVal sender As Object, ByVal e As System.EventArg
        If Me.SummaryCheckBox.Checked = True Then
            Me.SummaryGroupBox.Visible = True
        Else 'check box was deselected
            Me.SummaryGroupBox.Visible = False
        End If
    End Sub
```

Figure 5-56: Completed SummaryCheckBox Click event procedure

Now verify that the Click event procedures for the CheckAnswerButton and SummaryCheckBox controls are working correctly.

To test the application's code:

1 Save the solution, then start the application.

2 Type the correct answer to the addition problem appearing in the interface, then press **Enter** to select the Check Answer button, which is the default button on the form. The happy face icon and a new addition problem appear in the interface.

3 Click the **Display summary** check box to select it. A check mark appears in the check box, and the SummaryGroupBox control and its contents appear in the interface. Notice that the label controls within the group box indicate that you have made one correct response and zero incorrect responses.

4 Click inside the text box in which you enter the answer. Type an incorrect answer to the current addition problem, then press **Enter**. A neutral face icon appears in the interface, and a message box appears on the screen, as shown in Figure 5-57.

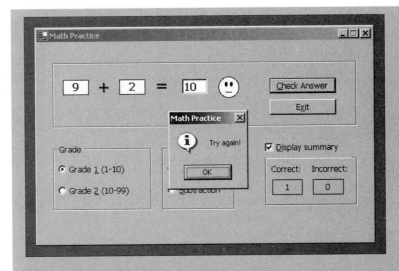

Figure 5-57: Result of entering an incorrect response to the addition problem

5   Click the **OK** button to close the message box. Notice that the number of incorrect responses changes from 0 to 1. Also notice that the incorrect answer is selected in the AnswerTextBox control. You can remove the incorrect answer simply by typing another answer in the text box.

6   Type the correct answer to the current addition problem, then press **Enter.** The number of correct responses changes from 1 to 2, and the happy face icon appears in the interface.

7   Click the **Display summary** check box to deselect it. The check mark is removed from the check box, and the SummaryGroupBox and its contents disappear from the interface.

8   Click the **Exit** button to end the application. When you return to the Code editor window, close the Output window.

9   Click **File** on the menu bar, and then click **Close Solution.**

You now have completed Tutorial 5. You can either take a break or complete the end-of-lesson questions and exercises.

S U M M A R Y

To select the existing text in a text box:

■   Use the SelectAll method. The method's syntax is *textbox*.**SelectAll()**, where *textbox* is the name of the text box whose text you want to select.

To display or hide a control:

■   Set the control's Visible property to the Boolean value True to display the control. Set the control's Visible property to the Boolean value False to hide the control.

To code a check box control's Click event procedure:

■   Use a selection structure to determine whether the check box was either selected or deselected by the user.

QUESTIONS

1. Which of the following statements selects all of the text contained in the NameTextBox control?
   a. `Me.NameTextBox.Select()`
   b. `Me.NameTextBox.SelectAll()`
   c. `Me.Select.NameTextBox()`
   d. `Me.SelectAll.NameTextBox()`
   e. None of the above.

2. Which of the following statements hides the DivisionPictureBox control?
   a. `Me.DivisionPictureBox.Hide`
   b. `Me.DivisionPictureBox.Hide = True`
   c. `Hide.DivisionPictureBox`
   d. `Hide.DivisionPictureBox = True`
   e. None of the above.

3. If a check box is deselected, its _____ property contains the Boolean value False.
   a. Checked
   b. Deselected
   c. On
   d. Value
   e. None of the above.

4. When coded, a check box's Click event procedure always will contain a selection structure that determines whether the check box is selected or deselected.
   a. True
   b. False

5. Like a check box, a radio button can be deselected by clicking it.
   a. True
   b. False

EXERCISES

The following list summarizes the GUI design guidelines you have learned so far. You can use this list to verify that the interfaces you create in the following exercises adhere to the GUI standards outlined in the book.

- Information should flow either vertically or horizontally, with the most important information always located in the upper-left corner of the screen.

- Maintain a consistent margin of two or three dots from the edge of the window.

- Try to create a user interface that no one notices.

- Related controls should be grouped together using white space, a GroupBox control, or a Panel control.

- Set the form's FormBorderStyle, ControlBox, MaximizeBox, MinimizeBox, and StartPosition properties appropriately:

  - A splash screen should not have a Minimize, Maximize, or Close button, and its borders should not be sizable.

  - A form that is not a splash screen should always have a Minimize button and a Close button, but you can choose to disable the Maximize button. Typically, the FormBorderStyle property is set to Sizable, but also can be set to FixedSingle.

- Position related controls on succeeding dots. Controls that are not part of any logical grouping may be positioned from two to four dots away from other controls.

- Buttons should be positioned either in a row along the bottom of the screen, or stacked in either the upper-right or lower-right corner.

- If the buttons are positioned at the bottom of the screen, then each button should be the same height; their widths, however, may vary.

- If the buttons are stacked in either the upper-right or lower-right corner of the screen, then each should be the same height and the same width.

- Use no more than six buttons on a screen.

- The most commonly used button should be placed first.

- The default button should be the button that is most often selected by the user, except in cases where the tasks performed by the button are both destructive and irreversible. The default button typically is the first button.

- Button captions should:

  - be meaningful
  - be from one to three words
  - appear on one line
  - be entered using book title capitalization

- Use labels to identify the text boxes in the interface, and position the label either above or to the left of the text box.

- Label text should:

  - be from one to three words
  - appear on one line
  - be left-justified
  - end with a colon (:)
  - be entered using sentence capitalization

- Labels that identify controls should have their BorderStyle property set to None.

- Labels that display program output, such as the result of a calculation, should have their BorderStyle property set to FixedSingle.

- Align controls to minimize the number of different margins.

- If you use a graphic in the interface, use a small one and place it in a location that will not distract the user.

- Use the Tahoma font for applications that will run on Windows 2000 or Windows XP.

- Use no more than two different font sizes, which should be 8, 9, 10, 11, or 12 point.

- Use only one font type, which should be a sans serif font, in the interface.

- Avoid using italics and underlining.

- Limit the use of bold text to titles, headings, and key items.

- Build the interface using black, white, and gray first, then add color only if you have a good reason to do so.

- Use white, off-white, light gray, pale blue, or pale yellow for an application's background, and black for the text.

- Limit the number of colors to three, not including white, black, and gray. The colors you choose should complement each other.

- Never use color as the only means of identification for an element in the user interface.

- Set each control's TabIndex property to a number that represents the order in which you want the control to receive the focus (begin with 0).

- A text box's TabIndex value should be one more than the TabIndex value of its identifying label.

- Assign a unique access key to each control (in the interface) that can receive user input (text boxes, buttons, and so on).

- When assigning an access key to a control, use the first letter of the caption or identifying label, unless another letter provides a more meaningful association. If you can't use the first letter and no other letter provides a more meaningful association, then use a distinctive consonant. Lastly, use a vowel or a number.

- Lock the controls in place on the form.

- Document the program internally.

- Use the Val function on any Text property involved in a calculation.

- Use the Format function to improve the appearance of numbers in the interface.

- In the InputBox function, use sentence capitalization for the *prompt*, and book title capitalization for the *title*.

- Use sentence capitalization for the optional identifying label in a group box control.

- MessageBox.Show method:

  - Use sentence capitalization for the *text* argument, but book title capitalization for the *caption* argument. The name of the application typically appears in the *caption* argument.

  - Avoid using the words "error," "warning," or "mistake" in the message.

  - Display the Warning Message icon ⚠ in a message box that alerts the user that he or she must make a decision before the application can continue. You can phrase the message as a question.

  - Display the Information Message icon ⓘ in a message box that displays an informational message along with an OK button only.

  - Display the Stop Message icon ⊗ when you want to alert the user of a serious problem that must be corrected before the application can continue.

  - The default button in the dialog box should be the one that represents the user's most likely action, as long as that action is not destructive.

■ Use the KeyPress event to prevent a text box from accepting inappropriate keys.

■ Radio buttons:

    ■ Use radio buttons when you want to limit the user to one of two or more related and mutually exclusive choices.

    ■ Use a minimum of two and a maximum of seven radio buttons in an interface.

    ■ Use sentence capitalization for the label entered in the radio button's Text property.

    ■ Assign a unique access key to each radio button in an interface.

    ■ Use a group box control (or a panel control) to create separate groups of radio buttons. Only one button in each group can be selected at any one time.

    ■ Designate a default radio button in each group of radio buttons.

■ Check boxes:

    ■ Use check boxes to allow the user to select any number of choices from a group of one or more independent and nonexclusive choices.

    ■ Use sentence capitalization for the label entered in the check box's Text property.

    ■ Assign a unique access key to each check box in an interface.

■ Test the application with both valid and invalid data (for example, test the application without entering any data, and test it by entering letters where numbers are expected).

---

1. In this exercise, you modify the selection structures contained in the Math Practice application.

    a. Use Windows to make a copy of the Math Solution folder, which is contained in the VBNET\Tut05 folder. Rename the folder Math Solution2.

    b. If necessary, start Visual Studio .NET. Open the Math Solution (Math Solution.sln) file, which is contained in the VBNET\Tut05\Math Solution2 folder. If the designer window is not open, right-click the form file's name in the Solution Explorer window, then click View Designer.

    c. Change the If...Then...Else statement in the SummaryCheckBox control's Click event procedure to a Select Case statement.

    d. Change the first selection structure in the CheckAnswerButton control's Click event procedure to an If...Then...Else statement.

    e. Change the second selection structure in the CheckAnswerButton control's Click event procedure to a Select Case statement.

    f. Change the If...Then...Else statement in the ProcessOperationRadioButtons procedure to a Select Case statement.

    g. Save the solution, then start the application. Test the application to verify that it is working correctly.

    h. Click the Exit button to end the application.

    i. Close the Output window, then close the solution.

2. In this exercise, you code an application for Willow Health Club. The application calculates a member's monthly dues.

    a. If necessary, start Visual Studio .NET. Open the Health Solution (Health Solution.sln) file, which is contained in the VBNET\Tut05\Health Solution folder. If the designer window is not open, right-click the form file's name in the Solution Explorer window, then click View Designer.

b. Declare a form-level variable named mintAdditional.

c. Code each check box's Click event procedure so that it adds the appropriate additional charge to the mintAdditional variable when the check box is selected, and subtracts the appropriate additional amount from the mintAdditional variable when the check box is deselected. The additional charges are $30 per month for tennis, $25 per month for golf, and $20 per month for racquetball. Each check box's Click event procedure should display the contents of the mintAdditional variable in the AdditionalLabel control, and also remove the contents of the TotalLabel control.

d. Code the Calculate button's Click event procedure so that it calculates the monthly dues. The dues are calculated by adding the basic fee to the total additional charge. Format the total due using the Currency format style.

e. When the user makes a change to the contents of the BasicTextBox, the application should remove the contents of the TotalLabel control. Code the appropriate event procedure.

f. Save the solution, then start the application. Test the application by entering 80 in the text box, and then selecting the Golf check box. The number 25 appears in the AdditionalLabel control. Click the Calculate button. $105.00 appears in the TotalLabel control.

g. Now select the Tennis and Racquetball check boxes and deselect the Golf check box. The number 50 appears in the AdditionalLabel control. Click the Calculate button. $130.00 appears in the TotalLabel control.

h. Click the Exit button to end the application.

i. Close the Output window, then close the solution.

3. In this exercise, you create an application for Washington High School. The application displays a class rank, which is based on the code entered by the user. Use the following information to code the application:

Code	Rank
1	Freshman
2	Sophomore
3	Junior
4	Senior

a. If necessary, start Visual Studio .NET. Create a blank solution named Washington Solution. Save the solution in the VBNET\Tut05 folder.

b. Add a Visual Basic .NET Windows Application project to the solution. Name the project Washington Project.

c. Assign the filename Washington Form.vb to the form file object.

d. Assign the name WashingtonForm to the Windows Form object.

e. When designing the interface, provide a text box for the user to enter the code, and a label control for displaying the rank.

f. Code the application appropriately. Allow the user to press only the numeric keys 1, 2, 3, and 4 and the Backspace key when entering the code. Also, set the text box's MaxLength property to the number 1; this allows the user to enter only one character in the text box.

g. When a change is made to the code entered in the text box, clear the contents of the label control that displays the rank.

h. Center the rank in the label control.

i. Save the solution, then start the application. Test the application using codes of 1, 2, 3, and 4. Also test the code using an empty text box (which should not display a rank in the label control). Additionally, try to enter characters other than 1, 2, 3, or 4 in the text box.

j. End the application.

k. Close the Output window, then close the solution.

4. In this exercise, you create an application for Barren Community Center. The application displays a seminar fee, which is based on the membership status and age entered by the user. Use the following information to code the application:

Seminar fee	Criteria
10	Club member younger than 65 years old
5	Club member at least 65 years old
20	Non-member

a. If necessary, start Visual Studio .NET. Create a blank solution named Barren Solution. Save the solution in the VBNET\Tut05 folder.

b. Add a Visual Basic .NET Windows Application project to the solution. Name the project Barren Project.

c. Assign the filename Barren Form.vb to the form file object.

d. Assign the name BarrenForm to the Windows Form object.

e. Design an appropriate interface. Use radio button controls for the status and age choices. Display the seminar fee in a label control. When the user clicks a radio button, clear the contents of the label control that displays the fee.

f. Code the application.

g. Save the solution, then start the application. Test the application appropriately.

h. End the application.

i. Close the Output window, then close the solution.

5. In this exercise, you create an application for Golf Pro, a U.S. company that sells golf equipment both domestically and abroad. Each of Golf Pro's salespeople receives a commission based on the total of his or her domestic and international sales. The application you create should allow the user to enter the amount of domestic sales and the amount of international sales. It then should calculate and display the commission. Use the following information to code the application:

Sales	Commission
1 – 100,000	2% * sales
100,001 – 400,000	2,000 + 5% * sales over 100,000
400,001 and over	17,000 + 10% * sales over 400,000

a. If necessary, start Visual Studio .NET. Create a blank solution named Golf Pro Solution. Save the solution in the VBNET\Tut05 folder.

b. Add a Visual Basic .NET Windows Application project to the solution. Name the project Golf Pro Project.

c. Assign the filename Golf Pro Form.vb to the form file object.

d. Assign the name GolfProForm to the Windows Form object.

e. Design an appropriate interface, then code the application. Keep in mind that the sales amounts may contain decimal places.

f. Save the solution, then start the application. Test the application using both valid and invalid data.

g. End the application.

h. Close the Output window, then close the solution.

6. In this exercise, you create an application for Marshall Sales Corporation. Each of the company's salespeople receives a commission based on the amount of his or her sales. The application you create should allow the user to enter the sales amount. It then should calculate and display the commission. Use the following information to code the application:

Sales	Commission
1 – 100,000	2% * sales
100,001 – 200,000	4% * sales
200,001 – 300,000	6% * sales
300,001 – 400,000	8% * sales
400,001 and over	10% * sales

   a. If necessary, start Visual Studio .NET. Create a blank solution named Marshall Solution. Save the solution in the VBNET\Tut05 folder.
   b. Add a Visual Basic .NET Windows Application project to the solution. Name the project Marshall Project.
   c. Assign the filename Marshall Form.vb to the form file object.
   d. Assign the name MarshallForm to the Windows Form object.
   e. Design an appropriate interface, then code the application. Keep in mind that the sales amount may contain decimal places.
   f. Save the solution, then start the application. Test the application using both valid and invalid data.
   g. End the application.
   h. Close the Output window, then close the solution.

7. In this exercise, you create an application for Jasper Springs Health Club. The application allows the user to enter a specific food's total calories and grams of fat. It then calculates and displays the food's fat calories (the number of calories attributed to fat) and its fat percentage (the ratio of the food's fat calories to its total calories). You can calculate the number of fat calories in a food by multiplying the number of fat grams contained in the food by the number nine, because each gram of fat contains nine calories. To calculate the fat percentage, you divide the food's fat calories by its total calories, and then multiply the result by 100.
   a. If necessary, start Visual Studio .NET. Create a blank solution named Jasper Solution. Save the solution in the VBNET\Tut05 folder.
   b. Add a Visual Basic .NET Windows Application project to the solution. Name the project Jasper Project.
   c. Assign the filename Jasper Form.vb to the form file object.
   d. Assign the name JasperForm to the Windows Form object.
   e. Design an appropriate interface, then code the application. Display the message "Low-fat food" if the fat percentage is less than or equal to 30%; otherwise, display the message "High-fat food".
   f. Save the solution, then start the application. Test the application using both valid and invalid data.
   g. End the application.
   h. Close the Output window, then close the solution.

8. In this exercise, you create an application that displays the number of daily calories needed to maintain your current weight. Use the following information to code the application:

   Moderately active female: total calories per day = weight multiplied by 12 calories per pound

Relatively inactive female: total calories per day = weight multiplied by 10 calories per pound

Moderately active male: total calories per day = weight multiplied by 15 calories per pound

Relatively inactive male: total calories per day = weight multiplied by 13 calories per pound

a. If necessary, start Visual Studio .NET. Create a blank solution named Calories Solution. Save the solution in the VBNET\Tut05 folder.

b. Add a Visual Basic .NET Windows Application project to the solution. Name the project Calories Project.

c. Assign the filename Calories Form.vb to the form file object.

d. Assign the name CaloriesForm to the Windows Form object.

e. Design an appropriate interface, then code the application.

f. Save the solution, then start the application. Test the application using both valid and invalid data.

g. End the application.

h. Close the Output window, then close the solution.

9. In this exercise, you create an application for Johnson Products. The application calculates and displays the price of an order, based on the number of units ordered and the customer's status (either wholesaler or retailer). The price per unit is as follows:

Wholesaler		Retailer	
Number of units	Price per unit ($)	Number of units	Price per unit ($)
1 – 4	10	1 – 3	15
5 and over	9	4 – 8	14
		9 and over	12

a. If necessary, start Visual Studio .NET. Create a blank solution named Johnson Solution. Save the solution in the VBNET\Tut05 folder.

b. Add a Visual Basic .NET Windows Application project to the solution. Name the project Johnson Project.

c. Assign the filename Johnson Form.vb to the form file object.

d. Assign the name JohnsonForm to the Windows Form object.

e. Design an appropriate interface, then code the application. Use a Select Case statement to determine the customer's status. Use an If...Then...Else statement to determine the price per unit.

f. Save the solution, then start the application. Test the application using both valid and invalid data.

g. End the application.

h. Close the Output window, then close the solution.

10. Jacques Cousard has been playing the lottery for four years and has yet to win any money. He wants an application that will select the six lottery numbers for him. Each lottery number can range from 1 to 54 only. (An example of six lottery numbers would be: 4, 8, 35, 15, 20, 3.)

a. If necessary, start Visual Studio .NET. Create a blank solution named Lottery Solution. Save the solution in the VBNET\Tut05 folder.

b. Add a Visual Basic .NET Windows Application project to the solution. Name the project Lottery Project.

c. Assign the filename Lottery Form.vb to the form file object.

d. Assign the name LotteryForm to the Windows Form object.

e. Design an appropriate interface, then code the application. (For now, do not worry if the lottery numbers are not unique. You learn how to display unique numbers in Tutorial 11.)

f. Save the solution, then start the application. Test the application.

g. End the application.

h. Close the Output window, then close the solution.

11. Ferris Seminars offers computer seminars to various companies. The owner of Ferris Seminars wants an application that the registration clerks can use to calculate the registration fee for each customer. Many of Ferris Seminars' customers are companies that register more than one person for a seminar. The registration clerk will need to enter the number registered for the seminar, then select either the Seminar 1 radio button or the Seminar 2 radio button. If a company is entitled to a 10 percent discount, the clerk will need to click the 10% discount check box. After the selections are made, the clerk will click the Calculate Total Due button to calculate the total registration fee. Seminar 1 is $100 per person, and Seminar 2 is $120 per person.

a. If necessary, start Visual Studio .NET. Open the Ferris Solution (Ferris Solution.sln) file, which is contained in the VBNET\Tut05\Ferris Solution folder. If the designer window is not open, right-click the form file's name in the Solution Explorer window, then click View Designer.

b. Code the application appropriately.

c. Save the solution, then start the application. Test the application.

d. End the application.

e. Close the Output window, then close the solution.

12. Western Veterinarians wants an application that its receptionist can use to display the doctor's fee for performing a specific medical procedure. Use the following information to code the application:

Procedure	Fee
Fecal Check	$5
Heartworm Test	15
Office Visit	15
Other Shots	5
Rabies Vaccination	15
Teeth Cleaning	50

a. If necessary, start Visual Studio .NET. Open the Western Solution (Western Solution.sln) file, which is contained in the VBNET\Tut05\Western Solution folder. If the designer window is not open, right-click the form file's name in the Solution Explorer window, then click View Designer.

b. Code the application appropriately.

c. Save the solution, then start the application. Test the application.

d. End the application.

e. Close the Output window, then close the solution.

13. Wholesome Veterinarians wants an application that its receptionist can use to display the total amount a customer owes. Use the following information to code the application:

Procedure	Fee
Fecal Check	$5
Heartworm Test	15
Office Visit	15
Other Shots	5
Rabies Vaccination	15
Teeth Cleaning	50

a. If necessary, start Visual Studio .NET. Open the Wholesome Solution (Wholesome Solution.sln) file, which is contained in the VBNET\Tut05\Wholesome Solution folder. If the designer window is not open, right-click the form file's name in the Solution Explorer window, then click View Designer.

    b.   Code the application appropriately.

    c.   Save the solution, then start the application. Test the application.

    d.   End the application.

    e.   Close the Output window, then close the solution.

Exercise 14 is a Discovery Exercise. Discovery Exercises, which may include topics that are not covered in this lesson, allow you to "discover" the solutions to problems on your own.

discovery ▶

14. In this exercise, you learn about a text box control's Enter event.

    a.   If necessary, start Visual Studio .NET. Open the Name Solution (Name Solution.sln) file, which is contained in the VBNET\Tut05\Name Solution folder. If the designer window is not open, right-click the form file's name in the Solution Explorer window, then click View Designer.

    b.   Start the application. Type your first name in the First text box, then press Tab. Type your last name in the Last text box, then press Tab. Click the Concatenate Name button. Your full name appears in the FullNameLabel control.

    c.   Press Tab twice to move the focus to the First text box. Notice that the insertion point appears after your first name in the text box. It is customary in Windows applications to have a text box's existing text selected (highlighted) when the text box receives the focus. You can select a text box's existing text by entering the SelectAll method in the text box's Enter event. (You also can enter the SelectAll method in the text box's GotFocus event. The Enter event occurs before the GotFocus event.)

    d.   Click the Exit button to end the application.

    e.   Open the Code editor window. Enter the SelectAll method in the Enter event procedure for the FirstTextBox and LastTextBox controls.

    f.   Save the solution, then start the application. Enter your first name in the First text box, then press Tab. Enter your last name in the Last text box, then press Tab. Click the Concatenate Name button. Your full name appears in the FullNameLabel control.

    g.   Press Tab twice to move the focus to the First text box. Notice that your first name is selected in the text box. Press Tab to move the focus to the Last text box. Notice that your last name is selected in the text box.

    h.   Click the Exit button to end the application.

    i.   Close the Output window, then close the solution.

Exercise 15 is a Debugging Exercise. Debugging Exercises provide an opportunity for you to detect and correct errors in an existing application.

debugging

15. In this exercise, you debug an existing application. The purpose of this exercise is to demonstrate the importance of testing an application thoroughly.

    a.   If necessary, start Visual Studio .NET. Open the Debug Solution (Debug Solution.sln) file, which is contained in the VBNET\Tut05\Debug Solution folder. If the designer window is not open, right-click the form file's name in the Solution Explorer window, then click View Designer. The application displays a shipping charge, which is based on the total price entered by the user. If the total price is greater than or equal to $100 but less than $501, the shipping charge is $10. If the total price is greater than or equal to $501 but less than $1001, the shipping charge is $7. If the total price is greater than or equal to $1001, the shipping charge is $5. No shipping charge is due if the total price is less than $100.

    b.   Start the application. Test the application using the following total prices: 100, 501, 1500, 500.75, 30, 1000.33. You will notice that the application does not display the correct shipping charge for some of these total prices.

    c.   Click the Exit button to end the application.

    d.   Correct the application's code, then save the solution and start the application. Test the application using the total prices listed in Step b.

    e.   Click the Exit button to end the application.

    f.   Close the Output window, then close the solution.

The Repetition Structure

Creating a Grade Calculator Application

case ▶ Next Monday is career day at your alma mater. Professor Carver, one of your computer programming instructors, has asked you to be a guest speaker in his Introduction to Programming class. You gladly accept this speaking engagement and begin planning your presentation. You decide to show the students how to create a program that calculates their grade in Professor Carver's class.

Previewing the Completed Application

Before creating the Grade Calculator application, you first preview the completed application.

To preview the completed application:

1   Use the Run command on the Windows Start menu to run the **Grade** (Grade.exe) file, which is contained in the VBNET\Tut06 folder on your computer's hard disk. The user interface for the Grade Calculator application appears on the screen.

2   Type your name in the Name text box. Click the **Project 1** check box to select it, then type **9** in the text box located to the right of the check box.

3   Click the **Midterm** check box to select it, then type **45** in the text box located to the right of the check box.

4   Click the **Display Grade** button. A grade of A appears in the Grade label control, as shown in Figure 6-1.

grade

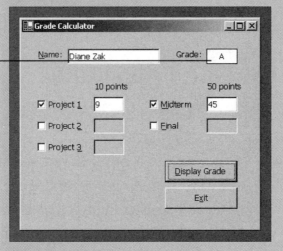

Figure 6-1: Grade shown in the Grade Calculator application

5   Press **Tab** twice to move the focus to the Name text box. Notice that the application highlights your name. You learn how to highlight the existing text in a text box in Lesson C.

6   Click the **Midterm** check box to deselect it. This removes the Midterm score (45) from the text box. It also removes the grade (A) from the label control.

7   Click the **Exit** button. A message box containing the message "Do you want to exit?" appears. Click the **No** button. Notice that the application remains open. You learn how to prevent a form from being closed in Lesson C.

8   Click the **Exit** button, then click the **Yes** button in the message box. The application closes.

The Grade Calculator application uses the repetition structure, an accumulator, and a collection. You learn about the repetition structure and accumulators in Lesson A. You learn about collections in Lesson B. You begin coding the application in Lesson B and complete it in Lesson C.

After completing this lesson, you will be able to:

- Code the repetition structure using the For...Next and Do...Loop statements
- Write pseudocode for the repetition structure
- Create a flowchart for the repetition structure
- Display a message in the Output window while an application is running
- Change the location and size of a control while an application is running
- Initialize and update counters and accumulators

The Repetition Structure (Looping)

The Repetition Structure

As you learned in Tutorial 1, the three programming structures are sequence, selection, and repetition. Every program contains the sequence structure, in which the program instructions are processed, one after another, in the order in which each appears in the program. Most programs also contain the selection structure, which you learned about in Tutorials 4 and 5. Recall that programmers use the selection structure when they need the computer to make a decision and then take the appropriate action based on the result of that decision.

In addition to including the sequence and selection structures, many programs also include the repetition structure. Programmers use the **repetition structure**, referred to more simply as a **loop**, when they need the computer to repeatedly process one or more program instructions until some condition is met, at which time the loop ends. For example, you may want to process a set of instructions—such as the instructions to calculate net pay—for each employee in a company. Or, you may want to process a set of instructions until the user enters a negative sales amount, which indicates that he or she has no more sales amounts to enter.

A repetition structure can be either a pretest loop or a posttest loop. In both types of loops, the condition is evaluated with each repetition, or iteration, of the loop. In a **pretest loop**, the evaluation occurs before the instructions within the loop are processed, while in a **posttest loop**, the evaluation occurs after the instructions within the loop are processed. Depending on the result of the evaluation, the instructions in a pretest loop may never be processed. The instructions in a posttest loop, however, always will be processed at least once. Of the two types of loops, the pretest loop is the most commonly used.

You code a repetition structure (loop) in Visual Basic .NET using one of the following statements: For...Next, Do...Loop, and For Each...Next. You learn about the For...Next and Do...Loop statements in this lesson, and about the For Each...Next statement in Lesson B.

The For...Next Statement

You can use the **For...Next statement** to code a loop whose instructions you want processed a precise number of times. The loop created by the For...Next statement is a pretest loop, because the loop's condition is evaluated before the instructions in the loop are processed. Figure 6-2 shows the syntax and an example of the For...Next statement. The example prompts the user to enter the name of a city, and then displays the name in a message box.

tip

As with the sequence and selection structures, you already are familiar with the repetition structure. For example, shampoo bottles typically include a direction that tells you to repeat the "apply shampoo to hair," "lather," and "rinse" steps until your hair is clean.

tip

Pretest and posttest loops also are called top-driven and bottom-driven loops, respectively.

You do not need to specify the name of the *counter* variable in the Next clause in a For...Next statement. However, doing so is highly recommended, because it makes your code more self-documenting.

You can use the Exit For statement to exit the For...Next statement prematurely—in other words, to exit it before it has finished processing. You may need to do so if the loop encounters an error when processing its instructions.

You can nest For...Next statements, which means that you can place one For...Next statement within another For...Next statement.

Syntax
For *counter* = *startvalue* **To** *endvalue* [**Step** *stepvalue*]   [*statements*] **Next** *counter*

Example

```
Dim intCount As Integer, strCity As String
For intCount = 1 To 3
    strCity = InputBox("Enter the city:", "City Entry")
    MessageBox.Show(strCity & " is city number " & intCount, _
          "City", MessageBoxButtons.OK, _
          MessageBoxIcon.Information)
Next intCount
```

Figure 6-2: Syntax and an example of the For...Next statement

The For...Next statement begins with the For clause and ends with the Next clause. Between the two clauses, you enter the instructions you want the loop to repeat. In Figure 6-2's example, the loop will repeat the InputBox function and MessageBox.Show method instructions.

In the syntax, *counter* is the name of the numeric variable that will be used to keep track of the number of times the loop instructions are processed. In the example shown in Figure 6-2, the name of the *counter* variable is intCount.

The *startvalue*, *endvalue*, and *stepvalue* items control how many times the loop instructions should be processed. The *startvalue* tells the loop where to begin, the *endvalue* tells the loop when to stop, and the *stepvalue* tells the loop how much to add to (or subtract from if the *stepvalue* is a negative number) the *counter* variable each time the loop is processed. If you omit the *stepvalue*, a *stepvalue* of positive 1 is used. In the example shown in Figure 6-2, the *startvalue* is 1, the *endvalue* is 3, and the *stepvalue* (which is omitted) is 1. Those values tell the loop to start counting at 1 and, counting by 1s, stop at 3—in other words, count 1, 2, and then 3. The loop shown in Figure 6-2's example will repeat the loop instructions three times.

The For clause's *startvalue*, *endvalue*, and *stepvalue* must be numeric and can be either positive or negative, integer or non-integer. If *stepvalue* is positive, then *startvalue* must be less than or equal to *endvalue* for the loop instructions to be processed. In other words, the instruction For intCount = 1 To 3 is correct, but the instruction For intCount = 3 To 1 is not correct, because you cannot count from 3 (the *startvalue*) to 1 (the *endvalue*) by adding increments of 1 (the *stepvalue*). If, on the other hand, *stepvalue* is negative, then *startvalue* must be greater than or equal to *endvalue* for the loop instructions to be processed. For example, the instruction For intCount = 3 To 1 Step –1 is correct, but the instruction For intCount = 1 To 3 Step –1 is not correct, because you cannot count from 1 to 3 by subtracting increments of 1.

When processed, the For...Next loop performs the following three tasks:

1. The loop initializes the *counter* (the numeric variable) to the *startvalue*. This is done only once, at the beginning of the loop.

2. If the *stepvalue* is positive, the loop checks to determine whether the value in the *counter* is greater than the *endvalue*. (Or, if the *stepvalue* is negative, the loop checks to determine whether the value in the *counter* is less than the *endvalue*.) If it is, the loop stops, and processing continues with the statement following the Next clause. If it is not, the instructions within the loop are processed and the next task, task 3, is performed. (Notice that the loop evaluates the condition before processing the statements within the loop.)

3. The loop adds the *stepvalue* to the *counter*. It then repeats tasks 2 and 3 until the *counter* is greater than (or less than, if the *stepvalue* is negative) the *endvalue*.

Figure 6-3 shows the flowchart and pseudocode corresponding to the code shown in Figure 6-2.

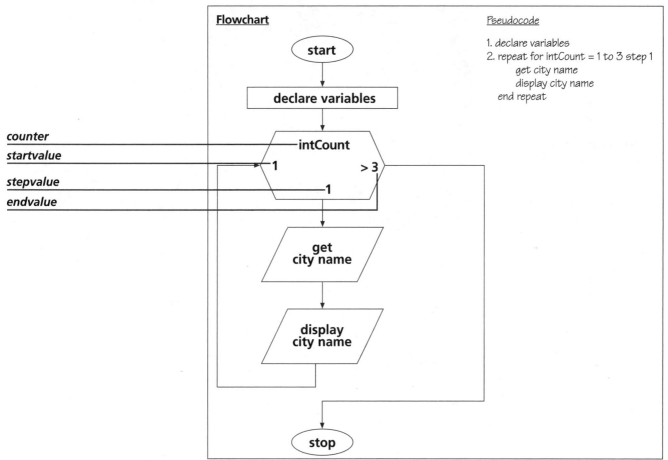

Figure 6-3: Flowchart and pseudocode for the code shown in Figure 6-2

tip

If the *stepvalue* is a negative number, a less-than sign (<) should precede the *end-value* in the hexagon, as a loop with a negative *step-value* stops when the value in the *counter* variable is less than the *endvalue*.

The For...Next loop is represented in a flowchart by a hexagon, which is a six-sided figure. Four values are recorded inside the hexagon: the name of the *counter* variable, the *startvalue*, the *stepvalue*, and the *endvalue*. Notice that the *endvalue* in Figure 6-3's hexagon is preceded by a greater-than sign (>); this is done to remind you that the loop stops when the value in the *counter* variable is greater than the *endvalue*.

On your computer's hard disk is an application that contains three examples of the For...Next statement.

To open the For Next application:

1 Start Microsoft Visual Studio .NET, if necessary, then close the Start Page window.

2 Click **File** on the menu bar, and then click **Open Solution**. The Open Solution dialog box opens. Open the **For Next Solution** (For Next Solution.sln) file, which is contained in the VBNET\Tut06\For Next Solution folder.

3 If the designer window is not open, right-click **For Next Form.vb** in the Solution Explorer window, then click **View Designer**.

4 Auto-hide the Toolbox, Solution Explorer, and Properties windows, if necessary. The For Next application's user interface is shown in Figure 6-4.

CarsPictureBox control ──────────────

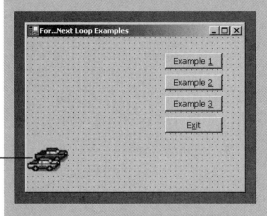

Figure 6-4: For Next application's user interface

The interface shown in Figure 6-4 contains one picture box control, which is named CarsPictureBox, and four button controls. Each of the button controls has been coded for you. First you view and then test the code entered in the Example 1 button's Click event procedure.

Example 1 Button

The Example 1 button's Click event procedure contains the code shown earlier in Figure 6-2. Recall that the code uses the For...Next statement to process the loop instructions, which get and display the name of a city, three times.

To view the Example 1 button's code, then test the code:

1 Right-click the **form**, and then click **View Code**. Figure 6-5 shows the code entered in the Example 1 button's Click event procedure.

```
Private Sub Example1Button_Click(ByVal sender As Object, ByVal e As System.EventArgs
    Dim intCount As Integer, strCity As String
    For intCount = 1 To 3
        strCity = InputBox("Enter the city:", "City Entry")
        MessageBox.Show(strCity & " is city number " & intCount, _
            "City", MessageBoxButtons.OK, _
            MessageBoxIcon.Information)
    Next intCount
End Sub
```

Figure 6-5: Example 1 button's Click event procedure

2 Start the application, then click the **Example 1** button. When the City Entry dialog box appears, type **Paris** and then press **Enter**. The message "Paris is city number 1" appears in a message box.

3 Press **Enter** to close the message box. The City Entry dialog box appears for a second time.

4 Type **London** in the dialog box and then press **Enter**. The message "London is city number 2" appears in a message box.

5 Press **Enter** to close the message box. The City Entry dialog box appears for a third time.

6 Type **Madrid** in the dialog box and then press **Enter**. The message "Madrid is city number 3" appears in a message box.

7 Press **Enter** to close the message box. The Example 1 button's Click event procedure ends.

8 Click the **Exit** button to end the application. When you return to the Code editor window, close the Output window.

Figure 6-6 describes how the computer processes the code entered in the Example 1 button's Click event procedure.

1. The computer creates and initializes the intCount and strCity variables in memory.

2. The For clause initializes the *counter*, intCount, to 1 (*startvalue*).

3. The For clause checks whether the value in intCount is greater than 3 (*endvalue*). It's not.

4. The InputBox function prompts the user to enter the name of a city. Assume the city "Paris" is entered.

5. The MessageBox.Show method displays the message "Paris is city number 1".

6. The Next clause adds 1 (*stepvalue*) to intCount, giving 2.

7. The For clause checks whether the value in intCount is greater than 3 (*endvalue*). It's not.

8. The InputBox function prompts the user to enter the name of a city. Assume the city "London" is entered.

9. The MessageBox.Show method displays the message "London is city number 2".

10. The Next clause adds 1 (*stepvalue*) to intCount, giving 3.

11. The For clause checks whether the value in intCount is greater than 3 (*endvalue*). It's not.

12. The InputBox function prompts the user to enter the name of a city. Assume the city "Madrid" is entered.

13. The MessageBox.Show method displays the message "Madrid is city number 3".

14. The Next clause adds 1 (*stepvalue*) to intCount, giving 4.

15. The For clause checks whether the value in intCount is greater than 3 (*endvalue*). It is, so the For...Next statement ends. Processing continues with the statement following the Next clause.

16. The End Sub statement ends the Click event procedure.

When the For...Next statement in the Example1Button Click event procedure ends, the value stored in the intCount variable is 4.

Figure 6-6: Processing steps for the code entered in the Example 1 button's Click event procedure

Next, view and test the code contained in the Example 2 button's Click event procedure.

Example 2 Button

Figure 6-7 shows the code contained in the Example 2 button's Click event procedure. Notice that the *startvalue* and *stepvalue* in the For...Next statement are decimal numbers. Also notice that the *startvalue* is greater than the *endvalue*, which is required when the *stepvalue* is a negative number, as it is here.

displays a message in the Output window

```
Private Sub Example2Button_Click(ByVal sender As Object, ByVal e As System.EventArgs
    Dim sngNumber As Single
    For sngNumber = 2.5 To 1 Step -0.5
        Debug.WriteLine(sngNumber)
    Next sngNumber
End Sub
```

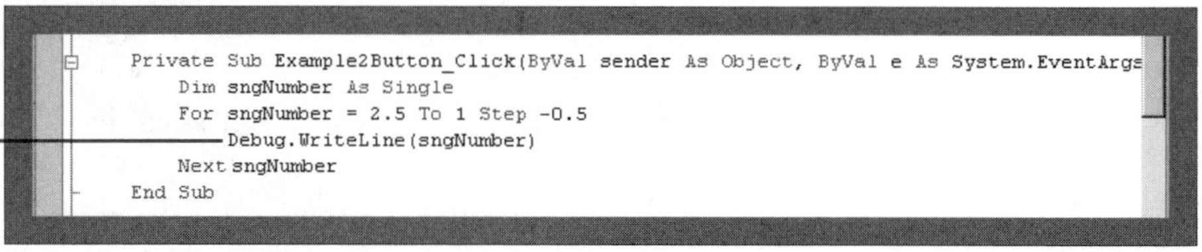

Figure 6-7: Example 2 button's Click event procedure

The code shown in Figure 6-7 contains a new method called Debug.WriteLine. You can use the **Debug.WriteLine method**, whose syntax is **Debug.WriteLine**(*message*), to display a message in the Output window while a procedure is being processed by the computer. The *message* argument can contain a literal constant, such as the string "Hello" or the number 5. It also can contain the name of a named constant, intrinsic constant, variable, or object. The Debug.WriteLine method shown in Figure 6-7 contains the name of a variable, sngNumber. The `Debug.WriteLine(sngNumber)` statement tells the computer to display the contents of the sngNumber variable in the Output window. In this case, the numbers 2.5, 2, 1.5, and 1 will be displayed. Observe how the Example 2 button's Click event procedure works.

To process the code contained in the Example 2 button's Click event procedure:

1 Start the application, then click the **Example 2** button. The procedure displays the numbers 2.5, 2, 1.5, and 1 in the Output window. Click the **Exit** button to end the application. The Output window is shown in Figure 6-8.

numbers displayed in the Output window

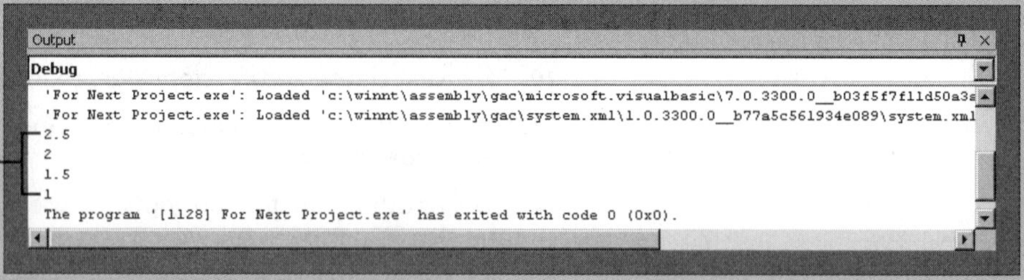

```
Output                                                              ↕ ×
Debug                                                                ▼
'For Next Project.exe': Loaded 'c:\winnt\assembly\gac\microsoft.visualbasic\7.0.3300.0__b03f5f7f11d50a3a ▲
'For Next Project.exe': Loaded 'c:\winnt\assembly\gac\system.xml\1.0.3300.0__b77a5c561934e089\system.xml
2.5
2
1.5
1
The program '[1128] For Next Project.exe' has exited with code 0 (0x0).                               ▼
◄                                                                                                     ►
```

Figure 6-8: Numbers displayed in the Output window

2 When you return to the Code editor window, close the Output window.

Figure 6-9 describes how the computer processes the code contained in the Example 2 button's Click event procedure.

1. The computer creates and initializes the sngNumber variable in memory.

2. The For clause initializes the *counter*, sngNumber, to 2.5 (*startvalue*).

3. The For clause checks whether the value in sngNumber is less than 1 (*endvalue*). It's not.

4. The Debug.WriteLine method displays the number 2.5 in the Output window.

5. The Next clause adds -0.5 (*stepvalue*) to sngNumber, giving 2.

6. The For clause checks whether the value in sngNumber is less than 1 (*endvalue*). It's not.

7. The Debug.WriteLine method displays the number 2 in the Output window.

8. The Next clause adds -0.5 (*stepvalue*) to sngNumber, giving 1.5.

9. The For clause checks whether the value in sngNumber is less than 1 (*endvalue*). It's not.

10. The Debug.WriteLine method displays the number 1.5 in the Output window.

11. The Next clause adds -0.5 (*stepvalue*) to sngNumber, giving 1.

12. The For clause checks whether the value in sngNumber is less than 1 (*endvalue*). It's not.

13. The Debug.WriteLine method displays the number 1 in the Output window.

14. The Next clause adds -0.5 (*stepvalue*) to sngNumber, giving .5.

15. The For clause checks whether the value in sngNumber is less than 1 (*endvalue*). It is, so the For...Next statement ends. Processing continues with the statement following the Next clause.

16. The End Sub statement ends the Click event procedure.

Figure 6-9: Processing steps for the code entered in the Example 2 button's Click event procedure

Finally, view and test the code contained in the Example 3 button's Click event procedure.

Example 3 Button

Figure 6-10 shows the code contained in the Example 3 button's Click event procedure.

changes the location of the control's left border

```
Private Sub Example3Button_Click(ByVal sender As Object, ByVal e As System.EventArgs
    Dim intX As Integer
    For intX = 0 To 275 Step 5
        Me.CarsPictureBox.SetBounds(intX, 0, 0, 0, BoundsSpecified.X)
    Next intX
End Sub
```

Figure 6-10: Example 3 button's Click event procedure

The Click event procedure shown in Figure 6-10 contains another new method called SetBounds. You can use the **SetBounds method** to change the location and/or size of a control while an application is running. Figure 6-11 shows the syntax and examples of the SetBounds method.

Syntax

control.**SetBounds(***x, y, width, height, specified***)**

specified argument	Meaning
BoundsSpecified.All	all arguments are specified
BoundsSpecified.Height	the *height* argument is specified
BoundsSpecified.Location	the *x* (left) and *y* (top) arguments are specified
BoundsSpecified.None	no arguments are specified
BoundsSpecified.Size	the *width* and *height* arguments are specified
BoundsSpecified.Width	the *width* argument is specified
BoundsSpecified.X	the *x* (left) argument is specified
BoundsSpecified.Y	the *y* (top) argument is specified

Examples and results

Example 1
```
Me.CarsPictureBox.SetBounds(25, 50, 0, 0, BoundsSpecified.Location)
```

Result
Positions the picture box at a location that is 25 pixels from the left edge of the form and 50 pixels from the top edge of the form. Leaves the control at its current size.

Example 2
```
Me.CarsPictureBox.SetBounds(25, 50, 0, 0, BoundsSpecified.All)
```

Result
Positions the picture box at a location that is 25 pixels from the left edge of the form and 50 pixels from the top edge of the form. Changes the width and height of the control to zero pixels.

Example 3
```
Me.CarsPictureBox.SetBounds(0, 0, 100, 0, BoundsSpecified.Width)
```

Result
Leaves the control at its current location and current height. Changes the width of the control to 100 pixels.

Figure 6-11: Syntax and examples of the SetBounds method

In the syntax, *control* is the name of the control whose location and/or size you want to change. You change the control's location by setting the SetBounds method's *x* and *y* arguments. The *x* argument specifies the location of the left edge of the control on the form, and the *y* argument specifies the location of the top edge of the control. You change the control's size by setting the SetBounds method's *width* and *height* arguments. The *x, y, width,* and *height* arguments are measured in pixels.

If you do not want to change the location of either the left or top edge of a control, or if you do not want to change the control's height or width, you simply set the appropriate argument to the number 0. For example, to keep the control's left border at its current location, you set the *x* argument to 0. Similarly, to keep the control at its current size, you set the *width* and *height* arguments to 0.

The *specified* argument in the SetBounds method is an intrinsic constant that indicates the arguments that you are specifying in the method. For example, to indicate that you are specifying the *height* argument only, you use the constant BoundsSpecified.Height as the *specified* argument. To indicate that only the *y* argument is specified in the SetBounds method, you use the constant BoundsSpecified.Y as the *specified* argument. Finally, to indicate that you are specifying both the *x* and *width* arguments, you use the Or operator to combine two constants in the *specified* argument, like this: BoundsSpecified.X Or BoundsSpecified.Width.

Study the three examples shown in Figure 6-11. In the first example, `Me.CarsPictureBox.SetBounds(25, 50, 0, 0, BoundsSpecified.Location)`, the *specified* argument indicates that only the arguments pertaining to the control's location are being specified; therefore, the method uses only the values appearing in the *x* and *y* arguments. Those values position the CarsPictureBox control at a location that is 25 pixels from the left edge of the form, and 50 pixels from the top edge of the form.

Example 2 in Figure 6-11 is almost identical to Example 1, except it uses BoundsSpecified.All as the *specified* argument. The BoundsSpecified.All setting indicates that all of the arguments are being specified in the SetBounds method. Like the SetBounds method in Example 1, the SetBounds method in Example 2 positions the CarsPictureBox control at a location that is 25 pixels from the left edge of the form, and 50 pixels from the top edge of the form. Unlike the SetBounds method in Example 1, however, the SetBounds method in Example 2 changes both the width and height of the picture box control to zero pixels. A control whose width and height are set to zero pixels is not visible on the form.

The third example shown in Figure 6-11, `Me.CarsPictureBox.SetBounds(0, 0, 100, 0, BoundsSpecified.Width)`, changes the width of the picture box control to 100 pixels. The location and height of the control remain at their current values.

In the Example 3 button's Click event procedure, the *counter* variable in the For...Next statement (intX) controls the value of the *x* argument in the SetBounds method. When you start the For Next application and click the Example 3 button, the For clause initializes the intX variable to the number 0 (the *startvalue*). Because the number 0 is not greater than the number 275 (the *endvalue*), the `Me.CarsPictureBox.SetBounds(intX, 0, 0, 0, BoundsSpecified.X)` statement positions the picture box at a location that is zero pixels from the left edge of the form. The Next clause then adds the number 5 (the *stepvalue*) to the value stored in the intX variable, giving 5. Because the number 5 is not greater than the number 275, the

`Me.CarsPictureBox.SetBounds(intX, 0, 0, 0, BoundsSpecified.X)` statement moves the picture box five pixels from the left edge of the form. Each time the loop is processed, the value stored in the intX variable is increased by five. As the value in the intX variable increases, the SetBounds method moves the picture box control farther away from the left edge of the form. When the intX variable contains a number that is greater than 275, the For...Next statement stops. In this example, the statement stops when the intX variable contains the number 280. Observe how the computer processes the code contained in the Example 3 button's Click event procedure.

> To process the code contained in the Example 3 button's Click event procedure:
>
> **1** Start the application, then click the **Example 3** button. The picture box control moves from the left side of the form to the right side of the form.
>
> **2** Click the **Exit** button to end the application. When you return to the Code editor window, close the Output window, then close the Code editor window.
>
> You are finished with this solution, so you can close it.
>
> **3** Click **File** on the menu bar, and then click **Close Solution**.

Recall that you also can use the Do...Loop statement to code a repetition structure in Visual Basic .NET.

The Do...Loop Statement

Unlike the For...Next statement, the **Do...Loop statement** can be used to code both a pretest loop and a posttest loop. Figure 6-12 shows two slightly different versions of the Do...Loop statement's syntax. You use the version shown in the first column to code a pretest loop, and the version shown in the second column to code a posttest loop. The figure also includes an example of using each syntax to display the numbers 1, 2, and 3 in the Output window.

You can use the `Exit Do` statement to exit the Do...Loop statement prematurely—in other words, to exit it before the loop has finished processing. You may need to do so if the loop encounters an error when processing its instructions.

You can nest Do...Loop statements, which means that you can place one Do...Loop statement within another Do...Loop statement.

As both examples shown in Figure 6-12 indicate, you do not type the braces ({}) or the pipe symbol (|) when entering the Do...Loop statement.

Do...Loop syntax (pretest loop)	Do...Loop syntax (posttest loop)

Do {While | Until} *condition*
    [*instructions to be processed either
    while the condition is true or until
    the condition becomes true*]
Loop
	Do
	    [*instructions to be processed either
	    while the condition is true or until
	    the condition becomes true*]
	Loop {While | Until} *condition*

Pretest loop example	**Posttest loop example**
``` Dim intCount As Integer = 1 Do While intCount <= 3 Debug.Writeline(intCount) intCount = intCount + 1 Loop ```	``` Dim intCount As Integer = 1 Do Debug.Writeline(intCount) intCount = intCount + 1 Loop Until intCount > 3 ```

Figure 6-12: Two versions of the Do...Loop statement's syntax, along with an example of using each version

Recall that the oval in a flowchart is the start/stop symbol, the rectangle is the process symbol, the parallelogram is the input/ output symbol, and the diamond is the selection/ repetition symbol.

The Do...Loop statement begins with the Do clause and ends with the Loop clause. Between both clauses, you enter the instructions you want the computer to repeat. In both examples shown in Figure 6-12, the computer will repeat the `Debug.WriteLine(intCount)` and `intCount = intCount + 1` instructions.

The {**While** | **Until**} portion of each syntax indicates that you can select only one of the keywords appearing within the braces—in this case, you can choose either the keyword While or the keyword Until. You follow the keyword with a *condition*, which can contain variables, constants, properties, functions, and operators. Like the *condition* used in the If...Then...Else statement, the *condition* used in the Do...Loop statement also must evaluate to a Boolean value—either True or False. The *condition* determines whether the computer processes the loop instructions. The keyword While indicates that the loop instructions should be processed while the *condition* is true. The keyword Until, on the other hand, indicates that the loop instructions should be processed until the *condition* becomes true. Notice that the keyword (either While or Until) and the *condition* appear in the Do clause in a pretest loop, but in the Loop clause in a posttest loop.

Figure 6-13 shows the flowcharts associated with the pretest and posttest loops shown in Figure 6-12; the pseudocode for each loop is shown in Figure 6-14.

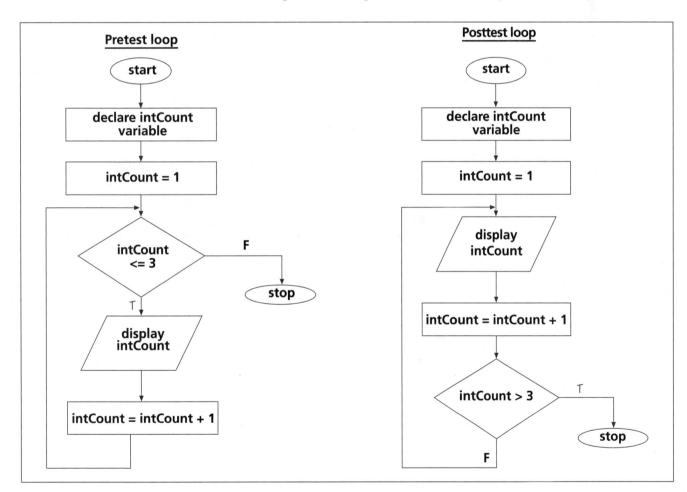

Figure 6-13: Flowcharts for the pretest and posttest loops shown in Figure 6-12

Pseudocode for the pretest loop	Pseudocode for the posttest loop
1. declare intCount variable	1. declare intCount variable
2. assign 1 to intCount variable	2. assign 1 to intCount variable
3. repeat while intCount < = 3	3. repeat
display intCount	display intCount
add 1 to intCount	add 1 to intCount
end repeat	end repeat until intCount > 3

Figure 6-14: Pseudocode for the pretest and posttest loops shown in Figure 6-12

Notice that the loop *condition* in both flowcharts shown in Figure 6-13 is represented by a diamond. As with the selection structure diamond, which you learned about in Tutorial 4, the repetition structure diamond contains a comparison that evaluates to either True or False only. The result of the comparison determines whether the instructions within the loop are processed.

Like the selection diamond, the repetition diamond has one flowline entering the diamond and two flowlines leaving the diamond. The two flowlines leaving the diamond should be marked with a "T" (for True) and an "F" (for False).

In the flowchart of the pretest loop shown in Figure 6-13, the flowline entering the repetition diamond, as well as the symbols and flowlines within the True path, form a circle or loop. In the posttest loop's flowchart shown in Figure 6-13, the loop is formed by all of the symbols and flowlines in the False path. It is this loop, or circle, that distinguishes the repetition structure from the selection structure in a flowchart.

On your computer's hard disk is an application that contains two examples of the Do...Loop statement. Both examples correspond to the code, flowcharts, and pseudocode shown in Figures 6-12 through 6-14.

To open the Do Loop application:

1 Click **File** on the menu bar, and then click **Open Solution**. The Open Solution dialog box opens. Open the **Do Loop Solution** (Do Loop Solution.sln) file, which is contained in the VBNET\Tut06\Do Loop Solution folder.

2 If the designer window is not open, right-click **Do Loop Form.vb** in the Solution Explorer window, then click **View Designer**. The Do Loop application's user interface is shown in Figure 6-15.

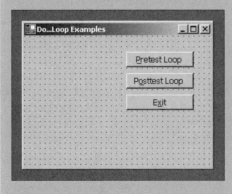

Figure 6-15: Do Loop application's user interface

The interface shown in Figure 6-15 contains three button controls. Each of the button controls has been coded for you. First you view and then test the code entered in the Pretest Loop button's Click event procedure.

Pretest Loop Button

The Pretest Loop button's Click event procedure contains the code to display the numbers 1, 2, and 3 in the Output window.

To view the Pretest Loop button's code, then test the code:

1 Right-click the **form**, and then click **View Code**. Figure 6-16 shows the code entered in the Pretest Loop button's Click event procedure.

pretest loop

```
Private Sub PretestButton_Click(ByVal sender As Object, ByVal e As System.EventArgs)
    Dim intCount As Integer = 1
    Do While intCount <= 3
        Debug.WriteLine(intCount)
        intCount = intCount + 1
    Loop
End Sub
```

Figure 6-16: Pretest Loop button's Click event procedure

2 Start the application, then click the **Pretest Loop** button. The computer processes the code in the button's Click event procedure, as described in Figure 6-17, and the numbers 1, 2, and 3 appear in the Output window.

1. The computer creates and initializes (to 1) the intCount variable in memory.
2. The Do clause checks whether the value in intCount is less than or equal to 3. It is.
3. The Debug.WriteLine method displays 1 (the contents of the intCount variable) in the Output window.
4. The `intCount = intCount + 1` statement adds 1 to intCount, giving 2.
5. The Loop clause returns processing to the Do clause (the beginning of the loop).
6. The Do clause checks whether the value in intCount is less than or equal to 3. It is.
7. The Debug.WriteLine method displays 2 (the contents of the intCount variable) in the Output window.
8. The `intCount = intCount + 1` statement adds 1 to intCount, giving 3.
9. The Loop clause returns processing to the Do clause (the beginning of the loop).
10. The Do clause checks whether the value in intCount is less than or equal to 3. It is.
11. The Debug.WriteLine method displays 3 (the contents of the intCount variable) in the Output window.
12. The `intCount = intCount + 1` statement adds 1 to intCount, giving 4.
13. The Loop clause returns processing to the Do clause (the beginning of the loop).
14. The Do clause checks whether the value in intCount is less than or equal to 3. It isn't, so the Do...Loop statement ends. Processing continues with the statement following the Loop clause.
15. The `End Sub` statement ends the Click event procedure.

Figure 6-17: Processing steps for the code entered in the Pretest Loop button's Click event procedure

3   Click the **Exit** button to end the application. When you return to the Code editor window, close the Output window.

Next, view and test the code entered in the Posttest Loop button.

Posttest Loop Button

The Posttest Loop button's Click event procedure also contains the code to display the numbers 1, 2, and 3 in the Output window. Figure 6-18 shows the code entered in the Posttest Loop button's Click event procedure.

posttest loop

```
Private Sub PosttestButton_Click(ByVal sender As Object, ByVal e As System.EventArgs
    Dim intCount As Integer = 1
    Do
        Debug.WriteLine(intCount)
        intCount = intCount + 1
    Loop Until intCount > 3
End Sub
```

Figure 6-18: Posttest Loop button's Click event procedure

To test the Posttest Loop button's code:

1   Start the application, then click the **Posttest Loop** button. The computer processes the code in the button's Click event procedure, as described in Figure 6-19, and the numbers 1, 2, and 3 appear in the Output window.

1. The computer creates and initializes (to 1) the intCount variable in memory.
2. The Do clause marks the beginning of the loop.
3. The Debug.WriteLine method displays 1 (the contents of the intCount variable) in the Output window.
4. The `intCount = intCount + 1` statement adds 1 to intCount, giving 2.
5. The Loop clause checks whether the value in intCount is greater than 3. It isn't, so the clause returns processing to the Do clause (the beginning of the loop).
6. The Debug.WriteLine method displays 2 (the contents of the intCount variable) in the Output window.
7. The `intCount = intCount + 1` statement adds 1 to intCount, giving 3.
8. The Loop clause checks whether the value in intCount is greater than 3. It isn't, so the clause returns processing to the Do clause (the beginning of the loop).
9. The Debug.WriteLine method displays 3 (the contents of the intCount variable) in the Output window.
10. The `intCount = intCount + 1` statement adds 1 to intCount, giving 4.
11. The Loop clause checks whether the value in intCount is greater than 3. It is, so the Do...Loop statement ends. Processing continues with the statement following the Loop clause.
12. The `End Sub` statement ends the Click event procedure.

Figure 6-19: Processing steps for the code entered in the Posttest Loop button's Click event procedure

2   Click the **Exit** button to end the application. When you return to the Code editor window, close the Output window.

Although it appears that the pretest and posttest loops produce the same results—in this case, for example, both loops display the numbers 1 through 3 in the Output window—that will not always be the case. In other words, the two loops are not always interchangeable. The difference between both loops will be more apparent in the next set of steps.

To observe the difference between the pretest and posttest loops:

1 Change the `Dim intCount As Integer = 1` statement in the PretestButton Click event procedure to **Dim intCount As Integer = 10**.

By setting the initial value of intCount to 10, the loop's condition (`intCount <= 3`) will evaluate to False, and the loop instructions will be skipped. Find out if that is, in fact, what happens.

2 Start the application, then click the **Pretest Loop** button. As expected, the numbers 1, 2, and 3 do not appear in the Output window. In this case, the loop instructions were not processed, because the loop's *condition* initially evaluated to False. Figure 6-20 describes how the computer processes the modified code in the Pretest Loop button's Click event procedure.

---

1. The computer creates and initializes (to 10) the intCount variable in memory.
2. The Do clause checks whether the value in intCount is less than or equal to 3. It isn't, so the Do...Loop statement ends. Processing continues with the statement following the Loop clause.
3. The End Sub statement ends the Click event procedure.

Figure 6-20: Processing steps for the modified code in the Pretest Loop button's Click event procedure

3 Click the **Exit** button to end the application.

Now make the same change to the Posttest Loop button's Click event procedure, then observe how the procedure handles this change.

4 Change the `Dim intCount As Integer = 1` statement in the PosttestButton Click event procedure to **Dim intCount As Integer = 10**.

5 Start the application, then click the **Posttest Loop** button. This time the number 10 appears in the Output window. The number 10 appears because the posttest loop's instructions are processed before its *condition* (`intCount > 3`) is evaluated. Figure 6-21 describes how the computer processes the modified code in the Posttest Loop button's Click event procedure.

---

1. The computer creates and initializes (to 10) the intCount variable in memory.
2. The Do clause marks the beginning of the loop.
3. The Debug.WriteLine method displays 10 (the contents of the intCount variable) in the Output window.
4. The `intCount = intCount + 1` statement adds 1 to intCount, giving 11.
5. The Loop clause checks whether the value in intCount is greater than 3. It is, so the Do...Loop statement ends. Processing continues with the statement following the Loop clause.
6. The End Sub statement ends the Click event procedure.

Figure 6-21: Processing steps for the modified code in the Posttest Loop button's Click event procedure

6 Click the **Exit** button to end the application. When you return to the Code editor window, close the Output window.

Now return the application to its original state.

7 Change the `Dim intCount As Integer = 10` statement in the PretestButton and PosttestButton Click event procedures to **Dim intCount As Integer = 1**.

8 Close the Code editor window. Click **File** on the menu bar, and then click **Save All**.

You are finished with this application, so you can close it.

9 Click **File** on the menu bar, and then click **Close Solution**.

Many times an application will need to display a subtotal, a total, or an average. To do so, you need to use a repetition structure that includes a counter, an accumulator, or both.

Using Counters and Accumulators

Counters and accumulators are used within a repetition structure to calculate subtotals, totals, and averages. A **counter** is a numeric variable used for counting something—such as the number of employees paid in a week. An **accumulator** is a numeric variable used for accumulating (adding together) something—such as the total dollar amount of a week's payroll.

Two tasks are associated with counters and accumulators: initializing and updating. **Initializing** means to assign a beginning value to the counter or accumulator. Although the beginning value usually is zero, counters and accumulators can be initialized to any number; the initial value you use will depend on the application. The initialization task typically is done before the loop is processed, because it needs to be done only once.

Updating, also called **incrementing**, means adding a number to the value stored in the counter or accumulator. The number can be either positive or negative, integer or non-integer. A counter is always incremented by a constant value—typically the number 1—whereas an accumulator is incremented by a value that varies. The assignment statement that updates a counter or an accumulator is placed within the loop in a procedure, because the update task must be performed each time the loop instructions are processed. You use both a counter and an accumulator in the Sales Express application, which you view and test in the next section.

tip

Counters are used to answer the question, "How many?"—for example, "How many salespeople live in Virginia?" Accumulators are used to answer the question, "How much?"—for example, "How much did the salespeople sell this quarter?"

The Sales Express Application

Assume that Sales Express wants an application that the sales manager can use to display the average amount the company sold during the prior year. The sales manager will enter the amount of each salesperson's sales. The application will use a counter to keep track of the number of sales amounts entered by the sales manager, and an accumulator to total those sales amounts. After all of the sales amounts are entered, the application will calculate the average sales amount by dividing the value stored in the accumulator by the value stored in the counter. It then will display the average sales amount on the screen. Figure 6-22 shows the flowcharts for two possible solutions to the Sales Express problem. The flowchart on the left uses a pretest loop, and the flowchart on the right uses a posttest loop.

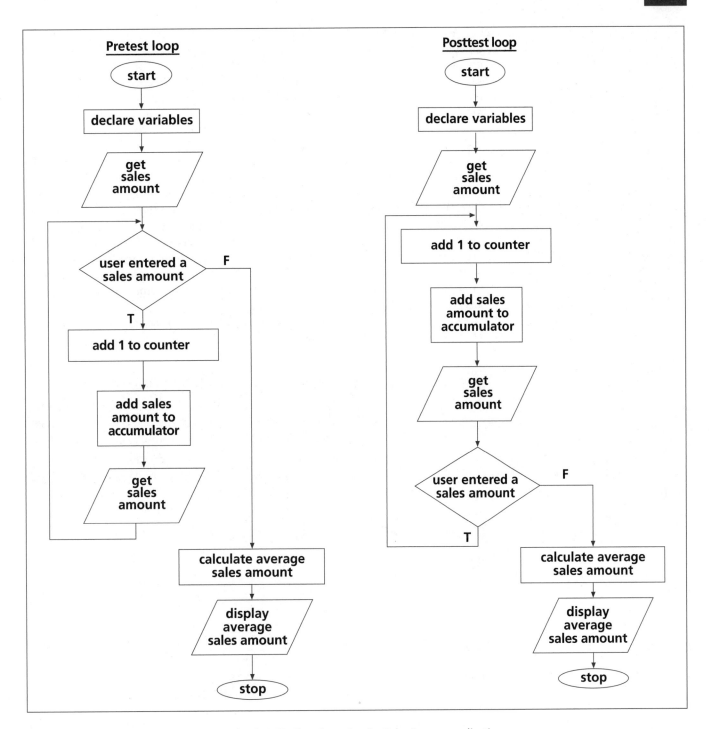

Figure 6-22: Flowcharts for the Sales Express application

The flowchart containing the pretest loop first declares the necessary variables, then gets a sales amount from the user. The loop in the flowchart then checks whether the user entered a sales amount. If the user did not enter a sales amount, the loop stops and the average sales amount is calculated and displayed. If, on the other hand, the user did enter a sales amount, the counter is incremented by one, the accumulator is incremented by the sales amount, and another sales amount is requested from the user. The flowchart then returns to the beginning of the loop, where the loop again checks whether the user entered a sales amount.

The flowchart containing the posttest loop also first declares the necessary variables and gets a sales amount from the user. The flowchart then increments both the counter by one and the accumulator by the sales amount before requesting another sales amount from the user. The loop in the flowchart then checks whether the user entered a sales amount; if he or she did not, the loop stops and the average sales amount is calculated and displayed. If, on the other hand, the user did enter a sales amount, the flowchart returns to the beginning of the loop and processes the loop instructions again.

Notice that both flowcharts shown in Figure 6-22 contain two "get sales amount" parallelograms. One of the parallelograms appears immediately above the loop in each flowchart, and the other appears within the loop in each flowchart. The "get sales amount" parallelogram that appears above the loop is referred to as the **priming read**, because it is used to prime (prepare or set up) the loop. In this case, the priming read will get only the first salesperson's sales amount from the user. In the pretest loop, this first value will determine whether the loop instructions are processed at all. The "get sales amount" parallelogram that appears within the loop in each flowchart will get the sales amounts for the remaining salespeople (if any) from the user.

On your computer's hard disk is an application that contains the code corresponding to the flowcharts shown in Figure 6-22.

To view the code associated with the flowcharts shown in Figure 6-22:

1   Click **File** on the menu bar, and then click **Open Solution**. The Open Solution dialog box opens. Open the **Sales Express Solution** (Sales Express Solution.sln) file, which is contained in the VBNET\Tut06\Sales Express Solution folder.

2   If the designer window is not open, right-click **Sales Express Form.vb** in the Solution Explorer window, then click **View Designer**. The Sales Express application's user interface is shown in Figure 6-23.

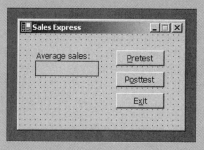

Figure 6-23: Sales Express application's user interface

The user interface shown in Figure 6-23 contains three button controls and two label controls. Each of the button controls has been coded for you. First, view and then test the code contained in the Pretest button's Click event procedure.

Pretest Button

The Pretest button's Click event procedure contains the code for the first flowchart shown in Figure 6-22.

To view the Pretest button's Click event procedure:

1   Right-click the **form**, and then click **View Code**. Figure 6-24 shows the Pretest button's Click event procedure.

```
Private Sub PretestButton_Click(ByVal sender As Object, ByVal e As System.EventArgs)
    Dim strSales As String
    Dim intNumSales As Integer   'counter
    Dim sngSumSales As Single    'accumulator
    Dim sngAverageSales As Single
    strSales = InputBox("Enter a sales amount. Click Cancel when finished.", _
        "Sales Entry")
    Do While strSales <> ""
        intNumSales = intNumSales + 1                   'update counter
        sngSumSales = sngSumSales + Val(strSales)    'update accumulator
        strSales = InputBox("Enter a sales amount. Click Cancel when finished.", _
            "Sales Entry")
    Loop
    sngAverageSales = sngSumSales / intNumSales
    Me.AvgLabel.Text = Format(sngAverageSales, "currency")
End Sub
```

Figure 6-24: Pretest button's Click event procedure

The procedure begins by declaring four variables: strSales, intNumSales, sngSumSales, and sngAverageSales. The strSales variable will store the sales amounts entered by the user. The intNumSales variable is the counter variable that will keep track of the number of sales amounts entered. The sngSumSales variable is the accumulator variable that the computer will use to total the sales amounts. The remaining variable, sngAverageSales, will store the average sales amount after it has been calculated.

Recall that counters and accumulators must be initialized, or given a beginning value; typically, the beginning value is the number zero. Because the Dim statement automatically assigns a zero to Integer and Single variables when the variables are created, you do not need to enter any additional code to initialize the intNumSales counter or the sngSumSales accumulator. If you want to initialize a counter or an accumulator to a value other than zero, however, you can do so either in the Dim statement that declares the variable or in an assignment statement. For example, to initialize the intNumSales counter variable to the number one, you could use either the declaration statement `Dim intNumSales As Integer = 1` or the assignment statement `intNumSales = 1` in your code.

After the variables are declared, the InputBox function in the procedure displays a dialog box that prompts the user to either enter a sales amount or click the Cancel button, which indicates that the user has no more sales amounts to enter. As you learned in Tutorial 3, the value returned by the InputBox function depends on whether the user clicks the dialog box's OK, Cancel, or Close button ⊠. If the user clicks the OK button, the InputBox function returns the value contained in the input area of the dialog box. However, if the user clicks either the Cancel button or the Close button, the InputBox function returns a zero-length (or empty) string.

In this case, when the user enters a sales amount and then clicks the OK button in the dialog box, the InputBox function stores the sales amount in the strSales variable. However, when the user fails to enter a sales amount before selecting the OK button, or when he or she selects either the dialog box's Cancel button or its Close button, the function stores a zero-length string ("") in the strSales variable.

tip

● ● ● ● ● ● ● ● ● ● ● ● ● ●

▶ Recall that the InputBox function's dialog box contains an input area and OK and Cancel buttons.

The Do clause in the Do...Loop statement then evaluates the *condition*, strSales <> "", to determine whether the loop instructions should be processed. If the strSales variable does not contain a zero-length string, the *condition* evaluates to True and the computer processes the loop instructions. If, on the other hand, the strSales variable contains a zero-length string, the *condition* evaluates to False and the computer skips over the loop instructions. Now take a closer look at the instructions within the loop.

The intNumSales = intNumSales + 1 instruction updates the counter variable by adding a constant value of one to it. Notice that the counter variable, intNumSales, appears on both sides of the assignment statement. The statement tells the computer to add one to the contents of the intNumSales variable, then places the result back in the intNumSales variable. The intNumSales variable's value will be incremented by one each time the loop is processed.

The sngSumSales = sngSumSales + Val(strSales) instruction updates the accumulator variable by adding a sales amount to it. Notice that the accumulator variable, sngSumSales, also appears on both sides of the assignment statement. The statement tells the computer to add the numeric equivalent of the strSales variable to the contents of the sngSumSales variable, then place the result back in the sngSumSales variable. The sngSumSales variable's value will be incremented by a sales amount, which will vary, each time the loop is processed.

After the counter and accumulator are updated, the InputBox function again prompts the user for another sales amount. Notice that the strSales = InputBox ("Enter a sales amount. Click Cancel when finished.", "Sales Entry") instruction appears twice in the code—before the Do...Loop statement and within the Do...Loop statement. Recall that the strSales = InputBox("Enter a sales amount. Click Cancel when finished.", "Sales Entry") instruction located above the loop is referred to as the priming read, and its task is to get only the first sales amount from the user. The strSales = InputBox("Enter a sales amount. Click Cancel when finished.", "Sales Entry") instruction located within the loop gets each of the remaining sales amounts (if any) from the user.

After the user enters another sales amount, the Loop clause sends the computer to the Do clause, where the loop's *condition* is tested again. If the *condition* evaluates to True, the loop instructions are processed again. If the *condition* evaluates to False, the loop stops and the instruction after the Loop clause is processed. That instruction calculates the average sales amount by dividing the contents of the accumulator variable (sngSumSales) by the contents of the counter variable (intNumSales). The result is assigned to the sngAverageSales variable. The next instruction in the procedure displays the average sales amount, formatted using the Currency format style, in the AvgLabel control.

tip

• • • • • • • • • • • • • • • •

▶ **If you forget to enter the second** strSales = InputBox("Enter a sales amount. Click Cancel when finished.", "Sales Entry") **instruction in the procedure, you will create an endless or infinite loop. To stop an endless loop, click Debug on the menu bar, and then click Stop Debugging.**

To test the code contained in the Pretest button's Click event procedure:

1 Start the application, then click the **Pretest** button.

2 Type 3000 in the Sales Entry dialog box and press **Enter**. The loop instructions add 1 to the intNumSales variable, giving 1, and also add 3000 to the sngSumSales variable, giving 3000. Then the user is prompted for another sales amount.

3 Type 4000 in the dialog box and press **Enter**. The loop instructions add 1 to the intNumSales variable, giving 2, and also add 4000 to the sngSumSales variable, giving 7000. Then the user is prompted for another sales amount.

Now click the Cancel button to stop the loop.

4 Click the **Cancel** button in the dialog box. The loop stops and the procedure calculates and displays the average sales amount, $3,500.00. The PretestButton Click event procedure then ends.

Now observe what happens when the user clicks the Pretest button and then selects the Cancel button before entering any sales amounts.

5 Click the **Pretest** button, then click the **Cancel** button. The intrinsic constant NaN, which stands for "Not a Number", appears in the AvgLabel control, as shown in Figure 6-25.

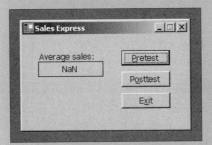

Figure 6-25: Result of clicking the Cancel button before entering any sales amounts

When you click the Cancel button immediately after clicking the Pretest button, the loop instructions in the Pretest button's Click event procedure are never processed, because the value in the strSales variable is equal to a zero-length string. (Recall that when the user selects the Cancel button in the InputBox function's dialog box, the function returns a zero-length string.) Because the loop instructions are not processed, the intNumSales and sngSumSales variables are not updated from their initial value, zero. When the computer processes the `sngAverageSales = sngSumSales / intNumSales` instruction, which appears after the Do...Loop statement in the procedure, it first tries to divide the contents of the sngSumSales variable (0) by the contents of the intNumSales variable (0) before assigning the result to the sngAverageSales variable. Because division by zero is mathematically impossible, the `sngSumSales / intNumSales` expression cannot be evaluated by the computer. When a Visual Basic .NET instruction attempts to divide the number zero by the number zero, the result is the constant NaN. The result of dividing any number other than zero by zero is the constant Infinity.

6 Click the **Exit** button to end the application. When you return to the Code editor window, close the Output window.

Before using a variable as the divisor in an expression, you can use a selection structure to determine whether the variable contains the number zero, and then take the appropriate action to avoid displaying the NaN or Infinity constants. For example, you will use a selection structure in the PretestButton Click event procedure to determine whether the value stored in the intNumSales variable is greater than zero. If it is, the selection structure will calculate and then display the average sales amount; otherwise, it will display the message "No sales" in the AvgLabel control.

To include a selection structure in the Pretest button's Click event procedure:

1 Modify the PretestButton Click event procedure, as shown in Figure 6-26.

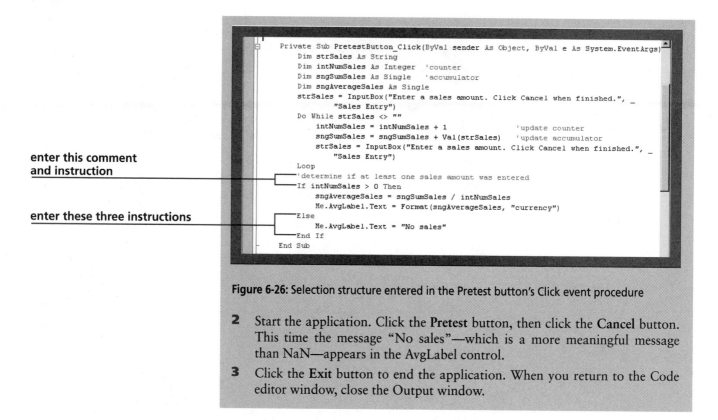

enter this comment
and instruction

enter these three instructions

```
Private Sub PretestButton_Click(ByVal sender As Object, ByVal e As System.EventArgs)
    Dim strSales As String
    Dim intNumSales As Integer   'counter
    Dim sngSumSales As Single    'accumulator
    Dim sngAverageSales As Single
    strSales = InputBox("Enter a sales amount. Click Cancel when finished.", _
        "Sales Entry")
    Do While strSales <> ""
        intNumSales = intNumSales + 1                'update counter
        sngSumSales = sngSumSales + Val(strSales)    'update accumulator
        strSales = InputBox("Enter a sales amount. Click Cancel when finished.", _
            "Sales Entry")
    Loop
    'determine if at least one sales amount was entered
    If intNumSales > 0 Then
        sngAverageSales = sngSumSales / intNumSales
        Me.AvgLabel.Text = Format(sngAverageSales, "currency")
    Else
        Me.AvgLabel.Text = "No sales"
    End If
End Sub
```

Figure 6-26: Selection structure entered in the Pretest button's Click event procedure

2 Start the application. Click the **Pretest** button, then click the **Cancel** button. This time the message "No sales"—which is a more meaningful message than NaN—appears in the AvgLabel control.

3 Click the **Exit** button to end the application. When you return to the Code editor window, close the Output window.

Now view the code contained in the Posttest button's Click event procedure.

Posttest Button

The Posttest button's Click event procedure contains the code for the second flow-chart shown in Figure 6-22. The procedure's code is shown in Figure 6-27. Notice that the loop *condition* appears in the Loop clause in this procedure, indicating that the loop is a posttest loop.

```
Private Sub PosttestButton_Click(ByVal sender As Object, ByVal e As System.EventArgs)
    Dim strSales As String
    Dim intNumSales As Integer   'counter
    Dim sngSumSales As Single    'accumulator
    Dim sngAverageSales As Single
    strSales = InputBox("Enter a sales amount. Click Cancel when finished.", _
        "Sales Entry")
    Do
        intNumSales = intNumSales + 1                'update counter
        sngSumSales = sngSumSales + Val(strSales)    'update accumulator
        strSales = InputBox("Enter a sales amount. Click Cancel when finished.", _
            "Sales Entry")
    Loop While strSales <> ""
    sngAverageSales = sngSumSales / intNumSales
    Me.AvgLabel.Text = Format(sngAverageSales, "currency")
End Sub
```

Figure 6-27: Posttest button's Click event procedure

To test the code contained in the Posttest button's Click event procedure:

1 Start the application, then click the **Posttest** button.

2 Type **3000** in the Sales Entry dialog box and press **Enter**. The loop instructions add 1 to the intNumSales variable, giving 1, and also add 3000 to the sngSumSales variable, giving 3000. Then the user is prompted for another sales amount.

3 Type **4000** in the dialog box and press **Enter**. The loop instructions add 1 to the intNumSales variable, giving 2, and also add 4000 to the sngSumSales variable, giving 7000. Then the user is prompted for another sales amount.

Now click the Cancel button to stop the loop.

4 Click the **Cancel** button in the dialog box. The loop stops and the procedure calculates and displays the average sales amount, $3,500.00. The PosttestButton Click event procedure then ends.

As you did with the pretest loop, observe what happens when the user clicks the Posttest button and then selects the Cancel button before entering any sales amounts.

5 Click the **Posttest** button, then click the **Cancel** button. The loop instructions first add 1 to the intNumSales variable, giving 1. They then add 0 (zero), which is the numeric equivalent of a zero-length string, to the sngSumSales variable, giving 0. Then the user is prompted for another sales amount.

Because the posttest loop's *condition* is not evaluated until after the second sales amount is entered, you will need to click the Cancel button again to stop the loop.

6 Click the **Cancel** button in the dialog box. The loop stops and $0.00 appears in the AvgLabel control before the PosttestButton Click event procedure ends. The $0.00 is the result of dividing the contents of the sngSumSales variable (0) by the contents of the intNumSales variable (1).

Because you can never be sure what a user might do while an application is running, it usually is safer to use a pretest loop instead of a posttest loop. Use a posttest loop only in situations where the loop instructions must be processed at least once.

7 Click the **Exit** button to end the application. When you return to the Code editor window, close the Output window, then close the Code editor window.

8 Click **File** on the menu bar, and then click **Close Solution** to close the solution.

You now have completed Lesson A. You can either take a break or complete the end-of-lesson questions and exercises before moving on to the next lesson.

SUMMARY

To have the computer repeat a set of instructions until some condition is met:

■ Use a repetition structure (loop). You can code a repetition structure in Visual Basic .NET using one of the following statements: For...Next, Do...Loop, and For Each...Next.

To use the For...Next statement to code a loop:

■ Refer to Figure 6-2 for the syntax of the For...Next statement. The For...Next statement can be used to code pretest loops only. In the syntax, *counter* is the name of the numeric variable that will be used to keep track of the number of times the loop instructions are processed. The *startvalue*, *endvalue*, and *stepvalue* items control how many times the loop instructions should be processed. The *startvalue*, *endvalue*, and *stepvalue* items must be numeric and can be positive or negative, integer or non-integer. If you omit the *stepvalue*, a *stepvalue* of positive 1 is used.

■ The For...Next statement performs the following three tasks:

1. The loop initializes the *counter* (the numeric variable) to the *startvalue*. This is done only once, at the beginning of the loop.

2. If the *stepvalue* is positive, the loop checks to determine whether the value in the *counter* is greater than the *endvalue*. (Or, if the *stepvalue* is negative, the loop checks to determine whether the value in the *counter* is less than the *endvalue*.) If it is, the loop stops, and processing continues with the statement following the Next clause. If it is not, the instructions within the loop are processed and the next task, task 3, is performed.

3. The loop adds the *stepvalue* to the *counter*. It then repeats tasks 2 and 3 until the *counter* is greater than (or less than, if the *stepvalue* is negative) the *endvalue*.

To flowchart a For...Next loop:

■ Use a hexagon that shows the name of the *counter*, the *startvalue*, the *stepvalue*, and the *endvalue*.

To display a message in the Output window while an application is running:

■ Use the Debug.WriteLine method. The syntax of the method is **Debug.WriteLine**(*message*), where *message* can contain a literal constant, as well as the name of a named constant, intrinsic constant, variable, or object.

To change the location and/or size of a control while an application is running:

■ Use the SetBounds method. The syntax of the method is *control*.**SetBounds**(*x*, *y*, *width*, *height*, *specified*). The *x* and *y* arguments specify the control's location, and the *width* and *height* arguments specify its size. The *x*, *y*, *width*, and *height* arguments are measured in pixels. If you do not want to change the location or size of a control, you set the appropriate argument to the number 0, and then set the *specified* argument accordingly. The *specified* argument indicates which of the first four arguments are specified in the SetBounds method. Refer to Figure 6-11 for a list of the constants used in the *specified* argument.

To use the Do...Loop statement to code a loop:

■ Refer to Figure 6-12 for the two versions of the Do...Loop statement's syntax. The Do...Loop statement can be used to code pretest and posttest loops. In a pretest loop, the loop condition appears in the Do clause; it appears in the Loop clause in a posttest loop.

■ The loop condition must evaluate to a Boolean value.

To flowchart the Do...Loop statement:

■   Use the selection/repetition diamond. The two flowlines leading out of the diamond should be marked with a "T" (for True) and an "F" (for False).

To use a counter:

■   Initialize the counter, if necessary.
■   Update the counter using an assignment statement within a repetition structure. You update a counter by incrementing (or decrementing) its value by a constant amount.

To use an accumulator:

■   Initialize the accumulator, if necessary.
■   Update the accumulator using an assignment statement within a repetition structure. You update an accumulator by incrementing (or decrementing) its value by an amount that varies.

Q U E S T I O N S

1.   Which of the following flowchart symbols represents the For...Next loop?
     a.   diamond
     b.   hexagon
     c.   oval
     d.   parallelogram
     e.   rectangle

2.   Which of the following flowchart symbols represents the *condition* in the Do...Loop statement?
     a.   diamond
     b.   hexagon
     c.   oval
     d.   parallelogram
     e.   rectangle

3.   Assuming intCount is a numeric variable, how many times will the `Debug.WriteLine(intCount)` instruction be processed?

```
For intCount = 1 to 6
        Debug.WriteLine(intCount)
Next intCount
```

     a.   0
     b.   1
     c.   5
     d.   6
     e.   7

4.   What is the value of intCount when the loop in Question 3 stops?
     a.   1
     b.   5
     c.   6
     d.   7
     e.   8

5. Assuming intCount is a numeric variable, how many times will the
    Debug.WriteLine(intCount) instruction be processed?

    ```
    For intCount = 4 to 11 Step 2
            Debug.WriteLine(intCount)
    Next intCount
    ```

    a. 0
    b. 3
    c. 4
    d. 5
    e. 12

6. What is the value of intCount when the loop in Question 5 stops?
    a. 4
    b. 6
    c. 10
    d. 11
    e. 12

7. When the *stepvalue* in a For...Next statement is positive, the instructions within the
    loop are processed only when the *counter* is _____ the *endvalue*.
    a. equal to
    b. greater than
    c. greater than or equal to
    d. less than
    e. less than or equal to

8. Which of the following is a valid For clause?
    a. `For intTemp = 1.5 To 5 Step .5`
    b. `For intTemp = 5 To 1 Step .25`
    c. `For intTemp = 1 To 3 Step -1`
    d. `For intTemp = 3 To 1`
    e. `For intTemp = 1 To 10`

9. The For...Next statement performs three tasks, as shown below. Put these tasks in their
    proper order by placing the numbers 1 through 3 on the line to the left of the task.

    _____ Adds the *stepvalue* to the *counter*.

    _____ Initializes the *counter* to the *startvalue*.

    _____ Checks to determine whether the value in the *counter* is greater (less) than
    the *endvalue*.

10. Assume that you do not know the precise number of times the loop instructions should
    be processed. You can use the _____ statement to code this loop.
    a. Do...Loop
    b. For...Next
    c. a or b

11. Assume that you know the precise number of times the loop instructions should be
    processed. You can use the _____ statement to code this loop.
    a. Do...Loop
    b. For...Next
    c. a or b

12. The _____ loop processes the loop instructions at least once, whereas the _____ loop instructions might not be processed at all.

    a.   posttest, pretest

    b.   pretest, posttest

13. Counters and accumulators must be initialized and _____.

    a.   added

    b.   counted

    c.   displayed

    d.   printed

    e.   updated

14. Which of the following statements will correctly update the counter variable named intNumber?

    a.   `intNumber = 0`

    b.   `intNumber = 1`

    c.   `intNumber = intNumber + intNumber`

    d.   `intNumber = intNumber + sngSales`

    e.   `intNumber = intNumber + 1`

15. Which of the following statements will correctly update the accumulator variable named sngTotal?

    a.   `sngTotal = 0`

    b.   `sngTotal = 1`

    c.   `sngTotal = sngTotal + sngTotal`

    d.   `sngTotal = sngTotal + sngSales`

    e.   `sngTotal = sngTotal + 1`

16. Which of the following clauses stops the loop when the value in the intAge variable is less than the number 0?

    a.   `Do While intAge >= 0`

    b.   `Do Until intAge < 0`

    c.   `Loop While intAge >= 0`

    d.   `Loop Until intAge < 0`

    e.   All of the above.

17. How many times will the `Debug.WriteLine(intCount)` instruction in the following code be processed?

```
Dim intCount As Integer
Do While intCount > 3
        Debug.WriteLine(intCount)
        intCount = intCount + 1
Loop
```

    a.   0

    b.   1

    c.   2

    d.   3

    e.   4

18. How many times will the `Debug.WriteLine(intCount)` instruction in the following code be processed?

```
Dim intCount As Integer
Do
        Debug.WriteLine(intCount)
        intCount = intCount + 1
Loop While intCount > 3
```

a. 0
b. 1
c. 2
d. 3
e. 4

Refer to Figure 6-28 to answer Questions 19 through 22.

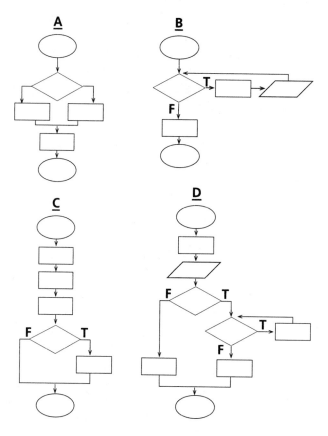

Figure 6-28

19. Which of the following programming structures are used in flowchart A in Figure 6-28? (Select all that apply.)

a. sequence
b. selection
c. repetition

20. Which of the following programming structures are used in flowchart B in Figure 6-28? (Select all that apply.)

a. sequence
b. selection
c. repetition

21. Which of the following programming structures are used in flowchart C in Figure 6-28? (Select all that apply.)
    a. sequence
    b. selection
    c. repetition

22. Which of the following programming structures are used in flowchart D in Figure 6-28? (Select all that apply.)
    a. sequence
    b. selection
    c. repetition

23. Assume that a program allows the user to enter one or more numbers. The first input instruction will get the first number only and is referred to as the _____ read.
    a. entering
    b. initializer
    c. priming
    d. starter

24. Which of the following statements can be used to change the width and height of the NameLabel control?
    a. `Me.NameLabel.Bounds(0, 0, 50, 60, BoundsSpecified.Width And BoundsSpecified.Height)`
    b. `Me.NameLabel.Bounds(50, 60, 0, 0, BoundsSpecified.Width Or BoundsSpecified.Height)`
    c. `Me.NameLabel.SetBounds(0, 0, 50, 60, BoundsSpecified.Width Or BoundsSpecified.Height)`
    d. `Me.NameLabel.SetBounds(0, 0, 50, 60, BoundsSpecified.Size)`
    e. Both c and d.

25. Which of the following statements can be used to change the location of the NameLabel control's top border on the form?
    a. `Me.NameLabel.Bounds(0, 50, 0, 0, BoundsSpecified.Top)`
    b. `Me.NameLabel.Bounds(0, 50, 0, 0, BoundsSpecified.X)`
    c. `Me.NameLabel.SetBounds(0, 50, 0, 0, BoundsSpecified.Top)`
    d. `Me.NameLabel.SetBounds(0, 50, 0, 0, BoundsSpecified.YBorder)`
    e. None of the above.

EXERCISES

1. Write a Visual Basic .NET Do clause that processes the loop instructions as long as the value in the intQuantity variable is greater than the number 0. Use the While keyword.

2. Rewrite the Do clause from Exercise 1 using the Until keyword.

3. Write a Visual Basic .NET Do clause that stops the loop when the value in the intStock variable is less than or equal to the value in the intReorder variable. Use the Until keyword.

4. Rewrite the Do clause from Exercise 3 using the While keyword.

5. Write a Visual Basic .NET Loop clause that processes the loop instructions as long as the value in the strLetter variable is either Y or y. Use the While keyword.

6. Rewrite the Loop clause from Exercise 5 using the Until keyword.

7. Write a Visual Basic .NET Do clause that processes the loop instructions as long as the value in the strName variable is not "Done" (in any case). Use the While keyword.

8. Rewrite the Do clause from Exercise 7 using the Until keyword.

9. Write a Visual Basic .NET assignment statement that updates the intQuantity counter variable by 2.

10. Write a Visual Basic .NET assignment statement that updates the intTotal counter variable by -3.

11. Write a Visual Basic .NET assignment statement that updates the intTotalPurchases accumulator variable by the value stored in the intPurchases variable.

12. Write a Visual Basic .NET assignment statement that subtracts 100 from the sngSales accumulator variable.

13. Assume that a procedure declares an Integer variable named intEvenNum and initializes it to 2. Write the Visual Basic .NET code for a pretest loop that uses the intEvenNum variable to display the even integers between 1 and 9 in the Output window. Use the For...Next statement.

14. Rewrite the pretest loop from Exercise 13 using the Do...Loop statement.

15. Change the pretest loop from Exercise 14 to a posttest loop.

16. Write the Visual Basic .NET code that corresponds to the flowchart shown in Figure 6-29. (Display the calculated result in the Output window.)

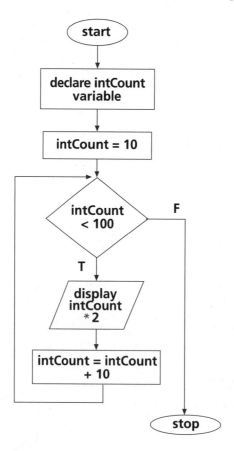

Figure 6-29

17. Write a For...Next statement that displays the numbers from 0 through 117, in increments of 9, in the Output window.

18. Write a For...Next statement that first calculates and then displays the square of the even numbers from 2 through 12 in the Output window.

19. Complete the following code, which should display the word "Hello" in the Output window 10 times:

```
Dim intCount As Integer = 1
Do _____
    Debug.WriteLine("Hello")
    intCount = intCount + 1
Loop
```

20. Complete the following code, which should display the word "Hello" in the Output window 10 times:

```
Dim intCount As Integer = 1
Do
    Debug.WriteLine("Hello")
    intCount = intCount + 1
Loop _____
```

21. What will the following code display in the Output window?

```
Dim intX As Integer
Do While intX < 5
    Debug.WriteLine(intX)
    intX = intX + 1
Loop
```

22. What will the following code display in the Output window?

```
Dim intX As Integer
Do
    Debug.WriteLine(intX)
    intX = intX + 1
Loop Until intX > 5
```

23. An instruction is missing from the following code. What is the missing instruction and where does it belong in the code?

```
Dim intNum As Integer = 1
Do While intNum < 5
    Debug.WriteLine(intNum)
Loop
```

24. An instruction is missing from the following code. What is the missing instruction and where does it belong in the code?

```
Dim intNum As Integer = 10
Do
    Debug.WriteLine(intNum)
Loop Until intNum = 0
```

25. The following code should display the commission (sngSales * .1) for each sales amount that is entered. The code is not working properly, because an instruction is missing. What is the missing instruction and where does it belong in the code?

```
Dim sngSales As Single
sngSales = Val(InputBox("Enter a sales amount", "Sales"))
Do While sngSales > 0
    Debug.WriteLine(sngSales * .1)
Loop
```

26. The following code should display the commission (sngSales * .1) for each sales amount that is entered. The code is not working properly. What is wrong with the code and how will you fix it?

```
Dim sngSales As Single
sngSales = Val(InputBox("Enter a sales amount", "Sales"))
Do
     sngSales = Val(InputBox("Enter a sales amount", "Sales"))
     Debug.WriteLine(sngSales * .1)
Loop Until sngSales <= 0
```

27. What will the following code display in the Output window?

```
Dim intTotEmp As Integer
Do While intTotEmp <= 5
     Debug.WriteLine(intTotEmp)
     intTotEmp = intTotEmp + 2
Loop
```

28. What will the following code display in the Output window?

```
Dim intTotEmp As Integer = 1
Do
     Debug.WriteLine(intTotEmp)
     intTotEmp = intTotEmp + 2
Loop Until intTotEmp >= 3
```

29. Write the Visual Basic .NET statement that changes the size of the FacePictureBox control to a width of 35 and a height of 50, and also the location of the control's left border to 10.

Exercise 30 is a Discovery Exercise. Discovery Exercises, which may include topics that are not covered in this lesson, allow you to "discover" the solutions to problems on your own.

discovery ▶   **30.** What is the difference between the Debug.WriteLine and Debug.Write methods?

LESSON B
objectives

After completing this lesson, you will be able to:

- Access the controls in the Controls collection
- Code the repetition structure using the For Each...Next statement
- Create an object variable
- Create a collection
- Create parallel collections
- Enable and disable a control

A control's index, which indicates its position in the Controls collection, is not the same as its TabIndex, which indicates its position in the tab order sequence.

When you use the toolbox to add controls to a form, the first control added to the form is initially assigned an index of 0 (zero) in the Controls collection. However, when you add the second control to the form, the second control is assigned an index of 0 (zero) and the first control's index is changed to 1 (one). This process occurs each time you add a new control to the form. Therefore, the last control added to a form is actually the first control in the Controls collection, because its index is zero.

Using Collections

The Controls Collection

The controls contained on a Windows form belong to the **Controls collection** in Visual Basic .NET. A **collection** is simply a group of one or more individual objects treated as one unit. The Controls collection, for example, contains one or more **Control objects**, which can be text boxes, labels, buttons, and so on.

Visual Basic .NET automatically assigns a unique number, called an **index**, to each Control object in the Controls collection. The index indicates the Control object's position in the collection. The first Control object in the Controls collection has an index of 0 (zero), the second has an index of 1 (one), and so on. You can refer to a Control object in the Controls collection using either the syntax **Controls.Item**(*index*) or the syntax **Controls**(*index*). In other words, specifying the Item property is optional in the syntax. In each syntax version, *index* is the Control object's index—in other words, its position number in the Controls collection.

Figure 6-30 shows three examples of using the Controls collection to refer to the controls on a form.

Examples and results
Example 1 `Me.MsgLabel.Text = Controls.Item(0).Name` **Result** displays (in the MsgLabel control) the name of the first control contained in the Controls collection

Example 2
`Dim intX As Integer`
`For intX = 0 To Controls.Count - 1`
`    MessageBox.Show(Controls.Item(intX).Name, "Name", _`
`        MessageBoxButtons.OK, MessageBoxIcon.Information)`
`Next intX`
 	
Result
displays (in message boxes) the name of each control contained in the Controls collection

Example 3
`Dim intX As Integer`
`Do While intX < Controls.Count`
`    If TypeOf Controls.Item(intX) Is TextBox Then`
`        Controls.Item(intX).Text = ""`
`    End If`
`    intX = intX + 1`
`Loop`
 	
Result
clears the contents of the text box controls on the form

Figure 6-30: Examples of using the Controls collection

The `Controls.Item(0)` portion of the statement shown in Example 1 refers to the first Control object in the Controls collection. You also could have used `Controls(0)` to refer to the first Control object. The statement in Example 1 displays the contents of the Control object's Name property in the MsgLabel control.

The Dim statement in Example 2 declares and initializes (to the number zero) an Integer variable named intX, which is used as the *counter* variable in the For...Next statement. The For clause indicates that the loop instructions should be performed for each Control object in the Controls collection, beginning with the Control object whose index is 0 (the *startvalue*) and ending with the Control object whose index is `Controls.Count - 1` (the *endvalue*). `Controls.Count` refers to the Controls collection's **Count property**, which stores the total number of Control objects in the collection. The *endvalue* in the For...Next statement must be one number less than the value stored in the Count property, because the index of the last Control object within the Controls collection is always one number less than the total number of Control objects in the collection. For example, if a form contains five controls, the Controls collection's Count property stores the number five, and the Control objects in the Controls collection have indexes of 0, 1, 2, 3, and 4. The code in Example 2 displays the name of each Control object in a message box.

Example 3 in Figure 6-30 shows how you can use a Do...Loop statement rather than a For...Next statement to refer to each Control object within the Controls collection. The Dim statement in Example 3 declares and initializes (to the number zero) an Integer variable named intX. The intX variable is a counter variable used to keep track of the number of times the loop instructions are processed. The `Do While intX < Controls.Count` clause indicates that the loop instructions should be processed while the value stored in the intX variable is less than the value stored in the Controls collection's Count property. You also could have written the Do clause in this pretest loop as `Do While intX <= Controls.Count - 1`, or as `Do Until intX = Controls.Count`.

Study the code that appears within the Do...Loop statement in Example 3. The If clause's *condition* uses the TypeOf...Is comparison operator, which you learned about in Tutorial 5, to determine whether the current Control object—Controls.Item(intX)— is a text box. If the *condition* evaluates to True, a zero-length string is assigned to the control's Text property; otherwise, the control's Text property is left as is. The `intX = intX + 1` instruction then updates the value stored in the counter variable, intX. You can use the code shown in Example 3 to clear the contents of any text boxes on a form.

As you already know, when you press the period while entering code in the Code editor window, the properties and methods associated with the current object appear in a list box. For example, when entering `Controls.Item(intX).Text` in the Code editor window, a list box appears when you press the period after typing the word "Controls" and when you press the period after typing the ending parentheses. The list box that appears when you press the period after typing the word "Controls" contains the properties and methods associated with the Controls collection; included in the listing are the Count and Item properties. The list box that appears when you press the period after typing the ending parentheses contains the properties and methods associated with an individual Control object in the Controls collection. Because the Controls collection can contain many different types of Control objects—such as text boxes, labels, and buttons—this listing includes only the properties and methods that are common to most controls, such as the Name and Text properties and the Focus method. It does not include properties and methods associated with only a few control types. For example, the listing does not include the BorderStyle property, because this property is not applicable to most controls. Therefore, you will not be able to use the instruction `Controls.Item(0).BorderStyle = BorderStyle.None` to change the BorderStyle property of the first control in the Controls collection, even if the control is a text box or label, both of which have a BorderStyle property. To change the BorderStyle property of a text box or label control in the Controls collection, you first must create an object variable, and then assign the address of the text box or label control to the object variable.

Object Variables

An **object variable** is a memory location that can store the address of an object. The address indicates where the object is located in the computer's internal memory. In most cases, you create an object variable using the syntax **Dim** *variablename* **As** *objecttype*. In the syntax, *variablename* is the name of the object variable and typically begins with the three-character ID "obj" (which stands for "object"). *Objecttype* is the type of object—for example, Control, TextBox, Button, or Label—whose address will be stored in the variable. The statement `Dim objStateTextBox As TextBox`, for instance, declares an object variable named objStateTextBox. Because the objStateTextBox variable is declared using the TextBox *objecttype*, it can store only the address of a text box control. Similarly, the statement `Dim objLabel As Label` declares an object variable named objLabel, which can store only the address of a label control.

Visual Basic .NET automatically initializes object variables to the keyword Nothing, which simply means that the object variable does not currently contain an address. You assign an object's address to an object variable using an assignment statement that follows the syntax *objectvariable* = *object*, where *objectvariable* is the name of an object variable, and *object* is the name of the object whose address you want assigned to the *objectvariable*. The statement `objStateTextBox = Me.StateTextBox`, for example, assigns the address of the StateTextBox control to the objStateTextBox variable. Likewise, the statement `objLabel = Controls.Item(1)` assigns the address of the second control in the Controls collection to the objLabel variable.

The *object* must be the same object type as the *objectvariable*. In other words, text boxes are assigned to object variables declared using the TextBox object type, and label controls are assigned to object variables declared using the Label object type. An error occurs if you attempt to store the address of a different type of *object* in the *objectvariable*.

When you assign a control from the Controls collection to a TextBox object variable, the Code editor displays a listing of text box properties and methods when you refer to the object variable in code. Similarly, when you assign a control from the Controls collection to a Label object variable, the Code editor displays the properties and methods for label controls. You observe how this works in the next set of steps.

tip

You also can assign the address of an object to an object variable when the object variable is declared. For example, the statement `Dim objLabel As Label = Me.NameLabel` declares the objLabel variable and assigns the address of the NameLabel control to the variable.

To use an object variable in code:

1 Start Microsoft Visual Studio .NET, if necessary, then close the Start Page window. Click **File** on the menu bar, and then click **Open Solution**. The Open Solution dialog box opens. Open the **Object Variable Solution** (Object Variable Solution.sln) file, which is contained in the VBNET\Tut06\Object Variable Solution folder.

2 If the designer window is not open, right-click **Object Variable Form.vb** in the Solution Explorer window, then click **View Designer**. Auto-hide the Toolbox, Solution Explorer, and Properties windows, if necessary. The Object Variable application's user interface is shown in Figure 6-31. The interface contains three label controls and two button controls.

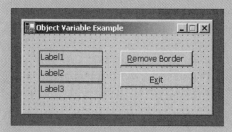

Figure 6-31: Object Variable application's user interface

3 Right-click the **form**, then click **View Code** to open the Code editor window.

The RemoveButton Click event procedure should remove the border from the three label controls. First try setting the BorderStyle property using the instruction `Controls.Item(intX).BorderStyle = BorderStyle.None`.

4 Click the blank line below the If clause in the RemoveButton Click event procedure, then press **Tab** four times to indent the line. Type **controls.item(intx).** (be sure to type the period after the ending parentheses). A listing of the properties and methods that are common to most controls appears, as shown in Figure 6-32. Notice that the BorderStyle property does not appear in the listing.

the BorderStyle property does not appear in the listing

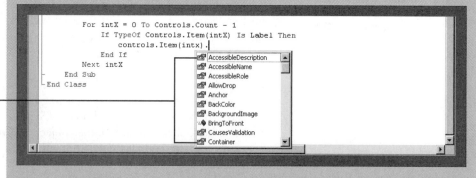

Figure 6-32: Listing of common properties and methods

5 Type **borderstyle = borderstyle.none** and press **Enter**. The Code editor displays a jagged line below `Controls.Item(intX).BorderStyle`. Place the mouse pointer on the jagged line, as shown in Figure 6-33. A message appears in a message box and indicates that 'borderstyle' is not a member of 'System.Windows.Forms.Control'. In other words, a Control object does not have a BorderStyle property.

```
For intX = 0 To Controls.Count - 1
    If TypeOf Controls.Item(intX) Is Label Then
        Controls.Item(intX).borderstyle = BorderStyle.None
                                   'borderstyle' is not a member of 'System.Windows.Forms.Control'.
    End If
Next intX
End Sub
```

Figure 6-33: Message displayed in the message box

6 Highlight the `Controls.Item(intX).borderstyle = BorderStyle.None` instruction, then press **Delete** to delete the instruction from the procedure.

Now use an object variable to change the BorderStyle property.

7 Click the blank line below the `Dim intX As Integer` instruction, then press **Tab** two times to indent the line. Type **dim objLabel as label** in the blank line.

8 Click the blank line below the If clause, then press **Tab** four times to indent the line. Type **objlabel = controls.item(intx)** and press **Enter**.

9 Type **objlabel.** (be sure to type the period). A listing of the properties and methods for a label control appears, as shown in Figure 6-34. Notice that the BorderStyle property is included in the listing.

BorderStyle property

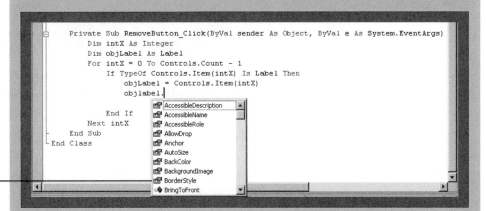

Figure 6-34: Listing of properties and methods for a label control

10 Click **BorderStyle** in the listing, then press **Tab**. Type **=**. The valid settings for the BorderStyle property appear in a list box. Click **BorderStyle.None** in the listing, and then press **Tab**. The completed procedure is shown in Figure 6-35.

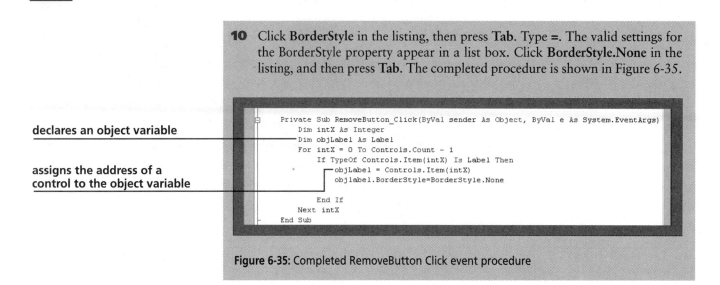

declares an object variable

assigns the address of a
control to the object variable

```
Private Sub RemoveButton_Click(ByVal sender As Object, ByVal e As System.EventArgs)
    Dim intX As Integer
    Dim objLabel As Label
    For intX = 0 To Controls.Count - 1
        If TypeOf Controls.Item(intX) Is Label Then
            objLabel = Controls.Item(intX)
            objlabel.BorderStyle=BorderStyle.None
        End If
    Next intX
End Sub
```

Figure 6-35: Completed RemoveButton Click event procedure

Now test the RemoveButton Click event procedure to verify that it is working correctly.

To test the RemoveButton Click event procedure:

1 Click **File** on the menu bar, and then click **Save All**. Click **Debug** on the menu bar, and then click **Start**.

2 Click the **Remove Border** button. The button's Click event procedure removes the border from the three label controls.

3 Click the **Exit** button to end the application. When you return to the Code editor window, close the Output window, then close the Code editor window.

You are finished with this application, so you can close it.

4 Click **File** on the menu bar, and then click **Close Solution**.

In addition to using For...Next and Do...Loop statements to refer to each control in the Controls collection, you also can use a For Each...Next statement.

The For Each...Next Statement

You can use the **For Each...Next statement** to code a loop whose instructions you want processed for each object in a collection. Figure 6-36 shows the syntax of the For Each...Next statement. It also shows how you can rewrite the code shown in Figure 6-35, as well as the code shown in Examples 2 and 3 in Figure 6-30, using a For Each...Next statement.

You can use the `Exit For` statement to exit the For Each...Next statement prematurely—in other words, to exit it before it has finished processing. You may need to do so if the loop encounters an error when processing its instructions.

You can nest For Each...Next statements, which means that you can place one For Each...Next statement nested within another For Each...Next statement.

Syntax

```
For Each element In group
      [statements]
Next element
```

Examples and results

Example 1
```
Dim objControl As Control, objLabel As Label
For Each objControl In Controls
      If TypeOf objControl Is Label Then
            objLabel = objControl
            objLabel.BorderStyle = BorderStyle.None
      End If
Next objControl
```

Result
removes the border from the label controls on the form

Example 2
```
Dim objControl As Control
For Each objControl In Controls
      MessageBox.Show(objControl.Name, "Name", _
            MessageBoxButtons.OK, MessageBoxIcon.Information)
Next objControl
```

Result
displays (in message boxes) the name of each control contained in the Controls collection

Example 3
```
Dim objControl As Control
For Each objControl In Controls
      If TypeOf objControl Is TextBox Then
            objControl.Text = ""
      End If
Next objControl
```

Result
clears the contents of the text box controls on the form

Figure 6-36: Syntax and examples of the For Each...Next statement

You also can use the For Each...Next statement to access the elements in an array, which is simply a collection of variables. You learn about arrays in Tutorial 11.

As Figure 6-36 indicates, the For Each...Next statement begins with the For Each clause and ends with the Next clause. Between the two clauses you enter the instructions that you want the loop to repeat for each object in the collection.

In the For Each...Next statement's syntax, *element* is the name of an object variable that the computer can use to keep track of each object in the collection, and *group* is the name of the collection. The object type of the *element* must match the type of objects contained in the *group*. For example, if the *group* contains TextBox objects, then the *element*'s object type must be TextBox. In Figure 6-36's examples, *element* is a Control object variable named objControl, and *group* is the Controls collection. (Recall that the Controls collection contains Control objects.)

The For Each clause first verifies that the *group* contains at least one object. If the *group* is empty—in other words, if the collection does not contain any objects—the instructions within the loop are skipped, and processing continues with the instruction following the Next clause. However, if the *group* does contain at least one object, the For Each clause assigns the address of the first object in the *group* to the *element* variable, and then the computer processes the instructions within the loop. The Next clause sends the computer to the beginning of the loop—the For Each clause—which checks whether the *group* contains another object. If it does, the address of the next object in the *group* is assigned to the *element* variable, and the loop instructions are processed again. This procedure is followed for each object in the *group*.

Next, learn how to show the For Each...Next loop in a flowchart and in pseudocode.

Including the For Each...Next Loop in a Flowchart and Pseudocode

Figure 6-37 shows the flowchart and pseudocode corresponding to the code shown in Example 1 in Figure 6-36.

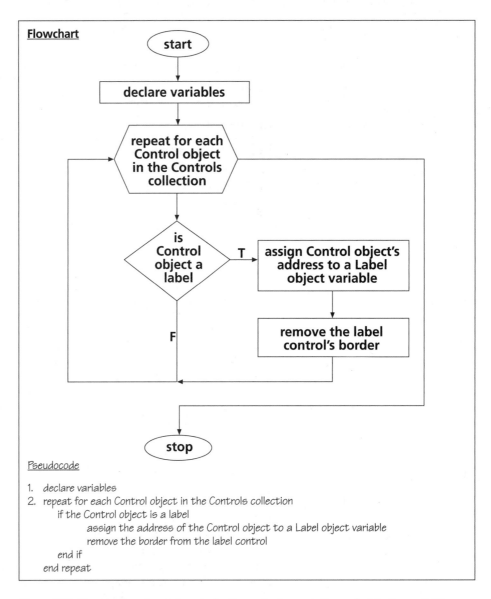

Figure 6-37: Flowchart and pseudocode for the code shown in Example 1 in Figure 6-36

Like the For...Next loop, the For Each...Next loop is represented in a flow-chart by a hexagon. Typically, the hexagon contains a message similar to "repeat for each *object* in the *collection*", where *collection* is the collection's name, and *object* is the type of object in the *collection*.

On your computer's hard disk is an application that contains three examples of the For Each...Next loop.

To open the For Each application:

1 Click **File** on the menu bar, and then click **Open Solution**. The Open Solution dialog box opens. Open the **For Each Solution** (For Each Solution.sln) file, which is contained in the VBNET\Tut06\For Each Solution folder.

2 If the designer window is not open, right-click **For Each Form.vb** in the Solution Explorer window, then click **View Designer**. Auto-hide the Toolbox, Solution Explorer, and Properties windows, if necessary. The For Each application's user interface is shown in Figure 6-38.

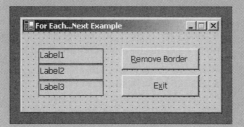

Figure 6-38: For Each application's user interface

The interface shown in Figure 6-38 contains five controls: three labels and two buttons. View and then test the code entered in the Remove Border button's Click event procedure.

To view and then test the code entered in the RemoveButton Click event procedure:

1 Right-click the **form**, and then click **View Code**. Figure 6-39 shows the code entered in the RemoveButton Click event procedure.

```
Private Sub RemoveButton_Click(ByVal sender As Object, ByVal e As System.EventArgs)
    Dim objControl As Control, objLabel As Label
    For Each objControl In Controls
        If TypeOf objControl Is Label Then
            objLabel = objControl
            objLabel.BorderStyle = BorderStyle.None
        End If
    Next objControl
End Sub
```

Figure 6-39: Code entered in the RemoveButton Click event procedure

2 Start the application, then click the **Remove Border** button. The border is removed from each label control.

3 Click the **Exit** button to end the application. When you return to the Code editor window, close the Output window, then close the Code editor window.

You are finished with this application, so you can close it.

4 Click **File** on the menu bar, and then click **Close Solution**.

Figure 6-40 describes how the computer processes the instructions entered in the Remove Border button's Click event procedure.

1. The computer creates and initializes (to Nothing) a Control object variable named objControl and a Label object variable named objLabel.

2. The For Each clause checks whether the Controls collection contains at least one Control object. It does, so the For Each clause assigns the address of the first Control object in the collection to the objControl variable.

3. The If clause determines whether the objControl variable contains the address of a label control. Assume that it does not. In that case, the If...Then...Else statement ends.

4. The Next clause returns processing to the beginning of the loop (the For Each clause).

5. The For Each clause checks whether the Controls collection contains another Control object. It does, so the For Each clause assigns the address of the second Control object in the collection to the objControl variable.

6. The If clause determines whether the objControl variable contains the address of a label control. Assume that it does. In that case, the instructions in the If...Then...Else statement's true path first assign the label control's address to the objLabel variable, and then set the label control's BorderStyle property to BorderStyle.None. Then the If...Then...Else statement ends.

7. The Next clause returns processing to the beginning of the loop (the For Each clause).

8. The For Each clause checks whether the Controls collection contains another Control object. It does, so the For Each clause assigns the address of the third Control object in the collection to the objControl variable.

9. The If clause determines whether the objControl variable contains the address of a label control. Assume that it does. In that case, the instructions in the If...Then...Else statement's true path first assign the label control's address to the objLabel variable, and then set the label control's BorderStyle property to BorderStyle.None. Then the If...Then...Else statement ends.

10. The Next clause returns processing to the beginning of the loop (the For Each clause).

11. The For Each clause checks whether the Controls collection contains another Control object. It does, so the For Each...Next statement assigns the address of the fourth Control object in the collection to the objControl variable.

12. The If clause determines whether the objControl variable contains the address of a label control. Assume that it does not. In that case, the If...Then...Else statement ends.

13. The Next clause returns processing to the beginning of the loop (the For Each clause).

14. The For Each clause checks whether the Controls collection contains another Control object. It does, so the For Each...Next statement assigns the address of the fifth Control object in the collection to the objControl variable.

15. The If clause determines whether the objControl variable contains the address of a label control. Assume that it does. In that case, the instructions in the If...Then...Else statement's true path first assign the label control's address to the objLabel variable, and then set the label control's BorderStyle property to BorderStyle.None. Then the If...Then...Else statement ends.

16. The Next clause returns processing to the beginning of the loop (the For Each clause).

17. The For Each clause checks whether the Controls collection contains another Control object. It does not, so the For Each...Next statement ends. Processing continues with the statement following the Next clause.

Figure 6-40: Processing steps for the code entered in the Remove Border button's Click event procedure

Next, you learn how to create your own collections in Visual Basic .NET.

Creating a User-Defined Collection

Visual Basic .NET automatically creates the Controls collection when you add controls to a form. You also can create your own collections, referred to as **user-defined collections**, in Visual Basic .NET. A user-defined collection allows you to group related controls together. For instance, you can create a collection of text boxes. Or, you can create a collection that contains the controls involved in a bonus calculation task.

You create a user-defined collection using the syntax *accessibility collectionname* **As New Collection**(), where *accessibility* is typically either the keyword Dim (for a local collection) or the keyword Private (for a form-level collection), and *collectionname* is the name of the collection. You then use the Collection object's Add method to add objects to the collection. The syntax of the Add method is *collection*.**Add**(*object*[, *key*]), where *collection* is the name of the collection, *object* is the name of the object, and *key* (which is optional) is a string that uniquely identifies the *object* in the *collection*. You can refer to an object in a user-defined collection using either the object's index or its *key*. Different from the Controls collection, the first control added to a user-defined collection has an index of 1 (one) rather than 0 (zero). Figure 6-41 shows examples of creating and adding objects to collections.

Examples

Example 1
```
Dim TextBoxCollection As New Collection()
TextBoxCollection.Add(Me.NameTextBox)
TextBoxCollection.Add(Me.AddressTextBox)
TextBoxCollection.Add(Me.StateTextBox)
```

Example 2
```
Private MyCollection As New Collection()
MyCollection.Add(Me.SalesTextBox, "Sales")
MyCollection.Add(Me.TotalSalesLabel, "Total")
MyCollection.Add(Me.CalculateButton, "Calculate")
```

Example 3
```
Dim ButtonCollection As New Collection()
Dim objControl As Control
For Each objControl In Controls
    If TypeOf objControl Is Button Then
        ButtonCollection.Add(objControl)
    End If
Next objControl
```

Figure 6-41: Examples of creating and adding objects to collections

The code shown in Example 1 in Figure 6-41 first creates a collection named TextBoxCollection, and then uses the Add method to add three TextBox objects to the collection. The NameTextBox is assigned an index of 1 (one), the AddressTextBox an index of 2, and the StateTextBox an index of 3. You use the index to refer to an object in the collection. For example, to display the contents of the NameTextBox in the Output window, you use either `Debug.WriteLine(TextBoxCollection.Item(1).Text)` or `Debug.WriteLine(TextBoxCollection(1).Text)`. (Recall that specifying the Item property is optional when referring to an object in a collection.)

The code shown in Example 2 in Figure 6-41 first creates a collection named MyCollection. It then uses the Add method to add three different types of objects to the collection: a text box, a label, and a button. Notice that the Add methods in this example include the *key* argument, which is assigned to the object (along with the index) when the object is added to the collection. For example, when the SalesTextBox is added to the collection, it is assigned the number 1 as its index and the string "Sales" as its *key*. Likewise, the TotalSalesLabel is assigned the number 2 and the string "Total", and the CalculateButton is assigned the number 3 and the string "Calculate". You can use either the index or the *key* to refer to an object in the MyCollection collection. For example, to display the contents of the TotalSalesLabel control in the Output window, you can use `Debug.WriteLine(MyCollection.Item(2).Text)`. Or, you can use `Debug.WriteLine(MyCollection.Item("Total").Text)`.

The Dim statements shown in Example 3 in Figure 6-41 create a collection named ButtonCollection and a Control object variable named objControl. The For Each...Next statement then repeats the loop instructions for each Control object in the Controls collection. The loop instructions first determine the object type of the Control object. If the Control object is a button, then the object is added to the ButtonCollection collection; otherwise, it is skipped over.

You can use the Collection object's Count property to determine the number of objects contained in a user-defined collection. The syntax of the Collection object's Count property is *collection*.**Count**, where *collection* is the name of the collection. For example, to display (in the Output window) the number of objects contained in the ButtonCollection, you use `Debug.WriteLine(ButtonCollection.Count)`.

In addition to the Add method, Visual Basic .NET also provides a Remove method, which you use to remove an object from a collection. The syntax of the Remove method is *collection*.**Remove**(*item*), where *collection* is the name of the collection, and *item* is either the index or *key* of the object you want to remove. For example, to remove the CalculateButton from the MyCollection collection, which is created in Example 2 in Figure 6-41, you use either `MyCollection.Remove(3)` or `MyCollection.Remove("Calculate")`.

You will use collections in the Grade Calculator application, which you begin coding in this lesson.

The Grade Calculator Application

Recall that your task in this tutorial is to create an application that Professor Carver's students can use to calculate their grade during the semester. A student must complete three projects (worth 10 points each) and a midterm and final (worth 50 points each). If the student accumulates at least 90% of the total points, he or she is assigned a grade of A; 80% is a B; 70% is a C; 60% is a D; and below 60% is an F. Open the Grade Calculator application, which is stored in the VBNET\Tut06\Grade Solution folder on your computer's hard disk.

To open the Grade Calculator application:

1 Click **File** on the menu bar, and then click **Open Solution**. The Open Solution dialog box opens. Open the **Grade Solution** (Grade Solution.sln) file, which is contained in the VBNET\Tut06\Grade Solution folder.

2 If the designer window is not open, right-click **Grade Form.vb** in the Solution Explorer window, then click **View Designer**.

3 Auto-hide the Toolbox, Solution Explorer, and Properties windows, if necessary. The Grade Calculator application's user interface is shown in Figure 6-42.

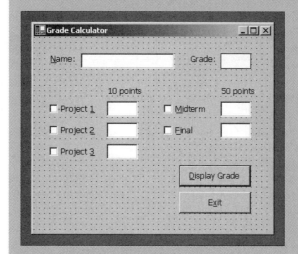

Figure 6-42: Grade Calculator application's user interface

The interface contains labels, check boxes, text boxes, and buttons. To determine the grade, the student needs simply to select the appropriate check boxes, then enter the scores in the corresponding text boxes, and then select the Display Grade button. The Display Grade button's Click event procedure displays the letter grade based on the work that has been completed so far.

Figure 6-43 shows the TOE chart for the Grade Calculator application.

Task	Object	Event

1. For each selected check box,
   a. add the score found in its associated text box to the total earned points accumulator
   b. if the check box is for a project, then add 10 to the total possible points accumulator; otherwise, add 50
2. calculate the ratio by dividing the value in the total earned points accumulator by the value in the total possible points accumulator
3. display the appropriate letter grade, based on the ratio, in the GradeLabel control
	DisplayButton	Click

End the application	ExitButton	Click
Assign the check boxes to a collection, and assign the project and test text boxes to a collection	GradeForm	Load
Verify that the user wants to exit the application, then take the appropriate action based on the user's response	GradeForm	Closing
Display the letter grade (from DisplayButton)	GradeLabel	None
Clear the contents of the GradeLabel control	Proj1TextBox, Proj2TextBox, Proj3TextBox, MidtermTextBox, FinalTextBox	TextChanged
Get and display the name and the project and test scores	NameTextBox, Proj1TextBox, Proj2TextBox, Proj3TextBox, MidtermTextBox, FinalTextBox	None
Highlight (select) the existing text	NameTextBox, Proj1TextBox, Proj2TextBox, Proj3TextBox, MidtermTextBox, FinalTextBox	Enter

1. If the user selects the check box
   a. enable the corresponding text box
   b. send the focus to the corresponding text box
2. If the user deselects the check box
   a. clear the contents of the corresponding text box
   b. disable the corresponding text box
	Proj1CheckBox, Proj2CheckBox, Proj3CheckBox, MidtermCheckBox, FinalCheckBox	Click

Figure 6-43: TOE chart for the Grade Calculator application

The ExitButton's Click event procedure and the TextChanged event procedure for the project and test text boxes have already been coded for you. In this lesson, you code the GradeForm's Load event procedure and the Click event procedure for the five check boxes. You code the remaining event procedures in Lesson C.

Coding the GradeForm's Load Event Procedure

According to the TOE chart shown in Figure 6-43, the GradeForm's Load event procedure is responsible for assigning the check boxes to a collection, and assigning the project and test text boxes to a different collection. Before you can make the assignments, you need to create the collections. The collections will be used by more than one procedure in the form, so you will declare them as form-level collections.

To declare two form-level collections, then begin coding the GradeForm's Load event procedure:

1 Right-click the **form**, and then click **View Code**.

2 Click the blank line below the comment `'declare form-level collections`. Press **Tab** to indent the line, then type **private mCheckBoxCollection as new collection()** and press **Enter**.

3 Type **private mTextBoxCollection as new collection()** and press **Enter**.

Now open the GradeForm's Load event procedure and assign the check boxes to the mCheckBoxCollection.

4 Click the **Class Name** list arrow, then click **(Base Class Events)** in the list. Click the **Method Name** list arrow, then click **Load** in the list. The template for the GradeForm's Load event procedure appears in the Code editor window.

5 Type the six lines of code shown in Figure 6-44.

enter these six lines of code

```
Private Sub GradeForm_Load(ByVal sender As Object, ByVal e As System.EventArgs) Hand
    'assign check boxes to form-level collection
    mCheckBoxCollection.Add(Me.Proj1CheckBox)
    mCheckBoxCollection.Add(Me.Proj2CheckBox)
    mCheckBoxCollection.Add(Me.Proj3CheckBox)
    mCheckBoxCollection.Add(Me.MidtermCheckBox)
    mCheckBoxCollection.Add(Me.FinalCheckBox)

End Sub
```

Figure 6-44: Partially completed Load event procedure

6 Click **File** on the menu bar, and then click **Save All**.

Before you can complete the GradeForm's Load event procedure, you need to learn about parallel collections.

Parallel Collections

tip

You also can create parallel collections using an object's Tag property rather than the Add method's *key* argument. You learn how to do so in Discovery Exercise 5 at the end of this lesson.

Each check box in the mCheckBoxCollection directly corresponds to a text box in the mTextBoxCollection. For example, the Proj1CheckBox is associated with the Proj1TextBox, the Proj2CheckBox with the Proj2TextBox, and so on. Collections whose objects are related in some way are called **parallel collections**. You can indicate to the computer that two collections are parallel collections by setting the *key* argument for each object in one of the collections to the name of the corresponding object in the other collection. In this case, for example, you will set the *key* argument for each text box in the mTextBoxCollection to the name of the corresponding object in the mCheckBoxCollection.

To complete the GradeForm's Load event procedure:

1 Type the additional six lines of code shown in Figure 6-45.

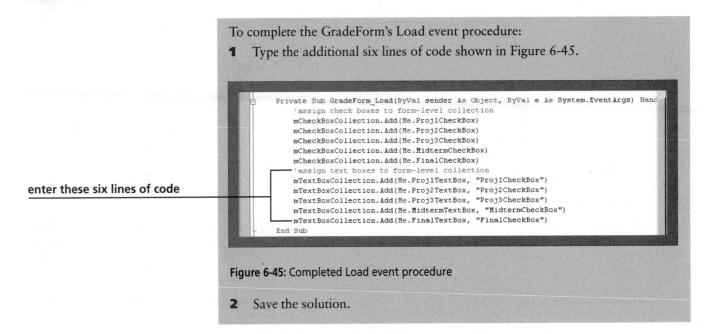

enter these six lines of code

```
Private Sub GradeForm_Load(ByVal sender As Object, ByVal e As System.EventArgs) Hand
        'assign check boxes to form-level collection
        mCheckBoxCollection.Add(Me.Proj1CheckBox)
        mCheckBoxCollection.Add(Me.Proj2CheckBox)
        mCheckBoxCollection.Add(Me.Proj3CheckBox)
        mCheckBoxCollection.Add(Me.MidtermCheckBox)
        mCheckBoxCollection.Add(Me.FinalCheckBox)
        'assign text boxes to form-level collection
        mTextBoxCollection.Add(Me.Proj1TextBox, "Proj1CheckBox")
        mTextBoxCollection.Add(Me.Proj2TextBox, "Proj2CheckBox")
        mTextBoxCollection.Add(Me.Proj3TextBox, "Proj3CheckBox")
        mTextBoxCollection.Add(Me.MidtermTextBox, "MidtermCheckBox")
        mTextBoxCollection.Add(Me.FinalTextBox, "FinalCheckBox")
    End Sub
```

Figure 6-45: Completed Load event procedure

2 Save the solution.

Next, code the Click event procedures for the check boxes.

Coding the Check Boxes' Click Event Procedures

The pseudocode shown in Figure 6-46 lists the tasks you want performed when the user clicks a check box.

Proj1CheckBox, Proj2CheckBox, Proj3CheckBox, MidtermCheckBox, FinalCheckBox

1. declare a check box object variable and a text box object variable

2. assign the address of the Click event procedure's sender parameter to the check box object variable

3. assign the address of the check box's associated text box to the text box object variable

4. if the user selected the check box
      enable the corresponding text box
      send the focus to the corresponding text box
  else
      clear the contents of the corresponding text box
      disable the corresponding text box
  end if

Figure 6-46: Pseudocode for each check box's Click event procedure

According to the pseudocode, each check box's Click event procedure should perform two tasks when the user selects the check box, and perform two different tasks when the user deselects the check box.

To begin coding each check box's Click event procedure:

1 Click the **Class Name** list arrow, then click **Proj1CheckBox** in the list. Click the **Method Name** list arrow, then click **Click** in the list. The template for the Proj1CheckBox's Click event procedure appears in the Code editor window.

2 Change the name of the procedure from `Proj1CheckBox_Click` to **ProcessCheckBoxes**.

3 Change the Handles portion of the procedure header as shown in Figure 6-47, then position the insertion point as shown in the figure.

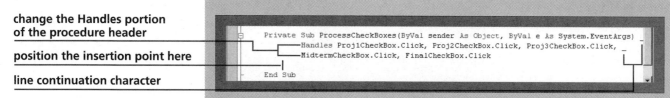

change the Handles portion of the procedure header

position the insertion point here

line continuation character

Figure 6-47: Changes made to the procedure header

The first step in the pseudocode is to declare two object variables.

4 Type **dim objCheckBox as checkbox, objTextBox as textbox** and press **Enter**.

Next, assign the address of the procedure's `sender` parameter to the objCheckBox variable.

5 Type **'assign sender parameter to object variable** and press **Enter**, then type **objcheckbox = sender** and press **Enter**.

Now assign, to the objTextBox variable, the address of the text box associated with the check box. You can do so using the assignment statement `objTextBox = mTextBoxcollection.Item(objCheckBox.Name)`. Notice that the statement uses the check box's name to access the appropriate text box. (Recall that you assigned a check box's name as the *key* for each text box in the mTextBoxCollection.)

6 Type **'assign corresponding text box to object variable** and press **Enter**, then type **objtextbox = mtextboxcollection.item(objcheckbox.name)** and press **Enter**.

Next, determine whether the user selected or deselected the check box. If the check box is selected, then its Checked property contains the Boolean value True.

7 Type **'if the user selected the check box** and press **Enter**, then type **if objcheckbox.checked = true then** and press **Enter**.

8 Save the solution.

If the user selected the check box, the procedure should enable the corresponding text box.

The Enabled Property

The **Enabled property** determines whether an object can respond to user-generated events, such as tabbing to the object or entering information into the object. When the Enabled property is set to its default value, True, the object can respond to a user-generated event. Setting the object's Enabled property to False prevents the object from responding to the user.

It is customary in Windows applications to disable objects that do not apply to the current state of the application. In the Grade Calculator application, for example, you do not want to allow the user to tab into the project and test text boxes, or enter information into those text boxes, until he or she selects the corresponding check box, which indicates that the project or test has been completed. Therefore, you will have the project and test text boxes disabled when the interface first appears on the screen. You will enable the appropriate text box when the user selects a check box, and disable the text box when the user deselects the check box.

To disable the project and test text boxes, then complete the ProcessCheckBoxes procedure:

1 Return to the designer window. Select the Proj1TextBox, Proj2TextBox, Proj3TextBox, MidtermTextBox, and FinalTextBox.

2 Set the Enabled property for the selected controls to **False**.

3 Click the **form** to deselect the controls, then return to the Code editor window.

4 The insertion point should be located in the blank line between the If and End If clauses. If necessary, press **Tab** three times to indent the line. Type **'enable the text box and send the focus to the text box** and press **Enter**.

5 Type **objtextbox.enabled = true** and press **Enter**, then type **objtextbox.focus()** and press **Enter**.

If the user deselected the check box, the procedure should clear the contents of the corresponding text box and then disable the text box.

6 Type the additional four lines of code shown in Figure 6-48, which shows the completed ProcessCheckBoxes procedure. (Be sure that the End If clause appears in the procedure.)

enter these four lines of code

```
Private Sub ProcessCheckBoxes(ByVal sender As Object, ByVal e As System.EventArgs) _
        Handles Proj1CheckBox.Click, Proj2CheckBox.Click, Proj3CheckBox.Click, _
        MidtermCheckBox.Click, FinalCheckBox.Click
    Dim objCheckBox As CheckBox, objTextBox As TextBox
    'assign sender parameter to object variable
    objCheckBox = sender
    'assign corresponding text box to object variable
    objTextBox = mTextBoxCollection.Item(objCheckBox.Name)
    'if the user selected the check box
    If objCheckBox.Checked = True Then
        'enable the text box and send the focus to the text box
        objTextBox.Enabled = True
        objTextBox.Focus()
    Else    'the user deselected the check box
        'clear the text box's contents and disable the text box
        objTextBox.Text = ""
        objTextBox.Enabled = False
    End If
End Sub
```

Figure 6-48: Completed ProcessCheckBoxes procedure

Now test the code you have entered so far.

To test the application's code:

1 Save the solution, then start the application.

2 Press **Tab** eight times. Notice that you can tab to only the Name text box, the check boxes, and the buttons on the form. You cannot tab to a text box that has its Enabled property set to False.

3 Click the **Project 1** check box. The text box situated to the right of the Project 1 check box is enabled, and the focus moves into the text box, as shown in Figure 6-49.

text box associated with the selected check box

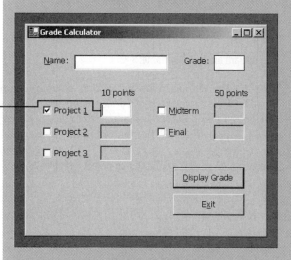

Figure 6-49: Text box is enabled and has the focus

4 Type **9** in the text box.

5 Click the **Midterm** check box. The text box situated to the right of the Midterm check box is enabled, and the focus moves into the text box. Type **45** in the text box.

6 Click the **Project 1** check box to deselect it. The contents of the text box are removed before the text box is disabled.

7 Click the **Midterm** check box to deselect it. The contents of the text box are removed before the text box is disabled.

8 Click the **Exit** button to end the application. When you return to the Code editor window, close the Output window, then close the Code editor window.

9 Click **File** on the menu bar, and then click **Close Solution** to close the solution.

You now have completed Lesson B. You finish coding the Grade Calculator application in Lesson C. For now, you can either take a break or complete the end-of-lesson questions and exercises before moving on to the next lesson.

S U M M A R Y

To refer to the controls on a form:

■ Use the Controls collection.

■ You refer to an individual control in the Controls collection using the Item property and the control's index. The first control in the Controls collection has an index of 0 (zero).

■ You can use a repetition structure to refer to each control within the Controls collection.

To determine the total number of controls in the Controls collection:

■ Use the Controls collection's Count property. The syntax of the Count property is **Controls.Count**.

To represent the For Each...Next loop in a flowchart:

■ Use a hexagon.

To declare an object variable:

■ Typically, you use the syntax **Dim** *variablename* **As** *objecttype* to declare an object variable. In the syntax, *variablename* is the name of the object variable and usually begins with the three-character ID "obj". *Objecttype* is the type of object—for example, Control, TextBox, Button, or Label—whose address will be stored in the variable.

To assign an object's address to an object variable:

■ Use an assignment statement that follows the syntax *objectvariable* = *object*, where *objectvariable* is the name of an object variable, and *object* is the name of the object whose address you want assigned to the *objectvariable*. The *object* must be the same object type as the *objectvariable*.

To repeat a set of instructions for each object in a collection:

■ Use the For Each...Next statement. Refer to Figure 6-36 for the syntax of the statement. The For Each...Next statement can be used to code pretest loops only. In the syntax, *element* is the name of the object variable used to refer to each object in the collection, and *group* is the name of the collection in which the object is contained. The *element*'s data type must be the same as the collection's data type.

■ The For Each...Next statement performs the following three tasks:
  1. The For Each clause checks whether the *group* contains at least one object.
  2. If the *group* is empty, the loop stops and processing continues with the statement following the Next clause. If the *group* is not empty, the address of the first object is assigned to the *element* variable, and the instructions within the loop are processed. The Next clause then returns processing to the beginning of the loop (the For Each clause).
  3. The For Each clause checks whether the *group* contains another object. If it does not, the loop stops and processing continues with the statement following the Next clause. If it does, the address of the object is assigned to the *element* variable, and the instructions within the loop are processed. The Next clause then returns processing to the beginning of the loop (the For Each clause). Task 3 is repeated for each object in the *group*.

To create and manipulate a user-defined collection:

■ You create a user-defined collection using the *accessibility collectionname* **As New Collection()**, where *accessibility* is typically either the keyword Dim or the keyword Private, and *collectionname* is the name of the collection.

■ Use the Add method to add an object to a collection. The syntax of the Add method is *collection*.**Add**(*object*[, *key*]). In the syntax, *collection* is the name of the collection, *object* is the name of the object you want to add to the *collection*, and *key* is a string that uniquely identifies the *object* in the *collection*.

- You can refer to an individual object in a user-defined collection using either the object's index or its *key*. The index of the first item in a user-defined collection is 1 (one).
- Use the Remove method to remove an object from a collection. The syntax of the Remove method is *collection*.**Remove**(*object*). In the syntax, *collection* is the name of the collection, and *object* is either the index or *key* of the object you want to remove.
- Use the Count property to determine the number of objects in a collection. The syntax of the Count property is *collection*.**Count**, where *collection* is the name of the collection.

To create parallel collections:

- Create two collections. When adding items to the collections, set the *key* argument for each object in one of the collections to the name of the corresponding object in the other collection.

To control whether an object can respond to user-generated events:

- If you want an object to respond to user-generated events, set the object's Enabled property to True (the default). To prevent an object from responding to user-generated events, set the object's Enabled property to False.

Q U E S T I O N S

1. Which of the following symbols represents the For Each...Next loop in a flowchart?
   a. diamond
   b. hexagon
   c. oval
   d. parallelogram
   e. rectangle

2. Assume that a form contains four labels, two text boxes, and two buttons. How many times will the computer process the Debug.WriteLine instruction in the following code?

   ```
   Dim intX As Integer
   For intX = 0 To Controls.Count - 1
       Debug.WriteLine(Controls.Item(intX).Name)
   Next intX
   ```

   a. 0
   b. 1
   c. 7
   d. 8
   e. 9

3. What is the value of intX when the loop in Question 2 stops?
   a. 1
   b. 5
   c. 7
   d. 8
   e. 9

4. Assume that a form contains four labels, two text boxes, and two buttons. How many times will the computer process the Debug.WriteLine instruction in the following code?

```
Dim intX As Integer, objButton As Button
For intX = 0 To Controls.Count - 1
     If TypeOf Controls.Item(intX) Is Button Then
          objButton = Controls.Item(intX)
            Debug.WriteLine(objButton.Name)
     End If
Next intX
```

   a. 0
   b. 1
   c. 2
   d. 7
   e. 8

5. Which of the following clauses indicates that the loop should be performed for each object in the ButtonCollection?

   a. `For intX = 0 To ButtonCollection.Count`
   b. `For intX = 0 To ButtonCollection.Count - 1`
   c. `For intX = 1 To ButtonCollection.Count`
   d. `For intX = 1 To ButtonCollection.Count - 1`
   e. Both b and c.

6. Which of the following clauses indicates that the loop should be performed for each object in the LabelCollection?

   a. `For Each objLabel In LabelCollection`
   b. `For Each objLabel In LabelCollection.Count`
   c. `For Each objLabel In LabelCollection.Count - 1`
   d. `For objLabel In LabelCollection`
   e. `For All objLabel In LabelCollection`

7. Which of the following statements adds the NameTextBox control to the TextBoxCollection?

   a. `Add.TextBoxCollection(Me.NameTextBox)`
   b. `Add(TextBoxCollection.Me.NameTextBox)`
   c. `TextBoxCollection.Add(Me.NameTextBox)`
   d. `TextBoxCollection(Add Me.NameTextBox)`
   e. `TextBoxCollection.NameTextBox.Add()`

8. Which of the following statements removes the first text box from the TextBoxCollection?

   a. `Remove.TextBoxCollection(0)`
   b. `Remove(TextBoxCollection(1))`
   c. `Remove.TextBoxCollection(1)`
   d. `TextBoxCollection.Remove(0)`
   e. `TextBoxCollection.Remove(1)`

9. Assume that an application contains two collections named LabelCollection and TextBoxCollection. Which of the following statements associates the IdNameLabel control (which is contained in the LabelCollection) with the FirstNameTextBox (which is contained in the TextBoxCollection?

   a. `Me.FirstNameTextBox.Add.TextBoxCollection("IdNameLabel")`
   b. `Me.IdNameLabel.Add.LabelCollection("FirstNameTextBox")`
   c. `TextBoxCollection.Add("IdNameLabel", Me.FirstNameTextBox)`
   d. `TextBoxCollection.Add(Me.FirstNameTextBox, "IdNameLabel")`
   e. Both a and b.

10. A unique number, called _____, is assigned to each object in a collection.
  a. an address
  b. a key
  c. an object number
  d. an object value
  e. an index

11. The index of the first control contained in the Controls collection is _____.
  a. 0
  b. 1

12. Assume that a procedure contains the statement `Dim ButtonCollection As New Collection()`. The first button contained in the ButtonCollection has an index of
_____.
  a. 0
  b. 1

13. Collections that have corresponding elements are called _____ collections.
  a. associated
  b. coordinated
  c. coupled
  d. matching
  e. parallel

14. To prevent an object from responding to user-generated events, set the object's _____ property to False.
  a. Enabled
  b. EventEnabled
  c. Prevent
  d. Response
  e. User

15. Assume that a procedure contains the following three lines of code:
`Dim ButtonCollection As New Collection()`,
`ButtonCollection.Add(Me.CalcButton, "Calculate")`, and
`ButtonCollection.Add(Me.ExitButton, "Exit")`. Which of the following can be used to refer to the first button in the ButtonCollection?
  a. `ButtonCollection.Item(0)`
  b. `ButtonCollection.Item(1)`
  c. `ButtonCollection.Item("Calculate")`
  d. Both a and c.
  e. Both b and c.

EXERCISES

1. In this exercise, you code an application that uses parallel collections to display an image.
  a. If necessary, start Visual Studio .NET. Open the Elements Solution (Elements Solution.sln) file, which is contained in the VBNET\Tut06\Elements Solution folder. If the designer window is not open, right-click the form file's name in the Solution Explorer window, then click View Designer.
  b. Create a collection for the five radio buttons on the form. Also create a collection for the five picture box controls that appear on the right side of the form. (Do not include the ImagePictureBox control in the picture box collection.)

c. Code the application so that it displays the appropriate image in the ImagePictureBox control when a radio button is selected. For example, when the user selects the SunRadioButton, display (in the ImagePictureBox control) the image contained in the SunPictureBox control.

d. Save the solution, then start the application. Test the application by clicking each radio button.

e. Click the Exit button to end the application.

f. Close the Output window, then close the solution.

2. In this exercise, you code an application that changes the color of the label controls on a form.

a. If necessary, start Visual Studio .NET. Open the Color Solution (Color Solution.sln) file, which is contained in the VBNET\Tut06\Color Solution folder. If the designer window is not open, right-click the form file's name in the Solution Explorer window, then click View Designer.

b. Code the BlueButton control's Click event procedure so that it sets the BackColor property of each label control to `Color.Blue`. Use the For...Next statement and the Controls collection.

c. Code the YellowButton control's Click event procedure so that it sets the BackColor property of each label control to `Color.Yellow`. Use the Do...Loop statement and the Controls collection.

d. Code the RedButton control's Click event procedure so that it creates a collection and assigns each label control to the collection. The procedure then should set the BackColor property of each control in the collection to `Color.Red`. Use the For Each...Next statement.

e. Save the solution, then start the application. Click the Blue button. The background color of the four label controls changes to blue. Click the Yellow button. The background color of the four label controls changes to yellow. Click the Red button. The background color of the four label controls changes to red.

f. Click the Exit button to end the application.

g. Close the Output window, then close the solution.

3. In this exercise, you code an application that hides and displays picture box controls.

a. If necessary, start Visual Studio .NET. Open the Faces Solution (Faces Solution.sln) file, which is contained in the VBNET\Tut06\Faces Solution folder. If the designer window is not open, right-click the form file's name in the Solution Explorer window, then click View Designer. The interface contains three picture box controls, two timer controls, and one button control. The Interval property for both timer controls is set to 500 milliseconds (1/2 of a second). Additionally, the DisplayTimer control's Enabled property is set to True, and the HideTimer control's Enabled property is set to False.

b. Create a form-level collection. In the form's Load event, assign each picture box control to the collection.

c. Code the DisplayTimer control's Tick event so that it displays one of the three faces every 500 milliseconds. In other words, when the application is started, the first face should appear after 500 milliseconds have elapsed. After another 500 milliseconds have elapsed, the second face should appear, and so on. When the three faces appear in the interface, the Tick event should disable the DisplayTimer control and enable the HideTimer control.

d. Code the HideTimer control's Tick event so that it hides one of the three faces every 500 milliseconds. Begin by hiding the last face and end by hiding the first face. When the three faces are hidden, the Tick event should disable the HideTimer control and enable the DisplayTimer control.

e. Save the solution, then start the application. The faces should appear, one at a time, in the interface. Then they should disappear, one at a time. This process should continue until you click the Exit button.

    f.   Click the Exit button to end the application.

    g.   Close the Output window, then close the solution.

Exercises 4 and 5 are Discovery Exercises. Discovery Exercises, which may include topics that are not covered in this lesson, allow you to "discover" the solutions to problems on your own.

discovery ▶   **4.** In this exercise, you learn more about the Controls collection.

    a.   If necessary, start Visual Studio .NET. Open the GroupBox Solution (GroupBox Solution.sln) file, which is contained in the VBNET\Tut06\GroupBox Solution folder. If the designer window is not open, right-click the form file's name in the Solution Explorer window, then click View Designer. The interface contains two label controls, two text box controls, two button controls, and one group box control.

    b.   Open the Code editor window. Notice that the Display button's Click event procedure displays (in a message box) the number of controls contained in the Controls collection.

    c.   Start the application, then click the Display button. The message box indicates that there are seven controls in the Controls collection. Click the OK button to close the message box, then click the Exit button to end the application.

    d.   Drag the IdFirstLabel and FirstTextBox controls into the group box control.

    e.   Save the solution. Start the application, then click the Display button. According to the message displayed in the message box, how many controls are contained in the Controls collection? What does this tell you about the controls contained in a GroupBox control?

    f.   Click the OK button. Click the Exit button to end the application.

    g.   Close the Output window, then close the solution.

discovery ▶   **5.** In this exercise, you learn how to use the Tag property to create parallel collections.

    a.   Use Windows to make a copy of the Grade Solution folder, which is contained in the VBNET\Tut06 folder. Change the name of the folder to Tag Solution.

    b.   If necessary, start Visual Studio .NET. Open the Grade Solution (Grade Solution.sln) file, which is contained in the VBNET\Tut06\Tag Solution folder. If the designer window is not open, right-click the form file's name in the Solution Explorer window, then click View Designer.

    c.   Assign the number 1 to the Tag property of the Proj1CheckBox, 2 to the Tag property of the Proj2CheckBox, 3 to the Tag property of the Proj3CheckBox, 4 to the Tag property of the MidtermCheckBox, and 5 to the Tag property of the FinalCheckBox.

    d.   Open the Code editor window. Remove the keys from the Add methods entered in the form's Load event procedure.

    e.   Modify the ProcessCheckBoxes procedure so that it uses the check box's Tag property rather than its Name property to access the appropriate text box.

    f.   Save the solution, then start the application. Verify that the check boxes work correctly.

    g.   Click the Exit button to end the application.

    h.   Close the Output window, then close the solution.

Completing the Grade Calculator Application

Coding the DisplayButton's Click Event Procedure

Recall that, to complete the Grade Calculator application, you still need to code the DisplayButton's Click event procedure, the GradeForm's Closing event procedure, and the Enter event procedure for the text boxes. You begin with the DisplayButton's Click event procedure. The pseudocode for this procedure is shown in Figure 6-50.

DisplayButton

1. declare variables

2. repeat for each check box in the mCheckBoxCollection
    if the check box is selected
        check box name:

Proj1CheckBox	add 10 to the total possible points accumulator
Proj2CheckBox	add 10 to the total possible points accumulator
Proj3CheckBox	add 10 to the total possible points accumulator
Other	add 50 to the total possible points accumulator

        assign the address of the associated text box to an object variable

        add the contents of the text box to the total earned points accumulator
    end if
  end repeat

3. if the total possible points is greater than zero
    calculate the ratio by dividing the total earned points by the total possible points

    ratio:

>= .9	display "A" in the GradeLabel control
>= .8	display "B" in the GradeLabel control
>= .7	display "C" in the GradeLabel control
>= .6	display "D" in the GradeLabel control
Other	display "F" in the GradeLabel control

  end if

Figure 6-50: Pseudocode for the DisplayButton's Click event procedure

To begin coding the DisplayButton's Click event procedure:

1 Start Microsoft Visual Studio .NET, if necessary, and then close the Start Page window. Click **File** on the menu bar, and then click **Open Solution**. The Open Solution dialog box opens. Open the **Grade Solution** (Grade Solution.sln) file, which is contained in the VBNET\Tut06\Grade Solution folder.

2 If the designer window is not open, right-click **Grade Form.vb** in the Solution Explorer window, then click **View Designer**. Auto-hide the Toolbox, Solution Explorer, and Properties windows, if necessary.

3 Right-click the **form**, and then click **View Code** to open the Code editor window. Click the **Class Name** list arrow, and then click **DisplayButton** in the list. Click the **Method Name** list arrow, and then click **Click** in the list. The template for the DisplayButton's Click event procedure appears in the Code editor window.

The first step in the pseudocode is to declare the necessary variables. The DisplayButton Click event procedure will use five variables.

4 Type **dim objCheckBox as checkbox, objTextBox as textbox** and press **Enter**. Then type **dim intPossible, intEarned as integer, sngRatio as single** and press **Enter**.

The procedure will use the two object variables to store the addresses of a check box and its associated text box. It will use the intPossible and intEarned variables to accumulate the total number of possible points and the total number of earned points, respectively. The sngRatio variable will store the result of dividing the intEarned variable by the intPossible variable.

Step 2 in the pseudocode is a loop whose instructions should be processed for each check box in the mCheckBoxCollection.

5 Type **for each objcheckbox in mcheckboxcollection** and press **Enter**.

Next, enter an If clause that checks whether the current check box is selected.

6 Type **if objcheckbox.checked = true then** and press **Enter**.

If the current check box is selected, then either 10 or 50 points should be added to the total possible points accumulator. The correct amount to add to the accumulator depends on the current check box's name. If the check box is named Proj1CheckBox, Proj2CheckBox, or Proj3CheckBox, then 10 points should be added to the accumulator, because each project is worth 10 points. However, if the check box is named MidtermCheckBox or FinalCheckBox, then 50 points should be added to the accumulator, because each test is worth 50 points.

7 Type the comment and Select Case statement shown in Figure 6-51, and then position the insertion point as shown in the figure. Be sure to type the control names in the Case statement using the capitalization shown in the figure.

enter the comment and Select Case statement

position the insertion point here

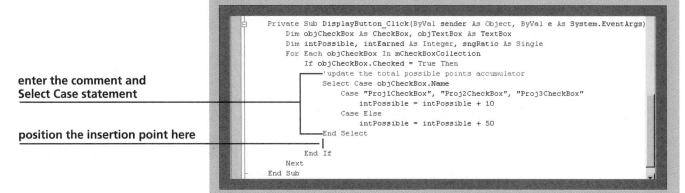

```
Private Sub DisplayButton_Click(ByVal sender As Object, ByVal e As System.EventArgs)
    Dim objCheckBox As CheckBox, objTextBox As TextBox
    Dim intPossible, intEarned As Integer, sngRatio As Single
    For Each objCheckBox In mCheckBoxCollection
        If objCheckBox.Checked = True Then
            'update the total possible points accumulator
            Select Case objCheckBox.Name
                Case "Proj1CheckBox", "Proj2CheckBox", "Proj3CheckBox"
                    intPossible = intPossible + 10
                Case Else
                    intPossible = intPossible + 50
            End Select

        End If
    Next
End Sub
```

Figure 6-51: Select Case statement entered in the procedure

Now assign, to an object variable, the address of the text box that is associated with the current check box.

8   Type **'assign text box address to object variable** and press **Enter**, then type **objtextbox = mtextboxcollection.item(objcheckbox.name)** and press **Enter**.

Now update the total earned points accumulator by adding the contents of the text box to it.

9   Type the comment and assignment statement shown in Figure 6-52. Also, change the **Next** clause to **Next objCheckBox**, and position the insertion point as shown in the figure.

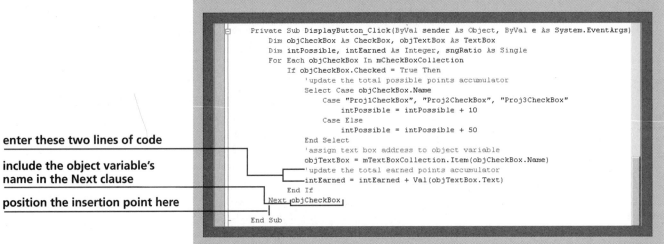

enter these two lines of code

include the object variable's name in the Next clause

position the insertion point here

```
Private Sub DisplayButton_Click(ByVal sender As Object, ByVal e As System.EventArgs)
    Dim objCheckBox As CheckBox, objTextBox As TextBox
    Dim intPossible, intEarned As Integer, sngRatio As Single
    For Each objCheckBox In mCheckBoxCollection
        If objCheckBox.Checked = True Then
            'update the total possible points accumulator
            Select Case objCheckBox.Name
                Case "Proj1CheckBox", "Proj2CheckBox", "Proj3CheckBox"
                    intPossible = intPossible + 10
                Case Else
                    intPossible = intPossible + 50
            End Select
            'assign text box address to object variable
            objTextBox = mTextBoxCollection.Item(objCheckBox.Name)
            'update the total earned points accumulator
            intEarned = intEarned + Val(objTextBox.Text)
        End If
    Next objCheckBox

End Sub
```

Figure 6-52: Current status of the DisplayButton Click event procedure

10   Click **File** on the menu bar, and then click **Save All**.

Step 3 in the pseudocode is to determine whether the total number of possible points, which is stored in the intPossible variable, is greater than zero and then assign a grade.

To complete the DisplayButton Click event procedure, then test the procedure:

1   The insertion point should be positioned below the **Next objCheckBox** clause. Type **'verify that the total number of possible points is greater than 0** and press **Enter**, then type **if intpossible > 0 then** and press **Enter**.

If total possible points are greater than zero, the procedure should calculate a ratio by dividing the total earned points by the total possible points.

2   Type **'calculate ratio** and press **Enter**, then type **sngratio = intearned / intpossible** and press **Enter**.

Finally, enter a Select Case statement that uses the ratio stored in the sngRatio variable to display the appropriate grade in the GradeLabel control.

3   Type the comment and Select Case statement shaded in Figure 6-53, which shows the completed DisplayButton Click event procedure.

```
Private Sub DisplayButton_Click(ByVal sender As Object, ByVal e As
System.EventArgs) Handles DisplayButton.Click
        Dim objCheckBox As CheckBox, objTextBox As TextBox
        Dim intPossible, intEarned As Integer, sngRatio As Single
        For Each objCheckBox In mCheckBoxCollection
            If objCheckBox.Checked = True Then
                'update the total possible points accumulator
                Select Case objCheckBox.Name
                    Case "Proj1CheckBox", "Proj2CheckBox", "Proj3CheckBox"
                        intPossible = intPossible + 10
                    Case Else
                        intPossible = intPossible + 50
                End Select
                'assign text box address to object variable
                objTextBox = mTextBoxCollection.Item(objCheckBox.Name)
                'update the total earned points accumulator
                intEarned = intEarned + Val(objTextBox.Text)
            End If
        Next objCheckBox
        'verify that the total number of possible points is greater than 0
        If intPossible > 0 Then
            'calculate ratio
            sngRatio = intEarned / intPossible
            'display grade
            Select Case sngRatio
                Case Is >= 0.9
                    Me.GradeLabel.Text = "A"
                Case Is >= 0.8
                    Me.GradeLabel.Text = "B"
                Case Is >= 0.7
                    Me.GradeLabel.Text = "C"
                Case Is >= 0.6
                    Me.GradeLabel.Text = "D"
                Case Else
                    Me.GradeLabel.Text = "F"
            End Select
        End If
    End Sub
```

enter the comment and Select Case statement

Figure 6-53: Completed DisplayButton Click event procedure

Now test the procedure to verify that it is working correctly.

4 Save the solution, then start the application.

5 Type your name in the Name text box. Click the **Project 1** check box to select it, then type 6 in the corresponding text box. Click the **Midterm** check box to select it, then type 50 in the corresponding text box. Press **Enter** to select the Display Grade button, which is the default button on the form. A grade of A appears in the GradeLabel control.

6 Click the **Project 2** check box, then type 5 in the corresponding text box.

7 Press **Tab** three times to move the focus to the Midterm text box. Notice that the existing text is not highlighted (selected) when you tab to the control. It is customary in Windows applications to highlight the existing text when a text box receives the focus. You learn how to fix this problem in the next section.

8 Click the **Midterm** check box to deselect it, then press **Enter**. A grade of F appears in the GradeLabel control.

GUI
Design Tips

Highlighting Existing Text

• It is customary in Windows applications to highlight, or select, the existing text in a text box when the text box receives the focus.

9 Click the Exit button to end the application. When you return to the Code editor window, close the Output window.

Next, you code each text box control's Enter event procedure.

Coding the Text Boxes' Enter Event Procedures

A text box control's **Enter event** occurs when the user tabs to the control, and when the Focus method is used in code to send the focus to the control. According to the Grade Calculator application's TOE chart (shown in Figure 6-43 in Lesson B), each text box control's Enter event is responsible for highlighting the existing text in the control.

To code each text box's Enter event procedure, then test the application:

1 Click the **Class Name** list arrow, then click **NameTextBox** in the list. Click the **Method Name** list arrow, then click **Enter** in the list. The template for the NameTextBox's Enter event procedure appears in the Code editor window.

2 Change the procedure's name from NameTextBox_Enter to **HighlightText**.

3 Change the Handles portion of the procedure header as shown in Figure 6-54, then position the insertion point as shown in the figure.

change the Handles portion of the procedure header

position the insertion point here

line continuation character

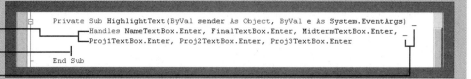

```
Private Sub HighlightText(ByVal sender As Object, ByVal e As System.EventArgs) _
    Handles NameTextBox.Enter, FinalTextBox.Enter, MidtermTextBox.Enter, _
    Proj1TextBox.Enter, Proj2TextBox.Enter, Proj3TextBox.Enter

End Sub
```

Figure 6-54: Changes made to the HighlightText procedure header

First create a TextBox object variable, and then assign the address of the procedure's `sender` parameter to the variable. This ensures that a complete list of the properties and methods of a text box appear when you are entering code.

4 Type **dim objTextBox as textbox** and press **Enter**, then type **objtextbox = sender** and press **Enter**.

Recall that you can use the SelectAll method to highlight (or select) the contents of a text box.

5 Type **objtextbox.** (be sure to type the period). A listing of the properties and methods for a text box appears. Click **SelectAll** in the list, then press **Tab**. Figure 6-55 shows the completed HighlightText procedure.

```
Private Sub HighlightText(ByVal sender As Object, ByVal e As System.EventArgs) _
    Handles NameTextBox.Enter, FinalTextBox.Enter, MidtermTextBox.Enter, _
    Proj1TextBox.Enter, Proj2TextBox.Enter, Proj3TextBox.Enter
    Dim objTextBox As TextBox
    objTextBox = sender
    objTextBox.SelectAll()
End Sub
```

Figure 6-55: Completed HighlightText procedure

> **6** Save the solution, then start the application.
>
> **7** Type your name in the Name text box. Click each check box and enter a value in its corresponding text box.
>
> **8** Press **Tab** several times. Notice that, when the focus enters a text box control, the control's existing text is highlighted.
>
> **9** Click the **Exit** button to end the application. When you return to the Code editor window, close the Output window.

The last procedure you need to code to complete the Grade Calculator application is the GradeForm's Closing event procedure.

Coding the GradeForm's Closing Event Procedure

A form's **Closing event** occurs when a form is about to be closed. You can close a form using either the Close button ☒ on its title bar, or the `Me.Close()` statement in code. According to the Grade Calculator application's TOE chart (shown in Figure 6-43 in Lesson B), the Closing event procedure is responsible for verifying that the user wants to exit the application, and then taking the appropriate action based on the user's response. Figure 6-56 shows the pseudocode for this procedure.

GradeForm

1. declare the intButton variable

2. ask the user whether he or she wants to exit the application, then assign the response to the intButton variable

3. if the user does not want to exit the application
       set the Cancel property of the procedure's e parameter to True
   end if

Figure 6-56: Pseudocode for the GradeForm's Closing event procedure

> To code the GradeForm's Closing event procedure:
>
> **1** Click the **Class Name** list arrow, then click **(Base Class Events)** in the list. Click the **Method Name** list arrow, then click **Closing** in the list. The template for the GradeForm's Closing event procedure appears in the Code editor window.
>
> First, declare the intButton variable.
>
> **2** Type **dim intButton as integer** and press **Enter**.
>
> Now use the MessageBox.Show method to ask the user if he or she wants to exit the application. Include Yes and No buttons and the Warning Message icon ⚠ in the message box. Designate the Yes button as the default button, and assign the user's response to the intButton variable.
>
> **3** Type **intbutton = messagebox.show("Do you want to exit?", "Grade Calculator", _** (be sure to type the line continuation character) and press **Enter**.
>
> **4** Press **Tab**, then type **messageboxbuttons.yesno, messageboxicon.exclamation, _** (be sure to include a space before the line continuation character) and press **Enter**.
>
> **5** Type **messageboxdefauitbutton.button1)** and press **Enter**.

If the user selects the No button in the message box, then the Closing procedure should prevent the form from being closed; you do so by setting the Cancel property of the procedure's **e** parameter to True.

6 Type the additional lines of code shown in Figure 6-57, which shows the completed Closing event procedure.

```
Private Sub GradeForm_Closing(ByVal sender As Object, ByVal e As System.ComponentMod
    Dim intButton As Integer
    intButton = MessageBox.Show("Do you want to exit?", "Grade Calculator", _
        MessageBoxButtons.YesNo, MessageBoxIcon.Exclamation, _
        MessageBoxDefaultButton.Button1)
    'if user selects the No button, cancel closing the form
    If intButton = MsgBoxResult.No Then
        e.Cancel = True
    End If
End Sub
```

enter these lines of code

**prevents the form
from being closed**

Figure 6-57: Completed Closing event procedure for the GradeForm

7 Save the solution, then start the application.

8 Click the **Close** button ☒ on the form's title bar. A message box containing the message "Do you want to exit?" appears on the screen. Click the **No** button. The form remains on the screen.

9 Click the **Exit** button. Here again, a message box containing the message "Do you want to exit?" appears on the screen. This time, click the **Yes** button. The application ends.

10 When you return to the Code editor window, close the Output window, then close the Code editor window. Click **File** on the menu bar, and then click **Close Solution**.

You now have completed Tutorial 6. You can either take a break or complete the end-of-lesson questions and exercises.

SUMMARY

To process code when the user tabs to a control, or when the Focus method is used in code to send the focus to the control:

■ Enter the code in the control's Enter event procedure.

To process code when a form is about to be closed:

■ Enter the code in the form's Closing event. The Closing event occurs when the user clicks the Close button ☒ on a form's title bar. It also occurs when the `Me.Close()` statement is used in code.

To prevent a form from being closed:

■ Set the Cancel property of the Closing event procedure's **e** parameter to True.

QUESTIONS

1. The _____ event is triggered when you click a form's Close button ☒.
   a. Close
   b. Closing
   c. FormClose
   d. FormClosing
   e. Unloading

2. The _____ event is triggered when you use the statement `Me.Close()` to close a form.
   a. Close
   b. Closing
   c. FormClose
   d. FormClosing
   e. Unloading

3. The _____ event occurs when the user tabs to a text box.
   a. Enter
   b. Focus
   c. Tab
   d. Tabbing
   e. None of the above.

4. Which of the following statements prevents a form from being closed?
   a. `e.Cancel = False`
   b. `e.Cancel = True`
   c. `e.Close = False`
   d. `sender.Cancel = True`
   e. `sender.Cancel = False`

5. Which of the following statements selects the contents of the text box whose address is stored in the objTextBox variable?
   a. `objTextBox.Enter()`
   b. `objTextBox.SelectText()`
   c. `SelectText(objTextBox)`
   d. `SelectAll.objTextBox()`
   e. None of the above.

EXERCISES

The following list summarizes the GUI design guidelines you have learned so far. You can use this list to verify that the interfaces you create in the following exercises adhere to the GUI standards outlined in the book.

- Information should flow either vertically or horizontally, with the most important information always located in the upper-left corner of the screen.

- Maintain a consistent margin of two or three dots from the edge of the window.

- Try to create a user interface that no one notices.

- Related controls should be grouped together using white space, a GroupBox control, or a Panel control.

- Set the form's FormBorderStyle, ControlBox, MaximizeBox, MinimizeBox, and StartPosition properties appropriately:

  - A splash screen should not have a Minimize, Maximize, or Close button, and its borders should not be sizable.

  - A form that is not a splash screen should always have a Minimize button and a Close button, but you can choose to disable the Maximize button. Typically, the FormBorderStyle property is set to Sizable, but also can be set to FixedSingle.

- Position related controls on succeeding dots. Controls that are not part of any logical grouping may be positioned from two to four dots away from other controls.

- Buttons should be positioned either in a row along the bottom of the screen, or stacked in either the upper-right or lower-right corner.

- If the buttons are positioned at the bottom of the screen, then each button should be the same height; their widths, however, may vary.

- If the buttons are stacked in either the upper-right or lower-right corner of the screen, then each should be the same height and the same width.

- Use no more than six buttons on a screen.

- The most commonly used button should be placed first.

- The default button should be the button that is most often selected by the user, except in cases where tasks performed by the user are both destructive and irreversible. The default button typically is the first button.

- Button captions should:

  - be meaningful
  - be from one to three words
  - appear on one line
  - be entered using book title capitalization

- Use labels to identify the text boxes in the interface, and position the label either above or to the left of the text box.

- Label text should:

  - be from one to three words
  - appear on one line
  - be left-justified
  - end with a colon (:)
  - be entered using sentence capitalization

- Labels that identify controls should have their BorderStyle property set to None.

- Labels that display program output, such as the result of a calculation, should have their BorderStyle property set to FixedSingle.

- Align controls to minimize the number of different margins.

- If you use a graphic in the interface, use a small one and place it in a location that will not distract the user.

- Use the Tahoma font for applications that will run on Windows 2000 or Windows XP.

- Use no more than two different font sizes, which should be 8, 9, 10, 11, or 12 point.

- Use only one font type, which should be a sans serif font, in the interface.

- Avoid using italics and underlining.

- Limit the use of bold text to titles, headings, and key items.

- Build the interface using black, white, and gray first, then add color only if you have a good reason to do so.

- Use white, off-white, light gray, pale blue, or pale yellow for an application's background, and black for the text.

- Limit the number of colors to three, not including white, black, and gray. The colors you choose should complement each other.

- Never use color as the only means of identification for an element in the user interface.

- Set each control's TabIndex property to a number that represents the order in which you want the control to receive the focus (begin with 0).

- A text box's TabIndex value should be one more than the TabIndex value of its identifying label.

- Assign a unique access key to each control (in the interface) that can receive user input (text boxes, buttons, and so on).

- When assigning an access key to a control, use the first letter of the caption or identifying label, unless another letter provides a more meaningful association. If you can't use the first letter and no other letter provides a more meaningful association, then use a distinctive consonant. Lastly, use a vowel or a number.

- Lock the controls in place on the form.

- Document the program internally.

- Use the Val function on any Text property involved in a calculation.

- Use the Format function to improve the appearance of numbers in the interface.

- In the InputBox function, use sentence capitalization for the *prompt*, and book title capitalization for the *title*.

- Use sentence capitalization for the optional identifying label in a group box control.

- MessageBox.Show method:

  - Use sentence capitalization for the *text* argument, but book title capitalization for the *caption* argument. The name of the application typically appears in the *caption* argument.

  - Avoid using the words "error," "warning," or "mistake" in the message.

■ Display the Warning Message icon ⚠ in a message box that alerts the user that he or she must make a decision before the application can continue. You can phrase the message as a question.

■ Display the Information Message icon ⓘ in a message box that displays an informational message along with an OK button only.

■ Display the Stop Message icon ⊗ when you want to alert the user of a serious problem that must be corrected before the application can continue.

■ The default button in the dialog box should be the one that represents the user's most likely action, as long as that action is not destructive.

■ Use the KeyPress event to prevent a text box from accepting inappropriate keys.

■ Radio buttons:

■ Use radio buttons when you want to limit the user to one of two or more related and mutually exclusive choices.

■ Use a minimum of two and a maximum of seven radio buttons in an interface.

■ Use sentence capitalization for the label entered in the radio button's Text property.

■ Assign a unique access key to each radio button in an interface.

■ Use a group box control (or a panel control) to create separate groups of radio buttons. Only one button in each group can be selected at any one time.

■ Designate a default radio button in each group of radio buttons.

■ Check boxes:

■ Use check boxes to allow the user to select any number of choices from a group of one or more independent and nonexclusive choices.

■ Use sentence capitalization for the label entered in the check box's Text property.

■ Assign a unique access key to each check box in an interface.

■ It is customary in Windows applications to disable objects that do not apply to the current state of the application.

■ It is customary in Windows applications to highlight, or select, the existing text in a text box when the text box receives the focus.

■ Test the application with both valid and invalid data (for example, test the application without entering any data, and test it by entering letters where numbers are expected).

1. In this exercise, you code an application for Colfax Industries. The application totals the sales made in four regions: North, South, East, and West.

    a. If necessary, start Visual Studio .NET. Open the Colfax Solution (Colfax Solution.sln) file, which is contained in the VBNET\Tut06\Colfax Solution folder. If the designer window is not open, right-click the form file's name in the Solution Explorer window, then click View Designer.

    b. Create a collection, then assign each text box to the collection.

    c. Code the Add button's Click event procedure so that it adds the four sales amounts together, and then displays the sum in the TotalSalesLabel control. Format the sum using the Currency format style.

d. Clear the contents of the TotalSalesLabel control when the contents of a text box changes.

e. Select the text in each text box when the user tabs into the control.

f. Code the form's Closing event so that it asks the user whether he or she wants to exit the application, and then takes the appropriate action based on the user's answer.

g. Save the solution, then start the application. Test the application by entering the following four sales amounts: 1000, 2000, 3000, and 4000. Click the Add button.

h. Click the Exit button to end the application, then click the Yes button.

i. Close the Output window, then close the solution.

2. In this exercise, you code an application that selects the appropriate state name when the user selects the name of a state capital. It also selects the appropriate capital name when the user selects the name of a state.

a. If necessary, start Visual Studio .NET. Open the Capitals Solution (Capitals Solution.sln) file, which is contained in the VBNET\Tut06\Capitals Solution folder. If the designer window is not open, right-click the form file's name in the Solution Explorer window, then click View Designer. The interface contains two groups of radio buttons. The first group contains state names, and the second group contains the names of state capitals.

b. Create a separate collection for each group of radio buttons, then assign each radio button to the appropriate collection.

c. When the user clicks a radio button in the state name group, the application should select the appropriate capital name radio button, and vice versa. For example, when you click the Colorado radio button, the application should select the Denver radio button. And, when you click the Madison radio button, the application should select the Wisconsin radio button.

d. Save the solution, then start the application. Test the application by clicking each radio button.

e. Click the Exit button to end the application.

f. Close the Output window, then close the solution.

3. In this exercise, you code an application for Gwen Industries. The application calculates and displays the total sales and bonus amounts.

a. If necessary, start Visual Studio .NET. Open the Gwen Solution (Gwen Solution.sln) file, which is contained in the VBNET\Tut06\Gwen Solution folder. If the designer window is not open, right-click the form file's name in the Solution Explorer window, then click View Designer.

b. Code the Calculate control's Click event procedure so that it allows the user to enter as many sales amounts as he or she wants to enter. (*Hint*: Use the InputBox function.) When the user has completed entering the sales amounts, the procedure should display the total sales in the TotSalesLabel control. It also should display a 10% bonus in the BonusLabel control.

c. When the user clicks either the Exit button or the form's Close button, the application should ask the user whether he or she wants to exit, and then take the appropriate action based on the user's response.

d. Save the solution, then start the application. Test the application by entering your name in the Name text box. Click the Calculate button, then enter the following six sales amounts: 600.50, 4500.75, 3500, 2000, 1000, and 6500.

e. Click the Exit button to end the application, then click the Yes button.

f. Close the Output window, then close the solution.

4. In this exercise, you create an application for Premium Paper. The application allows the sales manager to enter the company's income and expense amounts. The number of income and expense amounts may vary each time the application is started.

For example, the user may enter five income amounts and three expense amounts. Or, he or she may enter 20 income amounts and 30 expense amounts. The application should calculate and display the company's total income, total expense, and profit (or loss). Use the InputBox function to get the individual income and expense amounts.

a. If necessary, start Visual Studio .NET. Create a blank solution named Premium Solution. Save the solution in the VBNET\Tut06 folder.

b. Add a Visual Basic .NET Windows Application project to the solution. Name the project Premium Project.

c. Assign the filename Premium Form.vb to the form file object.

d. Assign the name PremiumForm to the Windows Form object.

e. Design an appropriate interface. Use label controls to display the total income, total expenses, and profit (loss). Display the calculated amounts using the Currency format style. If the company experienced a loss, display the amount of the loss using a red font; otherwise, display the profit using a black font. (*Hint*: Set the label control's ForeColor property to either `Color.Red` or `Color.Black`.)

f. Code the application appropriately.

g. Save the solution, then start the application. Test the application twice, using the following data:

First test: Income amounts: 57.75, 83.23
                       Expense amounts: 200
Second test: Income amounts: 5000, 6000, 35000, 78000
                       Expense amounts: 1000, 2000, 600

h. End the application.

i. Close the Output window, then close the solution.

Exercise 5 is a Discovery Exercise. Discovery Exercises, which may include topics that are not covered in this lesson, allow you to "discover" the solutions to problems on your own.

discovery ▶ 5. In this exercise, you code an application that allows you to play the Tic-Tac-Toe game.

a. If necessary, start Visual Studio .NET. Open the TicTacToe Solution (TicTacToe Solution.sln) file, which is contained in the VBNET\Tut06\TicTacToe Solution folder. If the designer window is not open, right-click the form file's name in the Solution Explorer window, then click View Designer. The interface contains nine label controls and two button controls. The New Game button's Click event procedure should clear the contents of the label controls and allow the user to play another game of Tic-Tac-Toe. The Exit button's Click event procedure should simply end the application.

b. Code the application appropriately.

c. Start the application, then test the application.

d. Click the Exit button to end the application.

e. Close the Output window, then close the solution.

Exercise 6 is a Debugging Exercise. Debugging Exercises provide an opportunity for you to detect and correct errors in an existing application.

debugging 6. In this exercise, you debug an existing application. The purpose of this exercise is to demonstrate common errors made when using collections.

a. If necessary, start Visual Studio .NET. Open the Debug Solution (Debug Solution.sln) file, which is contained in the VBNET\Tut06\Debug Solution folder. If the designer window is not open, right-click the form file's name in the Solution Explorer window, then click View Designer.

b. Open the Code editor window and study the existing code.

c. Start the application. Click the Example 1 button, which should display the words "Controls Collection" only in the three label controls. Notice that the Example 1 button is not working properly.

d. Click the bottom button to end the application.

e. Correct the Example 1 button's code, then save the solution and start the application. Click the Example 1 button, which should display the words "Controls Collection" in the three label controls.

f. Now click the Example 2 button, which should display the words "Label Collection" in the three label controls. An error message appears in a message box. Read the message, then click the Break button. The Code editor window highlights the instruction that is causing the error.

g. Click Debug on the menu bar, and then click Stop Debugging.

h. Correct the Example 2 button's code, then save the solution and start the application. Click the Example 2 button, which should display the words "Label Collection" in the three label controls.

i. Click the Exit button to end the application.

j. Close the Output window, then close the solution.

Sub and Function Procedures

Creating a Payroll Application

case ▶ Currently, Jefferson Williams, the payroll manager at Nelson Industries, manually calculates each employee's weekly gross pay, federal withholding tax (FWT), Social Security and Medicare (FICA) tax, and net pay—a very time-consuming process and one that is prone to mathematical errors. Mr. Williams has asked you to create an application that he can use to perform the payroll calculations both efficiently and accurately.

Previewing the Completed Application

Before creating the Payroll application, you first preview the completed application.

To preview the completed application:

1　Use the Run command on the Windows Start menu to run the **Payroll** (Payroll.exe) file, which is contained in the VBNET\Tut07 folder on your computer's hard disk. A copyright screen similar to the one that you created in Tutorial 1 appears on the screen. In a few seconds, the copyright screen closes and the user interface for the Payroll application appears on the screen. (Recall that the copyright screen from Tutorial 1 contains a timer control that removes the form from the screen after eight seconds have elapsed.)

2　Type your name in the Name text box.

3　Scroll down the Hours list box until you see the number 41, then click **41** in the list.

4　Scroll down the Rate list box until you see the number 10.50, then click **10.50** in the list.

5　Click the **Single** radio button, and then click **1** in the Allowances list box.

6　Click the **Calculate** button. The application calculates and displays the amount of your gross pay, federal withholding tax (FWT), Social Security and Medicare (FICA) tax, and net pay. See Figure 7-1.

your name will appear here

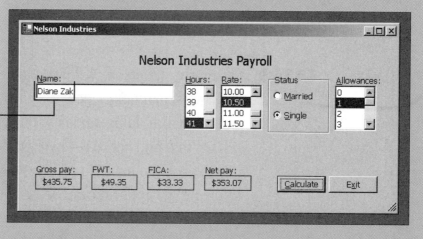

Figure 7-1: Payroll amounts shown in the Payroll application

7　Click the **Exit** button. The application closes.

The Payroll application uses list boxes and a user-defined Function procedure. You learn about user-defined procedures in Lesson A, and about list boxes in Lesson B. You begin coding the Payroll application in Lesson B and complete it in Lesson C.

After completing this lesson, you will be able to:

- Explain the difference between a Sub procedure and a Function procedure
- Create a procedure that receives information passed to it
- Explain the difference between passing data *by value* and *by reference*
- Create a Function procedure

Creating Sub and Function Procedures

Procedures

A **procedure** is a block of program code that performs a specific task. Procedures in Visual Basic .NET can be either Sub procedures or Function procedures. The difference between both types of procedures is that a **Function procedure** returns a value after performing its assigned task, whereas a **Sub procedure** does not return a value. Although you have been using Sub procedures since Tutorial 1, this lesson provides a more in-depth look into their creation and use. After exploring the topic of Sub procedures, you then learn how to create and use Function procedures.

Sub Procedures

There are two types of Sub procedures in Visual Basic .NET: event procedures and user-defined Sub procedures. Most of the procedures that you coded in previous tutorials were event procedures. An event procedure is simply a Sub procedure that is associated with a specific object and event, such as a button's Click event or a text box's KeyPress event. Recall that the computer automatically processes an event procedure when the event occurs.

You learned how to create a user-defined Sub procedure in Tutorial 5. Unlike an event procedure, a user-defined Sub procedure is independent of any object and event, and is processed only when called, or invoked, from code. Recall that you invoke a user-defined Sub procedure using the Call statement.

A Sub procedure can contain one or more parameters in its procedure header. Each parameter stores data that is passed to the procedure when it is invoked. For example, all event procedures contain two parameters: sender and e. The sender parameter contains the internal memory address of the object that raised the event, and the e parameter contains any additional information provided by the object. For instance, when a button's Click event occurs, the address of the button is passed to the Click event procedure and stored in the procedure's sender parameter. No additional information is passed when a Click event occurs, so no information is stored in a Click event procedure's e parameter.

Now consider what happens when the user types the letter B in a text box named NameTextBox. As you learned in Tutorial 4, typing a letter in a text box causes the text box's KeyPress event to occur. When the NameTextBox control's KeyPress event occurs, the address of the text box is passed to the KeyPress event procedure and stored in the procedure's `sender` parameter. Two additional items of information also are passed to the KeyPress event procedure. These items, `KeyChar="B"` and `Handled=False`, are stored in the procedure's `e` parameter. (Recall that the KeyChar property contains the character corresponding to the key that was pressed, and the Handled property determines whether the text box accepts the key contained in the KeyChar property.)

Like the procedure header for an event procedure, the procedure header for a user-defined Sub procedure also can include one or more parameters.

Including Parameters in a User-Defined Sub Procedure

Figure 7-2 shows the syntax you use to create a user-defined Sub procedure.

procedure header

procedure footer

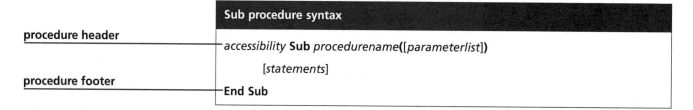

Sub procedure syntax

accessibility **Sub** *procedurename*(**[***parameterlist***]**)

    [*statements*]

End Sub

Figure 7-2: Syntax for creating a user-defined Sub procedure

As do all procedures, user-defined Sub procedures have both a procedure header and procedure footer. The procedure header begins with the procedure's *accessibility*, which determines from where in the application the procedure can be called (or accessed). *Accessibility* can be one of the following keywords: Private, Public, Protected, Friend, and Protected Friend. You use the keyword Private to indicate that only the procedures in the current form can access the procedure. You use the keyword Public when you want to allow unlimited access to the procedure. The process of creating Sub procedures using the keywords Protected, Friend, or Protected Friend is beyond the scope of this book.

Following *accessibility* in the procedure header is the keyword Sub, which identifies the procedure as a Sub procedure—one that does not return a value after performing its assigned task. After the keyword Sub is the *procedurename* and a set of parentheses that contains an optional *parameterlist*. The *parameterlist* lists the data type and name of memory locations used by the procedure to store the information passed to it. The *parameterlist* also specifies how each item of information is passed—either *by value* or *by reference*. You learn more about the *parameterlist*, as well as passing information *by value* and *by reference*, later in this lesson.

Unlike the procedure header, which varies with each procedure, the procedure footer for a Sub procedure is always `End Sub`. Between the procedure header and the procedure footer, you enter the instructions you want the computer to process when the procedure is invoked.

tip

As you learned in Tutorial 5, it is a common practice to begin a procedure's name with a verb.

Visual Basic .NET allows you to specify that an argument in the Call statement is optional. If the argument is not provided, a default value is used for the corresponding parameter in the *parameterlist*. You learn more about optional arguments in Discovery Exercise 11 at the end of this lesson.

As you learned in Tutorial 5, you can use the Call statement to call (or invoke) a Sub procedure. Recall that the syntax of the Call statement is **Call** *procedurename* ([*argumentlist*]), where *procedurename* is the name of the procedure you are calling, and *argumentlist* (which is optional) is a comma-separated list of arguments you want passed to the procedure. The number of arguments listed in the Call statement's *argumentlist* should agree with the number of parameters listed in the *parameterlist* in the procedure header. If the *argumentlist* includes one argument, then the procedure header should have one parameter in its *parameterlist*. Similarly, a procedure that is passed three arguments when called requires three parameters in its *parameterlist*. (Refer to the first tip on this page for an exception to this general rule.)

In addition to having the same number of parameters as arguments, the data type and position of each parameter in the *parameterlist* must agree with the data type and position of its corresponding argument in the *argumentlist*. For instance, if the argument is an integer, then the parameter in which the integer will be stored should have a data type of Integer, Short, or Long, depending on the size of the integer. Likewise, if two arguments are passed to a procedure—the first one being a String variable and the second one being a Single variable—the first parameter should have a data type of String and the second parameter should have a data type of Single.

You can pass a literal constant, named constant, keyword, or variable to a user-defined Sub procedure; in most cases, you will pass a variable.

Passing Variables

Each variable you declare in an application has both a value and a unique address that represents the location of the variable in the computer's internal memory. Visual Basic .NET allows you to pass either the variable's value (referred to as **passing by value**) or its address (referred to as **passing by reference**) to the receiving procedure. The method you choose—*by value* or *by reference*—depends on whether you want the receiving procedure to have access to the variable in memory—in other words, whether you want to allow the receiving procedure to change the contents of the variable.

Although the idea of passing information *by value* and *by reference* may sound confusing at first, it is a concept with which you already are familiar. To illustrate, assume that you have a savings account at a local bank. During a conversation with a friend, you mention the amount of money you have in the account. Telling someone the amount of money in your account is similar to passing a variable *by value*. Knowing the balance in your account does not give your friend access to your bank account; it merely gives your friend some information that he or she can use—perhaps to compare to the amount of money he or she has saved.

The savings account example also provides an illustration of passing information *by reference*. To deposit money to or withdraw money from your account, you must provide the bank teller with your account number. The account number represents the location of your account at the bank and allows the teller to change the account balance. Giving the teller your bank account number is similar to passing a variable *by reference*. The account number allows the teller to change the contents of your bank account, similar to the way the variable's address allows the receiving procedure to change the contents of the variable passed to the procedure.

First, learn how to pass a variable *by value*.

The internal memory of a computer is like a large post office, where each memory cell, like each post office box, has a unique address.

Passing Variables by Value

tip

In previous versions of Visual Basic, the default method for passing variables is *by reference*.

To pass a variable *by value* in Visual Basic .NET, you include the keyword ByVal, which stands for "by value", before the variable's corresponding parameter in the *parameterlist.* When you pass a variable *by value*, the computer passes only the contents of the variable to the receiving procedure. When only the contents are passed, the receiving procedure is not given access to the variable in memory, so it cannot change the value stored inside the variable. You pass a variable *by value* when the receiving procedure needs to *know* the variable's contents, but the receiving procedure does not need to *change* the contents. Unless specified otherwise, variables are passed *by value* in Visual Basic .NET.

Figure 7-3 shows two examples of passing variables *by value*. The *argumentlist* in each Call statement, and the *parameterlist* in each procedure header, are shaded in the figure.

Examples – passing *by value*

Example 1

```
Private Sub GetInfoButton_Click(ByVal sender As Object, _
           ByVal e As System.EventArgs) Handles GetInfoButton.Click
     Dim strName, strAge As String
     strName = InputBox("Pet's name:", "Name")
     strAge = InputBox("Pet's age (years):", "Age")
     Call DisplayMsg(strName, strAge)
End Sub


Private Sub DisplayMsg(ByVal strPet As String, ByVal strYears As String)
     Me.MessageLabel.Text = "Your pet " & strPet & " is " _
           & strYears & " years old."
End Sub
```

Example 2

```
Private Sub CalcButton_Click(ByVal sender As Object, _
           ByVal e As System.EventArgs) Handles CalcButton.Click
     Dim intRegion1, intRegion2 As Integer, sngBonusRate As Single
     intRegion1 = Val(Me.Region1TextBox.Text)
     intRegion2 = Val(Me.Region2TextBox.Text)
     sngBonusRate = Val(Me.BonusRateTextBox.Text)
     Call CalcAndDisplayBonus(intRegion1, intRegion2, sngBonusRate)
End Sub


Private Sub CalcAndDisplayBonus(ByVal intSale1 As Integer, _
                                ByVal intSale2 As Integer, _
                                ByVal sngRate As Single)
     Dim intTotal As Integer, sngBonus As Single
     intTotal = intSale1 + intSale2
     sngBonus = intTotal * sngRate
     Me.BonusLabel.Text = Format(sngBonus, "currency")
End Sub
```

Figure 7-3: Examples of passing variables *by value*

Notice that, in both examples, the number, data type, and sequence of the arguments in the Call statement match the number, data type, and sequence of the corresponding parameters in the procedure header. Also notice that the names of the parameters do not need to be identical to the names of the arguments to which they correspond. In fact, for clarity, it usually is better to use different names for the arguments and parameters.

Study closely the code shown in Example 1 in Figure 7-3. The GetInfoButton control's Click event procedure first declares two String variables named strName and strAge. The next two statements in the procedure use the InputBox function to prompt the user to enter the name and age (in years) of his or her pet. Assume that the user enters "Spot" as the name and "4" as the age. The computer stores the string "Spot" in the strName variable and the string "4" in the strAge variable.

Next, the `Call DisplayMsg(strName, strAge)` statement calls the DisplayMsg procedure, passing it the strName and strAge variables *by value*, which means that only the contents of the variables—in this case, "Spot" and "4"—are passed to the procedure. You know that the variables are passed *by value* because the keyword ByVal appears before each variable's corresponding parameter in the DisplayMsg procedure header. At this point, the computer temporarily leaves the GetInfoButton Click event procedure to process the code contained in the DisplayMsg procedure.

The first instruction processed in the DisplayMsg procedure is the procedure header. When processing the procedure header, the computer creates the strPet and strYears variables (which are listed in the *parameterlist*) in its internal memory, and stores the information passed to the procedure in those variables. In this case, the computer stores the string "Spot" in the strPet variable and the string "4" in the strYears variable. The strPet and strYears variables are local to the DisplayMsg procedure, which means they can be used only by the procedure.

After processing the DisplayMsg procedure header, the computer processes the assignment statement contained in the procedure. The assignment statement uses the values stored in the procedure's parameters—strPet and strYears—to display the appropriate message in the MessageLabel control. In this case, the statement displays the message "Your pet Spot is 4 years old."

Next, the computer processes the DisplayMsg procedure footer, which ends the DisplayMsg procedure. At this point, the strPet and strYears variables are removed from the computer's internal memory. (Recall that a local variable is removed from the computer's memory when the procedure in which it is declared ends.) The computer then returns to the GetInfoButton Click event procedure, to the statement immediately following the `Call DisplayMsg(strName, strAge)` statement. This statement, `End Sub`, ends the GetInfoButton Click event procedure. The computer then removes the procedure's local variables (strName and strAge) from its internal memory.

Now study closely the code shown in Example 2 in Figure 7-3. The CalcButton Click event procedure first declares two Integer variables named intRegion1 and intRegion2, and a Single variable named sngBonusRate. The next three statements in the procedure assign the contents of three text boxes to the variables. Assume that the user entered the number 1000 in the Region1TextBox, the number 3000 in the Region2TextBox, and the number .1 in the BonusRateTextBox. The computer stores the number 1000 in the intRegion1 variable, the number 3000 in the intRegion2 variable, and the number .1 in the sngBonusRate variable.

Next, the `Call CalcAndDisplayBonus(intRegion1, intRegion2, sngBonusRate)` statement calls the CalcAndDisplayBonus procedure, passing it three variables *by value*, which means that only the contents of the variables—in this case, 1000, 3000, and .1—are passed to the procedure. Here again, you know that the variables are passed *by value* because the keyword ByVal appears before each variable's corresponding parameter in the CalcAndDisplayBonus procedure header. At this point, the computer temporarily leaves the CalcButton Click event procedure to process the code contained in the CalcAndDisplayBonus procedure.

The first instruction processed in the CalcAndDisplayBonus procedure is the procedure header. When processing the procedure header, the computer creates the three local variables listed in the *parameterlist*, and stores the information passed to the procedure in those variables. In this case, the computer stores the number 1000 in the intSale1 variable, the number 3000 in the intSale2 variable, and the number .1 in the sngRate variable.

After processing the CalcAndDisplayBonus procedure header, the computer processes the statements contained in the procedure. The first statement declares two additional local variables named intTotal and sngBonus. The next statement adds the value stored in the intSale1 variable (1000) to the value stored in the intSale2 variable (3000), and assigns the sum (4000) to the intTotal variable. The third statement in the procedure multiplies the value stored in the intTotal variable (4000) by the value stored in the sngRate (.1) variable, and assigns the result (400) to the sngBonus variable. The fourth statement in the procedure displays the bonus, formatted using the Currency format style, in the BonusLabel control; in this case, the statement displays $400.00.

Next, the computer processes the CalcAndDisplayBonus procedure footer, which ends the CalcAndDisplayBonus procedure. At this point, the procedure's local variables—intSale1, intSale2, sngRate, intTotal, and sngBonus—are removed from the computer's internal memory. The computer then returns to the CalcButton Click event procedure, to the statement immediately following the Call statement. This statement, `End Sub`, ends the CalcButton Click event procedure. The computer then removes the intRegion1, intRegion2, and sngBonusRate variables from its internal memory.

Next, learn how to pass variables *by reference*.

Passing Variables by Reference

In addition to passing a variable's value to a procedure, you also can pass a variable's address—in other words, its location in the computer's internal memory. Passing a variable's address is referred to as passing *by reference*, and it gives the receiving procedure access to the variable being passed. You pass a variable *by reference* when you want the receiving procedure to change the contents of the variable.

To pass a variable *by reference* in Visual Basic .NET, you include the keyword ByRef, which stands for "by reference", before the name of the variable's corresponding parameter in the procedure header. The ByRef keyword tells the computer to pass the variable's address rather than its contents.

Figure 7-4 shows two examples of passing variables *by reference*. The *argumentlist* in each Call statement, and the *parameterlist* in each procedure header, are shaded in the figure.

Examples – passing *by reference*

Example 1
```
Private Sub DisplayButton_Click(ByVal sender As Object, _
        ByVal e As System.EventArgs) Handles DisplayButton.Click
    Dim strName, strAge As String
    Call GetInfo(strName, strAge)
    Me.MessageLabel.Text = "Your pet " & strName & " is " _
        & strAge & " years old."
End Sub


Private Sub GetInfo(ByRef strPet As String, ByRef strYears As String)
    strPet = InputBox("Pet's name:", "Name")
    strYears = InputBox("Pet's age (years):", "Age")
End Sub
```

Example 2
```
Private Sub BonusButton_Click(ByVal sender As Object, _
        ByVal e As System.EventArgs) Handles BonusButton.Click
    Dim intRegion1, intRegion2 As Integer, sngBonus As Single
    intRegion1 = Val(Me.Region1TextBox.Text)
    intRegion2 = Val(Me.Region2TextBox.Text)
    Call CalcBonus(intRegion1, intRegion2, .05, sngBonus)
    Me.BonusLabel.Text = Format(sngBonus, "currency")
End Sub


Private Sub CalcBonus(ByVal intSale1 As Integer, _
                      ByVal intSale2 As Integer, _
                      ByVal sngRate As Single, _
                      ByRef sngDollars As Single)
    Dim intTotal As Integer
    intTotal = intSale1 + intSale2
    sngDollars = intTotal * sngRate
End Sub
```

Figure 7-4: Examples of passing variables *by reference*

tip

••••••••••••••••••

You cannot determine by looking at the Call statement whether a variable is being passed *by value* or *by reference*. You must look at the procedure header to make the determination.

Notice that, in both examples, the number, data type, and sequence of the arguments in the Call statement match the number, data type, and sequence of the corresponding parameters in the procedure header. Also notice that the names of the parameters do not need to be identical to the names of the arguments to which they correspond.

Study closely the code shown in Example 1 in Figure 7-4. The DisplayButton Click event procedure first declares two String variables named strName and strAge. The next statement in the procedure calls the GetInfo procedure, passing it the strName and strAge variables *by reference*, which means that each variable's address in memory, rather than its contents, is passed to the procedure. You know that the variables are passed *by reference* because the keyword ByRef appears before each variable's corresponding parameter in the GetInfo procedure header. At this point, the computer temporarily leaves the DisplayButton Click event procedure to process the code contained in the GetInfo procedure.

The strName and strAge variables are local to the DisplayButton Click event procedure. The strPet and strYears variables, on the other hand, are local to the GetInfo procedure.

The first instruction processed in the GetInfo procedure is the procedure header. The ByRef keyword that appears before each parameter's name in the procedure header indicates that the procedure will be receiving the addresses of two variables. When you pass a variable's address to a procedure, the computer uses the address to locate the variable in memory. It then assigns the name appearing in the procedure header to the memory location. In this case, for example, the computer first locates the strName and strAge variables in memory; after doing so, it assigns the names strPet and strYears, respectively, to these locations. At this point, each of the two memory locations has two names: one assigned by the DisplayButton Click event procedure, and the other assigned by the GetInfo procedure.

After processing the GetInfo procedure header, the computer processes the two assignment statements contained in the procedure. Those statements prompt the user to enter the name and age of his or her pet, and then store the user's responses in the strPet and strYears variables. Assume that the user entered "Simba" as the name and "9" as the age. The computer stores the string "Simba" in the strPet variable and the string "9" in the strYears variable. Figure 7-5 shows the contents of memory after the two assignment statements in the GetInfo procedure are processed. Notice that changing the contents of the strPet and strYears variables also changes the contents of the strName and strAge variables, respectively. This is because the names refer to the same locations in memory.

memory location names	strName (DisplayButton Click event procedure) strPet (GetInfo procedure)	strAge (DisplayButton Click event procedure) strYears (GetInfo procedure)
memory location contents	Simba	9

Figure 7-5: Contents of memory after the two assignment statements in the GetInfo procedure are processed

As Figure 7-5 indicates, the two memory locations belong to both the DisplayButton Click event procedure and the GetInfo procedure. Although both procedures can access the two memory locations, each procedure uses a different name to do so. The DisplayButton Click event procedure, for example, uses the names strName and strAge to refer to these memory locations. The GetInfo procedure, on the other hand, uses the names strPet and strYears.

The End Sub statement in the GetInfo procedure is processed next and ends the procedure. At this point, the computer removes the strPet and strYears names assigned to the memory locations. Now, each memory location shown in Figure 7-5 has only one name.

The computer then returns to the DisplayButton Click event procedure, to the statement located immediately below the Call statement. This statement displays the message "Your pet Simba is 9 years old." in the MessageLabel control. Next, the computer processes the End Sub statement in the DisplayButton Click event procedure, which ends the procedure. The computer then removes the strName and strAge variables from its internal memory.

Now study the code shown in Example 2 in Figure 7-4. The BonusButton Click event procedure first declares two Integer variables named intRegion1 and intRegion2, and a Single variable named sngBonus. The next two statements assign the contents of two text boxes to the intRegion1 and intRegion2 variables. Assume that the user entered the numbers 500 and 200 in the text boxes. The computer stores the number 500 in the intRegion1 variable and the number 200 in the intRegion2 variable.

Next, the `Call CalcBonus(intRegion1, intRegion2, .05, sngBonus)` statement calls the CalcBonus procedure. The CalcBonus procedure header indicates that the first three arguments in the Call statement will be passed *by value*, whereas the last argument will be passed *by reference*. The items passed *by value* should be stored in the intSale1, intSale2, and sngRate variables. The item passed *by reference* should be stored in a variable named sngDollars.

When the computer processes the CalcBonus procedure header, it first creates the intSale1, intSale2, and sngRate variables in memory. It then stores the numbers 500, 200, and .05, respectively, in the variables. Next, the computer locates the sngBonus variable (which is declared in the BonusButton Click event procedure) in memory, and assigns the name sngDollars to the memory location.

After processing the CalcBonus procedure header, the computer processes the statements contained in the procedure. The first statement declares a local variable named intTotal. The next statement adds the value stored in the intSale1 variable (500) to the value stored in the intSale2 variable (200), and then assigns the sum (700) to the intTotal variable. The third statement in the procedure multiplies the value stored in the intTotal variable (700) by the value stored in the sngRate variable (.05), and then assigns the result (35) to the sngDollars variable. The `End Sub` statement in the CalcBonus procedure then ends the procedure. At this point, the computer removes the intSale1, intSale2, sngRate, and intTotal variables from its internal memory. It also removes the sngDollars name assigned to the sngBonus memory location.

When the CalcBonus procedure ends, the computer returns to the BonusButton Click event procedure, to the statement located immediately below the Call statement. This statement displays the number $35.00 in the BonusLabel control. Finally, the computer processes the `End Sub` statement in the BonusButton Click event procedure, which ends the procedure. The computer then removes the intRegion1, intRegion2, and sngBonus variables from its internal memory.

As you learned earlier, in addition to creating Sub procedures, you also can create Function procedures in Visual Basic .NET.

tip

Notice that you can pass a literal constant—in this case, the number .05—to a procedure. Literal constants are usually passed *by value* to a procedure.

Function Procedures

Like a Sub procedure, a **Function procedure**, typically referred to simply as a **function**, is a block of code that performs a specific task. However, unlike a Sub procedure, a function returns a value after completing its task. Some functions, such as the Val and InputBox functions, are intrinsic to Visual Basic .NET. Recall that the Val function returns the numeric equivalent of a string, and the InputBox function returns the user's response to a prompt that appears in a dialog box.

You also can create your own functions, referred to as **user-defined functions**, in Visual Basic .NET. After creating a user-defined function, you then can invoke it from one or more places in the application. You invoke a user-defined function in exactly the same way as you invoke a built-in function—simply by including the function's name in a statement. You also can pass (send) information to a user-defined function, and the information can be passed either *by value* or *by reference*.

Figure 7-6 shows the syntax you use to create a user-defined function. It also includes an example of using the syntax to create a user-defined function.

procedure header

procedure footer

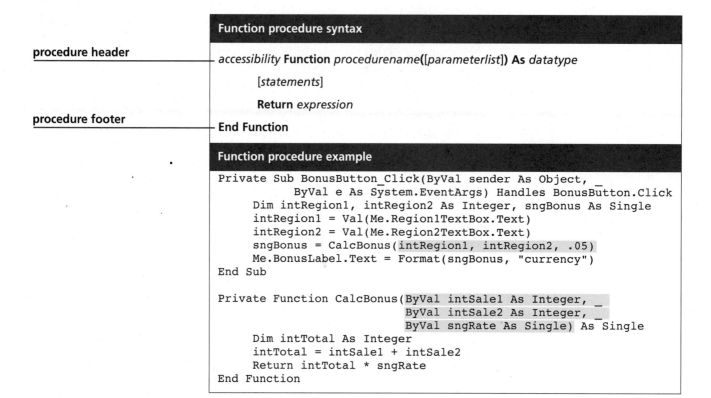

Function procedure syntax

accessibility **Function** *procedurename*(*[parameterlist]*) **As** *datatype*

    [statements]

    Return *expression*

End Function

Function procedure example

```
Private Sub BonusButton_Click(ByVal sender As Object, _
        ByVal e As System.EventArgs) Handles BonusButton.Click
    Dim intRegion1, intRegion2 As Integer, sngBonus As Single
    intRegion1 = Val(Me.Region1TextBox.Text)
    intRegion2 = Val(Me.Region2TextBox.Text)
    sngBonus = CalcBonus(intRegion1, intRegion2, .05)
    Me.BonusLabel.Text = Format(sngBonus, "currency")
End Sub

Private Function CalcBonus(ByVal intSale1 As Integer, _
                           ByVal intSale2 As Integer, _
                           ByVal sngRate As Single) As Single
    Dim intTotal As Integer
    intTotal = intSale1 + intSale2
    Return intTotal * sngRate
End Function
```

Figure 7-6: User-defined function syntax and example

tip

• • • • • • • • • • • • • • • •

Functions typically are called from statements that display the function's return value, use the return value in a calculation, or assign the return value to a variable.

Like Sub procedures, Function procedures have both a procedure header and procedure footer. The procedure header for a Function procedure is almost identical to the procedure header for a Sub procedure, except it includes the keyword Function rather than the keyword Sub. The keyword Function identifies the procedure as a Function procedure—one that returns a value after completing its task.

Also different from a Sub procedure header, a Function procedure header includes the As *datatype* clause. You use this clause to specify the data type of the value returned by the function. For example, if the function returns a string, you include As String at the end of the procedure header. Similarly, if the function returns a decimal number, you include As Single, As Decimal, or As Double at the end of the procedure header. The *datatype* you use depends on the size of the number, and whether you want the number stored with a fixed decimal point or a floating decimal point.

The procedure footer in a Function procedure is always End Function. Between the procedure header and the procedure footer, you enter the instructions you want the computer to process when the function is invoked. In most cases, the last statement in a Function procedure is **Return** *expression*, where *expression* represents the one and only value that will be returned to the statement that called the function. The data type of the *expression* in the Return statement must agree with the data type specified in the As *datatype* clause in the procedure header. The **Return statement** alerts the computer that the function has completed its task and ends the function after returning the value of its *expression*.

Study closely the example shown in Figure 7-6. The BonusButton Click event procedure first declares two Integer variables named intRegion1 and intRegion2, and a Single variable named sngBonus. The next two statements assign the contents of two text boxes to the intRegion1 and intRegion2 variables. Assume that the user entered the numbers 500 and 200 in the text boxes. The computer stores the number 500 in the intRegion1 variable and the number 200 in the intRegion2 variable.

Next, the `sngBonus = CalcBonus(intRegion1, intRegion2, .05)` statement calls the CalcBonus procedure, passing it the values 500, 200, and .05. The computer stores the values in the intSale1, intSale2, and sngRate variables, which appear in the CalcBonus procedure header.

After processing the CalcBonus procedure header, the computer processes the statements contained in the function. The first statement declares a local variable named intTotal. The next statement adds the value stored in the intSale1 variable (500) to the value stored in the intSale2 variable (200), and then assigns the sum (700) to the intTotal variable. The `Return intTotal * sngRate` statement in the function multiplies the value stored in the intTotal variable (700) by the value stored in the sngRate variable (.05), and then returns the result (35) to the statement that called the function—the `sngBonus = CalcBonus(intRegion1, intRegion2, .05)` statement in the BonusButton Click event procedure. After processing the Return statement, the CalcBonus function ends and the computer removes the intSale1, intSale2, sngRate, and intTotal variables from its internal memory.

The `sngBonus = CalcBonus(intRegion1, intRegion2, .05)` statement assigns the CalcBonus function's return value (35) to the sngBonus variable. The `Me.BonusLabel.Text = Format(sngBonus, "currency")` statement then displays $35.00 in the BonusLabel control. Finally, the computer processes the `End Sub` statement in the BonusButton Click event procedure, which ends the procedure. The computer then removes the intRegion1, intRegion2, and sngBonus variables from its internal memory.

The code shown in the example in Figure 7-6 is similar to the code shown in Example 2 in Figure 7-4. Both examples differ only in the way each assigns the appropriate bonus amount to the sngBonus variable. In Figure 7-6, the BonusButton Click event procedure calls a function to calculate the bonus amount, and then assigns the amount to the sngBonus variable. In Example 2 in Figure 7-4, on the other hand, the BonusButton Click event procedure passes the sngBonus variable *by reference* to the CalcBonus function. The CalcBonus function assigns the appropriate amount to the sngBonus variable. Both examples simply represent two different ways of performing the same task.

You now have completed Lesson A. You can either take a break or complete the end-of-lesson questions and exercises before moving on to the next lesson.

S U M M A R Y

To create a user-defined Sub procedure:

■   Refer to the syntax shown in Figure 7-2.

To create a user-defined Function procedure:

■   Refer to the syntax shown in Figure 7-6.

To pass information to a Sub or Function procedure:

■ Include the information in the Call statement's *argumentlist*. In the procedure header's *parameterlist*, include the names of memory locations that will store the information.

■ The number, data type, and sequence of the arguments listed in the Call statement's *argumentlist* should agree with the number, data type, and sequence of the parameters listed in the *parameterlist* in the procedure header.

To pass a variable *by value* to a procedure:

■ Include the keyword ByVal before the parameter name in the procedure header's *parameterlist*. Because only the value stored in the variable is passed, the receiving procedure cannot access the variable.

To pass a variable by reference:

■ Include the keyword ByRef before the parameter name in the procedure header's *parameterlist*. Because the address of the variable is passed, the receiving procedure can change the contents of the variable.

QUESTIONS

1. Which of the following is false?
   a. A Function procedure can return one or more values to the statement that called it.
   b. An event procedure is a Sub procedure that is associated with a specific object and event.
   c. A procedure can accept one or more items of data passed to it.
   d. The *parameterlist* in a procedure header is optional.
   e. At times, a memory location inside the computer's internal memory may have more than one name.

2. When the CodeRadioButton's Click event occurs, the address of the CodeRadioButton is stored in the event procedure's _____ parameter.
   a. `address`
   b. `button`
   c. `e`
   d. `object`
   e. `sender`

3. The items listed in the Call statement are called _____.
   a. arguments
   b. constraints
   c. events
   d. passers
   e. None of the above.

4. Each memory location listed in the *parameterlist* in the procedure header is referred to as _____.
   a. an address
   b. a constraint
   c. an event
   d. a parameter
   e. None of the above.

5. To determine whether a variable is being passed *by value* or *by reference* to a procedure, you will need to examine _____.
   a. the Call statement
   b. the procedure header
   c. the procedure footer
   d. the statements entered in the procedure
   e. Either a or b.

6. Which of the following statements can be used to call the CalcArea procedure, passing it two variables *by value*?
   a. `Call CalcArea(intLength, intWidth)`
   b. `Call CalcArea(ByVal intLength, intWidth)`
   c. `Call CalcArea(intLength, intWidth ByVal)`
   d. `Call ByVal CalcArea(intLength, intWidth)`
   e. `Call CalcArea(ByVal intLength, ByVal intWidth)`

7. Which of the following procedure headers receives the value stored in a String variable?
   a. `Private Sub DisplayName(strName As String)`
   b. `Private Sub DisplayName(ByValue strName As String)`
   c. `Private Sub DisplayName(ByRef strName As String)`
   d. `Private Sub DisplayName(strName ByVal As String)`
   e. None of the above.

8. Which of the following is a valid procedure header for a procedure that receives an integer first and a number with a decimal place second?
   a. `Private Sub CalcFee(intBase As Integer, sngRate As Single)`
   b. `Private Sub CalcFee(ByRef intBase As Integer, ByRef sngRate As Single)`
   c. `Private Sub CalcFee(ByVal intBase As Integer, ByVal sngRate As Single)`
   d. `Private Sub CalcFee(intBase As Integer ByVal, sngRate As Single ByVal)`
   e. None of the above.

9. A function procedure can return _____.
   a. one value only
   b. one or more values

10. The procedure header specifies the procedure's _____.
    a. accessibility
    b. name
    c. parameters
    d. type (either Sub or Function)
    e. All of the above.

11. Which of the following is false?
    a. In most cases, the number of arguments should agree with the number of parameters.
    b. The data type of each argument should match the data type of its corresponding parameter.
    c. The name of each argument should be identical to the name of its corresponding parameter.
    d. When you pass information to a procedure *by value*, the procedure stores the value of each item it receives in a separate memory location.
    e. The sequence of the arguments listed in the Call statement should agree with the sequence of the parameters listed in the procedure header.

12. Which of the following instructs a function to return the contents of the sngStateTax variable to the statement that called the function?

  a. `Restore sngStateTax`

  b. `Restore ByVal sngStateTax`

  c. `Return sngStateTax`

  d. `Return ByVal sngStateTax`

  e. `Return ByRef sngStateTax`

13. Which of the following is a valid procedure header for a procedure that receives the value stored in an Integer variable first and the address of a Single variable second?

  a. `Private Sub CalcFee(ByVal intBase As Integer, ByAdd sngRate As Single)`

  b. `Private Sub CalcFee(Val(intBase As Integer), Add(sngRate As Single))`

  c. `Private Sub CalcFee(ByVal intBase As Integer, ByRef sngRate As Single)`

  d. `Private Sub CalcFee(Value of intBase As Integer, Address of sngRate As Single)`

  e. None of the above.

14. Which of the following is a valid procedure header for a procedure that receives the number .09?

  a. `Private Function CalcTax(ByVal sngRate As Single) As Single`

  b. `Private Function CalcTax(ByAdd sngRate As Single) As Single`

  c. `Private Sub CalcTax(ByVal sngRate As Single)`

  d. `Private Sub CalcTax(ByAdd sngRate As Single)`

  e. Both a and c.

15. If the statement `Call CalcNet(sngNet)` passes the address of the sngNet variable to the CalcNet procedure, the variable is said to be passed _____.

  a. *by address*

  b. *by content*

  c. *by reference*

  d. *by value*

  e. *by variable*

16. Which of the following is false?

  a. When you pass a variable *by reference*, the receiving procedure can change its contents.

  b. When you pass a variable *by value*, the receiving function creates a local variable that it uses to store the passed value.

  c. Unless specified otherwise, all variables in Visual Basic .NET are passed *by value*.

  d. To pass a variable *by reference* in Visual Basic .NET, you include the keyword ByRef before the variable's name in the Call statement.

  e. None of the above.

17. Assume that a Sub procedure named CalcEndingInventory is passed the values stored in four Integer variables named intBegin, intSales, intPurchases, and intEnd. The procedure's task is to calculate the ending inventory, based on the beginning inventory, sales, and purchase amounts passed to the procedure. The procedure should store the result in the intEnd memory location. Which of the following procedure headers is correct?

  a. `Private Sub CalcEndingInventory(ByVal intB As Integer, ByVal intS As Integer, ByVal intP As Integer, ByRef intE As Integer)`

b. ```
    Private Sub CalcEndingInventory(ByVal intB As Integer,
    ByVal intS As Integer, ByVal intP As Integer, ByVal intE
    As Integer)
    ```
c.  ```
    Private Sub CalcEndingInventory(ByRef intB As Integer,
    ByRef intS As Integer, ByRef intP As Integer, ByVal intE
    As Integer)
    ```
d. ```
    Private Sub CalcEndingInventory(ByRef intB As Integer,
    ByRef intS As Integer, ByRef intP As Integer, ByRef intE
    As Integer)
    ```
e.  None of the above.

18. Which of the following statements should you use to call the CalcEndingInventory procedure described in Question 17?
    a.  ```
        Call CalcEndingInventory(intBegin, intSales, intPurchases,
        intEnd)
        ```
    b. ```
        Call CalcEndingInventory(ByVal intBegin, ByVal intSales,
        ByVal intPurchases, ByRef intEnd)
        ```
    c.  ```
        Call CalcEndingInventory(ByRef intBegin, ByRef intSales,
        ByRef intPurchases, ByRef intEnd)
        ```
    d. ```
        Call CalcEndingInventory(ByVal intBegin, ByVal intSales,
        ByVal intPurchases, ByVal intEnd)
        ```
    e.  ```
        Call CalcEndingInventory(ByRef intBegin, ByRef intSales,
        ByRef intPurchases, ByVal intEnd)
        ```

19. The memory locations listed in the *parameterlist* in a procedure header are local to the procedure and are removed from the computer's internal memory when the procedure ends.
    a. True
    b. False

20. What is the difference between a Sub procedure and a Function procedure?

EXERCISES

1. Write the Visual Basic .NET code for a Sub procedure that receives an integer passed to it. The procedure, named HalveNumber, should divide the integer by 2, and then display the result in the Output window.

2. Write the Visual Basic .NET code for a Sub procedure that prompts the user to enter the name of a city, and then stores the user's response in the String variable whose address is passed to the procedure. Name the procedure GetCity.

3. Write the Visual Basic .NET code for a Sub procedure that receives four Integer variables: the first two *by value* and the last two *by reference*. The procedure should calculate the sum and the difference of the two variables passed *by value*, and then store the results in the variables passed *by reference*. (When calculating the difference, subtract the contents of the second variable from the contents of the first variable.) Name the procedure CalcSumAndDiff.

4. Write the Visual Basic .NET code for a Sub procedure that receives three Single variables: the first two *by value* and the last one *by reference*. The procedure should divide the first variable by the second variable, and then store the result in the third variable. Name the procedure CalcQuotient.

5. Write the Visual Basic .NET code for a Function procedure that receives the value stored in an Integer variable named intNumber. The procedure, named DivideNumber, should divide the integer by 2, and then return the result (which may contain a decimal place).

6. Write an appropriate statement to call the DivideNumber function created in Exercise 5. Assign the value returned by the function to the sngAnswer variable.

7. Write the Visual Basic .NET code for a Function procedure that prompts the user to enter the name of a state, and then returns the user's response to the calling procedure. Name the procedure GetState.

8. Write the Visual Basic .NET code for a Function procedure that receives four integers. The procedure should calculate the average of the four integers, and then return the result (which may contain a decimal place). Name the procedure CalcAverage.

9. Write the Visual Basic .NET code for a Function procedure that receives two numbers that both have a decimal place. The procedure should divide the first number by the second number, and then return the result. Name the procedure CalcQuotient.

Exercises 10 and 11 are Discovery Exercises. Discovery Exercises, which may include topics that are not covered in this lesson, allow you to "discover" the solutions to problems on your own.

discovery ▶ **10.** In this exercise, you experiment with passing variables *by value* and *by reference*.

    a. If necessary, start Visual Studio .NET. Open the Passing Solution (Passing Solution.sln) file, which is contained in the VBNET\Tut07\Passing Solution folder. If the designer window is not open, right-click the form file's name in the Solution Explorer window, then click View Designer.

    b. Open the Code editor window. Study the application's existing code. Notice that the strName variable is passed *by value* to the GetName procedure.

    c. Start the application. Click the Display Name button. When prompted to enter a name, type your name and press Enter. Explain why the DisplayButton control's Click event procedure does not display your name in the NameLabel control. Click the Exit button to end the application.

    d. Modify the application's code so that it passes the strName variable *by reference* to the GetName procedure.

    e. Save the solution, then start the application. Click the Display Name button. When prompted to enter a name, type your name and press Enter. This time, your name appears in the NameLabel control. Explain why the DisplayButton control's Click event procedure now works correctly.

    f. Click the Exit button to end the application.

    g. Close the Output window, then close the solution.

discovery ▶ **11.** In this exercise, you learn how to specify that one or more arguments are optional in a Call statement.

    a. If necessary, start Visual Studio .NET. Open the Optional Solution (Optional Solution.sln) file, which is contained in the VBNET\Tut07\Optional Solution folder. If the designer window is not open, right-click the form file's name in the Solution Explorer window, then click View Designer.

b. Open the Code editor window. Study the application's existing code. Notice that the CalcButton control's Click event procedure contains two Call statements. The first Call statement passes three variables (sngSales, sngBonus, and sngRate) to the GetBonus procedure. The second Call statement, however, passes only two variables (sngSales and sngBonus) to the procedure. (Do not be concerned about the jagged line that appears below the second Call statement.) Notice that the sngRate variable is omitted from the second Call statement. You indicate that the sngRate variable is optional in the Call statement by including the keyword Optional before the variable's corresponding parameter in the procedure header. You also assign a default value that the procedure will use for the missing parameter when the procedure is called. In this case, you will assign the number .1 as the default value for the sngRate variable. (Optional parameters must be listed at the end of the procedure header.)

c. Change the `ByVal sngBonusRate As Single` in the procedure header to `Optional ByVal sngBonusRate As Single = .1`.

d. Save the solution, then start the application. Type the letter A in the Code text box, then type 1000 in the Sales text box. Click the Calculate button. When the Rate Entry dialog box appears, type .05 and press Enter. The `Call GetBonus(sngSales, sngBonus, sngRate)` statement calls the GetBonus procedure, passing it the number 1000, the address of the sngBonus variable, and the number .05. The GetBonus procedure stores the number 1000 in the sngTotalSales variable. It also assigns the name sngBonusAmount to the sngBonus variable, and stores the number .05 in the sngBonusRate variable. The procedure then multiplies the contents of the sngTotalSales variable (1000) by the contents of the sngBonusRate variable (.05), and assigns the result (50) to the sngBonusAmount variable. The `Me.BonusLabel.Text = Format(sngBonus, "currency")` statement then displays the number $50.00 in the BonusLabel control.

e. Now type the letter B in the Code text box, then type 2000 in the Sales text box. Click the Calculate button. The `Call GetBonus(sngSales, sngBonus)` statement calls the GetBonus procedure, passing it the number 2000 and the address of the sngBonus variable. The GetBonus procedure stores the number 2000 in the sngTotalSales variable, and assigns the name sngBonusAmount to the sngBonus variable. Because the Call statement did not supply a value for the sngBonusRate variable, the default value (.1) is assigned to the variable. The procedure then multiplies the contents of the sngTotalSales variable (2000) by the contents of the sngBonusRate variable (.1), and assigns the result (200) to the sngBonusAmount variable. The `Me.BonusLabel.Text = Format(sngBonus, "currency")` statement then displays the number $200.00 in the BonusLabel control.

f. Click the Exit button to end the application.

g. Close the Output window, then close the solution.

LESSON B

objectives

After completing this lesson, you will be able to:

- Add a list box to a form
- Add items to a list box
- Sort the contents of a list box
- Select a list box item from code
- Determine the selected item in a list box
- Round a number
- Code a list box's SelectedValueChanged event

Using a List Box Control

Completing the Payroll Application's User Interface

Recall that your task in this tutorial is to create a Payroll application for Jefferson Williams, the payroll manager at Nelson Industries. The application should allow Mr. Williams to enter an employee's name, hours worked, rate of pay, marital status (either "Married" or "Single"), and number of withholding allowances. The application should calculate the employee's weekly gross pay, federal withholding tax (FWT), Social Security and Medicare (FICA) tax, and net pay.

On your computer's hard disk is a partially completed Payroll application. You complete the application's user interface in this lesson.

To open the Payroll application:

1   Start Microsoft Visual Studio .NET, if necessary, and then close the Start Page window. Click **File** on the menu bar, and then click **Open Solution**. The Open Solution dialog box opens. Open the **Payroll Solution** (Payroll Solution.sln) file, which is contained in the VBNET\Tut07\Payroll Solution folder.

2   If the designer window is not open, right-click **Payroll Form.vb** in the Solution Explorer window, then click **View Designer**.

3   Auto-hide the Toolbox, Solution Explorer, and Properties windows, if necessary. The Payroll application's user interface is shown in Figure 7-7.

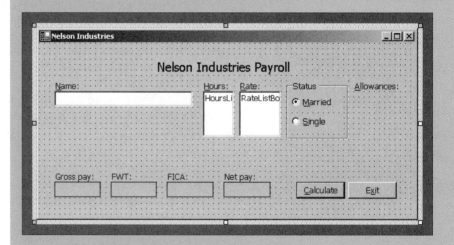

Figure 7-7: Payroll application's user interface

The interface contains one text box for the employee's name, and two list boxes for the employee's hours worked and pay rate. It also contains two radio buttons that allow the user to specify the employee's marital status. Missing from the interface is the list box that allows the payroll manager to select the number of withholding allowances.

Adding a List Box to a Form

You can use a **list box control** to display a list of choices from which the user can select zero choices, one choice, or more than one choice. The number of choices the user is allowed to select is controlled by the list box control's **SelectionMode property**. The default value for this property is One, which allows the user to select only one choice at a time in the list box. However, you also can set the property to None, MultiSimple, or MultiExtended. The None setting allows the user to scroll the list box, but not make any selections in it. The MultiSimple and MultiExtended settings allow the user to select more than one choice.

You can make a list box any size you want. If you have more items than fit into the list box, the control automatically displays scroll bars that you can use to view the complete list of items. The Windows standard for list boxes is to display a minimum of three selections and a maximum of eight selections at a time. In the next set of steps, you add the missing list box control to the Payroll application's user interface.

You learn how to use the MultiSimple and Multi-Extended settings in Discovery Exercise 7 at the end of this lesson.

If you have only two options to offer the user, you should use radio buttons instead of a list box.

To add a list box control to the form, then lock the controls and set the TabIndex property:

1 Click the **ListBox tool** [icon] in the toolbox, and then drag a list box control to the form. Position the list box control immediately below the Allowances: label. As you do with a text box, you use a label control to identify a list box. In this case, the Allowances label identifies the contents of the list box located below the label.

2 Set the ListBox1 control's Name property to **AllowListBox**. Set its Location property to **488, 72**, and set its Size property to **64, 68**. (Do not be concerned that the list box's name, AllowListBox, appears inside the list box. The name will not appear when you start the application.)

Now that the interface is complete, you can lock the controls on the form, and then set the TabIndex property for each control.

3 Right-click the **form**, then click **Lock Controls**.

4 Click **View** on the menu bar, and then click **Tab Order**. Use Figure 7-8 to set each control's TabIndex property to the appropriate value.

The AllowListBox, HoursListBox, and RateListBox controls on the form are instances of the ListBox class.

GUI
Design Tips

List Box Standards

- A list box should contain a minimum of three selections.
- A list box should display a minimum of three selections and a maximum of eight selections at a time.
- Use a label control to provide keyboard access to the list box. Set the label control's TabIndex property to a value that is one less than the list box's TabIndex value.

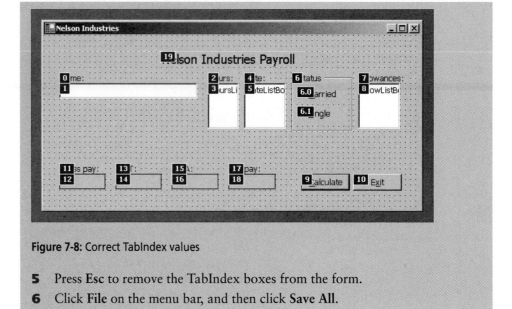

Figure 7-8: Correct TabIndex values

5 Press **Esc** to remove the TabIndex boxes from the form.

6 Click **File** on the menu bar, and then click **Save All**.

Next, learn how to specify the items to display in a list box.

Adding Items to a List Box

The items in a list box belong to a collection called the **Items collection.** The first item in the Items collection appears as the first item in the list box, the second item appears as the second item in the list box, and so on. As you learned in Tutorial 6, each item in a collection is identified by a unique number called an index. The first item in the Items collection—and, therefore, the first item in the list box—has an index of zero; the second item has an index of one, and so on.

You use the Items collection's **Add method** to specify the items you want displayed in a list box control. The syntax of the Add method is *object*.**Items.Add**(*item*), where *object* is the name of the control to which you want the item added, and *item* is the text you want displayed in the control. Figure 7-9 shows examples of using the Add method to display items in a list box.

tip

You also can use the Items collection's Insert method to add an item at a desired position in the list box. The syntax of the Insert method is *object*.**Items.Insert** (*position*, *item*). For example, the statement Me.NameListBox.Items. Insert(0, "Carol") inserts "Carol" as the first name in the NameListBox.

Examples	Results
`Me.AnimalListBox.Items.Add("Dog")`	displays the string "Dog" in the AnimalListBox
`Me.AgeListBox.Items.Add(35)`	displays the number 35 in the AgeListBox

`For sngRate = 0 To 5 Step .5`
`    Me.RateListBox.Items.Add(sngRate)`
`Next sngRate`
	displays the numbers from 0 through 5, in increments of .5, in the RateListBox

Figure 7-9: Examples of using the Items collection's Add method

▶ As you learned in Tutorial 4, ASCII stands for American Standard Code for Information Interchange and is the coding scheme used by microcomputers to represent the characters on your keyboard.

▶ If a list box's Sorted property is set to True, the items 1, 2, 3, and 10 will appear in the following order in the list box: 1, 10, 2, and 3. This is because items in a list box are treated as strings rather than as numbers, and strings are sorted based on the ASCII value of the leftmost character in the string.

GUI
Design Tips

Order of List Box Items

- List box items are either arranged by use, with the most used entries appearing first in the list, or sorted in ascending order.

The `Me.AnimalListBox.Items.Add("Dog")` statement shown in Figure 7-9 adds the string "Dog" to the AnimalListBox. The `Me.AgeListBox.Items.Add (35)` statement adds the number 35 to the AgeListBox. The `Me.RateListBox.Items.Add(sngRate)` statement in the For...Next loop displays numbers from zero through five, in increments of .5, in the RateListBox.

When you use the Add method to add an item to a list box, the position of the item in the list depends on the value stored in the list box's **Sorted property**. If the Sorted property contains its default value, False, the item is added to the end of the list. However, if the Sorted property is set to True, the item is sorted along with the existing items, and then placed in its proper position in the list. Visual Basic .NET sorts the list box items in ascending ASCII order, which means that numbers are sorted first, followed by uppercase letters, and then lowercase letters.

Whether you display the list box items in sorted order, or display them in the order in which they are added to the list box, depends on the application. If several list items are selected much more frequently than other items, you typically leave the list box's Sorted property set to False, and then add the frequently used items first, so that the items appear at the beginning of the list. However, if the list box items are selected fairly equally, you typically set the list box's Sorted property to True, because it is easier to locate items when they appear in a sorted order.

You will use the Items collection's Add method to add the appropriate items to the three list boxes in the Payroll application's user interface. Because you want each list box to display its values when the interface first appears on the screen, you will enter the appropriate Add methods in the form's Load event procedure. Recall that the Load event occurs when an application is started and the form is loaded into the computer's internal memory. The computer automatically executes the instructions contained in the Load event procedure when the Load event occurs.

To add items to the list boxes in the Payroll application's user interface:

1 Right-click the **form**, then click **View Code** to open the Code editor window.

Notice that two event procedures have already been coded for you. The ExitButton Click event procedure contains the `Me.Close()` statement, which ends the application. The NameTextBox Enter event procedure contains the `Me.NameTextBox.SelectAll()` statement, which selects the existing text in the text box when the user tabs to the control, and when the Focus method is used in code to send the focus to the control.

2 Click the **Class Name** list arrow, and then click (**Base Class Events**) in the list. Click the **Method Name** list arrow, and then click **Load** in the list. The Code template for the Payroll form's Load event procedure appears in the Code editor window.

3 Type **dim intHours, intAllow as integer, sngRate as single** and press **Enter**.

The payroll manager at Nelson Industries wants the HoursListBox to display numbers from one through 50, because that is the minimum and maximum number of hours an employee can work. The easiest way to display those values is to use a For...Next loop.

4 Type the comment and For...Next loop shown in Figure 7-10, then position the insertion point as shown in the figure.

enter these four lines
of code

position the insertion
point here

```
Private Sub PayrollForm_Load(ByVal sender As Object, ByVal e As System.EventArgs) Ha
    Dim intHours, intAllow As Integer, sngRate As Single
    'display hours worked
    For intHours = 1 To 50
        Me.HoursListBox.Items.Add(intHours)
    Next intHours

End Sub
```

Figure 7-10: Code for displaying values in the HoursListBox

The payroll manager wants the RateListBox to display pay rates from 6.00 through 12.00, in increments of .50. You will format the rates using the Standard format style, so that each rate contains two decimal places.

5 Type the comment and For...Next loop shown in Figure 7-11, then position the insertion point as shown in the figure.

enter these four lines
of code

position the insertion
point here

```
Private Sub PayrollForm_Load(ByVal sender As Object, ByVal e As System.EventArgs) Ha
    Dim intHours, intAllow As Integer, sngRate As Single
    'display hours worked
    For intHours = 1 To 50
        Me.HoursListBox.Items.Add(intHours)
    Next intHours
    'display pay rates
    For sngRate = 6 To 12 Step 0.5
        Me.RateListBox.Items.Add(Format(sngRate, "standard"))
    Next sngRate

End Sub
```

Figure 7-11: Code for displaying values in the RateListBox

Next, display numbers from 0 through 10 in the Allowances list box.

6 Type the comment and For...Next loop shown in Figure 7-12, then position the insertion point as shown in the figure.

enter these four lines
of code

position the insertion
point here

```
Private Sub PayrollForm_Load(ByVal sender As Object, ByVal e As System.EventArgs) Ha
    Dim intHours, intAllow As Integer, sngRate As Single
    'display hours worked
    For intHours = 1 To 50
        Me.HoursListBox.Items.Add(intHours)
    Next intHours
    'display pay rates
    For sngRate = 6 To 12 Step 0.5
        Me.RateListBox.Items.Add(Format(sngRate, "standard"))
    Next sngRate
    'display withholding allowances
    For intAllow = 0 To 10
        Me.AllowListBox.Items.Add(intAllow)
    Next intAllow

End Sub
```

Figure 7-12: Code for displaying values in the AllowListBox

Now test the code in the Load event procedure.

7 Click **File** on the menu bar, and then click **Save All**. Click **Debug** on the menu bar, and then click **Start**. See Figure 7-13.

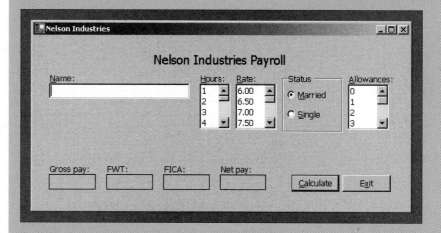

Figure 7-13: List boxes shown in the interface

8 Scroll down each of the list boxes to verify that each contains the appropriate values.

9 Scroll to the top of the Rate list box, then click **6.00** in the list. Notice that when you select an item in a list box, the item appears highlighted in the list. Additionally, the item's value (in this case, the number 6.00) is stored in the RateListBox control's SelectedItem property, and the item's index (in this case, the number 0) is stored in the RateListBox control's SelectedIndex property. You learn more about the SelectedItem and SelectedIndex properties in the next section.

10 Click the **Exit** button. When you return to the Code editor window, close the Output window.

If a list box allows the user to select only one item at a time, it is customary in Windows applications to have one of the items in the list box selected when the interface appears. You can accomplish this task using either a list box's SelectedItem property or its SelectedIndex property. (If a list box allows the user to select more than one item at a time, it is customary to have no items selected in the list when the interface appears.)

The SelectedItem and SelectedIndex Properties

A list box's **SelectedItem property** and its **SelectedIndex property** can be used both to determine the item selected in the list box and to select a list box item from code. Figure 7-14 shows examples of using these properties.

SelectedItem property examples	Results
Example 1 `Debug.WriteLine(Me.AllowListBox.SelectedItem)`	displays the contents of the AllowListBox control's SelectedItem property in the Output window
Example 2 `If Me.HoursListBox.SelectedItem > 40 Then`	compares the contents of the HoursListBox control's SelectedItem property with the number 40 to determine whether the selected item's value is greater than 40
Example 3 `Me.RateListBox.SelectedItem = 7.00`	selects the number 7.00 in the RateListBox control
SelectedIndex property examples	**Results**
Example 4 `Debug.WriteLine(Me.AllowListBox.SelectedIndex)`	displays the contents of the AllowListBox control's SelectedIndex property in the Output window
Example 5 `If Me.HoursListBox.SelectedIndex = 0 Then`	compares the contents of the HoursListBox control's SelectedIndex property with the number 0 to determine whether the first item is selected in the control
Example 6 `Me.RateListBox.SelectedIndex = 2`	selects the third item (7.00) in the RateListBox control

Figure 7-14: Examples of the SelectedItem and SelectedIndex properties

The statement shown in Example 1 in Figure 7-14 simply displays the contents of the AllowListBox control's SelectedItem property in the Output window. If the number 5 is selected in the control, the statement displays the number 5 in the Output window. In Example 2, the If clause compares the contents of the HoursListBox control's SelectedItem property with the number 40 to determine whether the employee worked more than 40 hours. You can use the `Me.RateListBox.SelectedItem = 7.00` statement shown in Example 3 to select the third item (in this case, the number 7.00) in the RateListBox.

Default List Box Item

- If a list box allows the user to make only one selection at a time, then a default item should be selected in the list box when the interface first appears. The default item should be either the most used selection or the first selection in the list. However, if a list box allows more than one selection at a time, you do not select a default item.

The statement shown in Example 4 in Figure 7-14 displays the contents of the AllowListBox control's SelectedIndex property in the Output window. If the second item is selected in the control, the statement displays the number 1 in the Output window. In Example 5, the If clause compares the contents of the HoursListBox control's SelectedIndex property with the number 0 to determine whether the first item is selected in the control. You can use the `Me.RateListBox.SelectedIndex = 2` statement shown in Example 6 to select the third item (in this case, the number 7.00) in the RateListBox.

As mentioned earlier, if a list box allows the user to select only one item at a time, it is customary in Windows applications to have an item in the list box selected when the interface appears. The selected item, called the **default list box item**, should be either the most used selection or, if all of the selections are used fairly equally, the first selection in the list. In the Payroll application, you will select the number 40 in the Hours list box, because most of the employees at Nelson Industries work 40 hours. In the Rate and Allowances list boxes, you will select the first item in the list, because the selections in these list boxes are used fairly equally.

To select a default item in each list box, then test the Load event procedure:

1 The insertion point should be positioned below the `Next intAllow` clause in the PayrollForm Load event procedure. Type **'select a default item in each list box** and press **Enter**.

First, use the SelectedItem property to select the number 40 in the Hours list box.

2 Type **me.hourslistbox.selecteditem = 40** and press **Enter**.

Next, use the SelectedIndex property to select the first item in the Rate and Allowances list boxes.

3 Type the two additional instructions shown in Figure 7-15, which shows the completed Load event procedure.

enter these two lines of code

```
Private Sub PayrollForm_Load(ByVal sender As Object, ByVal e As System.EventArgs) Ha
    Dim intHours, intAllow As Integer, sngRate As Single
    'display hours worked
    For intHours = 1 To 50
        Me.HoursListBox.Items.Add(intHours)
    Next intHours
    'display pay rates
    For sngRate = 6 To 12 Step 0.5
        Me.RateListBox.Items.Add(Format(sngRate, "standard"))
    Next sngRate
    'display withholding allowances
    For intAllow = 0 To 10
        Me.AllowListBox.Items.Add(intAllow)
    Next intAllow
    'select a default item in each list box
    Me.HoursListBox.SelectedItem = 40
    Me.RateListBox.SelectedIndex = 0
    Me.AllowListBox.SelectedIndex = 0
End Sub
```

Figure 7-15: Completed Load event procedure

Now test the Load event procedure to verify that it is working correctly.

4 Save the solution, then start the application. A default item is selected in each list box, as shown in Figure 7-16.

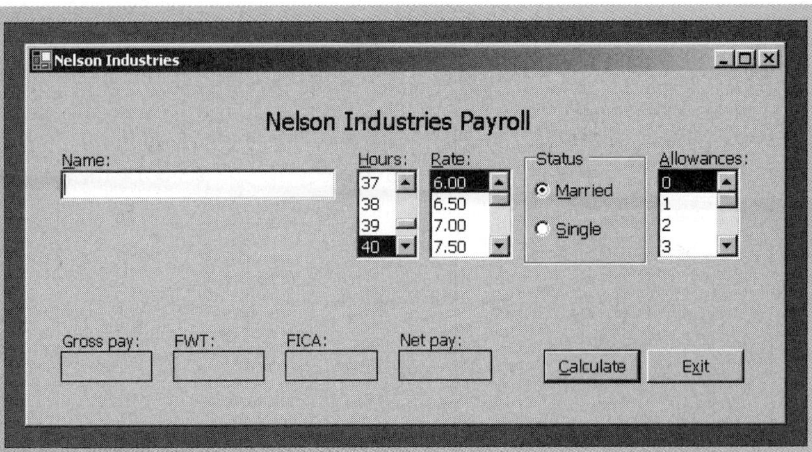

Figure 7-16: Default list box items selected in the interface

5 Click the **Exit** button to end the application. When you return to the Code editor window, close the Output window.

In addition to the ExitButton Click event procedure, the NameTextBox Enter event procedure, and the PayrollForm Load event procedure, several other procedures in the Payroll application also need to be coded. These procedures are shaded in the TOE chart shown in Figure 7-17.

Task	Object	Event
1. Calculate gross pay 2. Calculate federal withholding tax (FWT) 3. Calculate Social Security and Medicare (FICA) tax 4. Calculate net pay 5. Display gross pay, FWT, FICA, and net pay in GrossLabel, FwtLabel, FicaLabel, and NetLabel controls	CalculateButton	Click
End the application	ExitButton	Click
Display the gross pay, FWT, FICA, and net pay (from CalculateButton)	GrossLabel, FwtLabel, FicaLabel, NetLabel	None
Clear the contents of the GrossLabel, FwtLabel, FicaLabel, and NetLabel controls	NameTextBox	TextChanged
	HoursListBox, RateListBox, AllowListBox	SelectedValueChanged
	MarriedRadioButton, SingleRadioButton	Click
Highlight (select) the existing text	NameTextBox	Enter

Figure 7-17: TOE chart for the Payroll application

Task	Object	Event
Get and display the name, hours worked, pay rate, marital status, and number of withholding allowances	NameTextBox, HoursListBox, RateListBox, MarriedRadioButton, SingleRadioButton, AllowListBox	None
1. Fill HoursListBox, RateListBox, and AllowListBox controls with data 2. Select a default item in each list box	PayrollForm	Load

Figure 7-17: TOE chart for the Payroll application (continued)

First, code the CalculateButton Click event procedure.

Coding the CalculateButton Click Event Procedure

Figure 7-18 shows the pseudocode for the CalculateButton control's Click event procedure.

```
CalculateButton
1. declare variables
2. assign the item selected in the HoursListBox to a variable
3. assign the item selected in the RateListBox to a variable
4. if the hours worked are less than or equal to 40
       calculate gross pay = hours worked * pay rate
   else
       calculate gross pay = 40 * pay rate + (hours worked - 40) * pay rate * 1.5
   end if
5. call a function to calculate the FWT
6. calculate the FICA tax = gross pay * 7.65%
7. round the gross pay, FWT, and FICA tax to two decimal places
8. calculate the net pay = gross pay - FWT - FICA
9. display the gross pay, FWT, FICA, and net pay in the GrossLabel, FwtLabel, FicaLabel, and
   NetLabel controls
```

Figure 7-18: Pseudocode for the CalculateButton control's Click event procedure

To begin coding the CalculateButton control's Click event procedure:

1 Click the **Class Name** list arrow, and then click **CalculateButton** in the list. Click the **Method Name** list arrow, and then click **Click** in the list. The Code template for the CalculateButton Click event procedure appears in the Code editor window.

Step 1 in the pseudocode is to declare the variables. The CalculateButton Click event procedure will use one Integer variable to store the number of hours worked, and five Single variables to store the pay rate, gross pay, FWT, FICA tax, and net pay amounts.

2   Type **dim intHours as integer** and press **Enter**, then type **dim sngRate, sngGross, sngFwt, sngFica, sngNet as single** and press **Enter**.

Step 2 in the pseudocode is to assign to a variable the item that is selected in the HoursListBox, and Step 3 is to assign to a variable the item that is selected in the RateListBox. Recall that the item selected in a list box is stored in the list box's SelectedItem property.

3   Type **'assign selected items to variables** and press **Enter**.

4   Type **inthours = me.hourslistbox.selecteditem** and press **Enter**, then type **sngrate = me.ratelistbox.selecteditem** and press **Enter**.

Step 4 in the pseudocode is a selection structure that first compares the number of hours worked to the number 40, and then calculates the gross pay based on the result.

5   Type **'calculate gross pay** and press **Enter**, then type **if inthours <= 40 then** and press **Enter**.

If the number of hours worked is less than or equal to 40, then the procedure should calculate the gross pay by multiplying the number of hours worked by the pay rate.

6   Type **snggross = inthours * sngrate** and press **Enter**.

If, on the other hand, the number of hours worked is greater than 40, then the employee is entitled to his or her regular pay rate for the hours worked up to and including 40, and then time and one-half for the hours worked over 40.

7   Press **Backspace** to cancel the indentation, then type **else** and press **Enter**.

8   Type the additional line of code shown in Figure 7-19, then position the insertion point as shown in the figure.

enter this line of code

position the insertion point here

```
Private Sub CalculateButton_Click(ByVal sender As Object, ByVal e As System.EventArg
    Dim intHours As Integer
    Dim sngRate, sngGross, sngFwt, sngFica, sngNet As Single
    'assign selected items to variables
    intHours = Me.HoursListBox.SelectedItem
    sngRate = Me.RateListBox.SelectedItem
    'calculate gross pay
    If intHours <= 40 Then
        sngGross = intHours * sngRate
    Else
        sngGross = 40 * sngRate + (intHours - 40) * sngRate * 1.5
    End If
End Sub
```

Figure 7-19: Current status of the CalculateButton Click event procedure

9   Save the solution.

Step 5 in the pseudocode shown in Figure 7-18 is to call a function to calculate the FWT (federal withholding tax). Before entering the appropriate instruction, you will create the function, which you will name GetFwtTax.

Coding the GetFwtTax Function

The amount of federal withholding tax (FWT) to deduct from an employee's weekly gross pay is based on the employee's filing status—either single (including head of household) or married—and his or her weekly taxable wages. You calculate the weekly taxable wages by first multiplying the number of withholding allowances by $55.77 (the value of a withholding allowance for the year 2001), and then subtracting the result from the weekly gross pay. For example, if your weekly gross pay is $400 and you have two withholding allowances, your weekly taxable wages are $288.46 (400 minus 111.54, which is the product of 2 times 55.77). You use the weekly taxable wages, along with the filing status and the weekly Federal Withholding Tax tables, to determine the amount of tax to withhold. Figure 7-20 shows the 2001 weekly FWT tables.

FWT Tables – Weekly Payroll Period

Single person (including head of household)

If the taxable wages are:		The amount of income tax to withhold is		
Over	But not over	Base amount	Percentage	Of excess over
	$ 51	0		
$ 51	$ 552	0	15%	$ 51
$ 552	$1,196	$ 75.15 plus	28%	$ 552
$1,196	$2,662	$ 255.47 plus	31%	$1,196
$2,662	$5,750	$ 709.93 plus	36%	$2,662
$5,750		$1,821.61 plus	39.6%	$5,750

Married person

If the taxable wages are:		The amount of income tax to withhold is		
Over	But not over	Base amount	Percentage	Of excess over
	$ 124	0		
$ 124	$ 960	0	15%	$ 124
$ 960	$2,023	$ 125.40 plus	28%	$ 960
$2,023	$3,292	$ 423.04 plus	31%	$2,023
$3,292	$5,809	$ 816.43 plus	36%	$3,292
$5,809		$1,722.55 plus	39.6%	$5,809

Figure 7-20: Weekly FWT tables for 2001

Notice that both tables shown in Figure 7-20 contain five columns of information. The first two columns list various ranges, also called brackets, of taxable wage amounts. The first column—the Over column—lists the amount that a taxable wage in that range must be over, and the second column—the But not over column—lists the maximum amount included in the range. The remaining three columns (Base amount, Percentage, and Of excess over) tell you how to calculate the tax for each range. For example, assume that you are married and your weekly taxable wages are $288.46. Before you can calculate the amount of your tax, you need to locate your taxable wages in the first two columns of the Married table. In this case, your taxable wages fall within the $124 through $960 range. After locating the range that contains your taxable wages, you then use the remaining three columns in the table to calculate your tax. According to the table, taxable wages in the $124 through $960 bracket have a tax of 15% of the amount over $124; therefore, your tax is $24.67, as shown in Figure 7-21.

Taxable wages	$	288.46
Of excess over	–	124.00
		164.46
Percentage	*	.15
		24.67
Base amount	+	0.00
Tax	$	24.67

Figure 7-21: FWT calculation for a married taxpayer with taxable wages of $288.46

As Figure 7-21 indicates, you calculate the tax first by subtracting 124 (the amount shown in the Of excess over column) from your taxable wages of 288.46, giving 164.46. You then multiply 164.46 by 15% (the amount shown in the Percentage column), giving 24.67. You add the amount shown in the Base amount column—in this case, 0—to that result, giving $24.67 as your tax.

Now assume that your taxable wages are $600 per week and you are single. Figure 7-22 shows how the correct tax amount of $88.59 is calculated.

Taxable wages	$ 600.00
Of excess over	–552.00
	48.00
Percentage	* .28
	13.44
Base amount	+ 75.15
Tax	88.59

Figure 7-22: FWT calculation for a single taxpayer with taxable wages of $600

To calculate the federal withholding tax, the GetFwtTax function needs to know the employee's gross pay amount, as well as his or her marital status and number of withholding allowances. The function will get the gross pay amount from the CalculateButton Click event procedure, which will pass the value stored in its sngGross variable when it calls the function. The function can use the Checked properties of the Married and Single radio buttons to determine the marital status, and the AllowListBox control's SelectedItem property to determine the number of withholding allowances. After the GetFwtTax function calculates the appropriate federal withholding tax, it will return the tax amount to the CalculateButton Click event procedure. Figure 7-23 shows the pseudocode for the GetFwtTax function.

```
GetFwtTax function
1.  declare variables
2.  assign the item selected in the AllowListBox to a variable
3.  calculate the taxable wages = gross pay – number of withholding allowances * 55.77
4.  if the SingleRadioButton is selected
        taxable wages value:
            <= 51
                tax = 0
            <= 552
                calculate tax = 0.15 * (taxable wages - 51)
            <= 1196
                calculate tax = 75.15 + 0.28 * (taxable wages - 552)
            <= 2662
                calculate tax = 255.47 + 0.31 * (taxable wages - 1196)
            <= 5750
                calculate tax = 709.93 + .36 * (taxable wages - 2662)
            other
                calculate tax = 1821.61 + 0.396 * (taxable wages - 5750)
    else
        taxable wages value:
            <= 124
                tax = 0
            <= 960
                calculate tax = 0.15 * (taxable wages - 124)
            <= 2023
                calculate tax = 125.4 + 0.28 * (taxable wages - 960)
            <= 3292
                calculate tax = 423.04 + 0.31 * (taxable wages - 2023)
            <= 5809
                calculate tax = 816.43 + .36 * (taxable wages - 3292)
            other
                calculate tax = 1722.55 + 0.396 * (taxable wages - 5809)
    end if
5.  return tax
```

Figure 7-23: Pseudocode for the GetFwtTax function

To code the GetFwtTax function:

1   Insert two blank lines above the `End Class` statement, which appears as the last line in the Code editor window.

Recall that the CalculateButton Click event procedure will pass to the GetFwtTax function the value stored in the sngGross variable. In this case, you are passing the variable's value rather than its address because you do not want the GetFwtTax function to change the contents of the variable. You will store the value passed to the function in a Single variable named sngWeekPay.

2   In the blank line immediately above the `End Class` statement, type **private function GetFwtTax(byval sngWeekPay as single) as single** and press **Enter**. Notice that the Code editor automatically enters the procedure footer (`End Function`) for you.

Step 1 in the pseudocode shown in Figure 7-23 is to declare the variables. In addition to the sngWeekPay variable, which is declared in the procedure header, the GetFwtTax function will use an Integer variable named intAllow to store the number of withholding allowances. The procedure also will use a Single variable named sngTaxWages to store the taxable wages amount, and a Single variable named sngTax to store the federal withholding tax amount.

3   Type **dim intAllow as integer, sngTaxWages, sngTax as single** and press **Enter**.

Step 2 in the pseudocode is to assign the item that is selected in the AllowListBox to a variable. The selected item represents the number of the employee's withholding allowances.

4   Type **'assign number of withholding allowances to a variable** and press **Enter**, then type **intallow = me.allowlistbox.selecteditem** and press **Enter**.

Now calculate the taxable wages by multiplying the number of withholding allowances by $55.77, and then subtracting the result from the gross pay amount.

5   Type **'calculate taxable wages** and press **Enter**, then type **sngtaxwages = sngweekpay - intallow * 55.77** and press **Enter**.

Next, determine whether the SingleRadioButton is selected.

6   Type **'determine marital status, then calculate FWT** and press **Enter**, then type **if me.singleradiobutton.checked = true then** and press **Enter**. Notice that the Code editor enters the `End If` clause for you.

If the SingleRadioButton is selected, the procedure should calculate the federal withholding tax using the information from the Single tax table.

7   Type the Select Case statement shown in Figure 7-24, then position the insertion point as shown in the figure.

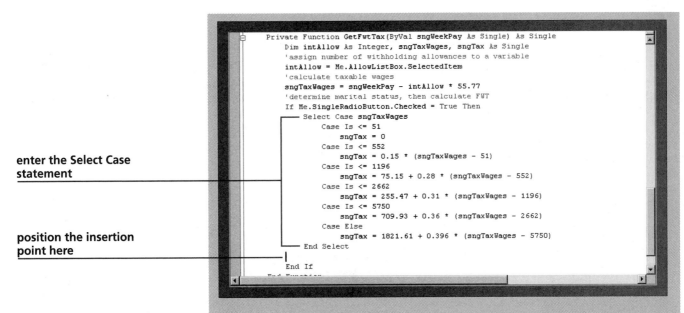

```
Private Function GetFwtTax(ByVal sngWeekPay As Single) As Single
    Dim intAllow As Integer, sngTaxWages, sngTax As Single
    'assign number of withholding allowances to a variable
    intAllow = Me.AllowListBox.SelectedItem
    'calculate taxable wages
    sngTaxWages = sngWeekPay - intAllow * 55.77
    'determine marital status, then calculate FWT
    If Me.SingleRadioButton.Checked = True Then
        Select Case sngTaxWages
            Case Is <= 51
                sngTax = 0
            Case Is <= 552
                sngTax = 0.15 * (sngTaxWages - 51)
            Case Is <= 1196
                sngTax = 75.15 + 0.28 * (sngTaxWages - 552)
            Case Is <= 2662
                sngTax = 255.47 + 0.31 * (sngTaxWages - 1196)
            Case Is <= 5750
                sngTax = 709.93 + 0.36 * (sngTaxWages - 2662)
            Case Else
                sngTax = 1821.61 + 0.396 * (sngTaxWages - 5750)
        End Select
    End If
    End Function
```

enter the Select Case statement

position the insertion point here

Figure 7-24: FWT calculations for taxpayers whose marital status is Single

If the SingleRadioButton is not selected, it means that the MarriedRadioButton is selected. In that case, the procedure should calculate the federal withholding tax using the information from the Married tax table.

8 Type **else** and press **Tab**, then type **'MarriedRadioButton is selected** and press **Enter**.

9 Type the Select Case statement shown in Figure 7-25, then position the insertion point as shown in the figure.

```
    Else    'MarriedRadioButton is selected
        Select Case sngTaxWages
            Case Is <= 124
                sngTax = 0
            Case Is <= 960
                sngTax = 0.15 * (sngTaxWages - 124)
            Case Is <= 2023
                sngTax = 125.4 + 0.28 * (sngTaxWages - 960)
            Case Is <= 3292
                sngTax = 423.04 + 0.31 * (sngTaxWages - 2023)
            Case Is <= 5809
                sngTax = 816.43 + 0.36 * (sngTaxWages - 3292)
            Case Else
                sngTax = 1722.55 + 0.396 * (sngTaxWages - 5809)
        End Select
    End If

    End Function
End Class
```

enter the Select Case statement

position the insertion point here

Figure 7-25: FWT calculations for taxpayers whose marital status is Married

The last step in the pseudocode shown in Figure 7-23 is to return the federal withholding tax amount, which is stored in the sngTax variable, to the statement that invoked the function.

10 Type **'return FWT** and press **Enter**, then type **return sngtax**. Figure 7-26 shows the completed GetFwtTax function.

```
Private Function GetFwtTax(ByVal sngWeekPay As Single) As Single
    Dim intAllow As Integer, sngTaxWages, sngTax As Single
    'assign number of withholding allowances to a variable
    intAllow = Me.AllowListBox.SelectedItem
    'calculate taxable wages
    sngTaxWages = sngWeekPay - intAllow * 55.77
    'determine marital status, then calculate FWT
    If Me.SingleRadioButton.Checked = True Then
        Select Case sngTaxWages
            Case Is <= 51
                sngTax = 0
            Case Is <= 552
                sngTax = 0.15 * (sngTaxWages - 51)
            Case Is <= 1196
                sngTax = 75.15 + 0.28 * (sngTaxWages - 552)
            Case Is <= 2662
                sngTax = 255.47 + 0.31 * (sngTaxWages - 1196)
            Case Is <= 5750
                sngTax = 709.93 + 0.36 * (sngTaxWages - 2662)
            Case Else
                sngTax = 1821.61 + 0.396 * (sngTaxWages - 5750)
        End Select
    Else    'MarriedRadioButton is selected
        Select Case sngTaxWages
            Case Is <= 124
                sngTax = 0
            Case Is <= 960
                sngTax = 0.15 * (sngTaxWages - 124)
            Case Is <= 2023
                sngTax = 125.4 + 0.28 * (sngTaxWages - 960)
            Case Is <= 3292
                sngTax = 423.04 + 0.31 * (sngTaxWages - 2023)
            Case Is <= 5809
                sngTax = 816.43 + 0.36 * (sngTaxWages - 3292)
            Case Else
                sngTax = 1722.55 + 0.396 * (sngTaxWages - 5809)
        End Select
    End If
    'return FWT
    Return sngTax
End Function
```

Figure 7-26: Completed GetFwtTax function

Recall that you still need to complete the CalculateButton Click event procedure.

Completing the CalculateButton Click Event Procedure

Now that you have created the GetFwtTax function, you can call the function from the CalculateButton Click event procedure. Calling the GetFwtTax function is Step 5 in the event procedure's pseudocode (shown earlier in Figure 7-18).

To complete the CalculateButton Click event procedure, then test the procedure:

1 Position the insertion point below the `End If` statement in the CalculateButton Click event procedure. If necessary, press **Tab** twice to align the insertion point with the letter E in the `End If` statement.

2 Type **'calculate FWT** and press **Enter**.

Recall that the CalculateButton Click event procedure needs to pass the value stored in its sngGross variable to the GetFwtTax function. The procedure should store the value returned by the function in the sngFwt variable.

3 Type **sngfwt = getfwttax(snggross)** and press **Enter**.

Step 6 in the pseudocode for the CalculateButton Click event procedure is to calculate the FICA tax by multiplying the gross pay amount by 7.65%.

4 Type **'calculate FICA tax** and press **Enter**, then type **sngfica = snggross * .0765** and press **Enter**.

Step 7 in the pseudocode is to round the gross pay, FWT, and FICA tax amounts to two decimal places. You can use Visual Basic .NET's **Math.Round function** to return a number rounded to a specific number of decimal places. The syntax of the Math.Round function is **Math.Round**(*value*[, *digits*]), where *value* is a numeric expression, and *digits*, which is optional, is an integer indicating how many places to the right of the decimal are included in the rounding. For example, `Math.Round(3.235, 2)` returns the number 3.24, but `Math.Round(3.234, 2)` returns the number 3.23. Notice that the Math.Round function rounds a number up only if the number to its right is 5 or greater; otherwise the Math.Round function truncates the excess digits. If the *digits* argument is omitted, the Math.Round function returns an integer.

5 Type **'round gross pay, FWT, and FICA tax** and press **Enter**. Type **snggross = math.round(snggross, 2)** and press **Enter**. Type **sngfwt = math.round(sngfwt, 2)** and press **Enter**. Type **sngfica = math.round(sngfica, 2)** and press **Enter**.

Step 8 in the pseudocode is to calculate the net pay by subtracting the FWT and FICA amounts from the gross pay amount.

6 Type **'calculate net pay** and press **Enter**, then type **sngnet = snggross - sngfwt - sngfica** and press **Enter**.

The last step in the pseudocode for the CalculateButton Click event procedure is to display the gross pay, FWT, FICA, and net pay in the appropriate label controls in the interface.

7 Type the additional five lines of code shaded in Figure 7-27, which shows the completed CalculateButton Click event procedure.

```
Private Sub CalculateButton_Click(ByVal sender As Object, ByVal e As
System.EventArgs) Handles CalculateButton.Click
    Dim intHours As Integer
    Dim sngRate, sngGross, sngFwt, sngFica, sngNet As Single
    'assign selected items to variables
    intHours = Me.HoursListBox.SelectedItem
    sngRate = Me.RateListBox.SelectedItem
    'calculate gross pay
    If intHours <= 40 Then
        sngGross = intHours * sngRate
    Else
        sngGross = 40 * sngRate + (intHours - 40) * sngRate * 1.5
    End If
    'calculate FWT
    sngFwt = GetFwtTax(sngGross)
    'calculate FICA tax
    sngFica = sngGross * 0.0765
    'round gross pay, FWT, and FICA tax
    sngGross = Math.Round(sngGross, 2)
    sngFwt = Math.Round(sngFwt, 2)
    sngFica = Math.Round(sngFica, 2)
    'calculate net pay
    sngNet = sngGross - sngFwt - sngFica
    'display calculated amounts
    Me.GrossLabel.Text = Format(sngGross, "currency")
    Me.FwtLabel.Text = Format(sngFwt, "currency")
    Me.FicaLabel.Text = Format(sngFica, "currency")
    Me.NetLabel.Text = Format(sngNet, "currency")
End Sub
```

enter these five
lines of code

Figure 7-27: Completed CalculateButton Click event procedure

Now test the CalculateButton Click event procedure and the GetFwtTax function to verify that both are working correctly.

8   Save the solution, then start the application.

Calculate the weekly gross pay, taxes, and net pay for Karen Douglas. Last week, Karen worked 40 hours. She earns $10 per hour, and her marital status is Married. She claims two withholding allowances.

9   Type **Karen Douglas** in the Name text box. Click **10.00** in the Rate list box, then click **2** in the Allowances list box. Click the **Calculate** button. The application calculates and displays Karen's gross pay, FWT, FICA, and net pay amounts, as shown in Figure 7-28.

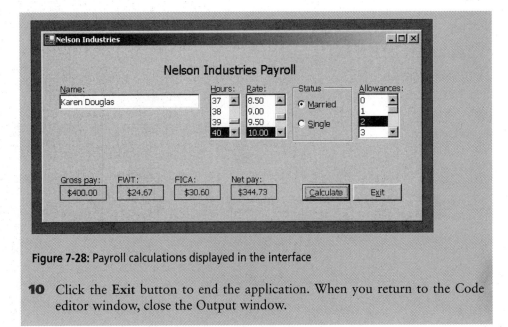

Figure 7-28: Payroll calculations displayed in the interface

10 Click the **Exit** button to end the application. When you return to the Code editor window, close the Output window.

When the user changes the value entered in the NameTextBox, or when he or she selects a different item in the HoursListBox, RateListBox, or AllowListBox, the Payroll application should clear the contents of the GrossLabel, FwtLabel, FicaLabel, and NetLabel controls in the interface. The contents of those label controls also should be cleared when the user selects a different radio button in the interface.

Clearing the Contents of the Label Controls

> **A list box's SelectedIndex-Changed event also occurs each time a different item is selected in a list box.**

According to the Payroll application's TOE chart (shown earlier in Figure 7-17), the contents of the GrossLabel, FwtLabel, FicaLabel, and NetLabel controls should be cleared when the NameTextBox control's TextChanged event occurs, or when either the MarriedRadioButton control's Click event or the SingleRadioButton control's Click event occurs. The label controls also should be cleared when the SelectedValueChanged event occurs for one of the list boxes in the interface. A list box's **SelectedValueChanged event** occurs each time a different value is selected in the list box.

To clear the appropriate label controls in the interface, then test the application:

1 Click the **Class Name** list arrow, then click **NameTextBox** in the list. Click the **Method Name** list arrow, then click **TextChanged** in the list. The template for the NameTextBox TextChanged event procedure appears in the Code editor window.

2 Change the name of the procedure from `NameTextBox_TextChanged` to **ClearLabels**.

3 Change the Handles portion of the ClearLabels procedure header as shown in Figure 7-29, then enter the four assignment statements shown in the figure.

change the Handles portion

enter these four lines
of code

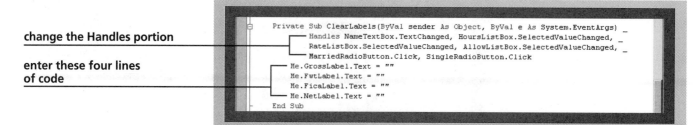

```
Private Sub ClearLabels(ByVal sender As Object, ByVal e As System.EventArgs) _
    Handles NameTextBox.TextChanged, HoursListBox.SelectedValueChanged, _
    RateListBox.SelectedValueChanged, AllowListBox.SelectedValueChanged, _
    MarriedRadioButton.Click, SingleRadioButton.Click
    Me.GrossLabel.Text = ""
    Me.FwtLabel.Text = ""
    Me.FicaLabel.Text = ""
    Me.NetLabel.Text = ""
End Sub
```

Figure 7-29: Completed ClearLabels procedure

Now test the ClearLabels procedure to verify that it is working correctly.

4   Save the solution, then start the application.

5   Type **Helen Stone** in the Name text box, then click the **Calculate** button.

6   Change the name in the Name text box to Helen Stoner. The **ClearLabels** procedure clears the gross pay, FWT, FICA, and net pay amounts from the label controls.

7   Click the **Calculate** button, then click the number **30** in the Hours list box. The ClearLabels procedure clears the gross pay, FWT, FICA, and net pay amounts from the label controls.

8   Click the **Calculate** button. On your own, verify that the gross pay, FWT, FICA, and net pay amounts are cleared from the label controls when you select a different pay rate, marital status, and number of withholding allowances.

9   Click the **Exit** button to end the application. When you return to the Code editor window, close the Output window, then close the Code editor window.

10   Click **File** on the menu bar, and then click **Close Solution** to close the solution.

You now have completed Lesson B. In Lesson C, you add to the Payroll application a copyright screen that is similar to the one you created in Tutorial 1. For now, you can either take a break or complete the end-of-lesson questions and exercises before moving on to the next lesson.

S U M M A R Y

To add a list box control to a form:

■   Use the ListBox tool ▦ in the toolbox.

To specify whether the user can select zero choices, one choice, or more than one choice in a list box:

■   Set the list box's SelectionMode property to None, One, MultiSimple, or MultiExtended.

To add items to a list box:

■   Use the Items collection's Add method. The syntax of the method is *object*.**Items.Add**(*item*), where *object* is the name of the control to which you want the item added, and *item* is the text you want displayed in the control.

To automatically sort the items in a list box:

■ Set the list box's Sorted property to True.

To determine the item selected in a list box, or to select a list box item from code:

■ Set either the list box's SelectedItem property or its SelectedIndex property.

To round a number to a specific number of decimal places:

■ Use the Math.Round function. The function's syntax is **Math.Round**(*value*[, *digits*]), where *value* is a numeric expression, and *digits*, which is optional, is an integer indicating how many places to the right of the decimal are included in the rounding. If the *digits* argument is omitted, the Math.Round function returns an integer.

To process code when a different value is selected in a list box:

■ Enter the code in the list box's SelectedValueChanged event procedure.

QUESTIONS

1. You use the _____ method to include items in a list box control.
   a. Add
   b. AddList
   c. Item
   d. ItemAdd
   e. ListAdd

2. You use the _____ property to specify whether the user can select zero or more choices from a list box.
   a. Choices
   b. Number
   c. Selection
   d. SelectionMode
   e. SelectionNumber

3. The items in a list box belong to the _____ collection.
   a. Items
   b. List
   c. ListBox
   d. Values
   e. None of the above.

4. The _____ property stores the index of the item that is selected in a list box.
   a. Index
   b. SelectedIndex
   c. SelectedItem
   d. Selection
   e. SelectionIndex

5. When you select an item in a list box, the item is stored in the list box's
   _____ property.
   a. Item
   b. SelectedItem
   c. Selection
   d. SelectionItem
   e. SelectionList

6. Which of the following adds the word DESK to a list box named OfficeListBox?
   a. `Me.OfficeListBox.Add("DESK")`
   b. `Me.OfficeListBox.AddItems("DESK")`
   c. `Me.OfficeListBox.Item.Add("DESK")`
   d. `Me.OfficeListBox.ItemAdd("DESK")`
   e. None of the above.

7. The second item in a list box has an index of _____.
   a. 1
   b. 2
   c. 3

8. Which of the following selects the number 3, which is the first item in a list box named
   TermListBox?
   a. `Me.TermListBox.SelectedIndex = 0`
   b. `Me.TermListBox.SelectedIndex = 3`
   c. `Me.TermListBox.SelectedItem = 0`
   d. `Me.TermListBox.SelectedItem = 3`
   e. Both a and d.

9. You use the _____ property to arrange list box items in ascending
   ASCII order.
   a. Alphabetical
   b. Arrange
   c. ASCII
   d. ListOrder
   e. Sorted

10. The _____ event occurs when the user selects a different value in a
    list box.
    a. ChangeItem
    b. ChangeValue
    c. SelectNewItem
    d. ValueChanged
    e. None of the above.

E X E R C I S E S

1. In this exercise, you modify the Payroll application so that it uses a user-defined Sub
   procedure rather than a Function procedure.
   a. Use Windows to make a copy of the Payroll Solution folder, which is contained in
      the VBNET\Tut07 folder. Change the name of the folder to Nelson Solution.
   b. If necessary, start Visual Studio .NET. Open the Payroll Solution (Payroll
      Solution.sln) file, which is contained in the VBNET\Tut07\Nelson Solution folder.

If the designer window is not open, right-click the form file's name in the Solution Explorer window, then click View Designer.

c. Modify the application's code so that it displays pay rates from 6.00 through 40.00, in increments of .50, in the Rate list box.

d. Change the GetFwtTax Function procedure to a user-defined Sub procedure, then modify the statement that calls the procedure.

e. Save the solution, then start the application. Test the application by entering Karen Douglas in the Name text box. Then click 10.00 in the Rate list box, and 2 in the Allowances list box. Click the Calculate button. The calculated amounts should be identical to those shown in Lesson B's Figure 7-28.

f. Click the Exit button to end the application.

g. Close the Output window, then close the solution.

2. In this exercise, you code an application that displays the telephone extension corresponding to the name selected in a list box. The names and extensions are shown here:

Smith, Joe	3388
Jones, Mary	3356
Adkari, Joel	2487
Lin, Sue	1111
Li, Vicky	2222

a. If necessary, start Visual Studio .NET. Open the Phone Solution (Phone Solution.sln) file, which is contained in the VBNET\Tut07\Phone Solution folder. If the designer window is not open, right-click the form file's name in the Solution Explorer window, then click View Designer.

b. Set the list box's Sorted property to True.

c. Code the form's Load event procedure so that it adds the five names shown above to the NamesListBox. Select the first name in the list.

d. Code the list box's SelectedValueChanged event procedure so that it assigns the item selected in the NameListBox to a variable. The procedure then should use the Select Case statement to display the telephone extension that corresponds to the name stored in the variable.

e. Save the solution, then start the application. Test the application by clicking each name in the list box.

f. Click the Exit button to end the application.

g. Close the Output window, then close the solution.

3. In this exercise, you modify the application that you coded in Exercise 2. The application will now assign the index of the selected item, rather than the selected item itself, to a variable.

a. Use Windows to make a copy of the Phone Solution folder, which is contained in the VBNET\Tut07 folder. Change the name of the folder to Phone2 Solution.

b. If necessary, start Visual Studio .NET. Open the Phone Solution (Phone Solution.sln) file, which is contained in the VBNET\Tut07\Phone2 Solution folder. If the designer window is not open, right-click the form file's name in the Solution Explorer window, then click View Designer.

c. Modify the list box's SelectedValueChanged event procedure so that it assigns the index of the item selected in the NameListBox to a variable. The procedure then should use the Select Case statement to display the telephone extension that corresponds to the index stored in the variable.

d. Save the solution, then start the application. Test the application by clicking each name in the list box.

e. Click the Exit button to end the application.

f. Close the Output window, then close the solution.

4. In this exercise, you code an application that allows the user to display an image that corresponds to the item selected in a list box.

    a. If necessary, start Visual Studio .NET. Open the Image Solution (Image Solution.sln) file, which is contained in the VBNET\Tut07\Image Solution folder. If the designer window is not open, right-click the form file's name in the Solution Explorer window, then click View Designer.

    b. Set the list box's Sorted property to True.

    c. Create a new form-level collection named mPictureBoxCollection.

    d. In the form's Load event procedure, add the CloudPictureBox, LightningPictureBox, RainPictureBox, SnowPictureBox, and SunPictureBox controls to the mPictureBoxCollection. After doing so, fill the ElementListBox with the following items: Cloud, Rain, Snow, Sun, and Lightning, then select the first item in the list. (*Hint*: When adding the picture boxes to the mPictureBoxCollection, assign a key to each picture box. Relate each picture box's key to the index of its associated item in the list box.)

    e. Code the list box's SelectedValueChanged event procedure so that it displays, in the ElementPictureBox control, the image that corresponds to the item selected in the list box.

    f. Save the solution, then start the application. Test the application by clicking each item in the list box.

    g. Click the Exit button to end the application.

    h. Close the Output window, then close the solution.

5. In this exercise, you modify the Grade application that you created in Tutorial 6 so that it uses a Function procedure to determine the grade.

    a. Use Windows to make a copy of the Grade Solution folder, which is contained in the VBNET\Tut06 folder. Change the name of the folder to GradeCalc Solution. Move the GradeCalc Solution folder to the VBNET\Tut07 folder.

    b. If necessary, start Visual Studio .NET. Open the Grade Solution (Grade Solution.sln) file, which is contained in the VBNET\Tut07\GradeCalc Solution folder. If the designer window is not open, right-click the form file's name in the Solution Explorer window, then click View Designer.

    c. Modify the application's code so that it uses a Function procedure to determine the student's grade. Return the grade to the DisplayButton Click event procedure, which should display the grade in the GradeLabel control.

    d. Save the solution, then start the application. Test the application to verify that it is working correctly.

    e. Click the Exit button to end the application.

    f. Close the Output window, then close the solution.

6. In this exercise, you modify the application that you coded in Exercise 5. The application will now use a user-defined Sub procedure rather than a Function procedure.

    a. Use Windows to make a copy of the GradeCalc Solution folder, which is contained in the VBNET\Tut07 folder. Change the name of the folder to GradeCalc2 Solution.

    b. If necessary, start Visual Studio .NET. Open the Grade Solution (Grade Solution.sln) file, which is contained in the VBNET\Tut07\GradeCalc2 Solution folder. If the designer window is not open, right-click the form file's name in the Solution Explorer window, then click View Designer.

    c. Modify the application's code so that it uses a Sub procedure rather than a Function procedure to determine the student's grade.

    d. Save the solution, then start the application. Test the application to verify that it is working correctly.

    e. Click the Exit button to end the application.

    f. Close the Output window, then close the solution.

Exercise 7 is a Discovery Exercise. Discovery Exercises, which may include topics that are not covered in this lesson, allow you to "discover" the solutions to problems on your own.

discovery ▶ 7. In this exercise, you learn how to create a list box that allows the user to select more than one item at a time.

   a. If necessary, start Visual Studio .NET. Open the Multi Solution (Multi Solution.sln) file, which is contained in the VBNET\Tut07\Multi Solution folder. If the designer window is not open, right-click the form file's name in the Solution Explorer window, then click View Designer. The interface contains a list box named NamesListBox. The list box's Sorted property is set to True, and its SelectionMode property is set to One.

   b. Open the Code editor window. Notice that the form's Load event procedure adds five names to the NamesListBox.

   c. Code the SingleButton Click event procedure so that it displays, in the ResultLabel control, the item that is selected in the NamesListBox. For example, if the user clicks Debbie in the list box and then clicks the Single Selection button, the name Debbie should appear in the ResultLabel control.

   d. Save the solution, then start the application. Click Debbie in the list box, then click Ahmad, and then click Bill. Notice that, when the list box's SelectionMode property is set to One, you can select only one item at a time in the list.

   e. Click the Single Selection button. The name "Bill" appears in the ResultLabel control.

   f. Click the Exit button to end the application, then close the Output window.

   g. Change the list box's SelectionMode property to MultiSimple. Save the solution, then start the application. Click Debbie in the list box, then click Ahmad, then click Bill, and then click Ahmad. Notice that, when the list box's SelectionMode property is set to MultiSimple, you can select more than one item at a time in the list. Also notice that you click to both select and deselect an item. (You also can use Ctrl+click and Shift+click, as well as press the Spacebar, to select and deselect items when the list box's SelectionMode property is set to MultiSimple.)

   h. Click the Exit button to end the application, then close the Output window.

   i. Change the list box's SelectionMode property to MultiExtended. Save the solution, then start the application.

   j. Click Debbie in the list box, then click Jim. Notice that, in this case, clicking Jim deselects Debbie. When a list box's SelectionMode property is set to MultiExtended, you use Ctrl+click to select multiple items in the list. You also use Ctrl+click to deselect items in the list. Click Debbie in the list, then Ctrl+click Ahmad, and then Ctrl+click Debbie.

   k. Next, click Bill in the list, then Shift+click Jim; this selects all of the names from Bill through Jim.

   l. Click the Exit button to end the application, then close the Output window.

   As you know, when a list box's SelectionMode property is set to One, the item selected in the list box is stored in the SelectedItem property, and the item's index is stored in the SelectedIndex property. However, when a list box's SelectionMode property is set to either MultiSimple or MultiExtended, the items selected in the list box are stored (as strings) in the SelectedItems property, and the indices of each item are stored (as integers) in the SelectedIndices property.

   m. Code the MultiButton Click event procedure so that it clears the contents of the ResultLabel control. The procedure should then display the selected names (which are stored in the SelectedItems property) on separate lines in the ResultLabel control.

   n. Save the solution, then start the application.

   o. Click Ahmad in the list box, then Shift+click Jim. Click the Multi-Selection button. The five names should appear on separate lines in the ResultLabel control.

   p. Click the Exit button to end the application.

   q. Close the Output window, then close the solution.

After completing this lesson, you will be able to:

- Add an existing form to a solution
- Add a new module to a solution
- Code the Sub Main procedure
- Create an instance of a form
- Display a form object using the ShowDialog method

Completing the Payroll Application

Adding an Existing Form to a Solution

In Tutorial 1, you created a copyright screen for Interlocking Software Company. Recall that the copyright screen is to be the splash screen for each custom application created by the company. The copyright screen identifies the application's author and copyright year and includes the Interlocking Software Company logo. In the next set of steps, you add the copyright screen to the Payroll application.

You also can click Project on the menu bar, and then click Add Existing Item to open the Add Existing Item – Payroll Project dialog box.

The Open button in the Add Existing Item – *projectname* dialog box also allows you to add to a solution a link to an existing file, rather than the file itself. You learn how to add a link in Discovery Exercise 2 at the end of this lesson.

To add the copyright screen to the Payroll application:

1 Start Microsoft Visual Studio .NET, if necessary, and then close the Start Page window. Click **File** on the menu bar, and then click **Open Solution**. The Open Solution dialog box opens. Open the **Payroll Solution** (Payroll Solution.sln) file, which is contained in the VBNET\Tut07\Payroll Solution folder.

2 If the designer window is not open, right-click **Payroll Form.vb** in the Solution Explorer window, then click **View Designer**. Auto-hide the Toolbox, Solution Explorer, and Properties windows, if necessary.

3 Click **File** on the menu bar, and then click **Add Existing Item**. The Add Existing Item – Payroll Project dialog box opens.

4 Open the Copyright Project folder, which is contained in the VBNET\Tut07\Copyright Solution folder on your computer's hard disk, and then click **Copyright Form.vb**.

5 Click the **Open** button to add the Copyright Form.vb file to the Payroll application.

6 Right-click **Copyright Form.vb** in the Solution Explorer window, then click **View Designer**. See Figure 7-30.

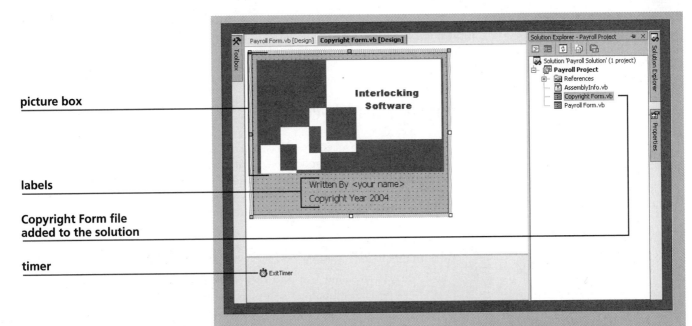

Figure 7-30: Copyright form

As Figure 7-30 indicates, the Copyright form contains a picture box, two labels, and a timer control.

7 Click the **AuthorLabel control** on the Copyright screen. Replace <your name> in the control's Text property with your name.

As you may recall, the timer control's Interval property is set to 8000 milliseconds, which means that the code in the control's Tick event procedure is processed every eight seconds. View the Tick event procedure's code.

8 Right-click the **Copyright form**, then click **View Code** to open the Code editor window. See Figure 7-31.

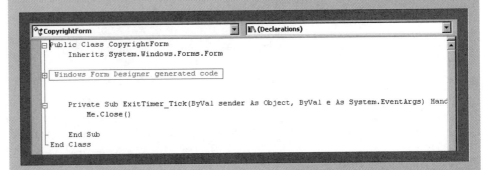

Figure 7-31: ExitTimer control's Tick event procedure

Notice that the ExitTimer control's Tick event procedure contains the statement `Me.Close()`, which closes the Copyright form.

9 Close the Code editor window, then close the Copyright form's designer window.

10 Click **File** on the menu bar, and then click **Save All**.

The Copyright form should be the first interface that appears when the Payroll application is started. When the ExitTimer control closes the Copyright form, the computer should display the Payroll form. You can control the display of both forms by coding the Sub Main procedure.

Coding the Sub Main Procedure

Sub Main is a special procedure in Visual Basic .NET, because it can be declared as the "starting point" for an application. In other words, you can tell the computer to process the Sub Main procedure automatically when an application is started. You enter the Sub Main procedure in a **module**, which is a file that contains code that is not associated with any specific object in the interface.

You also can click Project on the menu bar, and then click Add New Item to open the Add New Item – *projectname* dialog box.

To add a module and the Sub Main procedure to the Payroll application:

1 Click **File** on the menu bar, and then click **Add New Item**. The Add New Item – Payroll Project dialog box opens.

2 Click **Module** in the Templates list box. In the Name text box, change the module name from Module1.vb to **Payroll Module**.

3 Click the **Open** button to add the Payroll Module to the application, then temporarily display the Solution Explorer window. As Figure 7-32 indicates, a module begins with the module header and ends with the module footer.

module header

module footer

module file added to the solution

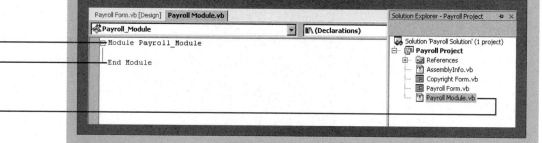

Figure 7-32: Payroll Module added to the application

Next, enter the Sub Main procedure's header and footer.

4 Position the insertion point in the blank line between the module's header and footer. Press **Tab** to indent the line, then type **Sub Main** and press **Enter**. Notice that the Code editor enters the procedure footer (`End Sub`) for you.

Now specify that the Sub Main procedure should be processed automatically when the application is started.

5 Right-click **Payroll Project** in the Solution Explorer window, and then click **Properties**. The Payroll Project Property Pages dialog box opens.

6 Click the **Startup object** list arrow, and then click **Sub Main** in the list. Click the **OK** button to close the dialog box.

Before you can complete the Sub Main procedure, you need to learn how to create an instance of a form.

Creating an Instance of a Form

If you look closely at the code shown earlier in Figure 7-31, you will notice that the code begins with the instruction `Public Class CopyrightForm` and ends with the instruction `End Class`. As you learned in Tutorial 1, a block of code that begins with the `Public Class` clause and ends with the `End Class` clause is called a class definition. Recall that a class definition, more simply referred to as a class, specifies (or defines) the attributes and behaviors of an object. The CopyrightForm class shown in Figure 7-31, for example, specifies the attributes and behaviors of a CopyrightForm object.

Figure 7-33 shows the code contained in the PayrollForm, with each procedure collapsed to make the figure more readable. Notice that the code contains the class definition for a PayrollForm object.

class definition

```
Public Class PayrollForm
    Inherits System.Windows.Forms.Form

    Windows Form Designer generated code

    Private Sub ExitButton_Click(ByVal sender As Object, ByVal e As System.EventArgs) Ha

    Private Sub NameTextBox_Enter(ByVal sender As Object, ByVal e As System.EventArgs) H

    Private Sub PayrollForm_Load(ByVal sender As Object, ByVal e As System.EventArgs) Ha

    Private Sub CalculateButton_Click(ByVal sender As Object, ByVal e As System.EventArg

    Private Function GetFwtTax(ByVal sngWeekPay As Single) As Single...

    Private Sub ClearLabels(ByVal sender As Object, ByVal e As System.EventArgs) ...
End Class
```

Figure 7-33: Code contained in the PayrollForm

When an application is started, Visual Basic .NET automatically processes the code contained in one object: the Startup object. For example, if the CopyrightForm is specified as the Startup object, Visual Basic .NET automatically processes the code contained in the CopyrightForm class definition. The code creates a CopyrightForm object and then displays the object on the screen. If you need to display a different form on the screen—for example, the PayrollForm—after the application is started, you first instruct the computer to create a PayrollForm object by processing the code entered in the PayrollForm class definition, and then instruct the computer to display the form object on the screen.

Similarly, if the PayrollForm is specified as the Startup object, Visual Basic .NET automatically processes the code contained in the PayrollForm class definition. In this case, the code creates a PayrollForm object and then displays the object on the screen. If you need to display a different form on the screen after the application is started, you first instruct the computer to create the form object by processing the code entered in the appropriate class definition, and then instruct the computer to display the form object on the screen.

When the Sub Main procedure is the Startup object, as it is in this case, neither the CopyrightForm class definition nor the PayrollForm class definition will be processed automatically. To allow the Payroll application to display the forms associated with these classes, the Sub Main procedure will need first to instruct the computer to create the objects, and then instruct the computer to display the objects on the screen.

You use the syntax **Dim** *variablename* **As New** *objecttype*() to instruct the computer to create an object from a class. In the syntax, *objecttype* is the name of the class, and *variablename* is the name of an object variable that will store the object's address. Storing the address in an object variable allows the computer to locate the object when it is referred to in code. The statement `Dim objCopyrightForm As New CopyrightForm()`, for example, instructs the computer to use the CopyrightForm class to create a CopyrightForm object. When the object is created, its address in the computer's internal memory is stored in an object variable named objCopyrightForm. Similarly, the statement `Dim objPayrollForm As New PayrollForm()` instructs the computer to use the PayrollForm class to create a PayrollForm object. When the object is created, its address in the computer's internal memory is stored in an object variable named objPayrollForm.

To create a CopyrightForm object and a PayrollForm object:

1 Enter the two Dim statements shown in Figure 7-34.

enter these two lines of code

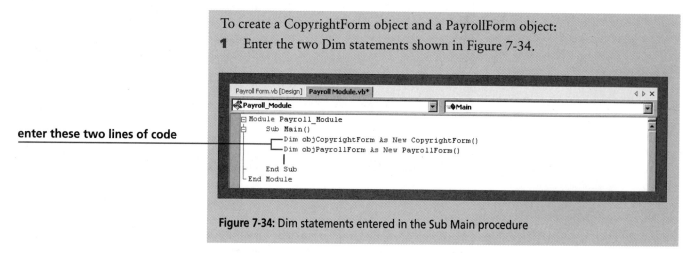

Figure 7-34: Dim statements entered in the Sub Main procedure

The Dim statements shown in Figure 7-34 create the CopyrightForm and PayrollForm objects and assign their addresses to object variables. However, they do not display the form objects on the screen. You use a form object's ShowDialog method to display the form objects.

Using a Form Object's ShowDialog Method

The form object's **ShowDialog method** allows you to display a form object on the screen. The syntax of the ShowDialog method is *form*.**ShowDialog**(), where *form* is the name of the object variable that contains the form object's address. For example, to display the CopyrightForm object, whose address is stored in the objCopyrightForm variable, you use the statement `objCopyrightForm.ShowDialog()`. Likewise, to display the PayrollForm object, whose address is stored in the objPayrollForm variable, you use the statement `objPayrollForm.ShowDialog()`.

To complete the Sub Main procedure:

1 Enter the two additional statements shown in Figure 7-35, which shows the completed Sub Main procedure.

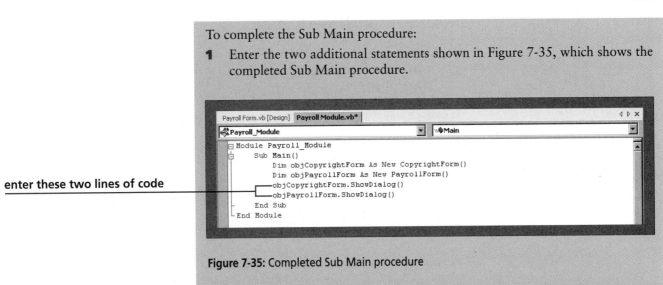

enter these two lines of code

Figure 7-35: Completed Sub Main procedure

2 Save the solution, then start the application. The Dim statements entered in the Sub Main procedure create a CopyrightForm object and a PayrollForm object. Then the `objCopyrightForm.ShowDialog()` statement displays the Copyright form on the screen. After eight seconds have elapsed, the `Me.Close()` statement in the ExitTimer control's Tick event procedure closes the CopyrightForm. The computer then returns to the Sub Main procedure to process the `objPayrollForm.ShowDialog()` statement, which displays the Payroll form on the screen.

3 Click the **Exit** button to close the Payroll form. The computer returns to the Sub Main procedure to process the `End Sub` instruction, which ends the procedure and the application.

4 When you return to the Code editor window, close the Output window, then close the Code editor window. Click **File** on the menu bar, and then click **Close Solution**.

You now have completed Tutorial 7. You can either take a break or complete the end-of-lesson questions and exercises.

SUMMARY

To add an existing item to an application:

■ Click File on the menu bar, and then click Add Existing Item. You also can click Project on the menu bar, and then click Add Existing Item.

To add a new item to an application:

■ Click File on the menu bar, and then click Add New Item. You also can click Project on the menu bar, and then click Add New Item.

To process code automatically when an application is started:

■ Add a module to the application, then create a Sub Main procedure in the module. Right-click the project's name in the Solution Explorer window, then click Properties. Click the Startup object list arrow, then click Sub Main in the list.

To create an instance of an object from a class:

■ Use the syntax **Dim** *variablename* **As New** *objecttype*(), where *objecttype* is the name of the class corresponding to the object you want to create, and *variablename* is the name of an object variable that will store the object's address.

To display a form object on the screen:

■ Use the form object's ShowDialog method. Its syntax is *form*.**ShowDialog**(), where *form* is the name of the object variable that contains the form object's address.

QUESTIONS

1. You can tell the computer to automatically process the code contained in the _____ procedure when an application is started.
   a. Auto
   b. AutoProcess
   c. Process
   d. Sub Main
   e. Sub Auto

2. The procedure from Question 1 is entered in a _____, which is a file that contains code that is not associated with any specific object in the interface.
   a. form
   b. global file
   c. module
   d. subroutine
   e. None of the above.

3. You can use the File menu to add both new and existing items to an application.
   a. True
   b. False

4. Which of the following statements creates an InventoryForm object and stores the object's address in an object variable named objInventoryForm?
   a. `Dim objInventoryForm As New Class()`
   b. `Dim objInventoryForm As New InventoryForm()`
   c. `Dim InventoryForm As New Object()`
   d. `Dim InventoryForm As New objInventoryForm()`
   e. None of the above.

5. Which of the following statements displays the InventoryForm object created in Question 4 on the screen?
   a. `InventoryForm.Display()`
   b. `InventoryForm.ShowDialog()`
   c. `objInventoryForm.Display()`
   d. `objInventoryForm.ShowDialog()`
   e. `objInventoryForm.ShowForm()`

E X E R C I S E S

The following list summarizes the GUI design guidelines you have learned so far. You can use this list to verify that the interfaces you create in the following exercises adhere to the GUI standards outlined in the book.

- Information should flow either vertically or horizontally, with the most important information always located in the upper-left corner of the screen.

- Maintain a consistent margin of two or three dots from the edge of the window.

- Try to create a user interface that no one notices.

- Related controls should be grouped together using white space, a GroupBox control, or a Panel control.

- Set the form's FormBorderStyle, ControlBox, MaximizeBox, MinimizeBox, and StartPosition properties appropriately:

    - A splash screen should not have a Minimize, Maximize, or Close button, and its borders should not be sizable.

    - A form that is not a splash screen should always have a Minimize button and a Close button, but you can choose to disable the Maximize button. Typically, the FormBorderStyle property is set to Sizable, but also can be set to FixedSingle.

- Position related controls on succeeding dots. Controls that are not part of any logical grouping may be positioned from two to four dots away from other controls.

- Buttons should be positioned either in a row along the bottom of the screen, or stacked in either the upper-right or lower-right corner.

- If the buttons are positioned at the bottom of the screen, then each button should be the same height; their widths, however, may vary.

- If the buttons are stacked in either the upper-right or lower-right corner of the screen, then each should be the same height and the same width.

- Use no more than six buttons on a screen.

- The most commonly used button should be placed first.

- The default button should be the button that is most often selected by the user, except in cases where the tasks performed by the button are both destructive and irreversible. The default button is typically the first button.

- Button captions should:

    - be meaningful
    - be from one to three words
    - appear on one line
    - be entered using book title capitalization

- Use labels to identify the text boxes in the interface, and position the label either above or to the left of the text box.

- Label text should:

    - be from one to three words

- appear on one line
- be left-justified
- end with a colon (:)
- be entered using sentence capitalization

- Labels that identify controls should have their BorderStyle property set to None.

- Labels that display program output, such as the result of a calculation, should have their BorderStyle property set to FixedSingle.

- Align controls to minimize the number of different margins.

- If you use a graphic in the interface, use a small one and place it in a location that will not distract the user.

- Use the Tahoma font for applications that will run on Windows 2000 or Windows XP.

- Use no more than two different font sizes, which should be 8, 9, 10, 11, or 12 point.

- Use only one font type, which should be a sans serif font, in the interface.

- Avoid using italics and underlining.

- Limit the use of bold text to titles, headings, and key items.

- Build the interface using black, white, and gray first, then add color only if you have a good reason to do so.

- Use white, off-white, light gray, pale blue, or pale yellow for an application's background, and black for the text.

- Limit the number of colors to three, not including white, black, and gray. The colors you choose should complement each other.

- Never use color as the only means of identification for an element in the user interface.

- Set each control's TabIndex property to a number that represents the order in which you want the control to receive the focus (begin with 0).

- A text box's TabIndex value should be one more than the TabIndex value of its identifying label.

- Assign a unique access key to each control (in the interface) that can receive user input (text boxes, buttons, and so on).

- When assigning an access key to a control, use the first letter of the caption or identifying label, unless another letter provides a more meaningful association. If you can't use the first letter and no other letter provides a more meaningful association, then use a distinctive consonant. Lastly, use a vowel or a number.

- Lock the controls in place on the form.

- Document the program internally.

- Use the Val function on any Text property involved in a calculation.

- Use the Format function to improve the appearance of numbers in the interface.

- In the InputBox function, use sentence capitalization for the *prompt*, and book title capitalization for the *title*.

- Use sentence capitalization for the optional identifying label in a group box control.

- MessageBox.Show method:

  - Use sentence capitalization for the *text* argument, but book title capitalization for the *caption* argument. The name of the application typically appears in the *caption* argument.

  - Avoid using the words "error," "warning," or "mistake" in the message.

  - Display the Warning Message icon ⚠ in a message box that alerts the user that he or she must make a decision before the application can continue. You can phrase the message as a question.

  - Display the Information Message icon ⓘ in a message box that displays an informational message along with an OK button only.

  - Display the Stop Message icon ✖ when you want to alert the user of a serious problem that must be corrected before the application can continue.

  - The default button in the dialog box should be the one that represents the user's most likely action, as long as that action is not destructive.

- Use the KeyPress event to prevent a text box from accepting inappropriate keys.

- Radio buttons:

  - Use radio buttons when you want to limit the user to one of two or more related and mutually exclusive choices.

  - Use a minimum of two and a maximum of seven radio buttons in an interface.

  - Use sentence capitalization for the label entered in the radio button's Text property.

  - Assign a unique access key to each radio button in an interface.

  - Use a group box control (or a panel control) to create separate groups of radio buttons. Only one button in each group can be selected at any one time.

  - Designate a default radio button in each group of radio buttons.

- Check boxes:

  - Use check boxes to allow the user to select any number of choices from a group of one or more independent and nonexclusive choices.

  - Use sentence capitalization for the label entered in the check box's Text property.

  - Assign a unique access key to each check box in an interface.

- List boxes:

  - A list box should contain a minimum of three selections.

  - A list box should display a minimum of three selections and a maximum of eight selections at a time.

> - Use a label control to provide keyboard access to the list box. Set the label control's TabIndex property to a value that is one less than the list box's TabIndex value.
> - List box items are either arranged by use, with the most used entries appearing first in the list, or sorted in ascending order.
> - If a list box allows the user to make only one selection at a time, then a default item should be selected in the list box when the interface first appears. The default item should be either the most used selection or the first selection in the list. However, if a list box allows more than one selection at a time, you do not select a default item.
> - It is customary in Windows applications to disable objects that do not apply to the current state of the application.
> - It is customary in Windows applications to highlight, or select, the existing text in a text box when the text box receives the focus.
> - Test the application with both valid and invalid data (for example, test the application without entering any data, and test it by entering letters where numbers are expected).

1. In this exercise, you add the copyright screen to the Grade application that you created in Tutorial 6.
   a. Use Windows to make a copy of the Grade Solution folder, which is contained in the VBNET\Tut06 folder. Change the name of the folder to MyGrade Solution. Move the MyGrade Solution folder to the VBNET\Tut07 folder.
   b. If necessary, start Visual Studio .NET. Open the Grade Solution (Grade Solution.sln) file, which is contained in the VBNET\Tut07\MyGrade Solution folder. If the designer window is not open, right-click the form file's name in the Solution Explorer window, then click View Designer.
   c. Add the Copyright form, which is contained in the VBNET\Tut07\Copyright Solution\Copyright Project folder, to the application.
   d. View the Copyright form in the designer window. Change <your name> in the AuthorLabel control's Text property to your name.
   e. Add a module named Grade Module to the application. Add a Sub Main procedure to the module. Code the Sub Main procedure so that it displays the Copyright form first, and then displays the Grade form.
   f. Change the Startup object to Sub Main.
   g. Save the solution, then start the application. The Copyright form should appear first on the screen. After eight seconds, the Copyright form should be removed from the screen and the Grade form should appear.
   h. Click the Exit button to end the application.
   i. Close the Output window, then close the solution.

Exercise 2 is a Discovery Exercise. Discovery Exercises, which may include topics that are not covered in this lesson, allow you to "discover" the solutions to problems on your own.

discovery ▶ 2. In this exercise, you learn how to include, in an application, a link to an existing file. When an application contains a link to a file, rather than the file itself, changes made to the linked file automatically appear in each application in which it is linked.

a. If necessary, start Visual Studio .NET. Open the Hoover Solution (Hoover Solution.sln) file, which is contained in the VBNET\Tut07\Hoover Solution folder. If the designer window is not open, right-click the form file's name in the Solution Explorer window, then click View Designer.

b. Click File on the menu bar, and then click Add Existing Item.

c. Open the First Screen Project folder, which is contained in the VBNET\Tu07\First Screen Solution folder. Click First Screen Form.vb in the list of filenames.

d. Click the Open button's list arrow, and then click Link File. This creates a link to the First Screen Form.vb file.

e. Right-click First Screen Form.vb in the Solution Explorer window, then click View Designer. Notice that the text "Hoover Industries" appears in the label control on the form.

f. Save the solution, then close the solution.

g. Open the First Screen Solution (First Screen Solution.sln) file, which is contained in the VBNET\Tut07\First Screen Solution folder. Right-click First Screen Form.vb in the Solution Explorer window, then click View Designer.

h. Change the contents of the label control from "Hoover Industries" to "Hoover Company".

i. Save the solution, then close the solution.

j. Open the Hoover Solution (Hoover Solution.sln) file, which is contained in the VBNET\Tut07\Hoover Solution folder. View the First Screen Form in the designer window. Notice that the First Screen Form in the Hoover application reflects the change you made to the form in Step h. This is because the Hoover application contains a link to the First Screen Form.vb file.

k. Close the solution.

Exercise 3 is a Debugging Exercise. Debugging Exercises provide an opportunity for you to detect and correct errors in an existing application.

debugging   3. In this exercise, you debug an existing application. The purpose of this exercise is to demonstrate a common error made when using functions.

a. If necessary, start Visual Studio .NET. Open the Debug Solution (Debug Solution.sln) file, which is contained in the VBNET\Tut07\Debug Solution folder. If the designer window is not open, right-click the form file's name in the Solution Explorer window, then click View Designer.

b. Open the Code editor window and study the existing code.

c. Start the application. Click 20 in the Length list box, then click 30 in the Width list box. Click the Calculate Area button, which should display the area of a rectangle having a length of 20 feet and a width of 30 feet. Notice that the application is not working properly.

d. Click the Exit button to end the application.

e. Correct the application's code, then save the solution and start the application. Click 20 in the Length list box, then click 30 in the Width list box. Click the Calculate Area button, which should display the area of a rectangle having a length of 20 feet and a width of 30 feet.

f. Click the Exit button to end the application.

g. Close the Output window, then close the solution.

Manipulating Strings

Creating a Hangman Game Application

case ▶ On days when the weather is bad and the students cannot go outside to play, Mr. Mitchell, who teaches second grade at Hinsbrook School, spends recess time playing a simplified version of the Hangman game with his class. Mr. Mitchell feels that the game is both fun (the students love playing the game) and educational (the game allows the students to observe how letters are used to form words). Mr. Mitchell has asked you to write an application that two students can use to play the game on the computer.

Mr. Mitchell's simplified version of the Hangman game requires two people to play. Currently, Mr. Mitchell thinks of a word that has five letters. He then draws five dashes on the chalkboard—one for each letter in the word. One student then is chosen to guess the word, letter by letter. If the student guesses a correct letter, Mr. Mitchell replaces the appropriate dash or dashes with the letter. For example, if the original word is *moose* and the student guesses the letter *o*, Mr. Mitchell changes the fives dashes on the chalkboard to *-oo--*. The game is over when the student guesses all of the letters in the word, or when he or she makes three incorrect guesses, whichever comes first.

Previewing the Completed Application

Before creating the Hangman Game application, you first preview the completed application.

To preview the completed application:

1 Use the Run command on the Windows Start menu to run the **Hangman** (Hangman.exe) file, which is contained in the VBNET\Tut08 folder on your computer's hard disk. The Hangman Game application's user interface appears on the screen.

Notice that the interface contains a File menu. You learn how to include a menu in an interface in Lesson B.

2 Click **File** on the menu bar, and then click **New Game**. When you are prompted to enter a word, type **puppy** and press **Enter**. A label control containing five dashes (hyphens)—one for each letter in the word "puppy"—appears in the application's interface. Also appearing in the interface are 26 label controls that contain the letters of the alphabet, and a label control that keeps track of the number of incorrect guesses made. See Figure 8-1.

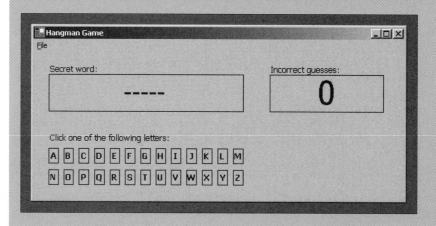

Figure 8-1 Label controls displayed in the user interface

Your first guess will be the letter "Y".

3   Click the **Y** label control. The application replaces the last dash in the interface with the letter "Y". This indicates that the letter "Y" is the last letter in the original word. Also notice that the application hides the Y label control to prevent the user from selecting it again.

Now guess the letter X.

4   Click the **X** label control. Because the letter X does not appear in the word "puppy", the application changes the number of incorrect guesses from zero to one. Additionally, the X label control is hidden from view.

5   Click the **P** label control. The application replaces three of the five dashes in the interface with the letter P, and hides the P label control from view.

6   Click the **U** label control. The application replaces the remaining dash in the interface with the letter U, and hides the U label control from view. The application then displays the message box shown in Figure 8-2.

message box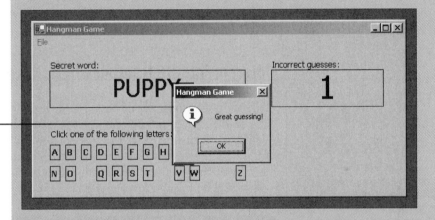

Figure 8-2 Message box displayed by the Hangman Game application

7   Click the **OK** button to close the message box. Click **File** on the menu bar, and then click **Exit** to end the application.

Before you can begin coding the Hangman Game application, you need to learn how to manipulate strings in Visual Basic .NET; you learn about string manipulation in Lesson A. You begin coding the Hangman Game application in Lesson B and complete it in Lesson C.

After completing this lesson, you will be able to:

- Determine the number of characters contained in a string
- Remove characters from a string
- Determine whether a string begins or ends with one or more specific characters
- Access characters from the beginning, middle, and end of a string
- Replace one or more characters in a string
- Insert characters within a string
- Search a string for one or more characters

tip

You also can use the Len function, which you learn about in Discovery Exercise 12 at the end of this lesson, to determine the number of characters contained in a string.

String Manipulation

Manipulating Strings in Visual Basic .NET

Many times, an application will need to manipulate (process) string data. For example, an application may need to verify that an inventory part number begins with a specific letter; or, it may need to determine whether the last three characters in an employee number are valid. In this tutorial, you learn several ways of manipulating strings in Visual Basic .NET. Begin by learning how to determine the number of characters contained in a string.

Determining the Number of Characters Contained in a String

In many applications, it is necessary to determine the number of characters contained in a string. For example, an application that expects the user to enter a 10-digit phone number needs to verify that the user entered the required number of characters. You can use a string's **Length property** to determine the number of characters contained in the string. The syntax of the Length property is shown in Figure 8-3 along with several examples of using the property.

Syntax
To determine the number of characters contained in a string: *string*.**Length**
Examples and results
Example 1 `Debug.WriteLine(Me.ZipTextBox.Text.Length)` **Result** displays in the Output window the number of characters contained in the ZipTextBox control's Text property

Example 2
`Dim strName As String = "Paul Blackfeather"`
`Debug.WriteLine(strName.Length)`
 	
Result
displays the number 17 in the Output window

Figure 8-3: Syntax and examples of the Length property

Examples and results

Example 3

```
Dim strPhone As String
strPhone = InputBox("10-digit phone number", "Phone")
Do While strPhone.Length = 10
      instructions to process when the loop condition evaluates to True
      strPhone = InputBox("10-digit phone number", "Phone")
Loop
```

Result

gets a phone number from the user, and then repeats the loop instructions while the number of characters contained in the phone number is equal to the number 10

Example 4

```
Dim strPart As String
strPart = InputBox("Part number", "Part Number")
If strPart.Length >= 4 Then
      instructions to process when the condition evaluates to True
End If
```

Result

gets a part number from the user, and then determines whether the part number contains at least four characters

---

Figure 8-3: Syntax and examples of the Length property (continued)

The statement shown in Example 1 in Figure 8-3, `Debug.WriteLine(Me.ZipTextBox.Text.Length)`, displays in the Output window the number of characters contained in the ZipTextBox control's Text property. (Recall that the Text property of a control is treated as a string.) Assuming the user enters the ZIP code 60111 in the ZipTextBox control, the statement displays the number five in the Output window.

The code shown in Example 2 assigns the string "Paul Blackfeather" to a String variable named strName. It then uses the strName variable's Length property to determine the number of characters contained in the variable, displaying the result in the Output window. In this case, the number 17 will appear in the Output window, because the strName variable contains 17 characters.

The code shown in Example 3 prompts the user to enter a 10-digit phone number, and stores the user's response in a String variable named strPhone. The `Do While strPhone.Length = 10` clause then compares the value stored in the strPhone variable's Length property to the number 10.

The code shown in Example 4 in Figure 8-3 prompts the user to enter a part number, and stores the user's response in a String variable named strPart. The `If strPart.Length >= 4 Then` clause then determines whether the strPart variable contains at least four characters.

Next, learn how to remove characters from a string.

Removing Characters from a String

At times, an application may need to remove one or more characters from an item of data entered by the user. For example, an application may need to remove a dollar sign from the beginning of a sales amount; or, it may need to remove a percent sign from the end of a tax rate.

You can use the **TrimStart method** to remove one or more characters from the beginning of a string. Similarly, you can use the **TrimEnd method** to remove one or more characters from the end of a string. To remove one or more characters from both the beginning and end of a string, you use the **Trim method**. Each method returns a string with the appropriate characters removed (trimmed).

Figure 8-4 shows the syntax of the TrimStart, TrimEnd, and Trim methods and includes several examples of using each method.

Syntax

To remove characters from the beginning of a string:	*string*.**TrimStart**[(*char*)]
To remove characters from the end of a string:	*string*.**TrimEnd**[(*char*)]
To remove characters from both the beginning and end of a string:	*string*.**Trim**[(*char*)]

Examples and results

Example 1
```
Dim strName As String
strName = Me.NameTextBox.Text.TrimStart
```

Result
assigns the contents of the NameTextBox control's Text property, excluding any leading spaces, to the strName variable

Example 2
```
Me.NameTextBox.Text = Me.NameTextBox.Text.TrimStart
```

Result
removes any leading spaces from the NameTextBox control's Text property

Example 3
```
Dim strName As String
strName = Me.NameTextBox.Text.TrimEnd
```

Result
assigns the contents of the NameTextBox control's Text property, excluding any trailing spaces, to the strName variable

Example 4
```
Dim strRate As String, sngRate As Single
strRate = InputBox("Rate:", "Rate")
sngRate = Val(strRate.TrimEnd("%", " "))
```

Result
assigns the contents of the strRate variable, excluding any trailing percent signs and spaces, to the sngRate variable

Example 5
```
Me.NameTextBox.Text = Me.NameTextBox.Text.Trim
```

Result
removes any leading and trailing spaces from the NameTextBox control's Text property

Example 6
```
Dim strNum As String
strNum = strNum.Trim("$", " ", "%")
```

Result
removes any leading and trailing dollar signs, spaces, and percent signs from the strNum variable

Figure 8-4: Syntax and examples of the TrimStart, TrimEnd, and Trim methods

In each syntax, *char* is a comma-separated list of characters that you want removed from the *string*. Notice that the *char* argument and its surrounding parentheses are optional in each syntax. If you omit the *char* argument and the parentheses, Visual Basic .NET assumes that you want to remove one or more spaces from the beginning and/or end of the *string*. In other words, the default value for the *char* argument is the space character (" ").

Study closely the examples shown in Figure 8-4. When processing the statement `strName = Me.NameTextBox.Text.TrimStart`, which is shown in Example 1, the computer first makes a temporary copy of the string stored in the NameTextBox control's Text property. It then removes any leading spaces from the temporary copy of the string, and then assigns the resulting string to the strName variable. Assuming the user enters the string " Karen" (two spaces followed by the name Karen) in the NameTextBox control, the `strName = Me.NameTextBox.Text.TrimStart` statement assigns the name "Karen" to the strName variable; however, the NameTextBox control's Text property still contains " Karen" (two spaces followed by the name Karen). After the statement is processed, the computer removes the temporary copy of the string from its internal memory.

Notice that the code shown in Example 1 does not remove the leading spaces from the NameTextBox control's Text property. To remove the leading spaces from the Text property, you use the statement shown in Example 2: `Me.NameTextBox.Text = Me.NameTextBox.Text.TrimStart`.

When processing the `strName = Me.NameTextBox.Text.TrimEnd` statement in Example 3, the computer first makes a temporary copy of the string stored in the NameTextBox control's Text property. It then removes any trailing spaces from the copied string, assigning the result to the strName variable. After the statement is processed, the computer removes the copied string from its internal memory. Assuming the user enters the string "Ned Yander   " (the name Ned Yander followed by four spaces) in the NameTextBox control, the `strName = Me.NameTextBox.Text.TrimEnd` statement assigns the name "Ned Yander" to the strName variable; however, the statement does not change the contents of the NameTextBox control's Text property.

When processing the `sngRate = Val(strRate.TrimEnd("%", " "))` statement in Example 4, the computer first makes a copy of the string stored in the strRate variable. It then removes any trailing percent signs and spaces from the copied string, and then assigns the resulting string, treated as a number, to the sngRate variable. For example, if the strRate variable contains the string "3 %" (the number 3, a space, and a percent sign), the `sngRate = Val(strRate.TrimEnd("%", " "))` statement assigns the number 3 to the sngRate variable, but it does not change the value stored in the strRate variable. Likewise, if the strRate variable contains the string "15% " (the number 15, a percent sign, and two spaces), the statement assigns the number 15 to the sngRate variable, but leaves the contents of the strRate variable unchanged.

You can use the statement shown in Example 5, `Me.NameTextBox.Text = Me.NameTextBox.Text.Trim`, to remove any leading and trailing spaces from the NameTextBox control's Text property. You can use the statement shown in Example 6, `strNum = strNum.Trim("$", " ", "%")`, to remove any leading and trailing dollar signs, spaces, and percent signs from the strNum variable.

At times, you may need to remove characters that are not located at the beginning or end of a string; for this, you use the Remove method.

The Remove Method

You can use the **Remove method** to remove one or more characters located anywhere in a string. Figure 8-5 shows the syntax of the Remove method and includes several examples of using the method. Like the TrimStart, TrimEnd, and Trim methods, the Remove method returns a string with the appropriate characters removed.

Syntax
To remove characters from anywhere in a string: *string*.**Remove**(*startIndex, count*)
Examples and results

Example 1
`Dim strName As String = "John Cober"`
`Me.NameTextBox.Text = strName.Remove(0, 5)`
 	
Result
assigns the string "Cober" to the NameTextBox control's Text property

Example 2
`Dim strName As String = "John"`
`Me.NameTextBox.Text = strName.Remove(2, 1)`
 	
Result
assigns the string "Jon" to the NameTextBox control's Text property

Example 3
`Dim strName As String = "Janis"`
`strName = strName.Remove(3, 2)`
 	
Result
assigns the string "Jan" to the strName variable

Figure 8-5: Syntax and examples of the Remove method

In the syntax, *startIndex* is the index of the first character you want removed from the *string*, and *count* is the number of characters you want removed. The first character in a string has an index of zero, the second character has an index of one, and so on. Therefore, to remove only the first character from a string, you use the number zero as the *startIndex*, and the number one as the *count*. To remove the fourth through eighth characters, you use the number three as the *startIndex*, and the number five as the *count*.

Study closely the three examples shown in Figure 8-5. When processing the statement `Me.NameTextBox.Text = strName.Remove(0, 5)`, which is shown in Example 1, the computer makes a copy of the string stored in the strName variable. It then removes the first five characters from the copied string; in this case, the computer removes the letters J, o, h, and n, and the space character. The computer then assigns the resulting string ("Cober") to the NameTextBox control's Text property before removing the copied string from its internal memory. The contents of the strName variable are not changed as a result of processing the `Me.NameTextBox.Text = strName.Remove(0, 5)` statement.

When processing the statement `Me.NameTextBox.Text = strName.Remove(2, 1)`, which is shown in Example 2, the computer makes a copy of the string stored in the strName variable. It then removes one character, beginning with the character whose index is 2, from the copied string. The character with an index of 2 is the third character in the string—in this case, the letter h. The computer then assigns the resulting string ("Jon") to the NameTextBox control's Text property. Here again, the statement `Me.NameTextBox.Text = strName.Remove(2, 1)` does not change the string stored in the strName variable.

You can use the `strName = strName.Remove(3, 2)` statement, which is shown in Example 3 in Figure 8-5, to remove two characters, beginning with the character whose index is 3, from the string stored in the strName variable. In this case, the letters i and s are removed, changing the contents of the strName variable from "Janis" to "Jan".

Next, learn how to determine whether a string begins or ends with a specific sequence of characters.

Determining Whether a String Begins or Ends with a Specific Sequence of Characters

In many applications, it is necessary to determine whether a string begins or ends with a specific character or characters. For example, an application may need to determine whether a phone number entered by the user begins with area code "312". Or, an application may need to determine whether a tax rate entered by the user ends with a percent sign.

Visual Basic .NET provides the **StartsWith method** for determining whether a specific sequence of characters occurs at the beginning of a string, and the **EndsWith method** for determining whether a specific sequence of characters occurs at the end of a string. Figure 8-6 shows the syntax of the StartsWith and EndsWith methods along with examples of using each method.

Syntax

To determine whether a specific sequence of characters occurs at the beginning of a string:
string.**StartsWith(***subString***)**

To determine whether a specific sequence of characters occurs at the end of a string:
string.**EndsWith(***subString***)**

Examples and results

Example 1
```
Dim strPay As String
strPay = InputBox("Pay rate", "Pay")
If strPay.StartsWith("$") = True Then
    strPay = strPay.TrimStart("$")
End If
```

Result
determines whether the string stored in the strPay variable begins with the dollar sign; if it does, the dollar sign is removed from the string

---

Figure 8-6: Syntax and examples of the StartsWith and EndsWith methods

Examples and results

Example 2
```
Dim strPhone As String
strPhone = InputBox("10-digit phone number", "Phone")
Do While strPhone.StartsWith("312") = True
    Debug.WriteLine(strPhone)
    strPhone = InputBox("10-digit phone number", "Phone")
Loop
```

Result
determines whether the string stored in the strPhone variable begins with "312"; if it does, the contents of the strPhone variable are displayed in the Output window and the user is prompted to enter another phone number

Example 3
```
Dim strCityState As String = UCase(Me.CityStateTextBox.Text)
If strCityState.EndsWith("CA") = True Then
    Debug.WriteLine("California customer")
End If
```

Result
determines whether the string stored in the strCityState variable ends with "CA"; if it does, the string "California customer" is displayed in the Output window

Example 4
```
Dim strName As String
strName = InputBox("Your name:", "Name")
If UCase(strName).EndsWith("SMITH") = False Then
    Debug.WriteLine(strName)
End If
```

Result
determines whether the string stored in the strName variable ends with "SMITH"; if it does not, the variable's value is displayed in the Output window

You can omit the equal sign and the Boolean value True from the If clause in Examples 1 and 3. In other words, you can write the If clauses as `If strPay.StartsWith("$") Then` and `If strCityState.EndsWith("CA") Then`.

You also can write the Do While clause in Example 2 as `Do While strPhone.StartsWith("312")`.

You also can write the If clause in Example 4 as `If Not UCase(strName).EndsWith("SMITH") Then`.

Figure 8-6: Syntax and examples of the StartsWith and EndsWith methods (continued)

In the syntax for the StartsWith and EndsWith methods, *subString* is the sequence of characters that you want the method to search for either at the beginning or end of the *string*. The StartsWith method returns the Boolean value True if *subString* is located at the beginning of *string*; otherwise, it returns the Boolean value False. Likewise, the EndsWith method returns the Boolean value True if *subString* is located at the end of *string*; otherwise, it returns the Boolean value False.

In the first example shown in Figure 8-6, the `If strPay.StartsWith("$")` `= True Then` clause determines whether the string stored in the strPay variable begins with the dollar sign. If it does, the `strPay = strPay.TrimStart("$")` statement removes the dollar sign from the variable's contents.

In the second example, the `Do While strPhone.StartsWith("312") =` `True` clause determines whether the string stored in the strPhone variable begins with "312". If it does, the contents of the variable are displayed in the Output window and the user is prompted to enter another phone number.

The code shown in Example 3 in Figure 8-6 displays the string "California customer" in the Output window if the string stored in the strCityState variable ends with "CA". The code shown in Example 4 displays the contents of the strName variable in the Output window, but only if the variable's contents do not end with "SMITH".

Next you learn how to access characters contained in a string.

Accessing Characters Contained in a String

At times, an application may need to access one or more characters contained in a string. For example, an application may need to determine whether the letter K appears as the third character in a string; or, it may need to display only the string's first five characters. You can use the **Substring method** to access any number of characters in a string. Figure 8-7 shows the syntax of the Substring method and includes several examples of using the method.

Syntax
To access one or more characters contained in a string: *string*.**Substring(***startIndex*[, *count*]**)**

Examples and results

Example 1
```
Dim strName As String = "Peggy Ryan"
strFirst = strName.Substring(0, 5)
strLast = strName.Substring(6)
```

Result
assigns "Peggy" to the strFirst variable, and assigns "Ryan" to the strLast variable

Example 2
```
Dim strSales As String
strSales = Me.SalesTextBox.Text
If strSales.StartsWith("$") = True Then
     strSales = strSales.Substring(1)
End If
```

Result
determines whether the string stored in the strSales variable begins with the dollar sign; if it does, assigns the contents of the variable, excluding the dollar sign, to the strSales variable

Example 3
```
Dim strRate As String, sngRate As Single
strRate = InputBox("Enter rate", "Tax Rate")
If strRate.EndsWith("%") = True Then
     sngRate = Val(strRate.Substring(0, strRate.Length — 1))
Else
     sngRate = Val(strRate)
End If
```

Result
determines whether the string stored in the strRate variable ends with the percent sign; if it does, assigns the contents of the strRate variable, excluding the percent sign and treated as a number, to the sngRate variable; otherwise, assigns the contents of the strRate variable, treated as a number, to the sngRate variable

Figure 8-7: Syntax and examples of the Substring method

tip

. . . .

You also can use the Left, Right, and Mid functions, which you learn about in Discovery Exercise 14 at the end of this lesson, to access characters contained in a string.

The Substring method contains two arguments: *startIndex* and *count*. *StartIndex* is the index of the first character you want to access in the *string*. The first character in a string has an index of zero, the second character has an index of one, and so on. The *count* argument, which is optional, specifies the number of characters you want to access. The Substring method returns a string that contains *count* number of characters, beginning with the character whose index is *startIndex*. If you omit the *count* argument, the Substring method returns all characters from the *startIndex* position through the end of the string.

Study closely the three examples shown in Figure 8-7. In Example 1, the statement `strFirst = strName.Substring(0, 5)` assigns the first five characters contained in the strName variable ("Peggy") to the strFirst variable. The statement `strLast = strName.Substring(6)` assigns all of the characters contained in the strName variable, beginning with the character whose index is 6, to the strLast variable. In this case, the statement assigns "Ryan" to the strLast variable.

Example 2's code uses the StartsWith method to determine whether the string stored in the strSales variable begins with the dollar sign. If it does, the statement `strSales = strSales.Substring(1)` assigns all of the characters from the strSales variable, beginning with the character whose index is 1, to the strSales variable. The `strSales = strSales.Substring(1)` statement is equivalent to the statement `strSales = strSales.Remove(0, 1)`, as well as to the statement `strSales = strSales.TrimStart("$")`.

The code shown in Example 3 in Figure 8-7 uses the EndsWith method to determine whether the string stored in the strRate variable ends with the percent sign. If it does, the statement `sngRate = Val(strRate.Substring(0, strRate.Length − 1))` assigns all of the characters contained in the strRate variable, excluding the last character (which is the percent sign), to the sngRate variable. The `sngRate = Val(strRate.Substring(0, strRate.Length − 1))` statement is equivalent to the statement `sngRate = Val(strRate.Remove(strRate.Length − 1, 1))`, as well as to the statement `sngRate = Val(strRate.TrimEnd("%"))`.

Next, learn how to replace a sequence of characters in a string with another sequence of characters.

Replacing Characters in a String

You can use the **Replace method** to replace a sequence of characters in a string with another sequence of characters. For example, you can use the Replace method to replace area code "800" with area code "877" in a phone number. Or, you can use it to replace the dashes in a Social Security number with the empty string. Figure 8-8 shows the syntax of the Replace method and includes several examples of using the method.

Syntax

To replace all occurrences of a sequence of characters in a string with another sequence of characters: *string*.**Replace(***oldValue*, *newValue***)**

Examples and results

Example 1
```
Dim strPhone As String = "1-800-111-0000"
Dim strNewPhone As String
strNewPhone = strPhone.Replace("800", "877")
```

Result
assigns the string "1-877-111-0000" to the strNewPhone variable

Example 2
```
Dim strSocial As String = "000-11-9999"
strSocial = strSocial.Replace("-", "")
```

Result
assigns the string "000119999" to the strSocial variable

Example 3
```
Dim strWord As String = "latter"
strWord = strWord.Replace("t", "d")
```

Result
assigns the string "ladder" to the strWord variable

Figure 8-8: Syntax and examples of the Replace method

tip

If the strPhone variable in Example 1 contained "1-800-111-0800", the string "1-877-111-0877" would be assigned to the strNewPhone variable, because the Replace method replaces all occurrences of *oldValue* with *newValue*.

In the syntax, *oldValue* is the sequence of characters that you want to replace in the *string*, and *newValue* is the replacement characters. The Replace method returns a string with all occurrences of *oldValue* replaced with *newValue*.

When processing the statement `strNewPhone = strPhone.Replace ("800", "877")`, which is shown in Example 1 in Figure 8-8, the computer first makes a copy of the string stored in the strPhone variable. It then replaces "800" with "877" in the copied string, and then assigns the result—in this case, "1-877-111-0000"—to the strNewPhone variable.

The `strSocial = strSocial.Replace("-", "")` statement in Example 2 replaces each dash (hyphen) in the string stored in the strSocial variable with a zero-length (empty) string. After the statement is processed, the strSocial variable contains the string "000119999".

In Example 3 in Figure 8-8, the statement `strWord = strWord.Replace ("t", "d")` replaces each letter "t" in the string stored in the strWord variable with the letter "d". The statement changes the contents of the strWord variable from "latter" to "ladder".

The Replace method replaces all occurrences of *oldValue* with *newValue*. At times, however, you may need to replace only a specific occurrence of *oldValue* with *newValue*; for this, you use the Mid statement rather than the Replace method.

The Mid Statement

You can use the **Mid statement** to replace a specified number of characters in a string with characters from another string. Figure 8-9 shows the syntax of the Mid statement and includes several examples of using the statement.

Syntax
To replace a specific number of characters in a string with characters from another string: **Mid(***targetString, start* [, *count*]**)** = *replacementString*
Examples and results

Example 1
`Dim strName As String = "Rob Smith"`
`Mid(strName, 7, 1) = "y"`
 	
Result
changes the contents of the strName variable to "Rob Smyth"

Example 2
`Dim strName As String = "Rob Smith"`
`Mid(strName, 7) = "y"`
 	
Result
changes the contents of the strName variable to "Rob Smyth"

Example 3
`Dim strName As String = "Ann Johnson"`
`Mid(strName, 5) = "Paul"`
 	
Result
changes the contents of the strName variable to "Ann Paulson"

Example 4
`Dim strName As String = "Earl Cho"`
`Mid(strName, 6) = "Liverpool"`
 	
Result
changes the contents of the strName variable to "Earl Liv"

Figure 8-9: Syntax and examples of the Mid statement

In the Mid statement's syntax, *targetString* is the string in which you want characters replaced, and *replacementString* contains the replacement characters. *Start* is the character position of the first character you want replaced in the *targetString*. The first character in the *targetString* is in character position one, the second is in character position two, and so on. The *count* argument, which is optional in the Mid statement, specifies the number of characters to replace in the *targetString*. If *count* is omitted, the Mid statement replaces the lesser of either the number of characters in the *replacementString*, or the number of characters in the *targetString* from position *start* through the end of the *targetString*.

Study closely the examples shown in Figure 8-9. In the first example, the statement `Mid(strName, 7, 1) = "y"` replaces the letter "i", which is located in character position seven in the strName variable, with the letter "y". After the statement is processed, the strName variable contains the string "Rob Smyth".

You also could have omitted the *count* argument and used the statement `Mid(strName, 7) = "y"`, which is shown in Example 2, to replace the letter "i" in the strName variable with the letter "y". Recall that when the *count* argument is omitted from the Mid statement, the statement replaces the lesser of either the number of characters in the *replacementString* (in this case, one) or the number of characters in the *targetString* from position *start* through the end of the *targetString* (in this case, three).

The `Mid(strName, 5) = "Paul"` statement in Example 3 replaces four characters in the strName variable, beginning with the character located in character position five in the variable (the letter J). Here again, because the *count* argument is omitted from the Mid statement, the statement replaces the lesser of either the number of characters in the *replacementString* (in this case, four) or the number of characters in the *targetString* from position *start* through the end of the *targetString* (in this case, seven). After the statement is processed, the strName variable contains the string "Ann Paulson".

The `Mid(strName, 6) = "Liverpool"` statement in Example 4 in Figure 8-9 replaces three characters in the strName variable, beginning with the character located in character position six in the variable (the letter C). Here again, because the *count* argument is omitted from the Mid statement, the statement replaces the lesser of either the number of characters in the *replacementString* (in this case, nine) or the number of characters in the *targetString* from position *start* through the end of the *targetString* (in this case, three). After the statement is processed, the strName variable contains the string "Earl Liv".

Now learn how to insert characters within a string.

Inserting Characters within a String

You can use the **Insert method** to insert characters within a string. For example, you can use the Insert method to insert an employee's middle initial within his or her name. Or, you can use it to insert parentheses around the area code in a phone number. Figure 8-10 shows the syntax of the Insert method and includes two examples of using the method.

Syntax
To insert characters within a string: *string*.**Insert**(*startIndex, value*)

Examples and results

Example 1
```
Dim strName As String = "Rob Smith"
Dim strNewName As String
strNewName = strName.Insert(4, "T. ")
```

Result
assigns the string "Rob T. Smith" to the strNewName variable

Example 2
```
Dim strPhone As String = "3120501111"
strPhone = strPhone.Insert(0, "(")
strPhone = strPhone.Insert(4, ")")
strPhone = strPhone.Insert(8, "-")
```

Result
changes the contents of the strPhone variable to "(312)050-1111"

Figure 8-10: Syntax and examples of the Insert method

In the syntax, *startIndex* specifies where in the *string* you want the *value* inserted. To insert the *value* at the beginning of the *string*, you use the number zero as the *startIndex*. To insert the *value* as the second character in the *string*, you use the number one as the *startIndex*, and so on. The Insert method returns a string with the appropriate characters inserted.

When processing the statement `strNewName = strName.Insert(4, "T. ")`, which is shown in Example 1 in Figure 8-10, the computer first makes a copy of the string stored in the strName variable, and then inserts the *value* "T. " (the letter T, a period, and a space) in the copied string. The letter T is inserted in *startIndex* position 4, which makes it the fifth character in the string. The period and space are inserted in *startIndex* positions 5 and 6, making them the sixth and seventh characters in the string. After the statement is processed, the strNewName variable contains the string "Rob T. Smith"; however, the strName variable still contains "Rob Smith".

In Example 2, the `strPhone = strPhone.Insert(0, "(")` statement changes the contents of the strPhone variable from "3120501111" to "(3120501111". The `strPhone = strPhone.Insert(4, ")")` statement then changes the contents of the variable from "(3120501111" to "(312)0501111", and the `strPhone = strPhone.Insert(8, "-")` statement changes the contents of the variable from "(312)0501111" to "(312)050-1111".

Finally, you learn how to search a string to determine whether it contains a specific sequence of characters.

Searching a String

You can use the **IndexOf method** to search a string to determine whether it contains a specific sequence of characters. For example, you can use the IndexOf method to determine whether the area code "312" appears in a phone number, or whether the street name "Elm Street" appears in an address. Figure 8-11 shows the syntax and several examples of the IndexOf method.

Syntax
To search a string to determine whether it contains a specific sequence of characters: *string*.**IndexOf**(*value*[, *startIndex*])
Examples and results

Example 1
`Dim strMsg As String = "Have a nice day", intIndex As Integer`
`intIndex = strMsg.IndexOf("nice", 0)`
 	
Result
assigns the number 7 to the intIndex variable

Example 2
`Dim strMsg As String = "Have a nice day", intIndex As Integer`
`intIndex = strMsg.IndexOf("nice")`
 	
Result
assigns the number 7 to the intIndex variable

Figure 8-11: Syntax and examples of the IndexOf method

Examples and results

Example 3
```
Dim strMsg As String = "Have a nice day", intIndex As Integer
intIndex = strMsg.IndexOf("Nice")
```

Result
assigns the number -1 to the intIndex variable

Example 4
```
Dim strMsg As String = "Have a nice day", intIndex As Integer
intIndex = UCase(strMsg).IndexOf("NICE")
```

Result
assigns the number 7 to the intIndex variable

Example 5
```
Dim strMsg As String = "Have a nice day", intIndex As Integer
intIndex = strMsg.IndexOf("nice", 5)
```

Result
assigns the number 7 to the intIndex variable

Example 6
```
Dim strMsg As String = "Have a nice day", intIndex As Integer
intIndex = strMsg.IndexOf("nice", 8)
```

Result
assigns the number -1 to the intIndex variable

Figure 8-11: Syntax and examples of the IndexOf method (continued)

You also can use the Instr function, which you learn about in Discovery Exercise 15 at the end of this lesson, to determine whether a string contains a specific sequence of characters.

In the syntax, *value* is the sequence of characters for which you are searching in the *string*, and *startIndex* is the index of the character at which the search should begin—in other words, *startIndex* specifies the starting position for the search. Recall that the first character in a string has an index of zero, the second character an index of one, and so on. Notice that the *startIndex* argument is optional in the IndexOf method's syntax. If you omit the *startIndex* argument, the IndexOf method begins the search with the first character in the *string*.

The IndexOf method searches for *value* within *string*, beginning with the character whose index is *startIndex*. If the IndexOf method does not find the *value*, it returns the number -1; otherwise, it returns the index of the starting position of *value* within *string*.

You can use either the `intIndex = strMsg.IndexOf("nice", 0)` statement in Example 1 in Figure 8-11, or the `intIndex = strMsg.IndexOf("nice")` statement in Example 2, to search for the word "nice" in the strMsg variable, beginning with the first character in the variable. In each case, the word "nice" begins with the eighth character in the variable. The eighth character has an index of seven, so both statements assign the number seven to the intIndex variable.

The IndexOf method performs a case-sensitive search, as Example 3 in Figure 8-11 indicates. In this example, the `intIndex = strMsg.IndexOf("Nice")` statement assigns the number -1 to the intIndex variable, because the word "Nice" is not contained in the strMsg variable.

You can use the `intIndex = UCase(strMsg).IndexOf("NICE")` statement shown in Example 4 to perform a case-insensitive search for the word "nice". The UCase function in the statement is processed first and temporarily converts the string stored in the strMsg variable to uppercase. The IndexOf method then searches the uppercase string for the word "NICE". The statement assigns the number seven to the intIndex variable because, ignoring case, the word "nice" begins with the character whose index is seven.

The intIndex = strMsg.IndexOf("nice", 5) statement in Example 5 searches for the word "nice" in the strMsg variable, beginning with the character whose index is five; that character is the second letter "a". The statement assigns the number seven to the intIndex variable, because the word "nice" begins with the character whose index is seven.

The intIndex = strMsg.IndexOf("nice", 8) statement in Example 6 searches for the word "nice" in the strMsg variable, beginning with the character whose index is eight; that character is the letter "i". Notice that the word "nice" does not appear anywhere in the "ice day" portion of the string stored in the strMsg variable. Therefore, the statement assigns the number -1 to the intIndex variable.

Figure 8-12 summarizes the string manipulation techniques you learned in the lesson.

Technique	Purpose
EndsWith method	determine whether a string ends with a specific sequence of characters
IndexOf method	search a string to determine whether it contains a specific sequence of characters
Insert method	insert characters within a string
Length property	determine the number of characters in a string
Mid statement	replace a specific number of characters in a string with characters from another string
Remove method	remove characters from anywhere in a string
Replace method	replace all occurrences of a sequence of characters in a string with another sequence of characters
StartsWith method	determine whether a string begins with a specific sequence of characters
Substring method	access one or more characters contained in a string
Trim method	remove characters from both the beginning and end of a string
TrimEnd method	remove characters from the end of a string
TrimStart method	remove characters from the beginning of a string

Figure 8-12: String manipulation techniques

You now have completed Lesson A. You can either take a break or complete the end-of-lesson questions and exercises before moving on to the next lesson.

S U M M A R Y

To determine the number of characters contained in a string:

■   Use the Length property in the following syntax: *string*.**Length**.

To remove one or more characters from the beginning and/or end of a string:

■ Use the TrimStart method to remove one or more characters from the beginning of a string. The method's syntax is *string*.**TrimStart**[(*char*)], where *char* is a comma-separated list of characters that you want removed from the *string*.

■ Use the TrimEnd method to remove one or more characters from the end of a string. The method's syntax is *string*.**TrimEnd**[(*char*)], where *char* is a comma-separated list of characters that you want removed from the *string*.

■ Use the Trim method to remove one or more characters from both the beginning and end of a string. The method's syntax is *string*.**Trim**[(*char*)], where *char* is a comma-separated list of characters that you want removed from the *string*.

■ The TrimStart, TrimEnd, and Trim methods return a string with the appropriate characters removed (trimmed).

To remove one or more characters from anywhere in a string:

■ Use the Remove method. The method's syntax is *string*.**Remove**(*startIndex, count*), where *startIndex* is the index of the first character you want removed from the *string*, and *count* is the number of characters you want removed. The first character in a string has an index of zero, the second character an index of one, and so on.

■ The Remove method returns a string with the appropriate characters removed.

To determine whether a specific sequence of characters occurs at either the beginning or end of a string:

■ Use the StartsWith method to determine whether a string begins with a specific sequence of characters. The method's syntax is *string*.**StartsWith**(*subString*), where *subString* is the sequence of characters that the method should search for at the beginning of the *string*. The StartsWith method returns the Boolean value True if *subString* is located at the beginning of *string*; otherwise, it returns the Boolean value False.

■ Use the EndsWith method to determine whether a string ends with a specific sequence of characters. The method's syntax is *string*.**EndsWith**(*subString*), where *subString* is the sequence of characters that the method should search for at the end of the *string*. The EndsWith method returns the Boolean value True if *subString* is located at the end of *string*; otherwise, it returns the Boolean value False.

To access one or more characters contained in a string:

■ Use the Substring method. The method's syntax is *string*.**Substring**(*startIndex*[, *count*]), where *startIndex* is the index of the first character you want to access in the *string*, and *count* (which is optional) specifies the number of characters to access.

■ The Substring method returns a string that contains *count* number of characters, beginning with the character whose index is *startIndex*. If you omit the *count* argument, the Substring method returns all characters from the *startIndex* position through the end of the string.

To replace all occurrences of a sequence of characters in a string with another sequence of characters:

■ Use the Replace method. The method's syntax is *string*.**Replace**(*oldValue, newValue*), where *oldValue* is the sequence of characters that you want replaced in the *string*, and *newValue* is the replacement characters.

■ The Replace method returns a string with all occurrences of *oldValue* replaced with *newValue*.

To replace a specific number of characters in a string with characters from another string:

■ Use the Mid statement. The statement's syntax is **Mid**(*targetString*, *start* [, *count*]) = *replacementString*, where *targetString* is the string in which you want characters replaced, and *replacementString* contains the replacement characters. *Start* is the character position of the first character you want replaced in the *targetString*. The first character in the *targetString* is in character position one, the second is in character position two, and so on. The *count* argument, which is optional, specifies the number of characters to replace in the *targetString*. If the *count* argument is omitted, the Mid statement replaces the lesser of either the number of characters in the *replacementString*, or the number of characters in the *targetString* from position *start* through the end of the *targetString*.

■ The Mid statement replaces *count* number of characters in *targetString*, beginning with the character in character position *start*. The characters are replaced with *replacementString*.

To insert characters within a string:

■ Use the Insert method. The method's syntax is *string*.**Insert**(*startIndex*, *value*), where *startIndex* specifies where in the *string* you want the *value* inserted. For example, to insert the *value* at the beginning of the *string*, you use the number zero as the *startIndex*.

■ The Insert method returns a string with the appropriate characters inserted.

To search a string to determine whether it contains a specific sequence of characters:

■ Use the IndexOf method. The method's syntax is *string*.**IndexOf**(*value*[, *startIndex*]), where *value* is the sequence of characters for which you are searching in the *string*, and *startIndex* (which is optional) specifies the index of the character at which the search should begin. If you omit the *startIndex* argument, the IndexOf method begins the search with the first character in the *string*.

■ The IndexOf method returns the number -1 if *value* is not contained on or after the character in position *startIndex* in *string*; otherwise, it returns the index of the starting position of *value* within *string*.

QUESTIONS

1. You can use the _____ to determine the number of characters in a string.
   a. Length method
   b. Length property
   c. NumChars property
   d. Size method
   e. Size property

2. Assume that the strAmount variable contains the string "$56.55". Which of the following removes the dollar sign from the variable's contents?
   a. `strAmount = strAmount.Remove("$")`
   b. `strAmount = strAmount.Remove(0, 1)`
   c. `strAmount = strAmount.TrimStart(0, 1)`
   d. `strAmount = strAmount.TrimStart("$")`
   e. Both b and d.

3. Assume that the strState variable contains the string "MI   " (the letters M and I followed by three spaces). Which of the following removes the three spaces from the variable's contents?
    a. `strState = strState.Remove(2, 3)`
    b. `strState = strState.Remove(3, 3)`
    c. `strState = strState.TrimEnd(2, 3)`
    d. `strState = strState.TrimEnd(3, 3)`
    e. Both a and c.

4. Which of the following removes any dollar signs and percent signs from the beginning and end of the string stored in the strAmount variable?
    a. `strAmount = strAmount.Trim("$", "%")`
    b. `strAmount = strAmount.Trim("$, %")`
    c. `strAmount = strAmount.TrimAll("$", "%")`
    d. `strAmount = strAmount.TrimAll("$, %")`
    e. None of the above.

5. The `strName = Me.NameTextBox.Text.TrimEnd` statement changes the contents of both the strName variable and the NameTextBox control.
    a. True
    b. False

6. The index of the first character in a string is _____.
    a. 0 (zero)
    b. 1 (one)

7. Which of the following can be used to determine whether the string stored in the strPart variable begins with the letter A?
    a. `strPart.Begins("A")`
    b. `strPart.BeginsWith("A")`
    c. `strPart.Starts("A")`
    d. `strPart.StartsWith("A")`
    e. `strPart.StartsWith = "A"`

8. Which of the following can be used to determine whether the string stored in the strPart variable ends with either the letter B or the letter b?
    a. `strPart.Ends("B, b")`
    b. `strPart.Ends("B", "b")`
    c. `strPart.EndsWith("B", "b")`
    d. `UCase(strPart).EndsWith("B")`
    e. `UCase(strPart).EndsWith = "B"`

9. Which of the following assigns the first three characters in the strPart variable to the strCode variable?
    a. `strCode = strPart.Assign(0, 3)`
    b. `strCode = strPart.Sub(0, 3)`
    c. `strCode = strPart.Substring(0, 3)`
    d. `strCode = strPart.Substring(1, 3)`
    e. None of the above.

10. Assume that the strWord variable contains the string "Bells". Which of the following changes the contents of the strWord variable to "Bell"?

    a. `strWord = strWord.Remove(strWord.Length - 1, 1)`
    b. `strWord = strWord.Substring(0, strWord.Length - 1)`
    c. `strWord = strWord.TrimEnd("s")`
    d. `strWord = strWord.Replace("s", "")`
    e. All of the above.

11. Which of the following changes the contents of the strZip variable from "60121" to "60323"?

    a. `Replace(strZip, "1", "3")`
    b. `strZip.Replace("1", "3")`
    c. `strZip = strZip.Replace("1", "3")`
    d. `strZip = strZip.Replace("3", "1")`
    e. None of the above.

12. Which of the following changes the contents of the strZip variable from "60537" to "60536"?

    a. `Mid(strZip, "7", "6")`
    b. `Mid(strZip, 4, "6")`
    c. `strZip = Mid(strZip, 4, "6")`
    d. `strZip.Mid("7", "6")`
    e. None of the above.

13. Which of the following changes the contents of the strWord variable from "men" to "mean"?

    a. `strWord = strWord.AddTo(2, "a")`
    b. `strWord = strWord.Insert(2, "a")`
    c. `strWord = strWord.Insert(3, "a")`
    d. `strWord = strWord.Replace(2, "a")`
    e. `strWord = strWord.Replace(3, "a")`

14. Assuming that the strMsg variable contains the string "Happy holidays", the `strMsg.IndexOf("day")` method returns _____.

    a. -1
    b. 0
    c. 10
    d. 11
    e. day

15. Assuming that the strMsg variable contains the string "Happy holidays", the `UCase(strMsg).IndexOf("Day")` method returns _____.

    a. -1
    b. 0
    c. 10
    d. 11
    e. Day

16. Assuming that the strMsg variable contains the string "Happy holidays", the `strMsg.IndexOf("days", 1)` method returns _____.

    a. -1
    b. 0
    c. 10
    d. 11
    e. None of the above.

17. Assume that the strMsg variable contains the string "Good morning". The statement `Mid(strMsg, 6) = "night"` changes the contents of the strMsg variable to _____.

    a.   Good mnight
    b.   Good mnightg
    c.   Good night
    d.   Good nightng
    e.   nightG

E X E R C I S E S

1. Write the Visual Basic .NET statement that displays in the Output window the number of characters contained in the strMsg variable.

2. Write the Visual Basic .NET statement that removes the leading spaces from the strCity variable.

3. Write the Visual Basic .NET statement that removes the leading and trailing spaces from the strNum variable.

4. Write the Visual Basic .NET statement that removes any trailing spaces, commas, and periods from the strAmount variable.

5. Write the Visual Basic .NET statement that uses the Remove method to remove the first two characters from the strName variable.

6. Write the Visual Basic .NET code that uses the EndsWith method to determine whether the string stored in the strRate variable ends with the percent sign. If it does, the code should use the TrimEnd method to remove the percent sign from the variable's contents.

7. Assume that the strPart variable contains the string "ABCD34G". Write the Visual Basic .NET statement that assigns the number 34 in the strPart variable to the strCode variable.

8. Assume that the strAmount variable contains the string "3,123,560". Write the Visual Basic .NET statement that assigns the contents of the variable, excluding the commas and treated as a number, to the sngAmount variable.

9. Write the Mid statement that changes the contents of the strWord variable from "mouse" to "mouth".

10. Write the Visual Basic .NET statement that uses the Insert method to change the contents of the strWord variable from "mend" to "amend".

11. Write the Visual Basic .NET statement that uses the IndexOf method to determine whether the strAddress variable contains the street name "Elm Street" (entered in uppercase, lowercase, or a combination of uppercase and lowercase). Begin the search with the first character in the strAddress variable, and assign the method's return value to the intIndex variable.

Exercises 12 through 15 are Discovery Exercises. Discovery Exercises, which may include topics that are not covered in this lesson, allow you to "discover" the solutions to problems on your own.

discovery ▶
12. In addition to using the Length property, you also can use the Len function to determine the number of characters contained in a string. The syntax of the Len function is **Len**(*string*). For example, you can rewrite Example 1 in Figure 8-3 as `Debug.WriteLine(Len(Me.ZipTextBox.Text))`. Rewrite Examples 2 through 4 in Figure 8-3 using the Len function.

discovery ▶ 13. In addition to using the TrimStart, TrimEnd, and Trim methods, you also can use the LTrim, RTrim, and Trim functions, respectively, to remove any leading and/or trailing spaces from a string. The syntax of the LTrim function is **LTrim**(*string*). The syntax of the RTrim function is **RTrim**(*string*), and the syntax of the Trim function is **Trim**(*string*). Each function returns a string with the appropriate spaces removed. For example, you can remove the leading spaces from the strName variable using the statement `strName = LTrim(strName)`.

    a. Write a statement that uses the LTrim function to remove the leading spaces from the NameTextBox control's Text property. The statement should assign the resulting string to the strName variable.

    b. Write a statement that uses the RTrim function to remove the trailing spaces from the strZip variable. The statement should assign the resulting string to the strZip variable.

    c. Write a statement that uses the Trim function to remove the leading and trailing spaces from the strNumber variable. The statement should assign the resulting string, treated as a number, to the sngNumber variable.

discovery ▶ 14. In addition to using the Substring method, you also can use the Left, Right, and Mid functions to access one or more characters in a string. The syntax of the Left function is **Left**(*string*, *length*), and the syntax of the Right function is **Right**(*string*, *length*). The Left function returns the leftmost *length* number of characters in the *string*, and the Right function returns the rightmost *length* number of characters in the *string*. For example, assuming the strName variable contains the string "Jose Tom Marsales", the statement `strFirstName = Left(strName, 4)` assigns the string "Jose" to the strFirstName variable, and the statement `strLastName = Right(strName, 8)` assigns the string "Marsales" to the strLastName variable.

The syntax of the Mid function is **Mid**(*string*, *start* [, *length*]). The Mid function returns *length* number of characters from a *string*, beginning with the *start* character. If *length* is omitted, the function returns all characters from the *start* position through the end of the *string*. The first character in a string is in character position one, the second is in character position two, and so on. For example, assuming the strName variable contains the string "Jose Tom Marsales", the statement `strMiddleName = Mid(strName, 6, 3)` assigns the string "Tom" to the strMiddleName variable.

    a. Assuming that the strProgName variable contains the string "Visual Basic .NET", what will the following functions return?

        1) `Left("January", 3)`

        2) `Right("January", 2)`

        3) `Left(strProgName, 6)`

        4) `Right(strProgName, 10)`

        5) `Mid("January", 2, 1)`

        6) `Mid("January", 4, 2)`

        7) `Mid(strProgName, 8, 1)`

        8) `Mid(strProgName, 8)`

    b. Write the Left function that returns the first three characters contained in the strPart variable.

    c. Write the Right function that returns the last character contained in the strPart variable.

    d. Write the Mid function that returns the second through fifth characters contained in the strPart variable.

discovery ▶ **15.** In addition to using the IndexOf method, you also can use the Instr ("in string") function to determine whether a specific sequence of characters appears in a string. The syntax of the Instr function is **Instr**(*start, string1, string2*[, *compare*]), where *start* specifies the character position at which the search should begin. The first character in a string is in character position one, the second is in character position two, and so on. *String1* in the syntax is the string to be searched, and *string2* is the sequence of characters being sought. The *compare* argument, which is optional, indicates whether the function should perform a case-sensitive or case-insensitive search. If the *compare* argument is either omitted or set to the number zero, the function performs a case-sensitive search. If the *compare* argument is set to the number one, on the other hand, the function performs a case-insensitive search. If *string2* is not contained within *string1*, then the Instr function returns the number zero; otherwise, it returns the starting character position of *string2* within *string1*. For example, the `Instr(1, "Have a nice day", "nice", 0)` function returns the number eight, and the `Instr(1, "Have a nice day", "nice", 10)` function returns the number zero.

    a. Assuming that the strMsg variable contains the string "Don't forget to VOTE for your favorite candidate", what will the following Instr functions return?

      1) `Instr(1, strMsg, "vote", 0)`

      2) `Instr(1, strMsg, "vote", 1)`

      3) `Instr(10, strMsg, "vote", 1)`

      4) `Instr(10, strMsg, "vote", 0)`

After completing this lesson, you will be able to:

■ Add a main menu control to a form

■ Add menu elements to a main menu control

■ Assign access keys and shortcut keys to menu elements

■ Code a menu item's Click event procedure

Using a Main Menu Control

Completing the Hangman Game Application's User Interface

Recall that your task in this tutorial is to create a simplified version of the Hangman game for Mr. Mitchell, who teaches second grade at Hinsbrook School. On your computer's hard disk is a partially completed Hangman Game application. You complete the application's user interface in this lesson, and also begin coding the application.

To open the Hangman Game application:

1   Start Microsoft Visual Studio .NET, if necessary, and then close the Start Page window. Click **File** on the menu bar, and then click **Open Solution**. The Open Solution dialog box opens. Open the **Hangman Solution** (Hangman Solution.sln) file, which is contained in the VBNET\Tut08\Hangman Solution folder.

2   If the designer window is not open, right-click **Hangman Form.vb** in the Solution Explorer window, then click **View Designer**.

3   Auto-hide the Toolbox, Solution Explorer, and Properties windows, if necessary. The partially completed user interface for the Hangman Game application is shown in Figure 8-13.

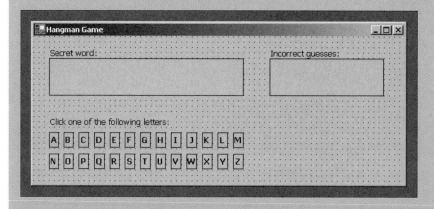

Figure 8-13: Partially completed interface for the Hangman Game application

The partially completed interface contains 31 label controls. You complete the interface by adding a main menu control to it

Adding a Main Menu Control to a Form

You use a **main menu control** to include one or more menus in an application. Each menu contains a **menu title**, which appears on the menu bar at the top of a Windows form. When you click a menu title, its corresponding menu opens and displays a list of options, called **menu items**. The menu items can be commands (such as Open or Exit), separator bars, or submenu titles. As in all Windows applications, clicking a command on a menu executes the command, and clicking a submenu title opens an additional menu of options; each of the options on a submenu is referred to as a **submenu item**. The purpose of a **separator bar** is to visually group together the related items on a menu or submenu. Figure 8-14 identifies the location of these menu elements.

separator bar

separator bar

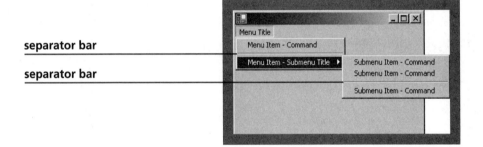

Figure 8-14: Location of menu elements

Although you can create many levels of submenus, it is best to use only one level in your application, because too many layers of submenus can be confusing to the user.

You learned about access keys in Tutorial 2. A menu title's access key allows the user to open the menu by pressing the Alt key in combination with the access key. A menu item's access key, however, allows the user to select the item simply by pressing the access key when the menu is open.

Each menu element is considered an object and has a set of properties associated with it. The most commonly used properties for a menu element are the Name and Text properties. The Name property is used by the programmer to refer to the menu element in code. The Text property, on the other hand, stores the menu element's caption, which is the text that the user sees when he or she is working with the menu. The caption indicates the purpose of the menu element. Examples of familiar captions for menu elements include Edit, Save As, Copy, and Exit.

Menu title captions should be one word only, with the first letter capitalized. Each menu title should have a unique access key. Menu item captions, on the other hand, can be from one to three words. Use book title capitalization for the menu item captions, and assign each menu item a unique access key. If a menu item requires additional information from the user, the Windows standard is to place an ellipsis (...) at the end of the caption. The ellipsis alerts the user that the menu item requires more information before it can perform its task.

When designing a menu, you must be sure to follow the standard conventions used in Windows applications. For example, the File menu is always the first menu on the menu bar, and typically contains commands for opening, saving, and printing files, as well as exiting the application. Cut, Copy, and Paste commands, on the other hand, are placed on an Edit menu, which typically is the second menu on the menu bar.

Before you can create a menu, you first must add a main menu control to the application.

To add a main menu control to the Hangman Game application:

1 Click the **MainMenu tool** 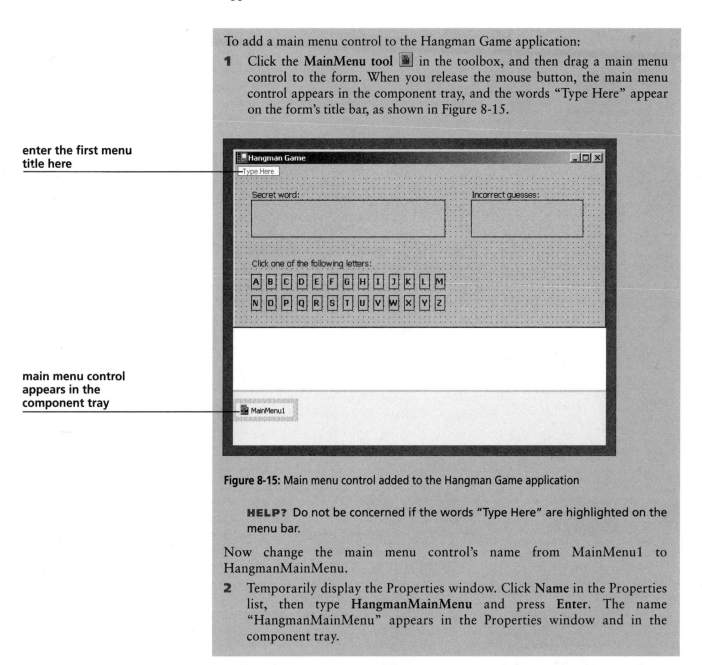 in the toolbox, and then drag a main menu control to the form. When you release the mouse button, the main menu control appears in the component tray, and the words "Type Here" appear on the form's title bar, as shown in Figure 8-15.

enter the first menu title here

main menu control appears in the component tray

Figure 8-15: Main menu control added to the Hangman Game application

HELP? Do not be concerned if the words "Type Here" are highlighted on the menu bar.

Now change the main menu control's name from MainMenu1 to HangmanMainMenu.

2 Temporarily display the Properties window. Click **Name** in the Properties list, then type **HangmanMainMenu** and press **Enter**. The name "HangmanMainMenu" appears in the Properties window and in the component tray.

You will include one menu—a File menu—on the Hangman Game application's menu bar. The File menu will contain three menu items: a New Game command, an Exit command, and a separator bar.

To create the File menu:

1   Click **Type Here** on the menu bar.

As is customary in Windows applications, you use the letter F as the File menu's access key.

2   Type **&File**. See Figure 8-16.

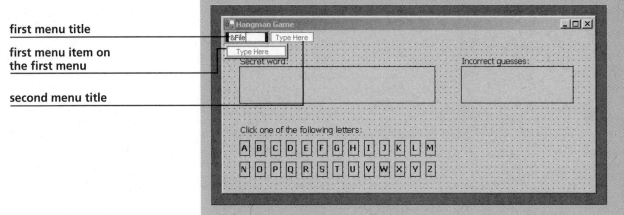

first menu title

first menu item on the first menu

second menu title

Figure 8-16: Menu title shown in the interface

Notice that the words "Type Here" appear below the File menu title and also to the right of the File menu title. The "Type Here" that appears below the menu title allows you to add a menu item to the File menu. The "Type Here" that appears to the right of the menu title allows you to add another menu title to the menu bar.

Now change the menu title's name to FileMenuTitle.

3   Press **Enter**, then click the **File** menu title. Temporarily display the Properties window. Click **Name** in the Properties list, and then type **FileMenuTitle** and press **Enter**.

Next, include a New Game menu item on the File menu. The letter N is the standard access key for the New option on a File menu.

4   Click the **Type Here** that appears below the File menu title, then type **&New Game**. Press **Enter**, then click the **New Game** menu item. Change the New Game menu item's name to **FileNewMenuItem**.

Now include an Exit menu item on the File menu. The letter X is the standard access key for the Exit option.

5   Click the **Type Here** that appears below the New Game menu item, and then type **E&xit**. Press **Enter**, then click the **Exit** menu item. Change the menu item's name to **FileExitMenuItem**.

Next, insert a separator bar between the New Game and Exit options on the File menu.

6   Right-click the **Exit** menu item. A context menu opens and displays options for deleting an existing menu item, inserting a new menu item, and inserting a separator bar. In this case, you want to insert a separator bar.

7   Click **Insert Separator**. Notice that the separator bar is inserted above the menu item that you right-clicked; in this case, it is inserted above the Exit menu item.

8 Change the separator bar's name to **FileSeparator**, then click the separator bar on the menu. The completed File menu is shown in Figure 8-17.

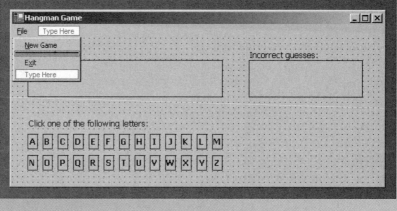

Figure 8-17: Completed File menu

In addition to assigning access keys to menu items, you also can assign shortcut keys.

Assigning Shortcut Keys

Shortcut keys appear to the right of a menu item and allow you to select an item without opening the menu. For example, in Windows applications you can select the Save command when the File menu is closed by pressing Ctrl + S. You should assign shortcut keys only to commonly used menu items. In the Hangman Game application, you will assign a shortcut key to the New Game option on the File menu.

> **tip**
>
> The difference between a menu item's access key and its shortcut key is that the access key can be used only when the menu is open, whereas the shortcut key can be used only when the menu is closed.

To assign a shortcut key to the New Game option:

1 Click the **New Game** menu item on the File menu. Temporarily display the Properties window, and then click **Shortcut** in the Properties list.

2 Click the **Shortcut** list arrow to display a list of shortcut keys. Scroll the list until you see CtrlN, then click **CtrlN** in the list. When you start the application and open the File menu, Ctrl+N will appear to the right of the New Game menu item. You verify that fact next.

3 Click **File** on Visual Basic .NET's menu bar, and then click **Save All**. Click **Debug** on the menu bar, and then click **Start**. Notice that the 31 label controls do not appear in the interface when the application is started; this is because their Visible properties are set to False.

4 Click **File** on the Hangman Game application's menu bar. The shortcut key, Ctrl+N, appears to the right of the New Game menu item, as shown in Figure 8-18.

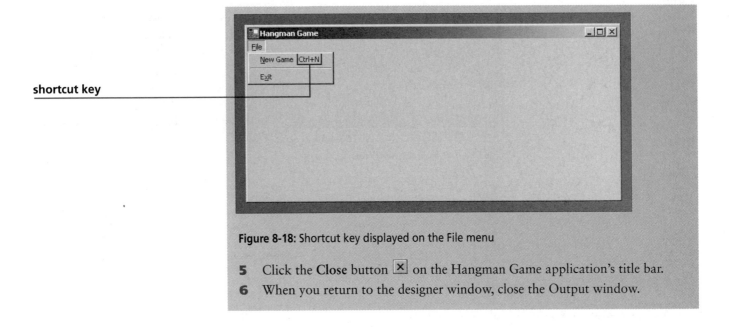

Figure 8-18: Shortcut key displayed on the File menu

5 Click the **Close** button ⊠ on the Hangman Game application's title bar.

6 When you return to the designer window, close the Output window.

Designing Menus

- Menu title captions, which appear on the menu bar, should be one word, with the first letter capitalized. Each menu title should have a unique access key.

- Menu item captions, which appear on a menu, can be from one to three words. Use book title capitalization and assign a unique access key to each menu item. Assign shortcut keys to commonly used menu items.

- If a menu item requires additional information from the user, place an ellipsis (...) at the end of the item's caption, which is entered in the item's Text property.

- Follow the Windows standards for the placement of menu titles and items.

- Use a separator bar to separate groups of related menu items.

Now that the interface is complete, you can begin coding the application. In this lesson, you code only the Exit menu item's Click event procedure. You code the remaining procedures in Lesson C.

Coding the Click Event Procedure for the Exit Menu Item

When the user clicks the Exit item on the File menu, the item's Click event procedure should simply end the Hangman Game application.

To code the Exit menu item's Click event procedure, then test the procedure:

1 Right-click the **form**, and then click **View Code** to open the Code editor window. For now, do not be concerned about the `'declare form-level variable` comment and the code template for the ProcessLetterLabels procedure.

2 Click the **Class Name** list arrow, and then click **FileExitMenuItem** in the list. Click the **Method Name** list arrow, and then click **Click** in the list. The code template for the FileExitMenuItem's Click event procedure appears in the Code editor window.

3 Enter the additional line of code shown in Figure 8-19.

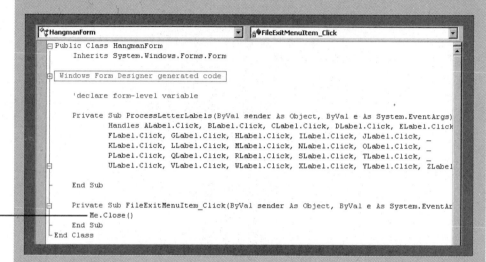

enter this line of code

Figure 8-19: Completed FileExitMenuItem Click event procedure

4 Save the solution, and then start the application.

5 Click **File** on the Hangman Game application's menu bar, and then click **Exit** to end the Hangman Game application. When you return to the Code editor window, close the Output window, then close the Code editor window.

6 Click **File** on Visual Basic .NET's menu bar, and then click **Close Solution**.

You now have completed Lesson B. You finish coding the Hangman Game application in Lesson C. For now, you can either take a break or complete the end-of-lesson questions and exercises before moving on to the next lesson.

SUMMARY

To add a main menu control to a form:

■ Use the MainMenu tool in the toolbox.

To create a menu:

■ Replace the words "Type Here" with the menu element's caption.
■ Assign a meaningful name to each menu element.
■ Assign a unique access key to each menu element, excluding menu items that are separator bars.

To insert a separator bar in a menu:

■ Right-click a menu item, and then click Insert Separator. The separator bar will be inserted above the menu item.

To assign a shortcut key to a menu item:

■ Set the menu item's Shortcut property.

Q U E S T I O N S

1. A menu can contain a _____.
   a. command
   b. menu title
   c. separator bar
   d. submenu title
   e. All of the above.

2. The horizontal line in a menu is called _____.
   a. a dashed line
   b. a hyphen
   c. a menu bar
   d. a separator bar
   e. an item separator

3. The underlined letter in a menu element's caption is called a(n) _____.
   a. access key
   b. dash
   c. menu key
   d. open key
   e. shortcut key

4. A(n) _____ key allows you to access a menu item without opening the menu.
   a. access
   b. dash
   c. menu item
   d. open
   e. shortcut

5. Which of the following is false?
   a. Menu titles appear on the menu bar.
   b. Menu titles should be one word only.
   c. Each menu title should have a unique access key.
   d. You should assign a shortcut key to commonly used menu titles.
   e. Menu items should be entered using book title capitalization.

6. Explain the difference between a menu item's access key and its shortcut key.

EXERCISES

1. In this exercise, you create a File menu and an Edit menu.
   a. If necessary, start Visual Studio .NET. Open the Menu Solution (Menu Solution.sln) file, which is contained in the VBNET\Tut08\Menu Solution folder. If the designer window is not open, right-click the form file's name in the Solution Explorer window, then click View Designer.
   b. Include a main menu control in the application. Change the control's name to PracticeMainMenu.
   c. Create the menu titles and menu items shown in Figure 8-20. Use appropriate names for the menu titles and menu items (including the separator bars).

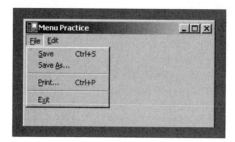

Figure 8-20

   d. Include the Undo, Paste, Copy, and Cut menu items on the Edit menu. Be sure to position the menu items in the correct order, and use a separator bar if appropriate. Also be sure to use the standard access keys and shortcut keys for the menu items. (*Hint*: You can use Visual Basic .NET's Edit menu to determine the standards for an Edit menu in a Windows application.)
   e. Code the Exit menu item so that it ends the application when the user clicks it.
   f. Save the solution, then start the application. Click File on the application's menu bar, and then click Exit to end the application.
   g. Close the Output window, then close the solution.

2. In this exercise, you include a menu in the Grade application that you created in Tutorial 6.
   a. Use Windows to make a copy of the Grade Solution folder, which is contained in the VBNET\Tut06 folder. Change the name of the folder to GradeMenu Solution. Move the GradeMenu Solution folder to the VBNET\Tut08 folder.
   b. If necessary, start Visual Studio .NET. Open the Grade Solution (Grade Solution.sln) file, which is contained in the VBNET\Tut08\GradeMenu Solution folder. If the designer window is not open, right-click the form file's name in the Solution Explorer window, then click View Designer.
   c. Add a File menu and a Display menu to the application. Include an Exit menu item on the File menu, and a Grade menu item on the Display menu. Allow the user to select the Grade menu item when the Display menu is not open.
   d. Move the Me.Close() statement from the Exit button's Click event procedure to the Exit menu item's Click event procedure, then remove the Exit button's Click event procedure from the Code editor window.
   e. Move the instructions contained in the Display Grade button's Click event procedure (excluding the procedure header and footer) to the Grade menu item's Click event procedure, then remove the Display Grade button's Click event procedure from the Code editor window.
   f. Remove the Display Grade and Exit buttons from the interface.

g. Save the solution, then start the application. Test the Grade menu item to verify that it is working correctly.

h. Click File on the application's menu bar, and then click Exit to end the application.

i. Close the Output window, then close the solution.

3. In this exercise, you include a menu in the Monthly Payment Calculator application that you created in Tutorial 4.

a. Use Windows to make a copy of the Payment Solution folder, which is contained in the VBNET\Tut04 folder. Change the name of the folder to PaymentMenu Solution. Move the PaymentMenu Solution folder to the VBNET\Tut08 folder.

b. If necessary, start Visual Studio .NET. Open the Payment Solution (Payment Solution.sln) file, which is contained in the VBNET\Tut08\PaymentMenu Solution folder. If the designer window is not open, right-click the form file's name in the Solution Explorer window, then click View Designer.

c. Add a File menu and a Calculate menu to the application. Include an Exit menu item on the File menu. Include two menu items on the Calculate menu: Annual Payment and Monthly Payment.

d. When the user clicks the Exit menu item, the application should end. When the user clicks the Annual Payment menu item, the application should calculate and display the annual payment. When the user clicks the Monthly Payment menu item, the application should calculate and display the monthly payment. Modify the application's code appropriately.

e. Remove the Calculate Monthly Payment and Exit buttons from the interface.

f. Save the solution, and then start the application. Test the Annual Payment and Monthly Payment menu items to verify that they are working correctly.

g. Click File on the application's menu bar, and then click Exit to end the application.

h. Close the Output window, and then close the solution.

Exercise 4 is a Discovery Exercise. Discovery Exercises, which may include topics that are not covered in this lesson, allow you to "discover" the solutions to problems on your own.

discovery ▶ 4. In this exercise, you learn about a menu item's Checked property.

a. If necessary, start Visual Studio .NET. Open the Check1 Solution (Check1 Solution.sln) file, which is contained in the VBNET\Tut08\Check1 Solution folder.

b. If the designer window is not open, right-click the form file's name in the Solution Explorer window, then click View Designer. The interface contains two label controls (IdCarsLabel and IdRocketLabel) and two picture boxes (CarsPictureBox and RocketPictureBox). It also contains a File menu and a Display menu. The File menu contains an Exit menu item, which already has been coded for you. The Display menu contains two options: Cars and Rocket.

In Windows applications, a check mark next to a menu item indicates that the menu item is active. For example, in Microsoft Word's Window menu, a check mark indicates which of several open documents is currently displayed on the screen. In the Check1 application, you will use the check mark to indicate which label and picture box is currently displayed on the screen.

c. Set the Visible property for the IdCarsLabel and CarsPictureBox controls to False.

d. Click the Rocket menu item, and then set the menu item's Checked property to True. Notice that a check mark appears next to the Rocket menu item.

e. Save the solution, and then start the application. Notice that only the IdRocketLabel and RocketPictureBox appear on the screen. Click the Display menu. Notice that a check mark appears next to the Rocket menu item.

f. Click File on the application's menu bar, and then click Exit to end the application. Close the Output window.

g. When the user clicks the Cars menu item, the item's Click event procedure should display the IdCarsLabel and the CarsPictureBox control, and hide the IdRocketLabel and RocketPictureBox controls. The procedure also should place a check mark next to the Cars menu item, and remove the check mark from the Rocket menu item. Code the Click event procedure for the DisplayCarsMenuItem.

h. When the user clicks the Rocket menu item, the item's Click event procedure should display the IdRocketLabel and the RocketPictureBox control, and hide the IdCarsLabel and CarsPictureBox controls. The procedure also should place a check mark next to the Rocket menu item, and remove the check mark from the Cars menu item. Code the Click event procedure for the DisplayRocketMenuItem appropriately.

i. Save the solution, and then start the application. Click Display, and then click Cars. Only the IdCarsLabel and CarsPictureBox controls appear on the screen. Click Display. A check mark appears next to the Cars menu item.

j. Click Rocket. Only the IdRocketLabel and RocketPictureBox controls appear on the screen. Click Display. A check mark appears next to the Rocket menu item.

k. Click File on the application's menu bar, and then click Exit to end the application.

l. Close the Output window, and then close the solution.

In the Check1 application, only one of the menu items can be selected at a time; recall that selecting one menu item on the Display menu deselected the other menu item on the menu. In the next application, however, the user can select some, none, or all of the menu items on a menu.

m. Open the Check2 Solution (Check2 Solution.sln) file, which is contained in the VBNET\Tut08\Check2 Solution folder. If the designer window is not open, right-click the form file's name in the Solution Explorer window, then click View Designer. The Check2 application's interface is identical to the Check1 application's interface.

n. Set the Visible property for the two label controls and two picture boxes to False.

o. Code the application so that it displays the IdRocketLabel and RocketPictureBox controls when the Rocket menu item is selected, and hides both controls when the Rocket menu item is deselected.

p. Code the application so that it displays the IdCarsLabel and CarsPictureBox controls when the Cars menu item is selected, and hides both controls when the Cars menu item is deselected.

q. Save the solution, and then start the application. No labels or picture boxes should appear in the interface. Open the Display menu. No check mark should appear next to either menu item on the Display menu.

r. Practice selecting and deselecting the Cars and Rocket menu items. When you select a menu item, its corresponding label and picture box should appear on the form, and a check mark should appear next to the menu item. When you deselect a menu item, its corresponding label and picture box should be hidden, and the check mark should be removed from the menu item.

s. Click File on the application's menu bar, and then click Exit to end the application.

t. Close the Output window, and then close the solution.

After completing this lesson, you will be able to:

■ Include the Substring method in a procedure
■ Include the Mid statement in a procedure
■ Include the IndexOf method in a procedure

Completing the Hangman Game Application

The Hangman Game Application

Recall that Mr. Mitchell has asked you to write an application that two students can use to play a simplified version of the Hangman game on the computer. The application should allow one of the students to enter a five-letter word, and then allow the other student to guess the word, letter by letter. The game is over when the second student guesses all of the letters in the word, or when he or she makes three incorrect guesses, whichever comes first.

To open the Hangman Game application:

1   Start Microsoft Visual Studio .NET, if necessary, and then close the Start Page window. Click **File** on the menu bar, and then click **Open Solution**. The Open Solution dialog box opens. Open the **Hangman Solution** (Hangman Solution.sln) file, which is contained in the VBNET\Tut08\Hangman Solution folder.

2   If the designer window is not open, right-click **Hangman Form.vb** in the Solution Explorer window, then click **View Designer**.

3   Auto-hide the Toolbox, Solution Explorer, and Properties windows, if necessary. The user interface for the Hangman Game application is shown in Figure 8-21. Recall that the File menu contains the New Game command, the Exit command, and a separator bar.

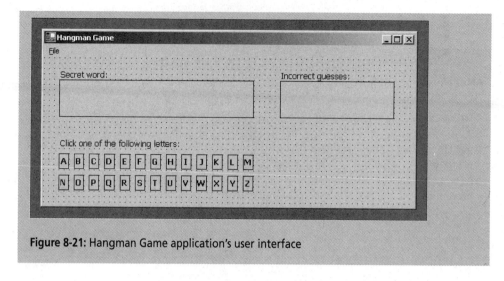

Figure 8-21: Hangman Game application's user interface

The TOE chart for the Hangman Game application is shown in Figure 8-22.

Task	Object	Event

1. Get the original word
2. Verify that the original word contains exactly five characters
3. If the original word contains exactly five characters
    a. Display the 31 label controls in the interface
    b. Display five dashes (hyphens) in the WordLabel control
    c. Display the number zero in the IncorrectGuessLabel control
4. If the original word does not contain exactly five characters, display an appropriate message
	FileNewMenuItem	Click

End the application	FileExitMenuItem	Click
Display the original word as hyphens and/or letters	WordLabel	None
Display the number of incorrect guesses	IncorrectGuessLabel	None
1. Search the original word for the letter stored in the label control's Text property 2. Replace the appropriate dashes in the WordLabel control with the letter 3. Keep track of the number of incorrect guesses, and display the number in the IncorrectGuessLabel control 4. Display the "Game Over" message	ALabel, BLabel, CLabel, DLabel, ELabel, FLabel, GLabel, HLabel, ILabel, JLabel, KLabel, LLabel, MLabel, NLabel, OLabel, PLabel, QLabel, RLabel, SLabel, TLabel, ULabel, VLabel, WLabel, XLabel, YLabel, ZLabel	Click

Figure 8-22: TOE chart for the Hangman Game application

Recall that you coded the FileExitMenuItem's Click event procedure in Lesson B. To complete the Hangman Game application, you need to code the Click event procedures for the FileNewMenuItem and the 26 label controls that contain the letters A through Z. Begin with the FileNewMenuItem's Click event procedure.

Coding the Click Event Procedure for the FileNewMenuItem

Each time the user wants to begin a new Hangman game, he or she will need to click File on the application's menu bar and then click New Game. Figure 8-23 shows the pseudocode for the FileNewMenuItem's Click event procedure.

```
FileNewMenuItem
1.  get the original word from the first student
2.  change the original word to uppercase
3.  if the original word contains exactly five characters
        change the Visible property for the 31 label controls to True
        display five dashes (hyphens) in the WordLabel control
        display the number zero in the IncorrectGuessLabel control
    else
        display an appropriate message in a message box
    end if
```

Figure 8-23: Pseudocode for the FileNewMenuItem's Click event procedure

To code the FileNewMenuItem's Click event procedure:

1   Right-click the **form**, and then click **View Code**.

First, declare a form-level variable named mstrWord. The application will use the mstrWord variable to store the original word, which is entered by the first student. The variable is declared as a form-level variable, rather than as a local variable, because it will be used by two procedures in the application—the FileNewMenuItem Click event procedure and the ProcessLetterLabels procedure.

2   Click the **blank line** below the comment `'declare form-level variable`, then press **Tab** to indent the line. Type **private mstrWord as string** and press **Enter**.

Now display the code template for the FileNewMenuItem Click event procedure.

3   Click the **Class Name** list arrow, and then click **FileNewMenuItem** in the list. Click the **Method Name** list arrow, and then click **Click** in the list. The code template for the FileNewMenuItem Click event procedure appears in the Code editor window.

According to the pseudocode shown in Figure 8-23, the Click event procedure should get the original word, and then change the word to uppercase.

4   Type the comment **'get original word** and press **Enter**, then type **mstrword = ucase(inputbox("Enter a 5-letter word", "Hangman Game"))** and press **Enter**.

Step 3 in the pseudocode is to determine whether the original word contains exactly five characters. As you learned in Lesson A, the number of characters contained in a string is stored in the string's Length property.

5   Type **'determine whether the original word contains exactly five characters** and press **Enter**, then type **if mstrword.length = 5 then** and press **Enter**.

If the original word contains exactly five characters, the procedure should change the Visible property for the 31 label controls to True. (As you may remember from Lesson B, the label controls do not appear in the interface when the application is started, because their Visible property is set to False in the Properties window.)

6 Type the additional five lines of code shown in Figure 8-24, then position the insertion point as shown in the figure.

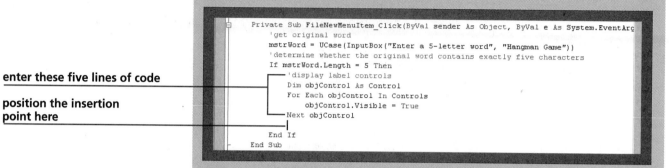

enter these five lines of code

position the insertion point here

```
Private Sub FileNewMenuItem_Click(ByVal sender As Object, ByVal e As System.EventArg
    'get original word
    mstrWord = UCase(InputBox("Enter a 5-letter word", "Hangman Game"))
    'determine whether the original word contains exactly five characters
    If mstrWord.Length = 5 Then
        'display label controls
        Dim objControl As Control
        For Each objControl In Controls
            objControl.Visible = True
        Next objControl

    End If
End Sub
```

Figure 8-24: Additional code entered in the FileNewMenuItem Click event procedure

The procedure also should display five dashes (hyphens) in the WordLabel control—one for each letter in the original word. It then should display the number zero in the IncorrectGuessLabel control.

7 Type **'display dashes** and press **Enter**, then type **me.wordlabel.text = "-----"** and press **Enter**.

8 Type **'set number of incorrect guesses to zero** and press **Enter**, then type **me.incorrectguesslabel.text = 0** and press **Enter**.

If the original word does not contain exactly five characters, the procedure should display an appropriate message.

9 Type the additional lines of code shown in Figure 8-25, which shows the completed FileNewMenuItem Click event procedure.

enter these four lines of code

```
Private Sub FileNewMenuItem_Click(ByVal sender As Object, ByVal e As System.EventArg
    'get original word
    mstrWord = UCase(InputBox("Enter a 5-letter word", "Hangman Game"))
    'determine whether the original word contains exactly five characters
    If mstrWord.Length = 5 Then
        'display label controls
        Dim objControl As Control
        For Each objControl In Controls
            objControl.Visible = True
        Next objControl
        'display dashes
        Me.WordLabel.Text = "-----"
        'set number of incorrect guesses to zero
        Me.IncorrectGuessLabel.Text = 0
    Else
        'display message
        MessageBox.Show("Please enter a 5-letter word", "Hangman Game", _
            MessageBoxButtons.OK, MessageBoxIcon.Information)
    End If
End Sub
```

Figure 8-25: Completed FileNewMenuItem Click event procedure

Now test the FileNewMenuItem Click event procedure to verify that it is working correctly.

To test the FileNewMenuItem Click event procedure:

1   Click **File** on the menu bar, and then click **Save All**. Click **Debug** on the menu bar and then click **Start**.

2   Click **File** on the Hangman Game application's menu bar, and then click **New Game**. The FileNewMenuItem Click event procedure displays a dialog box that prompts you to enter a five-letter word.

First, enter a word that has less than five characters.

3   Type **dog** and press **Enter**. The procedure displays the message "Please enter a 5-letter word" in a message box. Press **Enter** to close the message box.

4   Click **File** on the Hangman Game application's menu bar, and then click **New Game**.

Now enter a word that has more than five characters.

5   Type **balloon** and press **Enter**. The procedure displays the message "Please enter a 5-letter word" in a message box. Press **Enter** to close the message box.

6   Click **File** on the Hangman Game application's menu bar, and then click **New Game**.

Now type a word that has exactly five characters.

7   Type **basic** and press **Enter**. The procedure displays the 31 label controls in the interface. Notice that the WordLabel control contains five dashes, and the IncorrectGuessLabel control contains the number zero. See Figure 8-26.

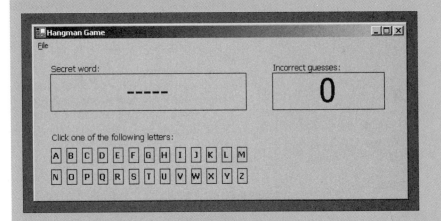

Figure 8-26: Result of entering a word that has exactly five characters

8   Click **File** on the Hangman Game application's menu bar, and then click **Exit**. When you return to the Code editor window, close the Output window.

Next, code the Click event procedures for the 26 label controls that contain the letters A through Z.

Coding the Label Controls that Contain the Letters of the Alphabet

After the first student enters a five-letter word, the second student then guesses the word, letter by letter. The second student indicates his or her letter choice by clicking one of the 26 label controls located at the bottom of the form; each of these label controls contains a letter of the alphabet. The pseudocode shown in Figure 8-27 identifies the tasks to be performed by the Click event procedures for the 26 label controls.

ALabel, BLabel, CLabel, DLabel, ELabel, FLabel, GLabel, HLabel, ILabel, JLabel, KLabel, LLabel, MLabel, NLabel, OLabel, PLabel, QLabel, RLabel, SLabel, TLabel, ULabel, VLabel, WLabel, XLabel, YLabel, ZLabel

1. declare variables
2. hide the letter (label control) that was clicked
3. assign the contents of the WordLabel control (which contains the current status of the guessed word) to the strPartialWord variable
4. repeat for each character in the original word
    if the character matches the letter selected by the user
        replace the dash in the strPartialWord variable with the selected letter

        assign True to the blnReplaced variable to indicate that a replacement was made in the strPartialWord variable
    end if
end repeat
5. if a replacement was made in the strPartialWord variable
    if the strPartialWord variable contains at least one dash
        display the contents of the strPartialWord variable in the WordLabel control
    else
        display the original word in the WordLabel control
        display the message "Great guessing!" in a message box
    end if
else
    add the number one to the number of incorrect guesses
    if the number of incorrect guesses equals three
        display the message "Game Over" in the WordLabel control

        display in a message box the message "Sorry, the word is" and the original word
    end if
end if

Figure 8-27: Pseudocode for the 26 label controls' Click event procedures

Because each Click event procedure must perform the same tasks, you will enter the appropriate code in a procedure named ProcessLetterLabels, and use the Handles section in the procedure header to associate the procedure with each of the 26 Click event procedures. The code template for the ProcessLetterLabels procedure is already entered in the Code editor window. You just need to translate the pseudocode shown in Figure 8-27 into the appropriate Visual Basic .NET code.

To begin translating the pseudocode shown in Figure 8-27:

1   Locate the ProcessLetterLabels procedure in the Code editor window, then position the insertion point as shown in Figure 8-28.

```
Private Sub ProcessLetterLabels(ByVal sender As Object, ByVal e As System.EventArgs)
          Handles ALabel.Click, BLabel.Click, CLabel.Click, DLabel.Click, ELabel.Click
     FLabel.Click, GLabel.Click, HLabel.Click, ILabel.Click, JLabel.Click, _
     KLabel.Click, LLabel.Click, MLabel.Click, NLabel.Click, OLabel.Click, _
     PLabel.Click, QLabel.Click, RLabel.Click, SLabel.Click, TLabel.Click, _
     ULabel.Click, VLabel.Click, WLabel.Click, XLabel.Click, YLabel.Click, ZLabel

     End Sub
```

position insertion point here

Figure 8-28: Correct location of the insertion point in the ProcessLetterLabels procedure

Step 1 in the pseudocode shown in Figure 8-27 is to declare the variables. The procedure will use five variables: objLetterLabel, strPartialWord, blnReplaced, intIndex, and strCharacter. The objLetterLabel variable will keep track of the label control that the user clicked. The strPartialWord variable will keep track of the current status of the guessed word. Initially, the strPartialWord variable will contain five dashes—one for each letter in the original word. However, when a letter selected by the user matches a character in the original word, the corresponding dash in the strPartialWord variable will be replaced with the letter. The blnReplaced variable will keep track of whether a replacement was made.

The intIndex variable will control the number of times the loop in Step 4 is processed. The loop will search the original word, character by character, to determine whether it contains the letter selected by the user. When performing the search, the loop will assign each character to the strCharacter variable.

2   Type **dim objLetterLabel as label, intIndex as integer, blnReplaced as boolean** and press **Enter**. Then type **dim strPartialWord, strCharacter as string** and press **Enter**.

Next, hide the label control (letter) that the user clicked; this prevents the user from selecting the letter again. The address of the selected label control is stored in the procedure's `sender` parameter. You can hide the label control by setting its Visible property to the Boolean value False.

3   Type **'hide the selected letter** and press **Enter**. Type **objletterlabel = sender** and press **Enter**, then type **objletterlabel.visible = false** and press **Enter**.

Now assign the contents of the WordLabel control, which contains the current status of the guessed word, to the strPartialWord variable.

4   Type **'assign current status of the guessed word to the strPartialWord variable** and press **Enter**. Type **strpartialword = me.wordlabel.text** and press **Enter**.

Step 4 in the pseudocode is a repetition structure that repeats its instructions for each character in the original word. In this case, the loop instructions need to be processed five times, because the original word contains five characters. The five characters have indexes of zero through four.

5   Type **'search for the selected letter in the original word** and press **Enter**, then type **for intindex = 0 to 4** and press **Enter**.

Now use the Substring method to access the current character in the original word, and then assign the character to the strCharacter variable.

6   Type **'assign current character to the strCharacter variable** and press **Enter**, then type **strcharacter = mstrword.substring(intindex, 1)** and press **Enter**.

Next, determine whether the character stored in the strCharacter variable matches the letter selected by the user.

7 Type **'determine whether current character matches the selected letter** and press **Enter**, then type **if strcharacter = objletterlabel.text then** and press **Enter**.

If a character in the original word matches the selected letter, then the procedure should replace the corresponding dash in the strPartialWord variable with the selected letter, and then assign the Boolean value True to the blnReplaced variable. For example, if the original word is SOFT and the user selects the letter F, then the third dash in the strPartialWord variable should be replaced with the letter F.

8 Type the additional four lines of code shown in Figure 8-29. Also, change the `Next` clause to `Next intIndex`, and verify that your code contains the `End If` clause. When you are finished, position the insertion point as shown in the figure.

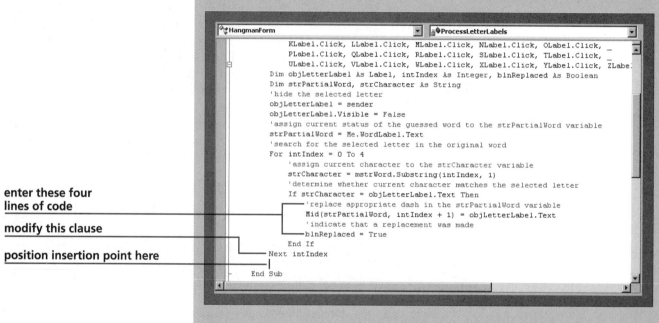

enter these four lines of code

modify this clause

position insertion point here

```
HangmanForm                                    ProcessLetterLabels
        KLabel.Click, LLabel.Click, MLabel.Click, NLabel.Click, OLabel.Click, _
        PLabel.Click, QLabel.Click, RLabel.Click, SLabel.Click, TLabel.Click, _
        ULabel.Click, VLabel.Click, WLabel.Click, XLabel.Click, YLabel.Click, ZLabel
    Dim objLetterLabel As Label, intIndex As Integer, blnReplaced As Boolean
    Dim strPartialWord, strCharacter As String
    'hide the selected letter
    objLetterLabel = sender
    objLetterLabel.Visible = False
    'assign current status of the guessed word to the strPartialWord variable
    strPartialWord = Me.WordLabel.Text
    'search for the selected letter in the original word
    For intIndex = 0 To 4
        'assign current character to the strCharacter variable
        strCharacter = mstrWord.Substring(intIndex, 1)
        'determine whether current character matches the selected letter
        If strCharacter = objLetterLabel.Text Then
            'replace appropriate dash in the strPartialWord variable
            Mid(strPartialWord, intIndex + 1) = objLetterLabel.Text
            'indicate that a replacement was made
            blnReplaced = True
        End If
    Next intIndex

    End Sub
```

Figure 8-29: Additional code entered in the ProcessLetterLabels procedure

9 Save the solution.

Step 5 in the pseudocode shown in Figure 8-27 is a selection structure that determines whether a replacement was made in the strPartialWord variable. If a replacement was made, then the blnReplaced variable will contain the Boolean value True.

To complete the ProcessLetterLabels procedure:

1 With the insertion point located as shown in Figure 8-29, type **'determine whether a replacement was made in the strPartialWord variable** and press **Enter**.

2 Type **if blnreplaced = true then** and press **Enter**.

If at least one dash was replaced in the strPartialWord variable, the procedure needs to determine whether any dashes remain in the variable. If the variable contains at least one dash, the current Hangman game should continue, because the user has not finished guessing the original word. In that case, the procedure should simply display the contents of the strPartialWord variable in the WordLabel control.

You can use the IndexOf method to determine whether the strPartialWord variable contains a dash. Recall that the IndexOf method returns the number -1 if the value for which you are searching is not contained in a string; otherwise, it returns the index of the starting location of the value within the string.

3 Type **'determine whether the strPartialWord variable contains a dash** and press **Enter**. Type **if strpartialword.indexof("-") > -1 then** and press **Enter**.

4 Type **me.wordlabel.text = strpartialword** and press **Enter**.

If, on the other hand, the strPartialWord variable does not contain any dashes, then the current Hangman game should end. In that case, the procedure should display the original word in the WordLabel control, and display the message "Great guessing!" in a message box.

5 Enter the additional lines of code shown in Figure 8-30, then position the insertion point as shown in the figure. (Be sure to verify that your code contains the End If clause.)

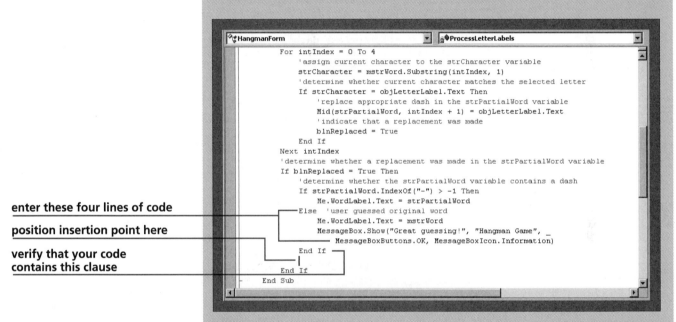

enter these four lines of code

position insertion point here

verify that your code contains this clause

```
For intIndex = 0 To 4
    'assign current character to the strCharacter variable
    strCharacter = mstrWord.Substring(intIndex, 1)
    'determine whether current character matches the selected letter
    If strCharacter = objLetterLabel.Text Then
        'replace appropriate dash in the strPartialWord variable
        Mid(strPartialWord, intIndex + 1) = objLetterLabel.Text
        'indicate that a replacement was made
        blnReplaced = True
    End If
Next intIndex
'determine whether a replacement was made in the strPartialWord variable
If blnReplaced = True Then
    'determine whether the strPartialWord variable contains a dash
    If strPartialWord.IndexOf("-") > -1 Then
        Me.WordLabel.Text = strPartialWord
    Else  'user guessed original word
        Me.WordLabel.Text = mstrWord
        MessageBox.Show("Great guessing!", "Hangman Game", _
            MessageBoxButtons.OK, MessageBoxIcon.Information)
    End If
End If
End Sub
```

Figure 8-30: Additional lines of code entered in the procedure

If no characters were replaced in the strPartialWord variable, then the ProcessLetterLabels procedure should add the number one to the number of incorrect guesses. If the number of incorrect guesses is three, then the current Hangman game should end, and the procedure should display the message "Game Over" in the WordLabel control, and display the message "Sorry, the word is", along with the original word, in a message box.

6 Enter the lines of code shaded in Figure 8-31, which shows the completed ProcessLetterLabels procedure. (Be sure to verify that your code contains the two End If clauses that appear above the End Sub clause.)

```
Private Sub ProcessLetterLabels(ByVal sender As Object, _
     ByVal e As System.EventArgs) Handles ALabel.Click, BLabel.Click, _
     CLabel.Click, DLabel.Click, ELabel.Click, FLabel.Click, GLabel.Click, _
     HLabel.Click, ILabel.Click, JLabel.Click, KLabel.Click, LLabel.Click, _
     MLabel.Click, NLabel.Click, OLabel.Click, PLabel.Click, QLabel.Click, _
     RLabel.Click, SLabel.Click, TLabel.Click, ULabel.Click, VLabel.Click, _
     WLabel.Click, XLabel.Click, YLabel.Click, ZLabel.Click
     Dim objLetterLabel As Label, intIndex As Integer, blnReplaced As Boolean
     Dim strPartialWord, strCharacter As String
     'hide the selected letter
     objLetterLabel = sender
     objLetterLabel.Visible = False
     'assign current status of the guessed word to the strPartialWord variable
     strPartialWord = Me.WordLabel.Text
     'search for the selected letter in the original word
     For intIndex = 0 To 4
         'assign current character to the strCharacter variable
         strCharacter = mstrWord.Substring(intIndex, 1)
         'determine whether current character matches the selected letter
         If strCharacter = objLetterLabel.Text Then
             'replace appropriate dash in the strPartialWord variable
             Mid(strPartialWord, intIndex + 1) = objLetterLabel.Text
             'indicate that a replacement was made
             blnReplaced = True
         End If
     Next intIndex
     'determine whether a replacement was made in the strPartialWord variable
     If blnReplaced = True Then
         'determine whether the strPartialWord variable contains a dash
         If strPartialWord.IndexOf("-") > -1 Then
             Me.WordLabel.Text = strPartialWord
         Else   'user guessed original word
             Me.WordLabel.Text = mstrWord
             MessageBox.Show("Great guessing!", "Hangman Game", _
                 MessageBoxButtons.OK, MessageBoxIcon.Information)
         End If
     Else
         Me.IncorrectGuessLabel.Text = Val(Me.IncorrectGuessLabel.Text) + 1
         If Val(Me.IncorrectGuessLabel.Text) = 3 Then
             Me.WordLabel.Text = "Game Over"
             MessageBox.Show("Sorry, the word is " & mstrWord, "Hangman Game", _
                 MessageBoxButtons.OK, MessageBoxIcon.Information)
         End If
     End If
End Sub
```

enter these lines of code

Figure 8-31: Completed ProcessLetterLabels procedure

Now test the procedure to verify that it is working correctly.

To test the ProcessLetterLabels procedure:

1   Save the solution, then start the application.

2   Click **File** on the application's menu bar, and then click **New Game**. When you are prompted to enter a word, type **moose** and press **Enter**.

First, observe what happens when the user guesses the original word.

3   Click the E label control. The ProcessLetterLabels procedure replaces the last dash in the WordLabel control with the letter E.

4   Click the O label control. The ProcessLetterLabels procedure replaces the second dash in the WordLabel control with the letter O, and also replaces the third dash with the letter O.

5   Click the M label control, then click the S label control. The ProcessLetterLabels procedure displays the message "Great guessing!" in a message box, as shown in Figure 8-32.

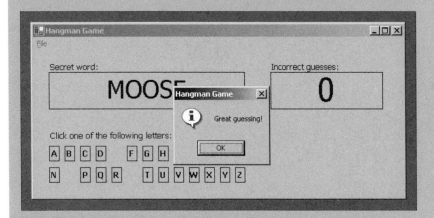

Figure 8-32: Result of guessing the original word

6   Click the **OK** button to close the message box.

7   Click **File** on the application's menu bar, and then click **New Game**. When you are prompted to enter a word, type **seven** and press **Enter**.

Now observe what happens when the user makes three incorrect guesses.

8   Click the **A** label control. The number one appears in the IncorrectGuessLabel control. Click the **B** label control, and then click the **C** label control. The ProcessLetterLabels procedure displays the message "Game Over" in the WordLabel control, and displays the message "Sorry, the word is SEVEN" in a message box, as shown in Figure 8-33.

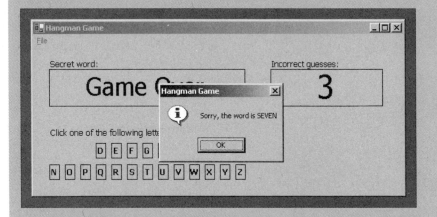

Figure 8-33: Result of making three incorrect guesses

9 Click the **OK** button to close the message box. Click **File** on the application's menu bar, and then click **Exit** to end the application.

10 When you return to the Code editor window, close the Output window, then close the Code editor window. Click **File** on the menu bar, and then click **Close Solution**.

You now have completed Tutorial 8. You can either take a break or complete the end-of-lesson questions and exercises.

SUMMARY

To access each character in a string:

■ Use the Substring method.

To replace a character in a string with another character:

■ Use the Mid statement.

To determine whether a specific character is contained in a string:

■ Use the IndexOf method.

QUESTIONS

1. Which of the following For clauses can be used to access each character contained in the strName variable, character by character? The variable contains 10 characters.
   a. `For intIndex = 0 To 10`
   b. `For intIndex = 0 To strName.Length`
   c. `For intIndex = 0 To strName.Length - 1`
   d. `For intIndex = 1 To 10`
   e. `For intIndex = 1 To strName.Length - 1`

2. Which of the following If clauses can be used to determine whether the strAmount variable contains a comma?
   a. `If strAmount.Contains(",") Then`
   b. `If strAmount.Substring(",") Then`
   c. `If strAmount.IndexOf(",") = 0 Then`
   d. `If strAmount.IndexOf(",") > -1 Then`
   e. None of the above.

3. Which of the following can be used to change the first letter in the strName variable from "K" to "C"?
   a. `Mid(strName, 0, "C")`
   b. `Mid(strName, 0) = "C"`
   c. `Mid(strName, 1, "C")`
   d. `Mid(strName, 1) = "C"`
   e. `strName = Mid(1, "C")`

4. Which of the following can be used to assign the fifth character in the strWord variable to the strLetter variable?
   a. `strLetter = strWord.Substring(4)`
   b. `strLetter = strWord.Substring(5, 1)`
   c. `strLetter = strWord(5).Substring`
   d. `strLetter = strWord.Insert(5, 1)`
   e. None of the above.

5. If the strWord variable contains the string "Irene Turner", the `strWord.IndexOf("r")` method returns _____.
   a. -1
   b. 2
   c. 3
   d. r
   e. None of the above.

EXERCISES

The following list summarizes the GUI design guidelines you have learned so far. You can use this list to verify that the interfaces you create in the following exercises adhere to the GUI standards outlined in the book.

- Information should flow either vertically or horizontally, with the most important information always located in the upper-left corner of the screen.

- Maintain a consistent margin of two or three dots from the edge of the window.

- Try to create a user interface that no one notices.

- Related controls should be grouped together using white space, a GroupBox control, or a Panel control.

- Set the form's FormBorderStyle, ControlBox, MaximizeBox, MinimizeBox, and StartPosition properties appropriately:

  - A splash screen should not have a Minimize, Maximize, or Close button, and its borders should not be sizable.

  - A form that is not a splash screen should always have a Minimize button and a Close button, but you can choose to disable the Maximize button. Typically, the FormBorderStyle property is set to Sizable, but also can be set to FixedSingle.

- Position related controls on succeeding dots. Controls that are not part of any logical grouping may be positioned from two to four dots away from other controls.

- Buttons should be positioned either in a row along the bottom of the screen, or stacked in either the upper-right or lower-right corner.

- If the buttons are positioned at the bottom of the screen, then each button should be the same height; their widths, however, may vary.

- If the buttons are stacked in either the upper-right or lower-right corner of the screen, then each should be the same height and the same width.

- Use no more than six buttons on a screen.

- The most commonly used button should be placed first.
- Button captions should:
  - be meaningful
  - be from one to three words
  - appear on one line
  - be entered using book title capitalization
- Use labels to identify the text boxes in the interface, and position the label either above or to the left of the text box.
- Label text should:
  - be from one to three words
  - appear on one line
  - be left-justified
  - end with a colon (:)
  - be entered using sentence capitalization
- Labels that identify controls should have their BorderStyle property set to None.
- Labels that display program output, such as the result of a calculation, should have their BorderStyle property set to FixedSingle.
- Align controls to minimize the number of different margins.
- If you use a graphic in the interface, use a small one and place it in a location that will not distract the user.
- Use the Tahoma font for applications that will run on Windows 2000 or Windows XP.
- Use no more than two different font sizes, which should be 8, 9, 10, 11, or 12 point.
- Use only one font type, which should be a sans serif font, in the interface.
- Avoid using italics and underlining.
- Limit the use of bold text to titles, headings, and key items.
- Build the interface using black, white, and gray first, then add color only if you have a good reason to do so.
- Use white, off-white, light gray, pale blue, or pale yellow for an application's background, and black for the text.
- Limit the number of colors to three, not including white, black, and gray. The colors you choose should complement each other.
- Never use color as the only means of identification for an element in the user interface.
- Set each control's TabIndex property to a number that represents the order in which you want the control to receive the focus (begin with 0).
- A text box's TabIndex value should be one more than the TabIndex value of its identifying label.
- Assign a unique access key to each control (in the interface) that can receive user input (text boxes, buttons, and so on).

- When assigning an access key to a control, use the first letter of the caption or identifying label, unless another letter provides a more meaningful association. If you can't use the first letter and no other letter provides a more meaningful association, then use a distinctive consonant. Lastly, use a vowel or a number.

- Lock the controls in place on the form.

- Document the program internally.

- Use the Val function on any Text property involved in a calculation.

- Use the Format function to improve the appearance of numbers in the interface.

- In the InputBox function, use sentence capitalization for the *prompt*, and book title capitalization for the *title*.

- The default button should be the button that is most often selected by the user, except in cases where the tasks performed by the button are both destructive and irreversible. The default button is typically the first button.

- Use sentence capitalization for the optional identifying label in a group box control.

- MessageBox.Show method:

  - Use sentence capitalization for the *text* argument, but book title capitalization for the *caption* argument. The name of the application typically appears in the *caption* argument.

  - Avoid using the words "error," "warning," or "mistake" in the message.

  - Display the Warning Message icon ⚠ in a message box that alerts the user that he or she must make a decision before the application can continue. You can phrase the message as a question.

  - Display the Information Message icon ⓘ in a message box that displays an informational message along with an OK button only.

  - Display the Stop Message icon ⊗ when you want to alert the user of a serious problem that must be corrected before the application can continue.

  - The default button in the dialog box should be the one that represents the user's most likely action, as long as that action is not destructive.

- Use the KeyPress event to prevent a text box from accepting inappropriate keys.

- Radio buttons:

  - Use radio buttons when you want to limit the user to one of two or more related and mutually exclusive choices.

  - Use a minimum of two and a maximum of seven radio buttons in an interface.

  - Use sentence capitalization for the label entered in the radio button's Text property.

  - Assign a unique access key to each radio button in an interface.

  - Use a group box control (or a panel control) to create separate groups of radio buttons. Only one button in each group can be selected at any one time.

  - Designate a default radio button in each group of radio buttons.

- Check boxes:

  - Use check boxes to allow the user to select any number of choices from a group of one or more independent and nonexclusive choices.

- Use sentence capitalization for the label entered in the check box's Text property.

- Assign a unique access key to each check box in an interface.

■ List boxes:

- A list box should contain a minimum of three selections.

- A list box should display a minimum of three selections and a maximum of eight selections at a time.

- Use a label control to provide keyboard access to the list box. Set the label control's TabIndex property to a value that is one less than the list box's TabIndex value.

- List box items are either arranged by use, with the most used entries appearing first in the list, or sorted in ascending order.

- If a list box allows the user to make only one selection at a time, then a default item should be selected in the list box when the interface first appears. The default item should be either the most-used selection or the first selection in the list. However, if a list box allows more than one selection at a time, you do not select a default item.

■ Menus:

- Menu title captions, which appear on the menu bar, should be one word, with the first letter capitalized. Each menu title should have a unique access key.

- Menu item captions, which appear on a menu, can be from one to three words. Use book title capitalization and assign a unique access key to each menu item. Assign shortcut keys to commonly used menu items.

- If a menu item requires additional information from the user, place an ellipsis (...) at the end of the item's caption, which is entered in the item's Text property.

- Follow the Windows standards for the placement of menu titles and items.

- Use a separator bar to separate groups of related menu items.

■ It is customary in Windows applications to disable objects that do not apply to the current state of the application.

■ It is customary in Windows applications to highlight, or select, the existing text in a text box when the text box receives the focus.

■ Test the application with both valid and invalid data (for example, test the application without entering any data, and test it by entering letters where numbers are expected).

1. In this exercise, you modify the Hangman Game application so that it allows the first student to enter a word that contains any number of characters.

   a. Use Windows to make a copy of the Hangman Solution folder, which is contained in the VBNET\Tut08 folder. Change the name of the folder to Revised Hangman Solution.

   b. If necessary, start Visual Studio .NET. Open the Hangman Solution (Hangman Solution.sln) file, which is contained in the VBNET\Tut08\Revised Hangman Solution folder. If the designer window is not open, right-click the form file's name in the Solution Explorer window, then click View Designer.

c. Modify the application's code appropriately. The number of incorrect guesses the user is allowed to make should be two less than the total number of characters in the original word. For example, if the original word contains seven characters, allow the user to make five incorrect guesses.

d. Save the solution, and then start the application. Click File on the application's menu bar, and then click New Game. Test the application using the word "telephone".

e. Click File on the application's menu bar, and then click Exit to end the application.

f. Close the Output window, and then close the solution.

2. In this exercise, you code an application that displays the color of an item.

a. If necessary, start Visual Studio .NET. Open the Color Solution (Color Solution.sln) file, which is contained in the VBNET\Tut08\Color Solution folder. If the designer window is not open, right-click the form file's name in the Solution Explorer window, then click View Designer.

b. The Display Color button should display the color of the item whose item number is entered by the user. All item numbers contain exactly five characters. All items are available in four colors: blue, green, red, and white. The third character in the item number indicates the item's color, as follows:

Character	Color
B or b	Blue
G or g	Green
R or r	Red
W or w	White

If the item number does not contain exactly five characters, or if the third character is not one of the characters listed above, the Display Color button should display an appropriate message in a message box.

c. Save the solution, and then start the application. Test the application using the following item numbers: 12x, 12b45, 99G44, abr55, 78w99, and 23abc.

d. Click the Exit button to end the application.

e. Close the Output window, and then close the solution.

3. In this exercise, you code an application that allows the user to enter a name (the first name followed by a space and the last name). The application then displays the name (the last name followed by a comma, a space, and the first name).

a. If necessary, start Visual Studio .NET. Open the Name Solution (Name Solution.sln) file, which is contained in the VBNET\Tut08\Name Solution folder. If the designer window is not open, right-click the form file's name in the Solution Explorer window, then click View Designer.

b. Code the Display New Name button appropriately.

c. Save the solution, and then start the application. Test the application using the following names: Carol Smith, Jose Martinez, and Sven Miller.

d. Click the Exit button to end the application.

e. Close the Output window, and then close the solution.

4. In this exercise, you code an application that allows the user to enter a phone number. The application then removes any hyphens and parentheses from the phone number before displaying the phone number.

a. If necessary, start Visual Studio .NET. Open the Phone Solution (Phone Solution.sln) file, which is contained in the VBNET\Tut08\Phone Solution folder. If the designer window is not open, right-click the form file's name in the Solution Explorer window, then click View Designer.

b. Code the Display New Number button appropriately.

c. Save the solution, and then start the application. Test the application using the following phone numbers: (555)-111-1111, 555-5555, and 123-456-1111.

d.   Click the Exit button to end the application.

e.   Close the Output window, and then close the solution.

5.   In this exercise, you code an application that allows the user to guess a letter chosen randomly by the computer.

a.   If necessary, start Visual Studio .NET. Open the Random Solution (Random Solution.sln) file, which is contained in the VBNET\Tut08\Random Solution folder. If the designer window is not open, right-click the form file's name in the Solution Explorer window, then click View Designer.

b.   Study the application's existing code. Notice that the Play Game button's Click event procedure assigns the letters of the alphabet to the strAlphabet variable. It also prompts the user to enter a letter, and stores the user's response in the strLetter variable. Complete the procedure by entering instructions to do the following:

■   generate a random integer that can be used to select one of the letters from the strAlphabet variable, and assign the selected letter to the strRandomLetter variable

■   verify that the user entered exactly one character

■   if the user did not enter exactly one character, display an appropriate message in a message box

■   if the user entered exactly one character, compare the lowercase version of the character to the letter stored in the strRandomLetter variable

■   allow the user to enter a character until he or she guesses the random letter stored in the strRandomLetter variable

■   if the character entered by the user is the same as the letter stored in the strRandomLetter variable, display the message "You guessed the correct letter."

■   if the letter stored in the strRandomLetter variable appears after the user's letter in the alphabet, display the message "The correct letter comes after the letter", followed by a space, the user's letter, and a period

■   if the letter stored in the strRandomLetter variable appears before the user's letter in the alphabet, display the message "The correct letter comes before the letter", followed by a space, the user's letter, and a period

c.   Save the solution, then start the application. Click the Play Game button, then enter one or more letters until the message "You guessed the correct letter." appears.

d.   Click the Exit button to end the application.

e.   Close the Output window, then close the solution.

Exercises 6 and 7 are Discovery Exercises. Discovery Exercises, which may include topics that are not covered in this lesson, allow you to "discover" the solutions to problems on your own.

discovery ▶   6.   In this exercise, you code an application that displays a message indicating whether a portion of a string begins with another string.

a.   If necessary, start Visual Studio .NET. Open the String Solution (String Solution.sln) file, which is contained in the VBNET\Tut08\String Solution folder. If the designer window is not open, right-click the form file's name in the Solution Explorer window, then click View Designer.

b.   The application allows the user to enter a name (first name followed by a space and the last name) and the search text. If the last name begins with the search text (entered in any case), the Display Message button should display the message "The last name begins with" followed by a space and the search text. If the characters in the last name come before the search text in the ASCII coding scheme, display the message "The last name comes before" followed by a space and the search text. Finally, if the characters in the last name come after the search text in the ASCII coding scheme, display the message "The last name comes after" followed by a space and the search text.

c.   Save the solution, then start the application. To test the application, enter Helga Swanson as the name, then use the following strings for the search text: g, ab, he, s, SY, sw, swan, and wan.

d.   Click the Exit button to end the application.

e.   Close the Output window, then close the solution.

7.   In this exercise, you learn how to use a ColorDialog control.

a.   If necessary, start Visual Studio .NET. Create a blank solution named Dialog Solution. Save the solution in the VBNET\Tut08 folder.

b.   Add a Visual Basic .NET Windows Application project to the solution. Name the project Dialog Project.

c.   Assign the filename Dialog Form.vb to the form file object.

d.   Assign the name DialogForm to the Windows Form object. Change the form's StartPosition property to CenterScreen. Change its Text property to Color Dialog Example.

e.   Change the project's Startup object to DialogForm.

f.   Add a label control to the interface. Name the label control ColorLabel. Set the label control's BorderStyle property to FixedSingle. Remove the contents of the label control's Text property.

g.   Add a MainMenu control to the interface. Name the control ColorMainMenu. Include two menu titles in the interface: File and Format. The File menu should contain an Exit option. The Format menu should contain a Color option. Use appropriate names and access keys for the menu titles and menu items.

h.   Add a ColorDialog control to the form.

i.   Code the File menu's Exit option so that it ends the application when it is clicked.

j.   Enter the following two lines of code in the Click event procedure for the Format menu's Color option:

```
Me.ColorDialog1.ShowDialog()
Me.ColorLabel.BackColor = Me.ColorDialog1.Color
```

k.   Close the Code editor window.

l.   Save the solution, then start the application. Click Format on the application's menu bar, and then click Color. The Color dialog box opens and displays a palette of colors. Click a color square, and then click the OK button. The background color of the ColorLabel control changes accordingly.

m.   Use the Exit option on the File menu to end the application.

n.   Close the Output window, then close the solution.

Exercise 8 is a Debugging Exercise. Debugging Exercises provide an opportunity for you to detect and correct errors in an existing application.

debugging

8. In this exercise, you debug an existing application. The purpose of this exercise is to demonstrate a common error made when manipulating strings.

   a. If necessary, start Visual Studio .NET. Open the Debug Solution (Debug Solution.sln) file, which is contained in the VBNET\Tut08\Debug Solution folder. If the designer window is not open, right-click the form file's name in the Solution Explorer window, then click View Designer.

   b. Open the Code editor window and study the existing code.

   c. Start the application. Enter Tampa, Florida in the Address text box, then click the Display City button. The button displays the letter T in a message box, which is incorrect; it should display the word Tampa. Click the Exit button to end the application.

   d. Correct the application's code, then save the solution and start the application.

   e. Enter Tampa, Florida in the Address text box, then click the Display City button. The button displays the word Tampa in a message box.

   f. Click the Exit button to end the application.

   g. Close the Output window, then close the solution.

Sequential Access Files and Printing

Creating the Carriage House Application

case ▶ Marge Bartowski is the Manager of Special Events at Carriage House, a nonprofit organization dedicated to enhancing the quality of life in the greater Scottsville community. Carriage House works in partnership with individuals, organizations, and businesses to provide educational, social, and cultural enrichment for people of all ages, interests, and backgrounds. Ms. Bartowski has asked you to develop an application that she can use to keep track of the special events scheduled for each month, and then print a Special Events report that lists the name, date, and price of each special event.

Previewing the Completed Application

Before creating the Carriage House application, you first preview the completed application.

To preview the completed application:

1 Use the Run command on the Windows Start menu to run the **Carriage** (Carriage.exe) file, which is contained in the VBNET\Tut09 folder on your computer's hard disk. The Carriage House application's user interface appears on the screen along with a dialog box that asks whether you want to create a new file. See Figure 9-1.

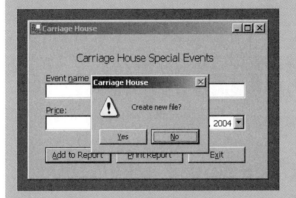

Figure 9-1: Carriage House application's user interface and dialog box

2 Click the **Yes** button. The application creates a sequential access file named preview.txt on your computer's hard disk.

3 Type **Art Show** in the Event name text box. Press **Tab**, then type 5 in the Price text box.

4 Click the **Date** list arrow button. A calendar for the month of February 2004 appears on the screen, as shown in Figure 9-2. (Do not be concerned if the date at the bottom of the calendar on your screen is different from the one shown in the figure.) The calendar is created by the DateTimePicker control.

**this date might be
different on your screen**

Figure 9-2: Calendar created by the DateTimePicker control

5   Click the number **11** in the calendar. The text "Wednesday, February 11, 2004" appears in the interface, as shown in Figure 9-3.

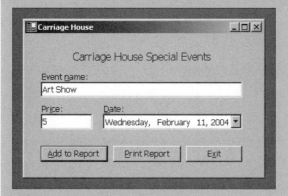

Figure 9-3: Date shown in the interface

6   Click the **Add to Report** button. The application adds the event's name, price, and date to the preview.txt file on your computer's hard disk. It also clears the text from the Event name and Price text boxes.

7   Type **Evening-tea Dance** in the Event name text box. Press **Tab**, then type **10** in the Price text box. Click the **Date** list arrow button, and then click the number **20** in the calendar for February 2004. Click the **Add to Report** button.

8   If your computer is connected to a printer, click the **Print Report** button. The application uses a PrintDocument control to print a report similar to the one shown in Figure 9-4.

```
┌─────────────────────────────────────────────────────────────────────────┐
│ Carriage House Special Events Report                                      │
│                                                                           │
│ Event                    Date                              Price          │
│ -----                    ----                              -----          │
│ Art Show                 Wednesday, February 11, 2004       5.00          │
│ Evening-tea Dance        Friday, February 20, 2004         10.00          │
└─────────────────────────────────────────────────────────────────────────┘
```

Figure 9-4: Report printed by the Carriage House application

9   Click the **Exit** button. The application closes.

You learn about sequential access files in Lesson A. The DateTimePicker control is covered in Lesson B, and the PrintDocument control is covered in Lesson C. You begin coding the Carriage House application in Lesson B and complete it in Lesson C.

LESSON A
objectives

After completing this lesson, you will be able to:

- Declare StreamReader and StreamWriter object variables
- Open a sequential access file
- Determine whether a sequential access file exists
- Write information to a sequential access file
- Align the text written to a sequential access file
- Read information from a sequential access file
- Determine whether the computer has finished reading a sequential access file
- Close a sequential access file

Sequential Access Files

File Types

In addition to getting information from the keyboard and sending information to the computer screen, an application also can get information from and send information to a file on a disk. Getting information from a file is referred to as "reading the file," and sending information to a file is referred to as "writing to the file." Files to which information is written are called **output files**, because the files store the output produced by an application. Files that are read by the computer are called **input files**, because an application uses the information in these files as input.

You can create three different types of files in Visual Basic .NET: sequential, random, and binary. The file type refers to how the information in the file is accessed. The information in a sequential access file is always accessed sequentially—in other words, in consecutive order from the beginning of the file through the end of the file. The information stored in a random access file can be accessed either in consecutive order or in random order. The information in a binary access file can be accessed by its byte location in the file. You learn about sequential access files in this tutorial and random access files in Tutorial 10. Binary access files are not covered in this book.

Using Sequential Access Files

A **sequential access file** is often referred to as a **text file**, because it is composed of lines of text. The text might represent an employee list, as shown in Example 1 in Figure 9-5. Or, it might be a memo or a report, as shown in Examples 2 and 3 in Figure 9-5.

Examples
Example 1 – employee list
Bonnel, Jacob Carlisle, Donald Eberg, Jack Hou, Chang
Example 2 – memo
To all employees: Effective January 1, 2004, the cost of dependent coverage will increase from $35 to $38.50 per month. Jefferson Williams Insurance Manager

Figure 9-5: Examples of sequential access files

Examples

Example 3 – report

```
ABC Industries Sales Report

State        Sales
California    15000
Montana       10000
Wyoming        7000
             -----
Total sales:  $32000
```

Figure 9-5: Examples of sequential access files (continued)

Sequential access files are similar to cassette tapes in that each line in the file, like each song on a cassette tape, is both stored and retrieved in consecutive order (sequentially). In other words, before you can record (store) the fourth song on a cassette tape, you first must record songs one through three. Likewise, before you can write (store) the fourth line in a sequential access file, you first must write lines one through three. The same holds true for retrieving a song from a cassette tape and a line of text from a sequential access file. To listen to the fourth song on a cassette tape, you must play (or fast-forward through) the first three songs. Likewise, to read the fourth line in a sequential access file, you first must read the three lines that precede it.

Figure 9-6 shows the procedure you follow when using a sequential access file in an application.

Sequential access file procedure

1. declare either a StreamWriter or StreamReader object variable

2. create a StreamWriter or StreamReader object by opening a file; assign the object's address to the object variable declared in Step 1

3. use the StreamWriter object to write one or more lines of text to the file, or use the StreamReader object to read one or more lines of text from the file

4. use the StreamWriter or StreamReader object to close the file

Figure 9-6: Procedure for using a sequential access file

Step 1 in Figure 9-6 is to declare either a StreamWriter or StreamReader object variable. The appropriate object variable to declare depends on whether you want to write information to the file or read information from the file.

Using StreamWriter and StreamReader Objects

In Visual Basic .NET, you use a **StreamWriter object** to write a sequence of characters—referred to as a **stream of characters** or, more simply, a **stream**—to a sequential access file. Similarly, you use a **StreamReader object** to read a stream (sequence of characters) from a sequential access file. Before you create the appropriate object, you first must declare an object variable to store the address of the object in the computer's internal memory. You use a StreamWriter object variable to store the address of a StreamWriter object, and a StreamReader object variable to store the address of a StreamReader object.

You declare StreamWriter and StreamReader object variables using the syntax *accessibility variablename* **As System.IO.***objecttype*. In the syntax, *accessibility* is typically either the keyword Dim or the keyword Private. The appropriate keyword to use depends on whether the object variable is a local or form-level variable. *Variablename* in the syntax is the name of the object variable, and *objecttype* is either StreamWriter or StreamReader. The statement `Dim objStreamWriter As System.IO.StreamWriter`, for example, declares a StreamWriter object variable named objStreamWriter. Similarly, the statement `Private objStreamReader As System.IO.StreamReader` declares a StreamReader object variable named objStreamReader.

After you declare the appropriate object variable, you then create a StreamWriter or StreamReader object and assign the object's address to the object variable. You create a StreamWriter or StreamReader object by simply opening a sequential access file.

The "IO" in the syntax stands for "Input/Output".

Opening a Sequential Access File

You use the syntax **System.IO.File.***method*(*filename*) to open a sequential access file named *filename*. When you open a sequential access file, the computer creates either a StreamReader or StreamWriter object, depending on the *method* specified in the syntax. Figure 9-7 lists the *methods* used to open sequential access files and includes a description of each *method*. The figure also indicates the type of object created by each *method*.

Method	Object created	Description
OpenText	StreamReader	opens an existing sequential access file for input, which allows the computer to read the information stored in the file; if the file does not exist, the computer displays an error message
CreateText	StreamWriter	opens a sequential access file for output, which creates a new, empty file to which data can be written; if the file already exists, its contents are erased before the new data is written
AppendText	StreamWriter	opens a sequential access file for append, which allows the computer to write new data to the end of the existing data in the file; if the file does not exist, the file is created before data is written to it

Figure 9-7: Methods used to open a sequential access file

The **OpenText method** opens an existing sequential access file for input and allows the computer to read the information stored in the file. If the file does not exist when the OpenText method is processed, the computer displays an error message in a message box. The OpenText method creates a StreamReader object and can be used to open input files only.

You use the **CreateText method** to create a new, empty sequential access file to which data can be written. If the file already exists, the computer erases the contents of the file before writing any data to it. You use the **AppendText method** when you want to add data to the end of an existing sequential access file. If the file does not exist, the computer creates the file for you. Unlike the OpenText method, the CreateText and AppendText methods create StreamWriter objects and are used to open output files only.

To complete Step 2 in the procedure shown in Figure 9-6, you assign the address of the object created by the OpenText, CreateText, or AppendText method to the object variable declared in Step 1. You make the assignment using the syntax *variablename* = **System.IO.File.***method*(*filename*), where *variablename* is the name of a StreamReader or StreamWriter object variable. Figure 9-8 shows examples of opening sequential access files.

Examples and results

Example 1
```
objStreamReader = System.IO.File.OpenText("a:\reports\pay.txt")
```

Result
opens for input the pay.txt file contained in the reports folder on the A drive; creates a StreamReader object and assigns its address to the objStreamReader object variable

Example 2
```
objStreamReader = System.IO.File.OpenText("pay.txt")
```

Result
opens the pay.txt file for input; creates a StreamReader object and assigns its address to the objStreamReader object variable

Example 3
```
objStreamWriter = System.IO.File.CreateText("memo.txt")
```

Result
opens the memo.txt file for output; creates a StreamWriter object and assigns its address to the objStreamWriter object variable

Example 4
```
objStreamWriter = System.IO.File.AppendText("sales.txt")
```

Result
opens the sales.txt file for append; creates a StreamWriter object and assigns its address to the objStreamWriter object variable

---

Figure 9-8: Examples of opening sequential access files

When the computer processes the statement shown in Example 1 in Figure 9-8, it first searches the reports folder on the A drive for a file named pay.txt. If it cannot locate the pay.txt file, the computer displays an error message in a message box; otherwise, it opens the file for input, creates a StreamReader object, and assigns the object's address to the objStreamReader variable. Notice that the statement shown in Example 2 is identical to the statement shown in Example 1, except the *filename* argument does not specify a folder path. If you do not include a folder path in the *filename* argument, the computer will search for the file in the current project's bin folder. For example, if the current project is stored in the VBNET\Tut09\Payroll Solution\Payroll Project folder, the computer will search for the pay.txt file in the VBNET\Tut09\Payroll Solution\Payroll Project\bin folder.

When processing the statement shown in Example 3, the computer searches the current project's bin folder for a file named memo.txt. If the memo.txt file exists, its contents are erased and the file is opened for output; otherwise, a new, empty file is created and opened for output. In addition to opening the memo.txt file, Example 3's statement also creates a StreamWriter object and assigns the object's address to the objStreamWriter variable.

When the computer processes the statement shown in Example 4, it searches the current project's bin folder for a file named sales.txt. If it locates the sales.txt file, the computer opens the file for append, which allows new information to be written to the end of the file. If the computer cannot locate the sales.txt file, it creates a new, empty file and opens the file for append. Example 4's statement also creates a StreamWriter object and assigns the object's address to the objStreamWriter variable.

The computer uses a file pointer to keep track of the next character either to read in or write to a file. When you open a file for input, the computer positions the file pointer at the beginning of the file, immediately before the first character. When you open a file for output, the computer also positions the file pointer at the beginning of the file, but recall that the file is empty. (As you learned earlier, opening a file for output tells the computer to create a new, empty file or erase the contents of an existing file.) However, when you open a file for append, the computer positions the file pointer immediately after the last character in the file. Figure 9-9 illustrates the position of the file pointer when files are opened for input, output, and append.

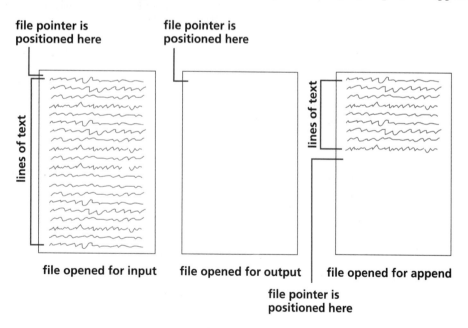

Figure 9-9: Position of the file pointer when files are opened for input, output, and append

Recall that the computer displays an error message if you use the OpenText method to open a file that does not exist. You can use the Exists method to determine whether a file exists before you attempt to open it.

Determining Whether a File Exists

The syntax of the Exists method is **System.IO.File.Exists(**_filename_**)**, where _filename_ is the name of the file whose existence you want to verify. The _filename_ argument can include an optional folder path; if the folder path is omitted, the computer searches for the file in the current project's bin folder.

The **Exists method** returns the Boolean value True if _filename_ exists; otherwise, it returns the Boolean value False. Figure 9-10 shows two examples of using the Exists method to determine whether the pay.txt file exists.

Examples and results

Example 1
```
If System.IO.File.Exists("pay.txt") = True Then
     objStreamReader = System.IO.File.OpenText("pay.txt")
     [instructions for processing the file]
Else
     MessageBox.Show("File does not exist", "Payroll", _
          MessageBoxButtons.OK, MessageBoxIcon.Information)
End If
```

Result
opens and then processes the pay.txt file if the file exists; otherwise, displays the "File does not exist" message in a message box

Example 2
```
If System.IO.File.Exists("pay.txt") = False Then
     MessageBox.Show("File does not exist", "Payroll", _
          MessageBoxButtons.OK, MessageBoxIcon.Information)
Else
     objStreamReader = System.IO.File.OpenText("pay.txt")
     [instructions for processing the file]
End If
```

Result
displays the "File does not exist" message in a message box if the pay.txt file does not exist; otherwise, opens and then processes the file

---

Figure 9-10: Examples of the Exists method

tip

You also can write the If clause shown in Example 1 as If System.IO.File. Exists("pay.txt") Then, and the If clause shown in Example 2 as If Not System.IO.File. Exists("pay.txt") Then.

Both examples shown in Figure 9-10 produce the same result and simply represent two different ways of accomplishing the same task.

Step 3 in the procedure shown earlier in Figure 9-6 is to use the StreamWriter object to write one or more lines of text to the file, or use the StreamReader object to read one or more lines of text from the file. First, learn how to write information to a sequential access file.

Writing Information to a Sequential Access File

You can use either the **Write method** or the **WriteLine method** to write information to a sequential access file. The syntax of the Write method is _variablename_.**Write(**_data_**)**, and the syntax of the WriteLine method is _variablename_.**WriteLine(**_data_**)**. In each syntax, _variablename_ is the name of a StreamWriter object variable, and _data_ is the information you want written to the file associated with the object variable. The difference between the two methods is the location of the file pointer after the *data* is written to the file. The **Write method** positions the file pointer at the end of the last character it writes to the file. The **WriteLine method**, on the other hand, positions the file pointer at the beginning of the next line in the file; it does so by appending a **line terminator character**, which is simply a carriage return followed by a line feed, to the end of the *data*. Figure 9-11 shows examples of using both methods to write information to sequential access files. The figure also indicates the placement of the file pointer after the method is processed.

Examples and results

Example 1
`objStreamWriter.Write("Hello")`
 	
Result
`Hello`

Example 2
`objStreamWriter.WriteLine("Hello")`
 	
Result
`Hello`

Example 3
`objStreamWriter.Write("The top salesperson is ")`
`objStreamWriter.WriteLine(strName & ".")`
`objStreamWriter.WriteLine()`
`objStreamWriter.Write("ABC Sales")`
 	
Result (assuming strName contains "Carolyn")
`The top salesperson is Carolyn.`
 	
`ABC Sales`

Example 4
`objStreamWriter.Write("Total price: ")`
`objStreamWriter.WriteLine(Format(intPrice, "currency"))`
 	
Result (assuming intPrice contains 25)
`Total price: $25.00`

Example 5
`objStreamWriter.WriteLine(Space(10) & "A" & Space(5) & "B")`
 	
Result
`          A     B`

file pointer (Example 1, after "Result")
file pointer (Example 2)
file pointer (Example 3)
file pointer (Example 4)
file pointer (Example 5)

Figure 9-11: Examples of the Write and WriteLine methods

The `objStreamWriter.Write("Hello")` statement in Example 1 writes the string "Hello" to the file and then positions the file pointer immediately after the last letter in the string, as indicated in the example. The `objStreamWriter.WriteLine("Hello")` statement in Example 2 writes the string "Hello" and a line terminator character to the file. The line terminator character positions the file pointer at the beginning of the next line in the file, as indicated in the example.

The first statement shown in Example 3, `objStreamWriter.Write ("The top salesperson is ")`, writes the string "The top salesperson is " to the file and then positions the file pointer after the last character in the string (in this case, after the space character). The next statement, `objStreamWriter. WriteLine(strName & ".")`, first concatenates the contents of the strName variable with a period; it then writes the concatenated string and a line terminator character to the file. The line terminator character moves the file pointer to the next line in the file. The third statement in Example 3, `objStreamWriter. WriteLine()`, writes only a line terminator character to the file; you can use this statement to insert a blank line in a file. The last statement in Example 3, `objStreamWriter.Write("ABC Sales")`, writes the string "ABC Sales" to the file, and then positions the file pointer after the last character in the string, as indicated in the example.

The two statements shown in Example 4 write the string "Total price: " and the contents of the intPrice variable (formatted using the Currency format style) on the same line in the file. The file pointer is then positioned at the beginning of the next line in the file.

Example 5 in Figure 9-11 shows how you can use the Space function to write a specific number of spaces to a file. The syntax of the Space function is **Space(***number***)**, where *number* represents the number of spaces you want to write. The `objStreamWriter.WriteLine(Space(10) & "A" & Space(5) & "B")` statement writes 10 spaces, the letter "A", five spaces, the letter "B", and the line terminator character to the file. After the statement is processed, the file pointer is positioned at the beginning of the next line in the file.

Next, learn how to use the PadLeft and PadRight methods to control the appearance of the text written to a file.

Using the PadLeft and PadRight Methods

You can use the PadLeft and PadRight methods to pad a string with a character until the string is a specified length. The syntax of the PadLeft method is *stringvariable*.**PadLeft**(*length*[, *character*]), and the syntax of the PadRight method is *stringvariable*.**PadRight**(*length*[, *character*]). In each syntax, *stringvariable* is the name of the String variable that contains the string you want to pad. *Length* is an integer that represents the desired length of the string—in other words, the total number of characters you want the string to contain. The *character* argument is the character that each method uses to pad the string until it reaches the desired *length*. Notice that the *character* argument is optional in each syntax; if omitted, the default *character* is the space character.

The **PadLeft method** pads the string on the left—in other words, it inserts the padded characters at the beginning of the string; doing so right-aligns the characters within the string. The **PadRight method**, on the other hand, pads the string on the right, which inserts the padded characters at the end of the string and left-aligns the characters within the string. Figure 9-12 shows examples of using the PadLeft and PadRight methods to pad strings.

Examples and results

Example 1
```
Dim strName As String = "Sue", strNewName As String
strNewName = strName.PadRight(10)
```

Result
assigns "Sue   " (the string "Sue" and seven spaces) to the strNewName variable

Example 2
```
Dim strName As String = "Sue"
strName = strName.PadRight(10)
```

Result
assigns "Sue   " (the string "Sue" and seven spaces) to the strName variable

Example 3
```
Dim sngNetPay As Single = 767.89, strNet As String
strNet = Format(sngNetPay, "currency")
strNet = strNet.PadLeft(15, "*")
```

Result
assigns "********$767.89" to the strNet variable

Example 4
```
Dim sngNetPay As Single = 767.89, strNet As String
strNet = Format(sngNetPay, "currency").PadLeft(15, "*")
```

Result
assigns "********$767.89" to the strNet variable

Example 5
```
Dim intNum as Integer = 42, strNum As String
strNum = intNum.ToString.PadLeft(5)
```

Result
assigns "   42" (three spaces and the string "42") to the strNum variable

Figure 9-12: Examples of the PadLeft and PadRight methods

When processing the `strNewName = strName.PadRight(10)` statement shown in Example 1, the computer first makes a copy of the string stored in the strName variable. It then pads the copied string with space characters until the string contains exactly 10 characters. In this case, the computer uses seven space characters, which it inserts at the end of the string. The computer then assigns the resulting string—"Sue   "—to the strNewName variable. Notice that the `strNewName = strName.PadRight(10)` statement does not change the contents of the strName variable. To assign "Sue   " to the strName variable, you would need to use the `strName = strName.PadRight(10)` statement shown in Example 2.

When processing the `strNet = Format(sngNetPay, "currency")` statement shown in Example 3 in Figure 9-12, the computer first makes a copy of the number stored in the sngNetPay variable. It then uses the Format function to format the number, and assigns the function's return value—the string $767.89"—to the strNet variable. The computer then processes the `strNet = strNet.PadLeft(15, "*")` statement. When processing the statement, it first makes a copy of the string stored in the strNet variable. It then pads the copied string with asterisks until the string contains exactly 15 characters. In this case, the computer inserts eight asterisks at the beginning of the string. The computer assigns the resulting string ("********$767.89") to the strNet variable.

The code shown in Example 4 produces the same result as the code shown in Example 3. Notice, however, that Example 4's code combines the Format function and the PadLeft method in one assignment statement, like this: `strNet = Format(sngNetPay, "currency").PadLeft(15, "*")`. When processing the statement, the computer first makes a copy of the number stored in the sngNetPay variable, and then uses the Format function to format the number. However, rather than assigning the resulting string ("$767.89") to the strNet variable, as it does in Example 3's code, the computer pads the "$767.89" string with asterisks before assigning the resulting string "********$767.89" to the strNet variable. Notice that the Format function is processed before the PadLeft method.

Example 5 in Figure 9-12 shows how you can use the **ToString method** to convert a number to a string, and then use the PadLeft method to pad the string with space characters. The ToString method's syntax is *variablename*.**ToString**, where *variablename* is the name of a numeric variable. When processing the `strNum = intNum.ToString.PadLeft(5)` statement, the computer first makes a copy of the number stored in the intNum variable. The ToString method tells the computer to convert the copied number to a string, and the PadLeft method tells the computer to pad the string with space characters until it contains exactly five characters. The computer assigns the resulting string ("   42") to the strNum variable. Here again, notice that the computer processes the ToString method before processing the PadLeft method.

You can use the PadLeft and PadRight methods to align columns of information in a sequential access file, as shown in Figure 9-13.

Examples and results

Example 1
```
For intRegion = 1 To 3
     strSales = InputBox("Sales amount", "Sales")
     strSales = Format(strSales, "standard")
     objStreamWriter.WriteLine(strSales.PadLeft(8))
Next intRegion
```

Result (assuming the user enters the following sales amounts: 645.75, 1200, 40.80
```
  645.75
1,200.00
   40.80
```

Figure 9-13: Examples of aligning columns in a sequential access file

Examples and results

Example 2
```
objStreamWriter.WriteLine("Name" & Space(11) & "Age")
strName = InputBox("Name:", "Name")
Do While strName <> ""
     strAge = InputBox("Age:", "Age")
     objStreamWriter.WriteLine(strName.PadRight(15) & strAge)
     strName = InputBox("Name:", "Name")
Loop
```

Result (assuming the user enters the following names and ages: Janice, 23, Sue, 67)
```
Name           Age
Janice         23
Sue            67
```

Figure 9-13: Examples of aligning columns in a sequential access file (continued)

Example 1's code shows how you can align a column of numbers by the decimal point. First, you use the Format function to ensure that each number in the column has the same number of digits to the right of the decimal point. You then use the PadLeft method to pad the number with spaces; this right-aligns the number within the column. Because each number has the same number of digits to the right of the decimal point, aligning each number on the right will, in effect, align each by its decimal point.

Example 2's code shows how you can align the second column of information when the first column contains strings whose lengths vary. To do so, you first use either the PadRight or PadLeft method to ensure that each string in the first column contains the same number of characters. You then concatenate the padded string to the information in the second column before writing the concatenated string to the file. The code shown in Example 2, for instance, uses the PadRight method to ensure that each name in the first column contains exactly 15 characters. It then concatenates the 15 characters with the age stored in the strAge variable, and then writes the concatenated string to the file. Because each name has 15 characters, each age will automatically appear beginning in character position 16 in the file.

Now learn how to read information from a sequential access file.

Reading Information from a Sequential Access File

You use the **ReadLine method** to read a line of text from a sequential access file. A **line** is defined as a sequence of characters followed by the line terminator character. The string returned by the ReadLine method contains only the sequence of characters contained in the line; it does not include the line terminator character.

The syntax of the ReadLine method is *variablename*.**ReadLine**(), where *variablename* is the name of a StreamReader object variable. Figure 9-14 shows examples of using the ReadLine method to read lines of text from a sequential access file.

Examples and results

Example 1
```
Debug.WriteLine(objStreamReader.Readline())
```

Result
reads a line from a sequential access file, and then displays the line (excluding the line terminator character) in the Output window

Example 2
```
strLine = objStreamReader.Readline()
```

Result
reads a line from a sequential access file, and then assigns the line (excluding the line terminator character) to the strLine variable

Example 3
```
Do Until objStreamReader.Peek = -1
    strLine = objStreamReader.ReadLine()
    MessageBox.Show(strLine, "Line", _
        MessageBoxButtons.OK, MessageBoxIcon.Information)
Loop
```

Result
reads a sequential access file, line by line; assigns each line (excluding the line terminator character) to the strLine variable and displays each line in a message box

Figure 9-14: Examples of the ReadLine method

The `Debug.WriteLine(objStreamReader.ReadLine())` statement shown in Example 1 reads a line of text from a sequential access file, and then displays the line, excluding the line terminator character, in the Output window. The `strLine = objStreamReader.ReadLine()` statement shown in Example 2 also reads a line of text from a sequential access file; however, it assigns the line, excluding the line terminator character, to the strLine variable.

In most cases, an application will need to read each line of text contained in a sequential access file, one line at a time. You can do so using a repetition structure along with the Peek method, as shown in Example 3 in Figure 9-14. The syntax of the Peek method is *variablename*.**Peek**, where *variablename* is the name of a StreamReader object variable. The **Peek method** "peeks" into the file to see whether it contains another character to read. If it does, the Peek method returns the character; otherwise, it returns the number -1. The `Do Until objStreamReader.Peek = -1` clause shown in Example 3 tells the computer to process the loop instructions, which read a line of text and then display the line (excluding the line terminator character) in a message box, until the Peek method returns the number -1, which indicates that there are no more characters to read.

The last step in the sequential access file procedure (shown earlier in Figure 9-6) is to use the StreamWriter or StreamReader object to close the file.

Closing a Sequential Access File

To prevent the loss of data, you should use the **Close method** to close a sequential access file as soon as you are finished using it. The syntax of the Close method is *variablename*.**Close()**, where *variablename* is the name of either a StreamReader or StreamWriter object variable. Figure 9-15 shows two examples of using the Close method to close sequential access files. The first example closes an input file, and the second example closes an output file.

Examples and results
Example 1 `objStreamReader.Close()` **Result** closes the file associated with the objStreamReader object
Example 2 `objStreamWriter.Close()` **Result** closes the file associated with the objStreamWriter object

Figure 9-15: Examples of the Close method

Now view an application that demonstrates most of what you have learned so far about files.

The File Application

On your computer's hard disk is an application that allows you to save information to and read information from a sequential access file.

To open the File application:

1   Start Microsoft Visual Studio .NET, if necessary, and then close the Start Page window. Click **File** on the menu bar, and then click **Open Solution**. The Open Solution dialog box opens. Open the **File Solution** (File Solution.sln) file, which is contained in the VBNET\Tut09\File Solution folder.

2   If the designer window is not open, right-click **File Form.vb** in the Solution Explorer window, then click **View Designer**.

3   Auto-hide the Toolbox, Solution Explorer, and Properties windows, if necessary. The File application's user interface is shown in Figure 9-16.

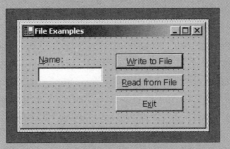

Figure 9-16: File application's user interface

The interface contains one text box, one label, and three buttons. You use the Write to File button to write the name entered in the Name text box to a sequential access file named file.txt. You use the Read from File button to read the file.txt file, line by line, and display each line in a message box. You use the Exit button to end the application.

First, view and test the code contained in the Write to File button's Click event procedure.

To view and test the Write to File button's Click event procedure:

1 Right-click the **form**, and then click **View Code**. Locate the WriteButton Click event procedure, which is shown in Figure 9-17.

```
Private Sub WriteButton_Click(ByVal sender As Object, ByVal e As System.EventArgs) F
    'declare a StreamWriter object variable
    Dim objStreamWriter As System.IO.StreamWriter
    'create a StreamWriter object by opening the file for append
    objStreamWriter = System.IO.File.AppendText("file.txt")
    'write a line of text to the file
    objStreamWriter.WriteLine(Me.NameTextBox.Text)
    'clear the Name text box, then send the focus to the text box
    Me.NameTextBox.Text = ""
    Me.NameTextBox.Focus()
    'close the file
    objStreamWriter.Close()
End Sub
```

Figure 9-17: WriteButton Click event procedure

Notice that the procedure declares a StreamWriter object variable named objStreamWriter. It then uses the AppendText method to both open the file.txt file and create a StreamWriter object. The procedure assigns the StreamWriter object's address to the objStreamWriter variable. Next, the procedure uses the WriteLine method to write the contents of the Name text box to the file.txt file. After clearing the contents of the Name text box and also sending the focus to the text box, the procedure uses the Close method to close the file.txt file.

2 Click **Debug** on the menu bar, and then click **Start**.

Use the application to enter three names in the file.txt file.

3 Type **Ned** in the Name text box, and then press **Enter** to select the Write to File button, which is the default button on the form. Type **Nancy** in the Name text box, and then press **Enter**. Type **Pamela** in the Name text box, and then press **Enter**.

4 Click the **Exit** button to end the application. When you return to the Code editor window, close the Output window.

Now verify that the three names were added to the file.txt file.

5 Click **File** on the menu bar, then point to **Open**, and then click **File**. The Open File dialog box opens.

6 Open the **bin** folder, which is contained in the VBNET\File Solution\File Project folder on your computer's hard disk. Click **file.txt** in the list of filenames, and then click the **Open** button. The contents of the file.txt file appear in a window, as shown in Figure 9-18. Notice that the WriteLine method writes each name on a separate line in the file.

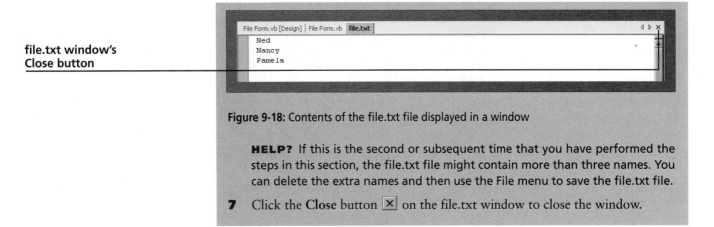

file.txt window's Close button

Figure 9-18: Contents of the file.txt file displayed in a window

> **HELP?** If this is the second or subsequent time that you have performed the steps in this section, the file.txt file might contain more than three names. You can delete the extra names and then use the File menu to save the file.txt file.

7 Click the **Close** button ☒ on the file.txt window to close the window.

Next, view and test the code contained in the Read from File button's Click event procedure.

To view and test the Read from File button's Click event procedure:

1 Locate the ReadButton Click event procedure, which is shown in Figure 9-19.

```
Private Sub ReadButton_Click(ByVal sender As Object, ByVal e As System.EventArgs) He
    'declare variables
    Dim strLine As String, objStreamReader As System.IO.StreamReader
    'determine whether the file.txt file exists
    If System.IO.File.Exists("file.txt") = True Then
        'create a StreamReader object by opening the file for input
        objStreamReader = System.IO.File.OpenText("file.txt")
        'process the loop instructions until there are no more characters to read
        Do Until objStreamReader.Peek = -1
            'read a line of text from the file
            strLine = objStreamReader.ReadLine()
            'display the line in a message box
            MessageBox.Show(strLine, "File Example", _
                MessageBoxButtons.OK, MessageBoxIcon.Information)
        Loop
        'close the file
        objStreamReader.Close()
    Else
        'display an appropriate message
        MessageBox.Show("The file.txt file does not exist.", "File Example", _
                    MessageBoxButtons.OK, MessageBoxIcon.Information)
    End If
End Sub
```

Figure 9-19: ReadButton Click event procedure

Notice that the procedure declares a StreamReader object variable named objStreamReader. It then uses the Exists method to determine whether the file.txt file exists. If the file does not exist, an appropriate message is displayed in a message box. However, if the file does exist, the procedure uses the OpenText method to both open the file and create a StreamReader object. The procedure assigns the StreamReader object's address to the objStreamReader variable. Next, the procedure uses a repetition structure, the Peek method, the ReadLine method, and the MessageBox.Show method to read each line in the file and display each line in a message box. Lastly, the procedure uses the Close method to close the file.txt file.

2 Click **Debug** on the menu bar, and then click **Start**.

Use the application to display the contents of the file.txt file, one line at a time, in a message box.

3 Click the **Read from File** button. The first name contained in the file.txt file, Ned, appears in a message box, as shown in Figure 9-20.

first name contained in the file

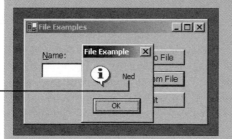

Figure 9-20: Message box showing the first name in the file

4 Click the **OK** button to close the message box. The second name contained in the file.txt file, Nancy, appears in a message box.

5 Click the **OK** button to close the message box. The third name contained in the file.txt file, Pamela, appears in a message box.

6 Click the **OK** button to close the message box. At this point, the ReadButton Click event procedure ends.

7 Click the **Exit** button to end the application. When you return to the Code editor window, close the Output window, then close the Code editor window.

8 Click **File** on the menu bar, and then click **Close Solution**.

You now have completed Lesson A. You can either take a break or complete the end-of-lesson questions and exercises before moving on to the next lesson.

SUMMARY

To use a sequential access file in an application:

■ Follow the procedure shown in Figure 9-6.

To declare a StreamWriter or StreamReader object variable:

■ Use the syntax *accessibility variablename* **As System.IO.***objecttype*, where *variablename* is the name of the object variable, and *objecttype* is either StreamWriter or StreamReader. *Accessibility* is typically either the keyword Dim or the keyword Private.

To open a sequential access file for input:

■ Use the syntax **System.IO.File.OpenText**(*filename*), where *filename* is the name of the file (including an optional folder path) that you want to open. If *filename* does not exist, the computer displays an error message in a message box.

■ The OpenText method creates a StreamReader object and allows the computer to read the file.

To open a sequential access file for append:

■ Use the syntax **System.IO.File.AppendText**(*filename*), where *filename* is the name of the file (including an optional folder path) that you want to open. If *filename* does not exist, the computer creates the file for you.

■ The AppendText method creates a StreamWriter object and allows the computer to write information to the end of the file.

To open a sequential access file for output:

■ Use the syntax **System.IO.File.CreateText**(*filename*), where *filename* is the name of the file (including an optional folder path) that you want to open. If *filename* exists, its contents are erased before any data is written to the file.

■ The CreateText method creates a StreamWriter object and allows the computer to write information to a new, empty file.

To assign the object created by the OpenText, CreateText, and AppendText methods to an object variable:

■ Use the syntax *variablename* = **System.IO.File**.*method*(*filename*), where *variablename* is the name of either a StreamReader or StreamWriter object.

To determine whether a file exists:

■ Use the Exists method. The method's syntax is **System.IO.File.Exists**(*filename*), where *filename* is the name of the file (including an optional folder path) whose existence you want to verify. The Exists method returns the Boolean value True if *filename* exists; otherwise, it returns the Boolean value False.

To write information to a sequential access file:

■ Use either the Write method or the WriteLine method.

■ The syntax of the Write method is *variablename*.**Write**(*data*), where *variablename* is the name of a StreamWriter object variable. The Write method writes the *data* to the file and then positions the file pointer at the end of the last character written.

■ The syntax of the WriteLine method is *variablename*.**WriteLine**(*data*), where *variablename* is the name of a StreamWriter object variable. The WriteLine method writes the *data* and a line terminator character to the file. The line terminator character positions the file pointer at the beginning of the next line in the file.

To write spaces to a sequential access file:

■ Use the Space function. The function's syntax is **Space**(*number*), where *number* represents the number of spaces you want to write.

To pad a string with a character until the string is a specified length:

■ Use the PadLeft method to pad a string on the left, and the PadRight method to pad a string on the right.

■ The syntax of the PadLeft method is *stringvariable*.**PadLeft**(*length*[, *character*]). The syntax of the PadRight method is *stringvariable*.**PadRight**(*length*[, *character*]). In each syntax, *stringvariable* is the name of the String variable that contains the string you want to pad. *Length* is an integer that represents the desired length of the string, and *character* is the character that each method uses to pad the string until it reaches the desired *length*. If the *character* argument is omitted, the default *character* is the space character.

■ The PadLeft method right-aligns the characters within a string, and the PadRight method left-aligns the characters.

To convert a number to a string:

■ Use the ToString method. The method's syntax is *variablename*.**ToString**, where *variablename* is the name of a numeric variable.

To read a line of text from a sequential access file:

■ Use the ReadLine method. The method's syntax is *variablename*.**ReadLine**(), where *variablename* is the name of a StreamReader object variable.
■ The ReadLine method returns a string that contains all of the characters in the line, excluding the line terminator character.

To determine whether a sequential access file contains another character to read:

■ Use the Peek method. The method's syntax is *variablename*.**Peek**, where *variablename* is the name of a StreamReader object variable.
■ If the file contains another character to read, the Peek method returns the character; otherwise, it returns the number -1.

To close a sequential access file:

■ Use the Close method. The method's syntax is *variablename*.**Close**(), where *variablename* is the name of either a StreamReader or StreamWriter object variable.

QUESTIONS

1. Which of the following creates an object variable that can be used when reading a sequential access file?
   a. `Dim objCharReader As System.IO.CharReader`
   b. `Dim objCharacterReader As System.IO.CharacterReader`
   c. `Dim objFileReader As System.IO.FileReader`
   d. `Dim objSequenceReader As System.IO.SequenceReader`
   e. `Dim objStreamReader As System.IO.StreamReader`

2. Which of the following opens the names.txt file and allows the computer to write information to the end of the existing data in the file?
   a. `System.IO.File.AddText("names.txt")`
   b. `System.IO.File.AppendText("names.txt")`
   c. `System.IO.File.CreateText("names.txt")`
   d. `System.IO.File.InsertText("names.txt")`
   e. `System.IO.File.OpenText("names.txt")`

3. The OpenText method creates a _____.
   a. StreamReader object
   b. StreamReader object variable
   c. StreamWriter object
   d. StreamWriter object variable
   e. Both a and c.

4. If the file you want to open exists, the _____ method erases the file's contents.
- a. AddText
- b. AppendText
- c. CreateText
- d. InsertText
- e. OpenText

5. If the file you want to open does not exist, the _____ method displays an error message in a message box.
- a. AddText
- b. AppendText
- c. CreateText
- d. InsertText
- e. OpenText

6. Which of the following can be used to determine whether the "employ.txt" file exists?
- a. `If System.IO.File.Exists("employ.txt") = True Then`
- b. `If System.IO.File("employ.txt").Exists = True Then`
- c. `If System.IO.Exists("employ.txt") = True Then`
- d. `If System.IO.Exists.File("employ.txt") = True Then`
- e. None of the above.

7. Which of the following can be used to write the string "Your pay is $56" to a sequential access file? (Assume that the intPay variable contains the number 56.)
- a. `objStreamWriter.Write("Your pay is $")`
  `objStreamWriter.WriteLine(intPay)`
- b. `objStreamWriter.WriteLine("Your pay is $" & intPay)`
- c. `objStreamWriter.Write("Your ")`
  `objStreamWriter.Write("pay is ")`
  `objStreamWriter.WriteLine("$" & intPay)`
- d. `objStreamWriter.WriteLine("Your pay is $" & intPay.ToString)`
- e. All of the above.

8. Which of the following can be used to write 15 space characters to a sequential access file?
- a. `objStreamWriter.WriteLine(Blank(15))`
- b. `objStreamWriter.WriteLine(Chars(15))`
- c. `objStreamWriter.WriteLine(Blank(15, " "))`
- d. `objStreamWriter.WriteLine(Space(15))`
- e. `objStreamWriter.WriteLine(Space(15, " "))`

9. Assume that the strState variable contains the string "Florida". Which of the following assigns six spaces followed by the contents of the strState variable to the strState variable?
- a. `strState = Space(6) & strState`
- b. `strState = strState.PadLeft(13)`
- c. `strState = strState.PadLeft(6)`
- d. Both a and b.
- e. Both a and c.

10. You use the _____ method to left-align the characters in a string.
- a. AlignLeft
- b. CharLeft
- c. PadLeft
- d. StringLeft
- e. None of the above.

11. Assume that the strMsg variable contains the string "Great job". Which of the following assigns the contents of the strMsg variable followed by four exclamation points (!) to the strNewMsg variable?

    a. `strNewMsg = strMsg.PadLeft(4, "!")`
    b. `strNewMsg = strMsg.PadLeft(13, "!")`
    c. `strNewMsg = strMsg.PadRight(4, "!")`
    d. `strNewMsg = strMsg.PadRight(13, "!")`
    e. `strNewMsg = strMsg.PadRight("!!!!")`

12. Which of the following assigns the contents of the intAge variable, converted to a string, to the strAge variable?

    a. `strAge = intAge.ToString`
    b. `strAge = String(intAge)`
    c. `strAge = ToString(intAge)`
    d. `strAge =  ToString.intAge`
    e. None of the above.

13. Which of the following reads a line of text from a sequential access file, and assigns the line (excluding the line terminator character) to the strText variable?

    a. `objStreamReader.Read(strText)`
    b. `objStreamReader.ReadLine(strText)`
    c. `strText = objStreamReader.ReadLine()`
    d. `strText = objStreamReader.ReadLine(line)`
    e. `strText = objStreamReader.Read(line)`

14. The Peek method returns _____ if the sequential access file does not contain any more characters to read.

    a. -1
    b. 0 (zero)
    c. 1 (one)
    d. the last character read
    e. the line terminator character

15. You can use the Close method to close files opened for _____.

    a. append
    b. input
    c. output
    d. All of the above.

EXERCISES

1. Write the statement to declare a local StreamReader object variable named objStreamReader.

2. Write the statement to open a sequential access file named jansales.txt for input. Assign the resulting StreamReader object to the objStreamReader variable.

3. Write the statement to open a sequential access file named firstQtr.txt for append. Assign the resulting StreamWriter object to the objStreamWriter variable.

4. Write the statement to open a sequential access file named febsales.txt for output. Assign the resulting StreamWriter object to the objStreamWriter variable.

5. Write the Visual Basic .NET code to determine whether the jansales.txt file exists. If it does, the code should display the string "File exists" in the Output window; otherwise, it should display the string "File does not exist" in the Output window.

6. Assume you want to write the string "Employee" and the string "Name" to the sequential access file associated with the objStreamWriter object variable. Each string should appear on a separate line in the file. Write the Visual Basic .NET code to accomplish this task.

7. Assume you want to write the contents of the strCapital variable followed by 20 spaces, the contents of the strState variable, and the line terminator character to the sequential access file associated with the objStreamWriter variable. Write the Visual Basic .NET code to accomplish this task.

8. Assume that the sngSales variable contains the number 2356.75. Write the statement to assign the contents of the sngSales variable, formatted using the Currency format style, to the strSales variable. The statement also should right-align the contents of the strSales variable, which should contain a total of 15 characters.

9. Assume you want the strAward variable to contain 10 characters, which should be right-aligned in the variable. Write the statement to accomplish this task. Use the asterisk character to pad the variable.

10. Write the statement that will ensure that the strName variable contains 30 characters, which should be left-aligned in the variable. Use the space character to pad the variable.

11. Write the statement to read a line of text from the sequential access file associated with the objStreamReader variable. Assign the line of text (excluding the line terminator character) to the strText variable.

12. Assume you want to read a sequential access file, line by line, and then display each line in the Output window. The file is associated with the objStreamReader variable. Write the Visual Basic .NET code to accomplish this task.

13. Write the statement to close the jansales.txt file, which is associated with the objStreamWriter variable.

14. In this exercise, you modify the File application that you viewed in the lesson. The modified application allows the user to either create a new file or append information to the end of an existing file.
    a. Use Windows to make a copy of the File Solution folder, which is contained in the VBNET\Tut09 folder. Change the name of the folder to Modified File Solution.
    b. If necessary, start Visual Studio .NET. Open the File Solution (File Solution.sln) file, which is contained in the VBNET\Tut09\Modified File Solution folder. If the designer window is not open, right-click the form file's name in the Solution Explorer window, then click View Designer.
    c. Open the Code editor window. Change the filename in the ReadButton Click event procedure from "file.txt" to "file2.txt". (You will need to change the name in four places.)
    d. Change the filename in the WriteButton Click event procedure from "file.txt" to "file2.txt".
    e. When the WriteButton Click event procedure is processed the first time, the procedure should determine whether the file2.txt exists before the file is opened. If the file exists, the procedure should use the MessageBox.Show method to ask the user if he or she wants to replace the existing file. Include Yes and No buttons in the message box. The procedure should take the appropriate action based on the user's response.
    f. Save the solution, then start the application. Type Jan in the Name text box, and then press Enter.

g.   Click the Exit button to end the application, then start the application again. Type Carol in the Name text box, and then press Enter. The application should ask if you want to replace the existing file. Click the No button.

h.   Click the Exit button to end the application, then use the File menu to open the file2.txt file in a window. The file should contain two names: Jan and Carol. Close the file2.txt window.

i.   Start the application again. Type Richard in the Name text box, and then press Enter. The application should ask if you want to replace the existing file. Click the Yes button.

j.   Click the Exit button to end the application, then use the File menu to open the file2.txt file in a window. The file should contain one name: Richard. Close the file2.txt window.

k.   Close the Output window, then close the solution.

Exercise 15 is a Discovery Exercise. Discovery Exercises, which may include topics that are not covered in this lesson, allow you to "discover" the solutions to problems on your own.

discovery ▶   **15.**   In this exercise, you learn about the Imports statement.

a.   Use Windows to make a copy of the File Solution folder, which is contained in the VBNET\Tut09 folder. Change the name of the folder to Imports File Solution.

b.   If necessary, start Visual Studio .NET. Open the File Solution (File Solution.sln) file, which is contained in the VBNET\Tut09\Imports File Solution folder. If the designer window is not open, right-click the form file's name in the Solution Explorer window, then click View Designer.

c.   Open the Code editor window. Change the filename in the ReadButton Click event procedure from "file.txt" to "file3.txt". (You will need to change the name in four places.)

d.   Change the filename in the WriteButton Click event procedure from "file.txt" to "file3.txt".

e.   Notice that "System.IO." appears in the Dim statements used to create the StreamWriter and StreamReader objects. It also appears in the statements used to open the file3.txt file, and in the statement used to determine whether the file3.txt file exists. System.IO is the name of a class; StreamWriter, StreamReader, File.OpenText, File.CreateText, File.AppendText, and File.Exists are members of the System.IO class.

f.   Remove each occurrence of "System.IO." (notice the period after IO) in the ReadButton Click and WriteButton Click event procedures. (*Hint*: Click Edit on the menu bar, then point to Find and Replace, and then click Replace. Type System.IO. in the Find what box, and leave the Replace with box empty.) Notice that, after removing each occurrence of "System.IO.", the Code editor displays a jagged line below the word StreamWriter, StreamReader, and File. Recall that a jagged line indicates that the Code editor does not recognize the underlined word.

g.   Insert a blank line above the statement Public Class FileForm, which is the first line of code. In the blank line, type Imports System.IO and press Enter. Notice that the Code editor removes the jagged lines from the code.

h.   Save the solution, then start the application. Test the application appropriately.

i.   Click the Exit button to end the application.

j.   Close the Output window, then close the solution.

LESSON B

objectives

After completing this lesson, you will be able to:

- Add a DateTimePicker control to a form
- Control the appearance of a DateTimePicker control
- Format the text that appears in a DateTimePicker control
- Set and retrieve the information stored in a DateTimePicker control
- Retrieve the system date and time
- Display a form immediately

Using a DateTimePicker Control

Completing the Carriage House Application's User Interface

Recall that your task in this tutorial is to create an application for Marge Bartowski, the Manager of Special Events at Carriage House. The application should allow Ms. Bartowski to keep track of the special events scheduled for each month, and then print a Special Events report that lists the name, date, and price of each event.

On your computer's hard disk is a partially completed Carriage House application. You complete the application's user interface in this lesson.

To open the Carriage House application:

1 Start Microsoft Visual Studio .NET, if necessary, and then close the Start Page window. Click **File** on the menu bar, and then click **Open Solution**. The Open Solution dialog box opens. Open the **Carriage** (Carriage.sln) file, which is contained in the VBNET\Tut09\Carriage folder.

2 If the designer window is not open, right-click **Carriage Form.vb** in the Solution Explorer window, then click **View Designer**.

3 Auto-hide the Toolbox, Solution Explorer, and Properties windows, if necessary. The Carriage House application's user interface is shown in Figure 9-21.

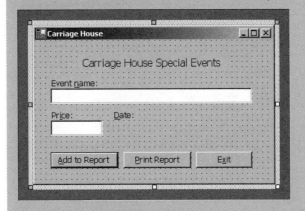

Figure 9-21: Carriage House application's user interface

The interface contains two text boxes for the event's name and price. Missing from the interface is a DateTimePicker control for selecting the date of the event, and a PrintDocument control for printing the Special Events report. You add the DateTimePicker control in this lesson, and the PrintDocument control in Lesson C.

Adding a DateTimePicker Control to a Form

The **DateTimePicker control** allows the user to select either a date or time, and then display the selected information in a specified format.

tip

▶ The DateTimePicker control on the form is an instance of the DateTimePicker class.

To add a DateTimePicker control to the form, then lock the controls and set the TabIndex property:

1 Click the **DateTimePicker tool** in the toolbox, and then drag a DateTimePicker control to the form. Position the control immediately below the Date: label. When you add a DateTimePicker control to the form, the control displays the current date according to your computer system's clock.

2 Set the DateTimePicker1 control's Name property to **EventDateTimePicker**. Set its Location property to **120, 120**, and set its Size property to **216, 23**.

3 Click the **form**. See Figure 9-22. (The date shown in the DateTimePicker control on your screen may be different from the date shown in the figure.)

the date on your screen might be different

Figure 9-22: DateTimePicker control shown in the interface

Now lock the controls on the form, and then set the TabIndex property for each control.

4 Right-click the **form**, and then click **Lock Controls**.

5 Click **View** on the menu bar, and then click **Tab Order**. Use Figure 9-23 to set each control's TabIndex property to the appropriate value.

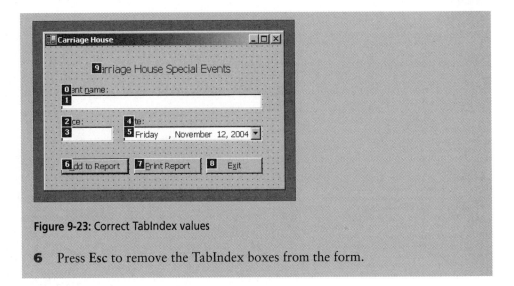

Figure 9-23: Correct TabIndex values

6   Press **Esc** to remove the TabIndex boxes from the form.

Now start the application and observe how the DateTimePicker control works.

To observe how the DateTimePicker control works:

1   Click **File** on the menu bar, and then click **Save All**. Click **Debug** on the menu bar, and then click **Start**.

Recall that the date displayed in the DateTimePicker control is the current date according to your computer system's clock. The date indicates the day of the week, the month name, the day number, and the year number. You can use the calendar feature of the DateTimePicker control to display a different date in the control.

2   Click the DateTimePicker control's **list arrow** button. A calendar for the current month opens, as shown in Figure 9-24. Notice that the current date appears at the bottom of the calendar. (Do not be concerned if your DateTimePicker control displays the calendar for a different month or year, or if the current date shown in the calendar is different from the one shown in Figure 9-24.)

right arrow button

list arrow button

left arrow button

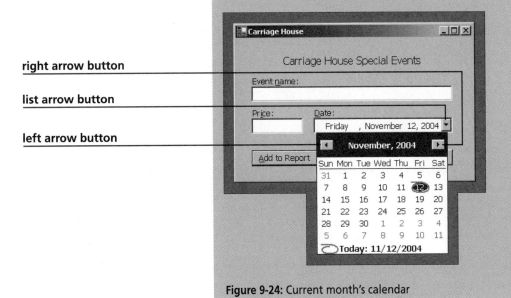

Figure 9-24: Current month's calendar

You can use the left and right arrow buttons located at the top of the calendar to display the calendar for the previous and next month, respectively.

3   Click the **left arrow** button several times, and then click the **right arrow** button several times. Each time you click the left arrow button, the previous month's calendar appears. Similarly, each time you click the right arrow button, the next month's calendar appears.

4   Use either the left arrow button or the right arrow button to display the calendar for February.

5   Click the number **11** in the calendar. "Wednesday, February 11, 2004" appears in the DateTimePicker control. (Do not be concerned if your DateTimePicker control displays a different year number or day of the week.)

You also can change the date displayed in the DateTimePicker control by clicking the month name, day number, or year number in the date, and then pressing the up and down arrow keys on your keyboard. You try this next.

6   Click **February** in the date; this highlights the name, as shown in Figure 9-25.

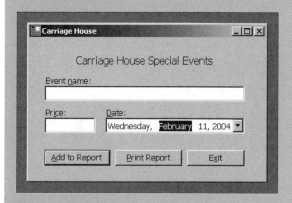

Figure 9-25: Month name highlighted in the DateTimePicker control

7   Press the **up arrow key** (↑) on your keyboard several times. Each time you press ↑, the name of the next month appears in the DateTimePicker control. Notice that the day of the week displayed in the control also changes.

8   Now press the **down arrow key** (↓) on your keyboard several times. Each time you press ↓, the name of the previous month appears in the DateTimePicker control. The day of the week displayed in the control also changes.

9   Click **11** (the day number) in the date, then press ↑ twice to change the day number to **13**.

You also can change the day and year number by clicking the current number and then simply typing a new number.

10   Click the **year number** in the date, then type **2000** to change the year number to 2000.

11   Click the **Exit** button to end the application. When you return to the designer window, close the Output window.

Next, you learn how to use the ShowUpDown property to control the appearance of the DateTimePicker control.

The ShowUpDown Property

The DateTimePicker control's **ShowUpDown property** determines whether a list arrow button or up and down arrow buttons appear on the control. If the property is set to its default value, False, the control contains a list arrow button. Recall that when you click the list arrow button while an application is running, the DateTimePicker control displays a calendar that you can use to select a date.

If, on the other hand, the ShowUpDown property is set to True, up and down arrow buttons appear on the control. You can use the buttons to change the date or time displayed in the DateTimePicker control. Unlike the list arrow button, however, the up and down arrow buttons do not display a calendar. Typically, you set a DateTimePicker control's ShowUpDown property to True when the control displays times, because a calendar is not required to set a time. A DateTimePicker control that displays dates, however, usually has its ShowUpDown property set to False, because this setting offers the user the convenience of selecting a date from a calendar. In the next set of steps, you observe the effect of setting the ShowUpDown property to True.

To observe the effect of setting the ShowUpDown property to True:

1 Change the EventDateTimePicker control's ShowUpDown property to **True**. Notice that up and down arrow buttons (rather than a list arrow button) appear on the control, as shown in Figure 9-26.

up and down
arrow buttons

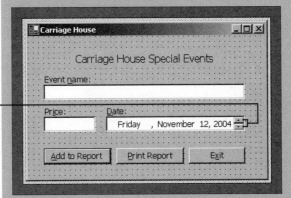

Figure 9-26: Effect of setting the ShowUpDown property to True

2 Start the application. Click the **year number** in the date; this highlights the year number.

3 Click the **up arrow** button on the control several times, and then click the **down arrow** button several times. Each time you click the up arrow button, the year number increases by one. Each time you click the down arrow button, the year number decreases by one.

4 Click the **Exit** button to end the application. When you return to the designer window, close the Output window.

Now return the EventDateTimePicker control's ShowUpDown property to its original setting.

5 Set the EventDateTimePicker control's ShowUpDown property to **False**.

In addition to controlling the appearance of the DateTimePicker control, you also can control the appearance of the text displayed in the control; you do so using the control's Format property.

The Format Property

You can use the **Format property** to control the format (style) of the date or time displayed in the DateTimePicker control. Figure 9-27 lists the valid settings for the Format property and describes the purpose of each setting. The figure also includes examples of dates and times formatted using each setting.

Setting	Purpose	Examples
Long	(default) displays a date using the Long format: dddd, MMMM dd, yyyy	Wednesday, February 11, 2004 Monday , November 08, 2004
Short	displays a date using the Short format: M/d/yyyy	2/11/2004 11/ 8/2004
Time	displays a time using the Time format: h:mm:ss tt	6:18:07 AM 10:09:15 PM
Custom	displays a date or time using the format specified in the CustomFormat property	Feb 11, Wednesday 6:18 AM

Figure 9-27: Settings for the DateTimePicker control's Format property

The Long setting is the default setting for the Format property and displays a date using the format "dddd, MMMM dd, yyyy". In the format, "dddd" represents the full name for the day of the week (for example, Monday) and "MMMM" represents the full name for the month (for example, January). The "dd" in the format represents a two-digit day number. If the day number contains only one digit, the day number is displayed with a leading zero; for instance, day number 3 is displayed as 03. The "yyyy" in the format represents the four-digit year number. As Figure 9-27 indicates, the Long setting displays the date "February 11, 2004" as "Wednesday, February 11, 2004". It displays the date "November 8, 2004" as "Monday   , November 08, 2004".

The Short setting displays a date using the format "M/d/yyyy", where "M" is a one- or two-digit month number, "d" is a one- or two-digit day number, and "yyyy" is a four-digit year number. If the month or day number contains only one digit, the number is displayed with a leading space character. As Figure 9-27 indicates, the Short setting displays the date "February 11, 2004" as " 2/11/2004", and the date "November 8, 2004" as "11/ 8/2004".

You use the Format property's Time setting to display a time (instead of a date) in the DateTimePicker control. The time is displayed using the format "h:mm:ss tt", where "h" is a one- or two-digit hour number, "mm" is a two-digit minute number, "ss" is a two-digit second number, and "tt" is either the abbreviation AM or the abbreviation PM. If the minute or second number contains only one digit, the number is displayed with a leading zero, as shown in the Time format examples in Figure 9-27.

You use the Format property's Custom setting when you want to display a date or time using a format other than Long, Short, or Time. When the Format property is set to Custom, Visual Basic .NET displays the date or time using the format entered in the CustomFormat property. For example, if the CustomFormat property contains the format "MMM dd, dddd", the DateTimePicker control displays the date "February 11, 2004" as "Feb 11, Wednesday". Similarly, if the CustomFormat property contains the format "h:mm tt", the DateTimePicker control displays the time "6:18:32 AM" as "6:18 AM". You learn more about the CustomFormat property in Discovery Exercise 8 at the end of this lesson.

In the next set of steps, you observe the effect of setting a DateTimePicker control's Format property to Short and Time.

To set the EventDateTimePicker control's Format property:

1 Click the **EventDateTimePicker** control, then set the Format property to **Short**. The EventDateTimePicker control uses the format "M/d/yyyy" to display the date.

Next, display the current time in the EventDateTimePicker control.

2 Set the Format property to **Time**. The EventDateTimePicker control displays the current time using the format "h:mm:ss tt".

Now return the Format property to its default setting.

3 Set the Format property to **Long**, which displays the date using the format "dddd, MMMM dd, yyyy".

You can use the Value property to set and retrieve the date and/or time stored in a DateTimePicker control.

The Value Property

When you add a DateTimePicker control to a form, Visual Basic .NET retrieves the current date and time from your computer system's clock, and assigns both values to the DateTimePicker control's **Value property**. You can verify that fact by viewing the Value property in the Properties list.

To view the EventDateTimePicker control's Value property:

1 Scroll the Properties list until you see the Value property, then click **Value**. Notice that the Value property contains the current month number, a slash, the current day number, another slash, and the current year number. It also contains the current hour number, a colon, the current minute number, and either the abbreviation AM or the abbreviation PM.

HELP? If you cannot see the entire contents of the Value property, simply rest your mouse pointer on the property's Settings box. A box appears and shows the contents of the Value property.

> If you do not change the value stored in the Value property, Visual Basic .NET retrieves the current date and time and assigns both to the Value property each time the application is either opened by the programmer or started by the user. If you want the Value property to contain a specific date/time instead of the current date/time, you simply enter the desired date/time in the Value property. Set the Value property to "7/5/2001 9:07 AM".
>
> **2** Type **7/5/2001 9:07 AM** in the Value property, and then press **Enter**. Now when the Carriage House application is either opened or started, the Value property will contain "7/5/2001 9:07 AM" rather than the current date and time.

In addition to setting the Value property in the Properties window, you also can set it from code. You do so by creating a DateTime object, and then assigning the object to the DateTimePicker control's Value property. A **DateTime object** is simply an object that represents a date and an optional time. Figure 9-28 shows the syntax you use to set the Value property from code and includes several examples of using the syntax.

Syntax
objectname.**Value = New DateTime(***year, month, day*[, *hour, minute, second*]**)**

Examples and results

Example 1
```
Me.PayDateTimePicker.Value = New DateTime(2004, 2, 3)
```

Result
assigns the date "2/3/2004" to the Value property

Example 2
```
Me.PayDateTimePicker.Value = New DateTime(2004, 9, 7, 5, 30, 18)
```

Result
assigns the date "9/7/2004" and the time "5:30:18 AM" to the Value property

Example 3
```
Me.PayDateTimePicker.Value = New DateTime(2001, 1, 6, 17, 30, 18)
```

Result
assigns the date "1/6/2001" and the time "5:30:18 PM" to the Value property

Figure 9-28: Syntax and examples of setting the Value property from code

In the syntax, *objectname* is the name of a DateTimePicker control. *Year*, *month*, and *day* are integers that represent the desired date, and *hour*, *minute*, and *second* are integers that represent the desired time. Notice that the *hour*, *minute*, and *second* arguments are optional in the syntax. Also notice that the time entry is based on a 24-hour clock, referred to as military time. In other words, you use "5,

30, 18" to enter the time "5:30:18 AM", but you use "17, 30, 18" to enter the time "5:30:18 PM".

When the user selects a different date in the DateTimePicker control, the date entry in the Value property is automatically replaced with the selected date. Likewise, when the user selects a different time in the DateTimePicker control, the time entry in the Value property is replaced with the selected time.

Next, learn how to retrieve the date and time information stored in the Value property.

Retrieving the Information Stored in the Value Property

You use the syntax *objectname*.**Value**, where *objectname* is the name of a DateTimePicker control, to access both the date and time stored in the control's Value property. To access only the date entry in the Value property, you use the syntax *objectname*.**Value**.*formatmethod*, where *formatmethod* is either ToLongDateString or ToShortDateString. The **ToLongDateString method** returns the date formatted using the Long format (dddd, MMMM dd, yyyy), and the **ToShortDateString method** returns the date formatted using the Short format (M/d/yyyy). Similarly, to access only the time entry in the Value property, you use the syntax *objectname*.**Value**.*formatmethod*, where *formatmethod* is either ToLongTimeString or ToShortTimeString. The **ToLongTimeString method** returns the time formatted using the Long format (h:mm:ss tt), and the **ToShortTimeString method** returns the time formatted using the Short format (h:mm tt). Figure 9-29 shows examples of retrieving the date and/or time stored in a DateTimePicker control's Value property.

Note: for these examples, assume that the Value property contains "11/12/2004 9:07 AM"	
Examples	**Results**
`Me.PayDateTimePicker.Value`	11/12/2004 9:07:00 AM
`Me.PayDateTimePicker.Value.ToLongDateString`	Friday, November 12, 2004
`Me.PayDateTimePicker.Value.ToShortDateString`	11/12/2004
`Me.PayDateTimePicker.Value.ToLongTimeString`	9:07:00 AM
`Me.PayDateTimePicker.Value.ToShortTimeString`	9:07 AM

Figure 9-29: Examples of retrieving the date and/or time stored in the Value property

In addition to retrieving the entire date and/or time stored in the Value property, you also can retrieve individual elements of the date and time. For instance, you can retrieve the month number in the date and the hour number in the time. You retrieve an element in the date or time using the syntax *objectname*.**Value**.*elementname*, where *objectname* is the name of a DateTimePicker control and *elementname* is the name of the element you want to retrieve. Figure 9-30 shows examples of retrieving individual date and time elements from the Value property.

Note: for these examples, assume that the Value property contains "11/12/2004 9:07 AM"	
Examples	**Results**
`Me.PayDateTimePicker.Value.Month`	11
`Me.PayDateTimePicker.Value.Day`	12
`Me.PayDateTimePicker.Value.Year`	2004
`Me.PayDateTimePicker.Value.DayOfWeek`	5
`Me.PayDateTimePicker.Value.DayOfWeek.ToString`	Friday
`Me.PayDateTimePicker.Value.DayOfYear`	317
`Me.PayDateTimePicker.Value.Hour`	9
`Me.PayDateTimePicker.Value.Minute`	7
`Me.PayDateTimePicker.Value.Second`	0

Figure 9-30: Examples of retrieving date and time elements

> **tip**
>
> ▶ If the date contained in the Value property falls on a Sunday, then *object-name*.Value.DayOfWeek results in the number zero.

You can use a DateTimePicker control's Text property to retrieve the date or time that appears in the control.

The Text Property

The text that appears in a DateTimePicker control is stored in the control's **Text property**. Visual Basic .NET automatically assigns to the Text property the contents of the Value property formatted using the setting specified in the Format property; this is illustrated in Figure 9-31.

Value property	**Format property**	**Text property**
11/12/2004 9:07 AM	Long	Friday, November 12, 2004
11/12/2004 9:07 AM	Short	11/12/2004
11/12/2004 9:07 AM	Time	9:07:00 AM
11/12/2004 9:07 AM	Custom	determined by the format entered in the CustomFormat property

Figure 9-31: Illustration of the Value, Format, and Text properties

As Figure 9-31 indicates, if the DateTimePicker control's Value property contains "11/12/2004 9:07 AM" and its Format property is set to Long, then Visual Basic .NET assigns the text "Friday, November 12, 2004" to the control's Text property. Recall that the contents of a DateTimePicker control's Text property appears in the control. However, if the Format property is set to Short, then Visual Basic .NET assigns the text "11/12/2004" to the Text property. It assigns the text "9:07:00 AM" to the Text property if the Format property is set to Time. The text assigned to the Text property when the Format property is set to Custom depends on the format entered in the control's CustomFormat property. (Recall that you learn more about the CustomFormat property in Discovery Exercise 8 at the end of this lesson.)

Unlike the Value property, the Text property allows you to retrieve the formatted text that appears in a DateTimePicker control. The statement `strDate = Me.PayDateTimePicker.Text`, for example, assigns the formatted text that appears in the PayDateTimePicker control to a String variable. The statement `objStreamWriter.WriteLine(Me.PayDateTimePicker.Text)` writes the formatted text to a sequential access file.

Before you begin coding the Carriage House application, you learn how to retrieve the system date and time.

Retrieving the System Date and Time

The **system date** is the current date according to your computer system's clock. You can retrieve the system date using the syntax **Today**[*.methodname*], where *methodname* (which is optional) is ToLongDateString, ToShortDateString, or ToString(*formatting characters*). Recall that the ToLongDateString method returns the date formatted using the Long format (dddd, MMMM dd, yyyy), and the ToShortDateString method returns the date formatted using the Short format (M/d/yyyy). To return the date formatted using a custom format, you use the ToString method. For example, if the current date is 10/23/2004, `Today.ToString("MMMM dd")` returns October 23. To retrieve an individual element in the system date, you use the syntax **Today**[*.elementname*], where *elementname* (which is optional) represents the name of the element to retrieve.

The **system time** is the current time according to your computer system's clock. You can retrieve the system time using the syntax **TimeOfDay**[*.methodname*], where *methodname* (which is optional) is ToLongTimeString, ToShortTimeString, or ToString(*formatting characters*). Recall that the ToLongTimeString method returns the time formatted using the Long format (h:mm:ss tt), and the ToShortTimeString method returns the time formatted using the Short format (h:mm tt). You use the ToString method to return the time formatted using a custom format. For example, if the current time is 7:30:23 PM, `TimeOfDay.ToString("h:mm")` returns 7:30. To retrieve an individual element in the system time, you use the syntax **TimeOfDay**[*.elementname*], where *elementname* (which is optional) represents the name of the element to retrieve.

Figure 9-32 shows examples of retrieving the system date, system time, and elements of the system date and time.

tip

You learn more about the *formatting characters* used to create a custom format in Discovery Exercise 8 at the end of this lesson.

Note: for these examples, assume that the system date is "9/6/2004" and the system time is "10:45:33 AM"

System date examples	Results
Today	9/6/2004
Today.ToShortDateString	9/6/2004
Today.ToLongDateString	Monday, September 6, 2004
Today.ToString("MMMM d")	September 6
Today.Month	9
Today.DayOfWeek.ToString	Monday

System time examples	Results
TimeOfDay	10:45:33 AM
TimeOfDay.ToLongTimeString	10:45:33 AM
TimeOfDay.ToShortTimeString	10:45 AM
TimeOfDay.ToString("hh tt")	10 AM
TimeOfDay.Hour	10

Figure 9-32: Examples of retrieving system date and time information

Now you can begin coding the Carriage House application. The TOE chart for the application is shown in Figure 9-33.

Task	Object	Event
1. Write the event name, price, and date to the sequential access file 2. Clear the contents of the NameTextBox and PriceTextBox controls 3. Send the focus to the NameTextBox control	AddButton	Click
1. Ask the user if he or she wants to create a new file 2. Create new sequential access file (if necessary)	CarriageForm	Load
End the application	ExitButton	Click
Select the existing text	NameTextBox, PriceTextBox	Enter
Get and display the event name, price, and date	NameTextBox, PriceTextBox, EventDateTimePicker	None
Use the ReportPrintDocument control to print the sequential access file	PrintButton	Click
1. Print the report heading 2. Read and print each line in the sequential access file	ReportPrintDocument	PrintPage

Figure 9-33: TOE chart for the Carriage House application

In this lesson, you code only the CarriageForm's Load event procedure and the AddButton's Click event procedure. You code the PrintButton's Click event procedure and the ReportPrintDocument's PrintPage procedure in Lesson C. (Recall that you add a PrintDocument control to the form in Lesson C.) The ExitButton's Click event procedure and the NameTextBox and PriceTextBox Enter event procedures have already been coded for you.

Coding the CarriageForm Load Event Procedure

The pseudocode for the CarriageForm Load event procedure is shown in Figure 9-34.

CarriageForm
1. declare variables
2. ask the user if he or she wants to create a new file
3. if the user wants to create a new file
      create a sequential access file named events.txt
      close the events.txt file
  end if
4. if the current month is not December
      display the first day of the next month in the EventDateTimePicker control
  else
      display January 1 of the next year in the EventDateTimePicker control
  end if

Figure 9-34: Pseudocode for the CarriageForm Load event procedure

To code the CarriageForm Load event procedure, then test the procedure:

1   Right-click the **form**, and then click **View Code** to open the Code editor window. Notice that the Code editor window contains the code for the ExitButton's Click event procedure. It also contains the code for a procedure named SelectText. The SelectText procedure is processed when the Enter event for either the NameTextBox or PriceTextBox control occurs.

2   Click the **Class Name** list arrow, and then click (**Base Class Events**) in the list. Click the **Method Name** list arrow, and then click **Load** in the list. The code template for the CarriageForm Load event procedure appears in the Code editor window.

The first step in the pseudocode is to declare the variables. The Load event procedure will use two variables: an Integer variable named intButton and a StreamWriter variable named objStreamWriter.

3   Type **dim intButton as integer, objStreamWriter as system.io.streamwriter** and press **Enter**.

Next, use the MessageBox.Show method to ask the user whether he or she wants to create a new file. Assign the user's response to the intButton variable.

4   Type '**determine whether the user wants to create a new file** and press Enter, then type **intbutton = messagebox.show("Create new file?", "Carriage House", _** and press **Enter**. (Be sure to type the line continuation character.)

5   Press **Tab**, then type **messageboxbuttons.yesno, messageboxicon.exclamation, _** and press **Enter**. (Be sure to include a space before the line continuation character.) Type **messageboxdefaultbutton.button2)** and press **Enter**.

If the user wants to create a new file, then the Load event procedure should open a file named events.txt for output. Recall that opening a file for output creates a new, empty file if the file does not exist. If the file does exist, opening the file for output erases the contents of the file. After opening the events.txt file for output, which simply ensures that the file is empty, the procedure should immediately close the file. As you learned in Lesson A, you should close a sequential access file as soon as you are finished using it. In this case, after the Load event procedure creates (or erases the contents of) the events.txt file, the procedure no longer needs the file.

6   Type the comment and selection structure shown in Figure 9-35, then position the insertion point as shown in the figure.

```
Private Sub CarriageForm_Load(ByVal sender As Object, ByVal e As System.EventArgs) B
    Dim intButton As Integer, objStreamWriter As System.IO.StreamWriter
    'determine whether the user wants to create a new file
    intButton = MessageBox.Show("Create new file?", "Carriage House", _
        MessageBoxButtons.YesNo, MessageBoxIcon.Exclamation, _
        MessageBoxDefaultButton.Button2)
    'create new sequential access file, if necessary
    If intButton = DialogResult.Yes Then
        objStreamWriter = System.IO.File.CreateText("events.txt")
        objStreamWriter.Close()
    End If

End Sub
```

enter these lines of code

position the insertion point here

Figure 9-35: Current status of the CarriageForm Load event procedure

In most cases, the events the user enters into the file take place during the month that follows the current month. For example, August events are entered in July, and September events are entered in August. January events are entered in December of the previous year. You can make it more convenient for the user to enter the event date by displaying the first day of the next month in the EventDateTimePicker control. This way the user needs to change only the day number in the date, and it ensures that the appropriate calendar appears when the user clicks the list arrow button.

7   Type the comment and selection structure shown in Figure 9-36.

```
Private Sub CarriageForm_Load(ByVal sender As Object, ByVal e As System.EventArgs) B
    Dim intButton As Integer, objStreamWriter As System.IO.StreamWriter
    'determine whether the user wants to create a new file
    intButton = MessageBox.Show("Create new file?", "Carriage House", _
        MessageBoxButtons.YesNo, MessageBoxIcon.Exclamation, _
        MessageBoxDefaultButton.Button2)
    'create new sequential access file, if necessary
    If intButton = DialogResult.Yes Then
        objStreamWriter = System.IO.File.CreateText("events.txt")
        objStreamWriter.Close()
    End If
    'display appropriate date
    If Me.EventDateTimePicker.Value.Month <> 12 Then
        Me.EventDateTimePicker.Value = New DateTime(Today.Year, Today.Month + 1, 1)
    Else
        Me.EventDateTimePicker.Value = New DateTime(Today.Year + 1, 1, 1)
    End If
End Sub
```

enter these lines of code

Figure 9-36: Additional code entered in the CarriageForm Load event procedure

Now test the procedure to verify that it is working correctly.

8   Click **File** on the menu bar, and then click **Save All**. Click **Debug** on the menu bar, and then click **Start**. The dialog box shown in Figure 9-37 appears on the screen.

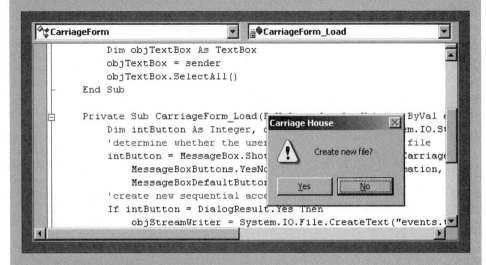

Figure 9-37: Dialog box created in the CarriageForm Load event procedure

9   Click the **No** button. The dialog box closes and the Carriage House application's user interface appears on the screen. The date displayed in the EventDateTimePicker control should be the first day of the month following the current month.

Notice that the CarriageForm does not appear on the screen until after you close the dialog box created by the MessageBox.Show method in the Load event procedure. This is because Visual Basic .NET does not display a form until all of the instructions in the form's Load event procedure are processed. However, you can use a form's Show method to tell Visual Basic .NET to display the form immediately. You enter the Show method in the next set of steps.

10 Click the **Exit** button to end the application. When you return to the Code editor window, close the Output window.

At times, as in the case of the Carriage House application, you may want a form to appear on the screen before all of the instructions in its Load event have been processed. You can do so using the form's Show method, which tells Visual Basic .NET to display the form on the screen immediately. The syntax of the form's Show method is simply **Me.Show()**.

To complete the CarriageForm Load event procedure, then test the procedure:

1   Type the additional comment and statement shown in Figure 9-38, which shows the completed CarriageForm Load event procedure.

enter these two lines of code

```
Private Sub CarriageForm_Load(ByVal sender As Object, ByVal e As System.EventArgs) F
    Dim intButton As Integer, objStreamWriter As System.IO.StreamWriter
    'display the form immediately
    Me.Show()
    'determine whether the user wants to create a new file
    intButton = MessageBox.Show("Create new file?", "Carriage House", _
        MessageBoxButtons.YesNo, MessageBoxIcon.Exclamation, _
        MessageBoxDefaultButton.Button2)
    'create new sequential access file, if necessary
    If intButton = DialogResult.Yes Then
        objStreamWriter = System.IO.File.CreateText("events.txt")
        objStreamWriter.Close()
    End If
    'display appropriate date
    If Me.EventDateTimePicker.Value.Month <> 12 Then
        Me.EventDateTimePicker.Value = New DateTime(Today.Year, Today.Month + 1, 1)
    Else
        Me.EventDateTimePicker.Value = New DateTime(Today.Year + 1, 1, 1)
    End If
End Sub
```

Figure 9-38: Completed CarriageForm Load event procedure

2 Save the solution, then start the application. This time, the CarriageForm is displayed first, followed by the dialog box, as shown in Figure 9-39.

Figure 9-39: CarriageForm and dialog box shown on the screen

3 Click the **Yes** button, which closes the dialog box and creates a sequential access file named events.txt.

4 Click the **Exit** button to end the application. When you return to the Code editor window, close the Output window.

Now verify that the Load event procedure created the events.txt file.

5 Click **File** on the menu bar, point to **Open**, and then click **File**. Open the **bin** folder, which is contained in the VBNET\Tut09\Carriage Solution\Carriage Project folder. Notice that the bin folder contains a file named events.txt. Click the **Cancel** button.

Finally, code the AddButton Click event procedure.

Coding the AddButton Click Event Procedure

The pseudocode for the AddButton Click event procedure is shown in Figure 9-40.

AddButton
1. declare variables
2. assign event name, price, and date to variables
3. open the events.txt file for append
4. write the event name, price, and date to the file
5. close the file
6. clear the contents of the NameTextBox and PriceTextBox controls
7. send the focus to the NameTextBox control

Figure 9-40: Pseudocode for the AddButton Click event procedure

tip

You also can use the statement `strDate = Me.EventDateTimePicker.Value.ToLongDateString` to assign the event date (formatted using the Long format) to the strDate variable.

To code the AddButton Click event procedure, then test the procedure:

1 Click the **Class Name** list arrow, and then click **AddButton** in the list. Click the **Method Name** list arrow, and then click **Click** in the list. The code template for the AddButton Click event procedure appears in the Code editor window.

The first step in the pseudocode is to declare the variables. The Click event procedure will use four variables: three String variables to store the input values (name, price, and date) and a StreamWriter variable for opening the events.txt file.

2 Type **dim strName, strPrice, strDate as string** and press **Enter**, then type **dim objStreamWriter as system.io.streamwriter** and press **Enter**.

Next, assign the event name, price, and date to the String variables. Format the price using the Standard format style to ensure that each price contains the same number of decimal places.

3 Type **strname = me.nametextbox.text** and press **Enter**. Type **strprice = format(me.pricetextbox.text, "standard")** and press **Enter**. Type **strdate = me.eventdatetimepicker.text** and press **Enter**.

Now open the events.txt file for append, then write the event name, price, and date in three separate columns in the file. After writing the information to the file, close the file.

4 Type the additional lines of code shown in Figure 9-41.

```
Private Sub AddButton_Click(ByVal sender As Object, ByVal e As System.EventArgs) Han
    Dim strName, strPrice, strDate As String
    Dim objStreamWriter As System.IO.StreamWriter
    strName = Me.NameTextBox.Text
    strPrice = Format(Me.PriceTextBox.Text, "standard")
    strDate = Me.EventDateTimePicker.Text
    'open the file, write the information, then close the file
    objStreamWriter = System.IO.File.AppendText("events.txt")
    objStreamWriter.WriteLine(strName.PadRight(30) _
        & strDate.PadRight(34) & strPrice.PadLeft(5))
    objStreamWriter.Close()

End Sub
```

enter these lines of code

Figure 9-41: Additional lines of code entered in the AddButton Click event procedure

The last two steps in the pseudocode shown in Figure 9-40 are to clear the contents of the text boxes and then send the focus to the NameTextBox control.

5   Type the additional lines of code shown in Figure 9-42, which shows the completed AddButton Click event procedure.

enter these lines of code

```
Private Sub AddButton_Click(ByVal sender As Object, ByVal e As System.EventArgs) Han
    Dim strName, strPrice, strDate As String
    Dim objStreamWriter As System.IO.StreamWriter
    strName = Me.NameTextBox.Text
    strPrice = Format(Me.PriceTextBox.Text, "standard")
    strDate = Me.EventDateTimePicker.Text
    'open the file, write the information, then close the file
    objStreamWriter = System.IO.File.AppendText("events.txt")
    objStreamWriter.WriteLine(strName.PadRight(30) _
        & strDate.PadRight(34) & strPrice.PadLeft(5))
    objStreamWriter.Close()
    'clear the contents of the text boxes, then send the focus to the NameTextBox
    Me.NameTextBox.Text = ""
    Me.PriceTextBox.Text = ""
    Me.NameTextBox.Focus()
End Sub
```

Figure 9-42: Completed AddButton Click event procedure

Now test the procedure to verify that it is working correctly.

6   Save the solution, then start the application. Click the **No** button in the dialog box.

7   Type **Flower Show** in the Event name text box, then type **10** in the Price text box. Click the **Add to Report** button.

8   Type **Festival of Lights** in the Event name text box, then type **5** in the Price text box. Select a different date in the DateTimePicker control, then click the **Add to Report** button.

9   Click the **Exit** button to end the application. When you return to the Code editor window, close the Output window.

Now verify that the AddButton's Click event procedure wrote the event information to the events.txt file.

10   Click **File** on the menu bar, point to **Open**, and then click **File**. Open the **events.txt** file, which is contained in the VBNET\Tut09\Carriage Solution\Carriage Project\bin folder. See Figure 9-43. (The event dates contained in your events.txt file might be different from the ones shown in the figure.)

your dates might be
different

Event Form.vb [Design] Event Form.vb **events.txt**			◁ ▷ ✕
Flower Show	Wednesday, December 01, 2004	10.00	
Festival of Lights	Thursday, December 16, 2004	5.00	

Figure 9-43: Contents of the events.txt file

11   Click the **Close** button ✕ on the events.txt window to close the window, then close the Code editor window. Click **File** on the menu bar, and then click **Close Solution** to close the solution.

You now have completed Lesson B. In Lesson C, you add a PrintDocument control to the Carriage House application. You also finish coding the application. For now, you can either take a break or complete the end-of-lesson questions and exercises before moving on to the next lesson.

S U M M A R Y

To add a DateTimePicker control to a form:

■ Use the DateTimePicker tool 📅 in the toolbox.

To control the format (style) of the date or time displayed in a DateTimePicker control:

■ Set the control's Format property to one of the three predefined formats: Long, Short, or Time. To use a customized format, set the Format property to Custom, and then enter the desired format in the control's CustomFormat property.

To retrieve the text that appears in a DateTimePicker control:

■ Use the control's Text property.

To retrieve both the date and time assigned to a DateTimePicker control:

■ Use the control's Value property.

To assign a date and an optional time to a DateTimePicker control's Value property:

■ Use the syntax *objectname*.**Value** = **New DateTime**(*year*, *month*, *day*[, *hour*, *minute*, *second*]). In the syntax, *objectname* is the name of the DateTimePicker control. *Year*, *month*, and *day* are integers that specify the desired date. *Hour*, *minute*, and *second* (which are optional) are integers that specify the desired time.

To retrieve an element of the date or time assigned to a DateTimePicker control:

■ Use the syntax *objectname*.**Value**.*elementname*, where *objectname* is the name of a DateTimePicker control, and *elementname* specifies the name of the element to retrieve.

To retrieve the current date, and then optionally display the date using a specified format:

■ Use the syntax **Today**[.*methodname*], where *methodname* (which is optional) is ToLongDateString, ToShortDateString, or ToString(*formatting characters*).

To retrieve an element of the current date:

■ Use the syntax **Today**[.*elementname*], where *elementname* (which is optional) represents the name of the element to retrieve.

To retrieve the current time, and then optionally display the time using a specified format:

■ Use the syntax **TimeOfDay**[.*methodname*], where *methodname* (which is optional) is ToLongTimeString, ToShortTimeString, or ToString(*formatting characters*).

To retrieve an element of the current time:

■ Use the syntax **TimeOfDay**[.*elementname*], where *elementname* (which is optional) represents the name of the element to retrieve.

To display a form immediately:

■   Use the form's Show method as follows: **Me.Show()**.

QUESTIONS

1. Which of the following is false?
   a. When a DateTimePicker control is added to a form, the current date and time are assigned to the control's Text property.
   b. When a DateTimePicker control is added to a form, the current date is displayed in the control.
   c. You can display the time in a DateTimePicker control.
   d. A calendar appears when you click the DateTimePicker control's list arrow.
   e. You can change the year displayed in the DateTimePicker control by clicking the year and then pressing either the up or down arrow key on your keyboard.

2. Which of the following determines whether the PayDateTimePicker control contains a July date?
   a. `If Me.PayDateTimePicker.Value.Month = 7 Then`
   b. `If Me.PayDateTimePicker.Month.Value = 7 Then`
   c. `If Me.PayDateTimePicker.Value.Month = "July" Then`
   d. `If Me.PayDateTimePicker.Month.Text = "July" Then`
   e. `If Me.PayDateTimePicker.Text.Month = 7 Then`

3. To display the time in a DateTimePicker control, set the control's _____ property to Time.
   a. Display
   b. Format
   c. TimeDisplay
   d. ToTime
   e. None of the above.

4. The formatted date that appears in a DateTimePicker control is stored in the control's _____ property.
   a. Date
   b. Display
   c. Format
   d. Value
   e. None of the above.

5. Which of the following assigns the date "October 2, 2004" to the PayDateTimePicker control?
   a. `Me.PayDateTimePicker.Value = New DateAndTime(2004, 2, 10)`
   b. `Me.PayDateTimePicker.Value = New DateAndTime(2004, 10, 2)`
   c. `Me.PayDateTimePicker.Value = New DateTime(2004, 2, 10)`
   d. `Me.PayDateTimePicker.Value = New DateTime(2004, 10, 2)`
   e. `Me.PayDateTimePicker.Value = New DateTime(10, 2, 2004)`

6. Which of the following assigns the date "June 5, 2005" and the time "4:40 AM" to the PayDateTimePicker control?
   a. `Me.PayDateTimePicker.Value = New DateAndTime(2005, 6, 5, 4, 40, 0)`
   b. `Me.PayDateTimePicker.Value = New DateAndTime(2005, 6, 5, 4, 40, 0, "AM")`

   c.   `Me.PayDateTimePicker.Value = New DateTime(2005, 6, 5, 4, 40, 0)`

   d.   `Me.PayDateTimePicker.Value = New DateTime(2005, 6, 5, 4, 40, 0, "AM")`

   e.   `Me.PayDateTimePicker.Value = New DateTime(6, 5, 2005, 4, 40, 0)`

7. Which of the following displays the current date using the Short format?

   a.   `Debug.WriteLine(CurrentDate.ToShortDate)`

   b.   `Debug.WriteLine(Date.ToShortDate)`

   c.   `Debug.WriteLine(Date.ToShortDateString)`

   d.   `Debug.WriteLine(TodaysDate.ToShortDateString)`

   e.   `Debug.WriteLine(Today.ToShortDateString)`

8. Which of the following displays the current time using the Long format?

   a.   `Debug.WriteLine(CurrentTime.ToLongTime)`

   b.   `Debug.WriteLine(Time.ToLongTime)`

   c.   `Debug.WriteLine(Time.ToLongTimeString)`

   d.   `Debug.WriteLine(TimeOfDay.ToLongTimeString)`

   e.   `Debug.WriteLine(Today.ToLongTimeString)`

9. Assume that today is Wednesday, May 25, 2004. Which of the following displays the string "Wednesday"?

   a.   `Debug.WriteLine(CurrentDate.DayOfWeek)`

   b.   `Debug.WriteLine(CurrentDate.WeekDay)`

   c.   `Debug.WriteLine(Date.DayName)`

   d.   `Debug.WriteLine(Today.DayOfWeek.ToString)`

   e.   `Debug.WriteLine(Today.WeekDay.ToString)`

10. Assume that the current time is 5:30 PM. Which of the following displays the minute number, 30?

   a.   `Debug.WriteLine(Time.Minute.ToString)`

   b.   `Debug.WriteLine(CurrentTime.Minute)`

   c.   `Debug.WriteLine(Time.Minute)`

   d.   `Debug.WriteLine(TimeOfDay.Minute)`

   e.   `Debug.WriteLine(Today.Minute)`

EXERCISES

1. In this exercise, you complete an application that saves names and birth dates to a sequential access file.

   a.   If necessary, start Visual Studio .NET. Open the Birthday Solution (Birthday Solution.sln) file, which is contained in the VBNET\Tut09\Birthday Solution folder. If the designer window is not open, right-click the form file's name in the Solution Explorer window, then click View Designer.

   b.   Add a DateTimePicker control to the form. Name the control BirthdayDateTimePicker. The control should display the date using the Short format.

   c.   Lock the controls on the form, then set the TabIndex property for each control.

   d.   The application allows the user to enter a person's name and birth date. Code the Add to File button's Click event procedure so that it writes the name and formatted birth date to a sequential access file named birthday.txt. The name and birth date should appear on the same line in the file, but in two separate columns.

The birth date should be right aligned in its column. The procedure also should send the focus to the NameTextBox control.

e. Save the solution, then start the application. Test the application by entering the following names and birth dates: Kareem Abdula, 4/6/1980, Jefferson Williams, 12/8/1978, Jessica Jones, 9/30/1982.

f. Click the Exit button to end the application.

g. Open the birthday.txt file, which is contained in the VBNET\Tut09\Birthday Solution\Birthday Project\bin folder. The file should contain two columns of information. The first column should contain three names, and the second column should contain three birth dates (formatted using the Short format). The birth dates should be right aligned in the column.

h. Close the Output window, then close the solution.

2. In this exercise, you complete an application that saves invoice numbers, dates, and amounts to a sequential access file.

a. If necessary, start Visual Studio .NET. Open the Invoice Solution (Invoice Solution.sln) file, which is contained in the VBNET\Tut09\Invoice Solution folder. If the designer window is not open, right-click the form file's name in the Solution Explorer window, then click View Designer.

b. Add a DateTimePicker control to the form. Name the control InvoiceDateTimePicker. The control should display the date using the Long format.

c. Lock the controls on the form, then set the TabIndex property for each control.

d. The application allows the user to enter an invoice number, amount, and date. Code the Save button's Click event procedure so that it writes the information entered by the user to a sequential access file named invoice.txt. Write the date using the Short format. The invoice number, amount, and date should appear on the same line in the file, but in three separate columns. Align the information appropriately. (Recall from Lesson A that you typically align a column of numbers by their decimal point.) The procedure also should send the focus to the NumberTextBox control.

e. Save the solution, then start the application. Test the application by entering the following invoice numbers, amounts, and dates (use the current year):

Number	Amount	Date
34NB	1389.56	2/4
124AC	6.35	11/24
12B	567	7/23

f. Click the Exit button to end the application.

g. Open the invoice.txt file, which is contained in the VBNET\Tut09\Invoice Solution\Invoice Project\bin folder. The file should contain three columns of information.

h. Close the Output window, then close the solution.

3. In this exercise, you complete an application that saves dates and times to a sequential access file.

a. If necessary, start Visual Studio .NET. Open the Appointment Solution (Appointment Solution.sln) file, which is contained in the VBNET\Tut09\Appointment Solution folder. If the designer window is not open, right-click the form file's name in the Solution Explorer window, then click View Designer.

b. Add two DateTimePicker controls to the form. Name the controls DateDateTimePicker and TimeDateTimePicker. The DateDateTimePicker control should display the date using the Long format. The TimeDateTimePicker control should display the time. Change the TimeDateTimePicker control's ShowUpDown property to True.

c. Lock the controls on the form, then set the TabIndex property for each control.

d. The application allows the user to keep track of his or her appointments. Code the Save button's Click event procedure so that it writes the information entered by the user to a sequential access file named appointment.txt. Write both the date and time using the Short format. The appointment description, date, and time should appear on the same line in the file, but in three separate columns. Align the information appropriately. The procedure also should send the focus to the AppointmentTextBox control.

e. Save the solution, then start the application. Test the application by entering the following appointments, dates (use the current year), and times:

Appointment	Date	Time
Lunch with Mary	7/5	11:30 AM
Sales meeting	7/19	8:30 AM
Harry Jacobs, ABC Industries	7/28	2:15 PM

f. Click the Exit button to end the application.

g. Open the appointment.txt file, which is contained in the VBNET\Tut09\Appointment Solution\Appointment Project\bin folder. The file should contain three columns of information.

h. Close the Output window, then close the solution.

4. In this exercise, you complete an application that saves dates to a sequential access file.

a. If necessary, start Visual Studio .NET. Open the Date Solution (Date Solution.sln) file, which is contained in the VBNET\Tut09\Date Solution folder. If the designer window is not open, right-click the form file's name in the Solution Explorer window, then click View Designer.

b. Add a DateTimePicker control to the form. Name the control DateDateTimePicker. The DateDateTimePicker control should display the date using the Short format.

c. Lock the controls on the form, then set the TabIndex property for each control.

d. The application allows the user to enter a date. Code the Write to File button's Click event procedure so that it writes the month name, day number, year number, and the day of the week name to a sequential access file named dates.txt. Use a user-defined function to convert the month number to the month name. The information should appear on the same line in the file, but in four separate columns. Align the information appropriately. The procedure also should send the focus to the DateDateTimePicker control.

e. Save the solution, then start the application. Test the application by entering the following dates (use the current year): 1/6, 3/12, 5/2, 9/23, and 11/7.

f. Click the Exit button to end the application.

g. Open the dates.txt file, which is contained in the VBNET\Tut09\Date Solution\Date Project\bin folder. The file should contain four columns of information.

h. Close the Output window, then close the solution.

5. In this exercise, you complete an application that saves names to a sequential access file.

a. If necessary, start Visual Studio .NET. Open the Names Solution (Names Solution.sln) file, which is contained in the VBNET\Tut09\Names Solution folder. If the designer window is not open, right-click the form file's name in the Solution Explorer window, then click View Designer.

b. The application allows the user to enter a first and last name. Code the Write to File button's Click event procedure so that it writes the last name followed by a comma and the first name to a sequential access file named names.txt. (For example, if the first name is Mary and the last name is Smith, the procedure should write Smith,Mary to the file.) The procedure also should send the focus to the FirstTextBox control.

   c.   Save the solution, then start the application. Test the application by entering the following names: Mary Smith, Carol Carter, Jeff Reise, and Sam Tenny.

   d.   Click the Exit button to end the application.

   e.   Open the names.txt file, which is contained in the VBNET\Tut09\Names Solution\Names Project\bin folder. The file should contain four lines of information.

   f.   Close the Output window, then close the solution.

6.   In this exercise, you modify the application that you coded in Exercise 5.

   a.   Use Windows to make a copy of the Names Solution folder, which is contained in the VBNET\Tut09 folder. Change the name of the folder to Modified Names Solution.

   b.   If necessary, start Visual Studio .NET. Open the Names Solution (Names Solution.sln) file, which is contained in the VBNET\Tut09\Modified Names Solution folder. If the designer window is not open, right-click the form file's name in the Solution Explorer window, then click View Designer.

   c.   Modify the Write to File button's Click event procedure so that it ensures that the first and last names begin with an uppercase letter before the names are written to the file. The remaining letters in the names should be lowercase.

   d.   Save the solution, then start the application. Test the application by entering the following names: mary smith, CAROL CARTER, JeFF rEISE, and Sam Tenny.

   e.   Click the Exit button to end the application.

   f.   Open the names.txt file, which is contained in the VBNET\Tut09\Modified Names Solution\Names Project\bin folder. The file should contain four lines of information. Each first and last name should begin with an uppercase letter; the remaining letters in the name should be lowercase.

   g.   Close the Output window, then close the solution.

7.   In this exercise, you complete an application that saves order numbers and shipping dates and times to a sequential access file.

   a.   If necessary, start Visual Studio .NET. Open the Ship Solution (Ship Solution.sln) file, which is contained in the VBNET\Tut09\Ship Solution folder. If the designer window is not open, right-click the form file's name in the Solution Explorer window, then click View Designer.

   b.   The application allows the user to enter an order number. Code the Shipped button's Click event procedure so that it writes the order number, the current date, and the current time to a sequential access file named shipped.txt. Use the Short format when writing the date and time. The order number, current date, and current time should appear on the same line in the file, but in three separate columns. Align the columns appropriately. After writing the order number, date, and time to the file, the procedure should clear the contents of the OrderTextBox, and then send the focus to the text box.

   c.   Save the solution, then start the application. Test the application by entering the following order numbers: AB456, NN893, ZYX123.

   d.   Click the Exit button to end the application.

   e.   Open the shipped.txt file, which is contained in the VBNET\Tut09\Ship Solution\Ship Project\bin folder. The file should contain three columns of information.

   f.   Close the Output window, then close the solution.

Exercises 8 and 9 are Discovery Exercises. Discovery Exercises, which may include topics that are not covered in this lesson, allow you to "discover" the solutions to problems on your own.

discovery ▶   **8.**   In this exercise, you learn how to create a custom format for a DateTimePicker control.

   a.   If necessary, start Visual Studio .NET. Open the Custom Solution (Custom Solution.sln) file, which is contained in the VBNET\Tut09\Custom Solution folder. If the designer window is not open, right-click the form file's name in the Solution Explorer window, then click View Designer.

b.   The interface contains two DateTimePicker controls named DateDateTimePicker and TimeDateTimePicker. Change both controls' Format property to Custom.

c.   Click Help on the menu bar, and then click Index. Display the Help screen for the DateTimePicker control's CustomFormat property. Study the information that appears on the Help screen. If your computer is connected to a printer, print the Help screen.

d.   Change the DateDateTimePicker control's CustomFormat property so that it displays the date in the following formats:

(1)   Jan 12 - Monday

(2)   1-12-04

(3)   01-12-2004

(4)   January 12

(5)   Mon

(6)   Day: Monday

e.   Change the TimeDateTimePicker control's CustomFormat property so that it displays the time in the following formats:

(1)   6:05 PM

(2)   6:05:00 P

(3)   18:05

(4)   06:05

(5)   Time: 6:05 PM

f.   Save the solution, then close the solution.

discovery ▶   9.   In this exercise, you learn about a DateTimePicker control's MaxDate and MinDate properties.

a.   If necessary, start Visual Studio .NET. Open the MaxMin Solution (MaxMin Solution.sln) file, which is contained in the VBNET\Tut09\MaxMin Solution folder. If the designer window is not open, right-click the form file's name in the Solution Explorer window, then click View Designer.

b.   You use a DateTimePicker control's MaxDate property to control the maximum date the user is allowed to select. Similarly, you use the control's MinDate property to control the minimum date the user is allowed to select. Set the DateTimePicker control's MaxDate and MinDate properties so that the user can select only dates from June 1, 2004 through June 30, 2004.

c.   Save the solution, then start the application. Try to use the up and down arrow keys on your keyboard to select a date that does not fall in the valid range. Also, click the DateTimePicker control's list arrow. The calendar for June 2004 opens. Try to use the left and right arrow keys on the calendar to display a different calendar.

d.   Click the Exit button to end the application.

e.   Close the Output window, then close the solution.

After completing this lesson, you
will be able to:

■ Add a PrintDocument control to
a form

■ Print text using the Print and
e.Graphics.DrawString methods

■ Code a PrintDocument control's
PrintPage event procedure

Completing the Carriage House Application

The Carriage House Application

To complete the Carriage House application, which you began coding in Lesson B, you need to add a PrintDocument control to the form, and then code the Print Report button's Click event procedure and the ReportPrintDocument control's PrintPage event procedure. First, open the Carriage House application.

To open the Carriage House application:

1   Start Microsoft Visual Studio .NET, if necessary, and then close the Start Page window. Click **File** on the menu bar, and then click **Open Solution**. The Open Solution dialog box opens. Open the **Carriage Solution** (Carriage Solution.sln) file, which is contained in the VBNET\Tut09\Carriage Solution folder.

2   If the designer window is not open, right-click **Carriage Form.vb** in the Solution Explorer window, then click **View Designer**.

3   Auto-hide the Toolbox, Solution Explorer, and Properties windows, if necessary.

Next, add a PrintDocument control to the form.

Adding a PrintDocument Control to the Form

Recall that Ms. Bartowski, the Manager of Special Events at Carriage House, wants the application to print a Special Events report. The report should list the name, date, and price of each event contained in the events.txt sequential access file. Before you can print a document within a Windows application, you need to add a **PrintDocument control** to the form.

To add a PrintDocument control to the form:

1   Click the **PrintDocument** tool 🖹 in the toolbox, then drag a PrintDocument control to the form. The PrintDocument1 control appears in the component tray, as shown in Figure 9-44. (The date shown in the DateTimePicker control on your screen might be different from the date shown in the figure.)

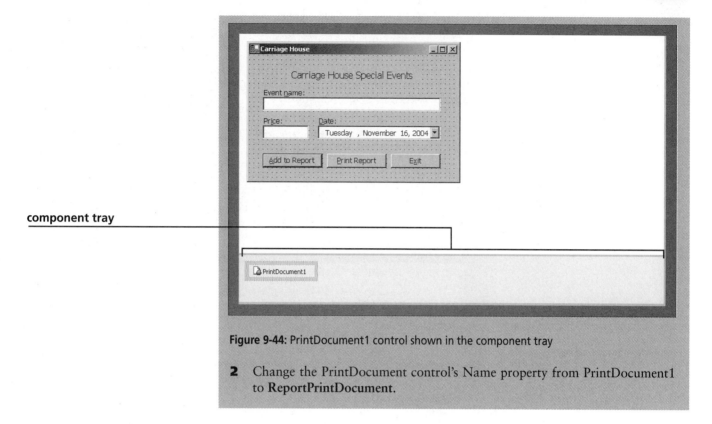

Figure 9-44: PrintDocument1 control shown in the component tray

2   Change the PrintDocument control's Name property from PrintDocument1 to **ReportPrintDocument**.

Now code the Print Report button's Click event procedure.

Coding the Print Report Button's Click Event Procedure

Figure 9-45 shows the pseudocode for the Print Report button's Click event procedure, which is responsible for using the ReportPrintDocument control to print the contents of the events.txt sequential access file.

```
PrintButton
if the events.txt file exists
        print the contents of the events.txt file
else
        display an appropriate message
end if
```

Figure 9-45: Pseudocode for the Print Report button's Click event procedure

To code the Print Report button's Click event procedure:

1   Right-click the **form**, and then click **View Code**.

2   Click the **Class Name** list arrow, and then click **PrintButton** in the list. Click the **Method Name** list arrow, and then click **Click** in the list. The code template for the PrintButton Click event procedure appears in the Code editor window.

3   Type **'print the file only if it exists** and press **Enter**, then type **if system.io.file.exists("events.txt") = true then** and press **Enter**.

If the events.txt file exists, the procedure should print the document. You print a document using the PrintDocument control's **Print method**. The method's syntax is *printdocument*.**Print**(), where *printdocument* is the name of a PrintDocument control.

4   Type **me.reportprintdocument.print()** and press **Enter**.

If the events.txt file does not exist, the procedure should display an appropriate message.

5   Type the additional lines of code indicated in Figure 9-46, which shows the completed PrintButton Click event procedure. Also verify that the procedure contains the **End If** clause.

enter these lines of code →

```
Private Sub PrintButton_Click(ByVal sender As Object, ByVal e As System.EventArgs)
    'print the file only if it exists
    If System.IO.File.Exists("events.txt") = True Then
        Me.ReportPrintDocument.Print()
    Else
        MessageBox.Show("File does not exist.", "Carriage House", _
            MessageBoxButtons.OK, MessageBoxIcon.Information)
    End If
End Sub
```

Figure 9-46: Completed PrintButton Click event procedure

The Print method causes the PrintDocument control's PrintPage event to occur. You use the **PrintPage event** to indicate the information you want to print, as well as how you want the information to appear in the printout.

Coding the PrintPage Event Procedure

In this case, the PrintPage event procedure should print the contents of the events.txt file in a report format. The report should contain a report header, which describes the contents of the report, and three columns of information. The first column should list the event names, the second column the event dates, and the third column the event prices. Figure 9-47 shows the pseudocode for the ReportPrintDocument control's PrintPage event procedure.

```
ReportPrintDocument
1.  declare variables
2.  print the report header
3.  open the events.txt file for input
4.  assign 10 to the intX variable, which controls the horizontal position of the text
5.  assign 70 to the intY variable, which controls the vertical position of the text
6.  repeat until there are no more characters to read
        read a line of text from the file
        print the line of text
        add 15 to the intY variable
    end repeat
7.  close the events.txt file
```

Figure 9-47: Pseudocode for the ReportPrintDocument PrintPage event procedure

> To begin coding the ReportPrintDocument PrintPage event procedure:
>
> **1** Click the **Class Name** list arrow, and then click **ReportPrintDocument** in the list. Click the **Method Name** list arrow, and then click **PrintPage** in the list. The code template for the ReportPrintDocument PrintPage event procedure appears in the Code editor window.
>
> First, declare the variables. The PrintPage event procedure will use four variables: a StreamReader variable for opening the events.txt file, a String variable for reading a line of text from the file, and two Integer variables for controlling the position of the text on the printed page.
>
> **2** Type **dim objStreamReader as system.io.streamreader, strLine as string** and press **Enter**, then type **dim intX, intY as integer** and press **Enter**.

The next step in the pseudocode is to print the report header. You use the e.Graphics.DrawString method to print text on the printer.

The e.Graphics.DrawString Method

You use the **e.Graphics.DrawString method** to print text on the printer. The method's syntax is **e.Graphics.DrawString(**_string_, **New Font(**_fontName, fontSize, fontStyle_**), Brushes.Black,** _horizontalPosition, verticalPosition_**)**. In the syntax, _string_ is the text to print. _FontName_, _fontSize_, and _fontStyle_ are the name, size, and style of the print font. The _horizontalPosition_ argument determines the location of the text from the left edge of the printed page, and the _verticalPosition_ controls the location of the text from the top edge of the printed page.

Some print fonts are proportionally spaced, while others are fixed-spaced, often referred to as mono-spaced. **Fixed-spaced fonts** use the same amount of space to print each character, whereas proportionally spaced fonts use varying amounts of space to print characters. For example, with a fixed-spaced font, such as Courier New, the wide letter W and the narrow letter l occupy the same amount of print space. However, with a proportionally spaced font, such as Microsoft Sans Serif, the letter W occupies more print space than the letter l does. In most cases, you use a fixed-spaced font when printing a report on the printer, because a fixed-spaced font allows you to align the text that appears in a printout.

Figure 9-48 shows the report header that should appear at the top of the Special Events Report.

report title

column headings

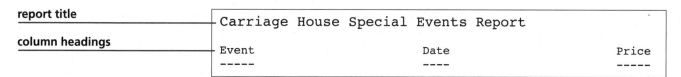

```
Carriage House Special Events Report

Event                        Date                  Price
-----                        ----                  -----
```

Figure 9-48: Special Events Report header

The first line in the report header contains the report title, which describes the contents of the report. An empty line follows the report title line. The third line in the report header contains the column headings, which identify the information listed in each column. The fourth line simply separates the column headings from the information listed in each column.

To continue coding the PrintPage event:

1 Type the lines of code indicated in Figure 9-49, then position the insertion point as shown in the figure.

enter these lines of code

position the insertion point here

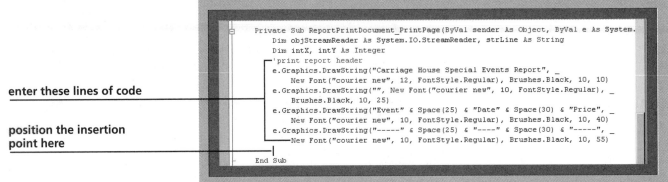

```
Private Sub ReportPrintDocument_PrintPage(ByVal sender As Object, ByVal e As System.
    Dim objStreamReader As System.IO.StreamReader, strLine As String
    Dim intX, intY As Integer
    'print report header
    e.Graphics.DrawString("Carriage House Special Events Report", _
        New Font("courier new", 12, FontStyle.Regular), Brushes.Black, 10, 10)
    e.Graphics.DrawString("", New Font("courier new", 10, FontStyle.Regular), _
        Brushes.Black, 10, 25)
    e.Graphics.DrawString("Event" & Space(25) & "Date" & Space(30) & "Price", _
        New Font("courier new", 10, FontStyle.Regular), Brushes.Black, 10, 40)
    e.Graphics.DrawString("-----" & Space(25) & "----" & Space(30) & "-----", _
        New Font("courier new", 10, FontStyle.Regular), Brushes.Black, 10, 55)

End Sub
```

Figure 9-49: Code to print the report header

The next step in the pseudocode shown in Figure 9-47 is to open the events.txt file for input.

2 Type **'open the file** and press **Enter**, then type **objstreamreader = system.io.file.opentext("events.txt")** and press **Enter**.

Next, assign the number 10 to the intX variable, which controls the horizontal position of the text on the printed page, and assign 70 to the intY variable, which controls the vertical position of the text on the printed page.

3 Type **'set the horizontal position of each line of text to be printed** and press **Enter**, then type **intx = 10** and press **Enter**.

4 Type **'set the vertical position of the next line of text to be printed** and press **Enter**, then type **inty = 70** and press **Enter**.

Now enter a loop whose instructions should be repeated until there are no more characters to read in the file. The loop instructions should read a line of text from the file, then print the line of text on the printer, and then add the number 15 to the intY variable. Updating the intY variable in this manner advances the printer to the next print line. When the repetition structure has finished processing, the PrintPage procedure should close the events.txt file.

5 Type the lines of code shaded in Figure 9-50, which shows the completed ReportPrintDocument PrintPage event procedure.

```
Private Sub ReportPrintDocument_PrintPage(ByVal sender As Object, ByVal e As
System.Drawing.Printing.PrintPageEventArgs) Handles ReportPrintDocument.PrintPage
    Dim objStreamReader As System.IO.StreamReader, strLine As String
    Dim intX, intY As Integer
    'print report header
    e.Graphics.DrawString("Carriage House Special Events Report", _
        New Font("courier new", 12, FontStyle.Regular), Brushes.Black, 10, 10)
    e.Graphics.DrawString("", New Font("courier new", 10, FontStyle.Regular), _
        Brushes.Black, 10, 25)
    e.Graphics.DrawString("Event" & Space(25) & "Date" & Space(30) & "Price", _
        New Font("courier new", 10, FontStyle.Regular), Brushes.Black, 10, 40)
    e.Graphics.DrawString("-----" & Space(25) & "----" & Space(30) & "-----", _
        New Font("courier new", 10, FontStyle.Regular), Brushes.Black, 10, 55)
    'open the file
    objStreamReader = System.IO.File.OpenText("events.txt")
    'set the horizontal position of each line of text to be printed
    intX = 10
    'set the vertical position of the next line of text to be printed
    intY = 70
    'repeat the loop instructions until there are no more characters to read
    Do Until objStreamReader.Peek = -1
        'read a line of text from the file, then print the line
        strLine = objStreamReader.ReadLine()
        e.Graphics.DrawString(strLine, _
            New Font("courier new", 10, FontStyle.Regular), _
            Brushes.Black, intX, intY)
        'update the vertical position of the next line to be printed
        intY = intY + 15
    Loop
    'close the file
    objStreamReader.Close()
End Sub
```

enter these
lines of
code

Figure 9-50: Completed ReportPrintDocument PrintPage event procedure

Now verify that the PrintButton Click event procedure and the ReportPrintDocument PrintPage event procedure work correctly.

6 Click **File** on the menu bar, and then click **Save All**. Click **Debug** on the menu bar, and then click **Start**. Click **No** in the dialog box.

7 If your computer is connected to a printer, click the **Print Report** button. The printer prints a report similar to the one shown in Figure 9-51. (The event dates in your report may be different from the dates shown in the figure.)

```
Carriage House Special Events Report

Event                          Date                              Price
-----                          ----                              -----
Flower Show          ┌─ Wednesday, December 01, 2004            10.00
Festival of Lights   └─ Thursday, December 16, 2004              5.00
```

your report might
show different dates

Figure 9-51: Special Events report

8 Click the **Exit** button to end the application. When you return to the Code editor window, close the Output window, then close the Code editor window.

9 Click **File** on the menu bar, and then click **Close Solution**.

You now have completed Tutorial 9. You can either take a break or complete the end-of-lesson questions and exercises.

S U M M A R Y

To print text within a Windows application:

- Include a PrintDocument control in the application.
- Use the Print method to print the document. The Print method's syntax is *printdocument*.**Print**(), where *printdocument* is the name of a PrintDocument control. The Print method invokes the control's PrintPage event.
- Use the PrintPage event procedure to indicate the information you want to print, as well as how you want the information to appear in the printout.
- Use the syntax **e.Graphics.DrawString**(*string*, **New Font**(*fontName*, *fontSize*, *fontStyle*), **Brushes.Black**, *horizontalPosition*, *verticalPosition*) to print the document. In the syntax, *string* is the text to print. *FontName*, *fontSize*, and *fontStyle* are the name, size, and style of the print font. The *horizontalPosition* argument determines the location of the text from the left edge of the printed page, and the *verticalPosition* controls the location of the text from the top edge of the printed page.

Q U E S T I O N S

1. You use the _____ method to print a document within a Windows application.
   a. DocumentPrint
   b. DocumentPrintPage
   c. PagePrint
   d. Print
   e. PrintPage

2. You use the _____ method to describe the text you want to print.
   a. e.Graphics.DrawString
   b. e.Graphics.Document
   c. e.Graphics.DocumentPrintPage
   d. e.Graphics.PrintDocument
   e. e.Graphics.PrintPage

3. The method from Question 2 allows you to specify the horizontal and vertical position of the text in the printout.
   a. True
   b. False

4. A _____ font uses varying amounts of space to print characters.
   a. changeable-spaced
   b. fixed-spaced
   c. permanent-spaced
   d. proportionally spaced
   e. varying-spaced

5. In most cases, you should use a _____ font to print a report.
  a. changeable-spaced
  b. fixed-spaced
  c. permanent-spaced
  d. proportionally spaced
  e. varying-spaced

E X E R C I S E S

The following list summarizes the GUI design guidelines you have learned so far. You can use this list to verify that the interfaces you create in the following exercises adhere to the GUI standards outlined in the book.

- Information should flow either vertically or horizontally, with the most important information always located in the upper-left corner of the screen.

- Maintain a consistent margin of two or three dots from the edge of the window.

- Try to create a user interface that no one notices.

- Related controls should be grouped together using white space, a GroupBox control, or a Panel control.

- Set the form's FormBorderStyle, ControlBox, MaximizeBox, MinimizeBox, and StartPosition properties appropriately:

  - A splash screen should not have a Minimize, Maximize, or Close button, and its borders should not be sizable.

  - A form that is not a splash screen should always have a Minimize button and a Close button, but you can choose to disable the Maximize button. Typically, the FormBorderStyle property is set to Sizable, but also can be set to FixedSingle.

- Position related controls on succeeding dots. Controls that are not part of any logical grouping may be positioned from two to four dots away from other controls.

- Buttons should be positioned either in a row along the bottom of the screen, or stacked in either the upper-right or lower-right corner.

- If the buttons are positioned at the bottom of the screen, then each button should be the same height; their widths, however, may vary.

- If the buttons are stacked in either the upper-right or lower-right corner of the screen, then each should be the same height and the same width.

- Use no more than six buttons on a screen.

- The most commonly used button should be placed first.

- Button captions should:
  - be meaningful
  - be from one to three words
  - appear on one line
  - be entered using book title capitalization
- Use labels to identify the text boxes in the interface, and position the label either above or to the left of the text box.
- Label text should:
  - be from one to three words
  - appear on one line
  - be left-justified
  - end with a colon (:)
  - be entered using sentence capitalization
- Labels that identify controls should have their BorderStyle property set to None.
- Labels that display program output, such as the result of a calculation, should have their BorderStyle property set to FixedSingle.
- Align controls to minimize the number of different margins.
- If you use a graphic in the interface, use a small one and place it in a location that will not distract the user.
- Use the Tahoma font for applications that will run on Windows 2000 or Windows XP.
- Use no more than two different font sizes, which should be 8, 9, 10, 11, or 12 point.
- Use only one font type, which should be a sans serif font, in the interface.
- Avoid using italics and underlining.
- Limit the use of bold text to titles, headings, and key items.
- Build the interface using black, white, and gray first, then add color only if you have a good reason to do so.
- Use white, off-white, light gray, pale blue, or pale yellow for an application's background, and black for the text.
- Limit the number of colors to three, not including white, black, and gray. The colors you choose should complement each other.
- Never use color as the only means of identification for an element in the user interface.
- Set each control's TabIndex property to a number that represents the order in which you want the control to receive the focus (begin with 0).
- A text box's TabIndex value should be one more than the TabIndex value of its identifying label.
- Assign a unique access key to each control (in the interface) that can receive user input (text boxes, buttons, and so on).

- When assigning an access key to a control, use the first letter of the caption or identifying label, unless another letter provides a more meaningful association. If you can't use the first letter and no other letter provides a more meaningful association, then use a distinctive consonant. Lastly, use a vowel or a number.

- Lock the controls in place on the form.

- Document the program internally.

- Use the Val function on any Text property involved in a calculation.

- Use the Format function to improve the appearance of numbers in the interface.

- In the InputBox function, use sentence capitalization for the *prompt*, and book title capitalization for the *title*.

- The default button should be the button that is most often selected by the user, except in cases where the tasks performed by the button are both destructive and irreversible. The default button typically is the first button.

- Use sentence capitalization for the optional identifying label in a group box control.

- MessageBox.Show method:

  - Use sentence capitalization for the *text* argument, but book title capitalization for the *caption* argument. The name of the application typically appears in the *caption* argument.

  - Avoid using the words "error," "warning," or "mistake" in the message.

  - Display the Warning Message icon ⚠ in a message box that alerts the user that he or she must make a decision before the application can continue. You can phrase the message as a question.

  - Display the Information Message icon ⓘ in a message box that displays an informational message along with an OK button only.

  - Display the Stop Message icon ⊗ when you want to alert the user of a serious problem that must be corrected before the application can continue.

  - The default button in the dialog box should be the one that represents the user's most likely action, as long as that action is not destructive.

- Use the KeyPress event to prevent a text box from accepting inappropriate keys.

- Radio buttons:

  - Use radio buttons when you want to limit the user to one of two or more related and mutually exclusive choices.

  - Use a minimum of two and a maximum of seven radio buttons in an interface.

  - Use sentence capitalization for the label entered in the radio button's Text property.

  - Assign a unique access key to each radio button in an interface.

  - Use a group box control (or a panel control) to create separate groups of radio buttons. Only one button in each group can be selected at any one time.

  - Designate a default radio button in each group of radio buttons.

- Check boxes:

  - Use check boxes to allow the user to select any number of choices from a group of one or more independent and nonexclusive choices.

  - Use sentence capitalization for the label entered in the check box's Text property.

- ■ Assign a unique access key to each check box in an interface.
- ■ List boxes:

  - ■ A list box should contain a minimum of three selections.
  - ■ A list box should display a minimum of three selections and a maximum of eight selections at a time.
  - ■ Use a label control to provide keyboard access to the list box. Set the label control's TabIndex property to a value that is one less than the list box's TabIndex value.
  - ■ List box items are either arranged by use, with the most used entries appearing first in the list, or sorted in ascending order.
  - ■ If a list box allows the user to make only one selection at a time, then a default item should be selected in the list box when the interface first appears. The default item should be either the most used selection or the first selection in the list. However, if a list box allows more than one selection at a time, you do not select a default item.

- ■ Menus:

  - ■ Menu title captions, which appear on the menu bar, should be one word, with the first letter capitalized. Each menu title should have a unique access key.
  - ■ Menu item captions, which appear on a menu, can be from one to three words. Use book title capitalization and assign a unique access key to each menu item. Assign shortcut keys to commonly used menu items.
  - ■ If a menu item requires additional information from the user, place an ellipsis (...) at the end of the item's caption, which is entered in the item's Text property.
  - ■ Follow the Windows standards for the placement of menu titles and items.
  - ■ Use a separator bar to separate groups of related menu items

- ■ It is customary in Windows applications to disable objects that do not apply to the current state of the application.

- ■ It is customary in Windows applications to highlight, or select, the existing text in a text box when the text box receives the focus.

- ■ Test the application with both valid and invalid data (for example, test the application without entering any data, and test it by entering letters where numbers are expected).

1. In this exercise, you modify the application that you coded in Exercise 1 in Lesson B. The modified application will allow the user to print the contents of the sequential access file.

   a. If necessary, start Visual Studio .NET. Open the Birthday Solution (Birthday Solution.sln) file, which is contained in the VBNET\Tut09\Birthday Solution folder. If the designer window is not open, right-click the form file's name in the Solution Explorer window, then click View Designer.

   b. Add a PrintDocument control and a Print button to the form. (Be sure to reset the TabIndex properties.) Code the application so that it prints the contents of the birthday.txt file. Display an appropriate message if the birthday.txt file does not exist.

   c. Save the solution, then start the application. Click the Print button.

   d. Click the Exit button to end the application.

   e. Close the Output window, then close the solution.

2. In this exercise, you modify the application that you coded in Exercise 2 in Lesson B. The modified application will allow the user to print the contents of the sequential access file.

    a. If necessary, start Visual Studio .NET. Open the Invoice Solution (Invoice Solution.sln) file, which is contained in the VBNET\Tut09\Invoice Solution folder. If the designer window is not open, right-click the form file's name in the Solution Explorer window, then click View Designer.

    b. Add a PrintDocument control and a Print button to the form. (Be sure to reset the TabIndex properties.) Code the application so that it prints the contents of the invoice.txt file. Include an appropriate heading above each column in the printout. Display an appropriate message if the invoice.txt file does not exist.

    c. Save the solution, then start the application. Click the Print button.

    d. Click the Exit button to end the application.

    e. Close the Output window, then close the solution.

3. In this exercise, you modify the application that you coded in Exercise 3 in Lesson B. The modified application will allow the user to print the contents of the sequential access file.

    a. If necessary, start Visual Studio .NET. Open the Appointment Solution (Appointment Solution.sln) file, which is contained in the VBNET\Tut09\Appointment Solution folder. If the designer window is not open, right-click the form file's name in the Solution Explorer window, then click View Designer.

    b. Add a PrintDocument control and a Print button to the form. (Be sure to reset the TabIndex properties.) Code the application so that it prints the contents of the appointment.txt file. Include an appropriate heading above each column in the printout. Display an appropriate message if the appointment.txt file does not exist.

    c. Save the solution, then start the application. Click the Print button.

    d. Click the Exit button to end the application.

    e. Close the Output window, then close the solution.

4. In this exercise, you modify the application that you coded in Exercise 4 in Lesson B. The modified application will allow the user to print the contents of the sequential access file.

    a. If necessary, start Visual Studio .NET. Open the Date Solution (Date Solution.sln) file, which is contained in the VBNET\Tut09\Date Solution folder. If the designer window is not open, right-click the form file's name in the Solution Explorer window, then click View Designer.

    b. Add a PrintDocument control and a Print button to the form. (Be sure to reset the TabIndex properties.) Code the application so that it prints the contents of the dates.txt file. Display an appropriate message if the dates.txt file does not exist.

    c. Save the solution, then start the application. Click the Print button.

    d. Click the Exit button to end the application.

    e. Close the Output window, then close the solution.

5. In this exercise, you modify the application that you coded in Exercise 5 in Lesson B. The modified application will allow the user to print the contents of the sequential access file.

    a. If necessary, start Visual Studio .NET. Open the Names Solution (Names Solution.sln) file, which is contained in the VBNET\Tut09\Names Solution folder. If the designer window is not open, right-click the form file's name in the Solution Explorer window, then click View Designer.

    b. Add a PrintDocument control and a Print button to the form. (Be sure to reset the TabIndex properties.)

c. Open the names.txt file, which is contained in the VBNET\Tut09\Names Solution\Names Project\bin folder. Notice that each line in the file contains a last name followed by a comma and a first name. Close the names.txt file.

d. Code the application so that it prints the contents of the names.txt file. Print the first name followed by a space and the last name. (For example, print Mary Smith.) Display an appropriate message if the names.txt file does not exist.

e. Save the solution, then start the application. Click the Print button.

f. Click the Exit button to end the application.

g. Close the Output window, then close the solution.

6. In this exercise, you modify the Carriage House application that you coded in the tutorial. The modified application will include the report heading in the sequential access file.

a. Use Windows to make a copy of the Carriage Solution folder, which is contained in the VBNET\Tut09 folder. Change the name of the folder to Modified Carriage Solution.

b. If necessary, start Visual Studio .NET. Open the Carriage Solution (Carriage Solution.sln) file, which is contained in the VBNET\Tut09\Modified Carriage Solution folder. If the designer window is not open, right-click the form file's name in the Solution Explorer window, then click View Designer.

c. Open the Code editor window and locate the ReportPrintDocument PrintPage event procedure. Remove the four statements that print the report heading. Also remove the 'print report header comment.

d. Modify the form's Load event procedure so that it writes the report heading to the events.txt file, but only if the user wants to create a new file. Include the current date and time in the report heading.

e. Save the solution, then start the application. Click the Yes button to indicate that you want to create a new file. Use the application to enter the following events, prices, and dates (use the current year):

Event	Price	Date
Swing Dance	8	10/5
Flower Show	5	10/10
Haunted House	10	10/25

f. Click the Print Report button, then click the Exit button to end the application.

g. Close the Output window, then close the solution.

7. In this exercise, you code an application that prints a multiplication table.

a. If necessary, start Visual Studio .NET. Open the Multiplication Solution (Multiplication Solution.sln) file, which is contained in the VBNET\Tut09\Multiplication Solution folder. If the designer window is not open, right-click the form file's name in the Solution Explorer window, then click View Designer.

b. Code the application so that it prints a multiplication table similar to the one shown in Figure 9-52. The first column of the table will always contain the numbers one through nine. The number in the third column, however, will be the number that the user enters in the Number text box. For example, if the user enters the number 12 in the Number text box, the number 12 should appear in the third column. If the user enters the number 3, the number 3 should appear in the third column.

```
┌─────────────────────────────────────────────────────────────┐
│ Multiplication Table                                        │
│                                                             │
│ 1       X       6       =       6                           │
│ 2       X       6       =       12                          │
│ 3       X       6       =       18                          │
│ 4       X       6       =       24                          │
│ 5       X       6       =       30                          │
│ 6       X       6       =       36                          │
│ 7       X       6       =       42                          │
│ 8       X       6       =       48                          │
│ 9       X       6       =       54                          │
└─────────────────────────────────────────────────────────────┘
```

Figure 9-52

    c. Save the solution, then start the application. Click the Print button.

    d. Click the Exit button to end the application.

    e. Close the Output window, then close the solution.

8. In this exercise, you code an application that assigns the contents of a sequential access file to a list box.

    a. If necessary, start Visual Studio .NET. Open the State Solution (State Solution.sln) file, which is contained in the VBNET\Tut09\State Solution folder. If the designer window is not open, right-click the form file's name in the Solution Explorer window, then click View Designer.

    b. Open the state.txt file, which is contained in the VBNET\Tut09\State Solution\State Project\bin folder. The file contains the names of five states. Close the file.

    c. Code the form's Load event procedure so that it reads the state.txt file and stores each state name in the StateListBox control.

    d. Save the solution, then start the application. The five state names appear in the list box.

    e. Click the Exit button to end the application.

    f. Close the Output window, then close the solution.

Exercise 9 is a Discovery Exercise. Discovery Exercises, which may include topics that are not covered in this lesson, allow you to "discover" the solutions to problems on your own.

discovery ▶ **9.** In this exercise, you modify the Carriage House application that you coded in the tutorial. The modified application will display a message informing the user that the file has been printed.

    a. Use Windows to make a copy of the Carriage Solution folder, which is contained in the VBNET\Tut09 folder. Change the name of the folder to EndPrint Carriage Solution.

    b. If necessary, start Visual Studio .NET. Open the Carriage Solution (Carriage Solution.sln) file, which is contained in the VBNET\Tut09\EndPrint Carriage Solution folder. If the designer window is not open, right-click the form file's name in the Solution Explorer window, then click View Designer.

    c. The PrintDocument control's EndPrint event occurs when the last page in the document has printed. Code the EndPrint event procedure so that it assigns the filename ("events.txt") to the PrintDocument control's DocumentName property. The procedure also should display the message "*filename* has finished printing", where *filename* is the name of the document. Display the message in a message box.

    d. Save the solution, then start the application. Click the No button to indicate that you do not want to create a new file. Click the Print Report button. The message "events.txt has finished printing" appears in a message box. Click the OK button to close the message box.

    e. Click the Exit button to end the application.

    f. Close the Output window, then close the solution.

Exercise 10 is a Debugging Exercise. Debugging Exercises provide an opportunity for you to detect and correct errors in an existing application.

debugging

10. In this exercise, you debug an existing application. The purpose of this exercise is to demonstrate a common error made when using files.

    a.   If necessary, start Visual Studio .NET. Open the Debug Solution (Debug Solution.sln) file, which is contained in the VBNET\Tut09\Debug Solution folder. If the designer window is not open, right-click the form file's name in the Solution Explorer window, then click View Designer.

    b.   Open the Code editor window and study the existing code.

    c.   Start the application. Type your name in the Name text box, then click the Write to File button.

    d.   Click the Exit button to end the application.

    e.   Open the debug.txt file, which is contained in the VBNET\Tut09\Debug Solution\Debug Project\bin folder. Notice that the file is empty. Close the debug.txt file.

    f.   Start the application. Type your name in the Name text box, then click the Write to File button. Type your name again in the Name text box, then click the Write to File button. An error message appears in a message box. Close the message box.

    g.   Correct the application's code, then save the solution and start the application. Type your name in the Name text box, then click the Write to File button. Type your name again in the Name text box, then click the Write to File button.

    h.   Click the Exit button to end the application.

    i.   Open the debug.txt file. Your name appears twice in the file.

    j.   Close the Output window, then close the solution.

Random Access Files

Creating a Seminar Application

case ▶ Each month, Mrs. Phelps teaches a three-day seminar called "Meditation and You" at the local high school. The classroom can accommodate 20 people, so the seminar is limited to a maximum of 20 participants. The seminar is designed to show participants how to use meditation to alleviate stress. Many local companies pay for their employees to attend the seminar, because they recognize the advantage of a happy workforce.

On the first day of the seminar, Mrs. Phelps assigns each participant a permanent seat in the classroom. She then records on a sheet of paper the seat number, the name of the participant, and the name of the company where the participant works. She has asked you to create an application that she can use to keep track of this information. The application should allow Mrs. Phelps to save the information to a file. It also should allow her to display the information associated with a specific seat number, remove a participant's information from the file, and print a Seminar Participant Report. The report should list the seat number, participant name, and company name.

Previewing the Seminar Application

Before creating the Seminar application, you first preview the completed application.

To preview the completed application:

1 Use the Run command on the Windows Start menu to run the **Seminar** (Seminar.exe) file, which is contained in the VBNET\Tut10 folder on your computer's hard disk. The Seminar application's user interface appears on the screen. See Figure 10-1.

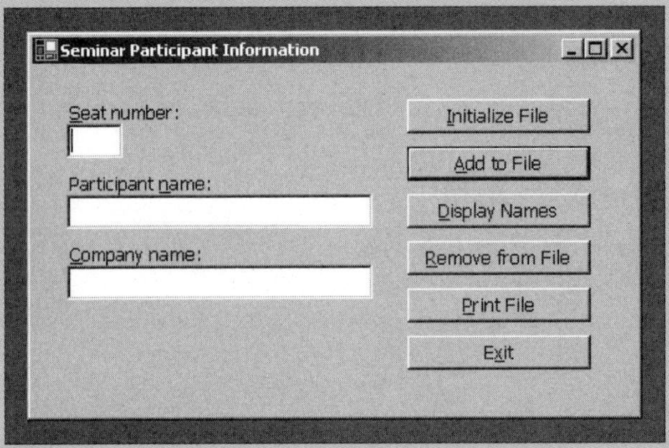

Figure 10-1: Seminar application's user interface

2 Click the **Initialize File** button. The message "Initialize the file?" appears in a message box. Click the **Yes** button. The Initialize File button's Click event procedure creates and initializes a random access file named preview.data on your computer's hard disk. It also displays the message "File was initialized" in a message box.

You learn how to create and initialize a random access file in Lesson A.

3 Click the **OK** button to close the message box.

Now add three seminar participants to the preview.data file.

4 Type 4 in the Seat number text box, then type **Xavier Martinez** in the Participant name text box. Type **ABC Corporation** in the Company name text box, then click the **Add to File** button.

5 Type 2 in the Seat number text box, then type **Carol Williams** in the Participant name text box. Type **Rogers Inc.** in the Company name text box, then click the **Add to File** button.

6 Type 7 in the Seat number text box, then type **Jack Johnson** in the Participant name text box. Type **K Enterprises** in the Company name text box, then click the **Add to File** button.

Next, display the participant and company names associated with seat number 4.

7 Type 4 in the Seat number text box, then click the **Display Names** button. The names "Xavier Martinez" and "ABC Corporation" appear in the Participant name and Company name text boxes, respectively.

Now remove the participant and company names associated with seat number 4 from the file.

8 Click the **Remove from File** button. To verify that the record was deleted from the file, type **4** in the Seat number text box, then click the **Display Names** button. Notice that no names appear in the Participant name and Company name text boxes.

Finally, print the Seminar Participant Report.

9 If your computer is connected to a printer, click the **Print File** button. A report similar to the one shown in Figure 10-2 prints on the printer.

```
                      Seminar Participant Report
 1
 2        Carol Williams              Rogers Inc.
 3
 4
 5
 6
 7        Jack Johnson                K Enterprises
 8
 9
10
11
12
13
14
15
16
17
18
19
20
```

Figure 10-2: Seminar Participant Report

10 Click the **Exit** button to end the application.

Before you can begin coding the Seminar application, you need to learn how to create and use a random access file; you learn about random access files in Lesson A. You begin coding the Seminar application in Lesson B and then complete it in Lesson C.

LESSON A
objectives

After completing this lesson, you will be able to:

■ Define the terminology used with random access files

■ Create a record structure

■ Open and close a random access file

■ Write data to and read data from a random access file

■ Initialize a random access file

■ Test for the end of a random access file

Random Access Files

Random Access Files Versus Sequential Access Files

In most of the applications you created in the previous tutorials, the data processed by the application was entered from the keyboard each time the application was started. This approach works fine in applications that require only a small amount of data. However, most real-world applications—such as payroll and inventory applications—process large amounts of data. Consider how time-consuming it would be to have a payroll clerk enter every employee's data—Social Security number, name, rate of pay, and so on—each time he or she processed the weekly payroll!

As you learned in Tutorial 9, in addition to getting data from the keyboard, an application also can get data from a file stored on the computer's disk. This means that, rather than having the payroll clerk enter the employee data each week, you can save the data to a file, and then instruct the payroll application to get its input data from there as often as needed.

In Tutorial 9, you learned how to save data to and read data from a sequential access file. In this tutorial, you learn how to save data to and read data from a random access file. Unlike a sequential access file, which typically is composed of lines of text, a random access file is composed of fields and records. A **field** is a single item of information about a person, place, or thing—for example, a Social Security number, a city, or a price. A **record** is a group of related fields that contain all of the necessary data about a specific person, place, or thing. The college you are attending keeps a student record on you. Your student record might contain the following fields: your Social Security number, name, address, phone number, credits earned, grades earned, grade point average, and so on. The place where you are employed also keeps a record on you. Your employee record might contain your Social Security number, name, address, phone number, starting date, salary or hourly wage, and so on. Figure 10-3 illustrates the concept of fields and records.

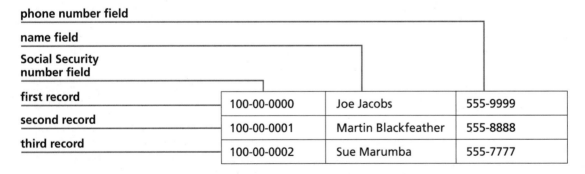

Figure 10-3: Illustration of fields and records

As you learned in Tutorial 9, a sequential access file is similar to a cassette tape in that each line in the file, like each song on a cassette tape, is both stored and retrieved in consecutive order from the beginning of the file to the end of the file. A random access file, on the other hand, is similar to a compact disc (CD) in that each record in the file, like each song on a CD, can be stored and retrieved in any order. This means, for example, that you can read or write the third record in a random access file without first reading or writing the two records that precede it.

As you know, each song on a CD is associated with a unique number. The number indicates the position of the song on the CD and allows you to access the song directly. Each record in a random access file also has a unique number, called a **record number**, that indicates its position in the file. The first record in the file is record number one; the second is record number two, and so on. You can directly access a record in a random access file by its record number. For this reason, random access files also are referred to as **direct access files**.

The ability to access a record directly allows quick retrieval of information, which accounts for the use of random access files for real-time activities, such as making airline reservations, looking up the prices of items at a store, and approving credit card purchases. You can access record number 500 in a random access file just as quickly as you can access record number one. Accessing record number 500 in a sequential access file would take much longer, because the computer would have to read the previous 499 records first.

Figure 10-4 shows the procedure you typically follow when using a random access file in an application. One exception to following this procedure is when a record contains only one field, and the field is not a String field. In that case, you do not need to create a record structure or declare a record variable; you can simply follow steps three through five in the procedure.

Random access file procedure
1. create a record structure 2. declare a record variable using the record structure 3. open the file 4. write one or more records to, or read one or more records from, the file 5. close the file

Figure 10-4: Procedure for using a random access file

Step 1 in the procedure shown in Figure 10-4 is to create a record structure.

Creating a Record Structure

Each record in a random access file must contain the same number of fields. Additionally, the names, data types, and lengths of the fields must be identical from record to record. You ensure that each record contains the exact same fields by creating a **record structure**. The record structure itself actually becomes a data type, called a **user-defined data type**, which is separate and distinct from the standard data types available in Visual Basic .NET.

You use the **Structure statement** to create a record structure in Visual Basic .NET. Figure 10-5 shows the syntax of the Structure statement and includes an example of using the statement to create a record structure named EmployStruc.

You also can include Function and Sub procedure declarations in a Structure statement. Additionally, you can declare the variables and procedures as Private rather than Public. You can learn more about the Structure statement by viewing its Help screen.

Syntax

Structure *structureName*
    [<**VBFixedString**(*length*)>] **Public** *fieldName1* **As** *datatype*
    [<**VBFixedString**(*length*)>] **Public** *fieldName2* **As** *datatype*
    [<**VBFixedString**(*length*)>] **Public** *fieldNameN* **As** *datatype*
End Structure

Example

```
Structure EmployStruc
                        Public intEmployNumber As Integer
    <VBFixedString(10)> Public strFirstName As String
    <VBFixedString(15)> Public strLastName As String
                        Public sngSalary As Single
End Structure
```

Figure 10-5: Syntax and example of the Structure statement

It is not necessary for a structure name to end with the five letters "Struc"; however, doing so helps to identify the record structure in code.

You also can create a record structure for storing records in an array. You learn about arrays in Tutorial 11. If the record structure is for an array, you do not need to specify the length of the String fields in the structure.

The Structure statement begins with the keyword Structure followed by the name of the record structure; the statement ends with the keywords End Structure. Between the Structure and End Structure keywords, you define the fields included in each record. Each field definition contains the keyword Public followed by the name of the field, the keyword As, and the field's *datatype*. The *datatype* identifies the type of data that the field will store and can be any of the standard data types available in Visual Basic .NET; it also can be another previously defined record structure (user-defined data type).

For all but the String data type, the data type you choose determines the length of the field. For example, if a field's data type is Boolean, Char, or Short, Visual Basic .NET automatically assigns a length of two bytes to the field. Visual Basic .NET assigns a length of four bytes to Integer and Single fields. Double, Long, and Date fields are assigned a length of eight bytes, and a Decimal field is assigned a length of 16 bytes. In the example shown in Figure 10-5, the intEmployNumber and sngSalary fields are assigned a length of four bytes each, because their data types are Integer and Single, respectively.

If a field's data type is String, then you must specify the length of the field. (Recall that the length of a field in a random access file must be identical from record to record.) You specify the field length by including the attribute <**VBFixedString**(*length*)>, where *length* is the number of characters to include in the field, at the beginning of the field definition. An **attribute** is simply an instruction that provides additional information for the Visual Basic .NET compiler. The <**VBFixedString**(*length*)> attribute, for instance, tells the compiler to create a fixed-length String field that contains *length* number of characters. Notice that two String fields are included in the EmployStruc record structure shown in Figure 10-5. The strFirstName field contains 10 characters, and the strLastName field contains 15 characters.

If the data assigned to a String field is shorter than the length of the field, Visual Basic .NET pads the unused space with blanks (spaces). For example, the seven-character string "Charles" is padded with three blanks before being stored in the 10-character strFirstName field. However, if the data assigned to a String field is longer than the length of the field, Visual Basic .NET crops (truncates) the data to fit the field. The twelve-character string "Penelope Ann" is cropped to a 10-character string—in this case, "Penelope A"—before being stored in the strFirstName field.

You create a form-level record structure by entering the Structure statement in the form's Declarations section. To create a global record structure—one that can be used by more than one form—you enter the Structure statement in a module file. (You learned about module files in Tutorial 7.)

The second step in the random access file procedure shown in Figure 10-4 is to declare a record variable using the record structure.

tip

•••••••••••••••••
Keep in mind that the Structure statement simply defines the record structure. It does not actually create the record variable or the field variables.

Declaring a Record Variable

Recall that a record structure is a user-defined data type. As you can with Visual Basic .NET's standard data types, you can use a user-defined data type (record structure) to declare a variable. The three-character ID for a variable declared as a user-defined data type is "udt". For example, the instruction `Dim udtEmploy As EmployStruc` declares an EmployStruc variable named udtEmploy, similar to the way the instruction `Dim intAge As Integer` declares an Integer variable named intAge. The difference, however, is that the variable declared as a user-defined data type, called a **record variable**, will itself contain one or more variables, called **field variables**. The instruction `Dim udtEmploy As EmployStruc`, for example, declares a record variable named udtEmploy and four field variables named intEmployNumber, strFirstName, strLastName, and sngSalary. In code, you refer to the entire record variable by its name—in this case, udtEmploy. To refer to the individual field variables, however, you must precede the field variable's name with the name of the record variable in which it is defined. You separate the record variable's name from the field variable's name with a period. As you learned in Tutorial 1, the period is called the dot member selection operator; in this case, it indicates that the field variable is a member of the record variable. The names of the field variables within the udtEmploy record variable are udtEmploy.intEmployNumber, udtEmploy.strFirstName, udtEmploy.strLastName, and udtEmploy.sngSalary.

After you create the record structure and declare the record variable, you then can open the random access file, which is Step 3 in the procedure shown in Figure 10-4.

Opening a Random Access File

In Visual Basic .NET, you use the **FileOpen function** to open either a new random access file or an existing random access file. Figure 10-6 shows the syntax and two examples of using the FileOpen function to open a random access file named employ.data.

Syntax
FileOpen(_filenumber, filename,_ **OpenMode.Random, [OpenAccess.ReadWrite, OpenShare.Shared,]** _recordLength_**)**

Examples

Example 1
```
FileOpen(1, "employ.data", OpenMode.Random, _
    OpenAccess.ReadWrite, OpenShare.Shared, 33)
```

Example 2
```
FileOpen(1, "employ.data", OpenMode.Random, _
    OpenAccess.ReadWrite, OpenShare.Shared, Len(udtEmploy))
```

Figure 10-6: Syntax and examples of the FileOpen function

In the syntax, _filename_ is the name of the file (including an optional folder path) you want to open, and is enclosed in quotation marks. If you do not include a folder path in the _filename_ argument, the computer searches for the file in the current project's bin folder. If the file does not exist, the FileOpen function creates the file; otherwise, it opens the existing file.

Filenumber in the FileOpen function's syntax is a positive integer that you assign to the file. Typically, you assign the number one to the first file opened, the number two to the second file opened, and so on. When the FileOpen function is processed, the computer associates the _filenumber_ with the file. You use the _filenumber_, rather than the _filename_, to refer to the file in other statements—such as statements that write information to and read information from the file. The _filenumber_ is associated with the file as long as the file is open. When the file is closed, the computer disassociates the _filenumber_ from the file.

The _recordLength_ argument in the FileOpen function's syntax specifies the length of each record in the file. _RecordLength_ must be a positive integer between 1 and 32767, inclusive. You can calculate the record length manually by simply adding together the length of each field in the record variable; or, you can use the **Len function** to have the computer calculate the record length for you. ("Len" stands for "length".) The syntax of the Len function is **Len(**_variablename_**)**, where _variablename_ is the name of the record variable. To calculate the length of the udtEmploy record variable, for example, you use `Len(udtEmploy)`. Notice that the first example shown in Figure 10-6 uses the number 33, which is the length of the udtEmploy record variable, as the _recordLength_ argument; in the second example, the function `Len(udtEmploy)` is used as the _recordLength_ argument.

The `OpenAccess.ReadWrite` argument in the FileOpen function's syntax indicates that the random access file can be both read from and written to. The `OpenShare.Shared` argument indicates that the file can be shared—in other words, other processes can use the file.

After opening the random access file, you then can move on to Step 4 in the random access procedure, which is to write records to the file or read records from the file. First, learn how to write records to a random access file.

Writing Records to a Random Access File

You use the **FilePut function** to write a record to a random access file. Figure 10-7 shows the syntax of the FilePut function and includes two example of using the function to write a record to the employ.data file, which was opened as file number one.

Syntax
FilePut(_filenumber, recordvariable[, recordnumber]_**)**

Examples and results
Example 1 `FilePut(1, udtEmploy, 1)`
Result writes the record as the first record in the file
Example 2 `FilePut(1, udtEmploy, 3)`
Result writes the record as the third record in the file

Figure 10-7: Syntax and examples of the FilePut function

The _filenumber_ argument in the syntax is the number assigned to the file in the FileOpen function. The _recordvariable_ argument is the name of the record variable that contains the record you want written to the file, and the _recordnumber_ argument is the number of the record you want written. If you do not include the _recordnumber_ argument in the FilePut function, the computer writes the record at the current location of the file pointer. (Recall from Tutorial 9 that the computer uses a file pointer to keep track of the next character to write in a file.)

The `FilePut(1, udtEmploy, 1)` function shown in Example 1 in Figure 10-7 writes the record contained in the udtEmploy record variable as the first record in the random access file opened as file number one. The `FilePut(1, udtEmploy, 3)` function shown in Example 2 writes the record as the third record in the random access file.

When a random access file is first created, you may find that it contains "garbage"—useless characters in places on the computer disk where records have not been written. This is due to the way your computer's operating system saves and deletes files from a disk. When you save a file to a disk, the sectors that contain the file are marked as "in use." When you delete a file, the regions (sectors) on the disk that contain the file are marked as "available," but the file is not really erased from the disk. Those sectors will contain the remains of old files until you write over that information. When you do not write information to each record in a random access file, the space reserved for the unwritten records can contain anything. The solution to this problem is to initialize the file—in other words, to clear the disk space for the file.

Initializing a Random Access File

You initialize a random access file by writing spaces to the String fields and a zero to the numeric fields. A random access file should be initialized before any records are written to it. If you initialize the file after records are written to it, the existing records will be overwritten with the spaces and zeros. However, a user may wish to initialize an existing file so that it can be reused for new data. In that case, a confirmation message should appear that lets the user confirm his or her intent.

Before you can initialize a random access file, you must estimate the maximum number of records the file will contain. Figure 10-8 shows the code that initializes a data file named employ.data for 10 records.

```
'declare variables
Dim udtEmploy As EmployStruc
Dim intRecordNum, intButton As Integer

'verify that the user wants to initialize the file
intButton = MessageBox.Show("Initialize the file?", _
    "Employee", MessageBoxButtons.YesNo, _
    MessageBoxIcon.Exclamation)
If intButton = DialogResult.Yes Then
    'assign spaces to String fields
    'and zero to numeric fields
    udtEmploy.intEmployNumber = 0
    udtEmploy.strFirstName = Space(10)
    udtEmploy.strLastName = Space(15)
    udtEmploy.sngSalary = 0

    'open the file
    FileOpen(1, "employ.data", OpenMode.Random, _
        OpenAccess.ReadWrite, OpenShare.Shared, _
        Len(udtEmploy))

    'use a loop to initialize the file
    For intRecordNum = 1 to 10
        FilePut(1, udtEmploy, intRecordNum)
    Next intRecordNum

    MessageBox.Show("File was initialized", _
        "Employee", MessageBoxButtons.OK, _
        MessageBoxIcon.Information)
Else
    MessageBox.Show("File was not initialized", _
        "Employee", MessageBoxButtons.OK, _
        MessageBoxIcon.Information)
End If
```

Figure 10-8: Code to initialize the employ.data file for 10 records

The code begins by declaring three variables: a record variable named udtEmploy and two Integer variables named intRecordNum and intButton. The udtEmploy variable is used to store the record—the employee number, first name, last name, and salary. The intRecordNum variable is used to keep track of the number of times the For...Next loop is processed. The intButton variable stores the user's response to the "Initialize the file?" question.

After declaring the variables, the code uses the MessageBox.Show method to display a dialog box that confirms the user's intent to initialize the file. If the user clicks the No button in the dialog box, the code displays the message "File was not initialized" in a message box. However, if the user clicks the Yes button in the dialog box, the code assigns the number zero to the numeric field variables in the record variable, and uses the Space function to assign the appropriate number of spaces to the String field variables. (Recall that you learned about the Space function in Tutorial 9.) The code then opens the employ.data file and uses a For...Next loop to initialize the file by writing 10 records to it. The code then displays the message "File was initialized" in a message box.

Next, learn how to read records from a random access file.

Reading Records from a Random Access File

You use the **FileGet function** to read a record from a random access file. Figure 10-9 shows the syntax of the FileGet function and includes two examples of using the function to read a record from the employ.data file, which was opened as file number one.

Syntax
FileGet(*filenumber, recordvariable*[, *recordnumber*]**)**
Examples and results
Example 1 FileGet(1, udtEmploy, 1) **Result** reads the first record in the file, and stores the record in the udtEmploy record variable
Example 2 FileGet(1, udtEmploy, 3) **Result** reads the third record in the file, and stores the record in the udtEmploy record variable

Figure 10-9: Syntax and examples of the FileGet function

The *filenumber* argument in the syntax is the number assigned to the file in the FileOpen function. The *recordvariable* argument is the name of the record variable that will store the record being read, and the *recordnumber* argument is the number of the record you want to read. If you do not include the *recordnumber* argument in the FileGet function, the computer reads the record at the current location of the file pointer. (Recall from Tutorial 9 that the computer uses a file pointer to keep track of the next character to read in a file.)

The FileGet(1, udtEmploy, 1) function shown in Example 1 in Figure 10-9 reads the first record from the random access file opened as file number one, and stores the record in the udtEmploy record variable. The FileGet(1, udtEmploy, 3) function shown in Example 2 reads the third record from the random access file and stores the record in the udtEmploy record variable.

At times, you might need to read each record in a random access file, stopping only when there are no more records to read.

Testing for the End of a Random Access File

You can use the **EOF function**, which stands for "end of file," to determine whether the file pointer is at the end of a random access file. The syntax of the EOF function is **EOF(***filenumber***)**, where *filenumber* is the number used in the FileOpen function to open the file. When the file pointer is at the end of the file, the EOF function returns the Boolean value True; otherwise, the function returns the Boolean value False. Figure 10-10 shows examples of using the EOF function to determine whether the file pointer is at the end of the employ.data file.

Examples and results

Example 1
```
Dim udtEmploy As EmployStruc, intRecordNum As Integer
Do Until EOF(1) = True
      intRecordNum = intRecordNum + 1
      FileGet(1, udtEmploy, intRecordNum)
      instructions to process the record
Loop
```

Result
repeats the loop instructions until the file pointer is at the end of the file

Example 2
```
Dim udtEmploy As EmployStruc, intRecordNum As Integer
Do Until EOF(1)
      intRecordNum = intRecordNum + 1
      FileGet(1, udtEmploy, intRecordNum)
      instructions to process the record
Loop
```

Result
same as Example 1

Example 3
```
Dim udtEmploy As EmployStruc, intRecordNum As Integer
Do While EOF(1) = False
      intRecordNum = intRecordNum + 1
      FileGet(1, udtEmploy, intRecordNum)
      instructions to process the record
Loop
```

Result
repeats the loop instructions while the file pointer is not at the end of the file

Example 4
```
Dim udtEmploy As EmployStruc, intRecordNum As Integer
Do While Not EOF(1)
      intRecordNum = intRecordNum + 1
      FileGet(1, udtEmploy, intRecordNum)
      instructions to process the record
Loop
```

Result
same as Example 3

Figure 10-10: Examples of the EOF function

The Do Until clause in Example 1 in Figure 10-10 tells the computer to repeat the loop instructions until the EOF function returns the Boolean value True. Notice that you can omit the "= True" text from the Do Until clause, as shown in Example 2. The Do While clause in Example 3 in the figure tells the computer to repeat the loop

You also can close two or more files by listing each file number, separated by commas, in the *filenumber* argument. For example, to close three files opened as file number one, file number three, and file number five, you use `FileClose(1, 3, 5)`.

instructions as long as (or while) the EOF function returns the Boolean value False. As Example 4 indicates, you can omit the "= False" text from the Do While clause by including the Not logical operator before the EOF function. (As you learned in Tutorial 4, the Not logical operator reverses the truth-value of a condition.)

The last step in the random access procedure shown in Figure 10-4 is to close the random access file.

Closing a Random Access File

You use the **FileClose function** to close a random access file. The syntax of the FileClose function is **FileClose([*filenumber*])**, where *filenumber* (which is optional) is the number assigned to the file in the FileOpen function. For example, to close the employ.data file, which was opened as file number one, you use `FileClose(1)`. If you do not include a *filenumber* in the FileClose function, the function closes all files that were opened with the FileOpen function.

You now have completed Lesson A. You can either take a break or complete the end-of-lesson questions and exercises before moving on to the next lesson. In Lesson B, you begin coding the Seminar application that you previewed at the beginning of the tutorial. You complete the application in Lesson C.

S U M M A R Y

To create a user-defined data type (record structure):

■ Use the Structure statement. The statement's syntax is
Structure *structureName*
        [<**VBFixedString**(*length*)>] **Public** *fieldName1* **As** *datatype*
        [<**VBFixedString**(*length*)>] **Public** *fieldName2* **As** *datatype*
        [<**VBFixedString**(*length*)>] **Public** *fieldNameN* **As** *datatype*
End Structure

To create or open a random access file:

■ Use the FileOpen function. The function's syntax is **FileOpen**(*filenumber*, *filename*, **OpenMode.Random**, [**OpenAccess.ReadWrite, OpenShare.Shared**,] *recordLength*).
■ *Filenumber* is an integer that you assign to the file. You use the *filenumber* to refer to the file in code.
■ *Filename* is the name of the file you want to create/open and can include an optional folder path. If you omit the folder path, the file is created/opened in the current project's bin folder.
■ **OpenMode.Random** indicates that the file is a random access file.
■ **OpenAccess.ReadWrite** indicates that the file can be both read from and written to.
■ **OpenShare.Shared** indicates that other processes can use the file.
■ *RecordLength* is the length of each record in the file and must be an integer in the range of 1 through 32767, inclusive.

To determine the size of a record:

■ Use the Len function. The function's syntax is **Len**(*variablename*), where *variablename* is the name of the record variable.

To write a record to an open random access file:

■ Use the FilePut function. The function's syntax is **FilePut**(*filenumber, recordvariable*[, *recordnumber*]), where *filenumber* is the number assigned to the file in the FileOpen function, *recordvariable* is the name of the record variable that contains the record you want written to the file, and *recordnumber* is the number of the record you want written. If you do not include the *recordnumber* argument in the FilePut function, the computer writes the record at the current location of the file pointer.

To initialize a String field variable to spaces:

■ Use the Space function. The function's syntax is **Space**(*number*), where *number* represents the number of spaces you want to assign to the variable.

To read a record from an open random access file:

■ Use the FileGet function. The function's syntax is **FileGet**(*filenumber, recordvariable*[, *recordnumber*]), where *filenumber* is the number assigned to the file in the FileOpen function, *recordvariable* is the name of the record variable that will store the record being read, and *recordnumber* is the number of the record you want to read. If you do not include the *recordnumber* argument in the FileGet function, the computer reads the record at the current location of the file pointer.

To determine whether the file pointer is at the end of a random access file:

■ Use the EOF function. The function's syntax **EOF**(*filenumber*), where *filenumber* is the number used in the FileOpen function to open the file. When the file pointer is at the end of the file, the EOF function returns the Boolean value True; otherwise, the function returns the Boolean value False.

To close a random access file:

■ Use the FileClose function. The function's syntax is **FileClose**([*filenumber*]), where *filenumber* (which is optional) is the number assigned to the file in the FileOpen function. If you do not include a *filenumber* in the FileClose function, the function closes all files that were opened with the FileOpen function.

QUESTIONS

1. You use the _____ statement to create a user-defined data type.
   a. Declare
   b. Define
   c. Record
   d. Structure
   e. UserType

2. Which of the following defines a 15-character String field variable named strCity?
    a. `Public strCity.PadLeft(15) As String`
    b. `Public strCity.Pad(15) As String`
    c. `Public strCity(15) As String`
    d. `<VBFixed(15)> Public strCity As String`
    e. `<VBFixedString(15)> Public strCity As String`

3. If you store the string "Chicago" (without the quotation marks) in a 15-character String field variable named strCity, what will Visual Basic .NET actually store in the strCity field variable?
    a. The string "Chicago" (with the quotation marks)
    b. The string "Chicago" (with the quotation marks) followed by six blank spaces
    c. The string "Chicago"
    d. The string "Chicago" followed by eight blank spaces
    e. Eight blank spaces followed by the string "Chicago"

4. You use the _____ function to create a random access file.
    a. FileCreate
    b. FileOpen
    c. Random
    d. RandomCreate
    e. RandomOpen

5. You use the _____ function to open an existing random access file.
    a. FileOpen
    b. OpenRandom
    c. OpenRandomFile
    d. RandomOpen
    e. None of the above.

6. You use the _____ function to write a record to a random access file.
    a. FilePut
    b. FileRecord
    c. FileWrite
    d. RecordWrite
    e. WriteRecord

7. You use the _____ function to read a record from a random access file.
    a. FileGet
    b. FileRead
    c. GetRecord
    d. ReadRecord
    e. RecordRead

8. Which of the following statements is valid? (The structure's name is ItemStruc. The record variable's name is udtItem. Each record contains 100 bytes.)
    a. `FileOpen(1, "item.data", OpenMode.Random,`
        `OpenAccess.ReadWrite, OpenShare.Shared, 100)`
    b. `FileOpen(1, "item.data", OpenMode.Random,`
        `OpenAccess.ReadWrite, OpenShare.Shared, Len(ItemStruc))`
    c. `FileOpen(1, "item.data", OpenMode.Random,`
        `OpenAccess.ReadWrite, OpenShare.Shared, Len(udtItem))`
    d. Both a and b.
    e. Both a and c.

9. Which of the following writes the udtStudent record, which consists of a last name and a first name, to a random access file?
   a. `FilePut(1, udtStudent, intRecordNumber)`
   b. `FilePut(1, udtStudent.strLast, udtStudent.strFirst)`
   c. `FilePut(1, udtStudent.strLast, udtStudent.strFirst, intRecordNumber)`
   d. `FileWrite(1, udtStudent, intRecordNumber)`
   e. `FileWrite(1, udtStudent.strLast, udtStudent.strFirst, intRecordNumber)`

10. Which of the following closes a random access file opened as file number 3?
    a. `Close(3)`
    b. `CloseFile(3)`
    c. `File(3).Close`
    d. `File.Close(3)`
    e. `FileClose(3)`

11. Which of the following returns the length of the udtStudent record?
    a. `Len(udtStudent)`
    b. `Length(udtStudent)`
    c. `RecLength(udtStudent)`
    d. `RecordLen(udtStudent)`
    e. `udtStudent(length)`

12. Which of the following assigns five spaces to a field variable named strRegion? The field variable is included in the udtStore record variable.
    a. `strRegion = Space(5)`
    b. `strRegion.udtStore = Space(5)`
    c. `udtStore = strRegion.Space(5)`
    d. `udtStore.strRegion = Space(5)`
    e. `Space(5) = udtStore.strRegion`

13. Which of the following tells the computer to repeat the loop instructions for each record in the file opened as file number one?
    a. `Do While Not EOF(1)`
    b. `Do Until EOF(1)`
    c. `Loop While Not EOF(1)`
    d. `Loop Until EOF(1)`
    e. All of the above.

Use the following information to answer Questions 14 through 18.

```
Structure CustomerStruc
        <VBFixedString(25)> Public strName As String
        <VBFixedString(12)> Public strPhone As String
                            Public sngSales As Single
End Structure
Dim udtCustomer As CustomerStruc
```

14. The name of the record variable is _____.
    a. CustomerStruc
    b. strName
    c. strPhone
    d. sngSales
    e. udtCustomer

15. The length of the sngSales field variable is _____.
   a. 2 bytes
   b. 4 bytes
   c. 8 bytes
   d. 16 bytes
   e. unknown

16. The length of the record variable is _____.
   a. 39 bytes
   b. 41 bytes
   c. 45 bytes
   d. 53 bytes
   e. unknown

17. In code, you refer to the strPhone field variable as _____.
   a. CustomerStruc.strPhone
   b. strPhone
   c. strPhone.udtCustomer
   d. strPhone.CustomerStruc
   e. udtCustomer.strPhone

18. Assume that the intNum variable contains the number 3. Which of the following statements reads the third customer record from a file opened as file number one?
   a. `FileGet(1, intNum, udtCustomer)`
   b. `FileGet(1, udtCustomer, intNum)`
   c. `FileGet(1, intNum, udtCustomer.strName,`
       `udtCustomer.strPhone, udtCustomer.sngSales)`
   d. `FileRead(1, udtCustomer.strName, udtCustomer.strPhone,`
       `udtCustomer.sngSales, intNum)`
   e. `FileRead(1, udtStudent, intNum)`

E X E R C I S E S

1. Write a Structure statement that defines a record structure named BookStruc. The record structure contains three fields: strTitle, strAuthor, and sngCost. The strTitle and strAuthor fields are String fields that contain 20 characters each. The sngCost field is a Single field.

2. Write a Structure statement that defines a record structure named TapeStruc. The record structure contains four fields: strName, strArtist, intSong, and strLength. The strName, strArtist, and strLength fields are 25-character, 20-character, and six-character String fields, respectively. The intSong field is an Integer field.

3. Write a Dim statement that declares a BookStruc variable named udtBook.

4. Write a Dim statement that declares a TapeStruc variable named udtTape.

5. Write a FileOpen function that opens a random access file named "books.data". Open the file as file number 1. The contents of the udtBook record variable will be written to the file.

6. Write a FileOpen function that opens a random access file named "tapes.data". Open the file as file number 1. The contents of the udtTape record variable will be written to the file.

7. Assume that the intRecNum variable contains the number five and the random access file was opened as file number one. Write a FilePut function that writes the contents of the udtBook record variable as the fifth record in the file.

8. Assume that the intRecNum variable contains the number two and the random access file was opened as file number one. Write a FilePut function that writes the contents of the udtTape record variable as the second record in the file.

9. Assume that the intRecNum variable contains the number three and the random access file was opened as file number one. Write a FileGet function that reads the third record in the file. The name of the record variable is udtBook.

10. Assume that the intRecNum variable contains the number five and the random access file was opened as file number one. Write a FileGet function that reads the fifth record in the file. The name of the record variable is udtTape.

11. Write the statement that closes the file opened as file number 1.

12. Assume that an application contains the following record structure:

```
Structure ComputerStruc
        <VBFixedString(5)> Public strName As String
        sngCost As Single
End Structure
```

  a. Write a Dim statement that declares a ComputerStruc variable named udtComputer.
  b. Write a FileOpen function that opens a random access file named "computer.data". Open the file as file number one.
  c. Write the code to initialize the computer.data file for 10 records.
  d. Write an assignment statement that assigns the name "IB-50" to the strName field variable.
  e. Write an assignment statement that assigns the number 2400 to the sngCost field variable.
  f. Assuming that the intRecNum variable contains the number five, write the FilePut function that writes the udtComputer record as the fifth record in the computer.data random access file.
  g. Assuming that the intRecNum variable contains the number five, write the FileGet function that reads the fifth record in the computer.data random access file.
  h. Write the assignment statements that assign the value in the strName field variable to the NameLabel control, and the value in the sngCost field variable to the CostLabel control.
  i. Write the statement that closes the computer.data file.

13. Assume that an application contains the following record structure:

```
Structure FriendStruc
        <VBFixedString(10)> Public strLast As String
        <VBFixedString(10)> Public strFirst As String
End Structure
```

a. Write a Dim statement that declares a FriendStruc variable named udtFriend.

b. Write a FileOpen function that opens a random access file named "friends.data". Open the file as file number one.

c. Write the code to initialize the friends.data file for five records.

d. Write an assignment statement that assigns the value in the FirstNameTextBox control to the strFirst field variable.

e. Write an assignment statement that assigns the value in the LastNameTextBox control to the strLast field variable.

f. Assuming that the intRecNum variable contains the number three, write the FilePut function that writes the udtFriend record as the third record in the friends.data random access file.

g. Assuming that the intRecNum variable contains the number three, write the FileGet function that reads the third record in the friends.data random access file.

h. Write the assignment statements that assign the value in the strLast field variable to the LastNameLabel control, and the value in the strFirst field variable to the FirstNameLabel control.

i. Write the statement that closes the friends.data file.

Exercise 14 is a Discovery Exercise. Discovery Exercises, which may include topics that are not covered in this lesson, allow you to "discover" the solutions to problems on your own.

discovery ▶ **14.** Display the Help screen for the FreeFile function. What is the purpose of the function? What does the function return?

After completing this lesson, you will be able to:

- Use a record structure in an application
- Initialize a random access file in an application
- Add records to a random access file
- Display a specific record contained in a random access file
- Verify that the record number is valid

Using a Random Access File in an Application

The Seminar Application

Recall that your task in this tutorial is to create a Seminar application that Mrs. Phelps can use to keep track of the participants enrolled in her "Meditation and You" seminar. The application should allow Mrs. Phelps to save each participant's name, as well as the name of the company where the participant is employed, to a file. It also should allow her to display the participant information associated with a specific seat number, remove a participant's information from the file, and print a report that lists the seat number, participant name, and company name.

On your computer's hard disk is a partially completed Seminar application. You begin coding the application in this lesson, and then complete the application in Lesson C.

To open the Seminar application:

1 Start Microsoft Visual Studio .NET, if necessary, and then close the Start Page window. Click **File** on the menu bar, and then click **Open Solution**. The Open Solution dialog box opens. Open the **Seminar Solution** (Seminar Solution.sln) file, which is contained in the VBNET\Tut10\Seminar Solution folder.

2 If the designer window is not open, right-click **Seminar Form.vb** in the Solution Explorer window, then click **View Designer**.

3 Auto-hide the Toolbox, Solution Explorer, and Properties windows, if necessary. The user interface for the Seminar application is shown in Figure 10-11.

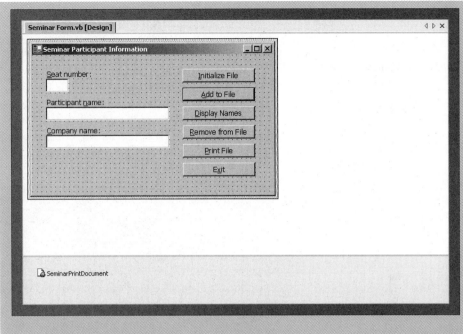

Figure 10-11: User interface for the Seminar application

The interface contains three labels, three text boxes, six buttons, and a PrintDocument control.

The TOE chart for the Seminar application is shown in Figure 10-12.

Task	Object	Event
Add a record to the random access file	AddButton	Click
Display the record associated with a seat number	DisplayButton	Click
End the application	ExitButton	Click
Initialize the participants.data random access file	InitializeButton	Click
Use the SeminarPrintDocument control to print the random access file	PrintButton	Click
Remove a record from the random access file	RemoveButton	Click
Print the Seminar Participant Report	SeminarPrintDocument	PrintPage
Clear the contents of the ParticipantTextBox and CompanyTextBox controls	SeatTextBox	TextChanged
Get and display the seat number, participant name, and company name	SeatTextBox, ParticipantTextBox, CompanyTextBox	None
Select the existing text	SeatTextBox, ParticipantTextBox, CompanyTextBox	Enter

Figure 10-12: TOE chart for the Seminar application

In this lesson, you code the Click event procedures for the InitializeButton, AddButton, and DisplayButton controls. You code the Click event procedures for the RemoveButton and PrintButton controls, as well as the PrintPage event for the SeminarPrintDocument control, in Lesson C. The remaining event procedures have already been coded for you.

The Seminar application will save each participant's name and the name of his or her company to a random access file. Recall that the first step in the procedure for using a random access file is to define the record structure for the records. In this case, the record structure will contain two String fields: one for the participant name and the other for the company name.

To create a record structure for the participant records:

1   Right-click the **form**, and then click **View Code** to open the Code editor window.

A form-level record structure is needed in this application, because the record structure will be used only by the procedures contained in the current form. Recall that you create a form-level record structure by entering the Structure statement in the Declarations section of the form.

2   In the blank line below the comment `'declare form-level record structure`, type the Structure statement shown in Figure 10-13.

enter these lines of code

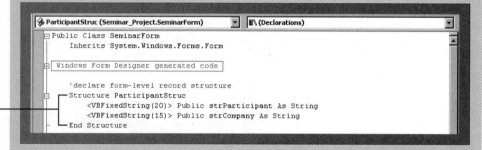

Figure 10-13: Structure statement entered in the Declarations section of the form

As you learned in Lesson A, before using a random access file you should initialize it to ensure that it does not contain garbage. This application provides the Initialize File button for this purpose. Mrs. Phelps can use the button to initialize the file at the beginning of each seminar.

Coding the InitializeButton Click Event Procedure

Figure 10-14 shows the pseudocode for the Initialize File button's Click event procedure.

```
InitializeButton
1. declare variables
2. verify that the user wants to initialize the file
3. if the user does not want to initialize the file
        display the message "File was not initialized" in a message box
   else
        assign 20 spaces to the strParticipant field variable
        assign 15 spaces to the strCompany field variable
        open a random access file named participants.data
        repeat 20 times
                write a record to the participants.data file
        end repeat
        close the participants.data file
        display the message "File was initialized." in a message box
   end if
```

Figure 10-14: Pseudocode for the InitializeButton Click event procedure

To code the InitializeButton Click event procedure:

1 Click the **Class Name** list arrow, and then click **InitializeButton** in the list. Click the **Method Name** list arrow, and then click **Click** in the list. The code template for the InitializeButton Click event procedure appears in the Code editor window.

The first step in the pseudocode shown in Figure 10-14 is to declare the variables. The InitializeButton Click event procedure will use three variables: two Integer variables named intSeat and intButton, and a ParticipantStruc variable named udtParticipant. The intSeat and udtParticipant variables will be used in a repetition structure to write 20 records to the participants.data file. The intButton variable will store the user's response to the "Initialize the file?" question.

2 Type **dim intSeat, intButton as integer, udtParticipant as participantstruc** and press **Enter**.

Next, verify that the user wants to initialize the file.

3 Type the comment and MessageBox.Show method shown in Figure 10-15, then position the insertion point as shown in the figure.

enter these lines of code

position the insertion point here

```
        Private Sub InitializeButton_Click(ByVal sender As Object, ByVal e As System.EventAr
            Dim intSeat, intButton As Integer, udtParticipant As ParticipantStruc
            'verify that the user wants to initialize the file
            intButton = MessageBox.Show("Initialize the file?", "Seminar Information", _
                MessageBoxButtons.YesNo, MessageBoxIcon.Exclamation, _
                MessageBoxDefaultButton.Button2)

        End Sub
```

Figure 10-15: Additional code entered in the procedure

If the user does not want to initialize the file, then the procedure should display the message "File was not initialized" in a message box. Otherwise, the procedure should assign 20 spaces to the strParticipant field variable and 15 spaces to the strCompany field variable, and then open a random access file named participants.data.

4 Type the selection structure shown in Figure 10-16, then position the insertion point as shown in the figure.

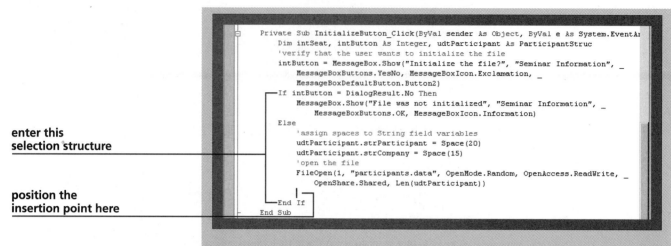

```
     Private Sub InitializeButton_Click(ByVal sender As Object, ByVal e As System.EventAr
         Dim intSeat, intButton As Integer, udtParticipant As ParticipantStruc
         'verify that the user wants to initialize the file
         intButton = MessageBox.Show("Initialize the file?", "Seminar Information", _
             MessageBoxButtons.YesNo, MessageBoxIcon.Exclamation, _
             MessageBoxDefaultButton.Button2)
      ┌─ If intButton = DialogResult.No Then
      │      MessageBox.Show("File was not initialized", "Seminar Information", _
      │          MessageBoxButtons.OK, MessageBoxIcon.Information)
      │  Else
      │      'assign spaces to String field variables
      │      udtParticipant.strParticipant = Space(20)
      │      udtParticipant.strCompany = Space(15)
      │      'open the file
      │      FileOpen(1, "participants.data", OpenMode.Random, OpenAccess.ReadWrite, _
      │          OpenShare.Shared, Len(udtParticipant))
      │          │
      └─ End If ┘
         End Sub
```

Figure 10-16: Selection structure entered in the procedure

Now use a repetition structure to write 20 records to the participants.data file. Then close the file and display the message "File was initialized" in a message box.

5   Type the additional lines of code shown in Figure 10-17, which shows the completed InitializeButton Click event procedure.

```
     Private Sub InitializeButton_Click(ByVal sender As Object, ByVal e As System.EventArgs) Handles
         Dim intSeat, intButton As Integer, udtParticipant As ParticipantStruc
         'verify that the user wants to initialize the file
         intButton = MessageBox.Show("Initialize the file?", "Seminar Information", _
             MessageBoxButtons.YesNo, MessageBoxIcon.Exclamation, _
             MessageBoxDefaultButton.Button2)
         If intButton = DialogResult.No Then
             MessageBox.Show("File was not initialized", "Seminar Information", _
                 MessageBoxButtons.OK, MessageBoxIcon.Information)
         Else
             'assign spaces to String field variables
             udtParticipant.strParticipant = Space(20)
             udtParticipant.strCompany = Space(15)
             'open the file
             FileOpen(1, "participants.data", OpenMode.Random, OpenAccess.ReadWrite, _
                 OpenShare.Shared, Len(udtParticipant))
         ┌─ 'initialize the file, then close the file
         │   For intSeat = 1 To 20
         │       FilePut(1, udtParticipant, intSeat)
         │   Next intSeat
         │   FileClose(1)
         │   MessageBox.Show("File was initialized", "Seminar Information", _
         └──── MessageBoxButtons.OK, MessageBoxIcon.Information)
         End If
         End Sub
```

Figure 10-17: Completed InitializeButton Click event procedure

Now test the InitializeButton Click event procedure to verify that it is working correctly.

To test the InitializeButton Click event procedure:

1   Click **File** on the menu bar, and then click **Save All**. Click **Debug** on the menu bar, and then click **Start**.

enter this selection structure

position the insertion point here

enter these lines of code

2 Click the **Initialize File** button. The message "Initialize the file?" appears in a message box. Click the **Yes** button. Because the participants.data file does not exist, the InitializeButton Click event procedure creates the file and then initializes it by writing 20 records to it. The message "File was initialized" appears in a message box.

3 Click the **OK** button to close the message box.

4 Click the **Exit** button to end the application. When you return to the Code editor window, close the Output window.

Now verify that the participants.data file was created and initialized.

5 Click **File** on the menu bar, point to **Open,** and then click **File.** The Open File dialog box opens. Open the **bin** folder, which is contained in the VBNET\Tut10\Seminar Solution\Seminar Project folder. Click **participants.data** in the list of filenames and then click the **Open** button. The participants.data file opens in a separate window. The file appears empty, because only spaces were written to it.

6 Click the **Close** button ☒ on the participants.data window to close the window.

Next, code the Add to File button's Click event procedure.

Coding the AddButton Click Event Procedure

According to the TOE chart shown in Figure 10-12, the AddButton Click event procedure is responsible for adding a participant record to the random access file. Figure 10-18 shows the pseudocode for the AddButton Click event procedure.

AddButton
1. declare an Integer variable named intSeat and a ParticipantStruc variable named udtParticipant
2. assign the seat number from the SeatTextBox to the intSeat variable
3. if the seat number is greater than 0 and less than 21
      assign the participant name from the ParticipantTextBox to the strParticipant field variable
      assign the company name from the CompanyTextBox to the strCompany field variable
      open the participants.data random access file
      write the record to the participants.data file
      close the participants.data file
   else
      display the message "The seat number must be from 1 through 20." in a message box
   end if
4. send the focus to the SeatTextBox

Figure 10-18: Pseudocode for the AddButton Click event procedure

To code the AddButton Click event procedure:

1 Click the **Class Name** list arrow, and then click **AddButton** in the list. Click the **Method Name** list arrow, and then click **Click** in the list. The code template for the AddButton Click event procedure appears in the Code editor window.

The first step in the pseudocode shown in Figure 10-18 is to declare two variables named intSeat and udtParticipant. The intSeat variable will store the participant's seat number, and the udtParticipant variable will store the participant's name and the name of his or her company.

2 Type **dim intSeat as integer, udtParticipant as participantstruc** and press **Enter**.

Now assign the participant's seat number, which is entered in the SeatTextBox control, to the intSeat variable.

3 Type **'assign the seat number to a variable** and press **Enter**, then type **intseat = val(me.seattextbox.text)** and press **Enter**.

Step 3 in the pseudocode shown in Figure 10-18 uses a selection structure to verify that the seat number, which is used as the record number, is valid. In this case, a valid seat (record) number must be a number from one through 20. Before writing a record to a random access file, you always should verify that the record number is valid; this ensures that the record will be written in the space saved for the file on the computer disk.

4 Type **'verify that the seat number is valid** and press **Enter**, then type **if intseat > 0 andalso intseat < 21 then** and press **Enter**.

If the seat number is valid, the procedure should assign the participant and company names to the field variables in the udtParticipant record variable. The participant and company names are entered in the ParticipantTextBox and CompanyTextBox controls, respectively, on the form.

5 Type **'assign names to field variables** and press **Enter**. Type **udtparticipant.strparticipant = me.participanttextbox.text** and press **Enter**, then type **udtparticipant.strcompany = me.companytextbox.text** and press **Enter**.

Now open the participants.data file and write the record to the file, then close the file.

6 Type the additional lines of code shown in Figure 10-19, then position the insertion point as shown in the figure.

```
Private Sub AddButton_Click(ByVal sender As Object, ByVal e As System.EventArgs) Han
    Dim intSeat As Integer, udtParticipant As ParticipantStruc
    'assign the seat number to a variable
    intSeat = Val(Me.SeatTextBox.Text)
    'verify that the seat number is valid
    If intSeat > 0 AndAlso intSeat < 21 Then
        'assign names to field variables
        udtParticipant.strParticipant = Me.ParticipantTextBox.Text
        udtParticipant.strCompany = Me.CompanyTextBox.Text
        'open the file
        FileOpen(1, "participants.data", OpenMode.Random, OpenAccess.ReadWrite, _
            OpenShare.Shared, Len(udtParticipant))
        'write the record, then close the file
        FilePut(1, udtParticipant, intSeat)
        FileClose(1)

    End If
End Sub
```

enter these lines of code

position the insertion point here

Figure 10-19: Additional code entered in the procedure

If the seat number is not valid, the procedure should display an appropriate message in a message box.

7 Type **else** and press **Enter**. Type **messagebox.show("The seat number must be from 1 through 20.", _** (be sure to include a space before the line continuation character) and press **Enter**.

8 Press **Tab**, then type **"Seminar Information", messageboxbuttons.ok, messageboxicon.information).**

The last step in the pseudocode shown in Figure 10-18 is to send the focus to the SeatTextBox.

9 Type the additional line of code shown in Figure 10-20, which shows the completed AddButton Click event procedure.

```vb
Private Sub AddButton_Click(ByVal sender As Object, ByVal e As System.EventArgs) Han
    Dim intSeat As Integer, udtParticipant As ParticipantStruc
    'assign the seat number to a variable
    intSeat = Val(Me.SeatTextBox.Text)
    'verify that the seat number is valid
    If intSeat > 0 AndAlso intSeat < 21 Then
        'assign names to field variables
        udtParticipant.strParticipant = Me.ParticipantTextBox.Text
        udtParticipant.strCompany = Me.CompanyTextBox.Text
        'open the file
        FileOpen(1, "participants.data", OpenMode.Random, OpenAccess.ReadWrite, _
            OpenShare.Shared, Len(udtParticipant))
        'write the record, then close the file
        FilePut(1, udtParticipant, intSeat)
        FileClose(1)
    Else
        MessageBox.Show("The seat number must be from 1 through 20.", _
            "Seminar Information", MessageBoxButtons.OK, MessageBoxIcon.Information)
    End If
    Me.SeatTextBox.Focus()
End Sub
```

enter this line of code ────────────

Figure 10-20: Completed AddButton Click event procedure

Now test the AddButton Click event procedure to verify that it is working correctly.

To test the AddButton Click event procedure:

1 Save the solution, then start the application.

First, try entering a record that contains an invalid seat number.

2 Type **34** in the Seat number text box, click the **Add to File** button. The procedure displays the message box shown in Figure 10-21.

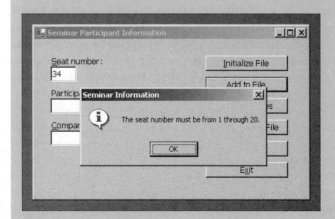

Figure 10-21: Message box displayed by the AddButton Click event procedure

3 Click the **OK** button to close the message box.

Recall that you can enter records in any order in a random access file. Enter record number 2 first.

4 Type **2** in the Seat number text box, then type **Thomas Jacob** in the Participant name text box. Type **Jacob Electric** in the Company name text box, then click the **Add to File** button. The AddButton Click event procedure writes the participant and company names as the second record in the participants.data file.

Now enter record number 1.

5 Type **1** in the Seat number text box. Type **Penelope Dombrowski** in the Participant name text box, then type **ABC Inc.** in the Company name text box. Press **Enter** to select the Add to File button, which is the default button on the form.

6 Click the **Exit** button to end the application. When you return to the Code editor window, close the Output window.

Next, verify that the records were written to the participants.data file.

7 Open the participants.data file. The file contains two records, as shown in Figure 10-22.

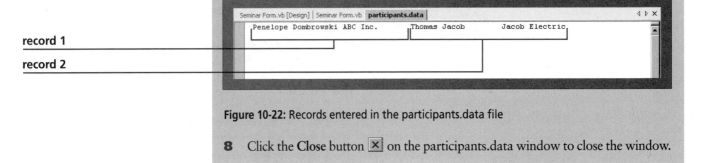

Figure 10-22: Records entered in the participants.data file

8 Click the **Close** button ☒ on the participants.data window to close the window.

The last procedure you code in this lesson is the Display Names button's Click event procedure.

Coding the DisplayButton Click Event Procedure

According to the TOE chart shown in Figure 10-12, the DisplayButton Click event procedure is responsible for displaying the record associated with a specific seat number. Figure 10-23 shows the pseudocode for the DisplayButton Click event procedure.

DisplayButton
1. declare an Integer variable named intSeat and a ParticipantStruc variable named udtParticipant
2. assign the seat number from the SeatTextBox to the intSeat variable
3. if the seat number is greater than 0 and less than 21
> open the participants.data random access file
> read the record from the participants.data file
> assign the participant name from the udtParticipant variable to the ParticipantTextBox
> assign the company name from the udtParticipant variable to the CompanyTextBox
> close the participants.data file

else
> display the message "The seat number must be from 1 through 20." in a message box

end if
4. send the focus to the SeatTextBox

Figure 10-23: Pseudocode for the DisplayButton Click event procedure

To code the DisplayButton Click event procedure:

1   Click the **Class Name** list arrow, and then click **DisplayButton** in the list. Click the **Method Name** list arrow, and then click **Click** in the list. The code template for the DisplayButton Click event procedure appears in the Code editor window.

The first step in the pseudocode shown in Figure 10-23 is to declare two variables named intSeat and udtParticipant. The intSeat variable will store the participant's seat number, and the udtParticipant variable will store the participant's record.

2   Type **dim intSeat as integer, udtParticipant as participantstruc** and press **Enter**.

Next, assign the seat number, which is entered in the SeatTextBox control, to the intSeat variable.

3   Type '**assign the seat number to a variable** and press **Enter**, then type **intseat = val(me.seattextbox.text)** and press **Enter**.

Step 3 in the pseudocode shown in Figure 10-23 uses a selection structure to verify that the seat number is valid. Recall that a valid seat number is a number in the range of 1 through 20, inclusive. Before reading a record from a random access file, you always should verify that the record number is valid to ensure that the information being read is actually part of the file.

4   Type '**verify that the seat number is valid** and press **Enter**, then type **if intseat > 0 andalso intseat < 21 then** and press **Enter**.

If the seat number is valid, the procedure should open the participants.data random access file, and then read the appropriate record from the file. The appropriate record is the one associated with the seat number stored in the intSeat variable.

5   Type the additional lines of code shown in Figure 10-24, then position the insertion point as shown in the figure.

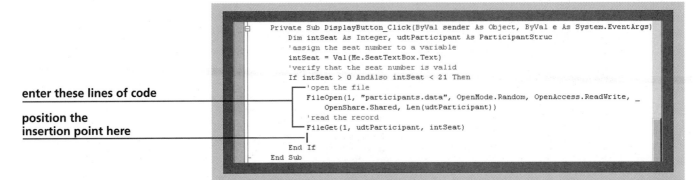

enter these lines of code

position the
insertion point here

Figure 10-24: Additional code entered in the procedure

Now assign the participant and company names, which are stored in the udtParticipant variable, to the ParticipantTextBox and CompanyTextBox controls, respectively. Use the TrimEnd method, which you learned about in Tutorial 8, to remove any spaces from the end of the names. (Recall that, if the data assigned to a String field is shorter than the length of the field, Visual Basic .NET pads the unused characters with spaces.)

6   Type **'assign field values to text boxes** and press **Enter**.

7   Type **me.participanttextbox.text = udtparticipant.strparticipant.trimend** and press **Enter**, then type **me.companytextbox.text = udtparticipant.strcompany. trimend** and press **Enter**.

Now close the file.

8   Type **'close the file** and press **Enter**, then type **fileclose(1)** and press **Enter**.

If the seat number is not valid, the procedure should display an appropriate message in a message box.

9   Press **Backspace** to cancel the indentation, then type **else** and press **Enter**. Type **messagebox.show("The seat number must be from 1 through 20.", _** (be sure to include a space before the line continuation character) and press **Enter**. Press **Tab**, then type **"Seminar Information", messageboxbuttons.ok, messageboxicon.information).**

The last step in the pseudocode shown in Figure 10-23 is to send the focus to the SeatTextBox.

10   Type the additional line of code shown in Figure 10-25, which shows the completed DisplayButton Click event procedure.

```
Private Sub DisplayButton_Click(ByVal sender As Object, ByVal e As System.EventArgs)
    Dim intSeat As Integer, udtParticipant As ParticipantStruc
    'assign the seat number to a variable
    intSeat = Val(Me.SeatTextBox.Text)
    'verify that the seat number is valid
    If intSeat > 0 AndAlso intSeat < 21 Then
        'open the file
        FileOpen(1, "participants.data", OpenMode.Random, OpenAccess.ReadWrite, _
            OpenShare.Shared, Len(udtParticipant))
        'read the record
        FileGet(1, udtParticipant, intSeat)
        'assign field values to text boxes
        Me.ParticipantTextBox.Text = udtParticipant.strParticipant.TrimEnd
        Me.CompanyTextBox.Text = udtParticipant.strCompany.TrimEnd
        'close the file
        FileClose(1)
    Else
        MessageBox.Show("The seat number must be from 1 through 20.", _
            "Seminar Information", MessageBoxButtons.OK, MessageBoxIcon.Information)
    End If
    Me.SeatTextBox.Focus()
End Sub
```

enter this line of code

Figure 10-25: Completed DisplayButton Click event procedure

Now test the DisplayButton Click event procedure to verify that it is working correctly.

To test the DisplayButton Click event procedure:

1 Save the solution, then start the application.

First, try displaying a record that contains an invalid seat number.

2 Type **34** in the Seat number text box, then click the **Display Names** button. The procedure displays the message "The seat number must be from 1 through 20." in a message box.

3 Click the **OK** button to close the message box.

Now display the information associated with seat number two.

4 Type **2** in the Seat number text box, then click the **Display Names** button. The procedure displays the name "Thomas Jacob" in the Participant name text box, and the name "Jacob Electric" in the Company name text box, as shown in Figure 10-26.

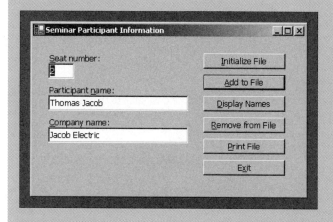

Figure 10-26: Record number two displayed in the interface

Next, display the information associated with seat number one.

5 Type **1** in the Seat number text box, then click the **Display Names** button. The procedure displays the name "Penelope Dombrowski" in the Participant name text box, and the name "ABC Inc." in the Company name text box.

Now enter a valid seat number, but one that is not associated with a participant record.

6 Type **4** in the Seat number text box, then click the **Display Names** button. Notice that no information appears in the Participant name and Company name text boxes. This indicates that the participants.data file does not contain any participant information for seat number four.

7 Click the **Exit** button to end the application. When you return to the Code editor window, close the Output window, then close the Code editor window.

8 Click **File** on the menu bar, and then click **Close Solution**.

You now have completed Lesson B. You can either take a break or complete the end-of-lesson questions and exercises before moving on to the next lesson. You finish coding the Seminar application in Lesson C.

SUMMARY

To create a form-level record structure:

■ Enter the Structure statement in the form's Declarations section.

To declare a local record variable:

■ Enter a Dim statement in a procedure. Use a record structure as the variable's data type.

To create or open a random access file:

■ Use the FileOpen function.

To determine the size of a record:

■ Use the Len function.

To write a record to an open random access file:

■ Use the FilePut function.

To initialize a String field variable to spaces:

■ Use the Space function.

To read a record from an open random access file:

■ Use the FileGet function.

To verify that the record number is valid:

■   Use a selection structure.

To close a random access file:

■   Use the FileClose function.

Q U E S T I O N S

1.   Which of the following statements is valid? (The structure's name is SalesPersonStruc. The record variable's name is udtSalesPerson.)
     a.   `FileOpen(1, "sales.data", OpenMode.Random,`
          `OpenAccess.ReadWrite, OpenShare.Shared)`
     b.   `FileOpen(1, "sales.data", OpenMode.Random,`
          `OpenAccess.ReadWrite, OpenShare.Shared,`
          `Len(udtSalesPerson))`
     c.   `FileOpen(1, "sales.data", OpenMode.Random,`
          `OpenAccess.ReadWrite, OpenShare.Shared,`
          `Len(SalesPersonStruc))`
     d.   `FileOpen(1, "sales.data", OpenMode.Random,`
          `OpenAccess.ReadWrite, OpenShare.Shared,`
          `Length(udtSalesPerson))`
     e.   `FileOpen(1, "sales.data", OpenMode.Random,`
          `OpenAccess.ReadWrite, OpenShare.Shared,`
          `Length(SalesPersonStruc))`

2.   Which of the following is false?
     a.   You use the FileClose function to close a random access file opened with the FileOpen function.
     b.   The Structure statement creates a record variable.
     c.   You should initialize a random access file before writing any records to it.
     d.   You use the FilePut function to write a record to a random access file.
     e.   Before accessing a record in a random access file, you should verify that the record number is valid.

3.   Assume that the udtSales record variable contains two field variables named strState and sngAmount. You use _____ to refer to the strState field variable in code.
     a.   strState
     b.   strState.udtSales
     c.   udtSales.strState
     d.   udtSales&strState
     e.   None of the above.

4.   Which of the following reads the fourth record in a file opened as file number one? (The structure's name is SalesStruc, and the record variable's name is udtSales.)
     a.   `FileGet(1, 4, SalesStruc)`
     b.   `FileGet(1, SalesStruc, 4)`
     c.   `FileGet(1, 4, udtSales)`
     d.   `FileGet(1, udtSales, 4)`
     e.   `FileGet(4, 1, udtSales)`

5. Assume that a file contains 10 records. Which of the following If clauses verifies whether the record number stored in the intNumber variable is valid for the file?

   a. `If intNumber > 0 AndAlso < 11 Then`

   b. `If intNumber > 0 AndAlso intNumber < 11 Then`

   c. `If intNumber >= 0 AndAlso intNumber <= 10 Then`

   d. `If intNumber > 0 OrElse intNumber < 11 Then`

   e. `If intNumber >= 0 OrElse intNumber <= 10 Then`

E X E R C I S E S

1. In this exercise, you modify the Seminar application that you began coding in the lesson. The modified application first verifies that the ParticipantTextBox contains an entry before writing the participant's record to the file.

   a. Use Windows to make a copy of the Seminar Solution folder, which is contained in the VBNET\Tut10 folder. Change the name of the folder to Seminar1 Solution.

   b. If necessary, start Visual Studio .NET. Open the Seminar Solution (Seminar Solution.sln) file, which is contained in the VBNET\Tut10\Seminar1 Solution folder. If the designer window is not open, right-click the form file's name in the Solution Explorer window, then click View Designer.

   c. Before writing the participant information to the participants.data file, the AddButton Click event procedure should verify that the user entered a name in the Participant name text box. If the text box contains a name, write the record to the file, and then display an appropriate message to the user. If the text box does not contain a name, do not write the record to the file; rather, simply display an appropriate message to the user. Make the appropriate modifications to the AddButton Click event procedure.

   d. Save the solution, and then start the application. Type 5 in the Seat number text box, then type SysCo in the Company name text box. Click the Add to File button. A message indicating that you must enter a name should appear in a message box. Close the message box.

   e. Type two spaces in the Participant name text box, then click the Add to File button. A message indicating that you must enter a name should appear in a message box. Close the message box.

   f. Type your name in the Participant name text box, then click the Add to File button. A message indicating that the record was saved should appear in a message box. Close the message box.

   g. Click the Exit button to end the application.

   h. Close the Output window, and then close the solution.

2. In this exercise, you modify the Seminar application that you began coding in the lesson. The modified application displays a message when the user clicks the Display Names button after entering a valid, but unassigned, seat number.

   a. Use Windows to make a copy of the Seminar Solution folder, which is contained in the VBNET\Tut10 folder. Change the name of the folder to Seminar2 Solution.

   b. If necessary, start Visual Studio .NET. Open the Seminar Solution (Seminar Solution.sln) file, which is contained in the VBNET\Tut10\Seminar2 Solution folder. If the designer window is not open, right-click the form file's name in the Solution Explorer window, then click View Designer.

   c. If the user enters a valid seat number, but the seat number has not been assigned to a participant, the DisplayButton Click event procedure should display the message "Seat number x is vacant.", where x is the seat number. Make the appropriate modifications to the procedure.

d. Save the solution, and then start the application. Type 5 in the Seat number text box, then click the Display Names button. The message "Seat number 5 is vacant." should appear in a message box. Close the message box.

e. Type 2 in the Seat number text box, then click the Display Names button. The names "Thomas Jacob" and "Jacob Electric" should appear in the Participant name and Company name text boxes, respectively.

f. Click the Exit button to end the application.

g. Close the Output window, and then close the solution.

3. In this exercise, you create an application that allows the user to keep track of the CDs that he or she owns. Each CD is numbered from 1 through 5.

a. If necessary, start Visual Studio .NET. Open the CD Solution (CD Solution.sln) file, which is contained in the VBNET\Tut10\CD Solution folder. If the designer window is not open, right-click the form file's name in the Solution Explorer window, then click View Designer.

b. In the form's Declarations section, define a record structure named CdStruc. The record structure should contain two 20-character String fields named strName and strArtist.

c. Code the InitializeButton Click event procedure so that it initializes a random access file named cds.data for five records. (Be sure to verify that the user wants to initialize the file.)

d. Code the WriteButton Click event procedure so that it writes the CD information (name and artist) to the file. Use the CD number as the record number. (Be sure to verify that the record number is valid.)

e. Code the DisplayButton Click event procedure so that it displays the CD information (name and artist) that corresponds to the CD number entered by the user. (Be sure to verify that the record number is valid.)

f. Save the solution, and then start the application. First, use the Initialize button to initialize the file. Next, use the Write button to write the following three records to the file.

CD number	CD name	Artist name
4	Western Way	Mingo Colfax
2	Country For All	Barbara Mender
1	Line Dancing	Helen Starks

g. Use the Display button to display the information for CD number two.

h. Enter an invalid CD number in the Number text box, then click the Write button. An appropriate message should display in a message box. Close the message box.

i. Enter an invalid CD number in the Number text box, then click the Display button. An appropriate message should display in a message box. Close the message box.

j. Click the Exit button to end the application.

k. Close the Output window, and then close the solution.

4. In this exercise, you create an application that allows the user to keep track of a company's monthly sales.

a. If necessary, start Visual Studio .NET. Open the Sales Solution (Sales Solution.sln) file, which is contained in the VBNET\Tut10\Sales Solution folder. If the designer window is not open, right-click the form file's name in the Solution Explorer window, then click View Designer.

b. In the form's Declarations section, define a record structure named SalesStruc. The record structure should contain a three-character String field named strMonthName and a Single field named sngSalesAmount.

c. Code the InitializeButton Click event procedure so that it initializes a random access file named sales.data for 12 records. (Be sure to verify that the user wants to initialize the file.)

    d. Code the WriteButton Click event procedure so that it writes the sales information (month name and sales amount) to the file. Use the month number as the record number. (Be sure to verify that the record number is valid.)

    e. Code the DisplayButton Click event procedure so that it displays (in a message box) the sales information (month name and sales amount) that corresponds to the month number entered by the user. (Be sure to verify that the record number is valid.)

    f. Save the solution, and then start the application. First, use the Initialize button to initialize the file. Next, use the Write button to record January sales of 500.75 and February sales of 1200 in the file.

    g. Use the Display button to display the information for month number one.

    h. Click the Exit button to end the application.

    i. Close the Output window, and then close the solution.

5. In this exercise, you modify the Seminar application that you began coding in the lesson. The modified application initializes the two field variables to the string "Unassigned" rather than to spaces.

    a. Use Windows to make a copy of the Seminar Solution folder, which is contained in the VBNET\Tut10 folder. Change the name of the folder to Seminar3 Solution.

    b. If necessary, start Visual Studio .NET. Open the Seminar Solution (Seminar Solution.sln) file, which is contained in the VBNET\Tut10\Seminar3 Solution folder. If the designer window is not open, right-click the form file's name in the Solution Explorer window, then click View Designer.

    c. Modify the InitializeButton Click event procedure so that it uses the string "Unassigned", rather than the Space function, to initialize the two field variables.

    d. Save the solution, and then start the application. Click the Initialize File button, then click the Yes button. Click the OK button to close the message box. Type 10 in the Seat number text box, then click the Display Names button. The string "Unassigned" should appear in both the Participant name and Company name text boxes.

    e. Click the Exit button to end the application.

    f. Close the Output window, and then close the solution.

Exercise 6 is a Discovery Exercise. Discovery Exercises, which may include topics that are not covered in this lesson, allow you to "discover" the solutions to problems on your own.

discovery ▶ **6.** In this exercise, you learn how numbers are saved to a random access file.

    a. If necessary, start Visual Studio .NET. Open the Savings Solution (Savings Solution.sln) file, which is contained in the VBNET\Tut10\Savings Solution folder. If the designer window is not open, right-click the form file's name in the Solution Explorer window, then click View Designer.

    b. Start the application. Click the Initialize File button. Type 1 in the Week number text box, then type Mary in the Name text box, and then type 25 in the Savings text box. Click the Write to File button. Type 2 in the Week number text box, then type Kevin in the Name text box, and then type 18 in the Savings text box. Click the Write to File button.

    c. Click the Exit button to end the application, then close the Output window.

    d. Start Notepad, which is the text editor that comes with the Windows operating system. Open the savings.data file, which is contained in the VBNET\Tut10\Savings Solution\Savings Project\bin folder. Notice that you can read the contents of the String field in both records; however, the contents of the Integer field in each record displays as strange-looking characters. The unusual characters appear because the numeric fields in a random access file are stored in a compressed format, called binary, which allows random access files to use less disk space than sequential access files when storing numbers. Because a text editor interprets all data it reads as text, the numbers appear as unusual characters because their binary codes are not associated with standard keyboard characters.

    e. Close Notepad, then close the Savings solution.

Completing the Seminar Application

Coding the Remaining Procedures in the Seminar Application

To complete the Seminar application, you need to code the Click event procedures for the RemoveButton and PrintButton controls, and the PrintPage event procedure for the SeminarPrintDocument control. Before you can code the procedures, you need to open the Seminar application.

To open the Seminar application:

1 Start Microsoft Visual Studio .NET, if necessary, and then close the Start Page window. Click **File** on the menu bar, and then click **Open Solution**. The Open Solution dialog box opens. Open the **Seminar Solution** (Seminar Solution.sln) file, which is contained in the VBNET\Tut10\Seminar Solution folder.

2 If the designer window is not open, right-click **Seminar Form.vb** in the Solution Explorer window, then click **View Designer**. The Seminar application's user interface appears on the screen.

3 Auto-hide the Toolbox, Solution Explorer, and Properties windows, if necessary.

The first procedure you code in this lesson is the RemoveButton Click event procedure.

Coding the RemoveButton Click Event Procedure

According to the TOE chart shown in Figure 10-12 in Lesson B, the RemoveButton Click event procedure is responsible for removing a record from the participants.data file. The appropriate record to remove depends on the seat number entered in the Seat number text box on the form. Figure 10-27 shows the pseudocode for the RemoveButton Click event procedure.

```
RemoveButton
1. declare an Integer variable named intSeat and a ParticipantStruc variable named
   udtParticipant
2. assign the seat number from the SeatTextBox to the intSeat variable
3. if the seat number is greater than 0 and less than 21
        open the participants.data random access file
        assign 20 spaces to the strParticipant field variable
        assign 15 spaces to the strCompany field variable
        write the record to the participants.data file
        close the participants.data file
   else
        display the message "The seat number must be from 1 through 20." in a message box
   end if
4. clear the contents of the SeatTextBox, ParticipantTextBox, and CompanyTextBox controls
5. send the focus to the SeatTextBox
```

Figure 10-27: Pseudocode for the RemoveButton Click event procedure

To code the RemoveButton Click event procedure:

1   Right-click the **form**, and then click **View Code** to open the Code editor window. Click the **Class Name** list arrow, and then click **RemoveButton** in the list. Click the **Method Name** list arrow, and then click **Click** in the list. The code template for the RemoveButton Click event procedure appears in the Code editor window.

The first step in the pseudocode shown in Figure 10-27 is to declare two variables named intSeat and udtParticipant. The intSeat variable will store the participant's seat number, and the udtParticipant variable will store the participant's name and the name of his or her company.

2   Type **dim intSeat as integer, udtParticipant as participantstruc** and press **Enter**.

Next, assign the participant's seat number, which is entered in the SeatTextBox control, to the intSeat variable.

3   Type **'assign the seat number to a variable** and press **Enter**, then type **intseat = val(me.seattextbox.text)** and press **Enter**.

Step 3 in the pseudocode shown in Figure 10-27 uses a selection structure to verify that the seat number, which is used as the record number, is valid. In this case, a valid seat (record) number must be a number from one through 20.

4   Type **'verify that the seat number is valid** and press **Enter**, then type **if intseat > 0 andalso intseat < 21 then** and press **Enter**.

If the seat number is valid, the procedure should open the participants.data file.

5   Type the comment and FileOpen function shown in Figure 10-28, then position the insertion point as shown in the figure.

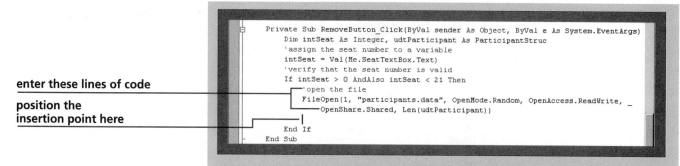

```
Private Sub RemoveButton_Click(ByVal sender As Object, ByVal e As System.EventArgs)
    Dim intSeat As Integer, udtParticipant As ParticipantStruc
    'assign the seat number to a variable
    intSeat = Val(Me.SeatTextBox.Text)
    'verify that the seat number is valid
    If intSeat > 0 AndAlso intSeat < 21 Then
        'open the file
        FileOpen(1, "participants.data", OpenMode.Random, OpenAccess.ReadWrite, _
            OpenShare.Shared, Len(udtParticipant))

    End If
End Sub
```

enter these lines of code

position the
insertion point here

Figure 10-28: Comment and FileOpen function entered in the procedure

Now remove the record associated with the seat number stored in the intSeat variable. You remove a record from a random access file simply by deleting the information stored in the record. In this case, for example, you will assign spaces to the two String field variables in the udtParticipant record variable, and then write the record variable to the file. The spaces will overwrite the existing information stored in the record. (If the file contains a numeric field variable, you assign a zero to the variable before writing the record to the file.)

6 Type 'delete the record information from the file and press **Enter**. Type **udtparticipant.strparticipant = space(20)** and press **Enter**, then type **udtparticipant.strcompany = space(15)** and press **Enter**.

7 Type **fileput(1, udtparticipant, intseat)** and press **Enter**.

Now close the file.

8 Type 'close the file and press **Enter**, then type **fileclose(1)** and press **Enter**.

If the seat number is not valid, the procedure should display an appropriate message in a message box.

9 Press **Backspace** to cancel the indentation, then type **else** and press **Enter**. Type **messagebox.show("The seat number must be from 1 through 20.", _** (be sure to include a space before the line continuation character) and press **Enter**. Press **Tab**, then type **"Seminar Information", messageboxbuttons.ok, messageboxicon.information)**.

The last two steps in the pseudocode shown in Figure 10-27 are to clear the contents of the three text boxes, and then send the focus to the SeatTextBox.

10 Type the additional lines of code shown in Figure 10-29, which shows the completed RemoveButton Click event procedure.

```
Private Sub RemoveButton_Click(ByVal sender As Object, ByVal e As System.EventArgs) Handles Remov
    Dim intSeat As Integer, udtParticipant As ParticipantStruc
    'assign the seat number to a variable
    intSeat = Val(Me.SeatTextBox.Text)
    'verify that the seat number is valid
    If intSeat > 0 AndAlso intSeat < 21 Then
        'open the file
        FileOpen(1, "participants.data", OpenMode.Random, OpenAccess.ReadWrite, _
            OpenShare.Shared, Len(udtParticipant))
        'delete the record information from the file
        udtParticipant.strParticipant = Space(20)
        udtParticipant.strCompany = Space(15)
        FilePut(1, udtParticipant, intSeat)
        'close the file
        FileClose(1)
    Else
        MessageBox.Show("The seat number must be from 1 through 20.", _
            "Seminar Information", MessageBoxButtons.OK, MessageBoxIcon.Information)
    End If
    'clear text boxes
    Me.SeatTextBox.Text = ""
    Me.ParticipantTextBox.Text = ""
    Me.CompanyTextBox.Text = ""
    Me.SeatTextBox.Focus()
End Sub
```

enter these lines of code ⎯⎯⎯⎯⎯

Figure 10-29: Completed RemoveButton Click event procedure

Now test the RemoveButton Click event procedure to verify that it is working correctly.

To test the RemoveButton Click event procedure:

1 Click **File** on the menu bar, and then click **Save All**. Click **Debug** on the menu bar, and then click **Start**.

First, enter two records.

2 Type **7** in the Seat number text box, then type your name in the Participant name text box. Type **TeleComp** in the Company name text box, then click the **Add to File** button.

3 Type **6** in the Seat number text box, then type **Perry Mays** in the Participant name text box. Type **TeleComp** in the Company name text box, then click the **Add to File** button.

Next, verify that your information was written as record number seven in the file.

4 Type **7** in the Seat number text box, then click the **Display Names** button. Your name and company information appear in the user interface.

Now remove record number seven's information from the file.

5 Click the **Remove from File** button.

6 To verify that the information stored in record number seven was removed from the file, type **7** in the Seat number text box, then click the **Display Names** button. Notice that your name and company information do not appear in the user interface.

Now delete the information stored in record number six.

7 Type **6** in the Seat number text box, then click the **Remove from File** button.

8 Click the **Exit** button to end the application. When you return to the Code editor window, close the Output window.

Next, code the PrintButton Click event procedure.

Coding the PrintButton Click Event Procedure

The PrintButton Click event procedure is responsible for using the SeminarPrintDocument control to print the contents of the random access file. Figure 10-30 shows the procedure's pseudocode.

```
PrintButton
1. if the participants.data file exists
        print the file
   else
        display the message "File does not exist." in a message box
   end if
```

Figure 10-30: Pseudocode for the PrintButton Click event procedure

To code the PrintButton Click event procedure:

1   Click the **Class Name** list arrow, and then click **PrintButton** in the list. Click the **Method Name** list arrow, and then click **Click** in the list. The code template for the PrintButton Click event procedure appears in the Code editor window.

2   Enter the code shown in Figure 10-31, which shows the completed PrintButton Click event procedure.

```
Private Sub PrintButton_Click(ByVal sender As Object, ByVal e As System.EventArgs) H
    'print the file if it exists
    If System.IO.File.Exists("participants.data") = True Then
        Me.SeminarPrintDocument.Print()
    Else
        MessageBox.Show("File does not exist.", "Seminar Information", _
            MessageBoxButtons.OK, MessageBoxIcon.Information)
    End If
End Sub
```

enter these lines of code

Figure 10-31: Completed PrintButton Click event procedure

3   Save the solution.

Finally, code the SeminarPrintDocument control's PrintPage event procedure.

Coding the SeminarPrintDocument PrintPage Event Procedure

The SeminarPrintDocument control's PrintPage event procedure is responsible for printing the Seminar Participant Report. The report should contain three columns of information. The first column should list the 20 seat numbers, and the second and third columns should list the corresponding participant and company names, which are stored in the participants.data file. Figure 10-32 shows the pseudocode for the SeminarPrintDocument control's PrintPage event procedure.

SeminarPrintDocument
1. declare an Integer variable named intSeat, a ParticipantStruc variable named udtParticipant, and a String variable named strLine
2. declare two Integer variables named intX and intY; initialize intX to 10 and intY to 20
3. print the report header
4. open the participants.data random access file
5. repeat for intSeat = 1 to 20
   read the record from the participants.data file

   assign the seat number, 10 spaces, the participant name, 10 spaces, and the company name to the strLine variable

   add 15 to the intY variable

   print the contents of the strLine variable
   end repeat
6. close the participants.data file

Figure 10-32: Pseudocode for the SeminarPrintDocument control's PrintPage event procedure

To code the SeminarPrintDocument PrintPage event procedure:

1 Click the **Class Name** list arrow, and then click **SeminarPrintDocument** in the list. Click the **Method Name** list arrow, and then click **PrintPage** in the list. The code template for the SeminarPrintDocument PrintPage event procedure appears in the Code editor window.

The first step in the pseudocode shown in Figure 10-32 is to declare three variables named intSeat, udtParticipant, and strLine. The intSeat variable will store the participant's seat number, and the udtParticipant variable will store the participant's name and the name of his or her company. The strLine variable will store the line of text you want printed on the printer.

2 Type **dim intSeat as integer, udtParticipant as participantstruc, strLine as string** and press **Enter**.

Step 2 in the pseudocode is to declare two Integer variables named intX and intY, initializing intX to the number 10 and intY to the number 20. The intX variable will be used to control the horizontal position of the text on the printed page, and the intY variable will be used to control the vertical position of the printed text.

3 Type **dim intX as integer = 10, intY as integer = 20** and press **Enter**.

Now print the report header, and then open the participants.data random access file.

4 Type the additional code shown in Figure 10-33, then position the insertion point as shown in the figure.

enter these lines of code

position the insertion point here

```
Private Sub SeminarPrintDocument_PrintPage(ByVal sender As Object, ByVal e As System
    Dim intSeat As Integer, udtParticipant As ParticipantStruc, strLine As String
    Dim intX As Integer = 10, intY As Integer = 20
    'print the report header
    e.Graphics.DrawString("Seminar Participant Report", _
        New Font("courier new", 10, FontStyle.Regular), Brushes.Black, _
        200, 10)
    'open the file
    FileOpen(1, "participants.data", OpenMode.Random, OpenAccess.ReadWrite, _
        OpenShare.Shared, Len(udtParticipant))

End Sub
```

Figure 10-33: Additional code entered in the procedure

Step 5 in the pseudocode shown in Figure 10-32 uses a loop to repeat a set of instructions 20 times—once for each valid seat (record) number.

5 Type **for intseat = 1 to 20** and press **Enter**.

The first instruction in the loop is to read a record from the participants.data file.

6 Type **'read a record** and press **Enter**, then type **fileget(1, udtparticipant, intseat)** and press **Enter**.

Next, assign the seat number, 10 spaces, the participant name, 10 spaces, and the company name to the strLine variable.

7 Type **'define the line of text to be printed** and press **Enter**. Type **strline = intseat.tostring.padleft(2) & space(10)** _ (be sure to include a space before the line continuation character) and press **Enter**. Press **Tab**, then type **& udtparticipant.strparticipant & space(10) & udtparticipant.strcompany** and press **Enter**.

Now add the number 15 to the intY variable, which controls the vertical position of the text on the printed page, and then print the line of text. Finally, close the participants.data file.

8 Type the additional code shown in Figure 10-34, which shows the completed SeminarPrintDocument PrintPage event procedure. Also, change the `Next` clause in the procedure to `Next intSeat`.

enter these lines of code
modify this line

```
Private Sub SeminarPrintDocument_PrintPage(ByVal sender As Object, ByVal e As System
    Dim intSeat As Integer, udtParticipant As ParticipantStruc, strLine As String
    Dim intX As Integer = 10, intY As Integer = 20
    'print the report header
    e.Graphics.DrawString("Seminar Participant Report", _
        New Font("courier new", 10, FontStyle.Regular), Brushes.Black, _
        200, 10)
    'open the file
    FileOpen(1, "participants.data", OpenMode.Random, OpenAccess.ReadWrite, _
        OpenShare.Shared, Len(udtParticipant))
    For intSeat = 1 To 20
        'read a record
        FileGet(1, udtParticipant, intSeat)
        'define the line of text to be printed
        strLine = intSeat.ToString.PadLeft(2) & Space(10) _
            & udtParticipant.strParticipant & Space(10) & udtParticipant.strCompany
        'print the line of text
        intY = intY + 15
        e.Graphics.DrawString(strLine, _
            New Font("courier new", 10, FontStyle.Regular), Brushes.Black, _
            intX, intY)
    Next intSeat
    FileClose(1)
End Sub
```

Figure 10-34: Completed SeminarPrintDocument PrintPage event procedure

Now test the PrintButton Click event procedure and the SeminarPrintDocument PrintPage event procedure to verify that both are working correctly.

To test the procedures:

1 Save the solution, then start the application.

2 Click the **Print File** button. A Seminar Participant Report similar to the one shown in Figure 10-35 prints on the printer. (Recall that you entered record number one and record number two in Lesson B.)

```
                        Seminar Participant Report
    1           Penelope Dombrowski           ABC Inc.
    2           Thomas Jacob                  Jacob Electric
    3
    4
    5
    6
    7
    8
    9
   10
   11
   12
   13
   14
   15
   16
   17
   18
   19
   20
```

Figure 10-35: Seminar Participant Report

3   Click the **Exit** button to end the application. When you return to the Code editor window, close the Output window, then close the Code editor window.

4   Click **File** on the menu bar, and then click **Close Solution**.

You now have completed Tutorial 10. You can either take a break or complete the end-of lesson questions and exercises.

S U M M A R Y

To remove a record from a random access file:

■   Delete the information stored in the record. To delete the information, assign spaces to the String field variables and the number zero to the numeric field variables, and then write the record variable to the file. The new record will overwrite the existing record in the file.

To print the contents of a random access file:

■   Use a loop to read and print each record in the file.

QUESTIONS

1. You remove a record from a random access file by deleting the information stored in the record.
   a. True
   b. False

2. Which of the following can be used to read each record contained in a random access file opened as file number one? (The file contains 10 records. The record variable's name is udtJobs.)
   a. ```
      For intNum = 1 To 10
            FileGet(1, udtJobs, intNum)
      Next intNum
      ```
   b. ```
      Dim intNum As Integer = 1
      Do Until EOF(1) = True
            FileGet(1, udtJobs, intNum)
      Loop
      ```
   c. ```
      Dim intNum As Integer = 1
      Do While Not EOF(1)
            FileGet(1, udtJobs, intNum)
            intNum = intNum + 1
      Loop
      ```
   d. Both a and c.
   e. All of the above.

3. Assume that the udtJobs record variable contains two field variables: strName and sngSalary. Which of the following assigns the contents of the strName field variable, 20 spaces, and the contents of the sngSalary field variable to a String variable named strLine?
   a. `strLine = strName & Space(20) & sngSalary.ToString`
   b. `strLine = strName.udtJobs & Space(20) & sngSalary.udtJobs.ToString`
   c. `strLine = "udtJobs.strName & Space(20) & udtJobs.sngSalary.ToString"`
   d. `strLine = udtJobs.strName, Space(20), udtJobs.sngSalary.ToString`
   e. None of the above.

# EXERCISES

The following list summarizes the GUI design guidelines you have learned so far. You can use this list to verify that the interfaces you create in the following exercises adhere to the GUI standards outlined in the book.
      ```

■ Information should flow either vertically or horizontally, with the most important information always located in the upper-left corner of the screen.

■ Maintain a consistent margin of two or three dots from the edge of the window.

■ Try to create a user interface that no one notices.

■ Related controls should be grouped together using white space, a GroupBox control, or a Panel control.

■ Set the form's FormBorderStyle, ControlBox, MaximizeBox, MinimizeBox, and StartPosition properties appropriately:

■ A splash screen should not have a Minimize, Maximize, or Close button, and its borders should not be sizable.

■ A form that is not a splash screen should always have a Minimize button and a Close button, but you can choose to disable the Maximize button. Typically, the FormBorderStyle property is set to Sizable, but also can be set to FixedSingle.

■ Position related controls on succeeding dots. Controls that are not part of any logical grouping may be positioned from two to four dots away from other controls.

■ Buttons should be positioned either in a row along the bottom of the screen, or stacked in either the upper-right or lower-right corner.

■ If the buttons are positioned at the bottom of the screen, then each button should be the same height; their widths, however, may vary.

■ If the buttons are stacked in either the upper-right or lower-right corner of the screen, then each should be the same height and the same width.

■ Use no more than six buttons on a screen.

■ The most commonly used button should be placed first.

■ Button captions should:

■ be meaningful
■ be from one to three words
■ appear on one line
■ be entered using book title capitalization

■ Use labels to identify the text boxes in the interface, and position the label either above or to the left of the text box.

■ Label text should:

■ be from one to three words
■ appear on one line
■ be left-justified
■ end with a colon (:)
■ be entered using sentence capitalization

■ Labels that identify controls should have their BorderStyle property set to None.

■ Labels that display program output, such as the result of a calculation, should have their BorderStyle property set to FixedSingle.

■ Align controls to minimize the number of different margins.

- If you use a graphic in the interface, use a small one and place it in a location that will not distract the user.

- Use the Tahoma font for applications that will run on Windows 2000 or Windows XP.

- Use no more than two different font sizes, which should be 8, 9, 10, 11, or 12 point.

- Use only one font type, which should be a sans serif font, in the interface.

- Avoid using italics and underlining.

- Limit the use of bold text to titles, headings, and key items.

- Build the interface using black, white, and gray first, then add color only if you have a good reason to do so.

- Use white, off-white, light gray, pale blue, or pale yellow for an application's background, and black for the text.

- Limit the number of colors to three, not including white, black, and gray. The colors you choose should complement each other.

- Never use color as the only means of identification for an element in the user interface.

- Set each control's TabIndex property to a number that represents the order in which you want the control to receive the focus (begin with 0).

- A text box's TabIndex value should be one more than the TabIndex value of its identifying label.

- Assign a unique access key to each control (in the interface) that can receive user input (text boxes, buttons, and so on).

- When assigning an access key to a control, use the first letter of the caption or identifying label, unless another letter provides a more meaningful association. If you can't use the first letter and no other letter provides a more meaningful association, then use a distinctive consonant. Lastly, use a vowel or a number.

- Lock the controls in place on the form.

- Document the program internally.

- Use the Val function on any Text property involved in a calculation.

- Use the Format function to improve the appearance of numbers in the interface.

- In the InputBox function, use sentence capitalization for the *prompt*, and book title capitalization for the *title*.

- The default button should be the button that is most often selected by the user, except in cases where the tasks performed by the button are both destructive and irreversible. The default button typically is the first button.

- Use sentence capitalization for the optional identifying label in a group box control.

- MessageBox.Show method:

  - Use sentence capitalization for the *text* argument, but book title capitalization for the *caption* argument. The name of the application typically appears in the *caption* argument.

- Avoid using the words "error," "warning," or "mistake" in the message.
- Display the Warning Message icon ⚠ in a message box that alerts the user that he or she must make a decision before the application can continue. You can phrase the message as a question.
- Display the Information Message icon ⓘ in a message box that displays an informational message along with an OK button only.
- Display the Stop Message icon ⊗ when you want to alert the user of a serious problem that must be corrected before the application can continue.
- The default button in the dialog box should be the one that represents the user's most likely action, as long as that action is not destructive.

- Use the KeyPress event to prevent a text box from accepting inappropriate keys.
- Radio buttons:

  - Use radio buttons when you want to limit the user to one of two or more related and mutually exclusive choices.
  - Use a minimum of two and a maximum of seven radio buttons in an interface.
  - Use sentence capitalization for the label entered in the radio button's Text property.
  - Assign a unique access key to each radio button in an interface.
  - Use a group box control (or a panel control) to create separate groups of radio buttons. Only one button in each group can be selected at any one time.
  - Designate a default radio button in each group of radio buttons.

- Check boxes:

  - Use check boxes to allow the user to select any number of choices from a group of one or more independent and nonexclusive choices.
  - Use sentence capitalization for the label entered in the check box's Text property.
  - Assign a unique access key to each check box in an interface.

- List boxes:

  - A list box should contain a minimum of three selections.
  - A list box should display a minimum of three selections and a maximum of eight selections at a time.
  - Use a label control to provide keyboard access to the list box. Set the label control's TabIndex property to a value that is one less than the list box's TabIndex value.
  - List box items are either arranged by use, with the most used entries appearing first in the list, or sorted in ascending order.
  - If a list box allows the user to make only one selection at a time, then a default item should be selected in the list box when the interface first appears. The default item should be either the most used selection or the first selection in the list. However, if a list box allows more than one selection at a time, you do not select a default item.

- Menus:

  - Menu title captions, which appear on the menu bar, should be one word, with the first letter capitalized. Each menu title should have a unique access key.

- Menu item captions, which appear on a menu, can be from one to three words. Use book title capitalization and assign a unique access key to each menu item. Assign shortcut keys to commonly used menu items.

- If a menu item requires additional information from the user, place an ellipsis (...) at the end of the item's caption, which is entered in the item's Text property.

- Follow the Windows standards for the placement of menu titles and items.

- Use a separator bar to separate groups of related menu items.

■ It is customary in Windows applications to disable objects that do not apply to the current state of the application.

■ It is customary in Windows applications to highlight, or select, the existing text in a text box when the text box receives the focus.

■ If an operation is destructive, prompt the user to verify that he or she wants to proceed with the operation.

■ Test the application with both valid and invalid data (for example, test the application without entering any data, and test it by entering letters where numbers are expected).

■ Display messages to inform the user of the status of important events.

1. In this exercise, you modify the Seminar application that you finished coding in the lesson. The modified application confirms that the user wants to remove a record.
   a. Use Windows to make a copy of the Seminar Solution folder, which is contained in the VBNET\Tut10 folder. Change the name of the folder to Seminar Remove Solution.
   b. If necessary, start Visual Studio .NET. Open the Seminar Solution (Seminar Solution.sln) file, which is contained in the VBNET\Tut10\Seminar Remove Solution folder. If the designer window is not open, right-click the form file's name in the Solution Explorer window, then click View Designer.
   c. Before it removes a record from the participants.data file, the RemoveButton Click event procedure should confirm that the user wants to remove the record. Make the appropriate modifications to the event procedure.
   d. Save the solution, and then start the application. Type 2 in the Seat number text box, then click the Remove from File button. A message box that confirms your intent to delete the record should appear on the screen. Delete the record. To verify that the record was deleted, type 2 in the Seat number text box, and then click the Display Names button.
   e. Type 1 in the Seat number text box, then click the Remove from File button. In this case, do not delete the record. To verify that the record was not deleted, type 1 in the Seat number text box, and then click the Display Names button.
   f. Click the Exit button to end the application.
   g. Close the Output window, and then close the solution.

2. In this exercise, you modify the Seminar application that you finished coding in the lesson. The modified application uses a Do...Loop statement rather than a For...Next statement in the SeminarPrintDocument PrintPage event.
   a. Use Windows to make a copy of the Seminar Solution folder, which is contained in the VBNET\Tut10 folder. Change the name of the folder to Seminar DoLoop Solution.
   b. If necessary, start Visual Studio .NET. Open the Seminar Solution (Seminar Solution.sln) file, which is contained in the VBNET\Tut10\Seminar DoLoop Solution folder. If the designer window is not open, right-click the form file's name in the Solution Explorer window, then click View Designer.

c. Replace the For...Next statement in the SeminarPrintDocument control's PrintPage event with a Do...Loop statement.

d. Save the solution, and then start the application. Click the Print File button.

e. Click the Exit button to end the application.

f. Close the Output window, and then close the solution.

3. In this exercise, you modify the Seminar application that you finished coding in the lesson. The modified application prints only the assigned seats in the Seminar Participant Report.

a. Use Windows to make a copy of the Seminar Solution folder, which is contained in the VBNET\Tut10 folder. Change the name of the folder to Seminar Print Solution.

b. If necessary, start Visual Studio .NET. Open the Seminar Solution (Seminar Solution.sln) file, which is contained in the VBNET\Tut10\Seminar Print Solution folder. If the designer window is not open, right-click the form file's name in the Solution Explorer window, then click View Designer.

c. Modify the SeminarPrintDocument PrintPage event so that it prints the seat numbers and names associated with only seats that have been assigned. Unassigned seat numbers should not appear in the report.

d. Save the solution, and then start the application. Type 12 in the Seat number text box. Type Carol Jones in the Participant name text box, then type Nelco in the Company name text box. Click the Add to File button.

e. Type 15 in the Seat number text box. Type Susan Creigh in the Participant name text box, then type Nelco in the Company name text box. Click the Add to File button.

f. Click the Print File button. The Seminar Participant Report should display the information for seat numbers 1, 2, 12, and 15 only.

g. Click the Exit button to end the application.

h. Close the Output window, and then close the solution.

4. In this exercise, you modify the Seminar application that you finished coding in the lesson. The modified application prevents duplicate participant names from being entered in the file.

a. Use Windows to make a copy of the Seminar Solution folder, which is contained in the VBNET\Tut10 folder. Change the name of the folder to Seminar Duplicate Solution.

b. If necessary, start Visual Studio .NET. Open the Seminar Solution (Seminar Solution.sln) file, which is contained in the VBNET\Tut10\Seminar Duplicate Solution folder. If the designer window is not open, right-click the form file's name in the Solution Explorer window, then click View Designer.

c. The AddButton Click event procedure should not allow any duplicate participant names to be entered in the participants.data file. Modify the procedure's code.

d. Save the solution, and then start the application. Type 4 in the Seat number text box. Type Roger Tau in the Participant name text box, then type XYZ in the Company name text box. Click the Add to File button.

e. Type 11 in the Seat number text box. Type Roger Tau in the Participant name text box, then type Hansen's in the Company name text box. Click the Add to File button. The AddButton Click event procedure should display a message informing you that the record cannot be added to the file. Close the message box.

f. Click the Exit button to end the application.

g. Close the Output window, and then close the solution.

5. In this exercise, you modify the application from Exercise 4. The modified application allows duplicate participant names to be entered in the file, but only if the participants are from different companies.

    a.   Use Windows to make a copy of the Seminar Duplicate Solution folder, which is contained in the VBNET\Tut10 folder. Change the name of the folder to Modified Seminar Duplicate Solution.

    b.   If necessary, start Visual Studio .NET. Open the Seminar Solution (Seminar Solution.sln) file, which is contained in the VBNET\Tut10\Modified Seminar Duplicate Solution folder. If the designer window is not open, right-click the form file's name in the Solution Explorer window, then click View Designer.

    c.   Currently, the AddButton Click event procedure does not allow any duplicate participant names to be entered in the participants.data file. Modify the procedure's code so that it allows duplicate participant names to be added to the file, but only if the participants are from different companies.

    d.   Save the solution, and then start the application. Type 13 in the Seat number text box. Type Jeff Strait in the Participant name text box, then type XYZ in the Company name text box. Click the Add to File button.

    e.   Type 16 in the Seat number text box. Type Jeff Strait in the Participant name text box, then type XYZ in the Company name text box. Click the Add to File button. The procedure should not allow you to add this record to the file. Close the message box.

    f.   Type 14 in the Seat number text box. Type Jeff Strait in the Participant name text box, then type Hansen's in the Company name text box. Click the Add to File button. The AddButton Click event procedure should allow you to add the record to the file.

    g.   Click the Exit button to end the application.

    h.   Close the Output window, and then close the solution.

6. In this exercise, you code an application that saves first and last names to a random access file, and then prints the names in a list format.

    a.   If necessary, start Visual Studio .NET. Open the Names Solution (Names Solution.sln) file, which is contained in the VBNET\Tut10\Names Solution folder. If the designer window is not open, right-click the form file's name in the Solution Explorer window, then click View Designer.

    b.   Create a record structure that contains two field variables: strFirst and strLast. Each field variable should contain 10 characters.

    c.   The Initialize button should initialize a random access file named names.data for five records. Code the button's Click event procedure.

    d.   The Save button should save the first and last names, which are entered in the text boxes, to the names.data random access file. Code the button's Click event procedure.

    e.   The Print button should print a list that contains two columns. In the first column, display the record number. In the second column, display the first name, followed immediately by a space and the last name. Code the button's Click event procedure and the NamePrintDocument's PrintPage event procedure.

    f.   Save the solution, and then start the application. Click the Initialize button.

    g.   Type 1 in the Record number text box. Type Karen in the First name text box, then type Landers in the Last name text box. Click the Save button.

    h.   Type 2 in the Record number text box. Type Jose in the First name text box, then type Martinez in the Last name text box. Click the Save button.

    i.   Type 3 in the Record number text box. Type Mary Ann in the First name text box, then type Kroner in the Last name text box. Click the Save button.

    j.   Click the Print button. The numbers 1 through 5 should appear in the first column of the listing. The names "Karen Landers", "Jose Martinez", and "Mary Ann Kroner" should appear in the second column of the listing.

    k.   Click the Exit button to end the application.

    l.   Close the Output window, and then close the solution.

Exercise 7 is a Discovery Exercise. Discovery Exercises, which may include topics that are not covered in this lesson, allow you to "discover" the solutions to problems on your own.

discovery ▶ 7. In this exercise, you modify the Seminar application that you finished coding in the lesson. The modified application allows the user to enter the name of the random access file.

    a. Use Windows to make a copy of the Seminar Solution folder, which is contained in the VBNET\Tut10 folder. Change the name of the folder to Seminar Filename Solution.

    b. If necessary, start Visual Studio .NET. Open the Seminar Solution (Seminar Solution.sln) file, which is contained in the VBNET\Tut10\Seminar Filename Solution folder. If the designer window is not open, right-click the form file's name in the Solution Explorer window, then click View Designer.

    c. In the form's Load event procedure, use the InputBox function to prompt the user to enter the name of the random access file. Store the user's response in a form-level variable named mstrFileName.

    d. Modify the application's code so that, rather than opening the participants.data file, it opens the file whose name is stored in the mstrFileName variable.

    e. Save the solution, and then start the application. Type seminar.data as the filename, then click the OK button. Click the Initialize File button. Click the Yes button, then click the OK button.

    f. Type 1 in the Seat number text box. Type Dan Williams in the Participant name text box, then type ABC Co in the Company name text box. Click the Add to File button.

    g. Type 2 in the Seat number text box. Type Sara Kling in the Participant name text box, then type ABC Co in the Company name text box. Click the Add to File button.

    h. Type 1 in the Seat number text box, then click the Display Names button.

    i. Click the Remove from File button to remove record number one from the file.

    j. Click the Print File button. The Seminar Participant Report should display the information for seat number two only.

    k. Click the Exit button to end the application.

    l. Close the Output window, and then close the solution.

Exercise 8 is a Debugging Exercise. Debugging Exercises provide an opportunity for you to detect and correct errors in an existing application.

debugging 8. In this exercise you debug an existing application.

    a. If necessary, start Visual Studio .NET. Open the Debug Solution (Debug Solution.sln) file, which is contained in the VBNET\Tut10\Debug Solution folder. If the designer window is not open, right-click the form file's name in the Solution Explorer window, then click View Designer.

    b. View the application's code. Notice that a jagged line appears below some of the lines of code. Correct the code to remove the jagged lines.

    c. Save the solution, then start the application. Click the Initialize button.

    d. Type 1 in the Record number text box, then type your first and last names in the appropriate text boxes on the form. Click the Save button. Correct any errors in the SaveButton Click event procedure. When the procedure is working correctly, enter your first and last names as record number one in the file.

    e. Type 1 in the Record number text box, then click the Display button. Correct any errors in the DisplayButton Click event procedure. When the procedure is working correctly, display the names associated with record number one in the file.

    f. Click the Exit button to end the application.

    g. Close the Output window, then close the solution.

Arrays

Creating a Tax Calculator Application

case ▶ John Blackfeather is the owner and manager of the Perrytown Gift Shop. Every Friday afternoon, Mr. Blackfeather calculates the weekly pay for his six employees. The most time-consuming part of this task, and the one prone to the most errors, is the calculation of the federal withholding tax (FWT). Mr. Blackfeather has asked you to create an application that he can use to quickly and accurately calculate the FWT.

Previewing the Tax Calculator Application

Before creating the Tax Calculator application, you first preview the completed application.

To preview the completed application:

1 Use the Run command on the Windows Start menu to run the **Perrytown** (Perrytown.exe) file, which is contained in the VBNET\Tut11 folder on your computer's hard disk. The Tax Calculator application's user interface appears on the screen.

First, calculate the FWT for a married employee who has taxable wages of $288.46.

2 Type **288.46** in the Taxable wages text box, then click the **Calculate Tax** button. The application calculates the FWT of $24.67, as shown in Figure 11-1.

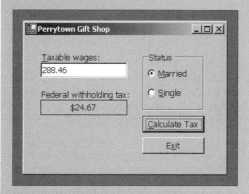

Figure 11-1: FWT for a married employee with taxable wages of $288.46

Next, calculate the FWT for a single employee who has taxable wages of $600.

3 Type **600** in the Taxable wages text box, then click the **Single** radio button. Click the **Calculate Tax** button. The application calculates the FWT of $88.59, as shown in Figure 11-2.

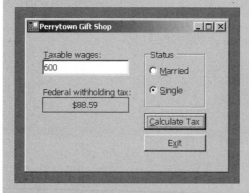

Figure 11-2: FWT for a single employee with taxable wages of $600

4 Click the **Exit** button to end the application.

Before you can begin coding the Tax Calculator application, you need to learn how to create and use an array. You learn about one-dimensional arrays in Lessons A and B, and two-dimensional arrays in Lesson C. You code the Tax Calculator application in Lesson C.

- Declare and initialize a one-dimensional array
- Assign data to a one-dimensional array
- Display the contents of a one-dimensional array
- Access an element in a one-dimensional array
- Search a one-dimensional array
- Compute the average of a one-dimensional array's contents
- Find the highest entry in a one-dimensional array
- Update the contents of a one-dimensional array
- Sort a one-dimensional array

▶ The variables in an array are stored in consecutive memory locations in the computer's internal memory.

▶ It takes longer for the computer to access the information stored in a disk file, because the computer must wait for the disk drive to locate the needed information and then read the information into internal memory.

Using a One-Dimensional Array

Arrays

All of the variables you have used so far have been simple variables. A **simple variable**, also called a **scalar variable**, is one that is unrelated to any other variable in memory. In many applications, however, you may need to reserve a block of related variables, referred to as an array.

An **array** is a group of variables that have the same name and data type and are related in some way. For example, each variable in the array might contain an inventory quantity, or each might contain a state name, or each might contain an employee record (name, Social Security number, pay rate, and so on). It may be helpful to picture an array as a group of small, adjacent boxes inside the computer's memory. You can write information to the boxes and you can read information from the boxes; you just cannot *see* the boxes.

Programmers use arrays to temporarily store related data in the internal memory of the computer. Examples of data stored in an array would be the federal withholding tax tables in a payroll program, and a price list in an order entry program. Storing data in an array increases the efficiency of a program, because data can be both written to and read from internal memory much faster than it can be written to and read from a file on a disk. Additionally, after the data is entered into an array, which typically is done at the beginning of the program, the program can use the data as many times as desired. A payroll program, for example, can use the federal withholding tax tables stored in an array to calculate the amount of each employee's federal withholding tax.

Although arrays in Visual Basic .NET can have as many as 60 dimensions, the most commonly used arrays are one-dimensional and two-dimensional. You learn about one-dimensional arrays in Lessons A and B, and two-dimensional arrays in Lesson C. Arrays having more than two dimensions, which are used in scientific and engineering applications, are beyond the scope of this book.

One-Dimensional Arrays

You can visualize a **one-dimensional** array as a column of variables. Each variable in a one-dimensional array is identified by a unique number, called a **subscript**, which Visual Basic .NET assigns to the variable when the array is created. The subscript indicates the variable's position in the array. The first variable in a one-dimensional array is assigned a subscript of 0 (zero), the second a subscript of 1 (one), and so on. You refer to each variable in an array by the array's name and the variable's subscript, which is specified in a set of parentheses immediately following the array name. For example, to refer to the first variable in a one-dimensional array named strStates, you use strStates(0)—read "strStates sub zero." Similarly, to refer to the third variable in the strStates array, you use strStates(2). Figure 11-3 illustrates this naming convention.

strStates(0)	Alaska
strStates(1)	Montana
strStates(2)	South Carolina
strStates(3)	Tennessee

Figure 11-3: Names of the variables in a one-dimensional array named strStates

Before you can use an array, you first must declare (create) it. Figure 11-4 shows two versions of the syntax you use to declare a one-dimensional array in Visual Basic .NET. The figure also includes examples of using each syntax.

You also can visualize a one-dimensional array as a row of variables, rather than as a column of variables.

A subscript is also called an index.

Syntax
Version 1 *accessibility arrayname*(*highestSubscript*) **As** *datatype*
Version 2 *accessibility arrayname*() **As** *datatype* = {*initialValues*}
Examples and results
Example 1 `Dim strCities(3) As String`
Result declares a four-element array named strCities; each element is automatically initialized to a zero-length (empty) string
Example 2 `Private intNumbers(5) As Integer`
Result declares a six-element array named intNumbers; each element is automatically initialized to the number zero
Example 3 `Private udtItems(4) As ItemStruc`
Result declares a five-element array named udtItems; assuming the ItemStruc data type contains two fields named strName and sngPrice, automatically initializes the strName field in each element to a zero-length (empty) string, and automatically initializes the sngPrice field in each element to the number zero
Example 4 `Private strStates() As String = {"Hawaii", "Alaska", "Maine"}`
Result declares and initializes a three-element array named strStates
Example 5 `Dim intScores() As Integer = {75, 9, 23, 6}`
Result declares and initializes a four-element array named intScores

Figure 11-4: Syntax versions and examples of declaring a one-dimensional array

In each syntax version, *accessibility* is typically either the keyword Dim (for a local array) or the keyword Private (for a form-level array). *Arrayname* is the name of the array, and *datatype* is the type of data the array variables, referred to as **elements**, will store. Recall that each of the elements (variables) in an array has the same data type. You can use any of the Visual Basic .NET data types you have learned so far to declare an array. You also can use a user-defined data type to declare an array.

In Version 1 of the syntax, *highestSubscript* is an integer that specifies the highest subscript in the array. When the array is created, it will contain one element more than the number specified in the *highestSubscript* argument; this is because the first element in an array has a subscript of zero. For instance, the statement `Dim strCities(3) As String`, which is shown in Example 1 in Figure 11-4, creates a local String array named strCities. The strCities array contains four elements with subscripts of 0, 1, 2, and 3. Similarly, the statement shown in Example 2, `Private intNumbers(5) As Integer`, creates a form-level Integer array named intNumbers. The intNumbers array contains six elements with subscripts of 0, 1, 2, 3, 4, and 5.

As mentioned earlier, in addition to using the standard data types available in Visual Basic .NET, you also can use a user-defined data type to declare an array. The statement shown in Example 3 in Figure 11-4, for instance, declares a form-level ItemStruc array named udtItems. The udtItems array contains five elements with subscripts of 0, 1, 2, 3, and 4. Each element contains two field variables: strName and sngPrice.

When you use the syntax shown in Version 1 to declare an array, Visual Basic .NET automatically initializes each element in the array when the array is created. If the array's data type is String, each element in the array is initialized to a zero-length (empty) string. Elements in a numeric array are initialized to the number zero, and elements in a Boolean array are initialized to the Boolean value False. Date array elements are initialized to 12:00 AM January 1, 0001. If the array's data type is a user-defined data type, the field variables that make up the data type are initialized in the same manner as single (scalar) variables.

You use the syntax shown in Version 2 in Figure 11-4 to declare an array and, at the same time, specify each element's initial value. You list the initial values in the *initialValues* section of the syntax, using commas to separate the values; you enclose the list in braces ({}). Notice that the syntax shown in Version 2 does not include the *highestSubscript* argument; rather, an empty set of parentheses follows the array name. Visual Basic .NET automatically calculates the highest subscript based on the number of values in the *initialValues* section. If the *initialValues* section contains five values, the highest subscript in the array is 4. Likewise, if the *initialValues* section contains 100 values, the highest subscript in the array is 99. Notice that the highest subscript is always one number less than the number of values listed in the *initialValues* section; this is because the first subscript in an array is the number zero.

The statement shown in Example 4 in Figure 11-4, `Private strStates() As String = {"Hawaii", "Alaska", "Maine"}`, declares a form-level array named strStates. The strStates array contains three elements with subscripts of 0, 1, and 2. When the array is created, Visual Basic .NET assigns the string "Hawaii" to the strStates(0) element, "Alaska" to the strStates(1) element, and "Maine" to the strStates(2) element. Similarly, the statement shown in Example 5, `Dim intScores() As Integer = {75, 9, 23, 6}`, declares a local array named intScores. The intScores array contains four elements with subscripts of 0, 1, 2, and 3. Visual Basic .NET assigns the number 75 to the intScores(0) element, 9 to the intScores(1) element, 23 to the intScores(2) element, and 6 to the intScores(3) element.

After declaring the array, you can use various methods to store data in the array.

Storing Data in a One-Dimensional Array

You can use a variety of ways to enter data into an array. The examples shown in Figure 11-5, for instance, can be used to enter data into the arrays declared in Figure 11-4.

Examples	Results

Example 1
`strCities(0) = "Madrid"`
`strCities(1) = "Paris"`
`strCities(2) = "Rome"`
	assigns the strings "Madrid", "Paris", and "Rome" to the strCities array, replacing the zero-length (empty) strings stored in the array

Example 2
`Dim intX As Integer`
`For intX = 1 To 6`
`    intNumbers(intX — 1) = intX * intX`
`Next intX`
	assigns the squares of the numbers from one through six to the intNumbers array, replacing the zeros stored in the array

Example 3
`Dim intX As Integer`
`Do While (intX <= 5 AndAlso Not EOF(1))`
`    FileGet(1, udtItems(intX), intX + 1)`
`    intX = intX + 1`
`Loop`
	reads the records from a random access file, and stores the data in the udtItems array, replacing the zero-length strings and zeros stored in the array

Example 4
`udtItems(0).sngPrice = _`
`    udtItems(0).sngPrice * 1.1`
	increases (by 10%) the price stored in the first element in the udtItems array

Example 5 `strStates(1) = "Virginia"`	assigns the string "Virginia" to the second element in the strStates array, replacing the string "Alaska"

Example 6
`intScores(0) = _`
`        Val(InputBox("Score:", "Scores"))`
	assigns the value entered by the user to the first element in the intScores array, replacing the value 75

Figure 11-5: Examples of entering data into a one-dimensional array

Study closely the examples shown in Figure 11-5. The three assignment statements shown in Example 1 assign the strings "Madrid", "Paris", and "Rome" to the strCities array, replacing the values assigned to the array elements when the array was created. The code shown in Example 2 assigns the squares of the numbers from one through six to the intNumbers array, writing over the array's initial values. Notice that the number one must be subtracted from the value stored in the intX variable when assigning the squares to the array; this is because the first array element has a subscript of zero rather than one.

Recall from Example 3 in Figure 11-4 that each element in the udtItems array contains two field variables: strName and sngPrice. The code shown in Example 3 in Figure 11-5 reads the names and prices from a random access file, and stores the information in the udtItems array, replacing the values stored in the array when the array was created. Example 4 shows how you can assign data to a field variable contained in an array element. In this case, the statement `udtItems(0).sngPrice = udtItems(0).sngPrice * 1.1` increases (by 10%) the price stored in the sngPrice field variable contained in udtItems(0) element.

In Example 5, the statement `strStates(1) = "Virginia"` assigns the string "Virginia" to the second element in the strStates array, replacing the string "Alaska" that was stored in the element when the array was created. The code shown in the last example in Figure 11-5 replaces the value stored in the first element in the intScores array (75) with the value entered by the user.

Now that you know how to declare and enter data into a one-dimensional array, you learn how to manipulate an array in a program.

Manipulating One-Dimensional Arrays

The variables (elements) in an array can be used just like any other variables. For example, you can assign values to them, use them in calculations, display their contents, and so on. In the next several sections, you view sample procedures that demonstrate how one-dimensional arrays are used in an application. More specifically, the procedures will show you how to perform the following tasks using a one-dimensional array:

1. Display the contents of an array
2. Access an array element using its subscript
3. Search the array
4. Calculate the average of the data stored in a numeric array
5. Find the highest value stored in an array
6. Update the array elements
7. Sort the array elements

Begin by viewing a procedure that displays the contents of a one-dimensional array.

Displaying the Contents of a One-Dimensional Array

Many times, a procedure will need simply to display the contents of an array used by the application. The DisplayMonths procedure shown in Figure 11-6, for instance, demonstrates how you can display the contents of the strMonths array in a list box named MonthsListBox.

Pseudocode

1. declare a String array named strMonths
2. declare an Integer variable named intX
3. repeat for each element in the strMonths array
   display the contents of the current array element in the MonthsListBox control
   end repeat

Visual Basic .NET code

```
Dim strMonths() As String = {"JAN", "FEB", "MAR", "APR", _
    "MAY", "JUN", "JUL", "AUG", "SEP", "OCT", "NOV", "DEC"}
Dim intX As Integer
For intX = 0 To 11
    Me.MonthsListBox.Items.Add(strMonths(intX))
Next intX
```

Results (displayed in a list box)

JAN
FEB
MAR
APR
MAY
JUN
JUL
AUG
SEP
OCT
NOV
DEC

Figure 11-6: DisplayMonths procedure

Notice that the loop in the procedure shown in Figure 11-6 stops when the intX variable contains the number 12, which is one number more than the highest subscript in the array.

The DisplayMonths procedure declares a 12-element String array named strMonths, using the names of the 12 months to initialize the array. The procedure also declares an Integer variable named intX. The procedure uses a loop, along with the intX variable, to display the contents of each array element in the MonthsListBox control. The first time the loop is processed, the intX variable contains the number zero, and the statement `Me.MonthsListBox.Items.Add` `(strMonths(intX))` displays the contents of the strMonths(0) element—JAN—in the MonthsListBox control. The statement `Next intX` then adds the number one to the value stored in the intX variable, giving one. When the loop is processed the second time, the statement `Me.MonthsListBox.Items.Add` `(strMonths(intX))` adds the contents of the strMonths(1) element—FEB—to the list box control, and so on. The computer repeats the loop instructions for each element in the strMonths array, beginning with the element whose subscript is zero and ending with the element whose subscript is 11. The computer stops processing the loop when the value contained in the intX variable is 12. As Figure 11-5 indicates, the procedure displays the names of the 12 months in a list box.

Next, you view a procedure that uses the array subscript to access the appropriate element in an array.

Using the Subscript to Access an Element in a One-Dimensional Array

Assume that XYZ Corporation pays its managers based on six different salary codes, 1 through 6. Each code corresponds to a different salary amount. You can use the procedure shown in Figure 11-7 to display the salary amount corresponding to the code entered by the user.

Pseudocode

1. declare an Integer array named intSalaries
2. declare an Integer variable named intCode
3. get the code from the user, and assign the code to the intCode variable
4. if the code stored in the intCode variable is not valid
       display the message "Invalid code" in a message box
    else
       display, in a message box, the array element located in position (intCode − 1)
    end if

Visual Basic .NET code

```
Dim intSalaries() As Integer = {25000, 35000, 55000, _
                                70000, 80200, 90500}
Dim intCode As Integer
intCode = Val(InputBox("Enter the salary code:", _
    "Salary Code"))
If intCode < 1 OrElse intCode > 6 Then
    MessageBox.Show("Invalid code", "Salary", _
              MessageBoxButtons.OK, MessageBoxIcon.Information)
Else
    MessageBox.Show(intSalaries(intCode - 1), "Salary", _
              MessageBoxButtons.OK, MessageBoxIcon.Information)
End If
```

Result (displayed in a message box)

55000   (assuming the user enters the number 3)
Invalid code   (assuming the user enters the number 8)

Figure 11-7: DisplaySalary procedure

The procedure shown in Figure 11-7 declares an Integer array named intSalaries, using six salary amounts to initialize the array. The salary amount for code 1 is stored in intSalaries(0). Code 2's salary amount is stored in intSalaries(1), and so on. Notice that the code is one number more than the array subscript with which it is associated.

After creating and initializing the array, the procedure declares an Integer variable named intCode. It then prompts the user to enter the salary code, storing the user's response in the intCode variable. The selection structure in the procedure determines whether the code entered by the user is invalid. In this case, invalid codes are numbers that are less than one or greater than six. If the code is not valid, the procedure displays an appropriate message; otherwise, it displays the corresponding salary from the intSalaries array. Notice that, to access the correct element in the intSalaries array, the number one must be subtracted from the contents of the intCode variable; this is because the code entered by the user is one number more than its associated array subscript. As Figure 11-7 indicates, the procedure displays the number 55000 if the user enters a code of 3. If the user enters a code of 8, the program displays the message "Invalid code".

In the next section, you learn how to search a one-dimensional array.

tip

Before accessing an array element, a procedure always should verify that the subscript is valid—in other words, that it is in range. If the procedure uses a subscript that is not in range, Visual Basic .NET displays an error message and the procedure ends abruptly.

Searching a One-Dimensional Array

Assume that the sales manager at Jacobsen Motors wants a procedure that allows him to determine the number of salespeople selling above a certain amount, which he will enter. To accomplish this task, the procedure will need to search the array, looking for values that are greater than the amount entered by the sales manager. The procedure shown in Figure 11-8 shows you how to search an array.

Pseudocode

1. declare an Integer array named intSales
2. declare Integer variables named intX, intCount, and intSearchFor
3. get the sales amount from the user, and assign the sales amount to the intSearchFor variable
4. repeat for each element in the intSales array
      if the value in the current array element is greater than the value in the intSearchFor variable
            add 1 to the intCount variable
      end if
   end repeat
5. display the contents of the intCount variable in a message box

Visual Basic .NET code

```
Dim intSales() As Integer = {45000, 35000, 25000, 60000, 23000}
Dim intX As Integer            'keeps track of subscripts
Dim intCount As Integer        'counter variable
Dim intSearchFor As Integer    'number to search for

intSearchFor = Val(InputBox("Enter sales to search for:", _
    "Sales"))
For intX = 0 To 4
    If intSales(intX) > intSearchFor Then
          intCount = intCount + 1
    End If
Next intX
MessageBox.Show("Count: " & intCount, "Sales", _
          MessageBoxButtons.OK, MessageBoxIcon.Information)
```

Results (displayed in a message box)

Count: 2   (assuming the user enters the number 40000)
Count: 0   (assuming the user enters the number 60000)

Figure 11-8: SearchArray procedure

The SearchArray procedure declares an Integer array named intSales, using five sales amounts to initialize the array. The procedure also declares three Integer variables named intX, intCount, and intSearchFor. After declaring the array and variables, the procedure prompts the user to enter a sales amount, and it stores the user's response in the intSearchFor variable. The loop in the procedure then repeats its instructions for each element in the array, beginning with the element whose subscript is zero and ending with the element whose subscript is four.

The selection structure in the loop compares the contents of the current array element with the contents of the intSearchFor variable. If the array element contains a number that is greater than the number stored in the intSearchFor variable, the selection structure's true path adds the number one to the value stored in the intCount variable. In this procedure, the intCount variable is used as a counter to keep track of the number of salespeople selling over the amount entered by the sales manager.

When the loop ends, which is when the intX variable contains the number five, the MessageBox.Show method displays the contents of the intCount variable in a message box. As Figure 11-8 indicates, the procedure displays the number two if the sales manager enters 40000 as the sales amount, and it displays the number zero if he enters 60000 as the sales amount.

Next, you learn how to calculate the average of the data stored in a numeric array.

Calculating the Average Amount Stored in a One-Dimensional Numeric Array

Professor Jeremiah wants a procedure that allows him to calculate and display the average test score earned by his students on the final exam. The DisplayAverage procedure shown in Figure 11-9 can be used to accomplish this task.

Pseudocode

1. declare an Integer array named intScores
2. declare Integer variables named intX and intTotal, and a Single variable named sngAvg
3. repeat for each element in the intScores array
       add the contents of the current array element to the intTotal variable
   end repeat
4. calculate the average score by dividing the contents of the intTotal variable by the number of array elements, and assign the result to the sngAvg variable
5. display the contents of the sngAvg variable in a message box

Visual Basic .NET code

```
Dim intScores() As Integer = {98, 100, 56, 74, 35}
Dim intX As Integer          'keeps track of subscripts
Dim intTotal As Integer      'accumulator variable
Dim sngAvg As Single         'average score
For intX = 0 To 4
     intTotal = intTotal + intScores(intX)
Next intX
sngAvg = intTotal / intScores.Length
MessageBox.Show("Average: " & sngAvg, "Average", _
        MessageBoxButtons.OK, MessageBoxIcon.Information)
```

Results (displayed in a message box)

Average: 72.6

Figure 11-9: DisplayAverage procedure

tip

You also can use the statement sngAvg = intTotal / intX to calculate the average test score in the DisplayAverage procedure.

The DisplayAverage procedure declares an Integer array named intScores, using five test scores to initialize the array. The procedure also declares two Integer variables named intX and intTotal, and a Single variable named sngAvg. The loop in the procedure adds the score contained in each array element to the intTotal variable. In this procedure, the intTotal variable is used as an accumulator to add up the test scores. When the loop ends, which is when the intX variable contains the number five, the statement sngAvg = intTotal / intScores.Length uses the array's Length property to calculate the average test score. The **Length property**, whose syntax is *arrayname*.Length, stores the number of array elements; in this case, it stores the number five, because the intScores array contains five elements. The DisplayAverage procedure then displays the average test score in a message box. As Figure 11-9 indicates, the program displays the number 72.6.

In the next section, you learn how to determine the highest value stored in a one-dimensional array.

Determining the Highest Value Stored in a One-Dimensional Array

Sharon Johnson keeps track of the amount of money she spends each week on groceries. She would like a procedure that allows her to display the highest amount spent in a week. Similar to the SearchArray procedure shown earlier in Figure 11-8, the DisplayHighest procedure will need to search the array. However, rather than looking in the array for values that are greater than a specific amount, the procedure will be looking for the highest amount in the array, as shown in Figure 11-10.

Pseudocode

1. declare a Single array named sngDollars
2. declare an Integer variable named intX and a Single variable named sngHigh
3. initialize the sngHigh variable to the contents of the first array element
4. initialize the intX variable to 1 (second subscript)
5. repeat while intX is less than the number of elements in the array
        if the value in the current array element is greater than the value in the
        sngHigh variable
            assign the current array element's contents to the sngHigh variable
        end if
        add 1 to the intX variable
    end repeat
6. display the contents of the sngHigh variable in a message box

Visual Basic .NET code

```
Dim sngDollars() As Single = {25.60, 30.25, 50, 20, 25.45}
Dim intX As Integer = 1   'begin search with second element
Dim sngHigh As Single     'highest value in the array
sngHigh = sngDollars(0)   'store first array value in sngHigh

Do While intX < sngDollars.Length
    If sngDollars(intX) > sngHigh Then
        sngHigh = sngDollars(intX)
    End If
    intX = intX + 1
Loop
MessageBox.Show("High: " & sngHigh, "Highest", _
        MessageBoxButtons.OK, MessageBoxIcon.Information)
```

Results (displayed in a message box)

High: 50

Figure 11-10: DisplayHighest procedure

Notice that the loop shown in Figure 11-10 searches the second through the last element in the array. The first element is not included in the search because it is already stored in the sngHigh variable.

The DisplayHighest procedure declares a Single array named sngDollars, and it initializes the array to the amounts that Sharon spent on groceries during the last five weeks. The procedure also declares an Integer variable named intX and a Single variable named sngHigh. The sngHigh variable is used to keep track of the highest value stored in the array, and is initialized using the value stored in the first array element. The intX variable is used to keep track of the array subscripts. Notice that the procedure initializes the intX variable to the number one, which is the subscript corresponding to the second element in the array.

The first time the loop in the procedure is processed, the selection structure within the loop compares the value stored in the second array element—sngDollars(1)—with the value stored in the sngHigh variable. (Recall that the sngHigh variable contains the same value as the first array element at this point.) If the value stored in the second array element is greater than the value stored in the sngHigh variable, then the statement `sngHigh = sngDollars(intX)` assigns the array element value to the sngHigh variable. The statement `intX = intX + 1` then adds the number one to the intX variable, giving 2. The next time the loop is processed, the selection structure compares the value stored in the third array element—sngDollars(2)—with the value stored in the sngHigh variable, and so on. When the loop ends, which is when the intX variable contains the number five, the procedure displays the contents of the sngHigh variable in a message box. As Figure 11-10 indicates, the procedure displays the number 50.

Next, learn how to update the values stored in a one-dimensional array.

Updating the Values Stored in a One-Dimensional Array

The sales manager at Jillian Company wants a procedure that allows her to increase the price of each item the company sells. She also would like the procedure to display each item's new price in a message box. The UpdateArray procedure shown in Figure 11-11 will perform these tasks.

Pseudocode

1. declare a Single array named sngPrices
2. declare an Integer variable named intX and a Single variable named sngIncrease
3. get the increase amount from the user, and store it in the sngIncrease variable
4. repeat for each element in the sngPrices array
    add the increase amount to the value stored in the current array element
    display the contents of the current array element in a message box
    end repeat

Visual Basic .NET code

```
Dim sngPrices() As Single = {150.35, 35.60, 75.75, 25.30}
Dim intX As Integer          'keeps track of subscripts
Dim sngIncrease As Single    'stores increase amount

sngIncrease = Val(InputBox("Increase amount:", "Increase"))
For intX = 0 To sngPrices.Length - 1
    sngPrices(intX) = sngPrices(intX) + sngIncrease
    MessageBox.Show("New Price: " & _
        Format(sngPrices(intX), "currency"), _
        "Prices", MessageBoxButtons.OK, _
        MessageBoxIcon.Information)
Next intX
```

Results (displayed in a message box)

New Price: $155.35   (assuming the user enters the number 5)
New Price: $40.60
New Price: $80.75
New Price: $30.30

Figure 11-11: UpdateArray procedure

The UpdateArray procedure declares a Single array named sngPrices, using four values to initialize the array. The procedure also declares an Integer variable named intX and a Single variable named sngIncrease. The procedure prompts the user to enter the amount of the increase, and stores the user's response in the sngIncrease variable. The loop in the procedure then repeats its instructions for each element in the array.

The first instruction in the loop, `sngPrices(intX) = sngPrices(intX)` `+ sngIncrease`, updates the contents of the current array element by adding the increase amount to it. The MessageBox.Show method then displays the updated contents in a message box. The loop ends when the intX variable contains the number four. Figure 11-11 shows the results of the procedure when the user enters the number five as the increase amount. Notice that each new price is five dollars more than the corresponding original price.

The last procedures you view in this lesson sort the data stored in a one-dimensional array.

Sorting the Data Stored in a One-Dimensional Array

At times, a procedure might need to arrange the contents of an array in either ascending or descending order. Arranging data in a specific order is called **sorting**. When an array is sorted in ascending order, the first element in the array contains the smallest value, and the last element contains the largest value. When an array is sorted in descending order, on the other hand, the first element contains the largest value, and the last element contains the smallest value.

You use the **Array.Sort method** to sort an array in ascending order. The method's syntax is **Array.Sort(***arrayname***)**, where *arrayname* is the name of the array to be sorted. The procedure shown in Figure 11-12 uses the Array.Sort method to sort the intNumbers array in ascending order.

Pseudocode

1. declare an Integer array named intNumbers
2. declare an Integer variable named intX
3. open the random access file named nums.data
4. repeat while intX is less than or equal to 5 and it is not the end of the nums.data file
  read a number from the file and store it in the current array element
  display the contents of the current array element in a message box
  add 1 to the intX variable
 end repeat
5. close the nums.data file
6. sort the intNumbers array in ascending order
7. repeat for each element in the intNumbers array
  display the contents of the current array element in a message box
 end repeat

Visual Basic .NET code

```
Dim intNumbers(5), intX As Integer

FileOpen(1, "nums.data", OpenMode.Random, _
    OpenAccess.ReadWrite, OpenShare.Shared, Len(intNumbers(0)))
Do While intX <= 5 AndAlso Not EOF(1)
    FileGet(1, intNumbers(intX), intX + 1)
    MessageBox.Show(intNumbers(intX), "Numbers", _
        MessageBoxButtons.OK, MessageBoxIcon.Information)
    intX = intX + 1
Loop
FileClose(1)

Array.Sort(intNumbers)   'sort the array in ascending order

For intX = 0 To 5
    MessageBox.Show(intNumbers(intX), "Numbers", _
        MessageBoxButtons.OK, MessageBoxIcon.Information)
Next intX
```

Figure 11-12: SortAscending procedure

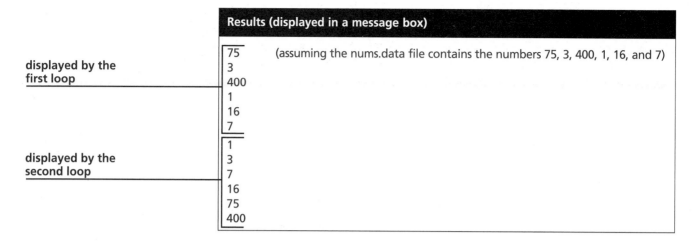

displayed by the first loop

displayed by the second loop

Results (displayed in a message box)
75   (assuming the nums.data file contains the numbers 75, 3, 400, 1, 16, and 7) 3 400 1 16 7
1 3 7 16 75 400

Figure 11-12: SortAscending procedure (continued)

If a random access file contains only one field and the field is not a String, you do not have to create a record structure to read data from or write data to the file.

The SortAscending procedure declares an Integer array named intNumbers and an Integer variable named intX. It then opens a random access file named nums.data. Notice that the length of the intNumbers(0) element is used as the record length in the FileOpen function. You can use the length of any of the elements in the intNumbers array; or, you can use the number four, because Visual Basic .NET assigns a length of four bytes to all Integer variables.

The first loop in the procedure repeats its instructions while the intX variable contains a value that is less than or equal to five and, at the same time, the computer has not reached the end of the nums.data file. The first instruction in the loop reads a number from the nums.data file and stores the number in the intNumbers array, in the element whose subscript is contained in the intX variable. The second instruction displays the contents of the current array element in a message box. The third instruction in the loop increases the value stored in the intX variable by one. The loop stops either when the value in the intX variable is six or when the computer reaches the end of the nums.data file, whichever occurs first. As Figure 11-12 indicates, if the nums.data file contains the numbers 75, 3, 400, 1, 16, and 7, the first loop displays the numbers 75, 3, 400, 1, 16, and 7 in a message box. When the first loop stops, the statement `FileClose(1)` closes the nums.data file.

The `Array.Sort(intNumbers)` statement in the SortAscending procedure sorts the numbers in the intNumbers array in ascending order. The second loop in the procedure then displays the contents of the intNumbers array in message boxes. As Figure 11-12 indicates, the second loop displays the numbers 1, 3, 7, 16, 75, and 400. Notice that the numbers appear in ascending order.

To sort an array in descending order, you first use the Array.Sort method to sort the array in ascending order, and then use the **Array.Reverse method** to reverse the array elements. The syntax of the Array.Reverse method is **Array.Reverse(***arrayname***)**, where *arrayname* is the name of the array whose elements you want reversed. The SortDescending procedure shown in Figure 11-13 sorts the contents of the strStates array in descending order, and then displays the contents of the array in message boxes.

Pseudocode

1. declare a String array named strStates
2. declare an Integer variable named intX
3. sort the strStates array in descending order
4. repeat for each element in the strStates array
        display the contents of the current array element in a message box
   end repeat

Visual Basic .NET code

```
Dim strStates() As String = _
    {"Colorado", "Hawaii", "Alaska", "Florida"}
Dim intX As Integer

Array.Sort(strStates)      'sort the array in ascending order,
Array.Reverse(strStates)   'then reverse the array elements

For intX = 0 To strStates.Length - 1
    MessageBox.Show(strStates(intX), "States", _
        MessageBoxButtons.OK, MessageBoxIcon.Information)
Next intX
```

Results (displayed in a message box)

Hawaii
Florida
Colorado
Alaska

Figure 11-13: SortDescending procedure

The SortDescending procedure declares a String array named strStates and an Integer variable named intX. It then uses the Array.Sort and Array.Reverse methods to sort the array elements in descending order. The loop in the procedure then displays the contents of the strStates array in message boxes. As Figure 11-13 indicates, the loop displays Hawaii, Florida, Colorado, and Alaska. Notice that the state names appear in descending alphabetical order.

You now have completed Lesson A. You can either take a break or complete the end-of-lesson questions and exercises before moving on to the next lesson. You learn more about one-dimensional arrays in Lesson B. In Lesson C, you learn about two-dimensional arrays, and you code the Tax Calculator application that you previewed at the beginning of the tutorial.

SUMMARY

To declare a one-dimensional array:

■ Use either of the following two syntax versions:
   Version 1: *accessibility arrayname*(*highestSubscript*) **As** *datatype*
   Version 2: *accessibility arrayname*() **As** *datatype* = {*initialValues*}
■ *Accessibility* is typically either the keyword Dim or the keyword Private. *Arrayname* is the name of the array, and *datatype* is the type of data the array variables will store. You can declare an array using any of Visual Basic .NET's standard data types; or, you can use a user-defined data type.

- The *highestSubscript* argument, which appears in Version 1 of the syntax, is an integer that specifies the highest subscript in the array. Using Version 1's syntax, Visual Basic .NET automatically initializes the elements (variables) in the array.
- The *initialValues* section, which appears in Version 2 of the syntax, is a list of values separated by commas and enclosed in braces. The values are used to initialize each element in the array.

To refer to a variable included in an array:

- Use the array's name followed by the variable's subscript. Enclose the subscript in a set of parentheses following the array name.

To determine the number of elements (variables) in an array:

- Use the array's Length property in the following syntax: *arrayname*.**Length**.

To sort the array elements in ascending order:

- Use the Array.Sort method. The method's syntax is **Array.Sort(***arrayname***)**.

To reverse the order of the elements included in an array:

- Use the Array.Reverse method. The method's syntax is **Array.Reverse(***arrayname***)**.

QUESTIONS

1. Which of the following is false?
   a. The elements in an array are related in some way.
   b. All of the elements in an array have the same data type.
   c. All of the elements in an array have the same subscript.
   d. All of the elements in an array have the same name.
   e. The first element in an array has a subscript of zero.

2. Elements in an array are identified by a unique _____.
   a. data type
   b. initial value
   c. order
   d. subscript
   e. symbol

3. Which of the following statements declares a one-dimensional array named sngPrices that contains five elements?
   a. `Dim sngPrices(4) As Single`
   b. `Dim sngPrices(5) As Single`
   c. `Dim sngPrices(4) As Single = {3.55, 6.70, 8, 4, 2.34}`
   d. `Dim sngPrices(5) As Single = {3.55, 6.70, 8, 4, 2.34}`
   e. Both b and d.

4. Assume that the strItem array is declared using the statement `Dim strItem(20) As String`. Also assume that the intX variable, which keeps track of the array subscripts, is initialized to the number zero. Which of the following Do clauses will process the loop instructions for each element in the array?
   a. `Do While intX > 20`
   b. `Do While intX < 20`
   c. `Do While intX >= 20`
   d. `Do While intX <= 20`
   e. `Do Until intX <= 20`

Use the following array, named intSales, to answer Questions 5 through 10. The array was declared with the following statement: `Dim intSales() As Integer = {10000, 12000, 900, 500, 20000}`.

| 10000 | 12000 | 900 | 500 | 20000 |

5. The statement `intSales(3) = intSales(3) + 10` will _____.
   a. replace the 500 amount with 10
   b. replace the 500 amount with 510
   c. replace the 900 amount with 10
   d. replace the 900 amount with 910
   e. result in an error

6. The statement `intSales(4) = intSales(4 - 2)` will _____.
   a. replace the 20000 amount with 900
   b. replace the 20000 amount with 19998
   c. replace the 500 amount with 12000
   d. replace the 500 amount with 498
   e. result in an error

7. The statement `Debug.WriteLine(intSales(0) + intSales(1))` will _____.
   a. display 0
   b. display 22000
   c. display 10000 + 12000
   d. display intSales(0) + intSales(1)
   e. result in an error

8. Which of the following If clauses can be used to verify that the array subscript, named intX, is valid for the intSales array?
   a. `If intSales(intX) >= 0 AndAlso intSales(intX) < 4 Then`
   b. `If intSales(intX) >= 0 AndAlso intSales(intX) <= 4 Then`
   c. `If intX >= 0 AndAlso intX < 4 Then`
   d. `If intX >= 0 AndAlso intX <= 4 Then`
   e. `If intX > 0 AndAlso intX < 4 Then`

9. Which of the following will correctly add 100 to each variable in the intSales array? (You can assume that the intX variable was initialized to the number zero.)
   a.
   ```
   Do While intX <= 4
         intX = intX + 100
   Loop
   ```
   b.
   ```
   Do While intX <= 4
         intSales = intSales + 100
   Loop
   ```

```
c.  Do While intSales < 5
        intSales(intX) = intSales(intX) + 100
    Loop
d.  Do While intX <= 4
        intSales(intX) = intSales(intX) + 100
        intX = intX + 1
    Loop
```
e. None of the above.

10. Which of the following statements sorts the intSales array in ascending order?

a. `Array.Sort(intSales)`
b. `intSales.Sort`
c. `intSales.Sort(Ascending)`
d. `Sort(intSales)`
e. `SortArray(intSales)`

Use the following array, named intNum, to answer Questions 11 through 16. The array was declared with the following statement: `Dim intNum() As Integer = {10, 5, 7, 2}`. Assume that the intTotal, intX, and sngAvg variables are initialized to the number zero.

10	5	7	2

11. Which of the following will correctly calculate and display (in the Output window) the average of the elements included in the intNum array?

a.
```
Do While intX < 4
    intNum(intX) = intTotal + intTotal
    intX = intX + 1
Loop
sngAvg = intTotal / intX
Debug.WriteLine(sngAvg)
```
b.
```
Do While intX < 4
    intTotal = intTotal + intNum(intX)
    intX = intX + 1
Loop
sngAvg = intTotal / intX
Debug.WriteLine(sngAvg)
```
c.
```
Do While intX < 4
    intTotal = intTotal + intNum(intX)
    intX = intX + 1
Loop
sngAvg = intTotal / intX - 1
Debug.WriteLine(sngAvg)
```
d.
```
Do While intX < 4
    intTotal = intTotal + intNum(intX)
    intX = intX + 1
Loop
sngAvg = intTotal / (intX - 1)
Debug.WriteLine(sngAvg)
```
e. None of the above.

12. The code in Question 11's answer a will display _____.
    a. 0
    b. 5
    c. 6
    d. 8
    e. None of the above.

13. The code in Question 11's answer b will display _____.
    a. 0
    b. 5
    c. 6
    d. 8
    e. None of the above.

14. The code in Question 11's answer c will display _____.
    a. 0
    b. 5
    c. 6
    d. 8
    e. None of the above.

15. The code in Question 11's answer d will display _____.
    a. 0
    b. 5
    c. 6
    d. 8
    e. None of the above.

16. Which of the following displays the number of elements included in the intNum array?
    a. `Debug.WriteLine(Len(intNum))`
    b. `Debug.WriteLine(Length(intNum))`
    c. `Debug.WriteLine(intNum.Len)`
    d. `Debug.WriteLine(intNum.Length)`
    e. None of the above.

17. Which of the following statements is false?
    a. Data stored in an array can be accessed faster than data stored in a disk file.
    b. Data stored in an array needs to be entered only once.
    c. Arrays allow the programmer to store information in internal memory.
    d. Arrays allow the programmer to use fewer variable names.
    e. Visual Basic .NET allows the programmer to create only one-dimensional and two-dimensional arrays.

18. The first subscript in a 25-element array is the number _____.

19. The last subscript in a 25-element array is the number _____.

20. `intQuantity(7)` is read _____.

EXERCISES

1. Write the statement to declare a local one-dimensional array named intNumbers. The array should have 20 elements.

2. Write the statement to store the value 7 in the second element contained in the intNumbers array.

3. Write the statement to declare a form-level one-dimensional array named mstrProducts. The array should have 10 elements.

4. Write the statement to store the string "Paper" in the third element contained in the mstrProducts array.

5. Write the statement to declare a local one-dimensional array named sngRates that has five elements. Use the following numbers to initialize the array: 6.5, 8.3, 4, 2, 10.5.

6. Write the code to display, in the Output window, the contents of the sngRates array. (The array has five elements.) Use the For...Next statement.

7. Rewrite the code from Exercise 6 using the Do...Loop statement.

8. Write the statement to sort the sngRates array in ascending order.

9. Write the statement to reverse the contents of the sngRates array.

10. Write the code to calculate the average of the elements included in the sngRates array. (The array has five elements.) Display the average in the Output window. Use the For...Next statement.

11. Rewrite the code from Exercise 10 using the Do...Loop statement.

12. Write the code to display, in the Output window, the largest number stored in the sngRates array. (The array has five elements.) Use the Do...Loop statement.

13. Rewrite the code from Exercise 12 using the For...Next statement.

14. Write the code to subtract the number one from each element in the sngRates array. (The array has five elements.) Use the Do...Loop statement.

15. Rewrite the code from Exercise 14 using the For...Next statement.

16. Write the code to multiply by two the number stored in the first element included in the intNum array. Store the result in the intDouble variable.

17. Write the code to add together the numbers stored in the first and second elements included in the intNum array. Display the sum in the Output window.

18. In this exercise, you code an application that displays the number of days in a month.
    a. If necessary, start Visual Studio .NET. Open the Month Solution (Month Solution.sln) file, which is contained in the VBNET\Tut11\Month Solution folder. If the designer window is not open, right-click the form file's name in the Solution Explorer window, then click View Designer.
    b. Open the Display Days button's Click event procedure. Declare a 12-element, one-dimensional array named intDays. Use the number of days in each month to initialize the array. (Use 28 for February.)
    c. Code the DisplayButton Click event procedure so that it displays (in a message box) the number of days in the month corresponding to the number entered by the user in the MonthTextBox control. For example, if the MonthTextBox control contains the number one, the procedure should display 31 in a message box. The procedure should display an appropriate message in a message box if the user enters an invalid number in the MonthTextBox control.

d. Save the solution, then start the application. Enter the number 20 in the MonthTextBox, then click the Display Days button. An appropriate message should appear in a message box. Close the message box.

e. Now test the application by entering numbers from 1 through 12 in the MonthTextBox. Click the Display Days button after entering each number.

f. Click the Exit button to end the application.

g. Close the Output window, then close the solution.

19. In this exercise, you code an application that displays the lowest value stored in an array.

a. If necessary, start Visual Studio .NET. Open the Lowest Solution (Lowest Solution.sln) file, which is contained in the VBNET\Tut11\Lowest Solution folder. If the designer window is not open, right-click the form file's name in the Solution Explorer window, then click View Designer.

b. Open the Display Lowest button's Click event procedure. Declare a 20-element, one-dimensional array named intScores. Assign the 20 numbers contained in the scores.data file to the array. The scores.data file is a random access file located in the VBNET\Tut11\Lowest Solution\Lowest Project\bin folder.

c. Code the DisplayButton Click event procedure so that it displays (in a message box) the lowest score stored in the array.

d. Save the solution, then start the application. Click the Display Lowest button. A message containing the lowest score (13) should appear in a message box. Close the message box.

e. Click the Exit button to end the application.

f. Close the Output window, then close the solution.

20. In this exercise, you code an application that updates each value stored in an array.

a. If necessary, start Visual Studio .NET. Open the Prices Solution (Prices Solution.sln) file, which is contained in the VBNET\Tut11\Prices Solution folder. If the designer window is not open, right-click the form file's name in the Solution Explorer window, then click View Designer.

b. In the form's Declarations section, declare a 10-element, one-dimensional array named sngPrices.

c. In the form's Load event procedure, assign the 10 prices stored in the prices.txt file to the sngPrices array. The prices.txt file is a sequential access file located in the VBNET\Tut11\Prices Solution\Prices Project\bin folder.

d. Open the Increase button's Click event procedure. The procedure should ask the user for a percentage amount by which each price should be increased. It then should increase each price by that amount, and then save the increased prices to a sequential access file named newprices.txt.

e. Save the solution, then start the application. Click the Increase button. Increase each price by 5%.

f. Click the Exit button to end the application.

g. Open the prices.txt and newprices.txt files. The prices contained in the newprices.txt file should be 5% more than the prices in the prices.txt file.

h. Close the Output window, then close the solution.

21. In this exercise, you modify the application from Exercise 20. The modified application allows the user to update a specific price.

a. Use Windows to make a copy of the Prices Solution folder, which is contained in the VBNET\Tut11 folder. Change the name of the folder to Prices2 Solution.

b. If necessary, start Visual Studio .NET. Open the Prices Solution (Prices Solution.sln) file, which is contained in the VBNET\Tut11\Prices2 Solution folder. If the designer window is not open, right-click the form file's name in the Solution Explorer window, then click View Designer.

c.   Open the Increase button's Click event procedure. Modify the procedure so that it also asks the user to enter a number from one through 10. If the user enters the number one, the procedure should update the first price in the array. If the user enters the number two, the procedure should update the second price in the array, and so on.

d.   Save the solution, then start the application. Click the Increase button. Increase the second price by 10%. Click the Increase button again. This time, increase the tenth price by 2%.

e.   Click the Exit button to end the application.

f.   Open the prices.txt and newprices.txt files. The second price contained in the newprices.txt file should be 10% more than the second price in the prices.txt file. The tenth price in the newprices.txt file should be 2% more than the tenth price in the prices.txt file.

g.   Close the Output window, then close the solution.

22. In this exercise, you code an application that displays the number of students earning a specific score.

a.   If necessary, start Visual Studio .NET. Open the Scores Solution (Scores Solution.sln) file, which is contained in the VBNET\Tut11\Scores Solution folder. If the designer window is not open, right-click the form file's name in the Solution Explorer window, then click View Designer.

b.   Open the Display button's Click event procedure. Declare a 20-element, one-dimensional array named intScores. Assign the 20 numbers contained in the scores.data file to the array. The scores.data file is a random access file located in the VBNET\Tut11\Scores Solution\Scores Project\bin folder.

c.   Code the DisplayButton Click event procedure so that it prompts the user to enter a score from zero through 100. The procedure then should display (in a message box) the number of students who earned that score.

d.   Save the solution, then start the application. Use the application to answer the following questions.

■   How many students earned a score of 72?

■   How many students earned a score of 88?

■   How many students earned a score of 20?

■   How many students earned a score of 99?

e.   Click the Exit button to end the application.

f.   Close the Output window, then close the solution.

23. In this exercise, you modify the application that you coded in Exercise 22. The modified application allows the user to display the number of students earning a score in a specific range.

a.   Use Windows to make a copy of the Scores Solution folder, which is contained in the VBNET\Tut11 folder. Change the name of the folder to Scores2 Solution.

b.   If necessary, start Visual Studio .NET. Open the Scores Solution (Scores Solution.sln) file, which is contained in the VBNET\Tut11\Scores2 Solution folder. If the designer window is not open, right-click the form file's name in the Solution Explorer window, then click View Designer.

c.   Open the Display button's Click event procedure. Modify the procedure so that it prompts the user to enter a minimum score and a maximum score. The procedure then should display (in a message box) the number of students who earned a score within that range.

    d.   Save the solution, then start the application. Use the application to answer the following questions.

       ■   How many students earned a score between 70 and 79, including 70 and 79?

       ■   How many students earned a score between 65 and 85, including 65 and 85?

       ■   How many students earned a score between 0 and 50, including 0 and 50?

    e.   Click the Exit button to end the application.

    f.   Close the Output window, then close the solution.

24. Jacques Cousard has been playing the lottery for four years and has yet to win any money. He wants an application that will select the six lottery numbers for him. Each lottery number can range from 1 through 54 only.

    a.   If necessary, start Visual Studio .NET. Open the Lottery Solution (Lottery Solution.sln) file, which is contained in the VBNET\Tut11\Lottery Solution folder. If the designer window is not open, right-click the form file's name in the Solution Explorer window, then click View Designer.

    b.   Open the Display Numbers button's Click event procedure. Code the procedure so that it displays six unique random numbers in the interface. (*Hint*: Store the numbers in a one-dimensional array.)

    c.   Save the solution, then start the application. Click the Display Numbers button several times. Each time you click the button, six unique random numbers between 1 and 54 (inclusive) should appear in the interface.

    d.   Click the Exit button to end the application.

    e.   Close the Output window, then close the solution.

25. In this exercise, you code an application that sorts (in ascending order) the values stored in a random access file.

    a.   If necessary, start Visual Studio .NET. Open the Sort Solution (Sort Solution.sln) file, which is contained in the VBNET\Tut11\Sort Solution folder. If the designer window is not open, right-click the form file's name in the Solution Explorer window, then click View Designer.

    b.   Open the Sort button's Click event procedure. Code the procedure so that it stores the 10 numbers (which are integers) contained in the unsorted.data file in an array. The unsorted.data file is a random access file contained in the VBNET\Tut11\Sort Solution\Sort Project\bin folder. The procedure should sort the numbers in ascending order, and then save the sorted numbers to a random access file named sorted.data.

    c.   Code the Print button's Click event procedure so that it prints the contents of the unsorted.data file followed by a blank line and the contents of the sorted.data file on the printer.

    d.   Save the solution, then start the application. Click the Sort button, then click the Print button.

    e.   Click the Exit button to end the application.

    f.   Close the Output window, then close the solution.

26. In this exercise, you modify the application that you coded in Exercise 25. This modified application sorts (in descending order) the values stored in a random access file.

    a.   Use Windows to make a copy of the Sort Solution folder, which is contained in the VBNET\Tut11 folder. Change the name of the folder to Sort2 Solution.

b. If necessary, start Visual Studio .NET. Open the Sort Solution (Sort Solution.sln) file, which is contained in the VBNET\Tut11\Sort2 Solution folder. If the designer window is not open, right-click the form file's name in the Solution Explorer window, then click View Designer.

c. Open the Sort button's Click event procedure. Modify the procedure so that it sorts the numbers in descending order.

d. Save the solution, then start the application. Click the Sort button, then click the Print button.

e. Click the Exit button to end the application.

f. Close the Output window, then close the solution.

Exercise 27 is a Discovery Exercise. Discovery Exercises, which may include topics that are not covered in this lesson, allow you to "discover" the solutions to problems on your own.

discovery ▶ **27.** In this exercise, you learn about the Array.GetUpperBound method.

a. Display the Help screen for the Array.GetUpperBound method. What is the purpose of the method?

b. Write the statement to display (in the Output window) the highest subscript included in a one-dimensional array named strItems.

More on One-Dimensional Arrays

Parallel One-Dimensional Arrays

Takoda Tapahe owns a small gift shop named Treasures. She has asked you to create an application that allows her to display the price of the item whose product ID she enters. Figure 11-14 shows a portion of the gift shop's price list.

Product ID	Price
BX35	13
CR20	10
FE15	12
KW10	24
MM67	4

Figure 11-14: A portion of the gift shop's price list

Recall that all of the variables in an array have the same data type. So how can you store a price list, which includes a string (the product ID) and a number (the price), in an array? One way of doing so is to use two one-dimensional arrays: a String array to store the product IDs and an Integer array to store the prices. Both arrays are illustrated in Figure 11-15.

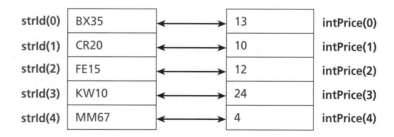

Figure 11-15: Illustration of a price list stored in two one-dimensional arrays

The arrays shown in Figure 11-15 are referred to as parallel arrays. **Parallel arrays** are simply two or more arrays whose elements are related by their position—in other words, by their subscript—in the arrays. The strId and intPrice arrays shown in Figure 11-15 are parallel because each element in the strId array corresponds to the element located in the same position in the intPrice array. For example, the first element in the strId array corresponds to the first element in the intPrice array. In other words, the item whose product ID is BX35 [strId(0)] has a price of $13 [intPrice(0)]. Likewise, the second elements in both arrays—the elements with a subscript of 1—also are related; the item whose product ID is CR20 has a price of $10. The same relationship is true for the remaining elements in both arrays. If you want to know an item's price, you simply locate the item's ID in the strId array and then view its corresponding element in the intPrice array. Figure 11-16 shows a procedure that displays the item's price based on the ID entered by the user.

Pseudocode

1. declare a String array named strId and an Integer array named intPrice
2. declare an Integer variable named intX and a String variable named strSearchFor
3. assign the product ID entered in the IdTextBox control, converted to uppercase, to the strSearchFor variable
4. repeat while intX is less than or equal to 4 and the value stored in the strSearchFor variable is not equal to the value stored in the current element in the strId array
       add 1 to intX
     end repeat
5. if the intX variable contains a number that is less than or equal to 4
       display, in a message box, the appropriate price from the intPrice array
     else
       display the message "Product ID is not valid" in a message box
     end if

Visual Basic .NET code

```
Dim strId() As String = {"BX35", "CR20", "FE15", "KW10", "MM67"}
Dim intPrice() As Integer = {13, 10, 12, 24, 4}
Dim intX As Integer, strSearchFor As String
strSearchFor = UCase(IdTextBox.Text)

'search the array
Do While intX <= 4 AndAlso strSearchFor <> strId(intX)
    intX = intX + 1
Loop
'determine whether the ID was located in the strId array
If intX <= 4 Then
    MessageBox.Show("Price: $" & intPrice(intX), "Treasures", _
        MessageBoxButtons.OK, MessageBoxIcon.Information)
Else
    MessageBox.Show("Product ID is not valid", "Treasures", _
        MessageBoxButtons.OK, MessageBoxIcon.Information)
End If
```

Results (displayed in a message box)

Price: $12   (assuming the user enters FE15 as the product ID)
Product ID is not valid   (assuming the user enters XX90 as the product ID)

Figure 11-16: DisplayPrice procedure using parallel one-dimensional arrays

The DisplayPrice procedure declares and initializes two parallel arrays: a five-element String array named strId and a five-element Integer array named intPrice. The procedure also declares an Integer variable named intX and a String variable named strSearchFor. After declaring the arrays and variables, the procedure assigns the contents of the IdTextBox control, converted to uppercase, to the strSearchFor variable.

The loop in the procedure continues to add the number one to the intX variable as long as the intX variable contains a value that is less than or equal to four and, at the same time, the product ID has not been located in the strId array. The loop stops when either of the following conditions is true: the intX variable contains the number five (which indicates that the loop reached the end of the array without finding the product ID) or the product ID is located in the array.

After the loop completes its processing, the selection structure in the procedure compares the value in the intX variable to the number four. If the intX variable's value is less than or equal to four, it indicates that the loop stopped processing because the product ID was located in the strId array. In that case, the MessageBox.Show method displays (in a message box) the corresponding price from the intPrice array. However, if the intX variable's value is not less than or equal to four, it indicates that the loop stopped processing because it reached the end of the array without finding the product ID; in that case, the message "Product ID is not valid" is displayed in a message box. As Figure 11-16 indicates, the procedure displays a price of $12 if the user enters FE15 as the product ID, and the message "Product ID is not valid" if the user enters XX90 as the product ID.

Using two parallel one-dimensional arrays is only one way of solving the price list problem; you also can use a one-dimensional array that contains records.

Storing Records in a One-Dimensional Array

Before you can store a record in a one-dimensional array, you first must create the record structure. As you learned in Tutorial 10, you create a record structure using the Structure statement. The Structure statement shown in Figure 11-17, for example, creates a record structure named ItemStruc that contains two fields: a String field named strId and an Integer field named intPrice. Notice that the record structure does not specify the length of the strId field. If the record structure is for an array rather than for a random access file, you do not need to specify the length of the String fields in the structure.

```
Structure ItemStruc
    Public strId As String
    Public intPrice As Integer
End Structure
```

Figure 11-17: Structure statement for the ItemStruc record structure

Recall that a record structure is actually a user-defined data type, which you can use to declare either a simple (scalar) variable or an array. The statement Dim udtItem As ItemStruc, for example, declares a local variable that can store one record only. Similarly, the statement Dim udtItems(4) As ItemStruc declares a local array that can store five records. An array that contains records is referred to as an **array of structures**.

Figure 11-18 shows how you can rewrite the DisplayPrice procedure shown in Figure 11-16 using a one-dimensional array of structures, rather than two parallel one-dimensional arrays. Changes made to the procedure shown in Figure 11-16 are shaded in Figure 11-18.

Pseudocode

1. declare an ItemStruc array named udtPriceList
2. declare an Integer variable named intX and a String variable named strSearchFor
3. assign IDs and prices to the udtPriceList array
4. assign the product ID entered in the IdTextBox control, converted to uppercase, to the strSearchFor variable
5. repeat while intX is less than or equal to 4 and the value stored in the strSearchFor variable is not equal to the value stored in the current array element's strId field
       add 1 to intX
   end repeat
6. if the intX variable contains a number that is less than or equal to 4
       display, in a message box, the appropriate price from the intPrice field in the array
   else
       display the message "Product ID is not valid" in a message box
   end if

Visual Basic .NET code

```
Dim udtItem(4) As ItemStruc
Dim intX As Integer, strSearchFor As String
'populate the array
udtItem(0).strId = "BX35"
udtItem(0).intPrice = 13
udtItem(1).strId = "CR20"
udtItem(1).intPrice = 10
udtItem(2).strId = "FE15"
udtItem(2).intPrice = 12
udtItem(3).strId = "KW10"
udtItem(3).intPrice = 24
udtItem(4).strId = "MM67"
udtItem(4).intPrice = 4
strSearchFor = UCase(IdTextBox.Text)

'search the array
Do While intX <= 4 AndAlso strSearchFor <> udtItem(intX).strId
     intX = intX + 1
Loop
'determine whether the ID was located in the udtItem array
If intX <= 4 Then
    MessageBox.Show("Price: $" & udtItem(intX).intPrice, _
    "Treasures", MessageBoxButtons.OK, _
    MessageBoxIcon.Information)
Else
    MessageBox.Show("Product ID is not valid", "Treasures", _
        MessageBoxButtons.OK, MessageBoxIcon.Information)
End If
```

Results (displayed in a message box)

Price: $12   (assuming the user enters FE15 as the product ID)
Product ID is not valid   (assuming the user enters XX90 as the product ID)

Figure 11-18: DisplayPrice procedure using a one-dimensional array of structures

Recall that in most procedures, the values stored in
an array come from a file
on the computer's disk.

The DisplayPrice procedure shown in Figure 11-18 uses the record structure (data type) created in Figure 11-17 to declare a five-element, one-dimensional array named udtItem. Each element in the array contains a record composed of two fields: a String field named strId and an Integer field named intPrice. The procedure also declares an Integer variable named intX and a String variable named strSearchFor. After declaring the array and variables, the procedure assigns the appropriate IDs and prices to the array. Assigning initial values to an array is referred to as **populating** the array. Notice that you refer to a field in an array variable using the syntax *arrayname(subscript).fieldname*. For example, you use udtItem(0).strId to refer to the strId field contained in the first element in the udtItem array. Likewise, you use udtItem(4).intPrice to refer to the intPrice field contained in the last element in the udtItem array.

After populating the udtItem array, the DisplayPrice procedure assigns the contents of the IdTextBox control, converted to uppercase, to the strSearchFor variable. The loop in the procedure then continues to add the number one to the intX variable as long as the intX variable contains a value that is less than or equal to four and, at the same time, the product ID has not been located in the current array element's strId field. The loop stops when either of the following conditions is true: the intX variable contains the number five (which indicates that the loop reached the end of the array without finding the product ID) or the product ID is located in the strId field in the array.

After the loop completes its processing, the selection structure in the procedure compares the value in the intX variable to the number four. If the intX variable's value is less than or equal to four, it indicates that the loop stopped processing because the product ID was located in the array. In that case, the MessageBox.Show method displays (in a message box) the corresponding price from the intPrice field in the array. However, if the intX variable's value is not less than or equal to four, it indicates that the loop stopped processing because it reached the end of the array without finding the product ID; in that case, the message "Product ID is not valid" is displayed in a message box. As Figure 11-18 indicates, the procedure displays a price of $12 if the user enters FE15 as the product ID, and the message "Product ID is not valid" if the user enters XX90 as the product ID.

You now have completed Lesson B. You can either take a break or complete the end-of-lesson questions and exercises before moving on to the next lesson. In Lesson C, you learn about two-dimensional arrays, and you code the Tax Calculator application that you previewed at the beginning of the tutorial.

S U M M A R Y

To create parallel one-dimensional arrays:

■ Create two one-dimensional arrays. When assigning values to both arrays, be sure that the value stored in each element in one array corresponds to the value stored in the same element in the other array.

To create an array of structures:

■ Use the Structure statement to create a record structure (user-defined data type). Then use the record structure to declare the array.

To refer to a field in an array variable that contains a record:

■ Use the syntax *arrayname(subscript).fieldname*.

Q U E S T I O N S

1. If the strState and strCapital arrays are parallel arrays, the capital of the state stored in the strState(0) variable is contained in the _____ variable.

2. Parallel arrays are related by their subscripts.
   a. True
   b. False

3. You use the _____ statement to create a user-defined data type.
   a. Datatype
   b. Define
   c. Record
   d. Structure
   e. UserType

4. You must specify the length of the String fields in a record structure created for an array.
   a. True
   b. False

5. Assume that each record in the udtInventory array contains two fields: a String field named strNumber and an Integer field named intQuantity. Which of the following assigns the inventory number "123XY" to the first element in the array?
   a. `strNumber(0).udtInventory = "123XY"`
   b. `udtInventory(0).strNumber = "123XY"`
   c. `udtInventory(1).strNumber = "123XY"`
   d. `udtInventory.strNumber(0) = "123XY"`
   e. `udtInventory.strNumber(1) = "123XY"`

E X E R C I S E S

1. In this exercise, you code an application that allows Professor Carver to display a grade based on the number of points he enters. The grading scale is shown below.

Minimum points	Maximum points	Grade
0	299	F
300	349	D
350	399	C
400	449	B
450	500	A

   a. If necessary, start Visual Studio .NET. Open the Carver Solution (Carver Solution.sln) file, which is contained in the VBNET\Tut11\Carver Solution folder. If the designer window is not open, right-click the form file's name in the Solution Explorer window, then click View Designer.

   b.　Store the minimum points in a five-element, one-dimensional Integer array named intPoints. Store the grades in a five-element, one-dimensional String array named strGrades. The arrays should be parallel arrays.

   c.　Code the Display Grade button's Click event procedure so that it searches the intPoints array for the number of points entered by the user, and then displays the corresponding grade from the strGrade array.

   d.　Save the solution, and then start the application. Enter 455 in the Points text box, then click the Display Grade button. A grade of A appears in the interface.

   e.　Enter 210 in the Points text box, then click the Display Grade button. A grade of F appears in the interface.

   f.　Click the Exit button to end the application.

   g.　Close the Output window, and then close the solution.

2.　In this exercise, you modify the application that you coded in Exercise 1. The modified application allows the user to change the grading scale when the application is started.

   a.　Use Windows to make a copy of the Carver Solution folder, which is contained in the VBNET\Tut11 folder. Change the name of the folder to Carver2 Solution.

   b.　If necessary, start Visual Studio .NET. Open the Carver Solution (Carver Solution.sln) file, which is contained in the VBNET\Tut11\Carver2 Solution folder. If the designer window is not open, right-click the form file's name in the Solution Explorer window, then click View Designer.

   c.　When the form is loaded into the computer's memory, the application should use the InputBox function to prompt the user to enter the total number of possible points—in other words, the total number of points a student can earn in the course. Modify the application's code to perform this task.

   d.　Modify the application's code so that it uses the grading scale shown below. (For example, if the user enters the number 500 in response to the InputBox function, the code should enter 450, which is 90% of 500, as the minimum number of points for an A. If the user enters the number 300, the code should enter 270, which is 90% of 300, as the minimum number of points for an A.)

Minimum points	Grade
Less than 60% of the possible points	F
60% of the possible points	D
70% of the possible points	C
80% of the possible points	B
90% of the possible points	A

   e.　Save the solution, and then start the application. Enter 300 as the number of possible points, then enter 185 in the Points text box. Click the Display Grade button. A grade of D appears in the interface.

   f.　Click the Exit button to end the application.

   g.　Start the application again. Enter 500 as the number of possible points, then enter 363 in the Points text box. Click the Display Grade button. A grade of C appears in the interface.

   h.　Click the Exit button to end the application.

   i.　Close the Output window, and then close the solution.

3. In this exercise, you code an application that allows Ms. Laury to display a shipping charge based on the number of items ordered by a customer. The shipping charge scale is shown below.

Minimum order	Maximum order	Shipping charge
1	10	15
11	50	10
51	100	5
101	99999	0

    a. If necessary, start Visual Studio .NET. Open the Laury Solution (Laury Solution.sln) file, which is contained in the VBNET\Tut11\Laury Solution folder. If the designer window is not open, right-click the form file's name in the Solution Explorer window, then click View Designer.

    b. Store the maximum order amounts in a four-element, one-dimensional Integer array named intOrder. Store the shipping charge amounts in a four-element, one-dimensional Integer array named intShip. The arrays should be parallel arrays.

    c. Code the Display Shipping Charge button's Click event procedure so that it searches the intOrder array for the number of items ordered by the user, and then displays the corresponding shipping charge from the intShip array. Display the shipping charge formatted using the Currency format style.

    d. Save the solution, and then start the application. Enter 65 in the Number ordered text box, then click the Display Shipping Charge button. A shipping charge of $5.00 appears in the interface.

    e. Enter 500 in the Number ordered text box, then click the Display Shipping Charge button. A shipping charge of $0.00 appears in the interface.

    f. Click the Exit button to end the application.

    g. Close the Output window, and then close the solution.

4. In this exercise, you modify the application that you coded in Exercise 1. The modified application uses a one-dimensional array of structures, rather than two parallel one-dimensional arrays.

    a. Use Windows to make a copy of the Carver Solution folder, which is contained in the VBNET\Tut11 folder. Change the name of the folder to Carver3 Solution.

    b. If necessary, start Visual Studio .NET. Open the Carver Solution (Carver Solution.sln) file, which is contained in the VBNET\Tut11\Carver3 Solution folder. If the designer window is not open, right-click the form file's name in the Solution Explorer window, then click View Designer.

    c. Create a form-level record structure that contains two fields: an Integer field for the minimum points and a String field for the grades.

    d. Use the record structure to declare a five-element, one-dimensional array named udtGradeScale. Modify the application's code so that it stores the grading scale in the udtGradeScale array.

    e. Modify the application's code so that it searches the udtGradeScale array for the number of points earned, and then displays the appropriate grade from the array.

    f. Save the solution, and then start the application. Enter 455 in the Points text box, then click the Display Grade button. A grade of A appears in the interface.

    g. Enter 210 in the Points text box, then click the Display Grade button. A grade of F appears in the interface.

    h. Click the Exit button to end the application.

    i. Close the Output window, and then close the solution.

5. In this exercise, you modify the application you coded in Exercise 3. The modified application uses a one-dimensional array of structures, rather than two one-dimensional parallel arrays.

   a. Use Windows to make a copy of the Laury Solution folder, which is contained in the VBNET\Tut11 folder. Change the name of the folder to Laury2 Solution.

   b. If necessary, start Visual Studio .NET. Open the Laury Solution (Laury Solution.sln) file, which is contained in the VBNET\Tut11\Laury2 Solution folder. If the designer window is not open, right-click the form file's name in the Solution Explorer window, then click View Designer.

   c. Create a form-level record structure that contains two Integer fields: one for the maximum order amounts and the other for the shipping charge amounts.

   d. Use the record structure to declare a four-element, one-dimensional array named udtShipScale. Modify the application's code so that it stores the shipping charge scale in the udtShipScale array.

   e. Modify the application's code so that it searches the udtShipScale array for the number of items ordered, and then displays the appropriate shipping charge from the array.

   f. Save the solution, and then start the application. Enter 65 in the Number ordered text box, then click the Display Shipping Charge button. A shipping charge of $5.00 appears in the interface.

   g. Enter 500 in the Number ordered text box, then click the Display Shipping Charge button. A shipping charge of $0.00 appears in the interface.

   h. Click the Exit button to end the application.

   i. Close the Output window, and then close the solution.

Exercise 6 is a Discovery Exercise. Discovery Exercises, which may include topics that are not covered in this lesson, allow you to "discover" the solutions to problems on your own.

discovery ▶ 6. In this exercise, you learn about the ReDim statement.

   a. Display the Help screen for the ReDim statement. What is the purpose of the statement?

   b. What is the purpose of the keyword Preserve?

   c. If necessary, start Visual Studio .NET. Open the ReDim Solution (ReDim Solution.sln) file, which is contained in the VBNET\Tut11\ReDim Solution folder. If the designer window is not open, right-click the form file's name in the Solution Explorer window, then click View Designer.

   d. Open the Code editor window and view the DisplayButton Click event procedure. Study the existing code, then modify the procedure so that it stores any number of sales amounts in the intSales array.

   e. Save the solution, then start the application. Click the Display Sales button, then enter the following sales amounts: 700, 550, 800, and 0. The button's Click event procedure should display each sales amount in a separate message box.

   f. Click the Display Sales button again, then enter the following sales amounts: 5, 9, 45, 67, 8, and 0. The button's Click event procedure should display each sales amount in a separate message box.

   g. Click the Exit button to end the application.

   h. Close the Output window, and then close the solution.

After completing this lesson, you will be able to:

- Create and initialize a two-dimensional array
- Store data in a two-dimensional array
- Manipulate a two-dimensional array

Using a Two-Dimensional Array

Two-Dimensional Arrays

As you learned in Lesson A, the most commonly used arrays are one-dimensional and two-dimensional. You learned about one-dimensional arrays in Lessons A and B. In this lesson, you learn about two-dimensional arrays.

Recall that you can visualize a one-dimensional array as a column of variables. A **two-dimensional array**, however, resembles a table in that the variables are in rows and columns. Figure 11-19 illustrates a two-dimensional array.

AC34	Shirt	Red
BD12	Coat	Blue
CP14	Blouse	White

Figure 11-19: Illustration of a two-dimensional array

Each variable (element) in a two-dimensional array is identified by a unique combination of two subscripts, which Visual Basic .NET assigns to the variable when the array is created. The subscripts specify the variable's row and column position in the array. Variables located in the first row in a two-dimensional array are assigned a row subscript of 0 (zero). Variables located in the second row are assigned a row subscript of 1 (one), and so on. Similarly, variables located in the first column in a two-dimensional array are assigned a column subscript of 0 (zero). Variables located in the second column are assigned a column subscript of 1 (one), and so on. You refer to each variable in a two-dimensional array by the array's name and the variable's row and column subscripts, which are separated by a comma and specified in a set of parentheses immediately following the array name. For example, to refer to the variable located in the first row, first column in a two-dimensional array named strProducts, you use strProducts(0, 0)—read "strProducts sub zero comma zero." Similarly, to refer to the variable located in the second row, third column in the strProducts array, you use strProducts(1, 2). Figure 11-20 illustrates this naming convention. Notice that the row subscript is listed first in the parentheses.

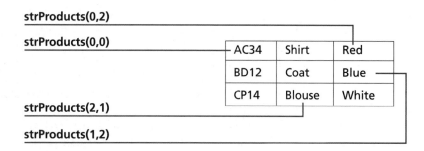

strProducts(0,2)

strProducts(0,0)

strProducts(2,1)

strProducts(1,2)

Figure 11-20: Names of some of the variables contained in the strProducts array

Recall that, before you can use an array, you first must declare (create) it. Figure 11-21 shows two versions of the syntax you use to declare a two-dimensional array in Visual Basic .NET. The figure also includes an example of using each syntax.

Syntax

Version 1
accessibility arrayname(*highestRowSubscript, highestColumnSubscript*) **As** *datatype*

Version 2
accessibility arrayname(,) **As** *datatype* = {{*initialValues*}, {*initialValues*}, …{*initialValues*}}

Examples and results

Example 1
```
Dim strCities(5, 3) As String
```

Results
declares a six-row, four-column array named strCities; each element is automatically initialized to a zero-length (empty) string

Example 2
```
Dim intScores(,) As Integer = {{75, 90}, _
                               {9, 25}, _
                               {23, 56}, _
                               {6, 12}}
```

Results
declares and initializes a four-row, two-column array named intScores

---

Figure 11-21: Syntax versions and examples of declaring a two-dimensional array

In each syntax version, *accessibility* is typically either the keyword Dim (for a local array) or the keyword Private (for a form-level array). *Arrayname* is the name of the array, and *datatype* is the type of data the array variables (elements) will store. Recall that each of the elements in an array has the same data type.

In Version 1 of the syntax, *highestRowSubscript* and *highestColumnSubscript* are integers that specify the highest row and column subscripts, respectively, in the array. When the array is created, it will contain one row more than the number specified in the *highestRowSubscript* argument, and one column more than the number specified in the *highestColumnSubscript* argument; this is because the first row subscript in a two-dimensional array is zero, and the first column subscript also is zero. When you use the syntax shown in Version 1 to declare a two-dimensional array, Visual Basic .NET automatically initializes each element in the array when the array is created.

You use the syntax shown in Version 2 in Figure 11-21 to declare a two-dimensional array and, at the same time, specify each element's initial value. Using Version 2's syntax, you include a separate *initialValues* section, enclosed in braces, for each row in the array. If the array has two rows, then the statement that declares and initializes the array should have two *initialValues* sections. If the array has five rows, then the declaration statement should have five *initialValues* sections.

Within the individual *initialValues* sections, you enter one or more values separated by commas. The number of values to enter corresponds to the number of columns in the array. If the array contains 10 columns, then each individual *initialValues* section should contain 10 values.

In addition to the set of braces that surrounds each individual *initialValues* section, notice in the syntax that a set of braces also surrounds all of the *initialValues* sections. Also notice that a comma appears within the parentheses that follow the array name. The comma indicates that the array is a two-dimensional array. (Recall that a comma is used to separate the row subscript from the column subscript in a two-dimensional array.)

Study closely the two examples shown in Figure 11-21. The statement shown in Example 1 creates a two-dimensional String array named strCities that has six rows and four columns. Visual Basic .NET automatically initializes each element in the array to a zero-length (empty) string. The statement shown in Example 2 creates a two-dimensional Integer array named intScores that has four rows and two columns. The statement initializes the intScores(0, 0) variable to the number 75, and the intScores(0, 1) variable to the number 90. The intScores(1, 0) and intScores(1, 1) variables are initialized to the numbers 9 and 25, respectively. The intScores(2, 0) and intScores(2, 1) variables are initialized to the numbers 23 and 56, respectively, and the inScores(3, 0) and intScores(3, 1) variables are initialized to the numbers 6 and 12, respectively.

After declaring the array, you can use various methods to store data in the array.

Storing Data in a Two-Dimensional Array

You can use a variety of ways to enter data into a two-dimensional array. The examples shown in Figure 11-22, for instance, can be used to enter data into the arrays declared in Figure 11-21.

Examples	Results

Example 1
```strCities(0, 0) = "Madrid"```
```strCities(0, 1) = "Paris"```
```strCities(0, 2) = "Rome"```
```strCities(0, 3) = "London"```
	assigns the strings "Madrid", "Paris", "Rome", and "London" to the elements contained in the first row in the strCities array, replacing the zero-length (empty) strings stored in the array

Example 2
```For intRow = 0 To 3```
```   For intColumn = 0 To 1```
```   intScores(intRow, intColumn) = 0```
```   Next intColumn```
```Next intRow```
	assigns the number zero to each element in the intScores array, replacing the numbers stored in the array

Figure 11-22: Examples of entering data into a two-dimensional array

The code shown in Example 1 in Figure 11-22 uses four assignment statements to assign values to the elements contained in the first row in the strCities array. The code shown in Example 2 uses a nested For...Next loop to assign the number zero to each element contained in the intScores array.

Next, view a procedure that displays the sum of the sales stored in a two-dimensional array.

Calculating the Sum of the Numbers Stored in a Two-Dimensional Array

Conway Enterprises has both domestic and international sales operations. The company's sales manager wants a procedure that allows her to display the total sales made by the company during a six-month period. The DisplaySales procedure shown in Figure 11-23 will accomplish this task.

Pseudocode

1. declare an Integer array named intSales
2. declare Integer variables named intRow, intCol, and intTotal
3. repeat for each row in the intSales array
       repeat for each column in the intSales array
           add the contents of the current array element to the intTotal variable
       end repeat
   end repeat
4. display the contents of the intTotal variable in a message box

Visual Basic .NET code

```
Dim intSales(,) As Integer = {{12000, 10000}, _
                              {45000, 56000}, _
                              {32000, 42000}, _
                              {67000, 23000}, _
                              {24000, 12000}, _
                              {55000, 34000}}
Dim intRow, intCol As Integer     'keeps track of subscripts
Dim intTotal As Integer           'accumulator variable

For intRow = 0 To 5
    For intCol = 0 To 1
        intTotal = intTotal + intSales(intRow, intCol)
    Next intCol
Next intRow
MessageBox.Show("Total: $" & intTotal, "Conway", _
        MessageBoxButtons.OK, MessageBoxIcon.Information)
```

two loops →

Results (displayed in a message box)

Total: $412000

Figure 11-23: DisplaySales procedure

The DisplaySales procedure declares and initializes a six-row, two-column Integer array named intSales. The company's domestic sales amounts are stored in the first column in each row in the array, and its international sales amounts are stored in the second column in each row. Notice that two loops are necessary to access each element in a two-dimensional array: one loop to keep track of the row number, and the other to keep track of the column number. According to Figure 11-23, the total sales made during the six months is $412000.

Now that you know how to use a two-dimensional array, you can begin coding the Tax Calculator application that you previewed at the beginning of the tutorial.

The Tax Calculator Application

Recall that your task in this tutorial is to create an application that John Blackfeather, the owner and manager of the Perrytown Gift Shop, can use to calculate the weekly federal withholding tax for his employees. On your computer's hard disk is a partially completed Tax Calculator application.

To open the Tax Calculator application:

1 Start Microsoft Visual Studio .NET, if necessary, and then close the Start Page window. Click **File** on the menu bar, and then click **Open Solution**. The Open Solution dialog box opens. Open the **Perrytown Solution** (Perrytown Solution.sln) file, which is contained in the VBNET\Tut11\Perrytown Solution folder.

2 If the designer window is not open, right-click **Perrytown Form.vb** in the Solution Explorer window, then click **View Designer**. The Tax Calculator application's user interface appears on the screen.

3 Auto-hide the Toolbox, Solution Explorer, and Properties windows, if necessary. See Figure 11-24.

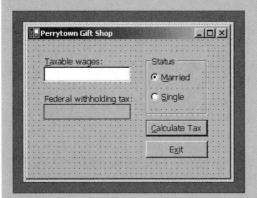

Figure 11-24: Tax Calculator application's user interface

To calculate the federal withholding tax, the user needs simply to enter the taxable wages in the Taxable wages text box and then click the Calculate Tax button.

The Tax Calculator application will use the tax tables shown in Figure 11-25 to calculate the appropriate federal withholding tax (FWT). Notice that the tax amount is based on an employee's taxable wages and his or her marital status.

FWT Tables – Weekly Payroll Period

Single person (including head of household)

If the taxable wages are:		The amount of income tax to withhold is		
Over	**But not over**	**Base amount**	**Percentage**	**Of excess over**
	$ 51	0		
$ 51	$ 552	0	15%	$ 51
$ 552	$1,196	$ 75.15 plus	28%	$ 552
$1,196	$2,662	$ 255.47 plus	31%	$1,196
$2,662	$5,750	$ 709.93 plus	36%	$2,662
$5,750		$1,821.61 plus	39.6%	$5,750

Married person

If the taxable wages are:		The amount of income tax to withhold is		
Over	**But not over**	**Base amount**	**Percentage**	**Of excess over**
	$ 124	0		
$ 124	$ 960	0	15%	$ 124
$ 960	$2,023	$ 125.40 plus	28%	$ 960
$2,023	$3,292	$ 423.04 plus	31%	$2,023
$3,292	$5,809	$ 816.43 plus	36%	$3,292
$5,809		$1,722.55 plus	39.6%	$5,809

Figure 11-25: Weekly FWT tables for 2001

Both tables shown in Figure 11-25 contain five columns of information. The first two columns list various ranges, also called brackets, of taxable wage amounts. The first column—the Over column—lists the amount that a taxable wage in that range must be over, and the second column—the But not over column—lists the maximum amount included in the range. The remaining three columns (Base amount, Percentage, and Of excess over) tell you how to calculate the tax for each range. For example, assume that you are married and your weekly taxable wages are $288.46. Before you can calculate the amount of your tax, you need to locate your taxable wages in the first two columns of the Married table. In this case, your taxable wages fall within the $124 through $960 range. After locating the range that contains your taxable wages, you then use the remaining three columns in the table to calculate your tax. According to the Married table, taxable wages in the $124 through $960 bracket have a tax of 15% of the amount over $124; therefore, your tax is $24.67.

You can use the weekly 2001 tax tables in the Tax Calculator application by simply storing each table in a separate two-dimensional array. To save you time, the application already contains the code to declare and initialize the arrays.

To view the code that declares and initializes the two-dimensional arrays:

1   Right-click the **form**, and then click **View Code** to open the Code editor window. The code to declare and initialize the arrays is located in the form's Declarations section, as shown in Figure 11-26. Notice that each array contains six rows and four columns. The four columns in each array correspond to the "But not over", "Base amount", "Percentage", and "Of excess over" columns in each table.

```
'declare form-level arrays
Private msngSingle(,) As Single = ((51, 0, 0, 0), _
                                    (552, 0, 0.15, 51), _
                                    (1196, 75.15, 0.28, 552), _
                                    (2662, 255.47, 0.31, 1196), _
                                    (5750, 709.93, 0.36, 2662), _
                                    (99999, 1821.61, 0.396, 5750))

Private msngMarried(,) As Single = ((124, 0, 0, 0), _
                                    (960, 0, 0.15, 124), _
                                    (2023, 125.4, 0.28, 960), _
                                    (3292, 423.04, 0.31, 2023), _
                                    (5809, 816.43, 0.36, 3292), _
                                    (99999, 1722.55, 0.396, 5809))
```

Figure 11-26: Code to declare and initialize the two-dimensional arrays

The last two zeroes in the first row in each array correspond to the empty blocks in the "Percentage" and "Of excess over" columns in the tax tables. The 99999 in the last row in each array represents the empty block in the "But not over" column in the tax tables. You can use any large number to represent the empty block in the "But not over" column, as long as the number is greater than the largest weekly taxable wage you expect the user to enter.

Figure 11-27 shows the TOE chart for the Tax Calculator application.

Task	Object	Event
1. Calculate the federal withholding tax 2. Display the federal withholding tax in the FwtLabel	CalculateButton	Click
End the application	ExitButton	Click
Display the federal withholding tax (from CalculateButton)	FwtLabel	None
Clear the contents of the FwtLabel	MarriedRadioButton, SingleRadioButton, TaxableTextBox	Click Click TextChanged
Get and display the taxable wages	TaxableTextBox	None
Select the existing text	TaxableTextBox	Enter

Figure 11-27: TOE chart for the Tax Calculator application

All of the event procedures listed in Figure 11-27, except the CalculateButton Click event procedure have already been coded for you.

Coding the CalculateButton Click Event Procedure

According to the TOE chart, the CalculateButton Click event procedure is responsible for calculating the federal withholding tax (FWT) and displaying the calculated amount in the FwtLabel control. Figure 11-28 shows the pseudocode for the procedure.

CalculateButton
1. declare a Single array named sngTaxTable
2. declare two Single variables named sngTaxable and sngFwt, an Integer variable named intRow, and a Boolean variable named blnFound
3. assign the taxable wages stored in the TaxableTextBox to the sngTaxable variable
4. if the Single radio button is selected
       assign the form-level msngSingle array to the sngTaxTable array
   else
       assign the form-level msngMarried array to the sngTaxTable array
   end if
5. repeat while the intRow variable is less than 6 and the blnFound variable contains False
       if the taxable wages stored in the sngTaxable variable are less than or equal to the
       value stored in the first column in the current row in the sngTaxTable array
           use the information stored in the second, third, and fourth columns in the
           sngTaxTable to calculate the federal withholding tax

           assign the value True to the blnFound variable
       else
           add 1 to the contents of the intRow variable
       end if
   end repeat
6. display the federal withholding tax in the FwtLabel control

---

Figure 11-28: Pseudocode for the CalculateButton Click event procedure

To code the CalculateButton Click event procedure:

1 Click the **Class Name** list arrow, and then click **CalculateButton** in the list. Click the **Method Name** list arrow, and then click **Click** in the list. The code template for the CalculateButton Click event procedure appears in the Code editor window.

The first step in the pseudocode is to declare an array and four variables.

2 Type **dim sngTaxTable(5, 3) as single** and press **Enter**. Type **dim sngTaxable, sngFwt as single, intRow as integer, blnFound as boolean** and press **Enter**.

Next, assign the taxable wages, which the user enters in the TaxableTextBox, to the sngTaxable variable.

3 Type '**assign taxable wages to a variable** and press **Enter**, then type **sngtaxable = val(me.taxabletextbox.text)** and press **Enter**.

Now determine whether the tax should be calculated using the information stored in the msngSingle or msngMarried array.

4 Type the comment and selection structure shown in Figure 11-29, then position the insertion point as shown in the figure.

```
Private Sub CalculateButton_Click(ByVal sender As Object, ByVal e As System.EventArg
    Dim sngTaxTable(5, 3) As Single
    Dim sngTaxable, sngFwt As Single, intRow As Integer, blnFound As Boolean
    'assign taxable wages to a variable
    sngTaxable = Val(Me.TaxableTextBox.Text)
    'determine appropriate array
    If Me.SingleRadioButton.Checked = True Then
        sngTaxTable = msngSingle
    Else
        sngTaxTable = msngMarried
    End If

End Sub
```

enter these lines of code ──────

position the insertion point here ──────

Figure 11-29: Comment and selection structure entered in the procedure

Now begin a loop that repeats its instructions while the intRow variable contains a value that is less than six (which indicates that there are more array elements to search) and, at the same time, the blnFound variable contains the value False (which indicates that the appropriate wage bracket has not yet been located).

5   Type '**search for the taxable wages in the first column in the array** and press **Enter**. Type **do while introw < 6 andalso blnfound = false** and press **Enter**.

If the taxable wages are less than or equal to the value stored in the first column in the current row in the sngTaxTable array, then use the information stored in the array's second, third, and fourth columns to calculate the federal withholding tax. Also assign the value True to the blnFound variable to indicate that the appropriate wage bracket was located.

6   Type the additional lines of code indicated in Figure 11-30, then position the insertion point as shown in the figure.

```
Private Sub CalculateButton_Click(ByVal sender As Object, ByVal e As System.EventArg
    Dim sngTaxTable(5, 3) As Single
    Dim sngTaxable, sngFwt As Single, intRow As Integer, blnFound As Boolean
    'assign taxable wages to a variable
    sngTaxable = Val(Me.TaxableTextBox.Text)
    'determine appropriate array
    If Me.SingleRadioButton.Checked = True Then
        sngTaxTable = msngSingle
    Else
        sngTaxTable = msngMarried
    End If
    'search for the taxable wages in the first column in the array
    Do While intRow < 6 AndAlso blnFound = False
        If sngTaxable <= sngTaxTable(intRow, 0) Then
            'calculate the FWT
            sngFwt = sngTaxTable(intRow, 1) + sngTaxTable(intRow, 2) _
                * (sngTaxable - sngTaxTable(intRow, 3))
            blnFound = True

        End If
    Loop
End Sub
```

enter these lines of code ──────

position the insertion point here ──────

Figure 11-30: Additional code entered in the procedure

If the correct wage bracket was not found in the current row in the sngTaxTable array, then the procedure should search the next row in the array. To do so, you need to add the number one to the contents of the intRow variable.

7   Type **else** and press **Enter**, then type **introw = introw + 1**.

The last step in the pseudocode shown in Figure 11-28 is to display the federal withholding tax in the FwtLabel control.

8 Type the two lines of code indicated in Figure 11-31, which shows the completed CalculateButton Click event procedure.

enter these two lines of code

```
Private Sub CalculateButton_Click(ByVal sender As Object, ByVal e As System.EventArgs) Handles Ca
    Dim sngTaxTable(5, 3) As Single
    Dim sngTaxable, sngFwt As Single, intRow As Integer, blnFound As Boolean
    'assign taxable wages to a variable
    sngTaxable = Val(Me.TaxableTextBox.Text)
    'determine appropriate array
    If Me.SingleRadioButton.Checked = True Then
        sngTaxTable = msngSingle
    Else
        sngTaxTable = msngMarried
    End If
    'search for the taxable wages in the first column in the array
    Do While intRow < 6 AndAlso blnFound = False
        If sngTaxable <= sngTaxTable(intRow, 0) Then
            'calculate the FWT
            sngFwt = sngTaxTable(intRow, 1) + sngTaxTable(intRow, 2) _
                * (sngTaxable - sngTaxTable(intRow, 3))
            blnFound = True
        Else
            intRow = intRow + 1
        End If
    Loop
    'display the FWT
    Me.FwtLabel.Text = Format(sngFwt, "currency")
End Sub
```

Figure 11-31: Completed CalculateButton Click event procedure

Now test the CalculateButton Click event procedure to verify that it is working correctly.

To test the CalculateButton Click event procedure:

1 Click **File** on the menu bar, and then click **Save All**. Click **Debug** on the menu bar, and then click **Start**.

First, calculate the FWT for a married taxpayer with taxable wages of $288.46.

2 Type **288.46** in the Taxable wages text box, then click the **Calculate Tax** button. The application calculates and displays a tax of $24.67.

Now calculate the FWT for a single taxpayer with taxable wages of $600.

3 Type 600 in the Taxable wages text box, then click the **Single** radio button. Click the **Calculate Tax** button. The application calculates and displays a tax of $88.59.

4 Click the **Exit** button to end the application. When you return to the Code editor window, close the Output window, then close the Code editor window.

5 Click **File** on the menu bar, and then click **Close Solution**.

You now have completed Tutorial 11. You can either take a break or complete the end-of lesson questions and exercises.

S U M M A R Y

To declare a two-dimensional array:

■ Use either of the following two syntax versions:
Version 1: *accessibility arrayname(highestRowSubscript, highestColumnSubscript)* **As** *datatype*
Version 2: *accessibility arrayname(,)* **As** *datatype* = {{*initialValues*}, {*initialValues*}, ...{*initialValues*}}

■ *Accessibility* is typically either the keyword Dim or the keyword Private. *Arrayname* is the name of the array, and *datatype* is the type of data the array variables will store. You can declare an array using any of Visual Basic .NET's standard data types; or, you can use a user-defined data type.

■ The *highestRowSubscript* and *highestColumnSubscript* arguments, which appear in Version 1 of the syntax, are integers that specify the highest row and column subscripts, respectively, in the array. Using Version 1's syntax, Visual Basic .NET automatically initializes the elements (variables) in the array.

■ The *initialValues* section in Version 2 of the syntax allows you to specify the initial values for the array. You include a separate *initialValues* section for each row in the array. Each *initialValues* section should contain the same number of values as there are columns in the array.

To refer to a variable included in a two-dimensional array:

■ Use the syntax *arrayname(rowSubscript, columnSubscript)*.

Q U E S T I O N S

1. The individual elements in a two-dimensional array are identified by a unique
   _____.
   a. combination of two subscripts
   b. data type
   c. order
   d. subscript
   e. Both a and b.

2. Which of the following statements creates a two-dimensional Single array named sngTemps that contains three rows and four columns?
   a. `Dim sngTemps(2, 3) As Single`
   b. `Dim sngTemps(3, 4) As Single`
   c. `Dim sngTemps(3, 2) As Single`
   d. `Dim sngTemps(4, 3) As Single`
   e. `Dim sngTemps(3)(4) As Single`

Use the following two-dimensional array, named intSales, to answer Questions 3 through 6.

10000	12000	900	500	20000
350	600	700	800	100

3. The statement `intSales(1, 3) = intSales(1, 3) + 10` will
    _____.

    a. replace the 900 amount with 910
    b. replace the 500 amount with 510
    c. replace the 700 amount with 710
    d. replace the 800 amount with 810
    e. result in an error

4. The statement `intSales(0, 4) = intSales(0, 4 - 2)` will _____.
    a. have no effect on the array
    b. replace the 20000 amount with 900
    c. replace the 20000 amount with 19998
    d. replace the 20000 amount with 19100
    e. result in an error

5. The statement `Debug.WriteLine(intSales(0, 3) + intSales(1, 3))` will
    _____.

    a. display 1300 in the Output window
    b. display 1600 in the Output window
    c. display intSales(0, 3) + intSales(1, 3) in the Output window
    d. display 0 in the Output window
    e. result in an error

6. Which of the following If clauses can be used to verify that the array subscripts named intRow and intCol are valid for the intSales array?
    a. `If intSales(intRow, intCol) >= 0 AndAlso intSales(intRow, intCol) < 5 Then`
    b. `If intSales(intRow, intCol) >= 0 AndAlso intSales(intRow, intCol) <= 5 Then`
    c. `If intRow >= 0 AndAlso intRow < 3 AndAlso intCol >= 0 AndAlso intCol < 6 Then`
    d. `If intRow >= 0 AndAlso intRow < 2 AndAlso intCol >= 0 AndAlso intCol < 5 Then`
    e. None of the above.

Use the following array, named intNum, to answer Questions 7 through 11.

10	200	50
300	25	30

7. Assume that a random access file contains the following numbers, in this order: 10, 200, 50, 300, 25, and 30. Which of the following nested loops fills the intNum array as shown above?

    a.
    ```
    For intCol = 0 To 2
        For intRow = 0 To 1
            FileGet(1, intNum(intRow, intCol))
        Next intRow
    Next intCol
    ```
    b.
    ```
    For intRow = 0 To 1
        For intCol = 0 To 2
            FileGet(1, intNum(intRow, intCol))
        Next intCol
    Next intRow
    ```

```
c.  For intRow = 0 To 2
        For intCol = 0 To 1
            FileGet(1, intNum(intRow, intCol))
        Next intCol
    Next intRow
d.  For intCol = 0 To 1
        For intRow = 0 To 2
            FileGet(1, intNum(intRow, intCol))
        Next intRow
    Next intCol
```

8. Show how the nested loops shown in Question 7's answer a fill the intNum array.

The code shown in Question 7's answer a will _____.
a.   fill the array correctly
b.   fill the array incorrectly
c.   result in an error

9. Show how the nested loops shown in Question 7's answer b fill the intNum array.

The code shown in Question 7's answer b will _____.
a.   fill the array correctly
b.   fill the array incorrectly
c.   result in an error

10. Show how the nested loops shown in Question 7's answer c fill the intNum array.

The code shown in Question 7's answer c will _____.
a.   fill the array correctly
b.   fill the array incorrectly
c.   result in an error

11. Show how the nested loops shown in Question 7's answer d fill the intNum array.

The code shown in Question 7's answer d will _____.
a. fill the array correctly
b. fill the array incorrectly
c. result in an error

12. Which of the following statements assigns the string "California" to the variable located in the third column, fifth row of a two-dimensional array named strStates?
a. `strStates(3, 5) = "California"`
b. `strStates(5, 3) = "California"`
c. `strStates(2, 4) = "California"`
d. `strStates(4, 2) = "California"`
e. None of the above.

E X E R C I S E S

The following list summarizes the GUI design guidelines you have learned. You can use this list to verify that the interfaces you create in the following exercises adhere to the GUI standards outlined in the book.

- Information should flow either vertically or horizontally, with the most important information always located in the upper-left corner of the screen.

- Maintain a consistent margin of two or three dots from the edge of the window.

- Try to create a user interface that no one notices.

- Related controls should be grouped together using white space, a GroupBox control, or a Panel control.

- Set the form's FormBorderStyle, ControlBox, MaximizeBox, MinimizeBox, and StartPosition properties appropriately:

    - A splash screen should not have a Minimize, Maximize, or Close button, and its borders should not be sizable.

    - A form that is not a splash screen should always have a Minimize button and a Close button, but you can choose to disable the Maximize button. Typically, the FormBorderStyle property is set to Sizable, but also can be set to FixedSingle.

- Position related controls on succeeding dots. Controls that are not part of any logical grouping may be positioned from two to four dots away from other controls.

- Buttons should be positioned either in a row along the bottom of the screen, or stacked in either the upper-right or lower-right corner.

- If the buttons are positioned at the bottom of the screen, then each button should be the same height; their widths, however, may vary.

- If the buttons are stacked in either the upper-right or lower-right corner of the screen, then each should be the same height and the same width.

- Use no more than six buttons on a screen.

- The most commonly used button should be placed first.

- Button captions should:
  - be meaningful
  - be from one to three words
  - appear on one line
  - be entered using book title capitalization
- Use labels to identify the text boxes in the interface, and position the label either above or to the left of the text box.
- Label text should:
  - be from one to three words
  - appear on one line
  - be left-justified
  - end with a colon (:)
  - be entered using sentence capitalization
- Labels that identify controls should have their BorderStyle property set to None.
- Labels that display program output, such as the result of a calculation, should have their BorderStyle property set to FixedSingle.
- Align controls to minimize the number of different margins.
- If you use a graphic in the interface, use a small one and place it in a location that will not distract the user.
- Use the Tahoma font for applications that will run on Windows 2000 or Windows XP.
- Use no more than two different font sizes, which should be 8, 9, 10, 11, or 12 point.
- Use only one font type, which should be a sans serif font, in the interface.
- Avoid using italics and underlining.
- Limit the use of bold text to titles, headings, and key items.
- Build the interface using black, white, and gray first, then add color only if you have a good reason to do so.
- Use white, off-white, light gray, pale blue, or pale yellow for an application's background, and black for the text.
- Limit the number of colors to three, not including white, black, and gray. The colors you choose should complement each other.
- Never use color as the only means of identification for an element in the user interface.
- Set each control's TabIndex property to a number that represents the order in which you want the control to receive the focus (begin with 0).
- A text box's TabIndex value should be one more than the TabIndex value of its identifying label.
- Assign a unique access key to each control (in the interface) that can receive user input (text boxes, buttons, and so on).

- When assigning an access key to a control, use the first letter of the caption or identifying label, unless another letter provides a more meaningful association. If you can't use the first letter and no other letter provides a more meaningful association, then use a distinctive consonant. Lastly, use a vowel or a number.

- Lock the controls in place on the form.

- Document the program internally.

- Use the Val function on any Text property involved in a calculation.

- Use the Format function to improve the appearance of numbers in the interface.

- In the InputBox function, use sentence capitalization for the *prompt*, and book title capitalization for the *title*.

- The default button should be the button that is most often selected by the user, except in cases where the tasks performed by the button are both destructive and irreversible. The default button typically is the first button.

- Use sentence capitalization for the optional identifying label in a group box control.

- MessageBox.Show method:

  - Use sentence capitalization for the *text* argument, but book title capitalization for the *caption* argument. The name of the application typically appears in the *caption* argument.

  - Avoid using the words "error," "warning," or "mistake" in the message.

  - Display the Warning Message icon ⚠ in a message box that alerts the user that he or she must make a decision before the application can continue. You can phrase the message as a question.

  - Display the Information Message icon ⓘ in a message box that displays an informational message along with an OK button only.

  - Display the Stop Message icon ⊗ when you want to alert the user of a serious problem that must be corrected before the application can continue.

  - The default button in the dialog box should be the one that represents the user's most likely action, as long as that action is not destructive.

- Use the KeyPress event to prevent a text box from accepting inappropriate keys.

- Radio buttons:

  - Use radio buttons when you want to limit the user to one of two or more related and mutually exclusive choices.

  - Use a minimum of two and a maximum of seven radio buttons in an interface.

  - Use sentence capitalization for the label entered in the radio button's Text property.

  - Assign a unique access key to each radio button in an interface.

  - Use a group box control (or a panel control) to create separate groups of radio buttons. Only one button in each group can be selected at any one time.

  - Designate a default radio button in each group of radio buttons.

- Check boxes:

  - Use check boxes to allow the user to select any number of choices from a group of one or more independent and nonexclusive choices.

- Use sentence capitalization for the label entered in the check box's Text property.
- Assign a unique access key to each check box in an interface.

■ List boxes:

- A list box should contain a minimum of three selections.
- A list box should display a minimum of three selections and a maximum of eight selections at a time.
- Use a label control to provide keyboard access to the list box. Set the label control's TabIndex property to a value that is one less than the list box's TabIndex value.
- List box items are either arranged by use, with the most used entries appearing first in the list, or sorted in ascending order.
- If a list box allows the user to make only one selection at a time, then a default item should be selected in the list box when the interface first appears. The default item should be either the most used selection or the first selection in the list. However, if a list box allows more than one selection at a time, you do not select a default item.

■ Menus:

- Menu title captions, which appear on the menu bar, should be one word, with the first letter capitalized. Each menu title should have a unique access key.
- Menu item captions, which appear on a menu, can be from one to three words. Use book title capitalization and assign a unique access key to each menu item. Assign shortcut keys to commonly used menu items.
- If a menu item requires additional information from the user, place an ellipsis (...) at the end of the item's caption, which is entered in the item's Text property.
- Follow the Windows standards for the placement of menu titles and items.
- Use a separator bar to separate groups of related menu items.

■ It is customary in Windows applications to disable objects that do not apply to the current state of the application.

■ It is customary in Windows applications to highlight, or select, the existing text in a text box when the text box receives the focus.

■ If an operation is destructive, prompt the user to verify that he or she wants to proceed with the operation.

■ Test the application with both valid and invalid data (for example, test the application without entering any data, and test it by entering letters where numbers are expected).

■ Display messages to inform the user of the status of important events.

1. Write the statement to declare a two-dimensional Decimal array named decBalances. The array should have four rows and six columns.

2. Write a loop that stores the number 10 in the decBalances array declared in Exercise 1. Use the For...Next statement.

3. Rewrite the loop from Exercise 2 using a Do...Loop statement.

4. Write the statement to assign the Boolean value True to the variable located in the third row, first column of the blnAnswers array.

5. In this exercise, you code an application that sums the values contained in a two-dimensional array.
   a. If necessary, start Visual Studio .NET. Open the Inventory Solution (Inventory Solution.sln) file, which is contained in the VBNET\Tut11\Inventory Solution folder. If the designer window is not open, right-click the form file's name in the Solution Explorer window, then click View Designer.
   b. Code the Display Total button's Click event procedure so that it adds together the values stored in the intInventory array. Display the sum in the TotalLabel control.
   c. Save the solution, and then start the application. Click the Display Total button to display the sum of the array values.
   d. Click the Exit button to end the application.
   e. Close the Output window, and then close the solution.

6. In this exercise, you code an application that sums the values stored in a two-dimensional array.
   a. If necessary, start Visual Studio .NET. Open the Conway Solution (Conway Solution.sln) file, which is contained in the VBNET\Tut11\Conway Solution folder. If the designer window is not open, right-click the form file's name in the Solution Explorer window, then click View Designer.
   b. Code the Display Totals button's Click event procedure so that it displays the total domestic sales, total international sales, and total company sales in the appropriate label controls.
   c. Save the solution, and then start the application. Click the Display Totals button. The button's Click event procedure should display domestic sales of $235000, international sales of $177000, and company sales of $412000.
   d. Click the Exit button to end the application.
   e. Close the Output window, and then close the solution.

7. In this exercise, you code an application that displays the number of times a value appears in a two-dimensional array.
   a. If necessary, start Visual Studio .NET. Open the Count Solution (Count Solution.sln) file, which is contained in the VBNET\Tut11\Count Solution folder. If the designer window is not open, right-click the form file's name in the Solution Explorer window, then click View Designer.
   b. Code the Display Count button's Click event procedure so that it displays the number of times each of the numbers from one through nine appears in the intNumbers array. (*Hint*: Store the counts in a one-dimensional array.)

    c.   Save the solution, and then start the application. Click the Display Count button to display the nine counts.

    d.   Click the Exit button to end the application.

    e.   Close the Output window, and then close the solution.

8.   In this exercise, you code an application that displays the highest score earned on the midterm exam and the highest score earned on the final exam.

    a.   If necessary, start Visual Studio .NET. Open the Highest Solution (Highest Solution.sln) file, which is contained in the VBNET\Tut11\Highest Solution folder. If the designer window is not open, right-click the form file's name in the Solution Explorer window, then click View Designer.

    b.   Code the Display Highest button's Click event procedure so that it displays (in the appropriate label controls) the highest score earned on the midterm exam and the highest score earned on the final exam.

    c.   Save the solution, and then start the application. Click the Display Highest button to display the highest scores earned on the midterm and final exams.

    d.   Click the Exit button to end the application.

    e.   Close the Output window, and then close the solution.

9.   MJ Sales employs 10 salespeople. The sales made by the salespeople during the months of January, February, and March are stored in a random access file named sales.data. The file contains 10 records, one for each salesperson. Each salesperson's record contains three fields. The first field contains the January sales amount, the second field contains the February sales amount, and the third field contains the March sales amount. The sales manager wants an application that allows him to print a Bonus Report showing each salesperson's number (1 through 10), total sales, and bonus amount. The report also should include the total bonus paid.

    a.   If necessary, start Visual Studio .NET. Open the MJ Solution (MJ Solution.sln) file, which is contained in the VBNET\Tut11\MJ Solution folder. If the designer window is not open, right-click the form file's name in the Solution Explorer window, then click View Designer.

    b.   Code the application so that it stores each saleperson's total sales and bonus amounts in a two-dimensional Single array named sngSales. The application also should print the Bonus Report.

    c.   Save the solution, and then start the application. Enter .1 in the Bonus rate text box, then click the Print Report button to print the Bonus Report on the printer.

    d.   Click the Exit button to end the application.

    e.   Close the Output window, and then close the solution.

Exercises 10 and 11 are Discovery Exercises. Discovery Exercises, which may include topics that are not covered in this lesson, allow you to "discover" the solutions to problems on your own.

discovery ▶ **10.**   In this exercise, you code an application that sorts the contents of a two-dimensional array.

    a.   If necessary, start Visual Studio .NET. Open the Names Solution (Names Solution.sln) file, which is contained in the VBNET\Tut11\Names Solution folder. If the designer window is not open, right-click the form file's name in the Solution Explorer window, then click View Designer.

    b.   Code the Sort button's Click event procedure so that it sorts the contents of the two-dimensional strUnsorted array. The procedure should store the sorted values in a one-dimensional array named strSorted.

    c. Code the Print button's Click event procedure so that it prints the contents of the strSorted array on the printer.

    d. Save the solution, and then start the application. Click the Sort button, then click the Print button.

    e. Click the Exit button to end the application.

    f. Close the Output window, and then close the solution.

discovery ▶ **11.** In this exercise, you modify the Tax Calculator application that you coded in Lesson C. The modified application passes the appropriate array to a function.

    a. Use Windows to make a copy of the Perrytown Solution folder, which is contained in the VBNET\Tut11 folder. Change the name of the folder to Modified Perrytown Solution.

    b. If necessary, start Visual Studio .NET. Open the Perrytown Solution (Perrytown Solution.sln) file, which is contained in the VBNET\Tut11\Modified Perrytown Solution folder. If the designer window is not open, right-click the form file's name in the Solution Explorer window, then click View Designer.

    c. Open the Code editor window. Remove any reference to the sngTaxTable array from the CalculateButton Click event procedure. Modify the selection structure so that it passes the taxable wages and the appropriate array—either msngSingle or msngMarried—to a user-defined function named CalcFwt.

    d. Create a user-defined function named CalcFwt. The function will need to accept the taxable wages and the array passed to it. Move the code that calculates the federal withholding tax from the CalculateButton to the CalcFwt function.

    e. Save the solution, then start the application. Use the application to display the tax for a married employee with taxable wages of $288.46. The application should display $24.67 as the tax. Now use the application to display the tax for a single employee with taxable wages of $600. The application should display $88.59 as the tax.

    f. Click the Exit button to end the application.

    g. Close the Output window, and then close the solution.

Exercise 12 is a Debugging Exercise. Debugging Exercises provide an opportunity for you to detect and correct errors in an existing application.

debugging **12.** In this exercise, you debug an existing application.

    a. If necessary, start Visual Studio .NET. Open the Debug Solution (Debug Solution.sln) file, which is contained in the VBNET\Tut11\Debug Solution folder. If the designer window is not open, right-click the form file's name in the Solution Explorer window, then click View Designer.

    b. View the application's code. The strNames array contains five rows and two columns. Column one contains five first names, and column two contains five last names. The DisplayButton Click event procedure should display the first and last names in the FirstListBox and LastListBox controls, respectively.

    c. Notice that a jagged line appears below some of the lines of code in the Code editor window. Correct the code to remove the jagged lines.

    d. Save the solution, then start the application. If an error message appears in a dialog box, click the Break button. Click Debug, then click Stop Debugging.

    e. Correct the errors in the application's code, then save the solution and start the application. Click the Display button to display the first and last names in the FirstListBox and LastListBox controls, respectively.

    f. Click the Exit button to end the application.

    g. Close the Output window, then close the solution.

Basic Tools Included in the Windows Forms Designer Toolbox

Tool icon	Tool name	Purpose
	Pointer	allows you to move and size forms and controls
	Button	displays a standard button that the user can click to perform actions
	CheckBox	displays a box that indicates whether an option is selected or deselected
	CheckedListBox	displays a scrollable list of items, each accompanied by a check box
	ColorDialog	displays the standard Windows Color dialog box
	ComboBox	displays a drop-down list of items
	ContextMenu	implements a menu that appears when the user right-clicks an object
	CrystalReport Viewer	allows a Crystal Report to be viewed in an application
	DataGrid	displays data in a series of rows and columns
	DateTimePicker	allows the user to select a single item from a list of dates or times
	DomainUpDown	displays a list of text items that users can scroll through using the up and down arrow buttons

(continued)

(continued)

Tool icon	Tool name	Purpose
	ErrorProvider	displays error information to the user in a nonintrusive way
	FontDialog	displays the standard Windows Font dialog box
	GroupBox	provides a visual and functional container for controls; similar to the Panel control, but can display a caption but no scroll bars
	HelpProvider	associates an HTML Help file with a Windows application
	HScrollBar	displays a horizontal scroll bar
	ImageList	stores images
	Label	displays text that the user cannot edit
	LinkLabel	adds a Web style link to a Windows Forms application
	ListBox	displays a list from which a user can select one or more items
	ListView	displays items in one of four views (text only, text with small icons, text with large icons, or report view)
	MainMenu	displays a menu while an application is running
	MonthCalendar	displays an intuitive graphical interface for users to view and set date information
	NotifyIcon	displays an icon for a process that runs in the background and would not otherwise have a user interface
	NumericUpDown	displays a list of numerals that users can scroll through with up and down arrow buttons
	OpenFileDialog	displays the standard Windows Open File dialog box
	PageSetupDialog	displays the standard Windows Page Setup dialog box
	Panel	provides a visual and functional container for controls; similar to a GroupBox control, but can display scroll bars but no caption
	PictureBox	displays graphics in bitmap, GIF, JPEG, metafile, or icon format
	PrintDialog	displays the standard Windows Print dialog box
	PrintDocument	prints a document within a Windows application
	PrintPreview Control	allows you to create your own Print Preview dialog box
	PrintPreviewDialog	displays the standard Windows Print Preview dialog box
	ProgressBar	indicates the progress of an action by displaying an appropriate number of rectangles arranged in a horizontal bar

(continued)

(continued)

Tool icon	Tool name	Purpose
	RadioButton	displays a button that indicates whether an option is selected or deselected
	RichTextBox	allows users to enter, display, and manipulate text with formatting
	SaveFileDialog	displays the standard Windows Save As dialog box
◄│►	Splitter	allows the user to resize a docked control while an application is running
	StatusBar	displays status information related to the object that has the focus
	TabControl	displays multiple tabs
	TextBox	accepts and displays text that the user can edit
	Timer	performs actions at specified time intervals
	ToolBar	displays menus and bitmapped buttons that activate commands
	ToolTip	displays text when the user points at an object
	TrackBar	allows a user to navigate through a large amount of information, or to visually adjust a numeric setting
	TreeView	displays a hierarchy of nodes that can be expanded or collapsed
	VScrollBar	displays a vertical scroll bar

Database Access Using a Windows Form

Accessing Data Stored in a Database

In order to maintain accurate records, most businesses store information about their employees, customers, and inventory in files called databases. In general, a **database** is simply an organized collection of related information stored in a file on a disk.

Many software packages exist for creating databases; some of the most popular are Microsoft Access, Oracle, and SQL Server. You can use Visual Basic .NET to access the data stored in these databases; this allows a company to create a standard interface in Visual Basic .NET that employees can use to access database information stored in a variety of formats. Instead of learning each database package's user interface, the employee needs to know only one interface. The actual format the database is in is unimportant and will be transparent to the user.

tip

You do not have to be a business to make use of a database. Many people use databases to keep track of their medical records, their compact disc collections, and even their golf scores.

> The databases are called relational because the information in the tables can be related in different ways.

> The column and row format used in a relational database is similar to the column and row format used in a spreadsheet.

In this appendix, you learn how to access the data stored in a Microsoft Access database. Databases created by Microsoft Access are relational databases. A **relational database** is one that stores information in tables, which are composed of columns and rows. Each column in a table represents a field, and each row represents a record. As you learned in Tutorial 10, a **field** is a single item of information about a person, place, or thing—such as a name, address, or phone number—and a **record** is a group of related fields that contain all of the necessary data about a specific person, place, or thing. A **table** is a group of related records. Each record in the group pertains to the same topic, and each contains the same type of information—in other words, the same fields.

A relational database can contain one or more tables. You could use a one-table database, for example, to store the information regarding the college courses you have taken. Each record in the table would contain a course ID (department and number), course title, number of credit hours, and grade. You would use a two-table database, on the other hand, to store information about your CD (compact disc) collection: one table to store the general information about each CD (the CD's name and the artist's name) and the other table to store the information about the songs on each CD (their title and track number). You would use a common field—for example, a CD number—to relate the records contained in both tables. Figure B-1 shows an example of both a one-table and a two-table relational database.

One-table college course relational database

ID	Title	Hours	Grade
CIS100	Intro to Computers	5	A
Eng100	English Composition	3	B
Phil105	Philosophy	5	C
CIS203	Visual Basic .NET	5	A

Two-table CD relational database

the two tables are related by the CD number

Number	Name	Artist
01	Western Way	Dolly Draton
02	Midnight Blue	Paul Elliot

Number	Song title	Track
01	Country	1
01	Night on the Road	2
01	Old Times	3
02	Lovely Nights	1
02	Colors	2
02	Heavens	3

Figure B-1: Example of a one-table and a two-table relational database

Storing data in a relational database offers many advantages. The computer can retrieve data stored in that format both quickly and easily, and the data can be displayed in any order. For example, the information in the CD database shown in Figure B-1 can be arranged by artist name, song title, and so on. A relational database also allows you to control how much information you want to view at a time. You can view all of the information in the CD database, or you can view only the information pertaining to a certain artist, or only the names of the songs contained on a specific CD.

In Visual Basic .NET, you use an OleDbDataAdapter object to access the data stored in a Microsoft Access database.

Adding an OleDbDataAdapter Object to a Windows Form

▶ "Ole" stands for "Object Linking and Embedding", and "Db" stands for "Database".

Carol Jones, the Personnel Manager at ABC Corporation, has asked you to create an application that she can use to display the employee numbers, names, and employment status (either full-time or part-time) of the company's 12 employees. The employee information is stored in a Microsoft Access database named employees, which is contained in the VBNET\AppB\ABC Solution\ABC Project\employees.mdb file on your computer's hard disk. You can use an OleDbDataAdapter object to access the information stored in the employees database. First, however, you need to open the partially completed ABC Corporation application.

To open the partially completed ABC Corporation application:

1. Start Microsoft Visual Studio .NET, if necessary, and then close the Start Page window. Click **File** on the menu bar, and then click **Open Solution**. The Open Solution dialog box opens. Open the **ABC Solution** (ABC Solution.sln) file, which is contained in the VBNET\AppB\ABC Solution folder.

2. If the designer window is not open, right-click **ABC Form.vb** in the Solution Explorer window, then click **View Designer**.

3. Auto-hide the Toolbox, Solution Explorer, and Properties windows, if necessary. The user interface for the ABC Corporation application is shown in Figure B-2.

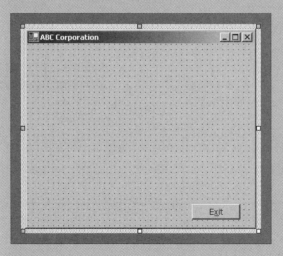

Figure B-2: User interface for the ABC Corporation application

Currently, the interface contains only an Exit button, which has already been coded for you.

You use the OleDbDataAdapter tool, which is located on the Data tab in the toolbox, to add an OleDbDataAdapter object to an application.

To add an OleDbDataAdapter object to the application, and then configure the object:

1 Temporarily display the toolbox, then click the **Data** tab. Click the **OleDbDataAdapter** tool, then drag an OleDbDataAdapter object to the form. The Welcome screen for the Data Adapter Configuration Wizard appears, as shown in Figure B-3.

OleDbDataAdapter tool

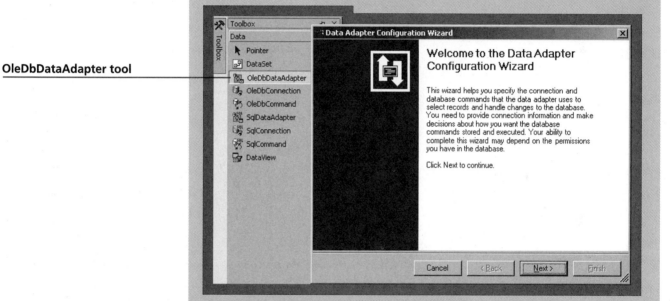

Figure B-3: Data Adapter Configuration Wizard welcome screen

As the welcome screen indicates, the wizard helps you specify the connection and database commands that the OleDbDataAdapter object uses to access the data in the database.

2 Click the **Next >** button. The Choose Your Data Connection screen appears, as shown in Figure B-4. You use this screen to specify the database that contains the data you want to access.

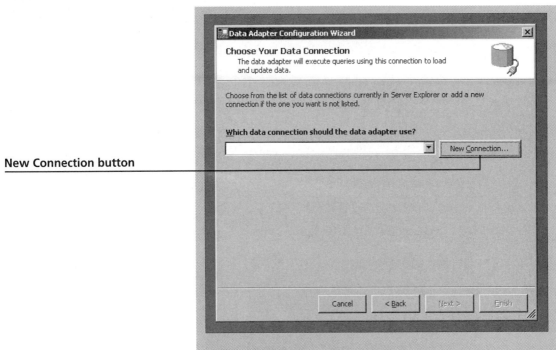

Figure B-4: Choose Your Data Connection screen

> **HELP?** Do not be concerned if the "Which data connection should the data adapter use?" list box contains text.

3   Click the **New Connection** button. The Data Link Properties dialog box opens.

4   Click the **Provider** tab on the Data Link Properties dialog box. You use the Provider tab to select the type of provider associated with the database you want to access. In this case, the database is a Microsoft Access database, so the correct provider to select is Microsoft Jet 4.0 OLE DB Provider.

5   Click **Microsoft Jet 4.0 OLE DB Provider**, as shown in Figure B-5.

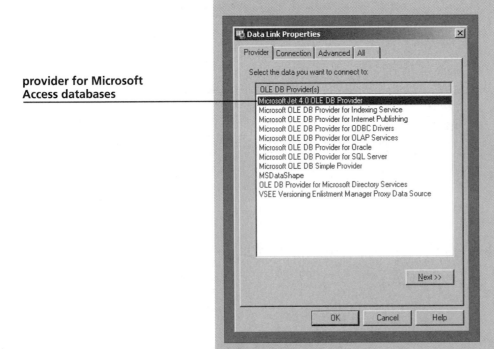

Figure B-5: Provider tab in the Data Link Properties dialog box

6   Click the **Next >>** button to display the Connection tab in the Data Link Properties dialog box, then click the **...** button next to the Select or enter a database name text box. The Select Access Database dialog box opens.

7   Click **employees.mdb**, which is located in the VBNET\AppB\ABC Solution\ABC Project folder on your computer's hard disk, and then click the **Open** button.

The Test Connection button on the Connection tab allows you to test the connection between the OleDbDataAdapter object and the employees.mdb database.

8   Click the **Test Connection** button. The Microsoft Data Link message box appears and displays the message "Test connection succeeded", as shown in Figure B-6.

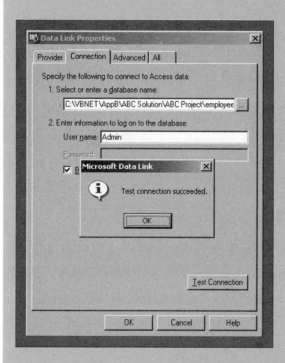

Figure B-6: Connection tab and Microsoft Data Link message box

> **HELP?** If the Microsoft Data Link Error message box appears with a message telling you that the test connection failed, click the OK button to close the message box. Verify that you entered the provider and the database name correctly, and then repeat Step 8.

9   Click the **OK** button to close the Microsoft Data Link message box, then click the **OK** button to close the Data Link Properties dialog box. You now have finished specifying the data connection. See Figure B-7.

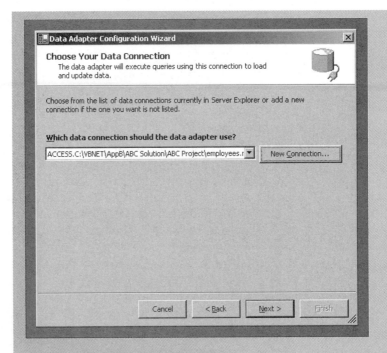

Figure B-7: Data connection shown in the Choose Your Data Connection dialog box

10 Click the **Next >** button. The Choose a Query Type screen appears, as shown in Figure B-8.

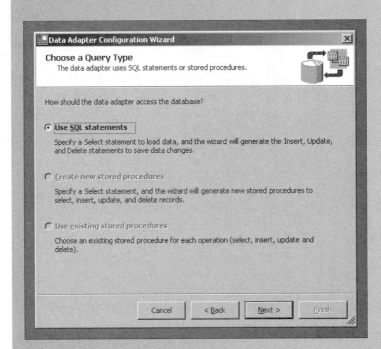

Figure B-8: Choose a Query Type screen

You use the Choose a Query Type screen to specify how the OleDbDataAdapter object should access the database. Notice that the Use SQL statements radio button is selected. You learn about SQL in the next section.

SQL

SQL, pronounced like the word *sequel*, stands for **Structured Query Language**. **SQL** is a set of commands that allows you to access and manipulate the data stored in many database management systems on computers of all sizes, from large mainframes to small microcomputers. You can use SQL commands to perform database tasks such as storing, retrieving, updating, deleting, and sorting data.

The most commonly used SQL command is the **Select statement**, which allows you to select the fields and records you want to view, as well as control the order in which the fields and records appear when displayed. The basic syntax of the Select statement is **select** *fields* **from** *table* [**where** *condition*] [**order by** *field*]. In the syntax, *fields* is one or more field names (separated by commas), and *table* is the name of the table containing the fields. For example, assume that each record in a table named tblPatron contains three fields: a numeric field named Seat and two String fields named Name and Phone. To view all of the fields and records stored in the table, you use the statement `select Seat, Name, Phone from tblPatron`. However, to view only the Name field for each record, you use the statement `select Name from tblPatron`.

The **where** *condition* portion of the Select statement's syntax is referred to as the **where clause** and allows you to limit the records that appear when displayed. For example, to display the name of the person associated with seat number three in the tblPatron table, you use the statement `select Name from tblPatron where Seat = 3`. Similarly, you use the statement `select Seat from tblPatron where Name = "Smith, Karen"` to display the seat number associated with the name "Smith, Karen". Notice that the where clause is optional in the Select statement.

The **order by** *field* portion of the Select statement's syntax is referred to as the **order by clause** and allows you to control the order in which the records appear when displayed. For example, the statement `select Name, Phone from tblPatron order by Name` displays the names and phone numbers in ascending alphabetical order by name. To display the names and phone numbers in descending alphabetical order by name, you use the statement `select Name, Phone from tblPatron order by Name desc`. ("Desc" stands for "descending".) Like the where clause, the order by clause is optional in the Select statement.

You can use the where and order by clauses in the same Select statement. For example, the statement `select Seat, Name, Phone from tblPatron where Seat > 20 order by Seat` displays, in seat number order, all records whose seat numbers are greater than 20.

In the ABC Corporation application, you will use the Select statement to display the employee numbers, names, and employment status (full-time or part-time) of each of the company's 12 employees.

tip

The SQL syntax, which refers to the rules you must follow to use the language, was accepted by the American National Standards Institute (ANSI) in 1986. You can use SQL in many database management systems and programming languages.

tip

The full syntax of the Select statement contains other clauses and options that are beyond the scope of this book.

To continue configuring the OleDbDataAdapter object:

1 Click the **Next >** button on the Choose a Query Type screen. The Generate the SQL statements screen appears, as shown in Figure B-9. You enter the appropriate Select statement in the "What data should the data adapter load into the dataset?" list box.

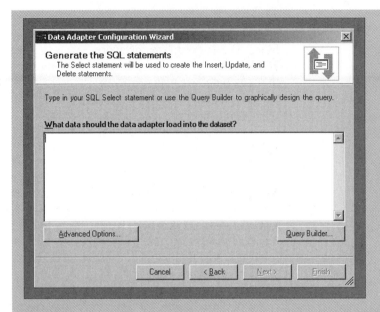

Figure B-9: Generate the SQL statements screen

You can enter the Select statement yourself, or you can have the Query Builder enter it for you. You will use the Query Builder.

2   Click the **Query Builder** button. The Query Builder and Add Table dialog boxes open. See Figure B-10.

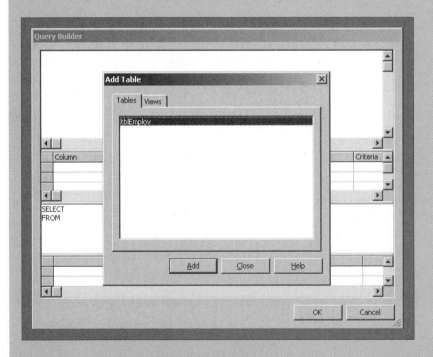

Figure B-10: Tables tab in the Add Table dialog box

The Tables tab in the Add Table dialog box contains the name of one table: tblEmploy. The tblEmploy table contains the employee information that you want to access.

3 Click the **Add** button to add the tblEmploy table to the Query Builder dialog box, then click the **Close** button to close the Add Table dialog box. The seven fields contained in the tblEmploy table appear in a list box in the Query Builder dialog box, as shown in Figure B-11. (The fields are listed in ascending alphabetical order and do not necessarily indicate their location within the employees.mdb file.)

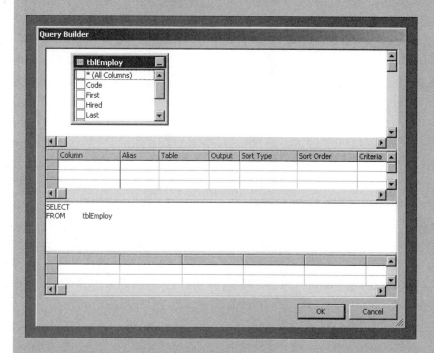

Figure B-11: Query Builder dialog box showing the fields contained in the tblEmploy table

Recall that Ms. Jones wants to display only the employee numbers, names, and employment status (full-time or part-time) of the 12 employees.

4 Click the **Number** check box, then click the **First** check box. Click the **Last** check box, then click the **Status** check box. Figure B-12 shows the completed Select statement in the Query Builder dialog box. The Select statement tells the OleDbDataAdapter object to select only four of the seven fields from the database.

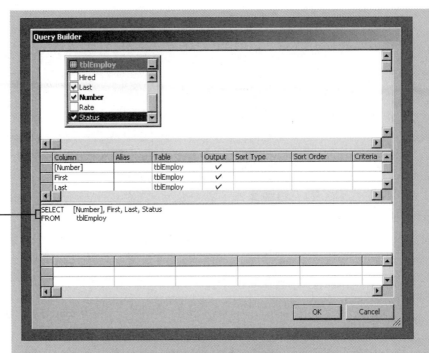

completed Select statement

Figure B-12: Completed Select statement in the Query Builder dialog box

5   Click the **OK** button to close the Query Builder dialog box. The Generate the SQL statements screen appears and displays the Select statement created by the Query Builder. See Figure B-13.

Figure B-13: Select statement entered in the Generate the SQL statements screen

6 Click the **Next >** button. The View Wizard Results screen appears and indicates that the "OleDbDataAdapter1" object was configured successfully. See Figure B-14.

Figure B-14: View Wizard Results screen

7 Click the **Finish** button. The Data Adapter Configuration Wizard adds an OleDbDataAdapter1 object and an OleDbConnection1 object to the component tray, as shown in Figure B-15.

objects added by the wizard

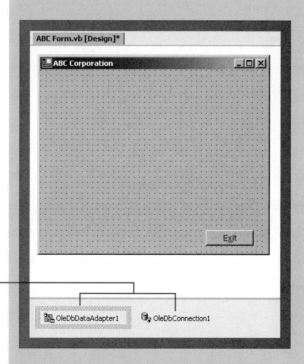

Figure B-15: Objects added to the component tray

8 Click **File** on the menu bar, and then click **Save All** to save the solution.

The next step in accessing the data stored in a Microsoft Access database is to create a data set.

Creating a Data Set

A **data set** is simply an object that represents the data you want to access. In this case, it represents the data contained in four of the fields in the tblEmploy table.

To create a data set:

1 Verify that the OleDbDataAdapter1 object is selected in the component tray, then temporarily display the Properties window. Three links appear below the Properties list in the Properties window: Configure Data Adapter..., Generate Dataset..., and Preview Data.... See Figure B-16.

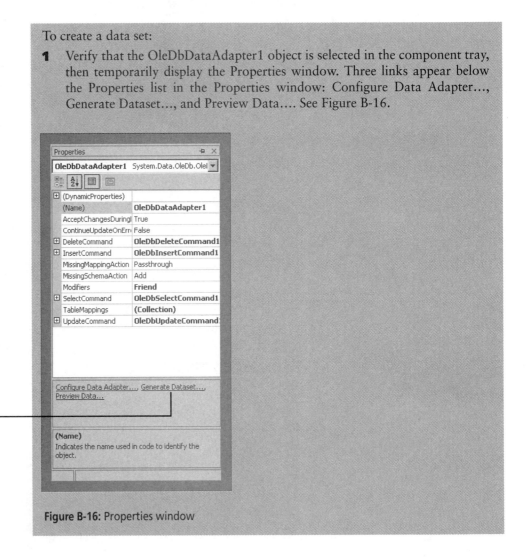

link

Figure B-16: Properties window

2 Click **Generate Dataset….** The Generate Dataset dialog box opens. Verify that the New radio button, the tblEmploy (OleDbDataAdapter1) check box, and the Add this dataset to the designer check box are selected, as shown in Figure B-17.

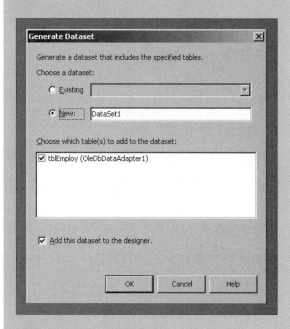

Figure B-17: Generate Dataset dialog box

3 Click the **OK** button to close the Generate Dataset dialog box. In a few moments, a DataSet object appears in the component tray. Change the DataSet object's Name property to **EmployDataSet**. See Figure B-18.

EmployDataSet object ————

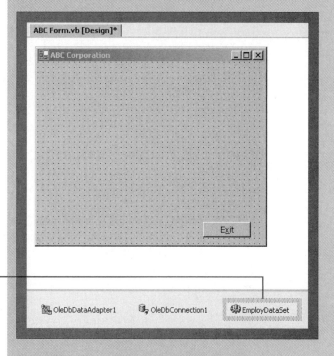

Figure B-18: EmployDataSet object added to the component tray

Next, you use the OleDbDataAdapter object's Fill method to fill the DataSet object with the appropriate data, which is determined by the Select statement you entered when configuring the OleDbDataAdapter object. The Fill method's syntax is *dataAdapter*.**Fill**(*dataSet*), where *dataAdapter* is the name of an OleDbDataAdapter object and *dataSet* is the name of a DataSet object. In most cases, you enter the Fill method in the form's Load event procedure.

4   Right-click the **form**, and then click **View Code**. Click the **Class Name** list arrow, and then click **(Base Class Events)**. Click the **Method Name** list arrow, and then click **Load**.

5   Type the line of code indicated in Figure B-19, which shows the completed Load event procedure.

enter this line of code

```
Private Sub AbcForm_Load(ByVal sender As Object, ByVal e As System.EventArgs) Handle
        Me.OleDbDataAdapter1.Fill(Me.EmployDataSet)
    End Sub
End Class
```

Figure B-19: Completed Load event procedure

6   Close the Code editor window, then save the solution.

Notice that the method for accessing the data stored in a Microsoft Access database is quite simple. You first drag an OleDbDataAdapter object to the form, and then use the Data Adapter Configuration Wizard to configure the object. Recall that the wizard adds the OleDbDataAdapter object and an OleDbConnection object to the component tray. You then use the Generate Dataset link, which appears in the OleDbDataAdapter object's Properties window, to generate the data set. Recall that the link adds a DataSet object to the component tray. Finally, you use the OleDbDataAdapter object's Fill method to fill the DataSet object with data.

You view the data contained in the DataSet object by connecting the object to one or more controls in the interface. Connecting a DataSet object to a control is called **binding**, and the connected controls are referred to as **bound controls**. In the ABC Corporation application, you will bind the EmployDataSet object to a DataGrid control.

Adding a DataGrid Control to the Form

When bound to a DataSet object, the **DataGrid control** displays the data from the DataSet object in a row and column format, similar to a spreadsheet. Each field in the DataSet object appears in a column in the DataGrid control, and each record appears in a row. The intersection of a row and a column in the DataGrid control is called a **cell**.

To add a DataGrid control to the form, and then bind the EmployDataSet object to the control:

1   Temporarily display the toolbox, then click the **Windows Forms** tab. Click the **DataGrid** tool 🔲, then drag a DataGrid control to the form.

2   Set the DataGrid control's Name property to **EmployDataGrid**. Set its Location property to **16, 16** and set its Size property to **320, 208**.

Now use the DataSource and DataMember properties to bind the EmployDataGrid control to the EmployDataSet object.

3 Set the EmployDataGrid control's DataSource property to **EmployDataSet**, and set its DataMember property to **tblEmploy**. The names of the four fields contained in the EmployDataSet appear as column headings in the EmployDataGrid control. See Figure B-20.

field names appear as column headings

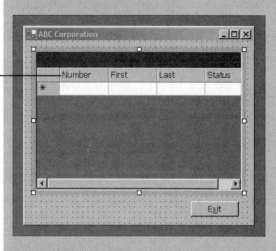

Figure B-20: EmployDataGrid control shown in the form

tip

You also could have set the DataGrid control's DataSource property to EmployDataSet.tblEmploy, and then left the Data-Member property empty.

Ms. Jones will not need to make any changes to the records displayed in the EmployDataGrid control, so you will set the control's ReadOnly property to True.

4 Set the EmployDataGrid control's ReadOnly property to **True**.

5 Right-click the **EmployDataGrid** control, and then click **Lock Controls**.

6 Set the EmployDataGrid control's TabIndex property to **0** (zero), and set the Exit button's TabIndex property to **1** (one).

7 Save the solution, then start the application. After several seconds, the employee numbers, names, and employment status for the 12 employees appear in the EmployDataGrid control, as shown in Figure B-21.

Figure B-21: Records displayed in the EmployDataGrid control

8 Try to enter a value in the current cell. You will not be able to enter a value, because the EmployDataGrid control's ReadOnly property is set to True.

9 Practice using the right, left, up, and down arrow keys on your keyboard to access a different cell in the EmployDataGrid control.

10 Click the **Exit** button to end the application. When you return to the designer window, close the Output window.

Next, you learn how to customize the appearance of the data displayed in the DataGrid control.

Customizing the Appearance of the DataGrid Control's Data

The DataGrid control provides many properties that you can use to control the appearance of its output. For example, the CaptionText property allows you to add a caption at the top of the control, immediately above the column headings. The ColumnHeadersVisible and RowHeadersVisible properties allow you to specify whether the column and row headings, respectively, should be shown or hidden. The GridLineColor property allows you to select the color of the gridlines displayed in the control. The DataGrid control also provides an AutoFormat link that allows you to select from a list of predefined formats for displaying data. In the next set of steps, you add a caption to the EmployDataGrid control, and also hide the row headings. Additionally, you select one of the control's predefined formats.

To customize the appearance of the EmployDataGrid control:

1 If necessary, click the **EmployDataGrid** control to select it.

First, display the text "ABC Corporation" at the top of the control.

2 Set the EmployDataGrid control's CaptionText property to **ABC Corporation**.

Next, remove the row headings, which appear in the first column of the control.

3 Set the EmployDataGrid control's RowHeadersVisible property to **False**.

Now use the AutoFormat link to select a predefined format.

4 Click the **AutoFormat** link, which appears below the Properties list in the Properties window for the EmployDataGrid control. The Auto Format dialog box opens, as shown in Figure B-22. The dialog box lists the names of the predefined formats and includes a preview of the selected format.

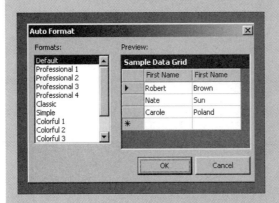

Figure B-22: Auto Format dialog box

Change the format from Default to Professional 4.

5 Click **Professional 4** in the Formats list box, and then click the **OK** button.

6 Save the solution, then start the application. The changes you made to the EmployDataGrid control are shown in Figure B-23.

Figure B-23: Changes shown in the EmployDataGrid control

7 Click the **Exit** button to end the application. When you return to the designer window, close the Output window.

8 Click **File** on the menu bar, and then click **Close Solution**.

You now have completed Appendix B.

Database Access Using a Web Form

Creating a Web-Based Application

As you learned in Tutorial 1, you can use Visual Basic .NET to create both Windows-based and Web-based applications. Recall that a Windows-based application has a Windows user interface and runs on a desktop computer. All of the applications you created in the tutorials in this book were Windows-based applications. A Web-based application, on the other hand, has a Web user interface and runs on a server. You access a Web-based application using your computer's browser. Examples of Web-based applications include e-commerce applications available on the Internet and employee handbook applications accessible on a company's intranet. You learn how to create a Web-based application in this appendix.

Jack Benton, the Personnel Manager at XYZ Corporation, has asked you to create a Web-based application that he can use to display the names of the company's 12 employees, as well as their employee numbers and hourly pay rates.

To create a Web-based application in Visual Basic .NET:

1 Start Microsoft Visual Studio .NET, if necessary, and then close the Start Page window. Click **File** on the menu bar, point to **New**, and then click **Blank Solution**. The New Project dialog box opens.

2 Change the name entered in the Name text box to **XYZ Solution**. If necessary, use the Browse button, which appears to the right of the Location text box, to open the **VBNET\AppC** folder on your computer's hard disk. See Figure C-1.

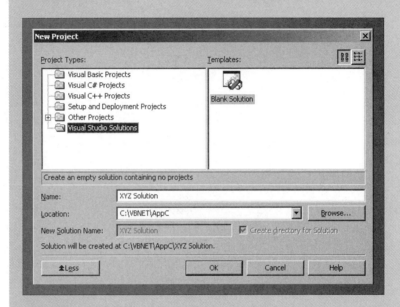

Figure C-1: New Project dialog box used to create a blank solution

3 Click the **OK** button to close the New Project dialog box. Visual Studio .NET creates a blank solution on your computer's hard disk.

4 Click **File** on the menu bar. Point to **Add Project**, and then click **New Project**. The Add New Project dialog box opens.

5 Verify that Visual Basic Projects is selected in the Project Types list box, then click **ASP .NET Web Application** in the Templates list box.

6 If necessary, change the entry in the Location text box to the URL of the Web server where you want to create your project. See Figure C-2.

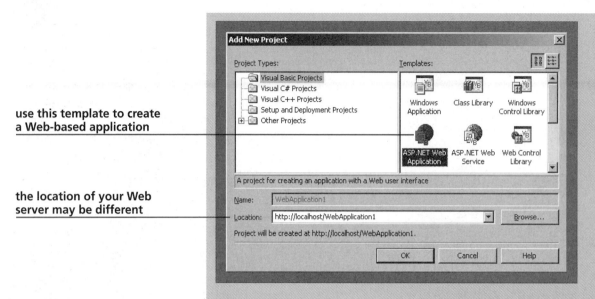

use this template to create
a Web-based application

the location of your Web
server may be different

Figure C-2: Completed Add New Project dialog box

7 Click the **OK** button to close the Add New Project dialog box. The Create New Web message box appears momentarily, and then a new Web form, also called a **Web page**, appears on the screen, as shown in Figure C-3. Notice that the default name for the Web form is WebForm1.aspx.

default name

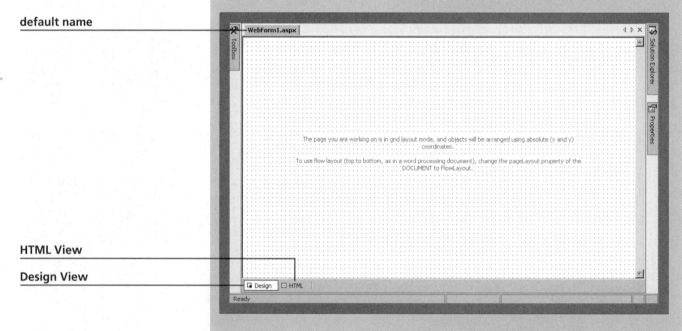

HTML View

Design View

Figure C-3: New Web form in Design View

> **HELP?** If the Web Access Failed dialog box appears on the screen, click the Try to open the project with FrontPage Server Extensions radio button, then click the OK button.

You use the Design and HTML buttons to view the Web page in either Design View or HTML View, respectively. Currently, you are viewing the Web page in Design View. Switching to HTML View allows you to view the HTML code that

Visual Basic .NET generates as you are creating the Web page. (HTML stands for Hypertext Markup Language, which is the language used to create Web pages.)

8 Click **File** on the menu bar, and then click **Save All** to save the solution.

The employee information you need to display in the Web-based application is stored in a database. You learn about databases in the next section.

Accessing Data Stored in a Database

To maintain accurate records, most businesses store information about their employees, customers, and inventory in files called databases. In general, a **database** is simply an organized collection of related information stored in a file on a disk.

Many software packages exist for creating databases; some of the most popular are Microsoft Access, Oracle, and SQL Server. You can use Visual Basic .NET to access the data stored in these databases; this allows a company to create a standard interface in Visual Basic .NET that employees can use to access database information stored in a variety of formats. Instead of learning each database package's user interface, the employee needs to know only one interface. The actual format the database is in is unimportant and will be transparent to the user.

In this appendix, you learn how to access the data stored in a Microsoft Access database. Databases created by Microsoft Access are relational databases. A **relational database** is one that stores information in tables, which are composed of columns and rows. Each column in a table represents a field, and each row represents a record. As you learned in Tutorial 10, a **field** is a single item of information about a person, place, or thing—such as a name, address, or phone number—and a **record** is a group of related fields that contain all of the necessary data about a specific person, place, or thing. A **table** is a group of related records. Each record in the group pertains to the same topic, and each contains the same type of information—in other words, the same fields.

A relational database can contain one or more tables. You could use a one-table database, for example, to store the information regarding the college courses you have taken. Each record in the table would contain a course ID (department and number), course title, number of credit hours, and grade. You would use a two-table database, on the other hand, to store information about your CD (compact disc) collection: one table to store the general information about each CD (the CD's name and the artist's name) and the other table to store the information about the songs on each CD (their title and track number). You would use a common field—for example, a CD number—to relate the records contained in both tables. Figure C-4 shows an example of both a one-table and a two-table relational database.

tip

You do not have to be a business to make use of a database. Many people use databases to keep track of their medical records, their compact disc collections, and even their golf scores.

tip

The databases are called relational because the information in the tables can be related in different ways.

tip

The column and row format used in a relational database is similar to the column and row format used in a spreadsheet.

One-table college course relational database

ID	Title	Hours	Grade
CIS100	Intro to Computers	5	A
Eng100	English Composition	3	B
Phil105	Philosophy	5	C
CIS203	Visual Basic .NET	5	A

Figure C-4: Example of a one-table and a two-table relational database

the two tables are related by the CD number

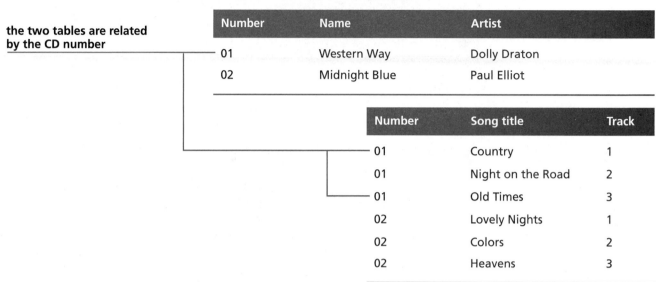

Two-table CD relational database

Number	Name	Artist
01	Western Way	Dolly Draton
02	Midnight Blue	Paul Elliot

Number	Song title	Track
01	Country	1
01	Night on the Road	2
01	Old Times	3
02	Lovely Nights	1
02	Colors	2
02	Heavens	3

Figure C-4: Example of a one-table and a two-table relational database (continued)

Storing data in a relational database offers many advantages. The computer can retrieve data stored in that format both quickly and easily, and the data can be displayed in any order. For example, the information in the CD database shown in Figure C-4 can be arranged by artist name, song title, and so on. A relational database also allows you to control how much information you want to view at a time. You can view all of the information in the CD database, or you can view only the information pertaining to a certain artist, or only the names of the songs contained on a specific CD.

The information pertaining to the 12 XYZ Corporation employees is stored in a Microsoft Access database named employees, which is contained in the VBNET\AppC\employees.mdb file on your computer's hard disk. In Visual Basic .NET, you use an OleDbDataAdapter object to access the data stored in a Microsoft Access database.

Adding an OleDbDataAdapter Object to a Web Form

You use the OleDbDataAdapter tool, which is located on the Data tab in the toolbox, to add an OleDbDataAdapter object to an application.

> **tip**
> ⚬⚬⚬⚬⚬⚬⚬⚬⚬⚬⚬⚬⚬
> "Ole" stands for "Object Linking and Embedding", and "Db" stands for "Database".

To add an OleDbDataAdapter object to the application, and then configure the object:

1 Temporarily display the toolbox, then click the **Data** tab. Click the **OleDbDataAdapter** tool [icon], then drag an OleDbDataAdapter object to the form. The Welcome screen for the Data Adapter Configuration Wizard appears, as shown in Figure C-5.

Figure C-5: Data Adapter Configuration Wizard welcome screen

As the welcome screen indicates, the wizard helps you specify the connection and database commands that the OleDbDataAdapter object uses to access the data in the database.

2 Click the Next > button. The Choose Your Data Connection screen appears, as shown in Figure C-6. You use this screen to specify the database that contains the data you want to access.

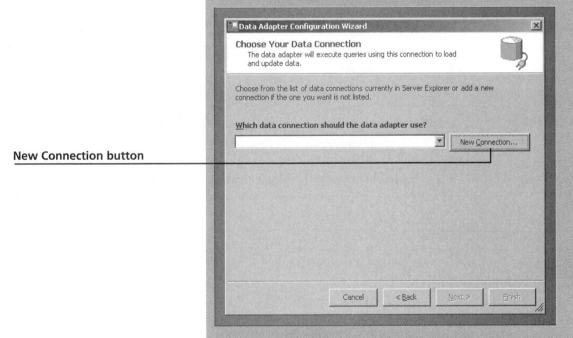

Figure C-6: Choose Your Data Connection screen

> **HELP?** Do not be concerned if the "Which data connection should the data adapter use?" list box contains text.

3   Click the **New Connection** button. The Data Link Properties dialog box opens.

4   Click the **Provider** tab on the Data Link Properties dialog box. You use the Provider tab to select the type of provider associated with the database you want to access. In this case, the database is a Microsoft Access database, so the correct provider to select is Microsoft Jet 4.0 OLE DB Provider.

5   Click **Microsoft Jet 4.0 OLE DB Provider**, as shown in Figure C-7.

Provider for Microsoft Access databases

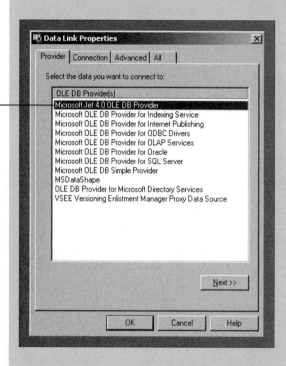

Figure C-7: Provider tab in the Data Link Properties dialog box

6   Click the **Next >>** button to display the Connection tab in the Data Link Properties dialog box, then click the **...** button next to the Select or enter a database name text box. The Select Access Database dialog box opens.

7   Click **employees.mdb**, which is located in the VBNET\AppC folder on your computer's hard disk, and then click the **Open** button.

The Test Connection button on the Connection tab allows you to test the connection between the OleDbDataAdapter object and the employees.mdb database.

8   Click the **Test Connection** button. The Microsoft Data Link message box appears and displays the message "Test connection succeeded.", as shown in Figure C-8.

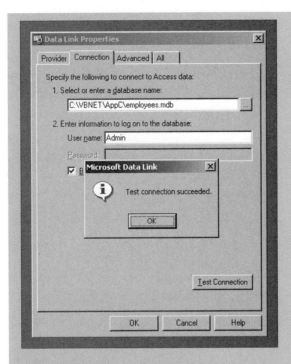

Figure C-8: Connection tab and Microsoft Data Link message box

HELP? If the Microsoft Data Link Error message box appears with a message telling you that the test connection failed, click the OK button to close the message box. Verify that you entered the provider and the database name correctly, and then repeat Step 8.

9 Click the **OK** button to close the Microsoft Data Link message box, then click the **OK** button to close the Data Link Properties dialog box. You now have finished specifying the data connection. See Figure C-9.

data connection

Figure C-9: Data connection shown in the Choose Your Data Connection dialog box

10 Click the **Next >** button. The Choose a Query Type screen appears, as shown in Figure C-10.

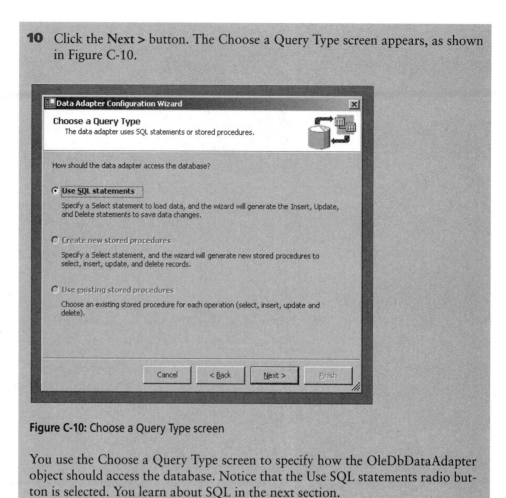

Figure C-10: Choose a Query Type screen

You use the Choose a Query Type screen to specify how the OleDbDataAdapter object should access the database. Notice that the Use SQL statements radio button is selected. You learn about SQL in the next section.

SQL

SQL, pronounced like the word *sequel*, stands for **Structured Query Language**. SQL is a set of commands that allows you to access and manipulate the data stored in many database management systems on computers of all sizes, from large mainframes to small microcomputers. You can use SQL commands to perform database tasks such as storing, retrieving, updating, deleting, and sorting data.

The most commonly used SQL command is the **Select statement**, which allows you to select which fields and records you want to view, as well as control the order in which the fields and records appear when displayed. The basic syntax of the Select statement is **select** *fields* **from** *table* [**where** *condition*] [**order by** *field*]. In the syntax, *fields* is one or more field names (separated by commas), and *table* is the name of the table containing the fields. For example, assume that each record in a table named tblPatron contains three fields: a numeric field named Seat and two String fields named Name and Phone. To view all of the fields and records stored in the table, you use the statement `select Seat, Name, Phone from tblPatron`. However, to view only the Name field for each record, you use the statement `select Name from tblPatron`.

The **where** *condition* portion of the Select statement's syntax is referred to as the **where clause** and allows you to limit the records that appear when displayed. For example, to display the name of the person associated with seat number three in the tblPatron table, you use the statement `select Name from tblPatron where Seat = 3`. Similarly, you use the statement `select Seat from tblPatron where Name = "Smith, Karen"` to display the seat number associated with the name "Smith, Karen". Notice that the where clause is optional in the Select statement.

The **order by** *field* portion of the Select statement's syntax is referred to as the **order by clause** and allows you to control the order in which the records appear when displayed. For example, the statement `select Name, Phone from tblPatron order by Name` displays the names and phone numbers in ascending alphabetical order by name. To display the names and phone numbers in descending alphabetical order by name, you use the statement `select Name, Phone from tblPatron order by Name desc`. ("Desc" stands for "descending".) Like the where clause, the order by clause is optional in the Select statement.

You can use the where and order by clauses in the same Select statement. For example, the statement `select Seat, Name, Phone from tblPatron where Seat > 20 order by Seat` displays, in seat number order, all records whose seat numbers are greater than 20.

In the XYZ Corporation application, you will use the Select statement to display the numbers, names, and hourly pay rates of each of the company's 12 employees.

To continue configuring the OleDbDataAdapter object:

1 Click the **Next >** button on the Choose a Query Type screen. The Generate the SQL statements screen appears, as shown in Figure C-11. You enter the appropriate Select statement in the "What data should the data adapter load into the dataset?" list box.

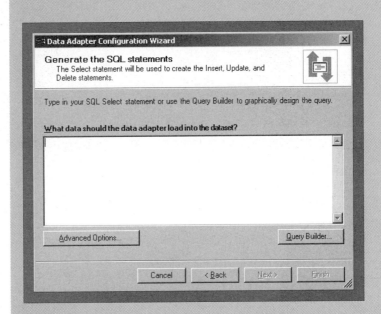

Figure C-11: Generate the SQL statements screen

You can enter the Select statement yourself, or you can have the Query Builder enter it for you. You will use the Query Builder.

2 Click the **Query Builder** button. The Query Builder and Add Table dialog boxes open. See Figure C-12.

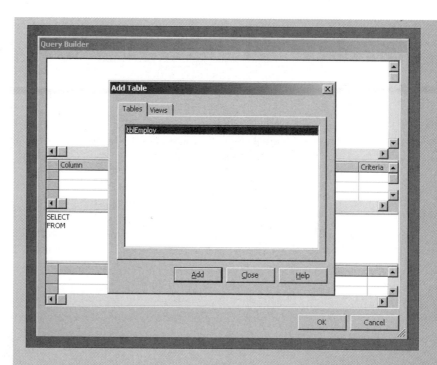

Figure C-12: Tables tab in the Add Table dialog box

The Tables tab in the Add Table dialog box contains the name of one table: tblEmploy. The tblEmploy table contains the employee information that you want to access.

3   Click the **Add** button to add the tblEmploy table to the Query Builder dialog box, then click the **Close** button to close the Add Table dialog box. The seven fields contained in the tblEmploy table appear in a list box in the Query Builder dialog box, as shown in Figure C-13. Not all of the field names are visible in the list box. You can scroll the list box to view the remaining field names. (The fields are listed in ascending alphabetical order and do not necessarily indicate their location within the employees.mdb file.)

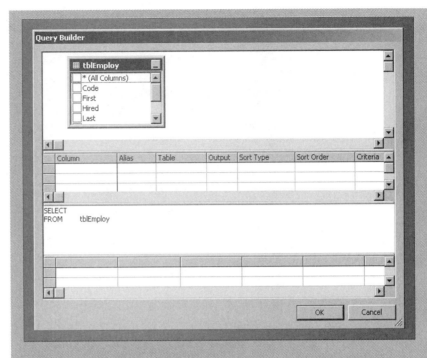

Figure C-13: Query Builder dialog box showing the fields contained in the tblEmploy table

Recall that Mr. Benton wants to display only the 12 employee numbers, names, and hourly pay rates.

4 Click the **Number** check box, then click the **Last** check box. Click the **First** check box, and then click the **Rate** check box. Figure C-14 shows the completed Select statement in the Query Builder dialog box. The Select statement tells the OleDbDataAdapter object to select only four of the seven fields from the database.

completed Select statement

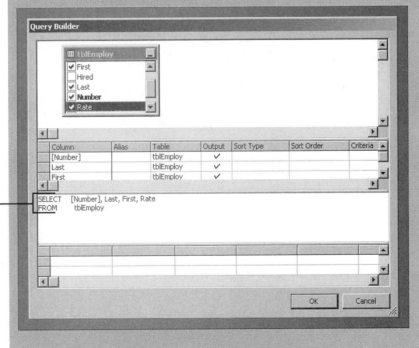

Figure C-14: Completed Select statement in the Query Builder dialog box

5   Click the **OK** button to close the Query Builder dialog box. The Generate the SQL statements screen appears and displays the Select statement created by the Query Builder. See Figure C-15.

Figure C-15: Select statement entered in the Generate the SQL statements screen

6   Click the **Next >** button. The View Wizard Results screen appears and indicates that the "OleDbDataAdapter1" object was configured successfully. See Figure C-16.

Figure C-16: View Wizard Results screen

7   Click the **Finish** button. The Data Adapter Configuration Wizard adds an OleDbDataAdapter1 object and an OleDbConnection1 object to the component tray, as shown in Figure C-17.

objects added by the wizard

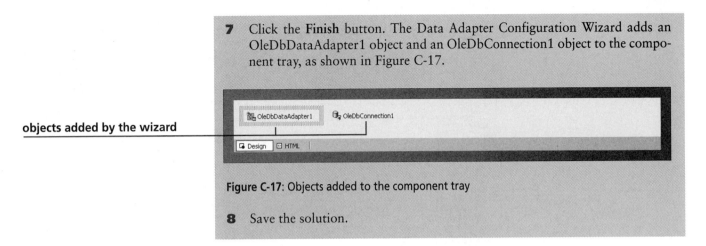

Figure C-17: Objects added to the component tray

8   Save the solution.

The next step in accessing the data stored in a Microsoft Access database is to create a data set.

Creating a Data Set

A **data set** is simply an object that represents the data you want to access. In this case, it represents the data contained in four of the fields in the tblEmploy table.

To create a data set:

1   If necessary, click the **OleDbDataAdapter1** object in the component tray, then temporarily display the Properties window. Three links appear below the Properties list in the Properties window: Configure Data Adapter..., Generate Dataset..., and Preview Data.... See Figure C-18.

link

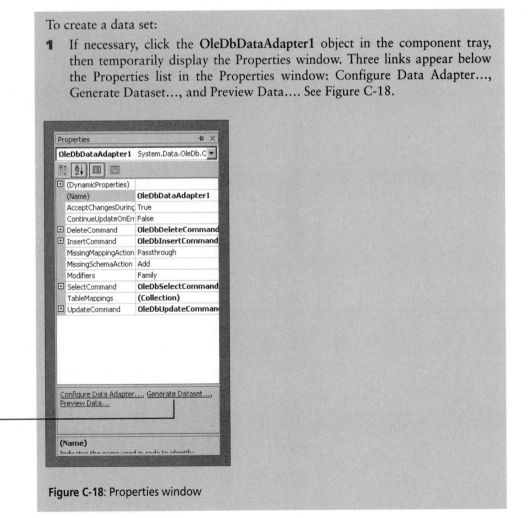

Figure C-18: Properties window

2 Click **Generate Dataset....** The Generate Dataset dialog box opens. Verify that the New radio button, the tblEmploy (OleDbDataAdapter1) check box, and the Add this dataset to the designer check box are selected, as shown in Figure C-19.

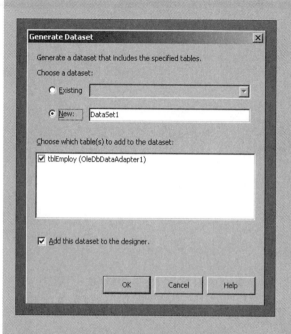

Figure C-19: Generate Dataset dialog box

3 Click the **OK** button to close the Generate Dataset dialog box. In a few moments, a DataSet object appears in the component tray. Change the DataSet object's Name property to **EmployDataSet**. See Figure C-20.

Figure C-20: EmployDataSet object added to the component tray

Next, you use the OleDbDataAdapter object's Fill method to fill the DataSet object with the appropriate data, which is determined by the Select statement you entered when configuring the OleDbDataAdapter object. The Fill method's syntax is *dataAdapter*.**Fill**(*dataSet*), where *dataAdapter* is the name of an OleDbDataAdapter object and *dataSet* is the name of a DataSet object. In most cases, you enter the Fill method in the Web page's Load event procedure.

4 Right-click the **form**, and then click **View Code**.

You want to fill the DataSet object with the appropriate data only when the Web page is loaded and accessed for the first time. When a Web page is loaded and accessed for the first time, its IsPostBack property contains the Boolean value False; otherwise, it contains the Boolean value True.

5 Type the selection structure indicated in Figure C-21.

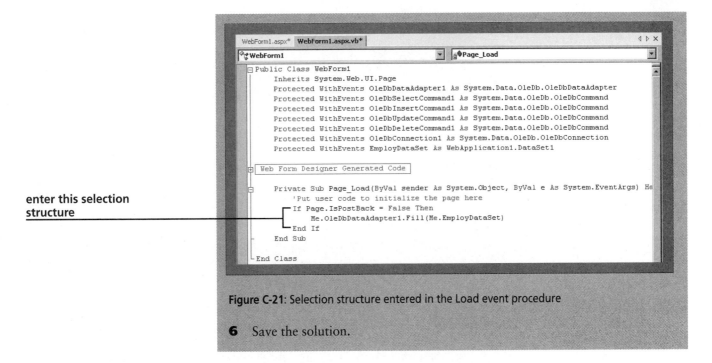

enter this selection structure

Figure C-21: Selection structure entered in the Load event procedure

6 Save the solution.

Notice that the method for accessing the data stored in a Microsoft Access database is quite simple. You first drag an OleDbDataAdapter object to the form, and then use the Data Adapter Configuration Wizard to configure the object. Recall that the wizard adds the OleDbDataAdapter object and an OleDbConnection object to the component tray. You then use the Generate Dataset link, which appears in the OleDbDataAdapter object's Properties window, to generate the data set. Recall that the link adds a DataSet object to the component tray. Finally, you use the OleDbDataAdapter object's Fill method to fill the DataSet object with data.

You view the data contained in the DataSet object by connecting the object to one or more controls in the interface. Connecting a DataSet object to a control is called **binding**, and the connected controls are referred to as **bound controls**. In the XYZ Corporation application, you will bind the EmployDataSet object to a DataGrid control.

Adding a DataGrid Control to the Form

When bound to a DataSet object, the **DataGrid control** displays the data from the DataSet object in a row and column format, similar to a spreadsheet. Each field in the DataSet object appears in a column in the DataGrid control, and each record appears in a row. The intersection of a row and a column in the DataGrid control is called a **cell**.

To add a DataGrid control to the form, and then bind the EmployDataSet object to the control:

1 Click the WebForm1.aspx tab. Temporarily display the Toolbox window, then click the **Web Forms** tab. Click the **DataGrid** tool ⊞, then drag a DataGrid control to the form.

2 Set the DataGrid control's ID property to **EmployDataGrid**.

3   Drag the EmployDataGrid control to the location indicated in Figure C-22. Set the control's Height property to **185px** and its Width property to **475px**, then click the EmployDataGrid control. (The "px" stands for "pixels".)

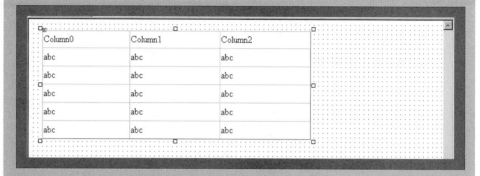

Figure C-22: Location and size of EmployDataGrid control

Now use the DataSource and DataMember properties to bind the EmployDataGrid control to the EmployDataSet object.

4   Set the EmployDataGrid control's DataSource property to **EmployDataSet**, and set its DataMember property to **tblEmploy**. Click the **EmployDataGrid** control. The names of the four fields contained in the EmployDataSet appear as column headings in the EmployDataGrid control. See Figure C-23.

field names appear
as column headings

Number	Last	First	Rate
0	abc	abc	0
1	abc	abc	0.1
2	abc	abc	0.2
3	abc	abc	0.3
4	abc	abc	0.4

Figure C-23: EmployDataGrid control shown in the form

Next, you need to use the DataGrid control's DataBind method to bind the control to the EmployDataSet object.

5   Click the **WebForm1.aspx.vb** tab. Enter the additional line of code indicated in Figure C-24, which shows the completed Load event procedure.

enter this line of code

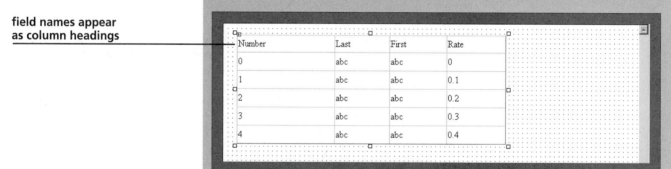

```
Private Sub Page_Load(ByVal sender As System.Object, ByVal e As System.EventArgs) H
    'Put user code to initialize the page here
    If Page.IsPostBack = False Then
        Me.OleDbDataAdapter1.Fill(Me.EmployDataSet)
        Me.EmployDataGrid.DataBind()
    End If
End Sub
```

Figure C-24: Completed Load event procedure

Next, view how the Web page (form) will appear when opened in your Web browser.

6 Save the solution. Click **Debug** on the menu bar, and then click **Start Without Debugging**. Maximize the Web page. After several seconds, the 12 employee numbers, names, and hourly pay rates appear in the EmployDataGrid control on the Web page, as shown in Figure C-25.

your Web server may be different

Number	Last	First	Rate
100	Benton	Jack	15
101	Jones	Carol	15
102	Ismal	Asaad	10
103	Rodriguez	Carl	12
104	Iovanelli	Sam	20
105	Nyugen	Thomas	8
106	Vine	Martha	9.5
107	Smith	Paul	17.5
108	Gerber	Wanda	21
109	Zonten	Mary	13.5
110	Sparrow	John	9
111	Krutchen	Jerry	9

Figure C-25: Records displayed in the EmployDataGrid control

7 Close the Web page. When you return to the Code editor window, close the Output window, then close the Code editor window.

Next, you learn how to customize the appearance of the data displayed in the DataGrid control.

Customizing the Appearance of the DataGrid Control's Data

The DataGrid control provides many properties that you can use to control the appearance of its output. For example, the ShowHeader property allows you to specify whether the column headings should be shown or hidden. The BackColor property allows you to select the background color for the control. The DataGrid control also provides an AutoFormat link that allows you to select from a list of predefined formats for displaying data. In the next set of steps, you select one of the grid control's predefined formats.

To customize the appearance of the EmployDataGrid control:

1 If necessary, click the **EmployDataGrid** control to select it. Click the **AutoFormat** link, which appears below the Properties list in the Properties window for the EmployDataGrid control. The Auto Format dialog box opens, as shown in Figure C-26. The dialog box lists the names of the predefined formats and includes a preview of the selected format.

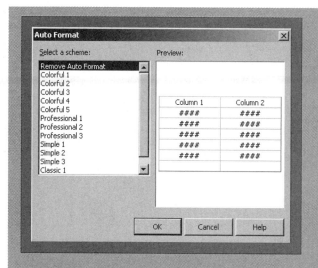

Figure C-26: Auto Format dialog box

Change the format to Colorful 4.

2   Click **Colorful 4** in the Select a scheme list box, and then click the **OK** button.

3   Save the solution. Click **Debug** on the menu bar, and then click **Start Without Debugging**. Maximize the Web page. Figure C-27 shows the EmployDataGrid control formatted to Colorful 4.

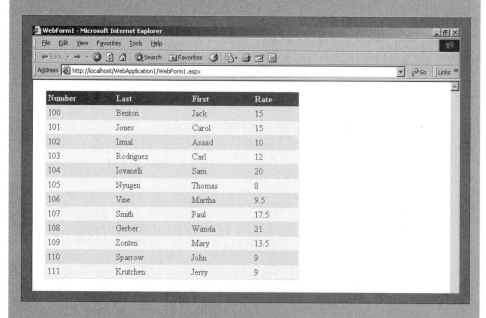

Figure C-27: EmployDataGrid control formatted to Colorful 4

4   Close the Web page. When you return to the designer window, close the Output window

5   Click **File** on the menu bar, and then click **Close Solution**.

You now have completed Appendix C.

Index

Symbols

& (ampersand), 112, 113, 183, 184
' (apostrophe), 130
* (asterisk), 34, 304
\ (backslash), 34
: (colon), 98
, (comma), 136, 138, 186
{} (curly braces), 370, 670
. (decimal point), 137
$ (dollar sign), 132, 138, 500
" (double quotes), B 126, 135, 186
... (ellipsis), 36, 517, 521
= (equal sign), 127
! (exclamation point), 305
> (greater-than sign), 363
- (hyphen), 305, 530
< (less-than sign), 363
() (parentheses), 63, 131–132, 139
| (pipe symbol), 370
+ (plus sign), 135, 184
% (percent sign), 132, 136, 137
. (period), 127, 189, 268
[] (square brackets), 127, 168,
    224, 304
_ (underscore), 134

A

ABC Form.vb, 726
ABC Solution.sln, 726
abstraction, defined, 6–7
AcceptButton property, 193
Access (Microsoft), 724–726,
    736, 745, 757. See also databases
access keys
    assigning, 112–113, 117–119
    described, 112
    Math Practice application
        and, 317, 319
    shortcut keys and, comparison
        of, 520
accessibility variablename syntax, 553
accumulators
    described, 376
    initializing, 376, 379
    updating/incrementing, 376, 380
Add Existing Item option, 479

Add method
    collections and, 403, 404, 407
    list box controls and, 454–455
ADD mnemonic, 3
Add New Project dialog box,
    24, 743–744
Add Table dialog box,
    732–733, 751–752
Add to File button, 639–640
Add to Report button, 549, 590
AddButton control, 589–591,
    634, 637–640
addition operator, 131–132, 233
AdditionRadioButton control,
    21, 318, 322–323, 330–332, 342
AddressTextBox control, 105,
    110, 114, 118
algorithms
    described, 289
    desk-checking, 289–294
    logical operators and, 289–291
    pseudo-random numbers
        and, 325
    reversing decisions and,
        292–293
Align option, 54
AllowListBox control, 453,
    456, 458–459, 465, 471
Alphabetic button, 25, 33
American National Standards
    Institute (ANSI), 731, 750
American Standard Code for
    Information Interchange
    (ASCII), 304, 455
ampersand (&), 112, 113, 183, 184
And operator, 230–236
AndAlso operator, 230–236, 291
ANSI (American National Standards
    Institute), 731, 750
AnswerPictureBox control,
    322, 343–344
AnswerTextBox control, 322
apostrophe ('), 130'
Appearance tab, 113
AppendText method, 553–554
applications. See also specific
    applications
        designing, 83–152

ending, 57–59
naming conventions for, 35
planning, 90–103
previewing, 154–155
running, 7–8
starting, 57–59, 118
tasks performed by,
    identifying, 91–98
arithmetic expressions. See also
    arithmetic operators
    basic description of, 131
    writing, 131–132
arithmetic operators, 131–132,
    233, 224, 225
arguments (listed by name)
    buttons argument, 255–256
    caption argument, 255–257
    char argument, 497
    character argument, 558
    count argument, 502, 505
    defaultButton argument,
        255–256
    defaultResponse argument, 186
    Due argument, 252–253
    filenumber argument, 621,
        623, 624
    FV argument, 252–253
    height argument, 368
    highestColumnSubscript
        argument, 701
    highestRowSubscript
        argument, 701
    horizontalPosition argument, 601
    icon argument, 255–256
    key argument, 407
    message argument, 366
    NPer argument, 252–254
    OpenAccess.ReadWrite
        argument, 620
    PV argument, 252–253
    Rate argument, 252–254
    recordLength argument, 620
    recordnumber argument,
        621, 623
    recordvariable argument,
        621, 623
    specified argument, 369

startIndex argument, 498, 502, 506, 507
text argument, 255–256
verticalPosition argument, 601
width argument, 368
x argument, 368
XPos argument, 186
y argument, 368
YPos argument, 186
Array.Reverse method, 680–681
arrays
accessing elements in, with the subscript, 674
average amount stored in, calculating, 676
calculating the sum of numbers in, 703–704
displaying the contents of, 672–673
highest value stored in, determining, 677–678
initializing elements in, 670
manipulating, 672–681
one-dimensional, 668–690
parallel, 691–693
searching, 675–676
sorting data in, 679–681
storing data in, 671–672, 693–695, 702–703
of structures, 693–695
Tax Calculator application and, 665–719
two-dimensional, 700–719
updating values in, 678–679
Array.Sort method, 679–681
As datatype clause, 444
ASCII (American Standard Code for Information Interchnage), 304, 455
assemblers, described, 3
assembly language, described, 2–3
AssemblyInfo.vb, 29, 30
assignment operator, 127, 162
assignment statements, 127–129, 133–134, 137, 161–162, 181
AutoSize property and, 61
described, 61
InputBox function and, 186, 188–189
making changes to, 204–205
newline characters and, 192
asterisk (*), 34, 304
attributes
described, 6, 618
hidden/exposed, 6–7
AuthorLabel control, 51–52, 61, 479
Auto Format dialog box, 741, 759–760

Auto Hide button, 18, 26–27, 30, 33
Auto Hide button affects active tab option, 18
AutoFormat link, 740, 759
AutoSize property, 51–53, 61
AvgLabel control, 381, 383

B

BackColor property, 35, 108, 759
background(s)
color, 9, 35, 107, 108, 759
for the Windows Form object, 35–36
BackgroundImage property, 35–36
backslash (\), 34
base classes
basic description of, 6–7
modifications to, 60
BASIC (Beginner's All-Purpose Symbolic Instruction Code), 3–4
behaviors, described, 6, 129
binary
access files, 553
operators, 131
binding, described, 757
Blank Solution template, 22–23
blnReplaced variable, 533
BlueTextBox control, 135, 180–181, 207–208
BonusButton control, 442, 445
BonusLabel control, 440
books, recommended, 10
Boolean data type, 157–160, 324, 345
conditions and, 224
random access files and, 618, 624
repetition structures and, 371
selection structures and, 224, 225
sequential access and, 556
strings and, 500
Boolean (logical) operators
basic description of, 230–236
selection structures and, 224, 288, 290–292
truth tables for, 230–234
borders
aligning, 98
styles for, 75–76, 109, 395, 396–398
BorderStyle property, 109, 395, 396–398
bottom-driven (posttest) loops
described, 362
Do...Loop statement and, 370–376

pretest loops and, observing the difference between, 375
Sales Express application and, 376–378
Browse button, 16, 22
browsers, 17, 741, 760. *See also* Object Browser
bugs. *See also* errors
described, 90
OOED applications and, 90
Build Action property, 32
Button tool, 56–57, 721
Button.PerformClick method, 333
buttons
assigning access keys to, 112–113
basic description of, 56–57
captions for, 98
classification of, as objects, 6
default, 193–194, 257
designating, 193–194
positioning, 98, 105, 106
sizing, 106
buttons argument, 255–256
ByRef keyword, 440, 442
Byte data type, 157, 159
ByVal keyword, 440

C

C (high-level language), 3
CalcAndDisplayBonus procedure, 440
CalcBonus procedure, 443
CalcButton control, 93–95, 105, 134, 170, 176–180, 439–440
InputBox function and, 187
modifying the code for, 201–205
newline characters and, 191–192
static variables and, 206
CalcComm procedure, 300–301
CalcPayButton control, 250–255, 259–261
Calculate button, 8, 170, 434, 472
Calculate Monthly Payment button, 218
Calculate Order button, 88, 118, 132–139, 154–155, 175, 185
access key for, 112
background color for, 108
designating, as the default button, 193–194
modifying the code for, 177–183, 201–204
Calculate Tax button, 705, 709

CalculateButton control, 404, 461–462, 465, 468–471, 707–709
Call statement
  Click event procedures and, 327–328
  Math Practice application and, 331, 333
  passing variables and, 438–439, 441
  Sub procedures and, 437, 438–439
CallGenerateAndDisplayNumbers statement, 327–329, 333
Cancel button, 185, 205
CancelButton property, 193
CancelKeys procedure, 271
capitalization. *See also* case sensitivity
  of elements, in the Code editor, 128
  sentence, 98, 105, 187, 247
  of variable names, 180
caption argument, 255–257
captions, 35, 255–257, 740
CaptionText property, 740
Carriage Form.vb, 573
Carriage House application
  Click event procedure for, 589–591
  completing, 598–612
  creating, 548–612
  DateTimePicker control for, 573–597
  Format property and, 578–579
  Load event procedure for, 585–589
  opening, 573
  previewing, 548–551
  PrintDocument control and, 598–599
  Print Report button for, 599–600
  ShowUpDown property and, 577–578
  Value property and, 579–582
Carriage House.sln, 573
Carriage.exe, 548
CarsPictureBox control, 364, 369
Case clause, 297–300, 302
Case Else clause, 297–298
Case selection structure, 296–300
case sensitivity, 236. *See also* capitalization
Categorized button, 33
cells
  described, 757
  DataGrid control and, 757

Center in Form option, 54
char argument, 497
Char data type, 157, 158, 159, 618
character argument, 558
characters. *See also* symbols
  accessing, 501–502
  at the beginning and end of strings, examining, 499–501
  comma-separated lists of, 497
  determining the number of, in strings, 494–495
  inserting, 505–506
  removing, from strings, 496–499
  replacing, in strings, 502–505
  specifying the number of, 504–505
  useless, in random access files, 621
Check Answer button, 282, 346
check box controls
  adding, 319–320
  Grade Calculator application and, 408–411
  Math Practice application and, 319–323, 340–345
  selecting/deselecting, 321
  standards for, 319–320
CheckAnswerButton control, 282, 322–323, 340–346
CheckBox tool, 319, 721
Checked property, 318, 324, 345
CheckedListBox control, 317, 721
Choose Your Data Connection dialog box, 730, 747, 749
Chr function, 190
City Entry dialog box, 365
CityTextBox control, 110
class definitions
  basic description of, 60–61
  Payroll application and, 481–482
Class Name list box, 61
Class View tab, 26
Class View window
  basic description of, 20
  closing, 26–27
classes. *See also* class definitions; classes (listed by name)
  base, 6–7, 60
  basic description of, 6–7
  data types as, 157
  derived, 6–7, 60
  inheritance and, 6–7, 60
  polymorphism and, 6
  representation of, by tools, 47

classes (listed by name). *See also* classes
  CopyrightForm class, 60–62
  DateTimePicker class, 574
  Form class, 28, 29, 60
  Integer class, 161
  Label class, 49
  ListBox class, 454
  PictureBox class, 55
  RadioButton class, 317
Clear procedure, 209
Clear Screen button, 113, 128–131, 134, 139, 178
ClearButton control, 94–95, 105, 302
ClearLabels procedure, 61–62, 74, 471–472
Click event procedure
  Carriage House application and, 589–591, 599–600
  constants and, 170
  Function procedures and, 445
  Grade Calculator application and, 364–374, 378–383, 396, 401, 405–411, 419–422
  Hangman Game application and, 521–522, 529–532
  InputBox function and, 187
  Math Practice application and, 323, 327–331, 340–347
  message boxes and, 259–260
  modifying the code for, 201–204
  Monthly Payment Calculator application and, 250–255, 259–260
  newline characters and, 191–192
  order screen and, 119, 129, 132–137
  random access files and, 634–644, 649–653
  sequential access and, 564–565
  Sub procedures and, 439, 460–471
  Tax Calculator application and, 707–709
  variables and, 161–168, 176–183, 206, 441, 442
Clipboard, 46, 128
Clipboard Ring tab, 46
Close button, 18, 25–27, 39, 58–59
  Closing event procedure and, 423–424
  InputBox function and, 186
Close button affects active tab only option, 18
Close method, 562–563, 565

COBOL, 3
code. *See also* Code editor window;
    source files
        garbage, in random access
            files, 621
        machine, use of the term, 2
        printing, 77, 140
        pseudo-, 84, 127
        sample segment of, 2
        templates, 22–24, 62
        viewing, 59–61
        writing, 59–64
Code editor window
    capitalization of elements in, 128
    color-coding in, 62, 130
    deleting code in, 74
    jagged lines below variable
        names in, 165
    opening, 59
    printing code from, 77, 140
    writing Visual Basic .NET code
        in, 59–64
collections
    creating and adding objects
        to, 403–404
    described, 393
    declaring, 407
    For Each...Next statement
        and, 398–403
    object variables and, 395–398
    parallel, 407–408
    user-defined, 403–404
    using, 393–416
colon (:), 98
color(s)
    background, 9, 35, 107, 108, 759
    -blindness, 107
    -coding, in the Code editor
        window, 62, 130
    of database displays, 759–760
    of internal documentation, 130
    of keywords, 130
    limiting the number of, 108
    subjectivity of, 107
    for user interfaces, selecting,
        107–108
Color dialog box, 9, 721
ColorDialog tool, 721
ColumnHeadersVisible property, 740
ComboBox control, 317
ComboBox tool, 721
comma (,), 136, 138, 186
comments, 129–131, 203, 204, 420
comparison (relational) operators
    basic description of, 225–229
    conditions and, 226, 227, 229

logical operators and, 233
selection structures and, 224,
    225–229, 300–305
compilers
    basic description of, 3
    attributes and, 618
component tray
    adding controls to, 73
    described, 73
Components tab, 46
concatenation operator, 183–185, 233
conditions
    as Boolean expressions, 224
    comparison operators and, 226,
        227, 229
    compound, 230–236
    described, 220–221
    truth tables and, 232–234
Connection tab, 729
Const application, 169–170
Const statement, 168–169
Constant Form.vb, 169
Constant Solution.sln, 169
constants
    creating, 156–174
    literal, 161, 224, 443
    Monthly Payment Calculator
        application and, 224, 253,
        258, 270
    selection structures and, 224
    using, 153–215
    viewing, with the Object
        Browser window, 190–191
ContextMenu tool, 721
Control Panel, 113
ControlBox property, 76–77
controls. *See also* controls (listed
    by name)
    aligning, 54
    borders for, 75–76, 98, 109,
        395, 396–398
    bound, 739, 757
    changing properties for, 52–54
    deleting, 50, 73
    grouping, using white space, 98
    hiding, 345
    locking, 111, 249–250, 320–321
    positioning, 52, 105–106,
        368–369
    sizing, 51–52, 55, 368–369
    working with, 45–71
controls (listed by name)
    AddButton control, 589–591,
        634, 637–640
    AdditionRadioButton control,
        21, 318, 322–323,
        330–332, 342

AddressTextBox control, 105,
    110, 114, 118
AllowListBox control, 453, 456,
    458–459, 465, 471
AnswerPictureBox control, 322,
    343–344
AnswerTextBox control, 322
AuthorLabel control, 51–52,
    61, 479
AvgLabel control, 381, 383
BlueTextBox control, 135,
    180–181, 207–208
BonusButton control, 442, 445
BonusLabel control, 440
CalcButton control, 93–95, 105,
    134, 170, 176–180, 187,
    191–192, 201–206, 439–440
CalcPayButton control,
    250–255, 259–261
CalculateButton control, 404,
    461–462, 465, 468–471,
    707–709
CarsPictureBox control, 364, 369
CheckAnswerButton control,
    282, 322–323, 340–346
CheckedListBox control,
    317, 721
CityTextBox control, 110
ClearButton control, 94–95,
    105, 302
ComboBox control, 317
CorrectLabel control, 322, 344
DataGrid control, 739–741,
    757–760
DateTimePicker control, 548,
    550, 573–597
DisplayButton control,
    419–422, 441–442, 634,
    640–644
DisplaySummaryCheckBox
    control, 282, 283, 319–321,
    340–347
EmployDataGrid control,
    739–741, 757–758
EqualPictureBox control, 322
EventDateTimePicker control,
    577, 579
ExitButton control, 61, 63,
    72–74, 94–95, 105, 187,
    406, 460
ExitTimer control, 73–74
FicaLabel control, 471–472
FwtLabel control, 471–472, 707
GetInfoButton control, 439
Grade1RadioButton control,
    322–323, 327–330

Grade2RadioButton control, 322–323, 327–330
GradeGroupBox control, 316, 318
GradeLabel control, 420–421
GrossLabel control, 471
HoursListBox control, 453, 456, 458–459, 471
IdPrincipalLabel control, 247, 249
IdRateLabel control, 247
IdTermLabel control, 247–248
IdTextBox control, 695
IncorrectGuessLabel control, 530, 531, 537
IncorrectLabel control, 322, 344
InfoGroupBox control, 249–250
InitializeButton control, 634–637
LetterTextBox control, 236
MathForm control, 322
MessageLabel control, 176–177, 182, 184–192, 205, 207–208
MsgLabel control, 303
NameTextBox control, 105, 114–117, 129–130, 436, 460, 471, 497, 498
NetLabel control, 471–472
Num1Label control, 322
Num2Label control, 322
OperationGroupBox control, 316–318
OperatorPictureBox control, 322, 330–331
Panel control, 96, 98, 394
PaymentLabel control, 254
PlusPictureBox control, 331
PriceTextBox control, 133, 180–181, 208
PrincipalTextBox control, 247, 249
PrintButton control, 653, 655
PrintDocument control, 598–599
RateListBox control, 453, 456–459, 471
RateTextBox control, 133, 180–181, 208, 247, 248
RemoveButton control, 396–398, 649–652
ReportPrintDocument control, 600–601
SalesButton control, 163–166
SalesLabel control, 163–166
SalesTextBox control, 302
SeminarPrintDocument control, 634, 653–656

StateTextBox control, 109–110, 129
SubtractionRadioButton control, 283, 317–318, 322, 330–332
SummaryCheckBox control, 316, 319, 321–323, 345–347
SumTextBox control, 128
SwapButton control, 228
TermTextBox control, 248
TotalBoardLabel control, 129, 133, 179, 182–183, 207–208
TotalPriceLabel control, 129, 182–183, 207–208
WordLabel control, 530, 531, 534, 535
YearLabel control, 51–52
YellowTextBox control, 135, 179–181, 208
Controls collection, 393–395, 402
Copy.exe, 16
Copyright Form.vb, 32, 37, 45, 479–480
Copyright Property Pages dialog box, 57–58
copyright screen
    adding graphics to, 55–56
    aligning controls on, 54
    buttons for, 56–57
    code, printing, 77
    completing, 72–82
    controls for, 45–71
    creating, 15–44
    instances of, creating, 481–482
    Payroll application and, 478–483
    previewing, 16
    removing the title bar from, 76
    sizing fonts for, 53
    timer control for, 72–77
Copyright Solution folder, 23, 24
Copyright Solution.sln, 23, 34, 37, 45
Copyright Solution.suo, 23
Copyright.exe, 57
CopyrightForm class, 60–62
CorrectLabel control, 322, 344
count argument, 502, 505
Count property, 394, 404
counter variable, 362–363, 365, 367, 369, 380, 393
counters
    described, 376–383
    initializing, 376, 379
    updating/incrementing, 376, 380
Courier font, 106
CreateText method, 553–554
CrystalReportViewer tool, 721
curly braces ({}), 370, 670

Currency format, 137–138, 254, 260, 440
CustomFormat property, 579, 583
Customize Toolbox dialog box, 48–49

D

Data Adapter Configuration Wizard, 726, 735, 738, 746–747, 754
Data Link Properties dialog box, 728–729, 747, 749
data sets
    creating, 736–739, 755–757
    described, 736
Data tab, 46
data types. *See also* data types (listed by name)
    arrays and, 670, 701
    described, 157
    random access files and, 617, 618–619
    Sub procedures and, 437
    selecting, for variables, 157–159
    user-defined, 617, 619
data types (listed by name). *See also* data types
    Boolean data type, 157–160, 224, 225, 324, 345, 371, 500, 556, 618, 624
    Byte data type, 157, 159
    Char data type, 157, 158, 159, 618
    Date data type, 157, 159, 618
    Decimal data type, 157, 158, 159, 179, 618
    Double data type, 157, 159, 618
    Integer data type, 157, 159, 179, 184
    Long data type, 157, 158, 159, 618
    Object data type, 157, 158–160, 168
    Short data type, 157, 158, 159, 179, 618
    Single data type, 157, 159, 179
    String data type, 157, 159–160, 184, 187, 618–619
data validation, 234
databases
    accessing data in, 724–741, 745–746
    data sets for, 736–739
    DataGrid control and, 739–741
    OleDbDataAdapter object and, 726–736
    relational, 725, 745–746

DataGrid control, 739–741, 757–760

DataGrid tool, 721, 757

DataMember property, 739, 758

DataSet object, 738–739

DataSource property, 739

date, system, retrieving, 583–585

Date data type, 157, 159, 618

DateTime object, 580

DateTimePicker class, 574

DateTimePicker control, 548, 550, 573–597
  adding, 574–579
  Format property and, 578–579
  ShowUpDown property and, 577–578
  Text property and, 582–583
  Value property and, 579–582

DateTimePicker tool, 574, 721

Debug Solution.sln, 664

debugging. *See also*
  Debug.WriteLine method
    described, 10, 139–140
    order screen and, 130, 139–140
    random access files and, 664
    strings, 545

Debug.WriteLine method, 366, 367, 373–374, 454

Decimal data type, 157, 158, 159, 179, 618

decimal point (.), 137

decision (selection) structures
  arrays and, 675
  Case structure, 296–300
  comparison operators and, 225–229, 300–305
  creating, 217–280
  described, 220–221
  four forms of, 221
  If/ElseIf/Else structure, 294–296
  LCase function and, 236–239
  logic errors in, 288–294
  logical operators and, 230–236
  Math Practice application and, 281–357
  nested, 284–288
  repetition structures and, 381–382
  UCase function and, 236–239
  using unnecessary, 293–294
  decisions. *See also* decision (selection) structures
  primary, 285, 286, 292–293
  secondary, 285, 292–293

declaration statements, 160–161, 169–170, 204

defaultButton argument, 255–256

defaultResponse argument, 186

derived classes
  basic description of, 6–7
  inheritance and, 60

Description pane, 32

desk-checking, 289–294, 298–299

dialog boxes
  Add New Project dialog box, 24, 743–744
  Add Table dialog box, 732–733, 751–752
  Auto Format dialog box, 741, 759–760
  Choose Your Data Connection dialog box, 730, 747, 749
  City Entry dialog box, 365
  Color dialog box, 9, 721
  Copyright Property Pages dialog box, 57–58
  creating, 185–190
  Customize Toolbox dialog box, 48–49
  Data Link Properties dialog box, 728–729, 747, 749
  Display Properties dialog box, 113
  Folder Options dialog box, 23
  Font dialog box, 53–54
  Generate Dataset dialog box, 737, 756
  Microsoft Data Link Error dialog box, 729, 748
  Name Entry dialog box, 154, 189, 192, 205–206
  New Project dialog box, 22, 743
  Open dialog box, 55
  Open File dialog box, 634
  Open Solution dialog box, 45, 479
  Options dialog box, 18, 19, 62
  Print dialog box, 77
  Query Builder dialog box, 733–735, 751–755
  Run dialog box, 7, 16
  Sales Entry dialog box, 380
  Scope Project Property Pages dialog box, 165
  Select Access Database dialog box, 729, 748
  Web Access Failed dialog box, 744

Dim keyword, 160, 166, 204, 670

Dim statement, 160–162, 166, 180, 204
  arrays and, 673, 701

collections and, 394, 404
  object variables and, 395
  Payroll application and, 482
  random access files and, 619
  repetition structures and, 379, 394, 404
  sequential access and, 553, 555

direct access files, 617. *See also* random access files

Display Grade button, 360, 405

Display icon, 113

Display Names button, 615, 643–644

Display Properties dialog box, 113

Display Sales button, 164–167

Display summary check box, 282, 283, 319–321, 346, 347

DisplayAverage procedure, 676

DisplayButton control, 419–422, 441–442, 634, 640–644

DisplayHighest procedure, 677

DisplayMessage procedure, 303–304

DisplayMonths procedure, 672–673

DisplayMsg procedure, 439

DisplayPrice procedure, 692–695

DisplaySales procedure, 703–704

DisplaySummaryCheckBox control, 282, 283, 319–321, 340–347

division operator, 131–132, 233

Do clause, 371, 380

Do Loop Form.vb, 372

Do Loop Solution.sln, 372

Do...Loop statement, 370, 380, 394

Do Until clause, 624

Do While clause, 500, 624

documentation. *See also* comments
  assembling, 140
  internal, 129–131

dollar sign ($), 132, 138, 500

DomainUpDown tool, 721

dot member selection operator, 34

double quotes ("), 126, 135, 186

Double data type, 157, 159, 618

Downloads link, 19

Due argument, 252–253

Dynamic Help tab, 27

Dynamic Help window
  basic description of, 20
  closing, 26–27
  opening, 26

E

e-commerce applications, 17, 741. *See also* order screen; Web-based applications

Edit menu
    Copy command, 128
    Paste command, 128
    Undo command, 108
Effects tab, 113
e.Graphics.DrawString method, 601–602
electronic switches, 2
ellipsis (. . .), 36, 517, 521
Else clause, 224
ElseIf clause, 301
EmployDataGrid control, 739–741, 757–758
EmployStruc record structure, 617
Enabled property, 72, 73, 409–410
encapsulation, defined, 6–7
End Class clause, 481
End Class statement, 323
End If clause, 600
End Sub keyword, 62
End Sub statement
    Grade Calculator application and, 367
    passing variables and, 442
    Math Practice application and, 330
    repetition structures and, 373
EndsWith method, 499–501, 508
endvalue item, 362–263, 366, 393
Enter event, 419–420, 422–423
Environment folder, 18, 62
EOF function, 623–625
equal sign (=), 127
equal to operator, 225–229, 233
EqualPictureBox control, 322
ErrorProvider tool, 722
errors. See also bugs
    database access and, 729
    logic, 139, 288–294
    rounding, 179
    sequential access and, 555
    syntax, 139
Event Report application, 585–586
EventDateTimePicker control, 577, 579
events. See also events (listed by name)
    associating procedures with, 208–209
    basic description of, 4, 59, 129
    identifying, 95–96
events (listed by name). See also
    Click event procedure; events
    Enter event, 419–420, 422–423
    KeyDown event, 268
    KeyPress event, 250, 267–272, 436

PrintPage event, 600–604, 634, 653–656
    SelectedValueChanged event, 471–472
    TextChanged event, 207–208, 250, 261–263, 302, 406
    Tick event, 72–73, 74
Example1Button, 364–366
Example2button, 366–367
Example3 button, 367–370
exclamation point (!), 305
.exe file extension, 57
executable files, described, 57
Exists method, 556, 565
Exit button, 56, 58–59, 61–63
    order screen and, 119, 126
    replacing, with a timer control, 72–77
Exit Do statement, 370
Exit For statement, 362, 399
ExitButton control, 61, 63, 94–95, 105, 187, 406
    deleting, 73–74
    list box controls and, 460
    replacing, with a timer control, 72–77
ExitTimer control, 73–74
Explorer, 23
exponentiation operator, 131–132, 233
External Help radio button, 18

F

false path, 222, 286–288
FicaLabel control, 471–472
fields
    data types and, 618
    described, 616
    initializing files and, 621–622
    record structures and, 167–618
    SQL and, 731
    Structure statement and, 618
file(s). See also source files
    hidden, 23
    input, 553
    -name extensions, 57
    output, 553
    renaming, the Properties window, 32–33
    view options for, 23, 30
File application, 563–566
File Form.vb, 563
File menu
    Add Project command, 23
    Close Solution command, 38

Exit command, 9, 77, 518–519, 521–522
    New Game command, 518–521, 529–532, 536
    Open Solution command, 38, 45
    Print command, 77
    Save All command, 37, 52
File Name property, 32
File Solution.sln, 563
FileClose function, 624
FileGet function, 623–625
FileNewMenuItem, 529–532
filenumber argument, 621, 623, 624
FileOpen function, 619–620, 623, 625, 651
FilePut function, 620–621
Fill method, 738, 756
Fixed format, 137–138
Fixed3D property setting, 75
FixedDialog property setting, 75
FixedSingle property setting, 75
FixedToolWindow property setting, 75
floating-point numbers, described, 158
flowcharts
    basic description of, 84, 222–224
    symbols in, 222–223
flowlines
    described, 222
    marking, 223
focus, controlling, 117–119, 129–130
Focus method, 129–130
Folder Options dialog box, 23
folders
    designating paths and, 34
    view options for, 29, 30
Font dialog box, 53–54
Font property, 52–54, 56
FontDialog tool, 722
fonts. See also text
    basic description of, 52
    button controls and, 56
    Code editor window and, 62
    design tips for using, 106
    fixed-spaced, 601
    measurement of, in points, 52
    overusing, 107
    printing and, 601
    sans serif, 54, 62, 106–107, 601
    selecting, for user interfaces, 106–108
    serif, 106–107
    size of, 52
    statements and, 224

For clause, 365, 367
For Each clause, 399, 402
For Each Solution.sln, 401
For Each...Next statement, 398–403
For Next application, 364–366
For Next Form.vb, 364, 401
For Next Solution.sln, 364
Form class, 28, 29, 60
Form Designer window, 25, 27
form file(s)
    described, 31
    objects, changing the name
      of, 32–33
Form1.vb, 25, 28–32
Form2.vb, 31
Format function, 137–138, 560–561
Format menu, 54
Format property, 578–579, 582
FormBorderStyle property, 74,
    75–76
form-level (module-level) variables
    creating, 166–168
    described, 162
forms. *See also* controls
    adding, to solutions, 479–480
    database access with, 724–760
    instances of, creating, 481–482
    naming conventions for,
      34–35, 744
Forms namespace, 34
For...Next statement
    Controls collection and, 394
    Grade Calculator application
      and, 362–370
    box controls and, 455, 456
    nested, 362
    random access files and, 622
frm prefix, for form names, 34–35
FrontPage Server Extensions, 744
Function keyword, 444
Function procedures
    creating, 435–451
    described, 435, 443–445
functions. *See also* functions (listed
    by name)
    described, 136
    passing information to, by value
      and by reference, 443
    user-defined, 443–445
functions (listed by name). *See also*
    functions
    Chr function, 190
    EOF function, 623–625
    FileClose function, 624
    FileGet function, 623–625
    FileOpen function, 619–620,
      623, 625, 651

FilePut function, 620–621
Format function, 137–138,
    560–561
GetFwtTax function, 463–470
InputBox function, 185–190,
    204–205, 365, 379–380
LCase function, 236–239
Len function, 620
MsgBox function, 255
Pmt function, 252–255
Rnd function, 326
Space function, 558, 622
Val function, 136–137,
    178–179, 186
FV argument, 252–253
FwtLabel control, 471–472, 707

G

garbage code, in random access
    files, 621
General tab, 46
Generate Dataset dialog box,
    737, 756
GenerateAndDisplayNumbers
    procedure, 323–327,
    329–332, 343
GeneratorRandom object, 325
Get Started link, 19, 20
Get Started pane, 20, 23
GetFwtTax function, 463–470
GetInfo procedure, 441, 442
GetInfoButton control, 439
Grade Calculator application
    check box controls for, 408–411
    collections and, 393–417
    completing, 419–431
    counters and, 376–383
    creating, 359–431
    Do...Loop statement and,
      370–376
    Enabled property and, 409–411
    For Each...Next statement and,
      398–403
    For...Next statement and,
      362–370
    opening, 405
    Pretest Loop button and, 372,
      373–374
    previewing, 360
    testing, 380
    TOE chart for, 405–406, 407
Grade Form.vb, 405, 419
grade procedure, 294–299
Grade Solution.sln, 405, 419
Grade1RadioButton control,
    322–323, 327–330

Grade2RadioButton control,
    322–323, 327–330
Grade.exe, 360
GradeForm, 407, 419–420,
    423–424
GradeGroupBox control, 316, 318
GradeLabel control, 420–421
graphics
    adding, to the copyright screen,
      55–56
    design tips for, 106
    overusing, 107
    selecting, for user interfaces, 106
    shipped with Visual
      Studio .NET, 36
    using too many, 106
greater than operator, 225–229, 233
greater than or equal to operator,
    225–229, 233
greater-than sign (>), 363
GridLineColor property, 740
GrossLabel control, 471
group box controls
    adding, 246–248
    Controls collection and, 394
    hiding, 345
    labeling, 246–247
    order screen and, 96, 98
    properties for, 247
GroupBox tool, 247, 722
GUI (graphical user interface), 4, 98

H

Handled property, 268
Handles keyword, 208
hand-tracing (desk-checking),
    289–294, 298–299
Hangman Form.vb, 516, 527
Hangman Game application
    completing, 527–545
    creating, 491–545
    IncorrectGuessLabel control for,
      530, 531, 537
    label controls for, 532–539
    main menu controls for,
      516–526
    opening, 516
    previewing, 492–493
    TOE chart for, 528–529
Hangman Solution.sln, 516, 527
Hangman.exe, 492
happy face icon, 283
Headlines link, 19
height argument, 368
Height property, 36

help
for closing solutions, 38
context-sensitive, displaying, 20
menu, managing windows with, 26
HelpProvider tool, 722
hidden files, 23
high-level languages, described, 3
highestColumnSubscript argument, 701
highestRowSubscript argument, 701
horizontalPosition argument, 601
HoursListBox control, 453, 456, 458–459, 471
HScrollBar tool, 722
hyphen (-), 305, 530

I

icon argument, 255–256
icons folder, 36
ID property, 757
IDE (integrated development environment)
basic description of, 17
executable files and, 57
familiarizing yourself with, 16–25
managing windows in, 26–28
opening the Code editor in, 60
windows in, list of, 20–21
IdPrincipalLabel control, 247, 249
IdRateLabel control, 247
IdTermLabel control, 247–248
IdTextBox control, 695
if selection structures, 220–244
if/Else selection structure, 221–224
If/ElseIf/Else selection structure, 294–296
if...then...else statement, 220–244, 301, 344
Image property, 55, 316
ImageList tool, 722
images
adding, to the copyright screen, 55–56
design tips for, 106
overusing, 107
selecting, for user interfaces, 106
shipped with Visual Studio .NET, 36
using too many, 106
IncorrectGuessLabel control, 530, 531, 537
IncorrectLabel control, 322, 344

index
described, 393
Remove method and, 498
user-defined collections and, 403, 404
IndexOf method, 506–508, 535
Infinity constant, 381
InfoGroupBox control, 249–250
Information Box, 9
Information Message icon, 257
inheritance, defined, 6–7, 60
Initialize File button, 614, 634–637
InitializeButton control, 634–637
input
files, described, 553
/output symbol, 223, 371
InputBox function, 185–190, 204–205
Grade Calculator application and, 365
repetition structures and, 365, 379–380
Insert method, 505–506, 508
instances, defined, 6–7
instantiation, defined, 6, 29, 30
instructions
defined, 2
mnemonics for, 2–3
intAge variable, 184
intBlue variable, 179, 180
intButton variable, 585, 622
intCode variable, 674
intCorrectAnswer variable, 341–343
intCount variable, 365, 373, 374, 675
Integer class, 161
Integer data type, 157, 159, 179, 184
integer division operator, 131–132, 233
integrated development environment (IDE)
basic description of, 17
executable files and, 57
familiarizing yourself with, 16–25
managing windows in, 26–28
opening the Code editor in, 60
windows in, list of, 20–21
intEmployNumber variable, 619
internal documentation, 129–131
interpreters, basic description of, 3
Interval property, 72, 73, 479
intFirst variable, 227
intIndex variable, 507–508, 533
intNum1 variable, 341–342
intNum2 variable, 341–342
intNumber variable, 162
intNumberCorrect variable, 341–342

intNumberIncorrect variable, 341–342
intNumOrdered variable, 300
intNumSales variable, 379–381
intRecordNum variable, 622
intRegion1 variable, 442, 445
intRegion2 variable, 442, 445
intSale1 variable, 440, 443, 445
intSale2 variable, 443, 445
intSales variable, 163, 165
intSearchFor variable, 675
intSecond variable, 227
intTemp variable, 228
intTotal variable, 440, 443, 676
IntTotalBoards variable, 179
intUserAnswer variable, 341–343
intX variable, 369–370, 394, 673, 675–679
intYellow variable, 179, 180
invalid data, described, 139
Is keyword, 300
IsComparison operator, 300–301
Items collection, 454, 455

J

Java, 5

K

key argument, 407
keys
access, 112–113, 117–119, 317, 319
shortcut, 520–521
user-defined collections and, 403
KeyChar property, 268–269
KeyDown event, 268
KeyPress event, 250, 267–272, 436
keywords. *See also* keywords (listed by name)
basic description of, 62
color of, 130
keywords (listed by name). *See also* keywords
ByRef keyword, 440, 442
ByVal keyword, 440
Dim keyword, 160, 166, 204, 670
End Sub keyword, 62
Function keyword, 444
Handles keyword, 208
Is keyword, 300
Nothing keyword, 331, 395
Private keyword, 62, 160, 166, 323, 436, 670
Public keyword, 62, 160

Static keyword, 160, 162
Sub keyword, 62, 444
To keyword, 299–300
Until keyword, 371
While keyword, 371

L

Label class, 49
label controls
  access keys and, 113
  aligning, 54
  BorderStyle property for, 109
  clearing the contents of, 471–472
  creating, 49–53
  font settings for, 52–54
  Hangman Game application
    and, 532–539
  naming, 50
  order screen and, 87, 95
  Payroll application and, 471–472
  providing keyboard access to list
    box controls with, 454
  purpose of, 49
  text for, aligning, 272–273
Label tool, 49–54, 722
LCase function, 236–239
Len function, 620
Length property, 494–495, 508, 676
Less button, 22
less than operator, 225–229, 233
less than or equal to operator,
  225–229, 233
less-than sign (<), 363
LetterTextBox control, 236
Like operator, 300, 303–305
line continuation character, 134, 184
line terminator character, 557, 561
LinkLabel tool, 722
list box controls
  adding, 453–461
  adding items to, 454–461
  default items in, 459
  Math Practice application
    and, 318
  Payroll application and,
    452–477
  SelectedIndex property and,
    457–461
  SelectedItem property and,
    457–461
  standards for, 454
List View option, 48
ListBox class, 454
ListBox tool, 453, 722
ListView tool, 722

literal constants, 161, 224, 443
Load event procedure
  Carriage House application and,
    585–589
  Math Practice application and,
    323, 332, 333–334
  modifying code in, 201–205
  order screen and, 176, 187,
    201–205
  repetition structures and, 406,
    407–408
local variables. *See also* static
  variables
  described, 162
  creating, 163–166
  scope of, 162–168
  Static keyword and, 162
Location property, 52, 55, 56
  DateTimePicker control
    and, 574
  list box controls and, 453
Lock Controls option, 111
locking controls, 111, 249–250,
  320–321
logic errors, 139, 288–294
logical (Boolean) operators
  basic description of, 230–236
  selection structures and, 224,
    288, 290–292
  truth tables for, 230–234
logos, adding, 55–56. *See also*
  graphics
Long data type, 157, 158, 159, 618
loops. *See also* repetition structures
  posttest, 362, 370–378
  pretest, 362, 370–378
  priming read and, 378
  stopping, 380–381

M

machine language, described, 2
main menu controls
  adding, 517–521
  described, 517
  Hangman Game application
    and, 516–526
MainMenu tool, 518, 722
Make Same Size option, 54, 110, 248
margins
  maintaining consistent, 106
  minimizing the number of
    different, 98, 105
Math Form.vb, 316, 340
Math Practice application
  check box controls for,
    319–323, 340–345

Click event procedure and, 323,
  327–331, 340–347
completing, 340–357
creating, 281–357
group box controls and, 316,
  318, 345
Load event procedure and, 323,
  332, 333–334
locking controls in, 320–321
opening, 316
previewing, 282–283
radio buttons for, 317–319,
  321, 330–332
sketch of, 315
Sub procedure and, 323–327
TabIndex property and,
  320–321
TOE chart for, 322–323, 327
user interface for, 315–322
Math Solution.sln, 316, 340
Math.exe, 282
MathForm control, 322
Maximize button, 76–77
MaximizeBox property, 76–77
measurement
  of fonts, in points, 52–54
  units of, setting, 53, 54
Me.Close method, 63, 73, 74,
  119, 423, 455
memory. *See also* variables
  addresses, 300–301, 437
  arrays and, 669
  Dynamic Help window and, 26
  loading applications into, 15, 333
  locating the Form class in, 34
  object references and, 300–301
  passing variables and, 440
  references and, 29
menu(s). *See also* menu controls;
  specific menus
  assigning shortcut keys to,
    520–521
  design tips for, 521
  classification of, as objects, 6
  sub-, 517
  titles for, 517, 321
menu controls. *See also* menus
  adding, 517–521
  described, 517
  Hangman Game application
    and, 516–526
message argument, 366
message box controls. *See also*
  MessageBox.Show method
  displaying, 255–261
  Hangman Game application
    and, 493

Monthly Payment Calculator application and, 255–261
MessageBox.Show method, 255–261, 435, 676, 679, 693
  Carriage House application and, 585, 587
  random access files and, 622, 634
  repetition structures and, 365, 423
  sequential access and, 565
MessageLabel control, 176–177, 182, 184–192, 205
  newline character and, 190, 191–192
  TextChanged event procedure and, 207–208
methods. *See also* methods (listed by name)
  basic description of, 63, 129
  names of, parentheses after, 63
methods (listed by name). *See also* methods
  Add method, 403, 404, 407, 454–455
  AppendText method, 553–554
  Array.Reverse method, 680–681
  Array.Sort method, 679–681
  Button.PerformClick method, 333
  Close method, 562–563, 565
  CreateText method, 553–554
  Debug.WriteLine method, 366, 367, 373–374, 454
  e.Graphics.DrawString method, 601–602
  EndsWith method, 499–501, 508
  Exists method, 556, 565
  Fill method, 738, 756
  Focus method, 129–130
  IndexOf method, 506–508, 535
  Insert method, 505–506, 508
  Me.Close method, 63, 73, 74, 119, 423, 455
  MessageBox.Show method, 255–261, 365, 423, 435, 565, 585, 587, 622, 634, 676, 679, 693
  OpenText method, 553–555, 565
  PadLeft method, 558–561
  PadRight method, 558–561
  Peek method, 562
  Print method, 600
  RadioButton.PerformClick method, 333

Random.Next method, 282, 325–327
Random.NextDouble method, 325
ReadLine method, 561–563
Remove method, 497, 498–499, 508
Replace method, 502–505, 508
SelectAll method, 344
SetBounds method, 368, 369
ShowDialog method, 482–483
StartsWith method, 499–501, 508
Substring method, 501–502, 508
ToLongDateString method, 583–585
ToLongTimeString method, 581, 583
ToShortDateString method, 581, 583–585
ToShortTimeString method, 581
ToString method, 560, 583–585
Trim method, 496–497, 498, 508
TrimEnd method, 496–497, 498, 508, 642
TrimStart method, 496–497, 498, 508
Write method, 556–561
WriteLine method, 556–561, 564
microcomputers, 455
Microsoft Access, 724–726, 736, 745, 757
Microsoft Data Link Error dialog box, 729, 748
Microsoft Developer Network (MSDN) Online Library, 19
Microsoft Development Environment window, 17–18
Microsoft FrontPage Server Extensions, 744
Microsoft Jet 4.0 OLE DB Provider, 728, 747–748
Microsoft Sans Serif font, 54, 62, 106–107, 601
Microsoft SQL Server, 724, 745
Microsoft Visual C++, 5
Microsoft Visual Studio .NET
  creating applications with, 21–28
  customizing, 17–21
  exiting, 39
  starting, 17–21
Microsoft Word, 93, 140
Mid statement, 504–505, 508
Midterm check box, 360
millisecond, definition of, 73

Minimize button, 76–77
MinimizeBox property, 76–77
Misc folder, 36
mnemonics, 2–3
module scope, 162
module-level (form-level) variables
  creating, 166–168
  described, 162
modulus operator, 131–132, 233
monitors, monochrome, 107
Monthly Payment Calculator application
  completing, 267–280
  creating, 217–280
  group box controls for, 246–248
  If...Then...Else statements and, 220–244
  KeyPress event and, 250, 267–272
  label controls for, 272–273
  locking controls for, 249–250
  message boxes and, 255–261
  Pmt function and, 252–255
  previewing, 218–219
  running, 7–9
  TextChanged event and, 261–263
  user interface for, 245–266
MonthlyCalendar tool, 722
More button, 22
MOV mnemonic, 3
MSDN Online Library, 19
MsgBox function, 255
MsgLabel control, 303
mstrSalesPerson variable, 187, 204
MUL mnemonic, 3
MultiExtended setting, 453
multiplication operator, 131–132, 233
MultiSimple setting, 453
My Profile link, 17, 19–20
My Profile pane, 17–18
MyCollection, 404

N

Name Entry dialog box, 154, 189, 192, 205–206
Name property, 34–35, 55–56, 73, 110
  DataGrid control and, 739
  DateTimePicker control and, 574
  list box controls and, 453
  main menu controls and, 517

named constants
  basic description of, 168–171
  creating, 156–174
  InputBox function and, 187
  selection structures and, 224
namespaces
  described, 29
  Form class and, 34
  references and, 29
NameTextBox control, 436, 460, 471
  order screen and, 105, 114–117, 129–130
  strings and, 497, 498
NaN constant, 381
negation operator, 131–132, 233, 254
nested selection structures, 284–288
NetLabel control, 471–472
New Blank Solution button, 21
New Connection button, 728, 747
New Project button, 23
New Project dialog box, 22, 743
newline character, 190
newvalue sequence, 503
Next clause, 362, 365, 367, 369, 399
Next Each clause, 402
not equal to operator, 225–229, 233
Not operator, 230–236
Nothing keyword, 331, 395
NotifyIcon tool, 722
NPer argument, 252–254
Num1Label control, 322
Num2Label control, 322
NumericUpDown tool, 722

O

objControl variable, 404
Object box, 31, 32, 34
Object Browser, 190–192, 270, 419
Object data type, 157, 158–160, 168
object references, 29, 300–301
Object Variable Form.vb, 396
Object Variable Solution.sln, 396
object variables
  basic description of, 395–398
  check box controls and, 409
  Grade Calculator application and, 419
  sequential access and, 555
objects
  assigning tasks to, 93–94
  associating procedures with, 208–209
  basic description of, 4, 5
  changing the name of, 32–33
  enabling/disabling, 409–411

identifying, 93–94
  naming conventions for, 50
  properties of, 31–33
objLetterLabel variable, 533
objPayrollForm variable, 482
objStateTextBox variable, 395
objStreamReader variable, 555
objStreamWriter variable, 555, 564, 585
OK button
  InputBox function and, 185, 186
  Monthly Payment Calculator application and, 256
oldvalue sequence, 503
OleDbConnection object, 735, 757
OleDbDataAdapter object, 726–736, 738, 745–757
OleDbDataAdapter tool, 746–747
one-dimensional arrays. *See also* arrays
  accessing elements in, with the subscript, 674
  average amount stored in, calculating, 676
  described, 668–690
  displaying the contents of, 672–673
  highest value stored in, determining, 677–678
  manipulating, 672–681
  parallel, 691–693
  searching, 675–676
  sorting data stored in, 679–681
  storing data in, 671–672, 693–695
  updating values in, 678–679
Online Community link, 19
OOD (object-oriented design), 5
OOED (object-oriented/event-driven) applications
  basic description of, 4–5
  building user interfaces for, 104–125
  planning, 90–103
  running, 87–89
  solving problems using, 86–87
OOED.exe, 87–88
OOP (object-oriented programming)
  terminology, 5–7
  Windows Form object and, 28
Open button, 479
Open dialog box, 55
Open File dialog box, 634
Open Solution dialog box, 45, 479
OpenAccess.ReadWrite argument, 620

OpenFileDialog tool, 722
OpenText method, 553–555, 565
OperationGroupBox control, 316–318
OperatorPictureBox control, 322, 330–331
operators. *See also* operators (listed by name)
  arithmetic, 131–132, 233, 224, 225
  basic description of, 131–132binary, 131
  unary, 131
operators (listed by name). *See also* operators
  addition operator, 131–132, 233
  And operator, 230–236
  AndAlso operator, 230–236, 291
  assignment operator, 127, 162
  concatenation operator, 183–185, 233
  division operator, 131–132, 233
  dot member selection operator, 34
  equal to operator, 225–229, 233
  exponentiation operator, 131–132, 233
  greater than operator, 225–229, 233
  greater than or equal to operator, 225–229, 233
  integer division operator, 131–132, 233
  IsComparison operator, 300–301
  less than operator, 225–229, 233
  less than or equal to operator, 225–229, 233
  Like operator, 300, 303–305
  modulus operator, 131–132, 233
  multiplication operator, 131–132, 233
  negation operator, 131–132, 233, 254
  not equal to operator, 225–229, 233
  Not operator, 230–236
  Or operator, 230–236
  OrElse operator, 230–236
  subtraction operator, 131–132, 233
  TypeOf...Is operator, 300, 302–303
  Xor operator, 230–236

options
  Add Existing Item option, 479
  Align option, 54
  Auto Hide button affects active tab option, 18
  Center in Form option, 54
  Close button affects active tab only option, 18
  List View option, 48
  Lock Controls option, 111
  Make Same Size option, 54, 110, 248
  Sort Items Alphabetically option, 47
  Tab Order option, 114, 115–116
Options dialog box, 18, 19, 62
Or operator, 230–236
Oracle, 725, 745
order by clause, 751
Order Form.vb, 126, 176, 193, 203
order screen
  backgrounds for, 107, 108
  building the user interface for, 104–124
  coding, 125–152
  constants and, 153–215
  creating, 83–152
  fonts for, 105–108 identifying events for, 94–96
  identifying objects for, 93–94
  identifying tasks for, 91–93
  margins for, 98, 105–106
  modifying the code for, 201–215
  OOED approach to, 85–89
  planning process for, 90–103
  procedure-oriented approach to, 84–89
  sketching the user interface for, 96–98
  variables and, 153–215
Order Solution.sln, 104, 126, 176, 203
OrElse operator, 230–236
output files, described, 553
Output window, 25

P

PadLeft method, 558–561
PadRight method, 558–561
PageSetupDialog tool, 722
Panel control, 96, 98, 394
Panel tool, 246, 722

parameters
  described, 62
  Sub procedures and, 435, 436–437
parentheses, 63, 131–132, 139
Pascal, Blaise, 159
Pascal (programming language), 159 Payment Form.vb, 246, 267–268
Payment Solution.sln, 267
Payment.exe, 218
PaymentLabel control, 254
Payroll application
  AllowListBox control in, 453, 456, 458–459, 465, 471
  completing, 479–484
  Copyright form and, 478–483
  creating, 433–489
  GetFwtTax function and, 463–468
  list box controls for, 452–477
  NameTextBox control for, 436, 460, 471
  passing variables and, 437–443
  previewing, 434–435
  TOE chart for, 460–461
Payroll Form.vb, 452, 479
Payroll Solution.sln, 452
Payroll.exe, 434
PayrollForm object, 481
Peek method, 562
Percent format, 137–138
percent sign (%), 132, 136, 137
period (.), 127, 189, 268
picture box controls
  adding, 55–56
  Grade Calculator application and, 364, 368–369
  positioning, 368–369
  removing graphics from, 331
  sizing, 368–369
PictureBox class, 55
PictureBox tool, 55–56, 722
pipe symbol (|), 370
pixels
  described, 36
  positioning controls in relation to, 52
plus sign (+), 135, 184
PlusPictureBox control, 331
Pmt function, 252–255
Pointer tool, 47, 721
points, measuring font size in, 52
polymorphism, 6
Posttest button, 382–383
Posttest Loop button, 374–376

posttest loops
  described, 362
  Do...Loop statement and, 370–376
  pretest loops and, observing the difference between, 375
  Sales Express application and, 376–378
precedence, order of, 131–132
Pretest button, 378–382
Pretest Loop button, 372, 373–374
pretest loops
  described, 362
  Do...Loop statement and, 370–376
  posttest loops and, observing the difference between, 375
  Sales Express application and, 376–378
PriceTextBox control, 133, 180–181, 208
primary decisions
  described, 285, 286
  reversing, 292–293
priming read, described, 378
PrincipalTextBox control, 247, 249
Print dialog box, 77
Print method, 600
Print Report button, 549, 599–601
PrintButton control, 653, 655
PrintDialog tool, 722
PrintDocument control, 598–599
PrintDocument tool, 598, 722
printing
  Carriage House application and, 548–612
  code, from the Code editor window, 77, 140
  e.Graphics.DrawString method and, 601–602
  PrintDocument control and, 598–599
  PrintPage event procedure and, 600–604, 634, 653–656
PrintPage event, 600–604, 634, 653–656
PrintPreviewControl tool, 722
Private keyword, 62, 160, 166, 323, 436, 670
ProblemGroupBox group box, 316
procedure(s). *See also* procedures (listed by name)
  accessibility of, 436
  associating, with events and objects, 208–209
  described, 435

footers for, 62, 436, 444
headers for, 62, 436, 441, 444
-oriented approach, 3–4, 84–89
scope, 162–168, 228
testing, 209, 381
procedures (listed by name). *See also*
  procedures
  CalcAndDisplayBonus proce-
    dure, 440
  CalcBonus procedure, 443
  CalcComm procedure, 300–301
  CancelKeys procedure, 271
  Clear procedure, 209
  ClearLabels procedure, 61–62,
    74, 471–472
  DisplayAverage procedure, 676
  DisplayHighest procedure, 677
  DisplayMessage procedure,
    303–304
  DisplayMonths procedure,
    672–673
  DisplayMsg procedure, 439
  DisplayPrice procedure,
    692–695
  DisplaySales procedure,
    703–704
  GenerateAndDisplayNumbers
    procedure, 323–327,
    329–332, 343
  GetInfo procedure, 441, 442
  grade procedure, 294–299
  ProcessCheckBoxes
    procedure, 410
  ProcessGradeRadioButtons
    procedure, 328–330
  ProcessLetterLabels procedure,
    532–537
  SearchArray procedure, 675
  SortAscending procedure,
    679–681
  SortDescending procedure, 681
  Sub procedure, 62, 323–327,
    435–451, 618
  Sub Main procedure, 480–481
  UpdateArray procedure,
    678–679
process symbols, 222, 371
ProcessCheckBoxes procedure, 410
ProcessGradeRadioButtons
  procedure, 328–330
ProcessLetterLabels procedure,
  532–537
processors, 26
profiles, described, 18
program, use of the term, 1
programmer, use of the term, 1

programming languages. *See also*
  specific languages
  described, 1
  history of, 1–7
ProgressBar tool, 722
Project Types list box, 22, 24
projects
  adding, to solutions, 24–25
  changing the properties
    of, 57–58
  defined, 21
  display of, in the Solution
    Explorer, 29–31
  naming, 24–25
properties. *See also* properties (listed
  by name)
  assigning values to, during run
    time, 127–129
  for controls, changing, 52–54
  viewing, in the Properties win-
    dow, 33–37
properties (listed by name). *See also*
  properties; Properties window
  AcceptButton property, 193
  AutoSize property, 51–53, 61
  BackColor property, 35,
    108, 759
  BackgroundImage property,
    35–36
  BorderStyle property, 109, 395,
    396–398
  Build Action property, 32
  CancelButton property, 193
  CaptionText property, 740
  Checked property, 318, 324,
    345
  ColumnHeadersVisible
    property, 740
  ControlBox property, 76–77
  Count property, 394, 404
  CustomFormat property,
    579, 583
  DataMember property,
    739, 758
  DataSource property, 739
  Enabled property, 72, 73,
    409–410
  File Name property, 32
  Font property, 52–54, 56
  Format property, 578–579, 582
  FormBorderStyle property, 74,
    75–76
  GridLineColor property, 740
  Handled property, 268
  Height property, 36

ID property, 757
Image property, 55, 316
Interval property, 72, 73, 479
KeyChar property, 268–269
Length property, 494–495,
  508, 676
Location property, 52, 55, 56,
  453, 574
MaximizeBox property, 76–77
MinimizeBox property, 76–77
Name property, 34–35, 55–56,
  73, 110, 453, 517, 574, 739
ReadOnly property, 740
RowHeadersVisible
  property, 740
SelectedIndex property,
  457–461
SelectedItem property,
  457–461, 465
SelectionMode property, 453
ShowHeader property, 759
ShowUpDown property,
  577–578
Size property, 36–37
SizeMode property, 55
Sorted property, 455
StartPosition property, 35
TabIndex property, 114–119,
  249–250, 320–321, 454,
  574–575, 740
Tag property, 407
TextAlign property, 272–273
UseMnemonic property, 113
Value property, 579–582
Visible property, 345, 529
Width property, 36
X property, 52
Y property, 52
Properties list, 31–32, 51, 110. *See*
  also Properties window
Properties tab, 30
Properties window. *See also*
  Properties list
  auto-hide feature, 30
  basic description of, 31–33
  displaying, 27
  scrolling in, 34
  viewing properties in, 33–37
pseudocode, defined, 84, 127
pseudo-random numbers, 325–327
Public Class clause, 481
Public keyword, 62, 160
PV argument, 252–253

Q

Query Builder, 732–735, 751–755
Query Builder dialog box, 733–735, 751–755
QuickBASIC, 84–85

R

radio button(s)
    adding, 317–318
    classification of, as objects, 6
    described, 317
    default, 318
    grouping, 318, 319
    selecting/deselecting, 321
    standards for, 319
RadioButton class, 317
RadioButton tool, 48, 317, 723
RadioButton.PerformClick method, 333
random access files
    basic description of, 613–664
    closing, 624
    declaring variables and, 619
    deleting, 621
    end of, testing for, 623–625
    estimating the maximum number of records in, 622
    garbage code in, 621
    initializing, 621–622
    opening, 619–620
    procedures for, 617
    reading records from, 623–625
    sequential access files versus, 616–619
    writing records to, 620–623
random numbers
    generating, 325–327
    pseudo-, 325–327
Random object, 282, 325–327
Randomize statement, 326
Random.Next method, 282, 325–327
Random.NextDouble method, 325
Rate argument, 252–254
RateListBox control, 453, 456–459, 471
RateTextBox control, 133, 180–181, 208, 247, 248
Read from File button, 565–566
ReadLine method, 561–563
ReadOnly property, 740
record(s)
    described, 616

maximum number of, in random access files, 622
reading, 623–625
storing, in arrays, 693–695
structures, 617
variables, declaring, 619
writing, to random access files, 620–623
recordLength argument, 620
recordnumber argument, 621, 623
recordvariable argument, 621, 623
reference, passing variables by, 437, 440–443, 445
References folder, 25, 29, 30
relational databases, 725, 745–746. *See also* databases
relational operators
    basic description of, 225–229
    logical operators and, 233
    selection structures and, 224, 225–229, 300–305
Remove Border button, 401–402
Remove from File button, 615, 652
Remove method, 497, 498–499, 508
RemoveButton control, 396–398, 649–652
repetition structures. *See also* looping
    collections and, 393–417
    counters and, 376–383
    Do...Loop statement and, 370–376
    For Each...Next statement and, 398–403
    For...Next statement and, 362–370
    Grade Calculator application and, 359–351
    object variables and, 395–398
    Pretest Loop button and, 372, 373–376
    testing, 380
Replace method, 502–505, 508
replacementString sequence, 504–505
ReportPrintDocument control, 600–601
Reset button, 49
Return statement, 444
RichTextBox tool, 723
Rnd function, 326
RowHeadersVisible property, 740
Run command, 7, 16
Run dialog box, 7, 16
run time, assigning values to properties during, 127–129

S

Sales Entry dialog box, 380
Sales Express application, 376–378
Sales Express Form.vb, 378
Sales Express Solution.sln, 378
SalesButton control, 163–166
SalesLabel control, 163–166
SalesTextBox control, 302
sans serif fonts, 54, 62, 106–107, 601. *See also* fonts
Save All button, 37, 111, 117
SaveFileDialog tool, 723
Scope application, 162–168
Scope Form.vb, 163
Scope Project Property Pages dialog box, 165
Scope Solution.sln, 163
SearchArray procedure, 675
searching
    arrays, 675–676
    case-sensitive, 507
    strings, 506–508
    for XML Web Services, 19–20
secondary decisions
    basic description of, 285
    reversing, 292–293
Select Access Database dialog box, 729, 748
Select Case statement, 297–302, 419
Select statement, 731, 735, 750–751
SelectAll method, 344
SelectedIndex property, 457–461
SelectedItem property, 457–461, 465
SelectedValueChanged event, 471–472
selection (decision) structures
    arrays and, 675
    Case structure, 296–300
    comparison operators and, 225–229, 300–305
    creating, 217–280
    described, 220–221
    four forms of, 221
    If/ElseIf/Else structure, 294–296
    LCase function and, 236–239
    logic errors in, 288–294
    logical operators and, 230–236
    Math Practice application and, 281–357
    nested, 284–288
    repetition structures and, 381–382
    UCase function and, 236–239
    using unnecessary, 293–294

SelectionMode property, 453
selection/repetition symbol, 223
selectorExpression, 297–298, 302–303
Seminar application
    completing, 649–664
    creating, 613–664
    opening, 632
    previewing, 614–615
    TOE chart for, 633–634, 640
Seminar Form.vb, 632, 649
Seminar Solution.sln, 632, 649
SeminarPrintDocument control, 634, 653–656
sender parameter, 301–303, 533
separator bars
    described, 517
    design tips for using, 521
    inserting, 519–520
    sequential access files
    aligning columns in, 558–561
    Carriage House application and, 548–612
    closing, 562–563
    described, 553
    determining the existence of, 556
    opening, 553–556
    PadLeft method and, 558–561
    PadRight method and, 558–561
    random access files versus, 616–619
    reading information from, 561–563
    using, 553–554
    writing information to, 556–561
Server Explorer tab, 26
Server Explorer window
    auto-hide features and, 26, 27
    basic description of, 20
    closing, 26–27
servers, 17, 741, 744
SetBounds method, 368, 369
Short data type, 157, 158, 159, 179, 618
short-circuit evaluation, 231
shortcut keys
    access keys and, comparison of, 520
    assigning, 520–521
Show All Files button, 25, 30
Show hidden files and folders radio button, 23
ShowDialog method, 482–483
ShowHeader property, 759
ShowUpDown property, 577–578

Single data type, 157, 159, 179
Single radio button, 434
Sizable setting, 75
SizableToolWindow setting, 75
Size property, 36–37
SizeMode property, 55
.sln file extension, 23
Smalltalk, 5
sngAverageSales variable, 379
sngBonus variable, 442, 445
sngHigh variable, 677–678
sngPrice variable, 179, 180–181, 670, 672
sngPrincipal variable, 251
sngRate variable, 179, 180–181, 251, 254, 440, 443
sngRatio variable, 420
sngSalary variable, 619
sngSalesTax variable, 179, 184
sngSubtotal variable, 179
sngSumSales variable, 379–381
sngTotalPrice variable, 179
Solution Explorer
    basic description of, 20, 29–31
    changing filenames with, 32–33
    display of blank solutions in, 22–23
    increasing the size of, 23, 27
    opening the Form Designer from, 25
    saving solutions in, 37
    view options, 25, 30
solutions
    adding projects to, 24–25
    adding forms to, 479–480
    closing, 38
    creating new, 21–22
    described, 21
    opening, 38
    saving, 37, 52, 111
Sort Items Alphabetically option, 47
SortAscending procedure, 679–681
SortDescending procedure, 681
Sorted property, 455
sorting
    data stored in arrays, 679–681
    described, 679
    list box items, 455
source files. *See also* source files (listed by name)
    described, 30
    as form files, 31
source files (listed by name). *See also* source files
    ABC Form.vb, 726
    AssemblyInfo.vb, 29, 30

Carriage Form.vb, 573
Constant Form.vb, 169
Copyright Form.vb, 32, 37, 45, 479–480
Do Loop Form.vb, 372
File Form.vb, 563
For Next Form.vb, 364, 401
Form1.vb, 25, 28–32
Form2.vb, 31
Grade Form.vb, 405, 419
Hangman Form.vb, 516, 527
Math Form.vb, 316, 340
Object Variable Form.vb, 396
Order Form.vb, 126, 176, 193, 203
Payment Form.vb, 246, 267–268
Payroll Form.vb, 452, 479
Sales Express Form.vb, 378
Scope Form.vb, 163
Seminar Form.vb, 632, 649
Space function, 558, 622
specified argument, 369
splash screens, 15, 56. *See also* copyright screenSplitter tool, 723
square brackets ([]), 127, 168, 224, 304
SQL (Structured Query Language)
    described, 731, 750–751
    Select statement, 731, 735, 750–751
SQL Server (Microsoft), 724, 745
Standard format, 137–138
Standard toolbar, 21, 23, 37
Start button, 7, 16
Start Page tab, 26
Start Page window, 17–19, 20, 23, 26–27
startIndex argument, 498, 502, 506, 507
StartPosition property, 35
start/stop symbol, 222, 371
StartsWith method, 499–501, 508
Startup object, 57, 481–482
startvalue item, 362, 366, 393
statements. *See also specific statements*
    blocks of, 224, 228
    copying, 128
StateTextBox control, 109–110, 129
Static keyword, 160, 162
static variables, 205–207
StatusBar tool, 723
stepvalue item, 362–363, 366, 369
Stop Message icon, 256, 257
strAge variable, 439, 441, 442

strCharacter variable, 533
strCity variable, 365
strCityState variable, 500, 501
strDate variable, 589
StreamReader object, 552–553, 556, 565
streams, of characters
  described, 552
  reading, 552–553, 556, 565
  writing, 552–561, 564, 585
StreamWriter object, 552–561, 564, 585
strFirstName field, 618
strFirstName variable, 184, 619
string(s)
  accessing characters in, 501–502
  adding, 135
  characters at the beginning/end of, examining, 499–501
  comparisons, 236–239, 303–305
  concatenating, 183–185, 558
  data type for, 157, 159–160, 184, 187, 618–619
  described, 126
  debugging, 545
  empty, 127
  inserting characters in, 505–506
  Like operator and, 303
  manipulating, 491–545
  number of characters contained in, determining, 494–495
  random access files and, 618–619
  removing characters from, 495–499
  replacing characters in, 502–505
  searching, 506–508
  sequential access and, 558
  Val function and, 136
  zero-length (empty), 127, 205, 379, 380
String data type, 157, 159–160, 184, 187, 618–619. *See also* strings
strLast variable, 502
strLastName variable, 184, 619
strLetter variable, 235, 304, 305
strMsg variable, 507, 508strName variable, 439, 441–442, 497–499, 505, 559, 670, 672
strNewName variable, 559
strNewPhone variable, 503
strNum variable, 497
strPart variable, 495
strPartialWorld variable, 533–535
strPay variable, 500

strPhone variable, 495, 503, 506
strRate variable, 497
strSales variable, 379, 380, 502
strSearchFor variable, 695
strState variable, 238–239
Structure statement, 617–618
Sub keyword, 62, 444
Sub procedure, 62, 618
  creating, 435–451
  described, 435
  including parameters in, 436–437
  user-defined, 323–327
Sub Main procedure, 480–481
submenu(s)
  disadvantages of, 517
  items, described, 517
subscript. *See also* index
  accessing elements in arrays with, 674
  described, 668–669
  verifying the validity of, 674
Substring method, 501–502, 508
subString sequence, 500
subtraction operator, 131–132, 233
SubtractionRadioButton control, 283, 317–318, 322, 330–332
SummaryCheckBox control, 316, 319, 321–323, 345–347
SumTextBox control, 128
.suo file extension, 23
SwapButton control, 228
symbols. *See also* characters
  & (ampersand), 112, 113, 183, 184
  ' (apostrophe), 130
  * (asterisk), 34, 304
  \ (backslash), 34
  : (colon), 98
  , (comma), 136, 138, 186
  {} (curly braces), 370, 670
  . (decimal point), 137
  $ (dollar sign), 132, 138, 500
  " (double quotes), 126, 135, 186
  ... (ellipsis), 36, 517, 521
  = (equal sign), 127
  ! (exclamation point), 305
  > (greater-than sign), 363
  - (hyphen), 305, 530
  < (less-than sign), 363
  () (parentheses), 63, 131–132, 139
  | (pipe symbol), 370
  + (plus sign), 135, 184
  % (percent sign), 132, 136, 137

. (period), 127, 189, 268
[] (square brackets), 127, 168, 224, 304
_ (underscore), 134
syntax
  described, 62
  errors, 139
system date/time, retrieving, 583–585
System namespace, 34
System tab, 108
System.Windows.Forms namespace, 29, 49

T

Tab Order option, 114, 115–116
TabControl tool, 723
TabIndex property, 114–119, 249–250
  databases and, 740
  DateTimePicker control and, 574–575
  list box controls and, 454
  Math Practice application and, 320–321
tables
  adding, 732–733, 751–752
  described, 725
  truth, 230–234
Tables tab, 732–733
Tag property, 407
Tahoma font, 54, 106
targetString sequence, 504–505
tasks
  assigning, to objects, 93–94
  identifying, 91–93
Tax Calculator application
  creating, 665–719
  opening, 704–705
  previewing, 666–667
  TOE chart for, 706–707
templates, 22–24, 62
Templates list box, 22
TermTextBox control, 248
Test Connection button, 729, 748
testing
  basic description of, 139–140
  database connections, 729, 748
  for the end of a random access file, 623–625
  the order screen, 130, 139–140
  the Pretest button, 380
  procedures, 209, 381
text. *See also* fonts; text box controls; Text property
  aligning, 272–273

captions, 35, 255–257, 740
for label controls, 272–273
text argument, 255–256
text box controls
 access keys and, 112–113, 117
 adding, 110–111
 BorderStyle property for, 109
 deleting, 110
 enabling, 409–411
 Enter events and, 422–423
 fonts for, 110
 Grade Calculator application
  and, 422–423
 labels identifying, 97–98
 order screen and, 87, 93, 95,
  97–98, 109–111
 properties for, 110–111
 selecting text in, 344
Text property, 35, 51–52, 76,
 177, 497
 check box controls and, 320
 DateTimePicker control and,
  582–583
 group box controls and, 246,
  247, 248
 LCase function and, 239
 main menu controls and, 517
 order screen, 109–110,
  112–113, 126, 128, 133,
  135, 156
 radio buttons and, 319
 strings and, 495
 UCase function and, 236
 Val function and, 178–179
 variables and, 166
TextAlign property, 272–273
TextBox tool, 110, 248, 723
TextChanged event, 207–208, 250,
 261–263, 302, 406
Tick event, 72–73, 74
time
 formats, 578–579
 system, retrieving, 583–585
timer controls, 56, 72–74, 479
Timer tool, 72–74, 723
title bar(s)
 buttons, disabling, 76–77
 captions, 28, 35
 filenames in, 35
 managing windows with, 26–27
 removing, 76
titles, for menus, 517, 321
To keyword, 299–300

TOE (Task, Object, Event) chart,
 87, 92–96, 125–126, 132
 assigning tasks from, to objects,
  93–94
 Calculate Order button and, 132
 completed, ordered by object,
  125–126
 described, 91
 drawing, 93
 entering tasks in, 92–93
 Event Report application,
  585–586
 Grade Calculator application,
  405–406, 407
 Hangman Game application,
  528–529
 Math Practice application,
  322–323, 327
 Monthly Payment Calculator
  application, 250
 order screen and, 175–176,
  201–204
 Payroll application, 460–461
 Seminar application, 633–634,
  640
 Tax Calculator application,
  706–707
ToLongDateString method, 583–585
ToLongTimeString method, 581, 583
ToolBar tool, 723
toolbox window. *See also* tools
 (listed by name)
 auto-hide feature and, 26, 27
 basic description of, 20, 45–49
 customizing, 48–49
 opening, 26
 sizing, 45–46
 tabs, 46
 tools included with, list of,
  721–723
tools (listed by name)
 Button tool, 56–57, 721
 CheckBox tool, 319, 721
 CheckedListBox control,
  317, 721
 ColorDialog tool, 721
 ComboBox tool, 721
 ContextMenu tool, 721
 CrystalReportViewer tool, 721
 DataGrid tool, 721, 757
 DateTimePicker tool, 574, 721
 DomainUpDown tool, 721
 ErrorProvider tool, 722
 FontDialog tool, 722

GroupBox tool, 247, 722
HelpProvider tool, 722
HScrollBar tool, 722
ImageList tool, 722
Label tool, 49–54, 722
LinkLabel tool, 722
ListBox tool, 453, 722
ListView tool, 722
MainMenu tool, 518, 722
MonthlyCalendar tool, 722
NotifyIcon tool, 722
NumericUpDown tool, 722
OleDbDataAdapter tool,
 746–747
OpenFileDialog tool, 722
PageSetupDialog tool, 722
Panel tool, 246, 722
PictureBox tool, 55–56, 722
Pointer tool, 47, 721
PrintDialog tool, 722
PrintDocument tool, 598, 722
PrintPreviewControl tool, 722
ProgressBar tool, 722
RadioButton tool, 48, 317, 723
RichTextBox tool, 723
SaveFileDialog tool, 723
Splitter tool, 723
StatusBar tool, 723
TabControl tool, 723
TextBox tool, 110, 248, 723
Timer tool, 72–74, 723
ToolBar tool, 723
ToolTip tool, 723
TrackBar tool, 723
TreeView tool, 723
VScrollBar tool, 723
ToolTip tool, 723
top-driven (pretest) loops
 described, 362
 Do...Loop statement and,
  370–376
 posttest loops and, observing the
  difference between, 375
 Sales Express application and,
  376–378
ToShortDateString method, 581,
 583–585
ToShortTimeString method, 581
ToString method, 560, 583–585
TotalBoardLabel control, 129, 133,
 179, 182–183, 207–208
TotalPriceLabel control, 129,
 182–183, 207–208
TrackBar tool, 723

TreeView tool, 723
Trim method, 496–497, 498, 508
TrimEnd method, 496–497, 498, 508, 642
TrimStart method, 496–497, 498, 508
true path
    described, 221, 222
    distinguishing, from the false path, 223
    selection structures and, 284, 285, 286
truth tables, 230–234
two-dimensional arrays. *See also* arrays
    calculating the sum of numbers stored in, 703–704
    described, 700–702
    storing data in, 702–703
TypeOf...Is operator, 300, 302–303

U

UCase function
    basic description of, 236–239
    Like operator and, 303, 304
    procedures and, 238–239
    searching strings and, 507
udtEmploy variable, 619–620, 622
udtParticipant variable, 638, 641, 642
unary operators, 131
underscore (_), 134
Until keyword, 371
UpdateArray procedure, 678–679
UseMnemonic property, 113
user interfaces
    color for, selecting, 107–108
    described, 17
    design elements for, planning and sizing, 106
    preparing to create, 104–110
    layout/organization of, 98
    sketches of, drawing, 96–98, 315

V

Val function, 136–137, 178–179, 186
valid data, described, 139
Value property, 579–582
variables. *See also* variables (listed by name)
    assigning data to, 161–162
    creating, 156–174
    described, 156
    declaring, 160–161, 204, 341, 619

naming, 159–160
passing, by reference, 437, 440–443, 445
passing, by value, 437–440
scope of, 161–168
selecting data types for, 157–159
simple (scalar), 668
storing information with, 156–160, 175–177
using, 153–215
variables (listed by name). *See also* variables
    blnReplaced variable, 533
    counter variable, 362–363, 365, 367, 369, 380, 393
    intAge variable, 184
    intBlue variable, 179, 180
    intButton variable, 585, 622
    intCode variable, 674
    intCorrectAnswer variable, 341–343
    intCount variable, 365, 373, 374, 675
    intEmployNumber variable, 619
    intFirst variable, 227
    intIndex variable, 507–508, 533
    intNum1 variable, 341–342
    intNum2 variable, 341–342
    intNumber variable, 162
    intNumberCorrect variable, 341–342
    intNumberIncorrect variable, 341–342
    intNumOrdered variable, 300
    intNumSales variable, 379–381
    intRecordNum variable, 622
    intRegion1 variable, 442, 445
    intRegion2 variable, 442, 445
    intSale1 variable, 440, 443, 445
    intSale2 variable, 443, 445
    intSales variable, 163, 165
    intSearchFor variable, 675
    intSecond variable, 227
    intTemp variable, 228
    intTotal variable, 440, 443, 676
    IntTotalBoards variable, 179
    intUserAnswer variable, 341–343
    intX variable, 369–370, 394, 673, 675–679
    intYellow variable, 179, 180
    mstrSalesPerson variable, 187, 204
    objControl variable, 404
    objLetterLabel variable, 533

    objPayrollForm variable, 482
    objStateTextBox variable, 395
    objStreamReader variable, 555
    objStreamWriter variable, 555, 564, 585
    sngAverageSales variable, 379
    sngBonus variable, 442, 445
    sngHigh variable, 677–678
    sngPrice variable, 179, 180–181, 670, 672
    sngPrincipal variable, 251
    sngRate variable, 179, 180–181, 251, 254, 440, 443
    sngRatio variable, 420
    sngSalary variable, 619
    sngSalesTax variable, 179, 184
    sngSubtotal variable, 179
    sngSumSales variable, 379–381
    sngTotalPrice variable, 179
    strAge variable, 439, 441, 442
    strCharacter variable, 533
    strCity variable, 365
    strCityState variable, 500, 501
    strDate variable, 589
    strFirstName variable, 184, 619
    strLast variable, 502
    strLastName variable, 184, 619
    strLetter variable, 235, 304, 305
    strMsg variable, 507, 508
    strName variable, 439, 441–442, 497–499, 505, 559, 670, 672
    strNewName variable, 559
    strNewPhone variable, 503
    strNum variable, 497
    strPart variable, 495
    strPartialWorld variable, 533–535
    strPay variable, 500
    strPhone variable, 495, 503, 506
    strRate variable, 497
    strSales variable, 379, 380, 502
    strSearchFor variable, 695
    strState variable, 238–239
    udtEmploy variable, 619–620, 622
    udtParticipant variable, 638, 641, 642
.vb file extension, 30
vbNewLine constant, 191
verticalPosition argument, 601
View tab, 23
View Wizard Results screen, 735, 754
Visible property, 345, 529
Visual C++ (Microsoft), 5

Visual Studio .NET (Microsoft)
    creating applications with,
        21–28
    customizing, 17–21
    exiting, 39
    starting, 17–21
VScrollBar tool, 723

W

Warning Message icon, 257, 423
Web Access Failed dialog box, 744
Web browsers, 17, 741, 760
Web Hosting link, 19
Web servers, 17, 741, 744
Web-based applications
    accessing data with, 745–746
    basic description of, 17, 741
    creating, 741–760
    data sets for, 755–757
    OleDbDataAdapter object and,
        745–755
What's New link, 19
where clause, 731, 750
While keyword, 371
white space, 98

width argument, 368
Width property, 36
windows
    auto-hiding, 26
    closing, 26
    increasing the size of, 23
    minimizing, 27
Windows Application template, 24
Windows Form Designer
    basic description of, 28
    code, viewing, 60–61
    displaying, 38
Windows Form object
    Background Image property
        and, 35–36
    base classes and, 60
    basic description of, 28
    border style of, 75–76
    changing the name of, 34–35
    properties for, 33–37
Windows Forms tab, 46–49
Windows namespace, 34
Wirth, Niklaus, 159
Word (Microsoft), 93, 140
WordLabel control, 530, 531,
    534, 535

Write to File button, 564
Write method, 556–561
WriteLine method, 556–561, 564

X

x argument, 368
X property, 52
XML Web Services, 19–20
XML Web Services link, 19–20
Xor operator, 230–236
XPos argument, 186

Y

y argument, 368
Y property, 52
YearLabel control, 51–52
YellowTextBox control, 135,
    179–181, 208
YPos argument, 186

Z

ZipTextBox control, 495